REFERENCE

Room use only

ROCKVILLE PUBLIC LIBRARY

D1064317

The
PACIFIC WAR
Encyclopedia

VOLUME II   M–Z

The
PACIFIC WAR
Encyclopedia

VOLUME II   M–Z

James F. Dunnigan and Albert A. Nofi

Facts On File, Inc.

THE PACIFIC WAR ENCYCLOPEDIA

Facts On File, Inc.
11 Penn Plaza
New York NY 10001

Library of Congress Cataloging-in-Publication Data

Dunnigan, James F.
    The Pacific war encyclopedia / James F. Dunnigan and Albert A. Nofi.
        p.   cm.
    Includes bibliographical references and index.
    ISBN 0-8160-3439-7 (set). — ISBN 0-8160-3437-0 (v. 1). — ISBN 0-8160-3438-9 (v. 2)
    1. World War, 1939–1945—Pacific Area—Encyclopedias. I. Nofi, Albert A. II. Title.
    D767.9.D86   1998
    940.54'099—dc21   97-15634

Facts On File books are available at special discounts when purchased in bulk quantities for businesses, associations, institutions or sales promotions. Please call our Special Sales Department in New York at 212/967-8800 or 800/322-8755.

You can find Facts On File on the World Wide Web at http://www.factsofile.com

Text design by Cathy Rincon
Cover design by Robert Yaffe
All photographic reproductions are from the National Archives.
Diagrams on pages 95 and 486 copyright © 1995 Combined Books, used with permission.
All other illustrations are from the authors' collections.
Maps by Karen Little and Dale Williams.

This book is printed on acid-free paper.

Printed in the United States of America

MP FOF 10 9 8 7 6 5 4 3 2 1

CONTENTS

Terms and Conventions Used in the Work

Times and Dates: It is important to recall that the International Date Line runs through the center of the Pacific Ocean, roughly along the 180th line of longitude. The date advances by one day when moving west across the line, but declines by one day when moving east. So the Japanese attack on PEARL HARBOR occurred on Sunday, 7 December 1941, in the United States and HAWAII, but on Monday, 8 December 1941, in Australia, Japan, and China. In addition, once the war began the United States went on "double daylight savings," or War Time, which further complicates reconciling the sequence of events. In this work all references to date and time will be made on the basis of the local situation.

Names: The spelling and forms of the names of persons and places are given in the style in which they appeared during the war. With the exception of particularly well-known persons (CHIANG KAI-SHEK, for example), East Asian names are usually in the European fashion, with family name second. For the more modern forms of some World War II place-names, see the Appendix.

Cross-references: Items mentioned in the text that are the subject of entries in this book have been indicated by SMALL CAPITAL LETTERS. At the end of many entries will be the names of entries of related interest.

References to specific military units (e.g., Seventh Infantry Division) should be checked under the main reference of the army in question: for example, US Army, Divisions, or Marine Corps, Divisions.

Aircraft References: Since Japanese aircraft were always referred to by their Allied code names, they have been referenced using these. Consult the table in "Aircraft, Japanese, Allied Code Names," for the appropriate entries. Technical details on the various aircraft—Allied and Japanese—are included in the Aircraft Tables.

Bibliographic References: Many entries include references to published materials, in abbreviated form. These should be checked against the bibliography and recommended reading list at the end of the volume. In the case of multivolume official histories, the reference entry includes only the series title. In most cases these references are to unusual or particularly valuable materials. Between the official histories and popular treatments, there are so many works on most operations that we have elected not to include references to them. References to campaigns are found in the bibliography. Similarly, there are usually no bibliographic references for individuals, ships, aircraft, and geographic locations.

Ship Descriptions: All major classes of warships have their own entries. In addition, there are master tables for each of the major categories of warship: aircraft carrier, battleship, cruiser, and destroyer. Submarines have been grouped under single entries for each of the principal nations. Most of the numerous classes of smaller vessels have been omitted.

In entries for particular classes of major warships there are short descriptions of the activities and fate of the most prominent members of the class. The years of laying down (when construction began), launching (when construction was sufficiently advanced for the still-incomplete vessel to be put into the water), and completion are given in parentheses, such as (1934–1936–1937). The date of laying down gives some idea as to the time the ship was designed, usually a year or so earlier. Launch date is important because at that point it is not likely that significant changes can be made in the ship without a virtual rebuilding. Completion date merely indicates the moment at which the ship is officially ready for service, after which a ship would normally spend a month or more on a "shakedown" cruise to determine any technical problems. In wartime, however, this cruise was sometimes omitted, or took place en route to the war zone. In descriptions of classes of minor warships the year of the laying down of the first vessels in the class is given, followed by that of the completion of the last to be built.

Abbreviations:

AA:	antiaircraft
A/C:	aircraft
Adm:	admiral
AFV:	armored fighting vehicles (tanks, APCs, etc.)
APC:	armored personnel carrier
Arm.:	armored
Art.:	artillery
ASW:	antisubmarine warfare
A/T:	antitank
BB:	battleship, including battle cruisers
Bde.:	brigade
BG:	brigadier general
Br.:	British/Britain
c.:	circa, about
CA:	heavy cruiser

CAP:	combat air patrol (aircraft maintained over a carrier, for defensive purposes)
Capt.:	captain
Cav.:	cavalry
CB:	large cruiser
CBI:	China-Burma-India Theater of Operations
Cdr.:	commander
CINCPAC:	Commander in Chief, Pacific (US Navy)
CL:	light cruiser
CLAA:	antiaircraft light cruiser (not introduced until after World War II)
CNO:	US Chief of Naval Operations
COL:	colonel
CPL:	corporal
CV:	aircraft carrier
CVE:	escort aircraft carrier
CVL:	light aircraft carrier
DD:	destroyer
DE:	destroyer escort
Div.:	division
Ens.:	ensign
ETO:	European Theater of Operations
Fr.:	French/France
Gen.:	general
Ger.:	German/Germany
GHQ:	general headquarters
GRT:	gross register ton, describes size of non-warships
HIJMS:	"His Imperial Japanese Majesty's Ship"
HMAS:	"His Majesty's Australian Ship"
HMNZ:	"His Majesty's New Zealand Ship"
HMS:	"His [Britannic] Majesty's Ship"
HNMS:	"Her Netherlands' Majesty's Ship"
IJN:	Imperial Japanese Navy
Inf.:	infantry
IX-:	US Navy type designation for a "miscellaneous" vessel, such as an historic relic or one performing a highly unusual mission, such as an "Aircraft Carrier, Training"
Jap.:	Japanese/Japan
JCS:	US Joint Chiefs of Staff

KIA:	killed in action
Knot:	KTS.; nautical mile per hour, equal to 1.15 land miles or 1.85 kilometers
LG:	lieutenant general
Lt:	lieutenant (1Lt, first lieutenant; 2Lt, second lieutenant)
LtCdr:	lieutenant commander
LTC:	lieutenant colonel
Maj.:	major
MG:	major general
mg.:	machine gun
Mtr.:	mortar
MPH:	miles per hour
na:	not available
Neth.:	Netherlands
PFC:	private first class
PBY:	Catalina multiengine floatplane used for reconnaissance
POW:	prisoner of war
PTO:	Pacific Theater of Operations
RAdm:	rear admiral
RAF:	Britain's Royal Air Force
RCT:	regimental combat team, a US task force consisting of an infantry regiment, an artillery battalion, and sundry support forces, about a third of a division
Recon:	reconnaissance
RN:	Britain's Royal Navy
SGT:	sergeant
SNLF:	special naval landing force, Japanese "Marines"
Sov.:	Soviet
SS:	submarine
Staff Sgt.:	staff sergeant
TF:	task force, group of warships traveling together
TG:	task group, portion of a naval TF
T/O&E:	table of organization and equipment, the officially prescribed organization of the allotments of troops and equipment in a military formation
US:	the United States
USAAF:	the United States Army Air Forces—more correctly, the Army Air Corps in the early part of the war, a change of nomenclature that we largely ignore
USAT:	"United States Army Transport"
USMC:	the US Marine Corps
USN:	the US Navy
USS:	"United States' Ship"
VAdm:	vice admiral

M

MacArthur, Douglas (1880–1964)

The son of Civil War hero Arthur MacArthur, who was awarded a MEDAL OF HONOR for bravery at Missionary Ridge, Douglas MacArthur graduated from West Point in 1903 with some of the highest grades ever recorded (as well as having the rather dubious distinction of being one of a handful of cadets in the history of the academy whose mother lived right outside the gate for four years). An engineer, he held a variety of staff and academic posts, but no troop commands (albeit that he got into action at Vera Cruz in 1914) until World War I, when he helped organize the 42nd "Rainbow" Division, composed of NATIONAL GUARD units from 26 states. As a staff officer, later deputy division commander, and for two days right at the end of the war acting division commander, MacArthur proved an able soldier, often going into action with the troops. After the war he reorganized West Point's academic and cadet discipline programs (and made a concerted effort to abolish hazing, which was only partially successful), served on the Billy Mitchell court-martial, commanded in the Philippines, and was chief of staff of the army in the early 1930s, violently suppressing the "Bonus March," apparently against orders from President Hoover. Despite this, Hoover's successor, FDR, kept MacArthur on for an extra year. In 1935 he went to the Philippines again to help organize the commonwealth's defense forces, and in 1938 resigned from the army in order to continue in the service of the commonwealth. When in mid-1941 the Philippine Armed Forces were activated by the president and merged into the US Armed Forces,

MacArthur was recalled to duty as a full general and placed in overall command. Caught napping by the onset of the war (he lost his entire air force on the ground nine hours after PEARL HARBOR), MacArthur seriously bungled the initial defense of the Philippines, but managed to salvage something from the disaster by a belated retreat to the BATAAN Peninsula.

In the closing days of the defense of Bataan, President ROOSEVELT awarded MacArthur a Medal of Honor and ordered him to turn command over to his principal subordinate, Jonathan WAINWRIGHT, and escape to Australia, to coordinate Allied efforts to carry on the war in the southwest Pacific. As a result, one night in February of 1942, MacArthur, some of his close aides, and a few others boarded several torpedo boats; the general himself was on *PT-41*, which successfully ran the Japanese blockade. Accompanying MacArthur were his wife, his son, and his son's nurse. Almost as soon as MacArthur had made good his escape, questions were raised as to why he brought along his family, albeit that the consequences of leaving them behind might have seriously impaired his abilities as a commander. Moreover, stories began to circulate that he had arranged to bring out not only members of his family, but also certain articles of furniture, including a refrigerator. The tale has proven extremely durable, but has no foundation in fact. None of those present, including the crews of the PT-BOATS, reported carrying anything unusual during the trip.

MacArthur assumed command of Allied forces in Australia, and shortly began an offensive that would eventually recover New Guinea and the

General Douglas MacArthur sports his twin trademarks, the cap of a Philippine field marshal and a corncob pipe, in a photograph taken during the Leyte landings, in October 1944.

Philippines. Army commander designate for the invasion of Japan, MacArthur instead commanded the occupation forces, and became virtual ruler of the country for several years.

In 1950 MacArthur assumed command of UN forces in Korea, planning the spectacularly successful Inchon Operation, but subsequently mismanaged the pursuit of the defeated North Korean Army and totally misread Chinese intentions, with disastrous results. After repeated warnings from President TRUMAN about unauthorized political statements, MacArthur was relieved of duty in April of 1951. Despite the belief by many that he would undertake a political career, he spent the rest of his life in retirement.

MacArthur was a commander of erratic capabilities. When he was good he was brilliant, but he was often careless and self-centered, which led to errors in planning. He also let his personal likes and dislikes, and particularly his love of publicity, interfere in his management of the war. From December of 1941 to March of 1942, 142 dispatches emanated from the headquarters of United States Army Forces in the Far East, of which 109 (76%) included the name of only one person, the theater commander, General Douglas MacArthur. MacArthur was so well known for his efforts to hog publicity that he once got an officer to undertake a difficult assignment by promising that if successful the man's name would appear in a press release.

He despised Marines and Australians, and made sure neither received any credit for operations in "his" theater. Even Robert EICHELBERGER, his most able subordinate, was almost fired after a newspaper accurately credited him with the victory at BUNA-GONA, and Eichelberger had to endure being on the shelf for almost a year.

MacArthur's reputation for being much more frugal with lives than Marine commanders is partially the product of the way in which CASUALTIES were classified. It was not uncommon for a campaign to be declared "over" in situations where the Marines would have declared the objective "secured," meaning that there was a lot of organized resistance still going on, but American control of the place was no longer in dispute. The protracted struggle for Luzon, for example, resulted in as many casualties as did OKINAWA, most of them after the campaign had been declared "over."

Although he despised the president, MacArthur seems never to have understood the extent to which FDR was responsible for creating his enormous reputation. It was Roosevelt who kept MacArthur on for an extra year as chief of staff of the army in 1934–35, who allowed him to accept the appointment as commander of the PHILIPPINE ARMY, who recalled him to active duty though overage in 1941, who made him commander of USAFFE, who ordered him out of CORREGIDOR, who awarded him the Medal of Honor, and so forth.

Although MacArthur was able to create the impression of intimacy with persons whom he wished to cultivate, he actually had no friends, merely a wide circle of acquaintances. His personality was such that people could not be indifferent to him; they either liked or hated him, attitudes often reflective of his purported political views. Generally regarded as a staunch conservative, MacArthur in fact appears to have had no genuine political principles, merely saying what seemed to please whomever he was speaking with (among other things he endorsed the American Civil Liberties Union). He was a masterful speaker, as can be seen from the proclamation he issued upon landing on Leyte on 20 October 1944:

> People of the Philippines, I have returned. By the Grace of Almighty God our forces stand on Philippine soil . . . Rally to me. Let the Indomitable spirit of Bataan and Corregidor lead on. As the lines of battle roll forward to bring you within the zone of operations, rise and strike! . . . For your homes and hearths, strike! For future generations of your sons and daughters, strike! In the name of your sacred dead, strike! Let no heart be faint. Let every arm be steeled. The guidance of divine God points the way. Follow in His name to the Holy Grail of righteous victory!

The MacArthurs are the only father and son to have both won the Medal of Honor. The "Defender of Australia, Liberator of the Philippines, Conqueror of Japan" is buried in a large monument at Norfolk, Virginia.

Ref: Rasor, *General Douglas MacArthur*; *Report of General MacArthur*.

Madras, India

A major commercial port, with a small naval base, Madras's location on the eastern coast of India made it vulnerable to Japanese carrier air raids in March 1942.

MAGIC

Completely independent of the ULTRA codebreaking project was an American effort to crack Japanese ciphers. This project was called MAGIC. Unlike the Germans, the Japanese did not use an Enigma machine, but rather a similar, but less capable device. They used older encryption methods, which could be (and constantly were) cracked by rooms full of clever and hardworking specialists. This was what American cryptanalysts did in the late 1930s and throughout the war. A US naval officer, Robert J. Rochefort, was the principal codebreaker for the Pacific Fleet for the entire war. Among his achievements was the breaking of the Japanese code JN25, which led to the American victory at MIDWAY. US naval officer Laurence F. Stafford and William Friedman were the two other men most responsible for breaking Japanese codes during the war. US Army codebreaker Friedman was head of the cryptanalysis bureau in the War Department. Friedman was chiefly responsible for breaking the Japanese PURPLE code. His wife, Elizabeth (1892–1980), was also a codebreaker of considerable ability.

As with ULTRA, MAGIC obtained timely results by reconstructing the Japanese cipher machine and automating the cracking of the coded messages. The Japanese, as a standard military practice, changed their codebooks from time to time, and this slowed down the deciphering of their messages by the Americans for several months. But, aside from that, secret Japanese radio messages were not very secret during the war. Some Japanese leaders were suspicious that their codes were compromised, but the American use of MAGIC information was done carefully, and the Japanese never took measures to completely change their cipher system.

MAGIC made possible two of the most crucial DECEPTIONS of the Pacific War. First, in June 1942 there was the ambush US carriers pulled off at Midway Island. A large Japanese fleet was headed for Midway, with the dual purpose of taking the island and drawing the remaining US fleet from HAWAII for a "decisive battle." Because of MAGIC intercepts, the Americans knew of the Japanese plans and set up an ambush with their outnumbered carriers. As a result, the Japanese were defeated. Having lost four of their large carriers, the Japanese were no longer able to do whatever they wanted in the Pacific.

The second deception involved yet another ambush. MAGIC intercepts informed the Americans of a visit to the SOLOMONS area by the commander of the Japanese Navy. This officer, Admiral Isoroku YAMAMOTO, was one of the most effective commanders the Japanese had. He had attended college in the United States and understood America better than most other Japanese leaders. Although opposed to war with the United States, Yamamoto nevertheless presided over the string of victories Japan enjoyed in the first seven months of the war. Yamamoto was known to be a superb leader and naval commander. While there was a risk that MAGIC would be compromised if Yamamoto's aircraft was attacked, the removal of Japan's best naval commander was considered worth the risk. So on April 18, 1943, long-range US P-38 fighters found and attacked Yamamoto's transport and its fighter escorts over the Solomons. The admiral died and with that Japan lost a naval commander who could have led Japanese forces in a much more effective defense. The Japanese did not suspect broken codes, but rather bad luck. There were many other lesser deceptions to come out of MAGIC. Knowledge of Japanese plans in many battles and preparations for battles enabled Allied forces to fight more effectively. MAGIC was particularly useful in the prosecution of the US submarine offensive against Japanese shipping. MAGIC intercepts indicated where valuable Japanese shipping would be, as well as the location of antisubmarine forces and other warships. Since subs depended on stealth and surprise for their success, MAGIC allowed US SUBMARINES to undertake their deceptions with maximum effectiveness and much less risk.

Ref: Boyd, *Hitler's Japanese Confidant*; Drea, *MacArthur's Ultra*; Lewin, *The American Magic*; Prados, *Combined Fleet Decoded*; Van Der Rhoer, *Deadly Magic*.

Mahan Class, US Destroyers

The largest interwar class of US destroyers (18 ships), the Mahans, built 1934–37, were ordered partially to stimulate the economy during the Great Depression. This was a useful "economy of force" measure employed by President F. D. ROOSEVELT to get some REARMAMENT money out of a penny-pinching and isolationist nation. They embodied many innovative ideas, including extreme high pressure boilers and a greatly enhanced TORPEDO complement, while reverting to the 5"/38 dual-purpose main battery of the FARRAGUT CLASS. They were very good ships (indeed, three more were built for Brazil) and very stable, taking the weight of numerous wartime upgrades to their antiaircraft capability with little difficulty. Six were lost in action.

Maizuru, Honshu

One of the four principal bases of the Imperial Navy, and the only one on the Sea of Japan, Maizuru specialized in the construction of destroyers and other light forces. It was the site of the Imperial Navy's Engineering Academy (candidates for line commissions went to Eta Jima, at KURE, while paymasters—whose duties included personnel and administrative matters—attended a third academy in Tokyo). It was also one of the four bases of the Special Navy Landing Force (SNLF).

Majuro, Marshall Islands

Despite a fairly extensive atoll, Majuro was of only limited importance on the eve of the war. Like most of the atolls in the area, its potential as a base was considerable. The Japanese neglected to fortify Majuro, and in January 1944 the United States just moved in, turning it into a forward base for operations elsewhere in the MARSHALL ISLANDS.

Makassar, Celebes, Netherlands East Indies

A small port, accessible to tramp steamers and coastal shipping, with some potential as a base for local control via small ships and long-range aircraft. It served as local Japanese headquarters from its capture in early 1942 until the end of the war.

Makatea, Society Islands

A useful atoll in the Society Islands, with no facilities of any sort. Strategically, its location on the northern edge of the archipelago made it of potential value if a threat were to develop from that direction. It remained in Allied hands throughout the war.

Makin, Gilbert Islands

A desolate island, with a British residence, a boat landing, and some shelter for ships, and room for a small airfield. Of value because it was one of the easternmost of the GILBERTS. It was raided by Marines on August 17–18, 1942 and occupied by US forces in late 1943.

See also CENTRAL PACIFIC CAMPAIGN; GILBERT ISLANDS; SMITHS, WAR OF THE.

Makin Island Raid, 1942

The US landing on GUADALCANAL on 7 August 1942 is rightly considered the first Allied offensive operation of the Pacific War. Ten days later, on August 17th, 221 US Marine "Raiders" landed on the Japanese-held island of Makin. The Marines, including Capt. James ROOSEVELT, the president's son, came ashore from *Argonaut* (SS-166) and *Nautilus* (SS-168), two of the largest SUBMARINES in the fleet (respectively 2,878 and 2,987 tons standard when surfaced). Aided by some of the local natives, and despite the intervention of Japanese aircraft summoned by radio from nearby islands, they destroyed a new seaplane reconnaissance base and killed most of the 90-man Japanese garrison,

including three men originally taken prisoner. The Marines lost 21 dead and 14 wounded. The island was quickly evacuated before Japanese reinforcements could arrive. Although some of the Marines—including Roosevelt—ended up staying on the island overnight, their final departure was in such haste that nine men were inadvertently left behind, and the Japanese murdered them.

The raid was mainly for propaganda purposes, although it did serve some military function. But the raid had an enormous impact on the subsequent fighting in the Pacific. The Japanese were alarmed at the vulnerability of dozens of similar island bases throughout the Pacific. The decision was made to increase the garrisons of these islands and to build the fortifications with which the Marines became so intimately acquainted during the rest of the war.

This was not the only case in which the Japanese reacted strongly to a minor American operation. The DOOLITTLE Raid (April 18, 1942, when 16 B-25 bombers flew from a carrier to bomb Japan) caused the Japanese to keep hundreds of combat aircraft in the Home Islands to prevent another attack, thereby greatly easing the plight of Allied forces elsewhere in the Pacific.

Malaya, Campaign for

The conquest of Malaya and its principal city, SINGAPORE, in February 1942 was one of the most spectacularly successful victories the Japanese were to achieve during World War II. Against a larger number of defending enemy infantry, and advancing 1,100 kilometers through jungle against a heavily fortified city, the Japanese emerged victorious in 55 days. It was a notable conquest, but one that resulted from serious misconceptions on both sides. The port of Singapore ("Lion City"), situated at the end of the Malay Peninsula and controlling the vital Straits of Malacca, had been a British possession since its founding in 1819. During the 1930s, Britain installed considerable coastal artillery and fortifications. But this was not as important as it appears. During the 1930s, naval warfare changed, with aircraft replacing large guns as the deciding weapon at sea. Moreover, Singapore was always defended by British control of the surrounding waters. Thus the key to the Japanese plan of conquest was to use superior airpower to control the seas around Singapore. This done, Japanese amphibious operations could proceed unhindered.

The Japanese troops had more combat experience and training than their British opponents, and were better led. But the Japanese underestimated the number of British troops they faced, while the British commander overestimated how many Japanese were attacking him. The Japanese also knew more about the British situation than the British knew of the Japanese invasion force. The Germans supplied copies of British strategic plans for Singapore and the Far East. They were obtained by a German U-boat commander from a British ship. HITLER expected Japan to declare war on Russia eventually, and provided support like this to ensure that such a declaration of war came to pass (it didn't.)

The British knew that Japanese combat units were on ships headed for Malaya in early December 1941. The British deployed their troops in the Malay Peninsula to confront any Japanese amphibious operations. Indeed, the British plan was to send one division into Thailand to disrupt Japanese operations if it came to war. An hour before the PEARL HARBOR attack, Japanese troops began landing in northern Malaya. Two Japanese divisions were coming by sea, while a third was marching overland through Thailand (which had agreed to allow passage of Japanese troops). Total Japanese troops sent into battle were about 100,000.

What the British did not know was how decisive Japanese aircraft would be. While the Japanese had available 560 modern combat aircraft, Britain was able to muster only 158 older and much less effective aircraft. Japanese planes quickly established air superiority. The British aircraft were destroyed within the first few days of the campaign. The British had two battleships operating out of Singapore, and these were promptly sunk by Japanese aircraft on 10 December. This was the first time that bat-

tleships under way at sea had been destroyed solely by air power. The British did not expect this, and had no way to counteract the resulting loss of sea control. On the other hand, even if Japanese aircraft had not sunk the two ships, there were enough Japanese battleships on call in the region to have done the job within a couple of days anyway, so that the Japanese would still have secured command of the seas. In any case, with HMSs *Prince of Wales* and *Repulse* gone, Malaya was wide open to invasion by sea. Japanese infantrymen were soon advancing down the Malay Peninsula, a 400-mile trek they would accomplish in six weeks against stiff opposition.

The British troops (one Indian, one Australian, and one mixed British/Malay division, plus some miscellaneous brigades) were generally new, inexperienced, and poorly trained. There were 138,700 of them, 38% more than the attacking enemy. Two of the Japanese divisions, the Fifth and 18th Infantry Divisions, had years of experience fighting in China, while the Imperial Guards Division, which had no combat experience, had undergone special training for Malaya. The Japanese were prepared, the British were not. The result was that British units were constantly out-fought and out-maneuvered during the fighting down the peninsula toward Singapore. The number of things the Japanese did right during this campaign and the number of things the British did wrong provide an interesting list of what it takes to win, or lose, a campaign.

Experienced troops. This is not always possible, as there isn't always a way to provide combat experience. But Japan had been fighting in China throughout the 1930s and was able to withdraw two experienced divisions from China for the invasion of Malaya. The third division used for the operation, the Imperial Guards Division, had no combat experience, but the troops were carefully selected for membership in that prestigious division and they were given extra jungle training before being sent into combat. Still, the other two combat experienced divisions, even without the special jungle training, did much better.

Engineer and logistics support. Knowing that the withdrawing forces would try to delay pursuit by destroying the bridges over Malaya's hundreds of rivers and streams, the attacking forces were given three independent engineer regiments, four bridging battalions, and seven bridging companies to supplement the engineer regiment each of the three divisions already had. Special exercises in early 1941 emphasized demolition and rebuilding of bridges. This attention to bridging paid off. River crossing and bridge repair units went with the forward elements all through the campaign and the ability to quickly get across river obstacles kept the British constantly off balance.

A railway rebuilding and maintenance brigade. This unit repaired and operated Malaya's main rail line, which ran north-south parallel to the Malay Peninsula's main hard-surface trunk road. There were also eight independent motor transport battalions and 10 independent motor transport companies. The railroad and truck units ensured that the advancing units did not have to halt because of a lack of fuel or ammunition. During the campaign's last act, the assault on Singapore Island, the supply units were able to provide the army's 440 artillery pieces with 1,000 rounds per field gun and 500 rounds per heavy gun. Once more, Japanese preparations had added speed to the assault and kept the British defense off balance.

Relentless pursuit of retreating units. The Japanese assumed that they would be able to defeat British units when they met them, but only speedy pursuit would prevent the British from fighting a lengthy delaying action that would increase Japanese losses. The Japanese rotated fresh units into the lead so that the troops fighting along the road would not tire and falter. Japanese tactics had their lead units spreading out from the road whenever they encountered resistance and moving quickly through the jungle to outflank the defenders. Once back on the road, the Japanese troops would want to move quickly to the next British position before the defenders could construct a well prepared defense. To this end, they equipped the infantry with 6,000 bicycles. The bicycles were a brilliant touch, for each bike could carry 60–80 pounds of equipment, food, and ammunition. The bikes could be walked across streams and past destroyed portions of the road. On the clear portions of the road the infantry on bicycles could move quickly, with units making over 20 kilometers an hour. The bicycle infantry, armed with rifles, grenades, and machine guns, would overcome small enemy units. Anything requiring more firepower might have to wait a few hours until the artillery and TANKS caught up. The bridging engineers enabled the tanks and truck-drawn artillery to keep up. British forces were unable to deal with any of these tactics and were repeatedly surprised at how hard it was to break contact as they fell back.

Tanks. While the Japanese were far behind the European nations in developing tanks, they did have them and used them to good effect in Malaya. Japan used two obsolescent tank models in Malaya, a light tank (with a 37mm gun) and a medium tank (with a 57mm gun). Although tanks could be used only on or near the one north-south road, and even though British forces had several effective antitank weapons, the Japanese tanks rampaged down the peninsula. Aggressive leadership by tank platoon commanders was the key. Junior lieutenants in several key engagements led a few tanks down the main road through the defenders, then pressed on without waiting for escorting infantry and shot up the defenders' rear areas. The tendency of junior armor officers to press on and exploit an initial breakthrough led to the rout of large British forces and cut weeks or months from the campaign. Timid use of tanks in Malaya would have made them practically useless.

The Japanese had one tank group of four regiments in Malaya. In effect, it was a tank division. Although the tank group was never used together as a single unit, it had over 200 tanks organized as follows:

ORGANIZATION OF THE 3RD TANK GROUP

Element	Medium Tanks	Light Tanks	Other MV
First Tank Regiment	37	20	91
Second Tank Regiment+	37	20	91
Sixth Tank Regiment	37	20	91
14th Tank Regiment	—	45	48
Tank Group Headquarters	5	5	(several)
Totals	116	110	321+

Other MV = Other motor vehicles. On January 29, 1942 this unit, less its light tank company, was sent to reinforce the units preparing to invade the Dutch East Indies.

The Japanese medium tank employed in Malaya was the Type 97 (1937), equipped with a 57mm low-velocity gun and two 7.7mm machine guns and had a crew of four. The light tank was the Type 95 (1935), mounting a short-barreled 37mm gun and one 7.7mm machine gun and had a crew of three. The armor on both tanks was quite light. The Type 95 tank could be shot up by heavy (12mm and up) machine guns. Both could easily be stopped by the standard British "2 pounder" (57mm) antitank gun.

The British had plenty of antitank guns and antitank MINES, but they did not use them properly. The antitank guns were largely organized into separate units that were constantly held in reserve while front-line units were overrun by Japanese tanks. The same was true of antitank mines; few were distributed to the front-line units. This was a command failure that, had it not occurred, would have made Japanese tanks much less effective.

Air force tactics. Making virtue of a necessity, Japanese combat aircraft did not operate in direct support of their ground units. The infantry and armor troops did not have enough radios to communicate with the aircraft and, because of all the jungle, it was difficult for pilots to tell friend from foe even if there was radio contact with the ground. So the Japanese initially used their qualitative and quantitative aircraft superiority to keep British aircraft out of action. After a week of pounding enemy air bases, Japanese fighters and bombers shifted much of their efforts to shooting up any British transport (road, rail, or sea) they spotted. This proved to be an excellent move, for the British found they could move safely only at night, while the Japanese could, and did, move around the clock.

Living off the land. Japanese forces traveled light. As a matter of policy, it was expected that enemy supplies and bases would be captured and immediately put to use. This was possible because of the high speed of the Japanese advance. In particular, several British air bases were overrun before they could be destroyed. In one case, the Japanese captured 100,000 gallons of aviation fuel. In several cases, Japanese aircraft were operating out of former British bases within 24 hours of capturing them, using British fuel and bombs. This allowed Japanese aircraft to operate closer to the fighting, making more sorties per day possible.

Amphibious operations. While we tend to think of World War II amphibious operations as US Marines storming ashore on some island, the more typical World War II example was putting a few hundred, or a few thousand, troops ashore on the mainland or on some large island. The Japanese had used these types of landings in China throughout the 1930s. The Japanese had a number of self-propelled 15-foot collapsible boats and 33-foot landing craft that were transported by truck and rail from southern Thailand to the west coast of Malaya right behind the advancing Japanese infantry. Along with a few boats captured on PENANG Island, this Japanese flotilla carried a reinforced infantry battalion of the Fifth Division (which had 20 years of experience with these landings) and made several landings behind the British front that disrupted the withdrawing enemy and made it easier to keep the Japanese advance moving. Later the Imperial Guards Division provided units for these landings and this led to the British abandoning Kuala Lumpur, the capital of the Federated Malay States. Thus, throughout the campaign the British had to worry about their open coastal flank.

One of the more decisive battles was on the Slim River, halfway down the Malay Peninsula and 80 miles north of Kuala Lumpur (the Malay capital). The British 11th Indian Division held the line with seven infantry battalions (three Indian, three Gurkha, and one British). On January 7, in a 24-hour battle starting shortly after midnight, one Japanese infantry regiment and less than 50 tanks took the 11th Indian Division apart. By the next day, only 1,150 of the troops in those seven infantry battalions were still available for action. The rest were dead, wounded, or for the most part either fleeing through the jungle or Japanese prisoners.

By the end of January, the Japanese were on the north shore of the narrow waterway that separates Malaya from Singapore Island. Despite the inevitability of the loss of Singapore, the British command insisted on pouring reinforcements into the island-city, including an entire new British division, the 18th. During the next two weeks, Japanese troops secured several beachheads on Singapore Island, and then fought their way toward the city, seizing the water reservoirs. At that point, with the Japanese beginning to penetrate the city itself, the British, deprived of drinking water, had no choice but to surrender. British losses were 8,000 killed in action and 130,000 taken prisoner, while Japanese dead totaled 10,000. Japan now possessed the best equipped port in Southeast Asia, complete with a system of coastal defense guns and shipyards that could repair any size ship.

The Japanese victory in Malaya had an enormous psychological impact on the British. For two years after this defeat, British commanders were extremely cautious, often overly cautious, in operations against the Japanese. In the longer term, the surrender of Singapore demonstrated to the local peoples that the Europeans were not invincible. This led to the rapid decolonialization of the region after the war.

Malaya, Federation of

Malaya is a peninsula about the size of Great Britain. For the most part covered by heavy jungles, its inhabitants were divided among native Malays, who were mostly Moslem, and Indians and Chinese who had settled there over the centuries. A British possession, Malaya was politically a federation of a number of semi-independent sultanates and several crown colonies.

It was rich in tin, as well as rubber and other tropical products, and the great port of Singapore was an important center of international commerce.

In 1941 the British were firmly in control. Although there was some nationalist sentiment among elements of the Malay population, the large Chinese and Indian communities were strongly committed to British rule.

The Japanese occupied Malaya in a swift campaign from December 1941 through February 1942, and ruthlessly exploited the country thereafter. By mid-1945, Allied—chiefly British—air raids and even naval raids were becoming common, in anticipation of a British plan to recover Malaya, with amphibious landings and an overland offensive from Siam, an operation that was scheduled to begin in late September.

Malaya, Resistance to the Japanese

This area, including SINGAPORE, was heavily garrisoned by the Japanese. A resistance movement sprang up anyway. GUERRILLA operations were most enthusiastically embraced by the Chinese population of Malaya, although there were also Malay and Indian (another local minority) guerrillas. The Chinese were the core of the resistance largely because of the depredations the Japanese were committing in China. The "overseas Chinese" maintained their language and traditions, as well as links with the homeland. Another item the Malay Chinese imported from China was communism, and the best disciplined partisans were communist led. Many native Malays and, to a lesser extent, Indians assisted the Japanese in fighting the guerrillas. This fighting continued after the war, when the Chinese communist guerrillas continued fighting. The British, like the Japanese, used Malay assistance to eventually put down the communist insurgency. This was something the Japanese were never able to do during the war. But the Japanese did manage to keep the guerrillas largely confined to the rural areas of Malaya.

Manchukuo

A Japanese puppet state established in 1932 comprising the region of Manchuria. From 1934 it was ostensibly ruled by Pu-yi, who as a boy had been deposed as the last emperor of China in 1911.

See also MANCHURIA.

Manchuria

The resource rich and industrially advanced northeastern regions of China, partially inhabited by the Manchu, a non-Chinese people who had given China its last imperial dynasty. In 1931 the Japanese invaded the region and set up the puppet "empire" of Manchukuo. Under Japanese rule, Manchuria was heavily exploited and settled by a surprisingly large number of Japanese, and even many migrants from China proper, who found peace under Japanese rule more attractive than the ongoing horrors of living in China. For most of the war it was a major training base for the Japanese Army, which maintained substantial forces there in anticipation of a Soviet invasion. Manchuria was more or less immune from the war, save for occasional bombing raids, until the Soviet Union invaded in August of 1945.

Manchuria, Campaign for, 1945

Japan and the Soviet Union had signed a non-aggression treaty in April 1941. But there was no love lost between the two, for Japan had defeated Russia in 1905 and taken a large chunk of Russian-controlled territory (actually, mostly Chinese territory that the Chinese were unable to control). The 1941 treaty was signed by the Japanese because they had found out, in several border battles during 1939, that they were outmatched by Soviet forces. The Soviets signed because they were preparing for a showdown with Germany and did not want any distractions in the Far East.

By 1945, the situation had changed. Over three years of war with America had left Japan weak. In May of 1945, Germany surrendered and the Soviet Union was free to use its armed forces elsewhere. In April 1945, Russia told Japan that the non-aggression treaty would not be renewed when it expired in April 1946. This led the Japanese to believe they were safe from a Soviet attack until that time. But in February 1945, Russia had promised its allies it would attack Japan three months after Germany surrendered. This promise was not made public. Germany surrendered on 8 May. It appeared that the Russian offensive would take place on or about 8 August 1945. It did.

A key factor in continued Japanese resistance was the forces Japan maintained in China and Manchuria. From early 1944 and into 1945, these forces had been on the offensive in China. The primary purpose of this fighting was to eliminate American air bases that could be used to bomb Japan, a moot point now that America had B-29 bases operating in the Mariana Islands. By the spring of 1945, Japanese forces deep inside China began to withdraw to Manchuria and Korea. Manchuria and Korea contained much of Japan's economic resources, as well as millions of Japanese colonists to see that the area stayed under Japanese control. Between the resources of Manchuria and Korea, and dogged resistance on the Japanese Home Islands, Japan felt it could keep fighting for years and eventually outlast the war-weary Allies. The key to all this was keeping the Russians from attacking. Diplomatic efforts to that end increased during 1945, but failed.

In early 1941 the Russians had 30 well equipped divisions in the Far East. This force contained 700,000 troops, 3,100 armored vehicles, and 4,100 combat aircraft. When Germany invaded in June of 1941, these divisions were quickly stripped of their best men and weapons and replaced, if at all, with less effective troops and equipment. For the rest of the war, the Russians used mainly older, younger, and less healthy local recruits to keep their Far East combat manpower at about one million troops. Artillery strength was increased, but armor strength averaged about 2,500 AFV and aircraft (mostly older models) strength fell to about 3,300. But once Germany was defeated, the Soviet troops went east again. Between May and August 1945, Russia sent 400,000 troops, 2,100 armored vehicles, and 17,000 trucks east. Combat aircraft strength was increased to some 4,600. By early August the Soviets had over 1.5 million troops (83 divisions) in the Far East. These were experienced soldiers who had defeated the Germans.

Japan's situation was rather less favorable. The army in Manchuria had 1.3 million troops, but a third of them were unreliable Korean and Chinese conscripts. These soldiers were organized into 37 infantry divisions and 40 independent regiments and brigades. There were only 1,200 TANKS, none of them anywhere near a match for Soviet armored vehicles. There were 1,900 Japanese combat aircraft available, and these matched Russian quality somewhat. But the Russians outnumbered the Japanese in the air two to one. Most of the Japanese troops were poorly trained and equipped. The best of them had been pulled back from China since June 1945. The Japanese had to defend a 4,500-kilometer front in Manchuria, and the math was against them. They had about 200 troops per kilometer of front and that wasn't going to be enough. Undaunted, the Japanese covered a thousand kilometers of this front with 17 fortified zones. This covered the routes that tanks were most likely to use. Some 8,000 bunkers and other fortifications were built in these zones. There was also a continuous series of bunkers and trenches along the entire border, but these were lightly manned and meant just to give a warning.

Although Japanese diplomats had noted the massive transfer of Russian combat units eastward since May 1945, Japan's leadership still thought they would be protected from a Russian attack until the non-aggression pact expired in April 1946. On August 8, 1945, Russia declared war on Japan.

Three Soviet Army groups invaded Manchuria and reached the Korean border in less than two weeks. Actually, a major part of the Russian attack took place on 6 August, as the Russian forces near the Pacific coast, faced with rather formidable Japanese defenses, got started early and achieved a high degree of surprise. Coming out of Mongolia and heading almost due east was the Russian Transbaikal Army Group, with 40 divisions, 654,000 troops and 2,400 tanks and assault guns, on a front of 580 kilometers. By August 14, units of this army group had advanced 250–450 kilometers into Japanese territory, making much headway once units were on the flat badlands of the Gobi Desert. By the end of August, this army group captured 220,000 Japanese troops. Next to the Transbaikal Army Group was the Second Far East Army Group, coming due south with 11 divisions, 337,000 troops and 1,200 armored vehicles, on a 480 kilometer front. By 14 August, units of this army group had advanced 50 to 200 kilometers through mountains and forests, and by the end of the month had captured 266,000 Japanese soldiers. Coming south along the Pacific coast was the First Far East Army Group with 32 divisions, 586,000 troops and 1,800 armored vehicles. By 14 August, units of this army group had advanced 120 to 150 kilometers and by the end of the month had captured 108,000 Japanese.

The Russian air force flew 14,000 combat sorties during August, and half as many noncombat sorties. Some 2,700 tons of bombs were dropped, plus 361 million cannon and a billion machine-gun rounds. Most of the Russian aircraft (2,497) were fighters, which, in addition to 808 ground attack aircraft and 1,364 bombers, spent most of their time pounding Japanese ground troops. The Japanese air force was swept from the skies during the first few days of the offensive. In support of parachute assaults, the 228 air force transports carried 16,000 troops, plus 4,800 tons of fuel, munitions, and other supplies.

RECORD COMBAT UNIT ADVANCES IN THE 20TH CENTURY

Force	War	Operation	Year	Advance	Duration	Rate
US 24th Inf.	Gulf	Iraq	1991	368 km.	4 days	92 km./day
British	WW I	Megiddo	1918	167 km.	3 days	56 km./day
Israeli	Six Day	Sinai	1967	220 km.	4 days	55 km./day
Russian	WW II	Manchuria	1945	300 km.	6 days	50 km./day
German	WW II	France	1940	368 km.	12 days	31 km./day
German	WW II	Russia	1941	700 km.	24 days	29 km./day
Allied	WW II	France	1944	880 km.	32 days	28 km./day

Note that smaller units have occasionally done even better over shorter periods.

It was surprise everywhere that hurt the Japanese the most. The Japanese generals mistakenly thought that the mountainous and wooded terrain along the border, as well as the immense size of Manchuria (500,000 square miles), would slow down the Russian attack. The combat-experienced Russian troops advanced over narrow mountain trails and through forests, avoiding the 17 Japanese fortified zones. For the most part, this shockingly fast advance paralyzed the Japanese troops on the border. Thus Russian armored units dashed past the border, leaving Japanese troops in their wake, to be captured or hunted down by following Soviet units.

But after a few days, resistance began to stiffen. Russian armored units were running out of fuel, and often had to halt and wait for supplies. Japanese units away from the border would barricade themselves within towns and fight it out to the last man. This type of resistance increased as the campaign went on. But the speed of the Russian advance made any kind of organized resistance useless. The Russian mechanized units were formidable, and these were the same units that had beaten the Germans at their own blitzkrieg game. The Japanese had nothing that could stop something like this, and only suicidal stubbornness with which to resist it.

Russian paratroopers landed on Japanese airfields to further paralyze resistance. After a week, Russian units were several hundred kilometers inside Manchuria. But the Russians were on a short leash because of resupply problems. It took them three weeks to traverse all of Manchuria (over 1,000 kilometers), and the Russians were unable to go much farther than Manchuria and northern Korea because of supply shortages. Most of the food and fuel for the troops had to come 4,500 miles over the Trans-Siberian Railroad. Nevertheless, the Russians did accomplish some record-breaking movement against armed opponents.

Although Japan announced its surrender on August 15, Japanese troops in Manchuria fought on for another week before their generals agreed to surrender. Even then, thousands of Japanese soldiers stayed in the woods, slowly making their way to the coast and what they hoped would be ships that would take them to Japan. Few ever got home.

The Soviet Union had ties to both major factions contending for primacy in China: the Nationalists and the Communists. Russia had signed a treaty with the Nationalists that called for the Soviets to evacuate Chinese territory within three weeks of the Japanese surrender. This the Russians did, but with a couple of twists. First, they left with all the industrial equipment they could carry off, and second, they gave most of the captured Japanese weapons to the Chinese communists. Meanwhile, the Chinese Red Army under Lin Piao took over villages and small towns, while CHIANG's Nationalist troops occupied the large cities in Manchuria. Chiang's Nationalist troops provided safe haven to Japanese civilians, which made great propaganda for the communists. Japanese civilians caught outside the safe havens were dealt with harshly by the Chinese. There were over 2 million Japanese civilians in Manchuria and many were never heard from again after 1945. Tens of thousands of Japanese refugees crossed the Yalu River trying to reach the ports farther south. Chinese mobs killed Japanese civilians by the thousands while many others died from starvation, disease, or exposure. Many more simply blended in with the local population.

On August 20, the Red Army moved into Korea. Within a week, Russian soldiers found themselves fighting Japanese stragglers moving down from Manchuria. The Japanese troops moved through the mountains, trying to reach the Sea of Japan and a ship for home. On August 24 Soviet troops occupied Pyongyang, the largest city in northern Korea, soon to become the capital of North Korea. On 1 September, the Korean People's Republic was established under Russian supervision. Russians also organized the roundup of Koreans who collaborated with the Japanese. Many were executed on the spot as crowds screamed "Kill the Jap lovers!" in reaction to 40 years of brutal Japanese occupation. On 8 September, US troops landed at CHEMULPO on the west coast. The US Military Government in Korea (USMGK) handed over police functions to former Japanese policemen. When word of this spread, nearly two million Koreans from the north (Japanese collaborators, landowners, Christians, and anti-communists) fled to South Korea.

There was a lot of settling of scores in the wake of the Manchurian Campaign. Hundreds of thousands of Japanese civilians, along with local collaborators, probably died from one cause (execution) or another (privation). The military costs were not that great, considering the size of the forces involved. Some two and a half million Russian and Japanese troops were in the area. There were another million Chinese troops who closed in as the campaign wound down and even Americans showed up toward the end. But the Soviets lost only 8,000 dead, one of their less bloody victories in World War II. Some 80,000 Japanese troops

were killed in the fighting, plus many more Japanese civilians. Some 600,000 Japanese were taken prisoner, and nearly 100,000 of these died in captivity (the rest were returned to Japan from labor camps in Russia, in the 1950s).

See also KURILE ISLANDS.

Ref: DuPuy, *Great Battles of the Eastern Front*; Glantz, *August Storm*.

Mandalay, Burma

Although possessed of some facilities as a river port, Mandalay's chief importance lay in the fact that it dominated central Burma. As such it was the principal objective of the Japanese invasion of Burma in 1942 and the British counteroffensive of 1944.

Mandates

Prior to World War I, the Caroline, MARSHALL, and Mariana Islands (save for GUAM, which belonged to the United States) were owned by Germany, which had bought them from Spain in 1898. In 1914 the Japanese moved in. In the early 1920s the League of Nations assigned the islands to Japan as a "mandate." Under the terms of a league mandate, the mandatory power was required to promote local development with the ultimate intention of granting independence. There were actually three classes of mandates, of which the Pacific mandates fell into the lowest, on the assumption that they were so backward they would take generations to become self-governing. The phrase "the Mandates" became commonplace when referring to the islands mandated to Japan. Various members of the British Commonwealth also held mandates over other former German territories in the Pacific Northeast New Guinea, the Solomon Islands, NAURU, and SAMOA—but these were not included in the phrase "the Mandates."

The Mandates are very small places, spread over an enormous amount of water. Together with the GILBERT ISLANDS and Guam, the Mandates totaled only some 2,100 square miles, spread across about three million square miles of ocean. The MARIA-

NAS are the largest group in surface area, about 700 square miles, of which Guam is slightly more than 200 square miles.

During and after World War II it was common to accuse the Japanese of having violated the league mandate and the naval DISARMAMENT TREATIES by fortifying the Mandates. However, the islands were regularly subjected to inspection until Japan withdrew from the league in 1936, and it is now clear that the Japanese did not begin to develop military installations in the islands until after that date, albeit that they technically forfeited their mandate by doing so.

Manila Bay, Luzon, Philippines

Including not only Manila, but also CAVITE and several other small ports, Manila Bay was a major commercial port with an extensive sheltered anchorage and extensive facilities to service shipping. There was also a small but well equipped US naval base at Cavite, and several important air bases in the area. The war left this area devastated.

Manpower, the Division Slice

Although the division is the principal combat formation of an army, it represents a relatively small proportion of an army's total strength. For example, at peak strength the US Army totaled some nine million men and women in World War II, of whom about two-thirds were in the Army Ground Forces or the Army Service Forces. The 89 divisions—68 infantry, 5 airborne, and 16 armored—in the army averaged about 13,800 men each. This totals only about 1.2 million men. The balance were helping to keep the front-line troops fighting.

For each division there were:

In the division itself, 13,800 men (on average) plus another 13,000 men in combat support and service units, 10,000 men in communications zone troops, and 20,000 men in miscellaneous status.

Combat support and service units provided extra artillery fire, engineer services, tank support, medical aid, and the like to the front-line troops, sometimes being on the front lines themselves.

Communications zone troops were the men and women (nurses, clerks) behind the front, who helped pass the ammunition and run the hospitals, as well as guard rear area installations, plus replacements, hospital patients, and the like. Miscellaneous status included troops in the United States in training, hospitals and headquarters personnel, and so forth.

Adding these troops to the division's brings the total up to about 56,800 men per division. This is referred to as a "division slice," the total number of troops in and supporting each division, all the way back to those in the recruiting stations back home. The US Army had the highest division slice in the war, partly because of its propensity for consuming enormous quantities of supplies, and partially because the Army Service Forces also supported Army Air Forces operations. In fact, if one includes the Army Air Forces, the US division slice rises to nearly 100,000.

The division slice varied by theater. That for troops in the Central Pacific was higher than that for those in the ETO. The six army divisions that took part in operations in the Central Pacific Theater had a division slice of about 76,000: 17,000 in the division, plus 28,000 in combat support and service units, and 11,000 in communications zone service forces, plus 20,000 in the United States.

The 60-odd divisions in Europe had a division slice of only about 60,000 men: 15,000 with the divisions (the 16 armored divisions were only about 60% the size of infantry divisions, and the airborne divisions even smaller), 15,000 in combat support and service units, 10,000 in communications zone forces, plus 20,000 in the United States.

Several other armies had problems with a burgeoning division slice. Initially, the Australian division slice was quite small, only 34,000 in the first half of 1942. However, during its mobilization in 1939–42, Australia had invested an inordinate amount of its manpower in combat units. A major part of these units served under British command in North Africa (Sixth, Seventh, and Ninth Divisions) and MALAYA (Eighth Division), and were supported by British combat support and service troops. The balance of the Australian divisions were serving in garrison in Australia into mid–1942, and thus needed little in the way of specialized support and service troops. Once the divisions in British service came home (less the eighth, lost at SINGAPORE) and, together with those at home, began to ship out to New Guinea and other operational theaters, Australia had to find support and service personnel for them. By mid–1945 the Australian division slice was 60,000.

The Japanese were very frugal with their division slice, preferring to put as many troops as possible in the front line. Early in the Pacific War it seems to have been as low as 25,000. Operationally, this proved to be a wasteful policy in the Pacific, as the troublesome geography and climate caused unsupported troops to waste away quickly in combat, which happened to the Japanese time after time. As the war went on the Japanese increased their division slice, until in the last year it was about 32,000 men, if one included the Imperial Army Air Force.

It's worth noting that the 173 divisions that Japan had, at least on paper, at the time of its surrender, amounted to only about as many combat troops as the 95 US divisions (89 army and 6 Marine) in existence at the time.

Ref: Greenberg, *The Ineffective Soldier*.

Manus, Admiralty Islands

A large island, with a modest anchorage and no port facilities. On paper, Manus was of great potential strategic value, being about 300 miles north of New Guinea and the same west of the BISMARCKS. It played a significant role in Operation CARTWHEEL and the NEW GUINEA campaign.

Mao Tse-tung (1893–1976)

Mao came from a prosperous peasant family in Hunan. He received an excellent traditional education but left school in 1911 to join Sun Yat-sen's revolutionary army. Discharged after about six months, Mao pursued a higher education, worked for a time as a librarian, and in 1921 helped found the Chinese Communist Party. For a time associated with the KOUMINTANG Party, Mao broke decisively with CHIANG KAI-SHEK in the late '20s and became a notable organizer and leader of GUERRILLA forces, and also an important theoretician of guerrilla warfare. Over the next 20 years Mao led communist forces in an on-again, off-again war against Chiang's Nationalist, pausing occasionally to fight the Japanese as well. After World War II the civil war resumed, to be concluded with a communist victory in 1949.

Maps

There were no reliable maps for many of the areas over which World War II was fought in Asia and the Pacific. Some regions, such as much of New Guinea, Burma, and BORNEO, had never been properly mapped. Others had been mapped years before, such as the Philippines, which were formally surveyed before World War I. So bad was the shortage of accurate maps and charts, that it was not uncommon for US forces in the South Pacific to operate with maps marked "U.S. Ex. Ex." This stood for the "United States Exploration Expedition," a major scientific survey conducted under the command of Lt. Charles Wilkes, USN, from 1838 to 1842. (Wilkes was later more famous for his precipitation of the "Trent Affair" during the Civil War; his great-grandson, RAdm John Wilkes, played a major role in the Normandy Invasion.) In the case of the BISMARCKS and SOLOMONS, despite several generations of German and British rule, many maps were barely updated versions of those produced by Bougainville, d'Entrecasteaux, La Perouse, Shortland, and other 18th century explorers. Needless to say, the available maps were often extremely inaccurate: To cite but one example, six different charts of Bougainville gave six different longitudes and latitudes for Cape Torokina, on the southwestern coast, not one of which was correct.

As the war went on, new maps were prepared and distributed and the situation improved. In addition to making use of traditional survey techniques, which could work only if a place was occupied by friendly personnel, cartographers employed a variety of innovative techniques in making new maps. Aerial photography using stereoscopic techniques was the principal tool used. However, since interpretation of the photographs was often difficult, the technique was supplemented in a variety of ways. Intelligence officers interviewed people who had visited or resided in the places being mapped, and also perused diaries, memoirs, and ship's logs. In some cases, SUBMARINES were used to survey coastal areas. On-site reconnaissance was also sometimes performed, with men landed from submarines to conduct investigations, often at some personal risk.

Initially, raw data was processed in the Pacific, and the resulting maps were then reproduced and distributed. It was later found to be more efficient, and the resulting product more accurate, if the data—and in some cases appropriate individuals—were shipped to Washington, to be processed by an increasingly efficient Hydrographic Office, which relied on hundreds of draughtsmen, or more often draughtswomen, to produce master maps. These maps could then be reproduced in the United States or in Australia, for final distribution.

One of the most interesting innovations during World War II was the preparation of three-dimensional maps and physical models of enemy-held islands. These were used to assist navy gunners and pilots to locate their assigned targets, and Marines and infantrymen to "see" up close what the ground would be like when they hit the beaches. Such maps and models were particularly popular with airmen, who were wont to "fly" their hands over them so that they could get a "feel" for the hills and valleys over which they would shortly be flying for real. By 1945, these relief maps and models had become a regular feature of island assaults. Even destroyers were supplied with them. This made sense, as destroyers often delivered vital fire support. Destroyers, because they drew less water,

could get in closer and provide more immediate support with their five-inch (127mm) guns.

Marcus Island

Although it possessed no port facilities, not even an anchorage, Marcus was valuable to the Japanese as a forward air base, since reconnaissance aircraft based there could reach far into the central Pacific, being located about 800 miles east of IWO JIMA and 1,200 northwest of WAKE ISLAND.

In practical terms Marcus figured small in the global conflict. Its only offensive use by the Japanese occurred in late 1941, when reconnaissance aircraft based there took part in the Wake Island operation. Otherwise, save for an occasional raid by the Pacific Fleet, including one in March 1942 during which the island was worked over by carrier aircraft and heavy cruiser gunfire, Marcus was bypassed during the war. By early 1945 the island was completely isolated, and the garrison suffered considerable privation, with outright starvation averted only by the Japanese surrender.

Marianas, Campaign for

Also known as the "Ladrones" ("Thieves") Islands, the Marianas are a chain of islands in the western Pacific Ocean, about 1,400 miles south of Japan. The total land area is less than 700 square miles, of which 200 comprise GUAM proper. The other two large islands, SAIPAN and TINIAN, account for nearly half of the rest of the land area. Inhabited by Micronesians, the islands were for centuries Spanish, but Guam was taken by the United States in 1898, and the balance sold to Germany, which lost them to Japan in 1914, after which they became part of the MANDATES. A great many Japanese settled in the islands before World War II.

The Allies' GILBERTS and MARSHALLS campaigns were largely preliminaries for the capture of the Marianas, the main goal of the CENTRAL PACIFIC CAMPAIGN. By capturing islands in the Marianas, the B-29 bombers just entering service would have bases from which to bomb Japan's cities and ports. This bombing campaign would either end the war or pave the way for the final act: the invasion of Japan itself.

It was understood that the Marianas campaign would involve some of the bloodiest fighting of the war. The islands to be invaded were larger and more heavily defended than any in the Gilberts or Marshalls. Even though the Japanese bases in the CAROLINES (to the south) were to be stripped of their aircraft and isolated, Japan was expected to use most of its remaining warships and aircraft to defend the Marianas. And they did.

Of the 15 Mariana Islands, stretching in a 435-mile arc in the central Pacific, only four were large enough, and in the right location, to be useful as B-29 bases. These were Saipan, Tinian, Rota, and Guam.

In late February 1944, right after TRUK had been blasted into ineffectiveness, American warships steamed into the Marianas for the first time since Guam had fallen to the Japanese in late 1941. Their purpose was to bomb Japanese bases and scout. Recon aircraft went in and took a lot of pictures, for the assault on these islands would take place in four months.

By early June, 535 American ships were closing in on the Marianas. They came from HAWAII, 3,500 miles distant, and from the forward base at ENIWETOK, a thousand miles away. On board were 127,000 combat troops, most of them Marines. Starting on 11 June, carrier aircraft hit Saipan. On June 13 the battleships closed in and bombarded. On June 15 two Marine divisions (the Second and Fourth) hit Saipan. The Japanese garrison of 29,000 troops was dug in and cut off from reinforcement. It would be another fight to the death.

While the land battle was under way, Japan sent out what was left of its fleet. Nine carriers, 46 other warships, and 473 aircraft went up against a US force of 15 carriers, 97 other warships, and 956 aircraft. While outnumbered in quantity and quality of warships, the Japanese had a few advantages. The naval Battle of the PHILIPPINE SEA (the area just to the west of the Marianas) was fought within range of Japanese island air bases and land-based

aircraft. While US carriers had earlier destroyed most Japanese land-based aircraft, more were always being brought in. Japanese carrier aircraft had a longer range than their American counterparts (560 to 350 miles for searching and 300 to 200 miles for attack).

From June 19 to 21 the naval battle raged. The Japanese were decisively beaten and lost three carriers and 480 aircraft. The United States lost no ships and a hundred aircraft, nearly half of those from running out of fuel on their way back from the last strike on the retreating Japanese.

The ground combat on Saipan went on to the end of June, with the army's 27th Infantry Division brought in on June 20 to expedite matters. The result was the usual one. Only about 1,800 of the 29,000-man Japanese garrison were taken prisoner. The rest died, along with 3,426 Americans from the three divisions eventually sent into the battle. Thousands of Japanese civilians, also perished, mostly by suicide.

On 21 July Guam was invaded by the Third Marine Division, the army's 77th Infantry Division, and, as a later reinforcement, by the First Marine Brigade. The 11,000-man Japanese garrison died, along with 1,435 Americans.

Tinian was invaded on July 24 by the Second and Fourth Marine Divisions and taken in seven days. Nearly all of the 8,000-man Japanese garrison perished, along with 389 Americans. Rota was left in Japanese hands, isolated and starving.

The Marianas campaign was over by mid-August of 1944. The Japanese carrier fleet was broken, although surviving battleships and cruisers would make suicide raids over the next year. More importantly, airfields for B-29s were under construction in the Marianas through the summer of 1944. By the fall of that year, American bombers would appear over Japanese cities in large numbers.

Marine Corps, US

For most of the nation's history the Marines were a very small force. So small, in fact, that until a provisional Marine battalion landed at Guantanamo Bay in Cuba on 10 June 1898, during the Spanish-American War, most Americans had never even heard of the Marine Corps. Up until that time, US Marines had served as shipboard specialists, much like marines in the world's other major navies for the last few centuries. Of course, the Marines also occasionally provided provisional battalions for service ashore. Usually the Marines did well in this business. Thus, a detachment of Marines (eight of them, plus a Marine officer and a Navy midshipman) helped storm Derna, in North Africa, on April 26, 1805 ("... To the shores of Tripoli ..."). A brigade of Marines and sailors were the only American troops who didn't run at the Battle of Bladensburg, on August 24, 1814, a disgraceful affair that resulted in the British capture of Washington. A battalion of Marines helped storm Mexico City on September 13, 1847 ("From the halls of Montezuma ..."). It wasn't all glory, however, as Marines did leave the field precipitously at Bull Run on July 21, 1861, an incident about which General VANDEGRIFT once said that the Marines must surely have been the last troops to flee the field.

Normally, Marines were organized as "detachments" on ships and at navy yards, only occasionally being formed into units of company-size and larger, on an ad hoc basis.

In 1911 all Marines not assigned to ships were formed into companies of 103 men (identical to US Army companies of that time). These companies were then organized into battalions (three companies) or regiments (10 companies) as needed. The cause of this reorganization was the Marines' fear of recurring bureaucratic and political efforts to abolish them by the army, and occasionally the navy. Thus the Marines began to seek a greater role for themselves than merely keeping order on warships, guarding naval bases, and occasionally landing in some remote place to "teach the natives a lesson." The Marines saw opportunities with the recent adoption of what became known as War Plan Orange, which envisioned the fleet advancing across the Pacific in the event of a war

with Japan. To effect such an advance islands would have to be occupied to serve as bases.

Although the Marines had previously never raised anything larger than a provisional regiment, quite early it was clear that the necessity of seizing islands from the Japanese as the fleet advanced across the Pacific in accordance with War Plan Orange would require the services of division-sized formations. As early as 1913 the Marines began to prepare for their role in War Plan Orange, creating the Advance Base Force. This was organized and trained to make amphibious landings. Over the years it did so several times, notably at Vera Cruz, in MEXICO, in Haiti, and in the Dominican Republic.

Still, on the eve of World War I the Marine Corps numbered only 13,700 men. During World War I the Corps grew rapidly, reaching 75,000 by late 1918. Two Marine brigades, about 25,000 men, served with the AEF in France. The Fourth Marine Brigade formed part of the Second Infantry Division, accumulating a distinguished record (Belleau Wood, for example). The other Marine brigade arrived later and, despite the efforts of Marine brass to create a Marine division, was used for rear-area security. After the Great War, the Corps was cut back to about 17,000 men. But the Advance Base Force, which had been redesignated a brigade, continued to exist, effecting occasional interventions but more importantly serving as a testbed for the development of amphibious doctrine, going through several name changes. Meanwhile, during the 1920s a regular Marine infantry regimental organization was developed. This was a small unit of only about 1,500 men.

The Marine Corps stayed small until the 1930s, when expansion began. On 1 February 1941 the Marines activated their first two divisions. By the end of the war they would have six.

As originally organized in 1941, a Marine division was quite similar to the army's contemporary infantry division. There were three rifle regiments of three battalions each, plus an artillery regiment (three battalions of 75mm guns and one of

105mm), plus supporting elements of reconnaissance, engineer, signal, service, and medical (supplied by the navy) troops. In addition, there were some formations specialized in amphibious warfare, like a US Navy "Beach and Shore" Battalion, to help get the troops ashore, and a "Defense" Battalion, intended to provided protection against attack from the sea and into a beachhead's rear.

A lot of changes in divisional organization took place even before the First Marine Division landed on GUADALCANAL on August 7, 1942. By then the on-paper 19,300 men of a Marine division had been reinforced by a tank battalion, a Navy Seabee battalion, and a 155mm artillery battalion, while the riflemen received an increased allocation of mortars (162) and light artillery (54 37mm anti-tank guns).

Although the basic organization of the division remained more or less unchanged for the rest of the war, equipment allocations continued to evolve, particularly in terms of automatic and semiautomatic weapons. By mid-1944 the division had over 16,000 M1 carbines or M1 rifles, 625 machine guns, and 45 submachine guns, not counting machine guns on TANKS and LVTs.

The Marines learned the hard way how useful it was to have many automatic weapons. When they first had to confront the reckless abandon of Japanese BANZAI attacks on Guadalcanal (1942), the Marines had to improvise. Some automatic weapons (machine guns and automatic rifles) were taken from all units and kept as a reserve in several trucks. When the signs of an imminent Japanese attack were detected (the Japanese were not always as stealthy as they could have been when preparing an attack), the trucks full of automatic weapons would be rushed to the threatened area and the troops promptly equipped with the needed additional firepower.

Although the number of mortars and 37mm guns fell slightly (to 153 and 36 respectively), the troops were lavishly provided with antitank rocket launchers (over 1,700) and flamethrowers, which had proven useful in "bunker busting."

As Marine Corps combat doctrine evolved, it was decided that each division should have an air wing associated with it (72 aircraft of various types) to provide air defense, ground support, and reconnaissance. In practice, however, only three air wings were fully formed and a fourth partially, so the "marriage" between ground and air elements was not as close as the Marine brass wished it to be, and Marines were often supported by navy airmen. On their own scale of evaluation, the Marine riflemen believed air support provided by Marines was best, followed by the navy, with the USAAF a distant third. There was something besides pride at work in this ranking. All Marine officers, including pilots, were trained as infantrymen. So Marine pilots supporting infantrymen were much more effective. Since these Marines trained the navy men in ground support, they were also pretty good. The Army Air Corps usually didn't want anything to do with ground support missions, and performed them only reluctantly, and thus with somewhat less effectiveness.

The Marines had the distinction of having most of the commando units in the Pacific. The army had formed six Ranger battalions, mostly for service in Europe, organized on the British model. The army Ranger units were not as successful as was hoped, and neither were their Marine counterparts in the Pacific. As good as these troops were, and they were very good, they were not supermen. Most of the fighting in the war required good infantry, not handpicked, highly trained COMMANDOS. The Marine commando units included several battal-

MARINE CASUALTIES IN WORLD WAR II	
Combat deaths	19,733
Wounds not mortal	67,207
Other deaths	4,778
*Prisoners of war	348
Total	92,066

*The prisoners of war figure omits c. 1,400 Marines captured by the Japanese in China in December 1941 and on Corregidor in May 1942.

STRENGTH OF THE MARINE CORPS			
Year	Officers	Enlisted	Total
1940	1,800	26,545	28,345
1941	3,339	51,020	54,359
1942	7,138	135,475	142,613
1943	21,384	287,139	308,523
1944	32,788	442,816	475,604
1945	37,067	437,613	474,680
1946	14,208	141,471	155,679

ions of "Raiders" and "Paramarines" (see MARINE CORPS, US, RAIDER BATTALIONS and MARINE CORPS US, PARAMARINES), but these were later disbanded and incorporated into the Sixth Marine Division.

The Marine Corps was a rather well-integrated force by the end of the war. There were many BLACK AMERICAN riflemen in its ranks by V-J Day. The Marines also used NAVAHO-speaking troops to provide a form of "code" the Japanese could not break. Many Japanese-speaking Japanese Americans also served in the ranks as translators. Both Navaho and Japanese-American Marines had to be provided with special bodyguards, lest over-enthusiastic white Marines think they were enemy infiltrators, not to mention the necessity of preventing the capture of the Navahos by Japanese troops, since as communications personnel they knew quite a bit more than the average Marine.

In the 50 years since World War II, Marine Corps strength has never fallen below 150,000 troops. This, incidentally, was the size of the entire US Army in the late 1930s.

Ref: Heinl, *Soldiers of the Sea*; *History of United States Marine Corps Operations in World War II*; Sherrod, *History of Marine Corps Aviation in World War II*; Wood, *Fourth Marine Division*.

Marine Corps, US, Defense Battalions

Recognizing that isolated island outposts would need to be defended and beachheads protected from enemy attack by sea, long before PEARL HARBOR the Marine Corps created a number of specialized battalions of varied organization, tailored to the peculiar defense needs of particular islands. In effect, defense battalions were portable coast defense organizations. Altogether, 20 defense battalions were raised by the end of 1943, including two composed primarily of black personnel, and 18 of them saw active service in the Pacific. However, as the nature of the war changed, the need for the defense battalions passed. By mid-1944 only four remained on active duty, and only three by the end of the war.

Although there was no "typical" defense battalion, they usually ran about a thousand men, and had five or more companies. The companies were a mix of coast defense batteries, with 5-inch guns, antiaircraft batteries, 3-inch guns or automatic weapons, a couple of rifle companies, and a service element. Depending upon circumstances, a defense battalion occasionally found itself with one or two tank platoons, and occasionally even with a few combat aircraft. The more notable defense battalions were:

First Defense Battalion. Some of the battalion was at Pearl Harbor on December 7, 1941, with substantial elements on JOHNSTON ISLAND and Palmyra, and about 40% was under Maj. James Devereaux (who later served many years in the Senate) on WAKE ISLAND, where it put up an heroic defense, its 5-inch guns accounting for a Japanese destroyer.

Third Defense Battalion. Beginning the war at Pearl Harbor, and serving later on MIDWAY during the June battle, the Third Battalion held the beaches for the First Marine Division on GUADALCANAL, and went on to fight on BOUGAINVILLE.

Ninth Defense Battalion. Joining the Third on Guadalcanal in late 1942, the Ninth took part in the New Georgia operation, and then fought on GUAM.

Ref: *History of United States Marine Corps Operations in World War II*.

Marine Corps, US, Divisions and Other Notable Formations

Although some Marines had lobbied to create a Marine Division during World War I, Marine divisions were first seriously projected in War Plan Orange shortly after World War I, once it became obvious that the movement of the fleet across the Pacific would require amphibious assaults on Japanese-held islands. Aside from some theoretical planning on the basis of experience derived from exercises, no actual divisions were raised until early 1941. Note that the figures on divisional CASUALTIES found below can be better appreciated if you keep in mind that most of them took place in the 18,000–man division's nine infantry battalions, each of which contained about 600 actual infantry (or other specialists always at the front). Divide the casualties by 10 to get a rough idea of how many losses the 600 infantry in each of these infantry battalions took: A third of the troops were taking most of the casualties. Many troops were wounded more than once. In the course of the war, some battalions had to replace nearly all their infantry at least once because of incapacitating wounds and deaths.

First Marine Division. The division was activated in February 1941 from a brigade of prewar regulars, the "Old Breed." These were very good men, since the Corps could be highly selective during the Depression. When war came, the division was filled out and dispatched to the South Pacific, to be "bloodied" on GUADALCANAL, where it made a legend of itself reclaiming the first territory from the Japanese. After surviving that, it fought in eastern New Guinea and NEW BRITAIN, serving alongside army units in the unglamorous jungle fighting that characterized the war in the southwest Pacific (where they received little press coverage, it being General MACARTHUR'S bailiwick).

In September 1944, the division finally got a chance to make the kind of amphibious landing that the Marines made famous in the Pacific. Unfortunately, they were sent against PELELIU, a heavily fortified island southeast of the Philippines. The resistance was greater than anyone expected, and the terrain totally unlike anything the troops were prepared for. The result was a hard-fought battle. To make matters worse, it was later realized that Peleliu could have been bypassed. Later, the division ended its Pacific career in the OKINAWA assault in April 1945. This turned into a three-month slugging match, one of the most grueling island assaults of the Pacific War. Overall, the First Marine Division had a hard time of it in the Pacific. At war's end it was earmarked for the projected invasion of Honshu in early 1946. Three weeks after the surrender of Japan, the First Marine Division was transferred to northern China on occupation duty. It returned to the United States in 1947. Casualties for the war totaled 19,284, of whom 5,435 (28.2%) were killed in action or died of their wounds. The First Marine Division had the highest losses of any US division—army or Marines—in the Pacific. Although eight divisions in the ETO suffered equal or greater losses—First, Third, Fourth, Ninth, 29th, 36th, 45th, and 90th—only one had a greater number of men killed in action. Eighteen men in the division received the MEDAL OF HONOR.

Second Marine Division. Although it was also formed in February of 1941, the First Division got priority on men and equipment and went into action first. The Second Division relieved the battered First on Guadalcanal during late 1942 and worked with army troops to finish running the Japanese out. With the Guadalcanal campaign over in early 1943, the division was withdrawn for retraining. Thus prepared, it mounted the first genuine Marine Corps amphibious assault at TARAWA, in November 1943. After this tough fight, the division had to be rebuilt and retrained for the SAIPAN invasion during June of 1944. Right after that it went on to storm TINIAN during July of 1944. In April 1945, the division ended its Pacific War career with the attack on Okinawa, in April 1945. Had it become necessary to invade Japan, the division would have formed part of the V Amphibious Corps during Operation Olympic in November 1945. The Second Marine Division served on occupation duty in Japan until early 1946, when it returned to the United States. Casualties totaled 11,482, including 2,729 combat deaths (23.8%). Eight men won the Medal of Honor

Third Marine Division. Activated in September 1942 from drafts made on the veteran First and Second Marine Divisions, the first case in which these divisions became "parents." About 40% of the men in each succeeding Marine division were drawn from the combat-seasoned veterans of the older outfits, a much higher margin of experienced troops than was the norm in most army divisions. The division had its first combat experience longside army troops in the SOLOMONS (BOUGAINVILLE) during 1943. Its first real island invasion was at GUAM, in 1944. Its final assault was against IWO JIMA in February 1945. Thereafter the division was on Guam, preparing for its role in Operation Olympic, as part of the V Amphibious Corps. By the time the division was inactivated, on Guam at the end of 1945, nearly 40,000 men had served in its ranks. Total casualties were 8,676, of whom 1,932 (22.3%) were battle-related deaths. Nine men earned the Medal of Honor

Fourth Marine Division. The division was formed in August 1943 by splitting up the already formed Third Marine Division and drawing veterans from the First and Second Divisions. It first saw action in February 1944 against Roi-Namur islands in KWAJALEIN. After receiving replacements and more training, it went on to invade Saipan and Tinian during the summer of 1944. Finally, the division participated in the assault on Iwo Jima in February 1945. The end of the war found the division preparing for its role in Operation Coronet, the proposed invasion of Honshu in early 1946. The division was inactivated in California in November 1945. It had been in combat only 63 of the 835 days since its activation. Casualties totaled 16,323, including 3,317 (20.3%) men killed in action or died of their wounds. Twelve men with the

division won the Medal of Honor. There were also 111 Navy Crosses, 646 Silver Stars, and 2,517 Bronze Stars.

Fifth Marine Division. Formed in January 1944, the Fifth Division participated in the Iwo Jima assault during February 1945. At the end of the war the division was preparing to take part in Operation Olympic as part of the V Amphibious Corps. After a brief tour of occupation duty in Japan, it returned to the United States, where it was inactivated in early 1946. Casualties were 8,563, including 2,113 (24.7%) battle-related deaths. Seventeen men won the Medal of Honor.

Sixth Marine Division. Although the Sixth Marine Division was formed in August 1944, and its only combat as a division was during the Okinawa Campaign in April–June 1945, most of its component elements had seen combat and had unusual histories. The Fourth Marine Regiment (see also, below) had been formed from the old Raider Battalions, which had seen action on Makin, Guadalcanal, and Bougainville in 1942–43. The regiment served as an independent unit in the occupation of Emirau Island, and as part of the First Provisional Marine Brigade on Guam in June of 1944. A second regiment, the 22nd, raised in early 1942, had occupied ENIWETOK Atoll in the MARSHALL ISLANDS as an independent unit, and at Guam was also part of the First Provisional Marine Brigade. The third regiment, the 29th, was newly formed, but one battalion, the First had seen action on Saipan as an independent unit. As a result, the cadre of the division was unusually well seasoned. The end of the war found the division preparing to participate in the March 1946 invasion of Honshu. The division's Fourth Marines was the first US unit to take up occupation duties in Japan, landing at Yokosuka on August 29. The division served on occupation duty in Japan for a short time, and then was transferred to support the First Marine Division in China, arriving in October 1945. The division was inactivated in China in April 1946. Casualties for the division as a whole, excluding losses by component units before the division was formed,

Gunners of the 14th Marines, Fourth Marine Division, shelling Japanese positions on Iwo Jima, February 1945. The littered position suggests that their 105mm howitzer has seen heavy use. The man on the left appears to be leaning on a tractor, the one on the right is removing a shell from its packaging.

totaled 8,227, of whom 1,637 (19.9%) were battle-related deaths. Two men won the Medal of Honor.

Fourth Marine Regiment. For many years stationed in Japanese-occupied SHANGHAI, the Fourth Marines was transferred to the Philippines in November of 1941. At the time it had only 800 men, the Corps letting it run down to that figure rather than risk losing more men in China should war break out. In the Philippines it was beefed up to about 1,200 men through the assignment of Marines from CAVITE and other naval installations. Although a well-trained, well-equipped outfit (it had M1 rifles rather than Springfields), the regiment spent the entire PHILIPPINE campaign on

CORREGIDOR, MacArthur disliking Marines. As a result, it was surrendered to the Japanese after being only lightly engaged. The regiment was re-formed in February 1944 from the old Marine Raiders (see Sixth Marine Division, above).

Ref: Heinl, *Soldiers of the Sea; History of United States Marine Corps Operations in World War II;* Wood, *Fourth Marine Division.*

Marine Corps, US, "Paramarines"

The Marine Corps became interested in creating a parachute element in 1940. By April of 1943 there were four battalions of "paramarines," three of which were fighting in the South Pacific as part of the First Marine Parachute Regiment. But by then the Marine brass had decided that "paramarines" were an unnecessary expense. Although the troops had performed well in combat, they never once made use of the parachute skills: All of the missions they performed could easily have been done by regular Marines. In December 1943 the First Marine Parachute Regiment was shipped to SAN DIEGO, where it was disbanded. In January of 1944 the paramarines were disbanded, and the men used to help form the Fifth Marine Division.

First Battalion: Organized in August 1941, it fought on GUADALCANAL in conjunction with the First Raider Battalion, and on Gavutu, Choiseul, and VELLA LAVELLA.

A patrol of Marines and scout dogs from the Second Raider Regiment somewhere on Bougainville, November or December 1943. Note the mud and jungle.

Second Battalion: Organized in August 1941, it fought in the central SOLOMONS and on Vella Lavella.

Third Battalion: Organized in 1942, it joined the other battalions on Vella Lavella.

Fourth Battalion: Organized in April 1943, it remained at San Diego until disbanded.

Ref: *History of United States Marine Corps Operations in World War II.*

Marine Corps, US, Raider Battalions

The notion of creating special battalions of Marines for the purpose of conducting lightning raids on isolated Japanese bases surfaced in 1941, inspired by the example of Britain's COMMANDOS and the effective use of small "hit-and-run" forces by the Chinese communists. The latter influence derived from the experience of Marine LTC Evans F. Carlson (1896–1947), who had been a US military observer in China with the communist Eighth Route Army in 1937–38. Carlson was a regular correspondent of President ROOSEVELT, having served as commander of the security detachment at Warm Springs, Georgia, and thus gained support at the highest levels. As a result, the Marine Corps began to organize what became known as Marine Raider Battalions. Eventually some 5,000 Marines were trained as raiders, and four battalions were raised. In March 1943 these were formed into the First Raider Regiment, which spun off its Second and Third Battalions to a provisional Second Regiment from September 1943.

First Raider Battalion: Organized in February 1942, from the First Separate Battalion, itself redesignated from the First Battalion, Fifth Marine Regiment, in January 1942, and commanded by LTC Merritt A. Edson. It spearheaded the assault on TULAGI at the onset of the GUADALCANAL Campaign, and went on to conduct many operations on Guadalcanal, usually combined with the First Parachute Battalion, most notably the Battle of Edson's Ridge (September 12–14, 1942), an action for which Edson and one of his men were awarded the MEDAL OF HONOR, and later fought on New Georgia in 1943.

Second Raider Battalion: Organized in February 1942 from the Second Separate Battalion, a newly created formation, and commanded by LTC Evans F. Carlson, with Capt. James Roosevelt as his executive officer. On August 17, 1942, about half the battalion, some 221 men, conducted a raid on MAKIN ISLAND, landing from two SUBMARINES. The battalion later served on Guadalcanal, conducting a grueling 30-day raid (November 4–December 4,

1942) which destroyed an entire Japanese regiment. Reinforced by the First Marine Dog Platoon, the first American canine unit to see action in the war, it supported the Third Marine Division landings on BOUGAINVILLE in late 1943. One man won the Medal of Honor.

Third Raider Battalion: Organized in SAMOA in September 1942 from individual volunteers, the Third Battalion took part in the unopposed occupation of the Russell Islands early in 1943, and went on to support the Third Marine Division's landings on Bougainville later that year. One man won the Medal of Honor.

Leathernecks of the Second Raider Regiment pose before a captured Japanese dugout at Cape Torokina, Bougainville, December 1943. Note the camouflage uniforms, which proved unsuitable for sustained wear.

Fourth Raider Battalion: Organized from volunteers in October 1942, under Maj. James Roosevelt, the Fourth Battalion fought on New Georgia in 1943.

By late 1943 the Marine brass were having second thoughts about the Raiders. Although they had performed well in combat, they had actually made only two raids, Carlson's raids on Makin and Guadalcanal. All their other missions could easily have been performed by regular Marine units. After thinking over the value of the investment in manpower, time, and training, the Marine brass decided to disband the Raiders. On February 1, 1944 the Raiders became the cadre of the reactivated Fourth Marine Regiment, which had been captured by the Japanese on CORREGIDOR in May 1942. The headquarters of the First Regiment became the headquarters of the new Fourth Marines, while the First, Third, and Fourth Raider Battalions became the First, Second, and Third Battalions, Fourth Marines, and the Second Raider Battalion became the Weapons Company, Fourth Marines.

Ref: *History of United States Marine Corps Operations in World War II.*

Marines, Japanese (Navy Ground Forces)

There was a bit of culture shock when America went to war with Japan. US troops knew little about Japan, and were forced to learn a lot in a short time once the shooting started. One of the "good news, bad news" surprises was the Special Naval Landing Forces (SNLF). Americans quickly assumed that these were Japanese marines, an elite force like the USMC; however, they were not as formidable as they were first thought to be.

As with most maritime powers, Japan had occasion to send troops ashore quickly when all they had available were warships sitting off the coast. In such cases the Japanese, like most navies, would simply arm sailors and have them land. If the warships involved were not going to move around or get into heavy combat themselves, a third or more of the crew could be sent ashore as infantry. For a

week or so, anyway. As recently as World War I (1914), America did the same thing, most obviously in MEXICO where sailors landed at Vera Cruz as infantry and seized the city. In continuation of this tradition, sailors still regularly train as riflemen. But the US Navy also had a few Marines on most major ships to send along with the sailors and contribute some expert advice on infantry operations. Marines (soldiers serving on board ships) were an ancient practice, as until the introduction of cannon, naval battles largely consisted of ships colliding and infantry fighting it out as if on land. When cannon came along, there was much less emphasis on infantry combat afloat. Some infantry troops remained on ships, and these evolved during the past few centuries into soldiers who served as guards on ships, helped man the big guns, and, when needed, went ashore to take care of infantry business. Since Japan got a late start in the navy business (in fact, it never owned a major sailing warship), it didn't develop marines in the traditional sense.

Yet Japan ran up against a need to land troops from warships along the Chinese coast in the 1920s their sailors worked relatively well because Japanese sailors were given infantry training as well as instruction in seamanship. However, the admirals were getting tired of seeing their ships stripped of sailors to take care of some emergency ashore and decided to do something about it. Thus was born the Special Naval Landing Forces in the late '20s. These were sailors trained and equipped to fight ashore. Their weapons were identical to those used by the army, and their uniforms were very similar. One of the differences, however, was the use of an anchor symbol on the steel HELMET instead of a star (which the army used.)

The SNLF was organized into large battalions (of 1,000 to 2,000 troops), containing a wide variety of weapons. Each of the four major Japanese naval bases (KURE, MAIZURU, SASEBO, and Yokosuka) was ordered to organize one or more of these units (called *Rikusentai* in Japanese). A dozen SNLF "battalions" were organized before and during the war, including a handful of parachute units. There were also several other types of specialized navy ground combat units. To put this in perspective, the US Marines during World War II organized some 100 battalion-sized combat units while only about three dozen (of all types) were created by the Japanese Navy's ground forces. Or, put another way, there were about five times as many American Marines as there were Japanese Navy ground troops.

After PEARL HARBOR, the SNLF spearheaded the Japanese Navy's offensive into the south and central Pacific. It was SNLF units that seized American islands such as Wake and the British GILBERTS. In cooperation with army troops, the SNLF, including paratroopers, also participated in the attacks on the Dutch East Indies (INDONESIA) and RABAUL (the major naval base just north of the SOLOMONS and Australia).

Because of the huge size of the Pacific battlefield, the Japanese Army and Navy had to divide the ground-fighting chores among themselves. In the wide open spaces (with few islands) of the central Pacific it was often an entirely navy show. The Japanese Navy had, in addition to all those warships, its own land-based aircraft and ground forces. But the navy was also forced to defend most of these islands against the expected American counterattack. For this purpose, the Japanese Navy organized special "island defense units." These were similar to the SNLF except that most of their weapons were antiaircraft guns for defending against air raids. The principal duty of these companies (100–200 men) and battalions (500–1,000 men) was the local defense of out of the way islands and their airfields. The Japanese had dozens of these islands garrisoned in this way. The aircraft they guarded were used to patrol the vast stretches of the Pacific that the Japanese held sway over early in the war.

The navy was also responsible for building these bases, or rebuilding ones they had captured. For this purpose they established naval construction battalions. These were similar in function to the US Navy's famed SEABEE battalions. The Japanese units were much less efficient, however, as they had little in the way of earth-moving equipment and special construction tools. Most work was done by hand, and about 80% of the personnel were Koreans or Taiwanese conscripted for this purpose. Actually, there were two types of naval construction battalions. One, the *Setsueitai* (or Combat Engineers), was about 30% Japanese and did the skilled work. These units had 800–1,300 troops. The other type were basically labor battalions, and only 10% of their strength (the supervisors) were Japanese.

When America began its drive across the central Pacific in late 1943, the first Japanese garrisons it attacked consisted largely of SNLF and other Japanese Navy ground forces. The closer the US Marines got to Japan, the more Japanese Army troops they encountered. General MACARTHUR, meanwhile, fought largely against Japanese Army units in his campaign from New Guinea to the Philippines, as did the British in Burma and the Chinese in China. Even in 1942, when the Marines came ashore at GUADALCANAL, they encountered a Japanese Navy construction battalion (whose largely Korean troops fled into the jungle rather than fight). When the Japanese mustered forces for their counterattack on Guadalcanal, it was with army troops.

Thus the SNLF were largely found as garrisons on small islands in the Pacific. Like the US Marines, the SNLF's main purpose was seizing forward bases for the navy, and then holding on to them. Beyond that, there were several significant differences between the SNLF and the American Marines (USMC).

1. The USMC had a long tradition of highly trained and disciplined assault troops. The USMC was always distinct from the sailors it served with. The SNLF were sailors trained and equipped as infantry.
2. The SNLF officers were simply naval officers assigned to land combat duty. USMC officers were strictly Marine officers. Thus the USMC leaders were far more expert at commanding infantry operations than their SNLF counterparts.

3. USMC units were specially equipped for amphibious warfare. While their gear included much that was identical to what the army used, where necessary unique weapons or equipment was developed. The SNLF had very little special equipment. In particular, the SNLF never had anything like the array of specialized amphibious equipment used by the USMC.

4. The USMC was primarily an amphibious assault force while the SNLF spent most of its time guarding bases. The USMC also had "base defense units," but these were a handful of defense battalions compared to nearly a hundred assault units.

5. The USMC, by tradition and training, was an elite force that was expected to, and usually did, successfully undertake very difficult assignments. The SNLF, on the other hand, was not even considered as capable as its army counterparts.

In short, there never were any Japanese marines. The SNLF was composed of sailors serving ashore as infantry.

Marquesas Islands

Comprised of 14 island (c. 400 square miles) in the Pacific Ocean about 900 miles northeast of Tahiti. Part of French Polynesia, the Marquesas early fell under Free French control. During the war they had some value as Allied air and naval bases.

Marshall, George C. (1880–1959)

George Catlett Marshall graduated from Virginia Military Institute in 1902 and entered the infantry. He served in the Philippine Insurrection, on various staffs, attended several schools, rising to captain by the time the United States entered World War I. Among the first American soldiers to go to France, Marshall proved an extremely able staff officer, rising rapidly to colonel, and engineering the extraordinary shift of American forces from the St.

Mihiel front to the Meuse-Argonne front late in 1918. After the war he rose steadily in the army, despite the hostility of Douglas MACARTHUR (having John J. Pershing as a patron probably saved his career). Marshall was named chief of staff in 1938 and retained the post through 1945, during which period he oversaw the expansion of the US Army from 125,000 men to over eight million. A meticulous planner and strategist of great vision, he was one of the principal architects of victory. Marshall was a man of great character, reserve, and dignity. Even FDR—who called everyone, including the king of England, by his first name—never addressed Marshall by his first name (he tried once, but Marshall's reaction was such that the president never did it again). Marshall was the first professional soldier ever to win the Nobel Prize for peace, which he received in 1953 for the Marshall Plan, a massive postwar economic assistance program that helped rebuild European economies shattered by the war.

Marshall's stepson, Allen T. Brown, was killed in action in Italy in 1944.

Marshall Islands Campaign

An archipelago in the central Pacific, the Marshalls lie nearly 2,200 miles southwest of HAWAII in the Pacific Ocean. There are actually two chains of islands, about 125 miles apart, comprising only about 70 square miles. Japan took them from Germany in 1914, and they formed part of the Mandated territories.

There was little economic development, but the Japanese began building bases in the islands in the late 1930s. The more notable of the islands are Majuro, ENIWETOK, and Bikini.

Two months after the GILBERT ISLANDS were taken, American amphibious forces moved on to their next target, the Marshalls. This was a very ambitious schedule, as the same amphibious units could not be used for the November 1943 Gilberts operation and then the January 1944 Marshalls attack. Amphibious units, both men and equipment, had to be rested and rebuilt after each assault. But the warships and aircraft were another matter. In 1943, American commanders had decided to maintain two sets of amphibious assault divisions (and their amphibious shipping) to work with one set of warships. The Japanese were not expecting this sort of high-speed approach to amphibious operations, so the January assault on the Marshalls came as a bit of a surprise.

Less of a surprise was the prompt use of airfields in the Gilberts to attack the easternmost islands of the Marshalls. By the end of January, all the Japanese airfields on these heavily fortified and garrisoned islands were destroyed. The well entrenched infantry were ready for any invasion, although none was expected for at least another month or so. But then the Americans did the unexpected. The US fleet went right past the heavily defended easternmost Marshall Islands and headed to KWAJALEIN, which has the largest lagoon of any CORAL atoll in the world. Kwajalein is a string of small islands, 60 miles long and about 20 miles wide. On one end is Kwajalein island. About 40 miles north along the chain of coral islands are the islands of Roi and Namur, linked by a causeway. Along the way, supply and repair ships were dropped off at one of the few unoccupied atolls in the area—Majuro. This provided a fleet base for damaged ships, plus some dry land on which to stockpile supplies. Then, on January 31 the Fourth Marine Division assaulted Roi and Namur (defended by 3,500 Japanese) while the army's Seventh Infantry Division went after Kwajalein and its 5,000-man garrison. By February 2, Roi and Namur were conquered. By February 5, Kwajalein Island was taken. The 41,000 US troops suffered 372 fatalities. The Japanese did much worse, with 7,870 out of 8,675 being killed.

Before going on, the US task force went after TRUK Island, a carrier and bombardment raid meant to shut down the principal Japanese naval base in the central Pacific. There was also a raid on PONAPE Island (600 miles from Kwajalein,) which was being used as a refueling base for aircraft flying from the Caroline islands (including Truk) to bomb US forces in the Marshalls. Truk was found with nearly 400 aircraft on its airfields and dozens of merchant and war ships in its harbor and surrounding waters. For three days, US carrier aircraft pounded the island and, in cooperation with American warships, hunted down Japanese ships. For the first time in history, a major naval base was shut down by carrier aircraft. Even the Japanese raid on PEARL HARBOR had not shut down the base. But this 1944 raid on Truk shut down Japan's largest naval base in the Pacific. Subsequent raids kept Truk out of action, although, after the February 1944 raid, the Japanese never again stationed large naval or air forces there.

The final stage of the Marshall Islands Campaign was the capture of Eniwetok atoll. This was 326 miles northwest of Roi and only a thousand miles from the Mariana Islands. Six infantry battalions were used for this (four Marine, two army). The first landing took place on February 17, and within a week 2,677 Japanese were dead and less than a hundred taken prisoner. Typically, only 339 Americans were killed.

The Marshall Islands Campaign left a number of large Japanese garrisons bypassed. This surprised the Japanese, but they soon realized that the Americans could get away with it. By placing large numbers of aircraft on nearby captured islands, the Americans could constantly patrol the surrounding waters and prevent any supplies from getting through to the bypassed Japanese garrisons. The initial air raids destroyed Japanese aircraft and airbase facilities, and subsequent raids were largely a form of armed reconnaissance. The isolated Japanese garrisons remained where they were until the end of the war. Many of the troops died from starvation or disease before they could hear the emperor's message to surrender, which all of these isolated garrisons did.

Ref: Heinl and Crown, *The Marshalls*.

Marston Mat

Also known as Pierced Steel Planking or Steel Matting, Marston Mats were large perforated steel sheets, easily handled by one man, which could be used to pave roads, runways, and anything else quickly, even if the undersurface was less than ideal for such use. Matting sufficient for a 3,000-foot runway weighed only 1,200 tons and could be laid by 100 unskilled workers in about 96 hours of steady work. This produced front-line airfields far faster than the Japanese thought possible, a fact brought home to them when American aircraft operating out of these new airfields began attacking Japanese targets.

Marston Mat proved particularly useful in tropical areas where there was light sand, and in the arctic where there were quaking bogs and muskeg, or other surfaces unsuited to the construction of airstrips, roads, and the like.

In fact, Marston Mat was used for an enormous variety of tasks, from building runways to improving traction on muddy jungle roads, to making improvised docks, to flooring buildings, and just about anything else the troops could think of.

Maryland Class, US Battleships

Although designed during World War I, the completion of these ships, indeed the laying down of two of them, was delayed in order to incorporate lessons learned during the war. Virtually identical to the CALIFORNIAS, save for their main armament (eight 16-inch guns rather than 12 14-inchers), the Marylands were the most powerful of the prewar American battleships, and formed the core of the battlefleet in the Pacific.

Colorado, BB-45 (1919–1921–1923), was refitting at SAN DIEGO when PEARL HARBOR was attacked, and thus was the least modernized of the three sisters. She served with the battle force that was scraped together to backstop the carriers during the MIDWAY Campaign, and then went on to support landings throughout the Pacific. Scrapped in 1959.

Maryland, BB-46 (1917–1920–1921), was lightly injured at Pearl Harbor and returned to the fleet rather quickly. She supported amphibious operations to the end of the war, taking a TORPEDO off SAIPAN in June 1944, getting off 48 16-inch

rounds at SURIGAO STRAIT, shortly after which she took a KAMIKAZE. Scrapped in 1959.

West Virginia, BB-45 (1920–1921–1923), was heavily damaged at Pearl Harbor, and so extensively rebuilt as to be more a sister of the Californias than the Marylands, with a 114-foot beam, which prevented her from passing through the PANAMA CANAL. She did not return to the fleet until September of 1944. She played a critical role at Surigao Strait, getting off numerous salvos, and supported amphibious operations through OKINAWA. Scrapped in 1959.

Mason, Robert (1904–1995)

US naval officer and codebreaker. A 1925 graduate of the US Naval Academy, during the 1930s Mason learned Japanese while attached to the US Embassy in Tokyo. Although he served in a variety of capacities both ashore and afloat in a career that spanned 45 years, his most important service was as an intelligence officer in the Office of the Chief of Naval Operations, in which capacity he oversaw the breaking of numerous Japanese codes, including MAGIC and PURPLE, work so secret that when decorated for it, his citation was virtually incomprehensible. During the Korean War, Mason, by then a rear admiral, commanded naval support operations. Possessed of an éidetic memory, in 1956 he won $100,000 on the television quiz show "The Big Surprise." He retired as an admiral in 1966.

Matsu Class, Japanese Destroyer Escorts

Even before US SUBMARINES began destroying the Japanese merchant marine, the Imperial Navy seems to have become uneasy about the availability of escorts. As a result, in 1942 the Matsu class was ordered. Eighteen units were laid down in 1943–44, launched before the end of 1944, and completed between April 1944 and January 1945. Somewhat more heavily armed than US DEs, they took a long time to build, the first unit not completing until April of 1944 and the last in January of 1945. A further 11 were canceled. They proved reasonably satisfactory and saw considerable service, seven becoming war losses: one to a mine, one to a submarine, two to aircraft, and three to surface ships.

McMorris, Charles H. (1890–1954)

Charles H. McMorris graduated from Annapolis in 1912. Through 1919 his career was almost entirely in destroyers, and toward the end of World War I he commanded the destroyer *Walke*. Between the wars he alternated between sea, administrative, and school assignments, rising to captain. Assigned to the staff of CINCPAC shortly before PEARL HARBOR, in May 1942, he assumed command of the heavy cruiser *San Francisco*, skippering her through some of the toughest fights in the GUADALCANAL Campaign. In November 1942 he was promoted to rear admiral and sent to command Task Force 16.6, in Alaskan waters, fighting the Battle of the KOMANDORSKI ISLANDS, the only purely ship-to-ship daytime action in the Pacific War. In June 1943 he became chief of staff to CINCPAC, in which post he remained until the end of the war. After the war he held various posts until retirement. Bright (his nickname was "Soc," short for "Socrates"), McMorris was also tactless and critical, which probably impeded his rise.

Medal of Honor

The fighting in the Pacific was different from that in other theaters of World War II. Infantry combat was the most dangerous form of fighting worldwide, but in the Pacific it was particularly lethal. The vast majority of the amphibious operations (one of the most dangerous and desperate forms of infantry combat) in World War II took place in the Pacific. The Pacific Theater was also characterized by the KAMIKAZE attacks on naval vessels, which offered further opportunities for men to earn the Medal of Honor.

Although only about a quarter of the nation's military forces were committed to the Pacific, they earned Medals of Honor awarded during the Sec-

MEDAL OF HONOR AWARDS BY THEATER AND SERVICE							
Branch	Total		(Post)	PTO	(Post)	ETO	(Post)
Army[+]		261	(128)	70	(44)	193	(84)
Army Air Forces		38	(18)	13	(6)	25	(12)
Coast Guard		1	(1)	1	(1)	0	(0)
Marine Corps		81	(47)	81	(47)	0	(0)
Navy		57	(27)	55	(26)	2	(1)
Total		441	(221)	220	124	220	(97)
Army	Artillery	1,688.4					
	Cavalry	594.4					
	Engineers	1,665.5					
	Infantry	800.4					
	Medical Corps	1,124.0					
Army Air Forces		861.0					
Coast Guard		574.0					
Navy		550.0					
Marines		368.9					

[+]Excluding the Army Air Forces, listed separately; Post = Posthumous

ond World War. Moreover, where 43.5% of the awards in the European Theater of Operations were posthumous, 62.3% were in the Pacific Theater, in each case counting only those who died as a consequence of the action that caused them to receive the award (in both theaters there were men who were killed subsequent to their battlefield heroism, but before they were decorated).

A look at the relationship between the number of awards and casualty rates among the various branches of the service is interesting.

These figures are based on the number of men in each branch who were killed in action, divided by the number of Medals of Honor that were awarded to members of that branch. The ratios

INFANTRYMEN AS MEDAL OF HONOR WINNERS				
Service	Theater	Awards	Infantry	(%)
Army	ETO	187	150	(80.2)
	PTO	69	60	(87.0)
Marines	PTO	81	64	(79.0)
Army and Marines	Both	337	274	(81.2)
All	Both	433	274	(63.3)

found on the two tables on page 413 were calculated in 1946, and so are not completely accurate, since several men have been awarded the Medal of Honor since then, in belated recognition of gallantry in action. The most dangerous job in the armed forces was infantryman, and it is worth recalling that most Marines were infantrymen.

Although the figures in the previous table do not suggest it, another very dangerous occupation was medic. Most medical personnel were more or less in the rear, and deaths among them were most likely to have been caused by artillery or air attacks, however, some medical personnel accompanied the troops, going right up to the front with the infantry. During World War II 16 medics earned the Medal of Honor, eight posthumously. Six recipients were with the army in the ETO, three of them posthumous. In the Pacific the army awarded three medics the Medal of Honor, one posthumously, and the navy, which supplied the medics for the Marines, decorated seven, four posthumously.

Both the oldest and the youngest winners of the Medal of Honor during World War II were in the Pacific. The oldest was General Douglas MACARTHUR, who was 64 when he was decorated for the heroic defense of the Philippines in early 1942. MacArthur was also the highest-ranking recipient in history, and the only one who was the son of a Medal of Honor winner, his father having received one for the Civil War. The youngest was PFC Jacklyn H. Lucas, who was just six days over 17 when he won the Medal of Honor on IWO JIMA, with the 26th Marines. Private Lucas had enlisted when UNDERAGE, and is apparently the youngest person to have won the Medal of Honor since the Civil War.

Other military specialties were much less dangerous. In the Army Air Forces the most common military specialty of Medal of Honor winners—pilot—represented 17 (44.4%) of the 38 recipients, all but three of them bomber pilots. It was not unusual for ACES to be awarded a Medal of Honor. The most common specialty in the navy—commanding officer—counted fully 22 (38.6%) of the

57 recipients, including commanders of squadrons, AIR GROUPS, ships, and SUBMARINES.

Incidentally, there is no absolute criteria for awarding the Medal of Honor. During World War II both services had different administrative mechanisms for processing Medal of Honor recommendations, and different regulations. Naval regulations permitted the award of the Medal of Honor for heroic deeds not connected with combat, and one man was so decorated during World War II.

See also BASILONE, JOHN; BONG, RICHARD I.; BOYINGTON, GREGORY; CALLAGHAN, DANIEL; DOOLITTLE, JAMES; DOSS, DESMOND; FLETCHER, FRANK; FRIENDLY FIRE, ALLIED PRISONER OF WAR DEATHS BY; JAPAN, ATTITUDE TOWARD THE ENEMY; KELLY, COLIN; MACARTHUR, DOUGLAS; MILLER, DORIE; O'CALLAGHAN, JOSEPH; PHILIPPINE SCOUTS; PORT CHICAGO MUTINY; ROOSEVELT FAMILY AT WAR; SCOTT, NORMAN; SHOUP, DAVID; VANDEGRIFT, ALEXANDER; WAINWRIGHT, JONATHAN; and divisional and unit entries under MARINE CORPS, US and UNITED STATES ARMY.

Medan, Sumatra, Netherlands East Indies

An important harbor, but lacking in extensive facilities and poorly sited for use as a base, Medan was occupied by the Japanese in early 1942. They used it as a local headquarters and transshipment point for the rest of the war.

Medical Service

Allied, and particularly American, medical services to the troops was extraordinarily extensive. Normally there was a medical battalion attached to every division, plus medical detachments in all elements of the division. Field treatment centers were set up just behind where heavy fighting was expected in order to render treatment quickly to badly wounded troops. It was known that speed was important, and throughout the Pacific War, procedures were improved to get intensive medical care to CASUALTIES faster and faster. This was accomplished by moving more medical personnel closer to the actual fighting.

Medics served with army and Marine infantry platoons. These first aid specialists were trained to give prompt care and make an accurate diagnosis of a wide range of battlefield injuries. That done, the wounded were quickly moved a few hundred meters (or less) to the rear and to an aid station manned by one or more MDs and more medics. Here the patient was given further diagnosis and treatment (including surgery, if needed). At that point, the casualty went offshore to a hospital ship, by truck to a field hospital, or, once airfields were available, could be flown to islands with even more extensive medical facilities. Larger hospitals were always quickly established on newly conquered territory, and patients were usually driven to these, accompanied by medics or nurses to provide needed care en route. As a result, even in the most difficult environments, such as New Guinea or Burma, an Allied soldier who was wounded, even seriously, had a very good chance of pulling through.

Amphibious operations had their own special requirements, because there was usually a very large

A wounded man is transferred from the carrier Bunker Hill *(CV-17), seriously damaged by a kamikaze attack, to the cruiser* Wilkes-Barre *(CL-90), off Okinawa on May 11, 1945. Rapid evacuation of the wounded was an important factor in keeping US combat deaths low.*

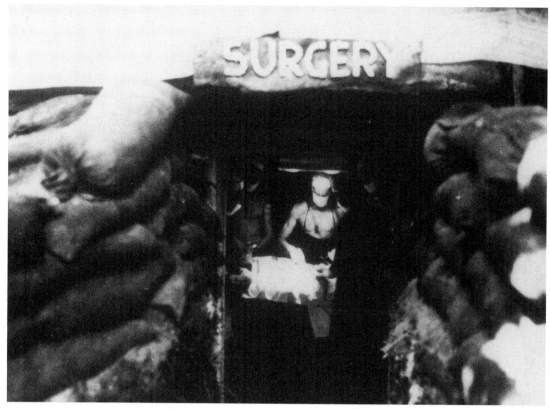

An underground operating room, somewhere on Bougainville, December 13, 1943. Such facilities, though crude, permitted quick treatment of the wounded, which saved numerous lives.

number of casualties in a short time, and these were on a beach or a short distance inland at a place where there were few medical facilities set up. To overcome these problems, the engineer units that went ashore to set up the supply system for the invading troops also included transportation units equipped and trained to evacuate casualties rapidly.

The Allies also had an advantage in their numerous hospital ships. Every service had some, and they were an ideal way to bring the latest medical technology as close as possible to the fighting. The introduction of AMPHIBIOUS VEHICLES (DUKWs and LVPs) made it easier to take casualties from the battlefields to the beach and then directly out to a waiting hospital ship.

While the industrialized Allied nations (United States, Britain, etc.) were able to supply a high degree of medical care, their Chinese allies were not. The Chinese Army rarely had more than a few thousand doctors to treat several million troops. There was also a severe shortage of medical equipment and supplies. The Chinese made do by creating two or three medical officers (who where not MDs) for each MD and training even more medics and nurses to at least render first aid on a prompt basis. This approach saved many lives, although a wound that required complex surgery was still a problem.

Most of the Allied medical effort did not go into caring for combat casualties, but into dealing with the high incidence of disease in the Pacific. Disease borne by numerous local insects was a major problem, and the solution was to kill the bugs and provide drinkable water and clean living conditions as much as possible in a combat zone. To this end, army and navy engineers spent a lot of time killing insects (the first major use of insecticides like DDT) and purifying water. When necessary, swamps were drained and thousands of prefabricated buildings were shipped to the Pacific, to supplement the even greater number of tents. Additional quantities of clothing, especially socks and boots, were shipped. "Trench foot" and various other conditions arising from feet kept in the water too often, could be best treated by having dry socks available. Boots tended to rot faster than the feet, so they had to be replaced quickly. Many Japanese troops, not so well supplied, ended up barefoot. On tropical battlefields, a pair of boots would often last but a few weeks.

In contrast, Japanese medical arrangements left much to be desired. During the Russo-Japanese War (1904–05) the medical service of the Japanese Army had attracted widespread admiration, but by the 1930s it had seriously deteriorated. While in theory each division was assigned three field hospitals, each with 180 litters and 45 ambulances, many divisions lacked more than the most rudimentary medical services. It was not uncommon for wholly untrained soldiers to be assigned as medical orderlies and nurses, or even, as happened increasingly toward the end of the war, for whole schools of untrained teenaged girls to be conscripted and shipped abroad to serve as nurses. Moreover, the few trained medical personnel in a unit often found themselves in the firing line, or taking part in BANZAI CHARGES. Of course, the increasingly successful US submarine campaign against Japanese shipping cut off distant garrisons from medical supplies, as well as food and ammunition. As a result, a wounded Japanese soldier stood little chance, tens of thousands perishing from relatively minor injuries, which went untreated by trained personnel.

See also JAPAN, ATTITUDE TOWARD WARFARE.

Melbourne, Australia

One of the most important ports in Australia, with a considerable capacity to service shipping, but only limited utility as a naval base, being on the country's southern coast. Its principal value in the war was as a supply base and manufacturing center.

Merrill's Marauders

See US ARMY, OTHER NOTABLE UNITS.

Meteor, British Jet Fighter

The Meteor was the world's first operational jet combat aircraft. Entering British service in the summer of 1944, eight days before the German Me-262, the Meteor promptly went to work shooting down German cruise missiles (V-1s). Armed with four 20mm cannon and able to fly higher and faster than any other fighter, the Meteor was limited only by small numbers (100 produced during the war) and the heavy maintenance load its two jet engines put on the ground crew. No Meteors served in the Pacific, but had the war against Japan continued beyond the summer of 1945, the Meteor would have been involved.

See also AIRCRAFT TYPES, DEVELOPMENT.

Mexico

Although relations between the United States and Mexico were severely strained in the first third of the 20th century, the "Good Neighbor" policy instituted by the ROOSEVELT administration in the mid-1930s had led to a considerable measure of reconciliation. Mexico declared war on the Axis in March 1942, partially in response to US urgings and partially as a result of persistent Axis submarine attacks on Mexican shipping. Through LEND-LEASE the Mexican armed forces were modernized and expanded. Although this affected all branches of the service, the only element of the Mexican armed forces to see action in the war was the air force. In cooperation with the United States, Mexico organized a special air wing of three squadrons. The 201st Squadron was a combat squadron equipped with P-47s; the 202nd, a replacement training squadron; and the 203rd was a primary training squadron. The 201st Squadron ("*Aguilas Aztecas*"—Aztec Eagles) arrived in the United States for advanced flight training in July 1944 and departed for the Philippines in March 1945. Attached to the Fifth Air Force and based at Clark Field on Luzon, the 201st Squadron performed reconnaissance, ground attack, and close air support operations against Japanese forces in the Philippines and on Formosa until August, when it was reassigned to the 13th Air Force and transferred to OKINAWA in anticipation of the invasion of Japan. Nine Mexican airmen were killed in action.

In addition to the men who served in the Mexican Armed Forces, an unknown number of Mexican citizens joined the US Armed Forces (by one estimate as many as 250,000, a figure that cannot be substantiated).

Although there was some discrimination against Mexicans, Mexican Americans, and other Hispanic Americans in the US Armed Forces during the war, it was relatively marginal. In fact, a number of Hispanic Americans attained relatively high rank, the most notable being MG Pedro del Valle (USMC), who commanded the First Marine Division on Okinawa; MG Terry de la Mesa Allen, who commanded the First Infantry Division in North Africa and Sicily, and the 104th Division in France and Germany; and MG Elwood R. Quesada (USAAF), who commanded the XIX Tactical Air Corps under Patton in Europe.

Midway Campaign

Midway comprises two small islands enclosed in an atoll, for a total land area of only about two square miles. The group, about 1,300 miles northwest of PEARL HARBOR, had only a limited anchorage. The only facilities available at the outbreak of war were a cable station, lighthouse, and Pan Am seaplane base, with a US Navy seaplane base under construction. It was valuable as a reconnaissance base and as the northernmost anchor of the Hawaiian chain. During the war the US Navy developed it into a modest air base and home port for SUBMARINES and light craft.

The Japanese began planning for a decisive, June 1942 battle in the vicinity of Midway shortly after the DOOLITTLE Raid on Tokyo in April. Indeed, the CORAL SEA operation was actually an integral part of the overall strategic plan, which was to bring about this battle. The intention was to smash the remnants of American naval power in the Pacific, and advance Japan's outer defensive perimeter more than a thousand miles farther by seizing the western ALEUTIANS, Midway Island, and, ultimately, FIJI, SAMOA, and NEW CALEDONIA, simultaneously severing the Allied lifeline between the US West Coast and Australia. Like the Pearl Harbor operation, the Midway operation was the brainchild of Isoroku YAMAMOTO. But it was neither as well planned nor as well executed.

Yamamoto's plan for the Midway operation was complex. The principal striking force would be Chuichi NAGUMO's First Air Fleet (the Pearl Harbor Striking Force), down to four fleet carriers (due to losses at Coral Sea), and two fast battleships, two heavy cruisers, a light cruiser, a dozen destroyers. This would be supported by an Advanced Force of 16 submarines. The actual capture of the objective would be the responsibility of the Midway Occupation Force of 5,000 troops in a dozen transports, supported by two battleships, a light carrier, two seaplane carriers, eight heavy cruisers, two light cruisers, and 20 destroyers, plus a dozen smaller warships, organized into seven task groups. Giving deep support was the Main Body, three battleships, a light carrier, two seaplane carriers, a light cruiser, and 17 destroyers. Then there was the Northern Area Force, comprising a support group of four battleships and two light cruisers, plus two light carriers, three heavy cruisers, three light cruisers, a dozen destroyers, three submarines, and about a dozen miscellaneous small warships, grouped in no less than six task groups, including two troop transports. All of these task groups, of course, had supply ships and oilers assigned. The plan was for the Northern Area Force to make a demonstration against the Aleutians, grabbing a couple of islands in an effort to divert American attention from the principal objective. While the US Navy raced northward to cope with the threat to the Aleutians, perhaps suffering losses to the Advanced Force, the Midway Occupation Force would take its objective under the protection of the First Air Fleet. Presumably, then the Americans would race south to relieve Midway, once more running the gauntlet of the Advanced Force, and right into an aerial ambush by the First Air Fleet. Should the Americans try for a surface action, the Main Body would be ready to come up from its supporting position, several hundred miles behind the First Air Fleet.

This plan may have looked fine on paper, but was seriously flawed. Not only was Japanese organization very complex, scattering task forces across half of the western Pacific, but the Aleutians operation also consumed too many resources for a proper diversion (90 carrier aircraft, a quarter of the approximately 350 available). Moreover, by early May, American Pacific commander Chester W. NIMITZ had a pretty good notion as to the identity of the principal Japanese objective, partially as a result of good guessing and partially as a result of fortuitous code breaking. Nimitz intended to counter Yamamoto's offensive by a careful concentration of everything he had, which admittedly was not much. He had three carriers (233 aircraft, only about a dozen fewer than those on Nagumo's four carriers), including YORKTOWN (mostly repaired from her Coral Sea damage), seven heavy cruisers, one light cruiser, and 17 destroyers. These were organized into two task forces under RAdm Frank J. FLETCHER, and supported by 19 submarines, plus as much shore-based air power as could be jammed onto Midway's tiny surface (60 navy and Marine combat aircraft plus 23 army B-26s and B-17s, plus about 32 Catalina patrol bombers), plus some Ma-

rines for a total of some 3,000 men. There were also three destroyers, some PT-BOATS, and some miscellaneous smaller warships assigned to patrol portions of the long chain of islets and atolls linking Midway with HAWAII (where the Japanese had once planned, and now planned again, to establish a temporary flying boat base using submarines).

Aware of the "threat" to the Aleutians, Nimitz grudgingly assigned five cruisers, 13 destroyers, six submarines, and some seaplane tenders, patrol boats, and minesweepers. He also ordered the carrier *Saratoga*, completing repairs from a torpedo hit, up from SAN DIEGO with her escorts, and ordered the battle fleet, composed of the more lightly damaged Pearl Harbor survivors plus reinforcements from the Atlantic, with an escort carrier, to sortie from SAN FRANCISCO Bay, where it was temporarily housed.

With Nimitz's approval, Fletcher deployed his carriers northeast of Midway, reasoning that the Japanese would most likely come from the northwest, the west, or the southwest. This conceded the initiative to the Japanese. Normally, giving away the initiative is a bad idea in war. But in this case it was perfectly reasonable, since in order to hit the Japanese one had to find them. Locating the enemy could be done by patrol planes reaching out from Midway or, failing that, by letting them hit something first. In this case, the "something" was Midway. And that is precisely what took place.

The Japanese hit the Aleutians on 3 June 1942 and by the 7th had occupied Attu and KISKA, there being no one there to oppose them. But Frank Fletcher had not, in the interim, "raced north." On 3 June a Catalina patrol bomber had spotted the Midway Occupation Force. Early the next morning another PBY spotted the Japanese carriers. So Fletcher knew where the enemy was, while they were still in ignorance of his location. At 6:30 A.M. Fletcher ordered Raymond SPRUANCE, commander of TF 16, to prepare to launch a strike against the Japanese carriers from *Enterprise* and *Hornet*, holding back his own YORKTOWN for a follow-up strike. Even as this strike was getting into the air, Nagumo hit Midway with 108 aircraft. Spotted by radar, the Japanese air strike met resistance from Midway-based fighters.

Now came the critical moment of the battle. When dispatching his strike against Midway, Nagumo had ordered a second strike readied in the event American carriers had to be attacked. Meanwhile the leader of the Midway strike returned, ahead of his colleagues, and urged that a second strike be made against Midway, in order to destroy the island as a useful base. As Nagumo mulled over this suggestion, Midway-based bombers hit the fleet. Although the air strike was a failure, inflicting no loss on the Japanese carriers and suffering heavily itself, it seems to have helped convince Nagumo to have another go at Midway (he may also have recalled that his failure to authorize a third strike at Pearl Harbor had had unfortunate results). Confident that the American carriers were nowhere in the vicinity, Nagumo ordered the 93 fueled and armed aircraft to be rearmed for another go at Midway. Fifteen minutes into this operation, a reconnaissance plane reported spotting American ships to the northwest. Nagumo dithered for another 15 minutes, then ordered the rearmament reversed, so that the 93 aircraft could be dispatched to attack these American vessels. Soon the hangar decks of the Japanese carriers were littered with ammunition, as general-purpose bombs were being removed from the aircraft while TORPEDOES and armor-piercing bombs were being loaded. And on their flight decks the four carriers were recovering the aircraft returning from the Midway strike.

Meanwhile, Spruance's TF 16 airstrikes had lifted off at about 7:00 A.M.: 116 fighters, dive bombers, and torpedo bombers.

About two hours later, Fletcher put 35 of his own *Yorktown* planes into the air as well. Spruance had calculated the odds closely. Aware of the Japanese air raid on Midway, he had estimated the time it would take for the attackers to return to their carriers, and launched his strike with the intention of catching the Japanese aircraft as they were rearming on deck. But he had a run of bad luck. Nagumo ordered a course change at 0905, just

as the last of the Midway strike planes were returning. This caused the *Hornet*'s fighters and dive bombers to miss the Japanese task force entirely. As a result, Torpedo Squadron 8—15 TBD1 DEVASTATORS—went in unsupported, with the loss of all the airplanes and all but one of the 45 crewmen to Zeros or antiaircraft fire. A similar fate awaited the *Enterprise* and *Yorktown* TBDs. Of 41 TBDs involved in attacks on the Japanese carriers only eight survived, and none scored a hit. By the time the *Yorktown* TBD strike had been beaten off, at 1024, the Japanese thought they had won the battle.

But within about 90 seconds the whole outcome of the battle was reversed. C. C. Wade McClusky arrived over Nagumo's carriers with 37 *Enterprise* dive bombers just as the last TBD was downed. With Nagumo's combat air patrol "on the deck" (at low altitude) from having annihilated the TBDs, McClusky's SBD DAUNTLESS attacks were largely unopposed and thus accurate. The SBD attack proved deadly. Within seconds KAGA and AKAGI took bombs to their hangar decks, which touched off ammunition and fueled aircraft, starting uncontrollable fires. Then, within seconds, *Yorktown*'s 17 SBD Dauntlesses showed up and put three 1,000–pound bombs neatly into the center of fueled and armed aircraft on SORYU's deck, turning her into an inferno as well. By 1030 Nagumo had lost three carriers, all burning uncontrollably. He ordered his last carrier, HIRYU, to launch a strike on *Yorktown*, while bringing up all available escorts to cover the ship.

Hiryu's strike, 50 fighters and bombers, followed the American aircraft home, arriving over *Yorktown* at about 1440 hours. A furious action ensued, as *Yorktown*'s CAP and escorts accounted for most of the Japanese attackers. But some got through, and the carrier took three bombs and two torpedoes. Not completely recovered from the damage she had taken at Coral Sea, *Yorktown* began to list dramatically and soon had to be abandoned. Admiral Fletcher shifted his flag to a cruiser and gallantly turned direction of the battle over to Spruance.

Having spotted *Hiryu*, at 1530 *Enterprise* launched 14 of her own and 10 of *Yorktown*'s SBDs. These jumped *Hiryu* at 1700. Nagumo's last carrier went down quickly after taking four hits. Apprised of the outcome of Midway within minutes of the loss of his carriers, Yamamoto reacted by ordering the Main Body and the light carriers in the Aleutians to the support of the now carrier-less First Air Fleet, a classic instance of "too little, too late." Save for some mopping up, the Battle of Midway was over, the Imperial Navy having lost four of its finest carriers and any chance to annihilate the US Navy in the Pacific.

Midway Campaign, Myths of

Midway, the second carrier battle of 1942, was the most decisive of the war. But not for the reasons the Japanese thought it would be, even if they had captured the place. In fact, the Battle of Midway would have turned into the "Siege of Midway" if the Americans had not known what the Japanese were up to or did not have forces available with which to ambush the Japanese. The Japanese plan was to seize Midway Island quickly and then advance down the chain of islands the thousand or so miles to HAWAII, forcing the US fleet to come out and do battle, so that it could then be decisively defeated. A base on Midway would provide an "unsinkable aircraft carrier" for the rest of the Japanese fleet to maneuver around, while the smaller US fleet was chopped to pieces. Midway was a massive operation, involving eight Japanese carriers plus numerous destroyers, cruisers, battleships, and SUBMARINES. The operation also involved landing Japanese troops on several undefended islands off Alaska as a diversion.

The US Navy had other ideas. If the Japanese had seized Midway, the United States would have put it under siege with long-range aircraft and submarines. Midway was over 2,000 miles from the Japanese Home Islands and quite isolated. It would have to be supplied by sea and the Japanese never fully grasped the problems of logistics in the Pacific War. A Japanese-held Midway Island would have turned into another of many Japanese logistics disasters. While the Japanese played down logistics, they played up the importance of "military honor." They felt the Americans would come out to defend Midway no matter what. The Americans felt otherwise.

Because the United States had broken many Japanese codes, the United States knew most of the Japanese plan and had all three of its available Pacific carriers stationed off Midway to ambush the Japanese. The US force was lucky, the Japanese force was sloppy, and four Japanese carriers were sunk to the loss of only one US carrier. The Japanese Navy never recovered from this because the United States built new carriers much faster than Japan. American admirals knew they would have to deal with the Japanese carriers eventually, especially the six heavy carriers. In June 1942, the United States had only three heavy carriers available for operations in the Pacific and would not receive the first of the two dozen new ESSEX CLASS heavy carriers until after the new year. The Americans had already resigned themselves to fighting a defensive battle until then, emphasizing submarines and land-based aircraft. Midway was an opportunity the Americans could not pass up, but only because they had the drop on the Japanese. Without the advantage of reading the coded Japanese messages, the United States would not have risked its three carriers against the Japanese. Midway would have fallen to the Japanese, but the effect of this success on the course of the war may actually have been relatively minimal.

Midway Class, US Aircraft Carriers

The culmination of US wartime carrier development, *Midway* and her two sisters were huge ships (so big they were classified as "CVB—Large Aircraft Carriers"), yet fast, far better protected than any previous US carriers, and with an enormous aircraft capacity (over 130 planes). Although built with considerable speed (22–23 months each), they began to enter service only at about the time that Japan surrendered. Rebuilt from time to time, the last one was not withdrawn from service until the end of the Cold War.

Midway, CVB-41 (1943–1945–1945), was commissioned eight days after the surrender of Japan. Scrapped, after much service, in the 1990s.

Franklin D. Roosevelt, CVB-42 (1943–1945–1945), originally to have been named *Coral Sea*, but renamed after the president's death. She was commissioned 25 days after Japan surrendered. Scrapped after much service, in the 1980s.

Coral Sea, CVB-43 (1944–1946–1947). Withdrawn from service after much service, in the 1980s.

Three other units were authorized, but were canceled in early 1945 before being laid down.

Mikawa, Gunichi

Gunichi Mikawa graduated from Japan's naval academy in 1911. He had a very distinguished career, attending various schools, serving as naval attaché in Paris, on staffs, and in command of ships. Early in the Pacific War he commanded battleship divisions and cruiser squadrons (as a vice admiral). He commanded the forces that defeated the Allies at the Battle of SAVO ISLAND (the most lopsided naval defeat in American history) and commanded surface forces throughout the battles for GUADAL-CANAL in 1942. Relieved in late 1943, as someone had to take the fall for Japan's steadily declining fortunes in the area after Savo, he went on to command the South West Area Fleet in early 1944 until US naval forces seized the area in late 1944.

Military Economics, Japan, 1933–1945

Japan was a rather recent arrival on the world stage in 1941, and the rest of the world didn't quite know what to make of it. What garnered attention was Japan's growing military prowess. From a defenseless, insular nation in the 1850s, Japan had modernized itself to the point where it was making war on China with Western weapons and techniques by the end of the 19th century. In 1905 Japan went on to defeat a European power, Russia. Allying it-

self with the Western Allies during World War I, Japan entered the 1920s as a recognized and proven major military power.

But something was missing, and that vital something was an economy that could support a world-class military machine. Until the 1930s, Japan had spent more effort on its armed forces than it had on industrializing. But while the rest of the world wallowed in the Great Depression of the 1930s, Japan made great strides in expanding its manufacturing capacity. Between 1930 and 1940, truck PRODUCTION increased nearly a hundredfold. Aircraft production went up nearly 12 times, shipbuilding increased five times, and steel production nearly tripled.

But it wasn't enough. Japan made these great strides by concentrating on the production of military goods. Much less progress was made in the civilian sector. This can be seen by the amount of government income spent on the armed forces. In the early 1930s, 29% was spent on the military. By 1940, the armed forces were taking two-thirds of the national budget. Moreover, the government had grabbed much of the increased production wealth for its own use. Between 1931 and 1940, government income increased 16 times.

To put all this in perspective, consider what America and Japan spent on armaments.

ARMAMENTS SPENDING (1995 BILLIONS)		
Year	U.S.	Japan
1935–38	$13.6	$18.1
1939	5.4	4.5
1940	14.5	9.0
1941	40.6	18.1
1942	181.0	27.2
1943	344.0	43.0
1944	380.0	55.0

Much of what Japan spent in the late 1930s went to prosecute the war in China. The territories Japan conquered in 1942 were also ruthlessly plundered through 1944. By 1945, US production was decreasing at a rapid clip and Japan's had fallen even more precipitously.

About a third of US spending went to the Pacific, while nearly half of Japanese spending went into mainland Asia operations (China, Burma, and the huge garrison in MANCHURIA watching the Russians). Moreover, Japan also had to face Britain in the Indian Ocean and Burma. Britain's wartime armaments spending was twice that of Japan, although less than 10% of it went to the Pacific.

It was America that was literally the "Arsenal of Democracy." Throughout the war, the United States alone represented 52% of worldwide (Allies and Axis) aircraft production, 36% of all artillery, 48% of all vehicles, and 61% of all shipbuilding. Add Britain, Canada (which produced at 30% of Japan's level), and Russia and you can see what dire straights the Japanese were in. Japan's only major ally, Germany, had total a armaments production that was only 50% of America's and had to deal with Russia, which spent about half as much as America. The Japanese disadvantage in armaments spending manifested itself differently depending on the branch of the military. The Japanese Navy was carefully built up during the 30 years before the war. Well designed ships and weapons plus skillful crews gave Japan an advantage at the beginning of the war. But the lack of resources did not allow for the replacement of wartime losses. Japanese admirals went into the war expecting to take up to 50% losses. When they suffered far less in the first few months, they got ambitious, and the result was a string of devastating defeats from Midway onward through the end of 1942. Japan didn't have the ability to replace those losses.

The Japanese air forces (both navy and army) were in a similar, although more complex, situation. Japan could build a lot of aircraft, but air force leaders were unwilling to lower their prewar PILOT selection standards. The result was that aircraft were replaced after heavy losses in 1942, but pilots were not. US air commanders did adapt their pilot training to wartime needs and were thus able to achieve air superiority in the Pacific from 1943 on. But even if Japan had implemented more efficient pilot training, it would have done little more than cause more losses to the Americans. The United States would still have had air superiority by 1943.

The Japanese army was least affected by Japan's armaments disadvantage. The army was the largest of the services and its principal restriction was a lack of shipping to get the troops where they were needed in the Pacific. The Japanese style of warfare was heavy on spirit and manpower while light on equipment. Against poorly trained and equipped troops, like the Chinese, this was quite successful. Against the lavishly equipped Americans, it was disastrous.

In China, the Japanese had air superiority and the Chinese had little artillery. The situation was just the opposite against the Allies in the Pacific. Against US troops, the Japanese encountered artillery fire the likes of which they had never experienced. Actually, American artillery, as used in World War II, was a radical new form of artillery use. In addition to prodigious use of ammunition (first seen in World War I), the Americans developed communications techniques that allowed many guns to bring their fire down on a single target more quickly than ever seen in the past. Japanese attacks, even when they had the element of surprise, were regularly blown to pieces by artillery fire. The Japanese learned to use their shovels and skill at fortification to defeat this gunfire when they were defending. But there was no way for a Japanese attack to avoid the devastating effect of the Yankee guns.

American troops were also lavishly equipped with machine guns and used them skillfully. This, combined with their artillery, demolished the Japanese offensive capability. Deprived of their ability to control battles with their fearless attacks, the Japanese were forced to defend. Even defending to the death did little for them, except to provide a means to "die honorably in battle." This did not win wars and as a result Japan lost lives. It was possible to trade lives for a lack of guns and ammunition. Later analysis (during the Korean War) showed that a regularly supplied Chinese Army could stalemate American air and artillery superiority by suffering five CASUALTIES for every American one. This was no help for the Japanese, because, unlike the Chinese in Korea, the garrisons of Pacific islands were cut off from reinforcement and supply when the US invasion fleet showed up. The Americans not only had material superiority, but they also knew how to use it.

The civilian leaders and navy admirals were generally aware of American production superiority. Most army generals were either ignorant of these realities or chose to ignore them. Unfortunately for Japan, the generals were running the government from the mid-1930s, and it was their view of things that determined national policy.

While many civilian and navy leaders had studied in the United States, few generals had done so. Those educated Japanese who had spent time in America came away with a clear understanding that the United States was an industrial powerhouse and not likely to back down from a fight. While the generals ruling Japan might acknowledge American industrial superiority, they dismissed the idea that Americans would not back down and ask for peace if sufficiently pummeled by Japanese military might. It was on this misunderstanding that Japan went to war, and lost everything.

Ref: Barnhart, *Japan Prepares for Total War*; Harries and Harries, *Soldiers of the Sun*.

Miller, Dorie (1919–1943)

A native of Waco, Texas, Dorie (actually Doris, sometimes rendered Dory) Miller enlisted in the navy in 1939, and was a mess attendant (steward's mate) 2nd class aboard the battleship *West Virginia* on December 7, 1941. At the start of the Japanese attack Miller first rendered assistance to the ship's captain, Mervyn S. Bennion, who was mortally wounded. After carrying Bennion to a place of relative safety, Miller manned a machine gun through the balance of the attack, being officially credited with downing two Japanese aircraft (and unofficially with six, albeit that accepting all the unofficial claims would presuppose that few of the

Japanese got away). For his heroism under fire, Miller was promoted mess attendant 1st class and decorated with the Navy Cross by Chester W. NIMITZ.

Returning to duty, Miller was serving aboard the escort carrier *LISCOMBE BAY* when the Japanese submarine *I-175* TORPEDOED her in the GILBERTS on November 24, 1943. The ship sank with great loss of life, over 640 of her 840 crewmen perishing, among them Miller.

Over the years there have been occasional proposals to upgrade Miller's Navy Cross to a MEDAL OF HONOR, on the grounds that he was denied one because of his race. While it is true that several black soldiers have belatedly been awarded the Medal of Honor for service in World War II, Miller's deeds—for which he achieved nationwide fame—were certainly in keeping with the tradi-

Dorie Miller, as depicted in a recruiting poster released shortly after his death in action off Makin Island on November 24, 1943.

tional criteria for the Navy Cross. On the other hand, a number of awards of the Medal of Honor were made primarily for political reasons, such as that to Douglas MACARTHUR

Miller's job, mess attendant or steward's mate, was the most common navy job assigned to BLACK AMERICANS, even black submariners, until well after the war. Although the navy was desegregated in the early 1950s, black sailors for higher skilled rates were slow to show up on many ships. In some cases, especially on smaller ships like destroyers, a newly assigned black specialist, like a radioman, might be the only black sailor on the vessel aside from the messmen. Some captains, wanting to avoid any racial tensions among an otherwise white crew, would give the black radioman the option of bunking with the messmen rather than in the other bunk areas where the rest of the sailors lived. More than one black sailor, realizing that the separate messmen bunking area was rather more comfortable, albeit segregated, than the rest of the crew quarters, opted for the "separate but unequal" accommodations. Since the messmen took care of the food for the officers, this also meant they had access to better chow than the rest of the crew. This, in addition to the better quarters, passed into history in 1970, when the messman rating was abolished.

Milne Bay, Papua

Milne Bay is an inlet on the easternmost end of Papua. Although it had very limited port facilities, it had a considerable anchorage and several nearby areas very suitable for airfield construction that gave it enormous potential value as a base. In late August 1942 the Japanese decided to capture Milne Bay before some 9,500 Allied troops (1,400 Americans, mostly engineers, 8,100 Australians) could complete an air base. Allied aerial reconnaissance detected the approach of a Japanese convoy on August 25, and the American and Australian troops made hasty preparations to resist the landings. The first Japanese troops, "marines" of the SNLF, came ashore about six miles east of the Allied defensive perimeter on the night of August 25–26, 1942. On the next night and that of the 28th–29th further contingents landed, until there were about 3,100 Japanese troops ashore. Surprisingly, the Japanese troops remained rather inactive, only a few skirmishes taking place, despite air strikes and naval shellings on the Allied positions. The first Japanese attack came at 0330 on 31 August, and it was easily beaten off, some 160 Japanese troops being killed as they attempted to cross one of the airfield clearings. Although the Allied command suspected that the Japanese would try again, they were wrong, for the Japanese troops essayed no further attacks. On September 5 the Japanese pulled out by sea. The Battle of Milne Bay was over. Milne Bay subsequently became an important air base for the Allies.

Minekaze Class, Japanese Destroyers

A Japanese World War I design, the Minekazes were comparable to the US "four stack" destroyers of the CLEMSON CLASS. Built 1918–23, they were obsolete even before the war. Two of the 15 ships in the class had been converted into high-speed transports, with reduced armament and speed, but able to carry 250 fully armed troops with landing craft, while a third had been fitted to serve as the command ship for a radio-controlled target vessel. All the units in the class saw considerable service in the war, 10 being lost in action.

Mines, Land

Land mines were one of the more feared weapons in the Pacific. Mines were usually detected only when victims stepped on them, and lost feet, legs, or lives. Mines were most frequently used on landing beaches and around heavily fortified Japanese positions. While the Japanese used a lot of mines, they did not have a very wide or sophisticated selection to choose from, compared with the Germans, or even the Americans. The most common mine was the 12-pound, saucer-shaped Model 93. It was used against both personnel and vehicles. This was done by varying the pressure device on the top of the mine to different degrees of sensitivity, from 7 to 250 pounds. More troublesome was the 107-pound, semi-spherical Model 96 mine. This was used on land or under a few feet of water, where it might encounter landing craft. Containing 46 pounds of explosive, the Model 96 would destroy any vehicle and most small landing craft. Another Japanese specialty was the Model 99 armor-piercing mine. However, this mine had to be placed against the side of a vehicle (or the metal door of a bunker) by a soldier who activated it, after which it would explode in five–six seconds. It was not entirely effective against heavier US TANKS and was often fatal to the user. The Model 99 weighed three pounds, contained 24 ounces of TNT, and had magnets on it to keep it attached to its intended target. The Japanese considered it a "grenade," and it was issued one per soldier when conditions warranted. The Japanese frequently improvised mines, using artillery shells, some even made from Russian stocks captured in 1905. These were relatively simple and not very effective, but could prove an annoyance to advancing Allied troops. One very odd antitank improvisation used relatively large-caliber naval shells (5-inch and up). A large hole was dug, into which the shell was placed. A Japanese soldier armed with a hammer then crouched down beside the shell and the whole was covered over with brush. The idea was that when an Allied tank drove over his position, the soldier was supposed to strike the detonator with the hammer. It is not known if any Allied vehicles were destroyed in this fashion, but Allied infantrymen caught a lot of Japanese troops assigned to this duty, and shot them before the hammer came down. The United States made only limited use of mines in the Pacific War.

Mines, Naval

Naval mines were first introduced during the mid-19th century. The TORPEDOES that Admiral David Glasgow Farragut "damned" at Mobile Bay in 1864 were actually mines. But for a long time the threat from mines was largely theoretical. Then came the Russo-Japanese War (1904–05), during which mines played a significant role. One battle was decided when the Russian flagship hit a mine and went down within minutes, taking with her the best Russian admiral of the day. Later the Japanese lost a third of their battleships to mines (their own mines) in one disastrous afternoon. Through and after World War I, mine technology developed steadily, so that during World War II a variety of mines was available. There were the original "contact mines," which go off when something hits them. New in World War II were magnetic mines, which detonate when large masses of steel pass by, and pressure mines, which go off if there is a change in water pressure, caused by a ship passing overhead. All of these could be delivered by surface ship, submarine, and, increasingly, by airplane.

Mines have generally been considered the weapon of the inferior naval power. And certainly no one has ever thought of them as a "warrior's weapon." In fact, many of the most perceptive naval commanders have tended to regard them with disdain. Despite this, the US Navy overcame its aversion to mines and used them extensively. Mines delivered by submarine and aircraft so effectively sealed off Japanese waters in 1945 as to completely shut down Japanese shipping, dealing the Japanese economy a deadly blow.

One reason that mines were so effective was that much Japanese shipping was actually carried by very small vessels, a response to Japan's long coastline and paucity of roads and railroads. Much of Japan's foodstuffs moved in small craft of 80 tons or less, which could easily run along coasts at night and hide in bays, rivers, and other inlets by day, where they could be CAMOUFLAGEd against American aircraft. Mines made this a problematic proposition. As a result, Japan began running short of food. Had Japan not surrendered in August 1945, many Japanese would have starved or frozen to death by the end of the next winter.

The Japanese also used mines effectively. Many US subs that never returned probably ran afoul of minefields planted off Japanese ports. The Japanese used mines extensively to defend their island bastions. These mines had to be cleared before the troops could hit the beach. This was dangerous work, with the minesweepers often operating under fire from Japanese shore batteries.

Some of the mines used against landing craft were planted like land mines. The 107-pound, Type 96 Japanese mine could be submerged under a few feet of water. Small landing craft and amphibious vehicles were the typical victims of this weapon. The only antidote was the UDT (Underwater Demolition Team) scuba divers the US Navy organized. UDT swimmers would go in at night, before an invasion, to disable mines and demolish other obstacles with explosives. This was, as one can imagine, very dangerous work. Sometimes the Japanese guarding the beaches were particularly alert and UDT CASUALTIES were very high. The UDT swimmers were an elite group and the only commando-type troops to be completely successful in the Pacific. The current US Navy SEAL teams are a direct descendant of the World War II-era UDTs.

Ref: Lott, *Most Dangerous Sea.*

Mitscher, Marc (1887–1947)

One of the most distinguished US naval officers in history, Marc Andrew Mitscher (1887–1947) graduated from Annapolis in 1910 and spent the next five years in battleships. In 1915 he took flight training, qualifying as a pilot the following year. During World War I he commanded various naval air stations. In 1919 he took part in an attempt to fly the Atlantic. Although his plane was forced down in the Azores by mechanical difficulties, another, *NC-4*, made it to Lisbon. Over the next few years he held various staff and air commands, and skippered a seaplane tender. In October of 1941 he became the first captain of the carrier *Hornet*, shortly rising to rear admiral in command of the *Hornet* task force, launching the DOOLITTLE bombers against Japan in April of 1942. After taking part in the Battle of MIDWAY, Mitscher for a time commanded a patrol wing, and in April of 1943 took command of all Allied air assets in the SOLOMONS.

The following January he was put in command of the newly formed Fast Carrier Task Force, TF 38/58. This he headed for most of the rest of the war, most notably in the Battle of the PHILIPPINE SEA, the Battle of LEYTE GULF, and ultimately in raids against the Japanese Home Islands. After the war Mitscher was promoted to full admiral. Continuing on active service, he died while in command of the Atlantic Fleet. Although overshadowed by HALSEY and, to a lesser extent, SPRUANCE, it was Mitscher who was responsible, under their overall direction, for the planning and execution of virtually all US carrier operations in the Pacific from January of 1944 onward.

Mogami Class, Japanese Heavy Cruisers.

Originally designed as light cruisers, mounting 15 6-inch guns ("A" on the light cruiser table), the Mogamis were refitted several times prior to being rebuilt in 1939–41. During this reconstruction they were converted to heavy cruisers mounting 10 8–inch guns ("B" on the heavy cruiser table). Despite shortcomings, they were tough ships.

Mogami (1931–1934–1935) helped cover operations in the East Indies early in the war, helping to sink *Houston* and PERTH in the Sunda Strait, and then escorted the First Air Fleet to Midway, where she was literally left a burning wreck after repeated US naval and marine air attacks. Remaining afloat, she managed to restore power, and returned to Japan for an extensive refit, lasting nearly a year, during which she was converted to something like the TONE CLASS, with six 8-inch guns in three turrets foreward, and a flight deck aft to operate a large number of floatplanes ("C" on the heavy cruiser table). She later accompanied Nishimura's squadron to SURIGAO STRAIT, where she was heavily damaged by gunfire and later sunk by dive bombers.

Mikuma (1931–1934–1935) was paired with *Mogami* from the start of the war until Midway, where on June 6, 1942 she was sunk by US Navy and Marine aircraft.

Suzuya (1933–1934–1937) operated with *Mogami* for much of the early part of the war, and then supported the battle force for most of the rest of the war, taking part in the action off SAMAR on 25 October 1944, during which she was sunk by carrier aircraft.

Kumano (1934–1936–1937) was paired with *Suzuya* until the action off Samar, in which she was severely damaged by air attack. She managed to escape, during which she took a TORPEDO from a submarine, and sought refuge in Dasoi Bay in the Philippines, where she was found and sunk by aircraft on 25 November 1944.

See also JAPAN, ATTITUDE TOWARD THE ENEMY; RECONNAISSANCE, NAVAL.

Mono, Bougainville

A small town with a sheltered anchorage but no facilities to supply or service ships; overshadowed as a potential base by RABAUL or KIETA, both nearby.

Montana Class, US Battleships

The five ships of the Montana Class were designed to succeed the IOWA CLASS battleships, being much larger and much more heavily armed, albeit at some sacrifice in speed. However, even before they were laid down it had become clear that the days of the battleship were numbered. Construction was suspended by order of President ROOSEVELT in April 1942, ostensibly as a result of a shortage of steel, and they were canceled in July 1943. Given the hull numbers BB-67 through BB-71, they were to have been named *Montana, Ohio, Maine, New Hampshire*, and *Louisiana*.

Morale

Happy, or less unhappy, troops are better fighters. Throughout history, military commanders have noted that cheering the troops up a bit improved their combat performance. At the very least, it reduced desertion and other forms of malingering. The Pacific War was no exception, even though the troops stuck on ships and sundry islands didn't

have the option of deserting. But the often horrendous physical conditions of this tropical battlefield did sap the will of the soldiers. Commanders quickly realized that they would have to cheer the lads up a bit from time to time in order to maintain morale and enthusiasm for the war.

As an example of what lengths American commanders would go to in the name of morale, consider that the US constructed on the 703.4 square miles of the MARIANA Islands and GUAM, 233 outdoor movie theaters, 65 staged theaters, 95 softball and 35 baseball fields, 225 volleyball and 30 basketball courts, and 35 boxing rings complete with seating for spectators, which works out to a total of 1.02 athletic facilities per square mile.

Danny Kaye entertains 4,000 leathernecks of the Fifth Marine Division on occupation duty at Sasebo, Japan. Literally hundreds of popular film and entertainment personalities made significant contributions to the war effort, promoting bond sales, making training films, and entertaining the troops in the field.

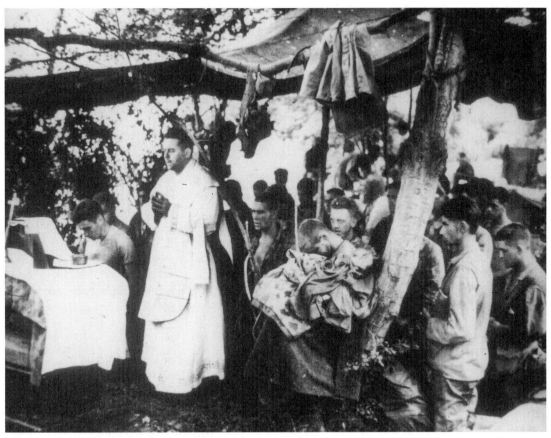

Using an improvised altar, a US Navy Roman Catholic chaplain conducts a field mass for Marines on Saipan, June 1944. Thousands of clergymen of all faiths were mobilized for service in the war, during which one earned a Medal of Honor.

The US Navy tried (and didn't always succeed) to provide a varied diet on board their ships. When possible, even ice cream was made on board. Army units were pulled out of battle when too many of their troops appeared to be getting punchy, and rear area rest facilities for the tired infantry were maintained. There were plenty of chaplains, entertainers, and other tangible evidence that the generals and admirals really cared.

America's allies also did what they could. To improve morale during the tedious New Guinea Campaign of World War II, an Australian officer offered a fortnight's home leave to whichever company in his brigade won a CAMOUFLAGE contest.

The result was an energetic competition, with the winners joyfully flying off for home. Unfortunately, upon arriving in Australia, the winning company, of the 39th Battalion, deserted almost to a man.

Japanese commanders tended to assume that morale was always high, regardless of circumstances, and that with their superior spirit Japanese troops could overcome all obstacles. As LG Renya Mutaguchi, commanding the Fifteenth Army in Burma put it shortly before his disastrous Imphal-Kohima Campaign in 1944, "Lack of weapons is no excuse for defeat." To be sure, raw courage and superior morale can win great victories against tremendous numerical and material odds. But as Inoguchi Rikihei, another Japanese soldier, observed, "Nothing is more destructive of morale than to learn of the enemy's superiority." As the war went on, the Japanese found themselves increasingly outclassed in material terms. No amount of élan could compensate for their inferiority. Toward the end of the war Japanese troops often went into action knowing that they could not possibly win. That they maintained their cohesion and discipline under such circumstances was extraordinary.

But the Japanese did make efforts to deal with troop morale. When there were foreigners about, they were preyed upon to provide more comfort for the troops. COMFORT WOMEN (non-Japanese women forced into prostitution) were one of the grimmer Japanese morale-building efforts, although the initial idea was to prevent the troops from rampaging and raping Chinese civilians in general.

The United States undertook a number of projects designed to undermine Japanese morale. Some of these were wholly impractical. For example, a study was made of the possibility of painting Mount Fuji red, which concluded that the project would consume so much paint, and so many aircraft that it might seriously impede the war effort.

Morotai, Moluccas, Netherlands East Indies

A small port, mostly suitable to coastal shipping, with no facilities. But it had some potential, and could be developed, particularly as an air base. The Japanese used it as a local base from 1942 onward.

Morison, Samuel Eliot (1887–1976)

Harvard scholar Morison became the principal historian of the US Navy in World War II when he suggested the assignment to fellow Harvard-man Franklin D. ROOSEVELT. He was well qualified for the job, being a seasoned sailor who had crossed the Atlantic under canvas, and a maritime historian of some note, his most famous work being a biography of Christopher Columbus, *Admiral of the Ocean Sea*. At one time or another Morison served in virtually all naval areas of operation, in eight different vessels, from battlewagons to Coast Guard cutters—though curiously never in a carrier—and was under fire often, as at KULA GULF, KOLOMBANGARA, and OKINAWA.

He began organizing and writing his 15-volume *History of United States Naval Operations in World War II* during the war, aided by a small staff, and later secured the cooperation of a number of former Japanese officers. The work is a remarkably literate, very complete treatment of the subject in sometimes extraordinary detail, which has stood the test of time rather well, despite the fact that he does not appear to have been privy to the existence of Ultra.

Quoque ipse miserrimi vidi, quorum pars magna fuit. ["These most grievous events I saw, and many of them I was."]

Mountbatten, Louis (1900–1979)

One of the youngest and most successful senior officers in the war, Louis Mountbatten's career was not harmed by his family connections. His father had been First Lord of the Admiralty for a time, and he himself was the uncle of Prince Philip of Greece and Denmark, during the war widely regarded as the prospective husband of Princess (later Queen) Elizabeth, which duly came to pass. A naval cadet and midshipman during World War I, by 1939 Mountbatten was a destroyer skipper. He commanded a British destroyer flotilla during the Norwegian Campaign and off Crete (Noel Coward's film *In Which We Serve* is loosely based on his exploits). In 1941 he was jumped several ranks and named head of Combined Operations, The Commandos. In order to enhance his already considerable clout he was simultaneously made a general and air marshal. In this role he oversaw numerous commando operations, and helped plan the raids on Dieppe and St.-Nazaire. From early 1943 he headed the Allied Southeast Asia Command, a post in which he rendered excellent service, being aided by a number of distinguished subordinates, most notably Bill SLIM. After the war he served as the last British viceroy of India, overseeing the British withdrawal and the partition. He later served in a variety of prominent military and civil posts, until his death by an IRA bomb in 1979. Mountbatten's abilities as a commander were considerable. Although his political connections helped smooth the way for him, he was an excellent administrator, could get along with the most sensitive egos, had a flair for the unusual, and possessed considerable charisma.

Munda, New Georgia, Solomon Islands

A well located peninsula off the island of New Georgia, in about the middle of the SOLOMONS, Munda had some plantation installations and a small port, of no particular importance. The plantation land was ideal for development into airfields. This the Japanese proceeded to do during the GUADALCANAL campaign, which led to US operations against New Georgia in 1943, Munda subsequently served as an Allied base.

Muskat, Oman

A small but decent harbor, with limited facilities and an important RAF base, Muskat, on the Persian Gulf of Oman, South Arabia, guarded the eastern approaches to the Persian Gulf, with its important oil resources and the Allied lifeline to Russia. It would have been the principal Japanese objective if the Imperial Navy had undertaken more extensive operations in the Indian Ocean. In October 1942 Japanese SUBMARINES briefly operated in the nearby Gulf of Oman, the farthest west in which the Imperial Navy conducted combat operations.

Mutsuki Class, Japanese Destroyers

The first Japanese destroyers designed after World War I, the Mutsukis were built 1923–27 and were refitted as fast transports early in the war. Despite this, they retained considerable antisubmarine and surface combat capability. All became war losses, most in the SOLOMONS.

MXY-7 Baka, Suicide Aircraft

The Japanese MXY-7 Baka was the ultimate KAMIKAZE aircraft. It was a rocket-propelled flying bomb that was carried underneath a bomber for most of its flight. When about 50 miles from the target area, the MXY-7 was released. The PILOT then guided the aircraft into a steep glide toward a target (at about 300 MPH). When near the enemy ships, the pilot aimed the aircraft right at its target and ignited the rocket for the last 30 seconds of the suicide flight. The rocket provided high enough speed to get past any defending fighters and anti-aircraft fire. While impressive on paper, the MXY-7 system didn't work. The lumbering bombers carrying the 1–1.5–ton rockets (there were two versions of the MXY-7) made easy targets for Allied interceptors. The high flying bombers (the MXY-7 needed some altitude before being dropped) were easily spotted by carrier radar. Those MXY-7s that did launch found that the new American proximity fuze shells, and heavy flak in general, presented a wall of exploding shells they had to fly through. But the Japanese had one thing right about the MXY-7. When it did hit a ship it was with devastating results. The speedy (over 500 MPH) rockets contained 1,300 or 2,600 pounds of explosive. It made quite a dent in whatever kind of ship it hit. Fortunately, only a few ships were hit by any of the 800 MXY-7s built.

See also KAMIKAZES, ROCKET POWERED.

N

N1K1 George, Japanese Fighter

The N1K1 George was originally developed as a Japanese floatplane fighter, but the floats were deleted and the N1K1 turned into a land-based naval fighter. The aircraft was fast, rugged, and extremely maneuverable. Entering combat in early 1944, it was quite a shock to Allied pilots. Like most other high-performance Japanese aircraft late in the war, the N1K1 suffered from repeated manufacturing defects and component failures. Only some 1,400 were produced.

See also AIRCRAFT TYPES, DEVELOPMENT.

Nachi Class, Japanese Heavy Cruisers

Good ships, designed with the experience of the FURUTAKAS and AOBAS in mind, the Nachis were much better protected, stabler, and somewhat faster vessels, being much larger (in violation of the 10,000–ton limit imposed by the naval limitation treaties). Despite this, like all Japanese ships they were rather cramped, having only 1.54 square meters of living space per man. Overall, they were tough ships, able to absorb considerable damage.

Nachi (1924–1927–1929) spent the early part of the war in the East Indies, where she fought in the JAVA SEA battles in February 1942, and operated against the British in the Indian Ocean later that year. She later fought in the KOMANDORSKI ISLANDS and at SURIGAO STRAIT, where she got away despite taking some hits and a collision with MOGAMI. Eleven days later, on 5 November 1944, she was sunk by carrier aircraft in Manila Bay.

Myoko (1924–1927–1929) began the war with *Nachi* in the East Indies, served as TAKAGI's flag-

ship in the CORAL SEA, ran TOKYO EXPRESS bombardment missions to GUADALCANAL, fought at EMPRESS AUGUSTA BAY and LEYTE GULF, where she took a TORPEDO and made for SINGAPORE. In mid-December 1944 she attempted to get home to Japan, to effect repairs, and was torpedoed off INDO-CHINA by *Bergall* (SS-320). She limped back to Singapore, where she was surrendered—still unrepaired—at the end of the war, and was scuttled by the British in 1946.

Haguro (1925–1925–1929) was one of the busiest of Japan's heavy cruisers. She began the war with *Nachi* and *Myoko* in the East Indies, played a critical role in the JAVA SEA battles, fought at the Coral Sea, at Empress Augusta Bay, and in the action against the escort carriers off SAMAR. She operated out of Singapore thereafter, and sank shortly after midnight on 16 May 1945 after taking eight torpedoes from British destroyers off PENANG in the Malacca Straits, having thus taken part in both the first and the last surface actions of the Pacific War.

Ashigara (1925–1928–1929) helped cover the Japanese invasion of the Philippines and East Indies and took part in the Indian Ocean operations. She had a minor role in Leyte Gulf, and took part in an abortive attempt to attack the landing force at LINGAYEN Gulf in January 1945, before retiring to Singapore again. On 8 June 1945 she took five torpedoes from the British T-Class submarine *Trenchant*, near the Banka Strait, off Java.

Nagano, Osami (1880–1947)

Osami Nagano was one of the senior Japanese naval admirals who got the fleet behind the idea of going to war with Britain and America. Nagano served as a military attaché in the United States just before World War I, but this did not change his attitude as a staunch Japanese nationalist. He failed to get Japan parity with Britain and America during the second London naval DISARMAMENT CONFERENCE in 1936, and pulled Japan out of the naval disarmament agreement. He served as navy minister, and then commander of the Combined Fleet during the 1930s. In early 1941 he became chief of the Naval General Staff. He was an enthusiastic supporter of the "strike south" (against Dutch oil fields) STRATEGY. Nagano went ahead with plans for the PEARL HARBOR strike despite the Foreign Ministry's continued efforts at diplomacy. He was an advocate of taking SAMOA to cut the American supply line to Australia, but the MIDWAY operation was selected instead. He was deposed by General TOJO in early 1944 when the army seized control of the Naval General Staff. He was tried as a war criminal after the war, but died of pneumonia during the trial. Nagano was smart but not a hard worker. He preferred to get others to do the work while he concentrated on politics (at which he was pretty good). When the war began, he was already in his 60s and losing his energy. Unable to wheel and deal as he once had, he lost his support in the Naval Staff and the Imperial Household as the war went on.

Nagara Class, Japanese Light Cruisers

Like all older Japanese cruisers, the Nagaras were small, lightly built, fast, and very obsolete by World War II standards. They spent most of the war as flotilla leaders, though one was converted into an antiaircraft cruiser.

Nagara (1920–1921–1922) led a destroyer flotilla during operations in the Philippines and East Indies, 1941–42, then with the First Air Fleet at MIDWAY, where she took NAGUMO and his staff off the burning AKAGI. She later served with Combined Fleet, and was lost off Kyushu on 7 August 1944 to *Croaker* (SS-246).

Natori (1920–1921–1922) led destroyers during operations in the East Indies and SOLOMONS, until sunk 18 August 1944 by *Hardhead* (SS-365) off SAMAR in the Philippines.

Yuru (1920–1922–1923) led a destroyer flotilla in the East Indies in 1941–42, and went on to fight in the Solomons, where she was severely damaged by Marine aircraft on 25 October 1942 near GUADALCANAL, and had to be sunk by Japanese destroyers. She was the first Japanese light cruiser to be sunk in the war.

Isuzu (1920–1921–1923) led destroyers with Combined Fleet and in the East Indies, where she was lost on 7 April 1945 by TORPEDOES from *Charr* (SS-328) and *Gabilan* (SS-252).

Kinu (1921–1922–1922) led destroyer flotillas, particularly with Combined Fleet, and later with carrier task forces until sunk by carrier air attack on 26 October 1944, in the aftermath of LEYTE GULF.

Abukuma (1921–1923–1925) led the destroyer flotilla that accompanied the PEARL HARBOR Strike Force, and spent most of the rest of the war with the battle fleet, though she did fight at the KOMANDORSKI ISLANDS. At SURIGAO STRAIT she was hit by a torpedo from *PT-137* on 25 October, and was sunk the next day off Los Negros, the Philippines, by air attack.

Nagasaki, Kyushu, Japan

Set at the head of a fine natural harbor, and partially surrounded by mountains, Nagasaki (population about 250,000 in 1940) was a major port and industrial city in western Kyushu, with extensive steel works and shipyards, the latter capable of building all classes of warships, up to carriers and battleships. The city was also the center of an important coal-mining area and was a major fishing port. The site of the local regional military district, in August 1945 Nagasaki was also the headquarters of an infantry brigade.

On 9 August 1945 Nagasaki was hit by the second ATOMIC BOMB. Some 65,000 to 75,000 people

Nagasaki, late 1945. The prominent structure is the Roman Catholic cathedral.

were killed or mortally wounded, and about a third of the city was left in ruins.

See also HIROSHIMA, THE PLOT.

Nagato Class, Japanese Battleships

Among the best older battleships in the world, the Nagatos were quite fast, well protected, and well armed. Under construction during the negotiations for the naval DISARMAMENT TREATIES, *Mutsu* was saved from the scrap heap when the Japanese negotiator observed that she had been paid for by the schoolchildren of Japan. The United States and Britain were allowed an increase in their battleship strength in compensation, the former retaining *Colorado* and *West Virginia*, originally slated to be scrapped, and the latter being allowed to build the two NELSON CLASS ships. Somewhat modernized

during the 1930s, like all Japanese battleships in the war, they saw little action.

Nagato (1917–1919–1920) spent most of the war with the battle force of Combined Fleet, initially as YAMAMOTO's flagship, until YAMATO became available. As a result, she was engaged only occasionally, taking some damage from a TORPEDO by *Skate* (SS-305) on Christmas Day, 1943. Her only serious action was against the escort carriers off SAMAR on October 25, 1944, during the Battle of LEYTE GULF. She ended the war relatively unscathed, the only surviving Japanese battleship, and was expended as a target during the 1946 Bikini atomic weapons trials.

Mutsu (1918–1920–1921) saw even less action than *Nagato*. On 8 June 1943 she was destroyed in HIROSHIMA harbor by an internal explosion, the nature of which has never been ascertained, but has generally been attributed to a new type of ammunition, the Mark 3 16–inch shell. This contained some 300 explosive submunitions (mini-bombs) and was designed for surface bombardment. It is believed that a Mark 3 round may have accidentally detonated in the ship's magazine, setting off a catastrophic explosion. The Mark 3 shell was withdrawn from service almost immediately after this incident.

Nagoya, Honshu, Japan

One of the principal bases of the Imperial Navy, a major port with extensive facilities to construct, repair, and service ships. Heavily bombed in 1944–1945.

Nagumo, Chuichi (1886–1944)

Chuichi Nagumo graduated from the Japanese naval academy in 1908, becoming a destroyerman and expert in TORPEDO warfare. During the 1920s he traveled in Europe and America, before returning to Japan to commence a series of increasingly important ship and squadron commands. Early in 1941 he was given the First Air Fleet, which he commanded in the attack on PEARL HARBOR. Although Japan's premier carrier admiral, Nagumo was not an able tactician or a bold leader. At Pearl Harbor his conservative nature caused him to refuse his staff's urging that a third strike be launched to hit the American fuel supplies and other targets at the now devastated base. However, in the following six months he added to his reputation by leading strikes against Allied bases in Australia and the Indian Ocean. His shortcomings didn't catch up with him until Midway, where his indecisiveness contributed to the loss of four Japanese carriers. He survived this debacle and continued to command carrier forces during 1942 as the Japanese attempted to retake GUADALCANAL. In these battles he again demonstrated a lack of drive and by the end of 1942 had been relegated to the command of the Sasebo Naval Base. In 1944, he was

given command of the forces defending SAIPAN. On July 7, 1944, he committed suicide as invading American forces completed their conquest of Saipan.

Naha, Okinawa

The principal port of Okinawa, Naha was small and cramped, and lacked important facilities, but did provide access to the island's several actual and many potential air bases. It was almost totally destroyed during the Okinawa Campaign.

Names, Battles, US versus Japanese

Many of the principal battles of the Pacific War have different names, depending upon whether the account is from the Allied side or the Japanese. Some examples are:

Allied Name of Battle	Japanese Name of Battle
Bandung Strait	Battle off Bali
Eastern Solomons	Second Battle of the Solomon Sea
Empress Augusta Bay	Gazelle Bay
Guadalcanal (Nov. '42)	Third Battle of the Solomon Sea
Komandorski Islands	Battle off Attu
Philippine Sea	Battle off the Marianas
Savo Island	First Battle of the Solomon Sea
Tassafaronga	Lunga Point
Unnamed	Battle of Horaniu

During the war there was occasionally more than one Allied name for a battle. The EASTERN SOLOMONS, for example, was sometimes referred to as the "Battle of the Stewart Islands." CAPE ESPERANCE was for a time officially known as the "Second Battle of Savo Island," the two November naval battles off GUADALCANAL being the "Third" and "Fourth," and TASSAFARONGA the "Fifth." But Santa Cruz is sometimes referred to as the "Third Battle of Savo Island," and Tassafaronga is also sometimes known as the Fourth or Sixth Battle of Savo Island. Similarly, the two naval battles of Guadalcanal (12–13 and 14–15 November 1942) are actually part of single air-sea battle that lasted

12–15 November, sometimes known to the Allies as the "Battle of the Solomons," and designated by the Japanese the "Third Battle of the Solomon Sea." The Battle of KOLOMBANGARA is sometimes referred to as the "Second Battle of Kolombangara," an otherwise unnamed engagement several weeks earlier in which several US cruisers and destroyers sank two Japanese destroyers off Vila, Kolombangara, being sometimes called the "First." To further complicate matters, Kolombangara is also occasionally referred to as the "Second Battle of KULA GULF" as well, since that took place in virtually the same waters!

National Guard

The National Guard constitutes the active militia of the individual states of the United States. Although neglected between the wars, it began to expand in the mid–1930s, and after the German invasion of Poland it was quietly expanded from 199,500 officers and men, so that by the summer of 1940 it comprised approximately 242,000 Guardsmen and was still growing. That September, the president began ordering National Guard units into federal service under special authority from Congress. This was accomplished in 22 increments, totaling as many as 63,646 officers and men in the first increment, down to as few as 362 in the last increment, in June 1941. A total of 297,754 National Guardsmen were taken into federal service, totaling 19,795 officers, 221 warrant officers, and 277,738 enlisted men. Only 1,032 of the prewar Guardsmen were refused induction. Although the accuracy of the figure is hard to confirm, by some estimates more than 75,000 (over 27%) of National Guard enlisted men eventually became officers during the war. In addition, Guard units won 148 Presidential Unit Citations, while individual Guardsmen were awarded 14 Medals of Honor, 50 Distinguished Service Crosses, 48 Distinguished Flying Crosses, and over 500 Silver Stars, testifying to the basic quality of National Guard manpower.

Although the preparedness, training, intelligence, and efficiency of the National Guard was generally—usually unjustly—denigrated by Regulars and the press, in fact it provided the nation with an immensely important pool of more or less trained men at a time when such were in short supply: The total Regular Army was only about 300,000 men at the time the Guard was federalized. It is worth noting that of the 12 divisions the army shipped overseas in 1942, eight were composed of National Guardsmen, and one included a National Guard regiment. Indeed, all seven of the divisions the army sent to the Pacific War in 1942 were composed at least partially of National Guardsmen (in order, the 27th, 41st, 32nd, American, 37th, and 43rd, which were followed by the 25th, which included a National Guard infantry regiment), as were two of the five divisions that went to the European Theater that year (the 34th and 29th, the others being the First, Third, and Ninth). By the end of the war, of 22 army divisions in the Pacific, 10.6 had their origins in the National Guard (48.2%), whereas of the 67 divisions that served in the European-Mediterranean-Middle Eastern Theater, only nine were from the National Guard (13.4%). Moreover, many of the so-called Regular Army and Reserve (i.e., draftee) divisions raised during the war were organized around cadres drawn from existing National Guard divisions. For example, the 30th Infantry Division (Guardsmen from the Carolinas, Georgia, and Tennessee), activated in September 1940, was actually down to only 2,100 officers and men exactly two years later, the balance of its manpower having been transferred to form the cadres of several new divisions. Of course, this meant that in fact much of the manpower of many ostensibly National Guard divisions was actually composed of draftees or volunteers, rather than Guardsmen.

To be sure, there were some problems with the National Guard units that first went into combat. Many of the troops were rather older than the optimal age for infantrymen, in their late 20s and early 30s or even older, rather than their late teens and early 20s. Then too, some National Guard personnel were not as well trained as they might have been. But then, as the disaster at Kasserine Pass in

North Africa in late 1942 demonstrated, neither were many old Regulars or new draftees. It's worth recalling that most armies—and most units—have problems upon first entering combat, and that the first US Army units to enter combat in the Pacific were National Guard units. Without the National Guard, getting ready would have taken longer.

Nauru Island, Central Pacific

Apart from some facilities to load phosphates, Nauru (8 square miles) lacked a port, although it could be said to have some value as a potential air base, lying south of the eastern CAROLINES and west of the GILBERTS, each only a few hundred miles distant. In 1942 it was under Australian administration when the Japanese walked in. Several times raided by U.S. naval aircraft, it remained under Japanese control until the end of the war.

Navaho Code Talkers, USMC

Early in 1942 the Marine Corps received a proposal to use Navaho Indians as communications technicians. By making use of their native tongue, an unwritten language virtually unknown by anyone but the Navaho, these men would be able to send radio and telephone messages without using codes, thereby facilitating communications. After tests, which demonstrated that this method of communication was faster than having to encode and then decode messages, the proposal was adopted. In September 1942 recruiting began for 200 Navaho to serve as communications specialists. The first group of recruits, 29 men, not only trained in radio and telephone communications, but also created a greatly expanded vocabulary for their language, inventing new words or adapting existing ones where the language lacked equivalent terms: Thus, Navaho for "turtle" was given the additional meaning of "tank."

The first Navaho code talkers reported for duty with Marine units in the Pacific in early 1943. That spring Marine commanders were asked their opinion of the program, and they universally praised it.

Navaho code talkers thereafter took part in every Marine operation for the rest of the war. Surprisingly, records as to the number of men so employed are imprecise. Estimates vary from about 375 to about 420. Attempts to determine the exact figure are futile, as many Navaho Marine veterans (altogether about 5,000 Navaho served in the armed forces during the war) subsequently claimed to have served as code talkers, but did not in fact do so.

Interestingly, before the outbreak of the war, Japanese intelligence suggested the possibility that the United States might use Indians as communications specialists. However, they decided that the language of choice was certain to be Lakota (Sioux), possibly because of the great military reputation of that nation. However, there were actually far more Navaho than Sioux, and they had proven pretty tough warriors as well, but had received less press coverage.

Naval Battles, Surface, in the Pacific

Before the Pacific War actually began, on 7 December 1941, surface combat was still expected to be the decisive form of naval action in the long-anticipated Japanese-American war. Certainly nothing that had occurred in the European war, which by then had been raging for more than two years, suggested otherwise.

However, PEARL HARBOR and the air-sea battles of CORAL SEA and MIDWAY in mid–1942 seemed to demonstrate that aircraft carriers now ruled the waves, rather than battleships and cruisers. But Coral Sea and Midway were followed by the EASTERN SOLOMONS and the SANTA CRUZ ISLANDS, which, together with some unfortunate torpedoings, effectively depleted everyone's carrier forces.

As a result, most of the naval actions from late 1942 until well into 1943 were surface engagements, occasionally influenced by the presence of aircraft. In fact, there were over a dozen major and several score minor engagements between battleships, cruisers, and destroyers during the Pacific War.

Aside from a number of surface actions in the Dutch East Indies in early 1942 and in the Philippines in 1944 virtually all of the remaining surface engagements took place in the Solomon Islands, notably in the vicinity of GUADALCANAL, where in the six months from August of 1942 through February of '43 there occurred five major and about 30 smaller surface engagements.

Before the war, the Japanese and the Americans had developed differing notions about surface combat. The Japanese, mindful of their probable numerical inferiority in a war with the United States, trained for night actions and stressed the use of TORPEDOES by both destroyers and cruisers. They preferred putting their heavier ships in the van, and were willing to use multiple columns, permitting the tactical independence of different squadrons operating together. All of these techniques were to make it easier for a smaller Japanese force to defeat a larger Allied one. And they worked.

The US Navy, in contrast, was fairly rigidly tied to the single line ahead formation, with destroyers at the van and rear and the heavier ships in the middle, all to operate under a single command. For all practical purposes, the US Navy saw no need to innovate or question what it was doing or what it was likely to face when surface naval combat occurred. Little attention was paid to Japanese preparations for the coming war, even though little effort would have been required to discover what the Japanese were doing to get ready. In fact, some military attachés in Tokyo did discern that the Japanese Navy was rather more effective than conventional wisdom in the West had it. These reports were generally ignored until it was too late.

When the two navies began to clash in surface actions, it quickly became apparent that the Japanese were superior. The battles did not conform to the USN's expectations. The extensive availability of land-based aircraft caused most surface battles to occur at night, since control of the air in daylight usually translated into victory. In night surface combat, the Japanese initially had an advantage. During peacetime they had trained hard for night

surface combat. They had evolved more realistic tactics for night combat and drilled their ships' crews relentlessly in all types of weather, regardless of CASUALTIES. In addition, they had developed superior optical equipment for range finding.

American sailors had received a more leisurely diet of daytime training exercises, marred by a contest-like atmosphere that resulted in training being conducted in the calmest possible weather, so that no ship would have an unfair advantage. Moreover, unlike their US counterparts, all Japanese cruisers carried torpedoes and many of them were provided with torpedo reloads. The cruiser crews were well trained in the use of torpedoes, something rare with torpedo equipped cruisers. The Japanese torpedoes were superior to all others in the world, being larger, more reliable, and longer ranged. The US admirals had generally neglected the use of the torpedo in surface combat, omitting it entirely from most cruisers, for example, and not getting enough practice in coordinating torpedo-armed destroyers with heavier ships during maneuvers.

So from the JAVA SEA battles (February 27–March 1, 1942) through the summer and fall battles around Guadalcanal, the Japanese were generally triumphant at night. American sailors had to undergo the same grueling training process as the Japanese before US surface ships could meet the Japanese on equal terms.

A lot of material changes in late 1942 helped the United States, but it was training that made the difference. Meanwhile, the USN gradually acquired superior ships, improved damage-control techniques, and found better communications methods. And it began to learn to use its torpedoes.

The torpedo was actually the most effective weapon used in the night battles, accounting for most of the ships lost. As it turned out, American destroyermen already knew how to make effective torpedo attacks, but had usually been kept on a tight leash by task force commanders intent on slugging it out. Given a chance to operate on their own they proved particularly effective in torpedo attacks, as at BALIKPAPAN (January 23–24, 1942) or CAPE ESPERANCE (October 11–12, 1942). Despite this, it was not until mid-1943 that US destroyers were routinely allowed to operate in conjunction with, rather than in line with, heavier ships.

Meanwhile, radar came along. Surprisingly, initially it may have actually handicapped US night fighting abilities. The first radars were inefficient, temperamental, and not at all understood by most senior officers. At times the presence of Japanese warships was first detected by lookouts, if it had not already been announced by the arrival of their shells, before they were detected by radar, at which point it was usually too late to do anything but die bravely. As radar improved and commanders who understood its capabilities and limitations (like Willis "Ching Chong China" LEE) came along, things began to improve, and American ships began to feel more comfortable in night actions. However, the Japanese remained formidable opponents. At KULA GULF (July 4–5, 1943) and KOLOMBANGARA (July 12–13, 1943) they gave better than they received, despite all the American ad-

vantages. But gradually they lost their edge, and in the last important surface actions of the war on anything like even terms, VELLA LAVELLA (August 6–7, 1943) and EMPRESS AUGUSTA BAY (November 2, 1943), the Japanese came off second best.

It had been a tough school, but the US Navy had learned, albeit the hard way. Learning how to fight while in combat is the hard way; learning during tough, realistic peacetime training is the easy way.

Naval War, World War II Outside the Pacific

Although Americans are wont to think that the naval war against Japan was where the seagoing action was during the Second World War, in fact the hottest maritime war was that against Germany and Italy, in terms of the loss not only of shipping, but also of major warships, destroyers, cruisers, carriers, and battlewagons.

Note, also, that the Axis actually inflicted and suffered losses in the Indian Ocean and the Pacific, where German and Italian SUBMARINES and surface raiders operated with some success against Allied shipping. The Axis accounted for a couple of warships in the Indian Ocean. For example, the German armed merchant raider *Kormoran* sank HMAS *Sydney* off Western Australia on Armistice Day, 1941, being sunk in turn as a result of damage

NAVAL FORCES IN THE PACIFIC, DECEMBER 1941

	Japanese	US	Allies	Totals
A/C: Carrier	545	280	—	280
A/C: Other	2,140	1,180	600	1,780
Carriers	10	3	0	3
Battleships	11	9	2	11
Heavy Cruisers	18	13	1	14
Light Cruisers	17	11	10	21
Destroyers	104	80	20	100
Submarines	67	73	13	86

Figures for carriers exclude ships working up (i.e., not yet fully operational) and escort carriers. Including these would raise the Japanese totals to 13 carriers with about 650 aircraft; US ships in these categories were all in the Atlantic. A/C indicates aircraft, with "Other" including non-naval land-based machines; US figures include aircraft in California, Washington, and Oregon. Allied battleship figures include one battlecruiser. The US allies were the British Commonwealth (Britain, Australia, New Zealand, Canada, and India) and the Netherlands. The United States also had its Atlantic Fleet, from which it quickly withdrew three carriers to improve the carrier odds in the Pacific, as well as a number of battleships and other vessels, but these were not available on 7 December 1941.

MAJOR WARSHIP LOSSES BY THEATER

Theater	Area	Number	Percent
European		856	58.9
	Atlantic	399	27.4
	Baltic/Black	126	8.7
	Mediterranean	331	22.8
Pacific		598	41.1
	Indian Ocean	25	1.7
	Pacific Ocean	573	39.4
Total		1,454	100.0

inflicted by her opponent. The Allies suffered no warship or merchant ship losses in the Atlantic at the hands of the Japanese.

See also GERMANY IN THE PACIFIC WAR; ITALY IN THE PACIFIC WAR.

Ref: Brown, *Warship Losses of World War Two*.

Ndeni, Santa Cruz Islands

Poorly suited to serve as a potential naval base, Ndeni did possess some possible value as an air base, helping to cover a wide area of the south-central Pacific, lying only about 400 miles east of GUADALCANAL and the same distance north of ESPIRITU SANTO. But the island was infected with a particularly virulent strain of malaria, which made it a dangerous place for foreigners. US forces reconnoitered the island for possible use as an air base in June 1942, and shortly thereafter the seaplane tender USS *Curtiss* arrived to establish a seaplane base. In October navy SEABEES laid out an airstrip, but construction never went beyond that stage, as malaria proved an insurmountable obstacle, causing numerous CASUALTIES and some deaths. Shortly after the Battle of the Santa Cruz Islands the project was abandoned. Not even COASTWATCHERS were left on the island, although Australian authorities did recruit men for labor service.

Nelson Class, British Battleships

Britain's Nelson Class had an odd design, to say the least. With three triple turrets forward of the superstructure ("C" turret, the third, was lower than "B" and could not fire ahead), intended to save weight, the Nelsons were the only battleships built during the "naval holiday" introduced by the DISARMAMENT TREATIES, and were actually rather successful. They were armored on the "Nevada" ("all or nothing") plan (See NEVADA CLASS, US BATTLESHIPS), which stressed enormous protection for vital areas and nothing at all elsewhere.

They were good ships, but very slow by World War II standards. They saw considerable service in the Indian Ocean.

Nelson (1922–1925–1927) spent most of the war in the North Sea, the Atlantic, and the Mediterranean. In late 1944 she joined the British Far Eastern Fleet, and supported British operations against Burma, MALAYA, and the Netherlands Indies until the surrender of Japan.

Rodney (1922–1925–1927) also spent most of the war in the ETO, the high point taking place on May 27, 1941 when, with HMS KING GEORGE V, she helped pound the German battleship *Bismarck* to destruction in the Atlantic. In late 1944 she accompanied *Nelson* to the Far East and served there until the end of the war.

Both ships were scrapped in 1948.

See also ROYAL NAVY.

Netherlands, The

Under German occupation from May 1940 to virtually the end of the war in Europe, the Netherlands could make only a limited contribution to the defense of its vast East Indian empire. There was a small army and air force in the NETHERLANDS EAST INDIES, but the main element of Dutch power in the region was the Royal Netherlands Navy, with three light cruisers, seven destroyers, and about 15 SUBMARINES. These put up a tough fight, only one light cruiser and seven submarines escaping the Japanese onslaught. Dutch influence on the Pacific War waned thereafter. Although a few Dutch ships always served with the British fleet in the Indian Ocean, while some reconnaissance aircraft as well as a small ground force operated out of Australia or those portions of Netherlands New Guinea not occupied by the Japanese, the Dutch played only a marginal military role in the Pacific. However, the large Dutch merchant marine proved of enormous value to the Allied cause. Of particular importance were the many small ships designed for inter-island trade in the East Indies, which escaped from the Japanese and helped support Australian and American operations in New Guinea waters.

Netherlands East Indies

Now called INDONESIA, these 3,000 islands stretch from Sumatra to western New Guinea, and total about 750,000 square miles. Some areas were well developed and densely populated (JAVA, Amboina, Bali), while others were thinly peopled, virtually virgin tropical forests (BORNEO, New Guinea). Rich in resources (oil, tin, rice, and more), the Netherlands East Indies constituted the core of the "Southern Resources Area" for which Japan was fighting.

When the Pacific War broke out the defense of the Netherlands East Indies was an impossible task. Although reinforced by some Australian and American troops and aircraft, the Dutch forces were greatly outnumbered by the Japanese. Moreover, the defense of the Indies was primarily a maritime problem, and the Allies could not commit ships and aircraft in numbers sufficient to do more than impede the Japanese advance. Nevertheless, Allied resistance was often fierce.

Under Japanese rule, the Netherlands East Indies were brutally exploited for their resources, to feed the Japanese economy. However, although they profited greatly from the tin and rubber produced in the Indies, the Japanese were never able to restore the oil fields to any sustained degree of PRODUCTION. In addition to material resources, the Japanese made extensive use of East Indians as slave laborers, many tens of thousands being shipped abroad. Most of these people did not survive the war.

In line with their "Asia for the Asiatics" policies, the Japanese supported local nationalist leaders, among them Sukarno, and promised eventual independence after the war. In fact, the nationalists who supported the Japanese were in league with those who took to the hills in presumed support of the Netherlands. The objective of both groups was the independence of the East Indies, not Japanese

or Dutch rule. Approximately 100,000 military and paramilitary personnel were organized by the collaborators ostensibly to support the Japanese. Shortly after the armistice of 15 August, these troops began clashing with Japanese forces, which were supposed to maintain "order" until relieved by Allied forces. When the British arrived, as surrogates for the Dutch, heavy fighting broke out as the erstwhile collaborationist troops began a full-scale insurrection against Dutch rule. This culminated in the eventual independence of Indonesia.

Netherlands East Indies Army

The bulk of the troops in the Dutch East Indian Army were locally raised. Organized, trained, and equipped primarily as a colonial constabulary, the army was badly scattered in numerous small garrisons, albeit that on paper two divisions and a division sized-task force existed. Total manpower was in the vicinity of 125,000, of whom about a fifth were Dutch, about as many more of mixed Dutch-Indonesian background or Indonesian Christians, and the rest natives of various cultural and ethnic backgrounds. When the Japanese came, the performance of the army was very uneven. Many units simply disintegrated, while others, particularly those with high proportions of Eurasian or native Christian troops, acquitted themselves well. Ultimately the difference didn't matter, as the defense of the Dutch East Indies was a naval problem; The destruction of the ABDA fleet at the end of February 1942 sealed the fate of the Netherlands East Indian Army.

Small elements of the Netherlands East Indies Army managed to maintain a GUERRILLA resistance on TIMOR with Australian assistance, before escaping to Australia in 1943, where they joined other elements that had escaped the collapse of Dutch power in the East Indies. Other detachments survived in the southern portions of Netherlands New Guinea, where the Japanese never reached. These enabled the Netherlands to maintain a token participation in the Pacific War. Although the Dutch government-in-exile authorized the creation of the First Netherlands East Indian Infantry Battalion for service on New Guinea, the primary role of the Netherlands ground forces (which included a lot of New Guineans and Indonesians under Dutch officers) was in providing scouts and guides for Australian troops. The only battalion-sized operation undertaken by the Netherlands East Indies Army was in support of the Australian landing at BALIKPAPAN.

Neutrality Acts, US

A series of laws enacted in the 1930s and designed to prevent the United States from being "dragged" into a war against its will. By the early 1930s a coterie of isolationist historians, political hacks of the far left and far right, and pacifists of various stripes, including many religious organizations, had established the notion that the American entry into World War I was due to a conspiracy on the part of the Allied powers and American bankers and munitions makers, the so-called "Merchants of Death." This theory attained its greatest influence as a result of the "Nye Commission." In 1934 Senator Gerald Nye headed an inquiry into the origins of American involvement in World War I. Calling only a handful of witnesses, all of them adherents of the "Merchants of Death" theory, the commission "proved conclusively" that Uncle Sam had been hustled into the war against his best interests. As a result, pacifist organizations applied pressure on Congress to enact a series of laws that would "insure" that the United States would never again go to war "against its will." These laws renounced the rights of neutrals in time of war, rights that had formed a cornerstone of American foreign policy since independence.

1935: Prohibited the sale or transport of munitions to belligerents by Americans, and withdrew American protection from citizens who traveled on belligerent ships or in war zones.
1936: Prohibited loans to belligerents.

1937: Modified the 1935 measure to permit "cash-and-carry" sales of certain goods to belligerents (i.e., they had to pay hard currency and take the goods away in their own ships).
1939: Authorized the president to prohibit US-flagships from entering "danger zones" in order to prevent international incidents likely to lead to war.

The Neutrality Acts were the culmination of the 1920s effort to legislate peace. Their primary effect was to encourage aggression. These laws helped convince both HITLER and the Japanese militarists that the United States lacked the moral courage for war.

The acts proved a serious impediment to assisting the Allies when World War II broke out. Only gradually, as the threat of Axis aggression grew, were the provisions of the law modified, culminating in LEND-LEASE.

Nevada Class, US Battleships

Old battleships, but well designed and a significant advance on the previous NEW YORK CLASS, they introduced a new armoring scheme, the "Nevada Plan," in which protection was on the "all or nothing" basis: Absolutely vital areas of the ship were given extremely heavy protection (13.5-inch side armor with 18 inches on the turret faces), while everything else was ignored. Both served with the ROYAL NAVY during World War I, although they saw no action. Between the wars they were extensively rebuilt.

Nevada, BB-36 (1912–1914–1916), was the only battleship to get underway during the PEARL HARBOR attack; she incurred heavy damage and was beached rather than risk having her sink in the narrow harbor entrance. Raised, she was extensively rebuilt and emerged as a very successful ship, in appearance surprisingly similar to the SOUTH DAKOTA CLASS. She saw action at Attu, then operated in the European Theater, helping support the Normandy invasion, and returned to the Pacific, where she continued to support amphibious operations. She took a KAMIKAZE off OKINAWA. After the war she was used as a target in the Bikini nuclear weapons tests, and finally sunk in weapons trials in 1948.

OKLAHOMA, BB-37 (1912–1914–1916), was struck hard below the waterline at Pearl Harbor and capsized. Hundreds of men trapped below were rescued through holes hastily cut in her bottom, but others could not be reached and died there. She became the object of one of the largest salvage operations in history, and after her hull was sealed while still under water, on 16 June 1943 she righted by a series of 21 bents, massive frames mounted right on her hull, linked to enormous winches ashore. It was determined that she was not worth repairing and she was sold for scrap. Shortly after the war she was being towed to the United States when she broke loose in a storm about 500 miles northwest of Hawaii, and was never seen again.

New Britain, Bismarck Archipelago

The largest of the BISMARCKS, an archipelago to the northeast of New Guinea, of which it was administratively a part under an Australian mandate dating from World War I. About 14,600 square miles, the island was very undeveloped and thinly inhabited, but RABAUL, the principal town, had a fine harbor, with numerous nearby sites suitable for airfields.

On January 26, 1942, Japanese troops landed on New Britain and seized the major anchorage at Simpson Harbor, Rabaul. The Japanese proceeded to make Rabaul a major military base. The Allies decided to bypass Rabaul rather than assault it directly. This approach, called operation CARTWHEEL required landing on New Britain Island to establish bases from which to isolate Rabaul. The first landings, by the US Army's 112th Cavalry Regiment, took place on 15 December 1943, 280 miles west of Rabaul itself. On December 26, the First Marine Division landed on the opposite side of the island from the army landing. The Japanese had a few thousand troops from their 17th Division on that part of New Britain, and these were either killed or forced back to the eastern (Rabaul) end of New Britain. By April 1943, the fighting was over on New Britain. The original invading troops were withdrawn, and a variety of other US Army and Australian units were sent to maintain a presence on New Britain until the end of the war, keeping watch on the Japanese pocket at Rabaul.

New Britain was a terrible place to campaign. Hot, humid, full of jungle and swamp, it was an unhealthy and very uncomfortable place to live. At the time, and ever since, it was suggested that no invasion of New Britain take place, for there was little the Japanese could do on the island once supplies of fuel and munitions could no longer get through.

New Caledonia

A French colony, New Caledonia is a group of islands about 750 miles east of Australia and 870

Marines struggle with a 3-foot surf as they wade ashore at Cape Gloucester, New Britain, December 26, 1943.

Cape Gloucester, January 1944, Marines armed with the Browning .50 caliber heavy machine gun. During January the Japanese launched several determined counterattacks on the Marine positions at Cape Gloucester. These were beaten off by machine-gun and artillery fire, and the Japanese withdrew into the jungle, abandoning their efforts to eject the Marines.

north of New Zealand, totaling about 7,400 square miles, most of it in New Caledonia proper (c. 6,500 square miles). Mountainous, but pleasantly tropical, the islands were thinly inhabited. When the Pacific War broke out the Free French administration placed them at the disposal of the United States, which used them as a staging area for the offensive into the SOLOMONS during 1942, developing the capital of NOUMEA into a major base.

New Guinea

The second largest island in the world (after Greenland), lying in the southwest Pacific, north of Australia and east of the NETHERLANDS EAST INDIES. The rugged, wet, tropical, and jungle-clad island is about 300,000 square miles. The population was very sparse: By one estimate there were only about 6,000 persons of European stock and 500,000 Melanesians in Papua, the southeastern quarter of the island. Much of New Guinea was largely unexplored on the eve of World War II. Mostly covered by jungle, there were virtually no roads, with a few airfields here and there hacked out of the jungle by ambitious miners. A rugged chain of mountains more or less completely divides the northern side of the island from the southern.

Extremes of climate are common in highland areas, with steamy, tropical days and chilly temperate nights making for an interesting contrast. A great many poisonous plants and animals were to be found, as well as a variety of interesting tropical diseases. Most of the inhabitants were Melanesians, belonging to numerous warlike tribes more or less living in the Neolithic Age and enormously suspicious of outsiders (those miners had not always been peaceful).

The western half of the island was owned by the Netherlands and administered as part of the Netherlands East Indies, although it was ethnically and culturally distinct from the other Dutch holdings. With the Japanese invasion, the Dutch presence in the island virtually evaporated. Although US and Australian forces paid lip service to Netherlands' sovereignty, they generally conducted themselves with little regard for the token Dutch presence.

Australia owned Papua, the southeastern quarter of the island, which was organized as a territory of the Commonwealth. It also controlled the northeastern portion of the island through a League of Nations MANDATE, which required it to prepare the territory for eventual independence. With the Japanese invasion, the administrative differences between the two Australian territories tended to become blurred.

The Japanese invaders were ill-prepared for what they found in New Guinea. Relations with the natives deteriorated rapidly. The Japanese penchant for casual massacre and their efforts to recruit COMFORT WOMEN rapidly drove even the most anti-white Papuans and New Guineans to support the king's men over the emperor's. As a result, for most of the protracted New Guinea Campaign— and fighting on the enormous island was more or less continuous from mid-1942 to the end of the war—the natives were generally friendly to the allies.

Prior to the outbreak of the war, Australia had developed rudimentary armed forces in both Papua and New Guinea, which were later merged into the PACIFIC ISLANDS REGIMENT.

New Guinea, Campaign for, 1942–43

While GUADALCANAL is generally regarded as the pivotal land battle in the first year of the Pacific War, it was actually only an extension of operations in New Guinea, which was the main campaign in the South Pacific.

New Guinea, a large tropical island north of Australia, was, before the war, controlled by Holland (the western half) and Australia (the rest). Smaller groups of islands extended to the northeast (the BISMARCKS) and southeast (the SOLOMONS, at virtually the tail end of which was Guadalcanal). All these were considered vital parts of the Japanese defensive system.

New Guinea was the scene of some of the longest and toughest ground combat of the Pacific War. The Japanese landed on the north coast of in early March 1942. The Australians (and later Americans) were on the south coast. Fighting first raged in the OWEN STANLEY MOUNTAINS, which form the rugged spine of New Guinea. This fighting combined the worst aspects of jungle and mountain combat. The Japanese had managed to struggle over the mountains against Australian rearguard resistance, but had been halted literally a few dozen miles north of PORT MORESBY, the principal Allied base in New Guinea. Then they fell back, in an agonizing retreat that cost the lives of many men.

By late 1942, the fighting was concentrated on Japanese positions on the north coast. This fighting continued into 1944 as the Japanese continually reinforced their battered forces, while American and Australian forces "leap frogged" their way along the coast, isolating Japanese strongpoints. The Allied objective was to push the Japanese off New Guinea and keep advancing west to the nearby Japanese-controlled oil fields. Japanese pockets in New Guinea were still being guarded into 1945. The fighting and maneuvering was constant, with dozens of amphibious landings and hundreds of battles on land and in the air. It was during this campaign that the US Army Air Force developed the successful tactic of using the twin-engine B-25 bomber to attack Japanese shipping.

New Guinea was something of a forgotten battle. Partially this was because of the way the media worked. New Guinea was almost wholly an army affair with few Marines and relatively little naval action. In addition, even more than Guadalcanal, New Guinea was a protracted, grinding jungle campaign, characterized by mud, heat, and disease. New Guinea was a tropical meatgrinder of constant combat through steaming jungles and steep mountains. All the aircraft operated from primitive, often mud-soaked airfields. While Guadalcanal was over in six months, New Guinea went on for years. In the eyes of the American public, New Guinea soon became dreary. That attitude carried on in the public's memory after the war.

Although the New Guinea fighting did more to cripple the Japanese armed forces, Guadalcanal still rated higher in the pantheon of Pacific battles.

Ref: *Australia in the Second World War: Series I, Army*, vols. 4 and 6; Prefer, *MacArthur's New Guinea Campaign*.

New Hebrides

Now called Vanuatu, a group of about 75 islands, atolls, and islets in the southwest Pacific, about a

Troops of the 163rd Infantry, 41st Infantry Division, land at Wadke Island, May 18, 1944, increasing the isolation of Japanese forces on New Guinea.

A US Signal Corps cameraman, T4 Ernani d'Emidio, took this shot of two of his comrades, Sgt. Carl Weinke and PFC Marjoram, as they waded in a stream in New Guinea on April 22, 1944. The terrain is fairly typical of the coastal areas of New Guinea, where fighting continued throughout the war.

thousand miles northeast of Australia. Three of the islands (Efate, ESPIRITU SANTO, and Tana) were of importance, and they comprised most of the 5,700 square miles of the group. Thinly inhabited by Melanesians (Port Vila, the capital and largest settlement, on Efate, had only about 1,500 inhabitants in 1942), the islands were jointly owned by Britain and France, and made a poor living off of tropical produce and fishing.

A small US force landed at Efate from NOUMEA, in NEW CALEDONIA, in March 1942. From May 1942, Efate began to be developed as a major base, and by July 1942 US troops were developing airstrips on Espiritu Santo, the largest and most northerly of the islands. With GUADALCANAL less than 600 miles to the northwest, Espiritu Santo soon became the most important US base in the South Pacific outside of Australia, and it remained so until the fighting moved up the chain of the SOLOMONS in 1943.

During the war there was no fighting in the New Hebrides. Japanese SUBMARINES were active in the area, however, and laid many MINES, which did cause some losses to Allied shipping. About 1,300 residents were recruited as labor troops. The war brought considerable prosperity to the islands, and a great deal of political and social change.

Ref: White and Lindstrom, *The Pacific Theater*.

New Mexico Class, US Battleships

The New Mexico Class battleships were substantially similar in design to the preceding PENNSYLVANIA CLASS, although much different in appearance. In the Atlantic in December of 1941, they were spared the trauma of PEARL HARBOR, and also the extensive modernization that the veterans of that disaster underwent, so that aside from numerous additions to their antiaircraft armament, they remained substantially unmodernized. All three were sent to the Pacific shortly after Pearl Harbor, where they formed part of the battle force that would have been all that remained had the Japanese won the carrier fight at MIDWAY. They spent the rest of the war supporting amphibious landings.

New Mexico, BB-40 (1915–1917–1918), was scrapped in 1947.

Mississippi, BB-41 (1915–1917–1917), fired one salvo at SURIGAO STRAIT, during the Battle of LEYTE GULF, and that the last one, after a cease-fire had been ordered. By some calculations these shells were the last rounds to strike *Yamashiro*, and so she has the distinction of being the last battlewagon to hit another in action. After the war she served as a test-bed for shipboard missile experimentation, until scrapped in 1957.

Idaho, BB-42 (1915–1917–1919), was scrapped in 1947.

New Orleans Class, US Heavy Cruisers

Representing a significant break with the earlier series of US heavy cruisers, the New Orleans Class were much better protected, among other things having a proper turret, rather than the turret-like gun shield that characterized earlier US heavy cruisers. In another divergence from earlier designs, the three 8–inch guns in each turret were mounted individually, rather than on a single sleeve. Although cramped, they were very good ships. They cost $14–15 million each. Despite their superior design, three of them became war losses in less than five minutes in the Battle of SAVO ISLAND on the night of August 9–10, 1942, no design being able to ensure against over-confidence, inexperience, bad luck, and a daring foe.

New Orleans, CA-32 (1931–1933–1934), escorted carrier task forces in the early months of the war, fighting at the CORAL SEA, Tassafaronga, (where she lost her bow), and Cape Engaño, among other actions. Scrapped in 1959.

Astoria, CA-34 (1930–1933–1934), escorted carrier task forces in the early months of the war, fighting at the Coral Sea, and later at Savo Island, where she was sunk.

Minneapolis, CA-36 (1931–1933–1934), helped escort carrier task forces in the early months of the war, was at the Coral Sea, Tassafaronga (like *New Orleans*, she lost her bow), and elsewhere. Scrapped in 1960.

Tuscaloosa, CA-37 (1931–1933–1934), served mostly in the Atlantic and ETO, supporting landings. Reached the Pacific in early 1945 and supported the fast carriers until the end of the war. Scrapped in 1959.

San Francisco, CA-38 (1931–1933–1934), survived Pearl Harbor with little damage, and went on to serve as Norman SCOTT's flagship at CAPE ESPERANCE, and Dan CALLAGHAN's in the First Naval Battle of GUADALCANAL, where the latter was killed, and the ship seriously damaged. Repaired, she returned to service and escorted fast carrier task forces until the end of the war. Scrapped in 1961.

Quincy, CA-39 (1933–1935–1936), was in the Atlantic at the start of the war. Shortly transferred to the Pacific, she supported the Guadalcanal landings and was sunk at Savo Island.

Vincennes, CA-44 (1934–1936–1937), was in the Atlantic when Pearl Harbor was attacked; she reached the Pacific in time to help cover the Guadalcanal landings and was sunk at Savo Island.

New York Class, US Battleships

America's first "super dreadnoughts," *New York* and *Texas* were a disappointment even when new. Although they served with Britain's Grand Fleet in 1917–18, they saw no combat in World War I. Modified somewhat between the world wars, by World War II they were not considered worth extensive reconstruction. Despite this, they saw considerable service. Until late 1944 both ships were in the European Theater, providing gunfire support for landings from North Africa to Normandy to the Riviera, *Texas* gaining the distinction of pounding a major coast defense installation at Cherbourg into rubble with only minor injury to herself, a rare occurrence in naval history. They then passed into the Pacific, where they rendered good service supporting the landings at IWO JIMA and OKINAWA.

New York (1911–1912–1914) was expended in the Bikini ATOMIC BOMB tests.

Texas (1911–1912–1914) is preserved as a war memorial near the San Jacinto battlefield in Texas.

New Zealand, Commonwealth of

Two large and numerous small islands about 1,200 miles east-southeast of Australia, New Zealand totals about 172,000 square miles. Possessed of an advanced agricultural economy, with some industry, in 1940 New Zealand was a self-governing member of the British Commonwealth. Despite having a population of only about 1.2 million, the New Zealand armed forces managed to reach a strength of 157,000 during the war, a remarkable 13.1% of the population under arms. Of these about 40,000 served in the Commonwealth, 75,000 in North Africa and Italy, and about 40,000 in the various Pacific campaigns.
Ref: Gillespie, *Official History of New Zealand in the Second World War, 1939–1945, The Pacific.*

New Zealand Army

On the outbreak of World War II, New Zealand, which had a very small regular army supported by a division's worth of militia (mostly World War I veterans), promptly raised a division of volunteers and dispatched it to the Mediterranean, where it covered itself with glory in North Africa and Italy. This left only the militia and some miscellaneous

units to guard against invasion. Attempts to raise another field division were only partially successful. As a result, New Zealand's contribution to the ground war in the Pacific was small, ultimately involving a number of brigade-sized actions in which the Kiwis greatly distinguished themselves.

New Zealand also maintained small garrisons on numerous tiny Pacific islands, such as Fanning, Norfolk, and the like, as well as provided the cadres and advisers for Fijian and TONGAN forces.

First New Zealand Division. A militia unit composed of World War I veterans, the division performed security and garrison duties in New Zealand during the war.

Second New Zealand Division. Raised in late 1940, the division was sent to North Africa in the spring of 1941, and saw almost continuous combat there, in Greece, and in Italy until the end of the war. It was commonly referred to as "the New Zealand Division."

Third New Zealand Division. Raised from volunteers in mid–1942, the division was never completely formed. Comprising only two brigades, it was committed to operations on VELLA LAVELLA in September 1943, then went into action in the Treasury Islands in October-November 1943 and the Green Islands in February 1944. Shortly afterward the division was stood down, and disbanded in April 1944.

Eighth New Zealand Brigade. Formed in the spring of 1941, the brigade was on garrison duty in the FIJI ISLANDS at the outbreak of the Pacific War. It formed the core about which the Third Division was activated, and saw extensive service in the Solomon Islands and NEW GUINEA.

14th New Zealand Brigade. Formed in October 1942 on Fiji as part of the new Third New Zealand Division, the brigade saw extensive service in the SOLOMONS.

15th New Zealand Brigade. This was activated briefly in 1943, to be the third brigade of the Third New Zealand Division. A shortage of manpower

caused the brigade to be disbanded on NEW CALE-
DONIA in early 1943.

Ref: Gillespie, *Official History of New Zealand in
the Second World War, 1939–1945, The Pacific.*

New Zealand Navy, Royal

The Royal New Zealand Navy was a small force,
never consisting of more than a few cruisers and
some corvettes (small destroyer-escort type vessels). It was a thoroughly professional force, however, and its ships fought in some of the toughest
actions of the war, HMNZS *Achilles* taking part in
the Battle of the River Plate in December 1939,
against the German "pocket battleship" *Graf Spee,*
while LEANDER was heavily damaged at Kolombangara in 1943. For most of the Pacific War the
RNZN served in the Solomons and East Indies, and
by the end of the war was operating virtually as an
integral part of the US Navy.

Ref: Gillespie, *Official History of New Zealand in
the Second World War, 1939–1945, The Pacific.*

Newcastle, Australia

A small but good harbor, with facilities to service
most merchant ships, albeit in limited numbers,
and an important air base, located on the northeastern coast of Australia, giving it some value as
a base for the domination of the CORAL SEA.

Nicobar Islands

South of the ANDAMANS and east of India, in the
Bay of Bengal. The 19 islands total only about 635
square miles. In 1940 they were a thinly inhabited,
primitive place, and were easily captured by the
Japanese, the British making no effort to defend
them. Nor did the British bother attempting to
eject the Japanese, so that their garrison was starving by the end of the war.

Niigata, Honshu, Japan

A small port, Niigata had a naval base suitable for
light forces and an air base.

Nimitz, Chester W., Sr. (1885–1966)

Chester W. Nimitz graduated from Annapolis in
1905 and embarked upon a career in SUBMARINES,
rising to command the Atlantic Fleet submarine
flotilla by 1912. The following year he toured various European nations, studying submarine development, and returned to build the first diesel
engine for the US Navy. During World War I he
served as chief of staff to the commander of Atlantic Fleet submarines. After the war he attended the
Naval War College, served on various staffs, and
rose steadily upward. At the time of PEARL HARBOR
he was chief of the Bureau of Navigation (i.e., personnel), from which post he was almost immedi-

*Admiral Chester W. Nimitz Sr., seen here decorating
Pearl Harbor hero Dorie Miller with the Navy Cross,
May 27, 1942.*

ately made commander of the Pacific Fleet, to which, in early 1942, he added command of all US forces in the central and North Pacific, as well as responsibility for coordinating operations with Douglas MACARTHUR in the southwest Pacific.

Nimitz oversaw all US operations in the Pacific for the entire war, approving STRATEGY, selecting personnel, ensuring the flow of men, ships, and materiel, and working with surprising smoothness with the egocentric MacArthur. After the war he was chief of naval operations until his retirement in late 1947. He later served as a special assistant to the secretary of the navy, as director of the UN plebiscite in Kashmir, and wrote a reasonably sound history of the Pacific War. A capable man, Nimitz was flexible in command and willing to listen to others, even when it annoyed him. Although a non-flyer, he recognized the logic behind John TOWERS' argument that all "black shoe" (non-aviation) officers should have a "brown shoe" (aviation) adviser and acted on it. His relaxed, almost informal style of command masked a great deal of toughness. Like his arch-foe YAMAMOTO, Nimitz had been injured in the service, and was missing the ring finger of his left hand. He had a schnauzer named Makalepa.

The admiral's son, LtCdr Chester W. Nimitz Jr., served in submarines in the Pacific, rising to command of *Hake* (SS-256), in which he accounted for a number of Japanese ships, including the destroyer *Kazagumo*. An occasional and forthcoming critic of his father's decisions, the younger Nimitz was also one of the officers instrumental in improving the malfunctioning US TORPEDO exploder during the war. After the war he rose to rear admiral.

Ning Hai Class, Chinese Light Cruisers

These Chinese light cruisers were to be built with Japanese assistance, which dried up during the project. Small for light cruisers, hardly larger than some oversized destroyers, and slow, their best trial speed only 24 knots, they were the largest, most modern, and most powerful ships in the Chinese Navy.

Both ships were sunk in the Yangtze River by Japanese air attacks on 23 September 1937. The sunken vessels were soon captured by the Japanese. Raised and repaired, they were turned over to the collaborationist Wang government in 1939. In 1943 the two ships were taken over by the Japanese Navy, and performed escort duties in the China Sea and in Japanese waters.

Ning Hai (1930–1931–1932) was built in a Japanese shipyard; after being transferred to the Japanese Navy in 1943 she was renamed *Ioshima*. She was sunk by the US submarine *Shad* (SS-235) while on convoy escort south of Honshu on 19 September 1944.

Ping Hai (1931–1935–1936) was built in a Chinese shipyard, initially with Japanese technical assistance, which was not forthcoming after 1933. The project languished until 1935, when the German Naval Mission to China took it over. As a result, she differed in some details from her sister, and had German antiaircraft guns, the Japanese having refused to deliver on the weapons originally ordered. She became *Yasoshima* in Japanese service and was sunk by US aircraft in Santa Cruz Bay, Luzon, on 25 November 1944.

Nishimura, Shoji (1889–1944)

Shoji Nishimura graduated from the Japanese naval academy in 1911. He had a satisfactory, but by no means distinguished career thereafter, rising slowly upward. At the beginning of the war he was a rear admiral. Nishimura commanded light cruiser and destroyer units through many of the 1941–42 operations, including the invasion of the Philippines and the East Indies. By 1944 he was a vice admiral and led the task force of two older battleships, one cruiser, and four destroyers that managed to avoid detection until it was in SURIGAO STRAIT and then headed for the American invasion force off Leyte. Nishimura kept coming despite enormous American fire. He went down with his flagship, the battleship *Yamashiro*, on 25 October 1944—". . . one of the least competent Japanese flag officers," according to Samuel Eliot MORISON.

Nixon, Richard M. (1913–1994)

A member of the Naval Reserve, Nixon went on active duty as a lieutenant junior grade in June 1942. He served in various administrative posts associated with naval aviation, and from January to June 1944 was commander of the South Pacific Combat Air Transport Command in the Northern SOLOMONS, in which capacity he earned a citation for "meritorious and efficient performance." He ended the war as a lieutenant commander on the staff of the Bureau of Aeronautics, in Washington. Entering politics, he became vice president under EISENHOWER (1953–61), lost the presidential election of 1960, won that of 1968 and that of 1972, but subsequently resigned due to the Watergate scandal in 1974.

Noemfoor Island

Just north of NEW GUINEA, Noemfoor had no port, but had a good anchorage and lots of room for airfields, which made it a valuable objective during MACARTHUR's drive up the New Guinea coast. The Allies developed it into an important base.

Norfolk Class, British Heavy Cruisers

The principal difference between the Norfolks and earlier British heavy cruisers lay in improved turret design and ammunition handling arrangements. The ships were involved in numerous actions in the Atlantic, including the final battle with the German battleship *Bismarck*, in May 1941, delivering the coup de grace with TORPEDOES.

Doresetshire (1927–1929–1930) joined the British Far Eastern Fleet in early 1942. On 5 April, while in company with HMS *Cornwall*, she was caught off CEYLON by Japanese carrier aircraft, who hit her with about 10 250–550 pound bombs, which caused a magazine explosion that sank her in about eight minutes.

Norfolk (1927–1928–1930) served in the ETO, once surviving two 11-inch rounds from the

German battleship *Scharnhorst*. Scrapped in 1950.
See also ROYAL NAVY.

Normandie, SS

French ocean liner, a floating art deco palace, and at some 85,000 GRT matched in size only by QUEEN MARY and *Queen Elizabeth*. Interned in the United States upon the fall of France in 1940, she was taken over by the navy, renamed *Lafayette*, and converted into a troop transport (alternate proposals were to convert her into a carrier, a fate suggested for several other liners, until the army convinced the navy of the desperate need for troop transport). While completing her fitting out at the 44th Street dock on the North River in New York a fire began in the former ballroom when a welder's torch ignited one of 15,000 kapok life jackets stored there. Within hours she had been reduced to a burned out, sunken wreck. Although raised, she was never repaired and was sold for scrap.

Arguably, had she entered service she might have helped shorten the war appreciably, since like the Queens she could carry a division's worth of manpower overseas at very high speed.

North Carolina Class, US Battleships

Designed within the limitations imposed by the naval DISARMAMENT TREATIES, the two ships of the North Carolina Class were arguably technically superior to those of the succeeding SOUTH DAKOTA CLASS. They were good sea boats, handy, relatively fast, and had a tremendous main battery.

North Carolina, BB-55 (1937–1940–1941), was the first US battleship to enter service since *West Virginia* in 1923. Built at the Brooklyn Navy Yard, she was nicknamed the "Show Boat" almost as soon as she entered service. She saw some escort duty in the Atlantic before going to the Pacific in June 1942. Her first combat mission was supporting the carriers covering the GUADALCANAL landings, and helping defend the carriers during the Battle of the EASTERN SOLOMONS. She took a torpedo on September 15, 1942, in the same attack that sank the carrier WASP and destroyer *O'Brien*, and did not return to service until early December. Although often escorting carrier task forces or providing cover for operations, she did not see combat again until the MARSHALL ISLANDS Campaign in early 1944. Thereafter she bombarded shore targets in several invasions, fought in the Battle of the PHILIPPINE SEA, and helped bombard OKINAWA and the Japanese Home Islands. She was laid up after the war, and eventually preserved as a war memorial at Wilmington, North Carolina.

Washington, BB-56 (1938–1940–1941), served with the ROYAL NAVY, covering convoys to Iceland and Northern Russia in the spring of 1942, and passed into the Pacific in midsummer. She supported operations in the SOLOMONS, most notably in the shootout with a Japanese squadron off Guadalcanal on November 14–15, 1942, when, using radar fire control, she put nine 16-inch rounds (of 117 fired) and 55 5-inch rounds into the Japanese *Kirishima* in a few minutes, turning her into a burning wreck—the largest sustained series of broadsides ever fired by a US battlewagon. She thereafter escorted carrier task forces and bombarded Japanese installations until the end of the war, when she was pressed into service as a troop transport. She was scrapped in 1961.

See also GUADALCANAL, NAVAL BATTLES.

Northampton Class, US Heavy Cruisers

The second version of the US "Treaty Cruiser," the Northamptons were somewhat better protected than the PENSACOLAS. This was achieved by dispensing with one 8-inch gun, reducing the total to nine mounted in three turrets, the weight saved on the fourth turret and tenth gun being put into protection. They cost about $12 million, slightly more than their predecessors. Prewar modifications removed their TORPEDO tubes but enhanced their antiaircraft protection. All saw hard service, notably as escorts to the fast carriers and during the GUADALCANAL campaign in 1942–43, and three became war losses. Despite their rather light protection, they were tough ships.

Northampton, CA-26 (1928–1928–1930), escorted carrier task forces at MIDWAY and SANTA CRUZ, then served in the Solomons, where she was sunk off SAVO ISLAND on 30 November 1942, during the Battle of TASSAFARONGA.

Chester, CA-27 (1928–1929–1930), saw extensive service during the war, and was seriously damaged by a torpedo from the submarine *I-176* on 20 October 1942, in the Solomons. Survived the war to be scrapped in 1959.

Louisville, CA-28 (1928–1930–1931), spent most of the war escorting carriers, and was broken up in 1960.

Chicago, CA-29 (1928–1930–1931), was fitted as a flagship; she survived numerous actions, including Savo Island, where she took a torpedo. She was sunk on 30 January 1943, during the Battle of the Russell Islands.

Houston, CA-30 (1928–1929–1930), was fitted as a flagship, and was serving as such for the Asiatic Fleet when the war broke out. She was heavily engaged in the struggle for the NETHERLANDS EAST INDIES in the early months of the war, proving herself an enormously valuable asset to the ABDA command. During one action her antiaircraft fire was so intense some observers thought she was on fire. After fighting in the Battle of the JAVA SEA (February 27, 1942), she was sunk in the Sunda Strait early on March 1, 1942, having absorbed at least four torpedoes and scores of 8-inch and 5-inch rounds, in what Samuel Eliot MORISON called one of the most "gallant fights in the history of the United States Navy."

Augusta, CA-31 (1928–1930–1931), also fitted as a flagship, was President ROOSEVELT's favorite ship (the famous picture of him reviewing the fleet in his long cape was taken on her bridge), and she took him to Argentia Bay for a conference with CHURCHILL that resulted in the Atlantic Charter. The only US prewar heavy cruiser not to see action in the Pacific, she served throughout the European War, offering gunfire support to landings from North Africa to Normandy. She was broken up for scrap in 1960.

See also JAPAN, ATTITUDE TOWARD THE ENEMY.

Noumea, New Caledonia

The capital of New Caledonia, Noumea had a fairly good port for the region, and was located so as to give it potential as a naval and air base for control of the CORAL SEA and the southern SOL-OMONS. Though cramped and of limited capacity, there were extensive sheltered anchorages in the area. There was a small French naval and air base. Noumea served as a vital forward base early in the war.

O

O'Callaghan, Joseph (1904–1964)

A Roman Catholic priest and chaplain, O'Callaghan was aboard the USS *Franklin* (CV-13) when she was hit and suffered over 700 men killed in a few minutes off the coast of Honshu on March 19, 1945. Fr. O'Callaghan organized fire fighting parties, helped heave burning ammunition overboard, and rescued the wounded, while also finding time to administer the last rites to the dying. He was awarded a MEDAL OF HONOR.

Officer Training, Japanese

Throughout history, in most armies the officers were generally taller than the troops. This was because the officers were usually recruited from the wealthier classes, folk who could afford a better diet. As a result, the officers tended to be taller than the less well fed troops. This was not the case in the Japanese Army. Officers had to pass through the dreaded military academy at Ichigaya. Here the day began at 5:30 A.M. and went on relentlessly until 10 P.M. at night (unless there was night training, in which case the cadets would simply lose a night's sleep). Most officers began their officer training at special military grammar and high schools. All stressed the same dedication to "spirit" rather than the mundane matters of flesh and blood. Physical training was a minor religion and, even in the winter, it was done barechested. Worst of all was the bland and skimpy rations. As a result, teenage cadets grew only half an inch in their adolescence, and gained about three pounds. The resulting officers were indeed a tough bunch, but their average size was 5 feet four inches and 128 pounds. Allied officers averaged nearly 30 pounds heavier and six inches taller. Postwar Japanese military officers are nearly as tall as Allied officers of that era, mainly because they are now fed better during training.

Oil

The war in the Pacific was started over oil. The Allies, mainly the Dutch, controlled the local supplies in Borneo and the NETHERLANDS EAST INDIES. In 1940, these areas produced 65 million barrels a year. At the time, the major global producer was the United States, with over 1.3 billion barrels a year. America and the Dutch Borneo fields were Japan's sole source of oil. When this supply was cut off in the summer of 1941, in an attempt to stop Japanese aggression, Japan responded by attacking America and seizing the Dutch oil fields in Borneo and Sumatra. Because of the demolition of many of the oil facilities, the Japanese were able to pump only 25.9 million barrels in 1942. By 1943 they were getting 49.6. The major problem then became getting the oil refined and back to Japan. American SUBMARINES proved capable of sinking Japanese tankers faster than new oil transports could be built. While warships could use the Borneo oil right out of the ground, trucks and aircraft needed refined product. It was easier to carry the refined products back to Japan, than to haul larger quantities of crude oil back to Japan-based refineries. But the ultimate bottleneck was tankers.

PREWAR JAPANESE ESTIMATE OF OIL AVAILABILITY AND CONSUMPTION (MILLIONS OF BARRELS)

War Year	Reserve	Production	Consumption*
1st	61.1	5.0	37.8
2nd	28.3	12.9	34.6
3rd	6.6	23.6	34.6
4th	4.4	30.0	34.6

*Note that the figures do not tally for the 3rd and 4th year, a "clerical error" the Japanese leadership appears to have overlooked.

JAPANESE COAL OIL PRODUCTION (MILLIONS OF BARRELS)

Year	Output
1937	0.03 (The goal was .15 bbl)
1941	1.50
1942	N/A
1943	1.05
1944	1.20
1945	N/A

In December of 1941 the Japanese had about 61 million barrels stockpiled, enough to run the armed forces for about two years at peacetime levels of consumption. In mid-'41 they made what they considered careful calculations as to their oil needs and resources in the coming war.

Although the Japanese had made what they thought were conservative estimates of wartime oil PRODUCTION and consumption, these proved wildly optimistic. For example, peacetime imports from the Dutch East Indies were about 17.7 million barrels a year. The Japanese estimated that in the first year of the war they would be able to import only about 15.4 million barrels, due to destruction of the facilities and whatnot, but that by the third year they could crank it up to about 30.0 million barrels. In fact, they were never able to even approach the prewar figure. There were several reasons for this. The destruction of production and storage facilities was greater than expected, although it could have been worse. In addition, the Japanese do not seem to have understood the complexities of the oil industry.

ACTUAL OIL AVAILABILITY AND CONSUMPTION (MILLIONS OF BARRELS)

End of	Reserve	Production	Consumption
1941	61.1	—	—
1942	52.86	12.5	51.92
1943	14.47	20.1	41.7
1944	−8.1	9.6	29.5
1945	−28.0		

They were short of technical personnel, various important chemicals, and spare parts, most of which were imported from Europe or America in the prewar period. Worse yet, one of the few cargo ships sunk early in the war was the one carrying Japanese refinery technicians and their equipment. As a result of all this they ran out of oil a lot faster than they expected.

The actual figures for oil production and consumption are quite interesting.

By the end of 1944 the Japanese had more or less run out of fuel. It is, however, interesting to note that their estimates for production in War Years 2 and 3 were not far off the mark. That they kept things going after 1944 is a testimony to their ability to scrounge unaccounted oil stocks. Where they failed was in estimating consumption, which was much higher than predicted. Surprisingly, there had been a minority opinion on this in the Japanese military. Although overruled before the war, this group had managed to convince the brass that an experimental coal oil production program might be useful in an emergency. Although the program was supposed to yield several million barrels a year, it never approached its goal, due largely to a lack of genuine interest and a shortage of resources.

In short, Japan began the war short of resources, and steadily fell further and further behind.

Okamura, Yasutsugu

Yasutsugu Okamura joined the Japanese Army in 1904. By the outbreak of the Pacific War he was commander of the North China Area Army and a full general. At the end of 1944 Okamura took command of all Japanese forces in China. At the end of the war he surrendered to CHIANG KAI-SHEK and spent several years assisting the Nationalist Chinese in their civil war with the communists, whom he fervently hated. His postwar service in China allowed him to return to Japan in 1949 and become involved in the creation of Japan's "Self Defense Forces."

Okinawa, Battle of

On April 1, 1945, Easter Sunday, the last major battle of World War II began. This was the American invasion of the island of Okinawa, one of the smaller islands that were considered part of the Japanese Home Islands. Actually, it wasn't, as Okinawa had maintained itself as an independent kingdom until the 1870s, when the Japanese forcibly annexed it. Okinawa had a population of half a million at the time of the invasion, plus a garrison of 110,000 troops. The American force was 287,000 strong, of which over 60% were combat troops in four army infantry and three Marine divisions. The Japanese had learned from earlier island battles. They now realized that it was not wise to resist on the beaches, where American warships could deliver devastating firepower at point-blank range. Better to build defenses inland, where Japanese troops could do their usual "fight to the death" routine to maximum effect. So it was on Okinawa.

The initial landings, by 60,000 troops in two army and two Marine divisions, were essentially unopposed. Japanese air attacks were there from the beginning, however. On the second day a Japanese airfield was captured and friendly aircraft began operating from it. By 4 April Japanese resistance became more determined. US troops were now encountering the massive Japanese fortification system inland. The bloodbath had begun and would continue until 22 June, when the battle was declared over, though some Japanese holdout troops remained active even after the war ended.

On 6 April, the first major KAMIKAZE attack was launched. Only 24 of 355 suicide planes got through, but they caused a lot of damage. So much antiaircraft fire was put out that eight US ships were damaged by FRIENDLY FIRE. On 7 April, a Japanese task force was intercepted by 900 US aircraft before it could reach Okinawa. Japan's largest battleship, the 72,000-ton YAMATO, was sunk, along with a cruiser and four destroyers. The Japanese also lost 54 escorting aircraft. Only 10 US aircraft were lost. During the entire Okinawa campaign, Japan lost at least 180 ships, from small subchasers and transports up to major warships.

During the first two weeks of April, US forces on Okinawa probed Japanese defenses and prepared for a major offensive. On April 18, Ernie PYLE, one of the most famous World War II reporters, was killed by a sniper on an island off Okinawa. On 19 April, US forces made a major push, accompanied by heavy naval gunfire and air bombardment. For the rest of April the fighting raged. But the well-dug-in Japanese could be routed only with great effort. The fighting continued into May, with a small Japanese amphibious force making a landing behind US lines on 3 May. This was in conjunction with many Japanese counterattacks. As scary as this was to US troops, it was easier to kill Japanese troops out in the open than in their fortifications.

Throughout May, Japanese air attacks on US ships off Okinawa continued, with over 1,100 Japanese aircraft destroyed. On 5 May, the Japanese air attacks had their greatest success, sinking 17 US ships in 24 hours. The Japanese lost 131 aircraft in this effort. Their kamikaze tactics, first used six months earlier in the Philippines, were employed to maximum effect off Okinawa. Nearby airfields in Japan, as well as the supply of planes and pilots, also made it possible to use non-suicide aircraft attacks. Despite the hundreds of US carrier aircraft available, the Japanese did much damage to American shipping. Some 4,200 Japanese aircraft (1,900 of them kamikaze), went after the US fleet sinking 36 ships (all but two by kamikaze) and damaging 368 (only 164 by kamikaze). Overall, the Japanese

With the devastated ruins of recently captured Naha in the background, Sixth Marine Division commander, MG Lemuel Shepherd (1896–1990)—later the 22nd commandant of the Marine Corps—consults a map, late May 1945.

lost 7,830 aircraft during the Okinawa battle, versus US losses of some 800 planes.

The fighting on the ground remained intense for the first three weeks of May, but then two weeks of heavy rains came and this slowed operations down as US troops struggled to move supplies forward in the mud. Under cover of the rain, the Japanese landed paratroopers on 24 May. This desperate tactic was used against an American airfield on Okinawa, but succeeded in destroying only a few aircraft. On 28 May, the Japanese launched their last major air raid. Over a hundred Japanese aircraft were shot down and only one US ship was sunk.

On 5 June, a TYPHOON (Pacific hurricane) hit the US fleet off Okinawa. Severe damage was in-flicted on four battleships, eight carriers, seven cruisers, and 11 destroyers. Dozens of support ships were damaged. As the typhoon passed away, so did the rains. On 17 June, after two weeks of heavy fighting, the last line of Japanese fortifications was breached. The commander of the Japanese garrison, General KURIBAYASHI then committed suicide. On June 20, Japanese soldiers and civilians began to surrender in groups, something that had rarely happened before. In one case, a thousand Japanese gave up. Still, over 100,000 Japanese troops had fought to the death. On June 22, the battle for Okinawa was declared officially over.

The US Navy suffered its greatest number of CASUALTIES (some 10,000) in one operation while off Okinawa. Japanese deaths, including civilians, were well over 150,000. Some 7,000 Japanese troops surrendered, but thousands of civilians committed suicide rather than be captured. America suffered 12,281 combat deaths (including 4,907 navy). Over 50,000 Americans were wounded, plus over 14,000 combat fatigue casualties and nearly 30,000 noncombat casualties. It was the bloodiest campaign of the Pacific War. The high casualty rate of the Okinawa battle was a major factor in the decision to drop the ATOMIC BOMB on Japan. It was thought that an invasion of the main Japanese Home Islands would be even bloodier than Okinawa.

Okinawa, Ryukyu Islands

The largest of the RYUKYU ISLANDS (about 450 square miles) was the first victim of Japanese imperialism, the native dynasty being deposed in the 1870s and the islands forcibly incorporated into Japan. The site of important Japanese military installations by 1945, the principal reason for the American landings in the spring of that year was to seize the island as an advanced base for the pending invasion of Japan.

Olongapo, Luzon, Philippines

An important American naval base in the Philippines, Olongapo, on the northwestern side of Luzon, had a fair-sized harbor and considerable facilities to effect all but the most extensive repairs. It was also relatively isolated from Manila, the principal center of American military power in the islands, and only lightly defended. Hastily evacuated during the early stages of the Japanese invasion, whatever could not be withdrawn was sabotaged.

Omaha Class, US Light Cruisers

Although quite old, and no longer a match for contemporary light cruisers, the 10 Omahas, built 1918–25, were excellent ships, well designed, reliable, fast, maneuverable, and very seaworthy, even by World War II standards, albeit cramped. They gave excellent service in all theaters and, surprisingly, none became a war loss. Most served in the Atlantic and ETO, but several were heavily engaged in the Pacific:

Raleigh, CL-7 (1920–1922–1924), survived PEARL HARBOR with moderate damage and later served in the ALEUTIANS. Scrapped in 1946.

Richmond, CL-9 (1920–1921–1923), served in the Pacific for virtually the entire war, mostly in northern waters, where she took part in the Battle of the KOMANDORSKI ISLANDS. Scrapped in 1946.

Marblehead, CL-12 (1920–1923–1924), began the war with the Asiatic Fleet, and was so severely damaged off JAVA in February 1942 that she had to be sent home. She served thereafter in the Atlantic. Scrapped in 1945.

Onishi, Takejiro (1891–1945)

Takejiro Onishi, one of the militaristic "wild men" and the driving force behind Japanese carrier aviation, graduated from the naval academy in 1912. After flight training he was thrown out of the Naval College because of his enthusiasm for gambling and chasing women and went off to study in Britain and France for two years beginning in 1918. As one of the first Japanese naval aviators, he spent much of the 1920s and 1930s laying the foundation for the great carrier force that would forever change the nature of naval warfare, meanwhile finding time to become an ACE in China. Onishi not only

helped organize and train the carrier force, but was also instrumental in establishing much of the industrial base necessary to build and sustain it. He became a rear admiral in 1939, after having commanded land-based naval aviation units. In 1941 he worked on the plan for attacking PEARL HARBOR. His outspokenness about dumping battleships and building more aircraft and carriers prevented him from getting sea commands, and as a result he spent most of the war directing the construction of naval weapons and munitions. He became a vice admiral in 1944 and was given command of Japanese naval air forces in the Philippines. He went along with KAMIKAZE tactics because he was pragmatic, not because he believed the quasi-religious rhetoric. Onishi organized kamikaze operations in the Philippines through the end of 1944, when ordered to move himself and his staff to Taiwan. There he organized more kamikaze units, some of which operated during the battle for OKINAWA. When the emperor ordered the armed forces to surrender on August 15, 1945, Onishi chose suicide instead.

Order of Battle, Divisional, Outline

Although ground combat in the Pacific War was one of relatively small battles, the basic ground combat unit was still the division. Often the divisions were broken up to provide garrisons or assault forces for the many small islands fought over, but everyone still kept score by counting divisions. The divisions in the Pacific varied in size from about 4,500 men (Chinese) to as many as 20,000 (US Marines), depending upon their arm of service and nationality. Regardless of size, however, a division was supposed to be a more or less self-contained combat formation of all arms (infantry, armor, artillery, support troops) capable of some degree of sustained independent operations. The principal differences among the numerous types of division (infantry, armor, parachute, marine, and so forth) were due to the specialized missions to which they were dedicated. The vast majority of all divisions in the Pacific were infantry divisions. The US Marine division was basically an infantry division that was beefed up for amphibious assaults. There was a US parachute division in the Pacific and the Japanese had some armored divisions in China. But, overall, it was an infantry war.

This table summarizes the number of divisions available to each of the belligerent powers as of the beginning of the indicated year, regardless of location. "Pre" gives strength in September of 1939, and "End" at the end of the war (September 1945).

ASIATIC-PACIFIC THEATER OF OPERATIONS

	Pre	1940	1941	1942	1943	1944	1945	End
Australia	0	7	9	7	8	7	7	7
Britain	0	1	1	2	2	1	1	1
China				c. 250–300				
India	3	5	6	9	11	11	14	14
Japan	36	36	39	73	84	100	145	197
New Zealand	0	1	0	1	1	0	0	0
United States								
Army	2	2	3	3	9	13	21	21
Marine	0	0	2	3	5	6	6	6
USSR	32	30	30	25	25	35	45	65

By way of comparison with the rest of the war, here are the divisions involved elsewhere.

EUROPEAN-MEDITERRANEAN-MIDDLE EASTERN THEATER

	Pre	1940	1941	1942	1943	1944	1945	End
Australia	0	0	1	3	1	0	0	0
Brazil	0	0	0	0	0	1	1	1
Britain	9	33	34	36	37	36	30	30
Bulgaria	12	14	14	16	23	29	29	20
Canada	0	1	3	5	8	6	6	6
Finland	14	17	19	20	20	20	12	12
France	86	105	0	0	5	7	14	14
Germany	78	189	235	261	327	347	319	375
Hungary	6	7	10	16	19	22	23	30
India	0	0	4	5	5	5	4	4
Italy	66	73	64	89	86	2	9	10
New Zealand	0	0	1	1	1	1	1	1
Poland:								
Western Front	43	2	2	2	2	5	5	5
Eastern Front	–	0	0	0	0	1	12	17
Romania	11	28	33	31	33	32	24	24
S. Africa	0	0	3	3	3	4	3	1
US Army	0	0	0	0	8	17	57	68
USSR	170	180	210	240	340	390	478	411

Since several countries (e.g., the United States, the British Commonwealth, and the USSR) had forces in both theaters, their overall strength is summarized in the following table:

GLOBAL SUMMARY FOR THE TWO-THEATER ALLIES

	Pre-1940	1940	1941	1942	1943	1944	1945	End
Australia	0	7	10	10	9	7	7	7
Britain	9	34	35	38	39	37	31	31
India	3	5	10	14	16	16	18	18
New Zealand	0	1	1	2	2	1	1	1
United States								
Army	8	8	37	73	90	89	89	89
Marine	0	0	2	3	5	6	6	6
USSR	194	200	220	250	350	400	488	491

Figures for most countries are approximate, showing divisions active at the start of the indicated year. In some cases the figures include separate brigades, lumped together on the basis of three brigades per division. All types of divisions are included except training formations, depot divisions, militia, and territorial units. No attempt has been made to modify the figures on the basis of actual strength, degree of training, scales of equipment, or state of readiness. Japanese figures exclude "satellite" forces, but German and Soviet ones include them. For example, in January of 1943 German totals include one Serbian-manned division, two Bosnian-manned ones, eight Croatian ones, and four Slovakian ones, not to mention German divisions formed from troops of other nationalities. German figures include air force, navy, and Waffen-SS ground divisions. British figures include divisions composed primarily of African personnel. Polish "Western" figures include original forces raised in 1939 and those raised in exile in the Middle East, Mediterranean, and Britain, while "Eastern" figures are those raised under Soviet control. French figures after 1940 include only Free French units, omitting Vichy divisions, about 16 by mid-1941, including those in colonies that later went over to the Free French. Italian figures post–1943 omit units of Mussolini's Italian Social Republic, which numbered four by 1944 and six by 1945.

Romanian figures for 1945 reflect forces fighting under Allied control.

In 1939–41 the Netherlands had nine divisions (plus about three more in the East Indies, also not shown), the Belgians 22, the Danes two, the Greeks about 22, and the Yugoslavs 34, before being overrun by the Germans. The Dutch, Belgian, and Greek governments-in-exile were unable to raise any divisions. The Danish divisions were disbanded by the Germans. The Yugoslav partisans under Tito raised some 24 "divisions" (including one Italian-manned) from about mid-1943 onward, after Italy switched sides, opening up the Adriatic to Allied shipping (and easier resupply of the Yugoslav forces). US theater figures omit units within the 48 states, the 13 PHILIPPINE ARMY divisions, activated in late 1941 and destroyed by March of 1942, and the many GUERRILLA divisions formed in the Philippines during the Japanese occupation, but do include the Regular Army Philippine Division, which was also destroyed in March of 1942. SIAM maintained four divisions through the war, although these saw little service.

Organization, Ground Combat Divisions, 1942

The Chinese division shown here was more or less the paper T/O&E for regular divisions of the "Central Army," the forces directly under CHIANG KAI-SHEK's control, and only about 10 of those had full allocations of men and equipment. Most divisions were not so well equipped, often lacking artillery. There were also many variants in the divisional T/O&E. Shown here is a "square" division, one with two brigades of two regiments each. Several divisions had one or even two additional brigades (6–12 additional battalions), and some were on a triangular model (three regiments), and there was also a group of divisions organized and rather lavishly equipped on a triangular model by the United States. These were supposed to have about 12,000 troops, but generally operated with 8,000 or so. To further complicate matters, the Chinese Army had

several series of divisions, each with its own numbering system, so that there were, for example, at least eight different units designated "First Division": There were regular divisions, "new" divisions, "honor" divisions, reserve divisions, provisional divisions, guerrilla divisions, training divisions, "temporary" divisions, and even a "Salt Tax Division."

The British 1941 infantry division shown here was more or less similar to those of the other Imperial and Commonwealth forces throughout the war, albeit that Australian and New Zealand divisions, which had some minor differences in organization, tended to be composed of better manpower. Note that, particularly during the early part

DIVISIONS OF THE PACIFIC WAR, 1942							
				U.S.		Japanese	
Army	Chinese	British	Phil.	Army	USMC	Type I	Type II
Men	10.9	17.5	8.2	15.5	19.3	15.5	12.0
Bns.:							
Inf.	12	10	9	9	9	9	6
Art.	1	5	3	4	6	3	1
Recon.	0	1	0.3	0.3	0.3	1	0
Engr.	1	1	1	1	2	1	1
Sig.	0	1	0.3	0.3	1	0.3	0.3
Equipment							
MG	54	867	54	280	680	412	270
Art.	24	72	36	72	60	70	16
A/T	0	48	0	109	54	8	0
Mtr.	24	218	24	138	162	108	72
Value	4	9	4	12	16	10	5

Key to the table: Under US, **Phil.** = units of the Philippine Commonwealth; **Army** = Army Divisions; **USMC** = Marine units; **Men** = the number of men in the division, in thousands; **Bns.** = the number of battalions of each type (.3 indicates a company): **Inf.** = infantry; **Art.** = artillery, including antitank and antiaircraft battalions; **Recon.** = reconnaissance; **Engr.** = Engineers; **Sig.** = signals, which in some armies were subsumed in the engineers; **Equipment** = excluding rifles: automatic rifles (BARs), carbines, submachine guns, pistols; **MG** = machine guns, excluding antiaircraft machine guns and automatic rifles, classed as light machine guns by the Chinese; **Art.** = artillery pieces, excluding antitank and antiaircraft pieces; **A/T** = antitank guns, also useful for "bunker busting"; **Mtr.** = mortars; **Value** = a rough mathematical calculation of the relative fighting power of each division, combining manpower, equipment, experience, organizational, and doctrinal factors.

of the war in Malaya and Burma, most of the British and Indian divisions committed to action were not at full strength, about 13,500 men being common, with equipment reduced in proportion. Commonwealth divisions often had some armored vehicles attached and were frequently supported by non-divisional resources.

Usually overlooked is the fact that the "American" troops defending the Philippines in 1941–42 were mostly locally recruited. Figures here are for the optimal paper strength of a Philippine Army division. The US Army division shown is on the basis of those that fought in New Guinea and GUADALCANAL during 1942, as is the Marine division. In general, it's important to keep in mind that the American divisions—both army and Marines—usually went into action with various attached combat and combat support units, such as tank battalions, with 72 light and medium TANKS, which are not shown in the table. The additional engineer battalion in the Marine division was a US Navy Seabee unit.

The Japanese Army had an extremely confusing organization. The two types of divisions (see page 461) didn't really exist at all. They are merely given to show some idea of the broad differences between divisions. Type I divisions were "triangular" formations (built around three regiments), while Type II divisions were "square" formations (four regiments). But in practice there were many variations in division strength. So many, in fact, that the Japanese themselves came to designate divisions in three classes: "A," overstrength and ready for action; "B," more or less at normal strength; and "C," weak, without artillery or other services. The actual details of each type (or of any of the half-dozen or so different varieties of brigades) could vary greatly. There were Type I divisions with as many as 26,000 men, and others as small as 12,000, and while some were fully motorized, such as the Fifth (15,340 men and over 1,000 motor vehicles, with no HORSES) or the Guards (12,650 men, over 900 motor vehicles, and no horses) when they spearheaded the conquest of MALAYA, most were "leg" outfits, in which the men walked and much of the equipment

was horse-drawn. There were Type II divisions as small as 8,000 men on occupation duty in China and as large as 22,000 men being used for offensive operations (the 18th Division in Malaya, which had just 33 motor vehicles and over 5,700 horses). In all armies, of course, there was some variation in divisional organization, but the Japanese were rather extreme in this regard.

Organization, Ground Combat Divisions, US, 1945

During the war a considerable evolution took place in divisional organization in all armies, sometimes formally and often informally. However, the changes to US units were greatest, partially because the increasing productivity of the "Arsenal of Democracy" permitted ever increasing upgrades of equipment. It would be impossible to trace all the changes in American divisional organization that took place during the war. For example, the US Army's standard infantry divisions underwent four official reorganizations between June of 1941 and September of 1945, with a fifth planned. The Marines went through seven reorganizations in roughly the same period. But some idea of the great changes that took place may be gained by comparing the official divisional tables of organization and equipment as they stood at the beginning of 1945 with the figures in the preceding entry.

Japanese divisions had not appreciably changed since 1942, save for an increased allocation of automatic weapons. British and Chinese divisions have been omitted, because there had been little change in their organization or equipment scales since 1942, albeit that the British divisions were more likely to be at full T/O&E rather than at about 70–75% and had a lot more light antitank weaponry. The PHILIPPINE ARMY, of course, had disappeared.

Changes in division manpower and weapons allocations were rooted in weapons developments, the growth in firepower, the increasing role of TANKS, and changes in the tactical situation, such as the greatly increased allocation of automatic

Type	Army	USMC
Men	14.0	17.5
Bns.:		
Tank	0	1
Inf.	9	9
Art.	4	6
Recon.	0.3	0.3
Engr.	1	2
Sig.	0.3	1
Equipment:		
MG	448	625
Art.	99	60
A/T	57	36
Mtr.	144	153
Tanks	0	46
Value	16	20

Key to the table: **Bns.** = battalions; **Inf.** = infantry; **Art.** = artillery; **Recon.** = reconnaissance; **Engr.** = engineer; **Sig.** = signal; **MG** = machine guns; **A/T** = antitank guns; **Mtr.** = mortar; **Value** = rough approximation of the relative combat value of the unit.

weapons. In addition, there was a desperate need to conserve manpower. By eliminating a single man from each infantry platoon, the US Army could realize a manpower savings of about 30 men per regiment, some 10,000 men on an army-wide basis. Similar small economies in the manpower of other elements could yield sufficient surplus personnel to allow the army to raise entire new divisions. Of course such changes often led to acrimonious disputes. Not every officer, for example, was sufficiently understanding as to want to lose a couple of clerks or drivers.

Note that equipment allocations were usually exceeded in the field, when units would scrounge up additional equipment, often adopting overrun enemy material. On GUADALCANAL and SAIPAN, for example, the US Marines made good use of some captured Japanese 37mm guns.

Organization, Higher Army Commands, Comparative

At the higher levels, US and British military organizational terminology differed from that employed by the Chinese and Japanese.

US/British	Chinese	Japanese
Army Group	War Area	General Army
Army	Army Group	Area Army
	Front Army	
	Route Army	
Corps	Army	Army
Division	Division	Division

Osaka, Honshu, Japan

One of the principal ports of Japan, with important naval and air base facilities.

Oshima, Hiroshi (1886–1975)

A former military officer, Oshima was the Japanese ambassador to Nazi Germany. Despite German racial attitudes (he was, after all, an "honorary Aryan"), Oshima was very well regarded by most senior German political and military leaders, including HITLER. As a result, he was privy to an enormous amount of critical information, which he shared with his superiors in Tokyo. As these were in the PURPLE diplomatic code, this proved of enormous value to the Allies, since the United States had broken the code. After the war Oshima, who was an enthusiastic supporter of Axis aggression, was tried as a war criminal. Sentenced to life imprisonment, he was released in 1955.

Ref: Boyd, *Hitler's Japanese Confidant.*

Otori Class, Japanese Fleet Torpedo Boats

Completed in the mid-1930s, the Otori class torpedo boats were much enlarged and improved versions of the unsuccessful TOMOZURU CLASS. When the American submarine warfare program began sinking Japanese shipping in enormous numbers they were pressed into service as improvised destroyer escorts. Like the Tomozurus they proved surprisingly effective in this role. Seven of the eight units of the class were lost in action.

Owen Stanley Mountains, Papua New Guinea

A spine of rugged mountains extending through the east-west axis of the easternmost portion of Papua New Guinea. With many peaks over 13,000 feet, the range is carved up into numerous valleys at all altitudes, plus occasional plateaus. The KOKODA TRAIL, the principal track traversing the range from Papua to northeastern New Guinea, crossed the mountains at an altitude of 7,000 feet. All of this is covered by lush tropical vegetation, the product of a rain forest climate. Rainfall averages over 80 inches a year. High humidity, frequent thick mist, and winter (June-August) nighttime temperatures in the 50s make for one of the more unhealthy climates on the planet.

Oyodo, Japanese Antiaircraft Cruiser

An enlarged version of AGANO, *Oyodo* (1941–1942–1943) was intended to serve as a flagship for submarine flotillas, for which she was supposed to have a sizable complement of floatplanes on a plan similar to that of the TONE CLASS heavy cruisers. During construction plans were changed, and she emerged with enhanced antiaircraft defenses, which were constantly improved during the war, so that by its end she was effectively an antiaircraft cruiser. She saw little action, most notably while taking part in the "bait" squadron during the Battle of LEYTE GULF. She was sunk in KURE Harbor by US naval aircraft on 28 July 1945.

Ozawa, Jisaburo (1886–1966)

Jisaburo Ozawa graduated from the naval academy in 1909, served in destroyers, went on to various service schools, and then made his mark as a surface warfare expert in the 1920s and 1930s. He was particularly skillful in the use of TORPEDOES, a weapon the Japanese Navy became noted for during the 1942 battles. By 1941 he was a vice admiral and commanded the surface forces that supported the invasions in MALAYA and the Dutch East Indies from late 1941 through early 1942. He became the commander of the Third Fleet at TRUK in late 1942. In early 1943, he commanded an unsuccessful attempt to destroy Allied air power in the New Guinea/Solomons area. Commanded Japanese forces during the summer 1944 BATTLE OF THE PHILIPPINE SEA. The result was the GREAT MARIANAS TURKEY SHOOT. Offered to resign after this, but was instead put in charge of Japanese naval forces that sortied to resist the American invasion of the Philippines in late 1944. This led to another defeat, and he returned to Japan with the few surviving ships. He served on the Naval General Staff for the remainder of the war. He died in 1966, at age 80. Ozawa was a classic "fighting admiral," but even these capabilities were not able to overcome the quantity and quality of naval forces America was able to muster. He was several inches taller than the average Japanese, but was actually rather modest in demeanor.

P

P-26 Peashooter, US Fighter

The P-26 Peashooter played only a minor role in the Pacific War, with some being used in the US defense of the Philippines in late 1941. The P-26 was the US Army's first all-metal monoplane fighter. It was in US service between 1934 and 1938, being replaced by the P-36 (which was itself quickly replaced by the P-40). The P-26 was the last army fighter with an open cockpit. It was a good performer, by 1930s standards. The Chinese Air Force bought some and with these P-26s shot down many Japanese aircraft. The Philippine Army Air Force also scored some victories with its handful of P-26s during the opening weeks of the war. Fewer than 200 P-26s were produced. Several continued to serve in the Guatemalan Air Force until 1957.

See also AIRCRAFT TYPES, DEVELOPMENT.

P-35, US Fighter

The P-35 was one of the many fighters produced in America during the 1930s that eventually saw Pacific combat while serving with American allies. In this case, the P-35 flew with the newly formed Philippine Army Air Force. These P-35s had originally been ordered by Sweden, but events in Europe prevented delivery. In the summer of 1941, 40 were sent to the Philippines where they were quickly lost during the Japanese invasion later that year. Lacking any armor or self-sealing fuel tanks, the P-35s didn't last long against the more maneuverable and better armed Japanese fighters.

See also AIRCRAFT TYPES, DEVELOPMENT.

When introduced in 1934 the P-26 was one of the hottest fighters in the world, but it was hopelessly obsolete by 1941. The first all-metal monoplane fighter with an air-cooled engine in US service, it retained an open cockpit and fixed landing gear, as well as requiring wire stays, not visible in this silhouette.

P-36 Hawk, US Fighter

The US P-36 Curtiss Hawk was obsolete when the war began. Even so, P-36s opposed the Japanese attack on PEARL HARBOR and managed to shoot down two enemy aircraft. While it looked fairly modern, and was a contemporary of the German Me-109, the P-36 was not as well designed and its performance was lower than most of the aircraft it faced in combat. While a very maneuverable and sturdy aircraft, it was relatively slow. The P-36 was built largely for export, and many nations received them (China, Thailand, France, South Africa, Argentina). Fewer than 400 were built, with PRODUCTION ending in early 1941.

See also AIRCRAFT TYPES, DEVELOPMENT.

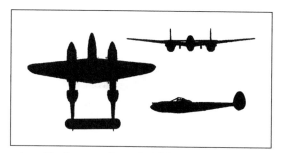

Arguably the most effective US fighter in the Pacific, the P-38 came in more than a dozen models, with numerous subvariants. Shown here is the P-38J, introduced in early 1944.

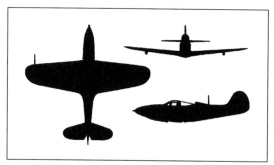

Although it proved a poor fighter, the P-39 Airacobra found its niche as a ground-attack aircraft, in which role it performed quite well.

P-38 Lightning, US Fighter

The Lockheed P-38 Lightning was one of the more successful American fighters, and the only one that was in PRODUCTION continuously from PEARL HARBOR through V-J Day. Over 9,000 were built. But the P-38 was unusual in many respects. It had twin engines, a characteristic that does not usually produce successful fighters. The P-38 succeeded by using its high speed and superior ceiling to dive on opponents with guns blazing. If this did not work, the P-38 was usually going fast enough to escape for another try. It was heavily armed, with 37mm or 20mm cannon, plus four .50 caliber machine guns. The twin engines were often a lifesaver, as the aircraft could fly on one engine. Large and sturdy, the P-38 could absorb more punishment than most other fighters. Lastly, the P-38 had exceptional range. Twelve-hour flights were not uncommon, at a time when most fighters carried only enough fuel to stay in the air for a few hours, which made the P-38 very useful as a reconnaissance aircraft. The major disadvantage of the P-38 was its lack of maneuverability at low altitudes. Despite this, there was always enough high-altitude work available to keep the P-38 busy throughout the war. By some reckoning the P-38 shot down more Japanese aircraft than any other fighter.

See also AIRCRAFT TYPES, DEVELOPMENT.

P-39 Airacobra, US Fighter

The P-39 Airacobra was another prewar US design that came up short when the shooting started. However, in this case it was the military's fault. The original 1936 design was for a speedy, heavily armed, and robust interceptor. But the generals insisted on a ground-support aircraft and the design was changed to meet those requirements. When fighters were desperately needed in the Pacific during 1942, the P-39 was among the few aircraft available. Pilots soon found out that if they could stay away from the Japanese Zeros, the P-39 was a very effective ground-attack aircraft. The 37mm cannon also made the P-39 an excellent "bomber buster." Over 7,000 were built, with PRODUCTION continuing into early 1943. Many were exported to allies, and the Russians were particularly fond of the P-39's ground-attack capabilities. A number of P-39s were produced in a special "export" version called the P-400, and some of these saw service with US Army pilots in the South Pacific.

See also AIRCRAFT TYPES, DEVELOPMENT.

P-40 Tomahawk, US Fighter

The US P-40 Tomahawk was a follow on to the P-36 Hawk and was a more effective aircraft. Actually, it was a P-36 with a more powerful engine and some other improvements. About 13,000 were built. Nevertheless, the P-40 was not quite as good as most of its opposition. The main reason that the P-40 was the most widely available fighter in 1942 was because America had waited so long to rearm. While not as capable as the contemporary Japanese Zero or German FW-190, the P-40 could hold its own if used properly. A sturdy aircraft, like its P-36 predecessor, P-40 PRODUCTION continued until late 1944. Most P-40s ended up being used as

fighter-bombers or as interceptors in secondary theaters (where first-line enemy fighters were unlikely to be encountered). Thousands were given to allies, for whom a P-40 was considered better than no fighter at all.

See also AIRCRAFT TYPES, DEVELOPMENT.

P-43, US Fighter

An experimental aircraft, similar in appearance to the P-47 and made by the same firm, Republic Aviation. First flew in 1940. Only 272 were built and some were supplied to Australia and China as part of the LEND-LEASE program.

See also AIRCRAFT TYPES, DEVELOPMENT.

P-47 Thunderbolt, US Fighter

The US P-47 Thunderbolt—nicknamed the "Jug"—was a very successful design, although it didn't enter service until late 1942 and didn't get to the Pacific until early 1944. Europe had priority on top-of-the-line air force aircraft, and European commitments had to be filled before any could be diverted to the Pacific. Over 15,000 were produced, and more were built after the war. Some were given

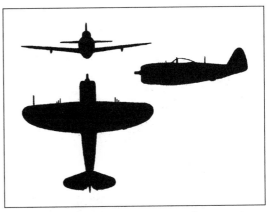

The P-40 Tomahawk was the US Army's principal fighter for most of the first year of the war. Although outclassed by many enemy fighters, it remained in production into 1944, fully 17 different models being developed: The P-40C is shown.

Introduced in 1942, the P-47D was the principal version of the Thunderbolt to see combat in the Pacific Theater, flying not only with USAAF squadrons, but also with the RAF in Burma and the Mexican Air Force in the Philippines.

to allies. The P-47 was one of the heaviest single-engine fighters of the war. It was quite modern in that the aircraft was literally designed around the most powerful engine available (2,000 horsepower initially, 2,300 and then 2,800 as the war went on). Most of those in the Pacific came with the more powerful engines. Its normal loaded weight of 7 to 8 tons was puny by modern standards, but it was a heavyweight in World War II. Carrying eight .50 caliber machine guns (and up to 3,000 pounds of bombs), the P-47 could inflict enormous damage on air or ground targets. Partly because of its own weight, the P-47 could take a lot of punishment and keep flying. It wasn't unusual for the P-47 to take dozens of machine gun and cannon shell hits and keep flying. Once pilots got used to the "heft" of the P-47, they loved it. At high altitudes, the P-47 was quite nimble. Its weight allowed it to dive away from trouble at high speed. With drop tanks, the P-47 was widely used as a bomber escort. The Japanese never came up with anything that could overwhelm the P-47.

See also AIRCRAFT TYPES, DEVELOPMENT.

P-51 Mustang, US Fighter

The US P-51 Mustang was the thoroughbred of World War II fighters. It was designed at the request of the British. An extraordinary airplane,

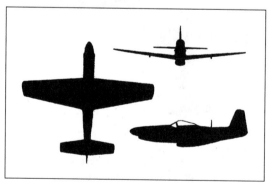

The final production version of the P-51, the P-51H, was introduced in 1945 and was primarily employed as an escort for B-29 missions over Japan.

many consider the P-51 the best of the lot. Unfortunately, few got to the Pacific. The P-51 arrived on the Pacific scene in late 1944, primarily to serve as an escort for long-range B-29 bombers. The P-51 was more agile than the P-47 and had a longer range. It weighed about half as much as the P-47 and had about half the firepower (six .50 caliber machine guns). Nevertheless, the P-51 could carry a 2,000-ton bombload. About 16,000 were delivered and PRODUCTION continued after the war. Mustang was the British name, the Americans originally calling it the Apache.

See also AIRCRAFT TYPES, DEVELOPMENT.

P-59 Airacomet, US Jet Fighter

The P-59 Airacomet was America's first jet fighter. Work began in 1941 using technology from the British. Although it performed satisfactorily, the design was never considered capable enough for combat use. Nearly 200 were built by late 1945 for use as trainers. The technology was transferred to Lockheed, which used it to produce the more successful postwar P-80 fighter. Had the design gone better, the P-59 could have been deployed by late 1944. Most would probably have ended up in Europe but, if the situation had warranted, could have appeared in the Pacific.

See also AIRCRAFT TYPES, DEVELOPMENT.

P-61 Black Widow, US Night Fighter

The US P-61 Black Widow was a night fighter, a 15-ton, two-engine aircraft designed specifically to carry a large radar and heavy armament (four 20mm cannon). The pilot and radar operator would seek out and destroy enemy bombers trying to hide in the darkness. Unfortunately, development only began after noting the problems the British were having with night bombers in late 1940. The first flight was just before PEARL HARBOR. Thus P-61s didn't reach the front until 1943, and the Pacific Theater didn't get them until the summer of 1944. While there were few German aircraft still operating at night, the Japanese were

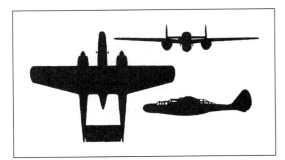

Introduced in mid-1944, the P-61B began to see service in the Pacific late that year, supplementing the older "A" model, which had been at the front since the spring of 1944.

another matter. Several Pacific P-61 pilots became aces for shooting five or more Japanese bombers trying to attack at night. Only about 700 were built.

See also AIRCRAFT TYPES, DEVELOPMENT.

P-63 Kingcobra, US Fighter

The P-63 Kingcobra was a much improved version of the earlier P-39. Some 3,300 were produced between 1943 and 1945. Most of them (2,400) were sent to Russia (already an enthusiastic user of the P-39) and another 300 were given to the French. US forces took the remainder but did not use them in combat. This was another of those aircraft that could have shown up in the Pacific. As it was, the P-63 did fly for the French in Vietnam in the late 1940s.

See also AIRCRAFT TYPES, DEVELOPMENT.

P-66, US Fighter

A prewar fighter made by the Vultee Corporation, it was not impressive and 129 of the 144 produced in 1939 and 1940 were sent to China. Originally ordered by Sweden, exports to that nation were prohibited by the US government.

See also AIRCRAFT TYPES, DEVELOPMENT.

P-80, US Jet Fighter

Test-flown in mid-1945, this was the US jet design most likely to have seen combat if the war had dragged into mid–1946. Army Air Force ACE Richard I. BONG was killed test-flying one in 1945.

See also AIRCRAFT TYPES, DEVELOPMENT.

P-400, US Fighter

A special "export" version of the P-39 designed for poverty-stricken countries. A number of them were shipped to the South Pacific in 1942 due to the desperate shortage of aircraft, and they performed with surprising effectiveness during the GUADAL-CANAL Campaign.

See also AIRCRAFT TYPES, DEVELOPMENT.

P1Y1 Frances, Japanese Bomber

The P1Y1 Frances was the Japanese Navy's most modern bomber, entering service during the summer of 1943. Faster, better armed and more robust than earlier models, the P1Y1 could outrun many Allied fighters at low altitudes. Hampered by shortages of fuel, spare parts, and skilled crews, about 1,100 were built (including night fighter versions).

See also AIRCRAFT TYPES, DEVELOPMENT.

Pacific Islanders, Japanese Subjects

Japan controlled most of the MARIANAS and all of the MARSHALL and CAROLINE ISLANDS from 1914, when it seized them from Germany. Under a League of Nations MANDATE from 1920, Japanese rule in the islands was surprisingly benevolent. For the most part Japanese exploitation of the larger islands was lightly supervised by the league until Japan withdrew from the organization in the mid–1930s. Japanese rule brought considerable economic prosperity to the natives of some islands, generally the larger, more fertile, and occasionally mineral-rich "high" islands (those of volcanic origins, such as SAIPAN or PONAPE, rather than the numerous "low" CORAL atolls). The Japanese also brought schools, hospitals, and other useful installations. Of course, the emphasis was on "Japanizing" the natives. On some islands this proved highly successful. For example, when the CHINA INCIDENT broke out in 1937, many men on Saipan, Rota, Ponape, and PALAU offered themselves for the emperor's service.

Although there was considerable recruiting of labor troops in the islands during World War II, the emperor never made any systematic attempt to recruit combat troops among his South Seas subjects. Nevertheless, small contingents of men from Palau and Ponape did enter imperial service as combat troops. Although the Palauans did not see active service, a platoon of Ponapans did. Some 20 men were sent to New Guinea in 1943, where they saw considerable action. Only three men survived.

However, with some exceptions, when US troops landed on one of the Japanese-mandated islands the local people either welcomed the invaders or maintained a certain distance. The principal exception was on Saipan, where many of the natives joined—voluntarily or otherwise—the thousands of Japanese residents who committed mass suicide rather than surrender.

Ref: White and Lindstrom, *The Pacific Theater*.

Pacific Islanders, Resistance to the Japanese

The Japanese overran most of the SOLOMONS, the BISMARCKS, many of the other islands in the southwest Pacific, and much of New Guinea rather easily, there being nothing much to oppose them. The local populations were Melanesian, stone age people with Negroid features, descended from Southeast Asians. Some of these peoples were Christians, and many spoke PIDGIN, a form of English. They had relatively long experience of colonial rule under the British, Dutch, Australians, or New Zealanders.

By the late 1930s many of the more educated elements, particularly clergymen and local tribal leaders, were expressing some dissatisfaction with the colonial powers. Despite this, for the most part

these "stout black fellows," cooperated quite freely with their Commonwealth overlords in resisting the Japanese. This was partially out of loyalty, but mostly out of self-interest. A few weeks of Japanese domination usually convinced even the most hardened anti-British islander that the king's men were easier to get along with than the emperor's.

To be sure, in a few instances the Japanese were able to recruit among the native peoples, notably on New Guinea and BOUGAINVILLE, where tribal rivalries were strong. And many of the islanders tried desperately to remain neutral, in some cases even returning downed pilots to their appropriate comrades with the deliberate intention of convincing both the Allies and the Japanese that they were friendly.

On several islands local hostility to colonial domination broke into open rebellion upon the withdrawal of most whites in the early months of 1942, even when there was no Japanese presence. In the LOUISIADES, for example, a local man named Buriga prophesied that if the people rose up and killed all the remaining whites and all persons of mixed race, the traditional gods of the islands would return, bringing with them many good things. The rebellion cost the lives of several whites, including representatives of the ANGAU. After the return of Australian forces in some strength, over 150 local people were arrested. Tried for treason to the Crown, nine men, including Buriga, were sentenced to be hanged, and many others to imprisonment. Buriga cheated the executioner by hanging himself in his cell, but the other eight men were publicly executed. The revolt, in fact, attracted few supporters, most of the people of the islands being much in terror of the rebels.

The peoples of the Pacific suffered severely during the war. Not only were many brutalized, killed and some even eaten by the Japanese, but others were also killed during the fighting, particularly by Allied air attacks, which often struck innocent villages that just happened to be behind Japanese lines.

Without the cooperation of these islanders, the task of ejecting the Japanese from the southwest

Pacific would have been far more difficult. Coast-watching operations, in which Commonwealth officers kept tabs on Japanese fleet and air movements from jungle-covered islands, would have been impossible without the assistance of the islanders. The islanders also reconnoitered Japanese positions, helped rescue downed flyers, and occasionally knocked off Japanese troops. The Allies offered a bounty for dead Japanese and live Allied pilots, a form of transaction the avid hunters among the islanders could appreciate. Many a downed Allied pilot was shocked to be confronted by a group of stone age warriors, one of whom would inquire in a British accent, "Are you all right, chap?" A great many islanders were killed, and many were subsequently decorated by the various Allied governments and awarded pensions for their wartime service.

The war had a profound effect on the peoples of the South Pacific in other ways. In addition to the devastation, it brought an extraordinary measure of prosperity and many luxury goods. At the same time, it undermined the authority of the colonial powers to an enormous extent.

One of the most pervasive influences on social change in Pacific societies was the US armed forces. Since the Americans had no vested interests to protect in the islands—they were there because the war was there, and they mostly wanted to be elsewhere—they tended to ignore the niceties of colonial hierarchy. The casual informality of Americans, their generosity (especially with regard to food, the sharing of which has an important religious meaning in many cultures), their tendency to treat everyone as an equal, their objections to calling grown men "boys," and the fact that Americans supervising native laborers never struck them (a common practice of British, Australian, or New Zealand foremen), all greatly impressed the islanders. That the US armed forces included many BLACK AMERICANS (not to mention some Chinese Americans, Hawaiian Americans, Native Americans, and even Japanese Americans) was a particularly important influence on the peoples of the South Pacific. If anything, the colonial powers had maintained a stricter racial separation than was common in even the most segregated parts of the United States. On many islands the "boys" were not permitted to wear Western clothing, drink alcohol, or even eat European foods, let alone eat at the same table with whites. The apparent equality among the various types of Americans (the uniform clothing, similar occupations, common equipment, identical rations, and even the presence of nonwhite officers) caused many islanders to perceive a racial equality that, of course, did not actually exist. This had an important impact on postwar political developments on many of the South Pacific islands, where even today Americans are immensely popular.

See also GUERRILLA WARS; PACIFIC ISLANDS REGIMENT; SOLOMON ISLANDS DEFENCE FORCE.

Ref: White and Lindstrom, *The Pacific Theater*.

Pacific Islands Regiment

Shortly before the Pacific War broke out, the Australian colonial authorities created the Papua Light Infantry from local police forces in Papua. This force was composed of locally recruited enlisted men under Australian officers, with commands usually given in PIDGIN. By the outbreak of the war the Papua Light Infantry was at about the strength of a battalion. In addition, several companies had been raised in the mandated territory of Northeast NEW GUINEA. The New Guinea Defence Force ultimately totaled four battalions. These forces proved invaluable to the Allied cause, not merely as guides, scouts, and GUERRILLAS, but also as combat troops, the Papua Light Infantry taking a major part in the brutal KOKODA TRAIL Campaign in mid- and late 1942.

In February 1945 the two forces were united into the Pacific Islands Regiment. By then all of the NCOs and many warrant officers were Papua-New Guineans. The merger was not achieved without some acrimony. The Papua Light Infantry had worn European-style uniforms, shorts and shirts with insignia on the collars, in colonial terms symbolic of very high status. When the Pacific Islands

Regiment was formed, the prescribed uniform was that of the New Guinea Defence Force, kilt-like laplaps (lavalavas) with insignia of rank on the skirt. Many veterans of the Papua Light Infantry objected to this symbolic lowering of their status, and there was some indiscipline in the ranks, including an incident in which three Australian officers were injured in a riot. Tensions festered for several months, before order was restored, when the Australian military authorities acknowledged that they had made a mistake.

By the end of the war there were three active battalions in the Pacific Islands Regiment (one each was serving on BOUGAINVILLE, New Guinea, and NEW BRITAIN) plus two more being formed. A total of 3,500 Papuans and New Guineans served in the Pacific Islands Regiment during the war, and it accumulated 11 battle honors. Thousands of other Papua-New Guineans served as combatants in other organizations, including the ANGAU, the police, special operations forces, the Australian militia, and as guides for Allied troops. Although inactivated shortly after the war, the regiment was subsequently reactivated in the late 1940s, and became the basis of the Papua-New Guinea armed forces when the combined territories achieved their independence.

See also FIJI ISLANDS; TONGA.

Ref: Sinclair, *To Find a Path*; White and Lindstrom, *The Pacific Theater*.

Pacific War, the Course of the War

The Pacific War did not simply start at PEARL HARBOR, then move west until Japan was reached. The fighting took place over a third of the Earth's surface and often simultaneously, thousands of miles apart. Understanding how this came to be requires that we take a look at the reasons why Japan decided to start the war.

Many of Japan's top military leaders realized that they could not win a long war against the United States. But that was not enough to keep Japan from entering World War II. Since the 1920s, the government had been increasingly dom-

inated by army officers who had involved Japan in its aggressive war in China that had led to the oil embargo by the Western nations. This last action put the Japanese generals on the spot. They could not afford to abandon their operations in China, as that was their principal justification for running the government. But they could not ignore the oil embargo either, as the Western countries controlled the world's oil supply and without oil the Japanese armed forces would be largely crippled within a year.

For the military, it was a case of use it or lose it. The Japanese generals convinced themselves that some chance of military victory in the Pacific was preferable to guaranteed impotence from a lack of oil. The generals saw the embargo as an offensive move, and their military response as a defensive reaction. While the Imperial Navy's admirals did not exercise nearly as much control over the government, they went along with the generals. Japan was a maritime nation, it depended on control of the seas. The generals recognized this and the navy budget was relatively large throughout the 20 years preceding Pearl Harbor. But the generals were in firm control of the government and the admirals followed the generals' lead.

The basic plan for the Pacific War was to destroy the Allied forces in the region, seize all the Allied colonies and possessions, and then sue for peace on favorable terms. It was felt (though not all Japanese leaders believed it) that the Allies would prefer some kind of settlement to a long war in the Pacific. It was a desperate gamble, which at first appeared to be working.

The Japanese had a high opinion of their own military prowess. This attitude certainly helped, because the numbers didn't look quite so favorable. Most of the Japanese Army was tied down in China. Only about a quarter of a million ground troops could be scraped together for the Pacific offensive. Japan's target list was impressive: the Philippines, sundry central Pacific islands, the NETHERLANDS EAST INDIES (modern INDONESIA), NEW GUINEA and nearby island groups, INDOCHINA (Vietnam and environs), MALAYA (Malaysia and SINGAPORE), Thailand, Burma, and parts of India. In these territories there were over half a million Allied troops. But it was more than numbers that counted. Many of the Allied troops were either poorly trained, inexperienced or both, and many were locally recruited and were not necessarily completely happy with the rule of the "Mother Country."

The Vichy French troops in Indo-China were neutral (and, technically, allies of Japan, because of Vichy France's relationship with Japan's ally, Nazi Germany). SIAM (Thailand) was pro-Japanese, primarily out of fear rather than enthusiasm for the Japanese cause.

But the biggest asset the Japanese Army had was the Japanese Navy. The Pacific War began with the Allies and Japan having a rough parity in naval forces, and Japanese carrier superiority, as well as larger and more capable air forces.

The Japanese plan for conquering the Pacific was to be executed with naval superiority, and barely sufficient ground forces. Most of the Japanese target areas were not heavily garrisoned. The British had large forces in Singapore, as did the United States in the Philippines. But the nearby Japanese forces were better trained and led and had superior air support. Many Allied territories were held by token forces, and all the Japanese had to do was walk in and take over.

The initial Japanese attacks in December 1941 and January 1942 soon overwhelmed all resistance. The Japanese used their naval superiority to isolate Allied forces. This not only cut the Allied forces off from resupply and reinforcement, it also allowed the Japanese to take care of Allied forces one at a time. For example, Japanese troops took care of Malaya before going on to the Netherlands East Indies and Burma.

What stopped the Japanese eventually, and slowed them down in the meantime, was a lack of merchant shipping to move the troops and supplies forward. In the first six months of the war, Japan had seized all the central Pacific islands, all of what is now called Indonesia, all of southeast Asia except for western Burma and most of New Guinea

and the adjacent islands. In less than half a year, Japan's carriers attacked targets from the Hawaiian Islands to southern India, going almost halfway around the world in the process. Japan's fleet, and particularly its carriers, were what protected the relatively small Japanese ground forces from retribution by Allied land, air, or naval forces.

But in May, with more US carriers in the Pacific, Japan began to lose carriers. First, a light carrier was lost in the Battle of the CORAL SEA and a heavy carrier damaged. A month later, four heavy carriers were lost at MIDWAY. That essentially evened up the carrier situation in the Pacific, despite the United States's loss of two carriers (one each at Coral Sea and Midway). Equally important was the United States pouring land-based aircraft into the theater. This restricted where the Japanese carriers, and their ships in general, could operate with relative safety.

Had they not lost five carriers in the first seven months of the war, the Japanese planned to keep pushing their defensive perimeter outward. These planned conquests (as far south as the FIJI ISLANDS and, eventually, HAWAII to the east and India and the Persian Gulf in the west) would be garrisoned slowly (because of the lack of cargo ships) by troops withdrawn from China and new units raised in Japan. The Japanese Army had misgivings about these expansion plans, even though it agreed with the navy about the need to grab as much territory as possible as a prelude to the eventual peace negotiations with the Allies. The army did draw the line at an attempt to land in Australia. That nation was simply too large for the Japanese Army's scant resources to handle, particularly in light of the hostile population there.

But in the spring of 1942, there was much optimism and little clear thought at Japanese military headquarters. The early victories had been more spectacular than even the most enthusiastic Japanese militarists envisioned. For a few months, anything seemed possible. But after Midway, reality again set in. However, the worst news was not the loss of the carriers at Midway, but the refusal of the Allies to negotiate. Pearl Harbor had wakened the sleeping tiger (as many Japanese officers who had studied in America had warned) and America now wanted vengeance.

Japanese who knew a bit about world economics and US history knew that the Americans would not rest until Japan was a smoldering ruin, and the Americans were quite capable of Japan's destruction. No one in Tokyo would ever admit this publicly until near the end. But it was now clear, the Americans were on the offensive.

In August 1942, the United States landed a Marine division on GUADALCANAL and seized an unfinished Japanese airfield. Meanwhile, to the northwest the Japanese were continuing to fight over possession of NEW GUINEA. The Guadalcanal battle lasted six months and resulted in a Japanese defeat. This was but one of a series of battles in this area that took Allied troops right up the Solomon chain of islands, past RABAUL, across New Guinea, and on toward the Philippines by late 1944. Meanwhile, the fighting on New Guinea continued into 1945.

During late 1942 there were a series of carrier battles that demonstrated US capabilities in carrier warfare and killed many of Japan's hard-to-replace carrier pilots.

Meanwhile, two other fronts gave the Japanese still more trouble. In Burma, the Japanese offensive had stalled by mid-1942. Noting that the Allies were building railroad, truck, and air routes into China, the Japanese eventually tried in 1943–44 to push the British back into India and away from any access to China. But the forces were more evenly matched now and the Japanese offensives failed. By early 1945, the Allies were on the offensive and eventually pushed the Japanese out of most of Burma. While Burma was a stalemate the Japanese could afford, the third prong of the Allied counteroffensive led right to Tokyo. In late 1943, the United States began the series of amphibious operations in the Central Pacific that would, eight months later, seize islands close enough to Japan for B-29 bombers to reach Tokyo and other Home Island cities. Trying to defeat this offensive, in the summer of 1944, the rebuilt Japanese carrier force

was destroyed once and for all in the Battle of the PHILIPPINE SEA (the GREAT MARIANAS TURKEY SHOOT). In late 1944 the Philippines were retaken. In early 1945, islands even closer to Japan were taken and the bombing campaign against Japanese industry and population intensified.

By the summer of 1945, Japan was isolated and broken.

Ref: Collier, *The War in the Far East*; Cook and Cook, *Japan at War*; Dower, *War without Mercy*; Dunnigan and Nofi, *Victory at Sea*; Hoyt, *Japan's War*; Ienaga, *The Pacific War*; MacIntyre, *The Battle for the Pacific*; Ready, *Forgotten Allies*; Spector, *Eagle Against the Sun*; Van der Vat, *The Pacific Campaign*.

Palau Group, Caroline Islands

The westernmost group of the CAROLINE ISLANDS, about 600 miles east of the Philippines, the Palau Group are "high" islands, primarily volcanic in origin rather than CORAL atolls. There are hundreds of them, but they amount to only about 175 square miles. In Japanese hands since World War I, the Palaus were among the most developed of the MANDATES, and some 30,000 Japanese civilians set up residence there during the 1920s and 1930s, establishing a fairly modern community on Koror, in the central part of the archipelago. There were also about 5,000 Melanesian Palauans.

The Palaus figured early in US war planning, being one of the places earmarked for occupation under the various incarnations of War Plan Orange. In the 1920s the eccentric, and alcoholic, Colonel Pete Ellis (USMC) resided in the islands in disguise, attempting to spy on Japanese military installations, which he was convinced existed there in violation of the naval DISARMAMENT TREATIES and the League of Nations MANDATES. Ellis died of alcoholism in 1923 (though some attribute his death to poisoning by Japanese Intelligence). In fact, the Japanese did not begin intensive military development in the Palaus until the late 1930s, after they had left the League of Nations. The war initially had little impact on the islands. During it upward of 50,000 Japanese troops were stationed in the islands, most of whom were left to "wither on the vine" as US forces island-hopped across the Pacific. From March of 1944, the islands were subjected to American aerial and naval bombardment on numerous occasions, which succeeded in destroying several airfields and other military installations. The two southernmost large islands, Anguar and PELELIU, were invaded by US forces in late 1944, and there was particularly heavy fighting on the latter. During the last year of the war there was considerable privation and some starvation in the islands.

After nearly 30 years of Japanese rule, many of the Palauans were devoted to the emperor. A large number of men volunteered for labor service, and many were shipped to New Guinea, where they supervised work gangs composed of local natives. Late in the war some Palauans volunteered for military service, forming a "suicide commando" that saw no action.

Ironically, after the war, when the United States took control of the Palaus under a United Nations trusteeship, the islanders proved distinctly unhappy. Prosperous under Japanese rule, if only because the Japanese invested heavily in the islands, particularly after they began to develop them as military bases, the Palauans found the United States much less generous.

Ref: White and Lindstrom, *The Pacific Theater.*

Palau Islands, Campaign for

The Palaus, located midway between the CAROLINES and Philippines, were to be the target of the US central Pacific offensive, before the carriers and amphibious ships turned north and went after Japan itself. At the last minute, it was argued that invading the Palaus was no longer necessary, but Admiral NIMITZ ordered the operations to go ahead anyway. The campaign took place from September to October 1944, cost the lives of some 2,000 Americans, and centered largely around the Battle for PELELIU Island.

At the time, in late 1944, there was no unambiguous way to know that avoiding the Palaus would have been all right. As it turned out, the air bases in the Palaus were not needed because of ineffective Japanese airpower in the area and the unexpectedly rapid advance of Allied forces from the south and across the central Pacific. No one realized that the Japanese were particularly well fortified in Peleliu. This was one of the few campaigns that was fought unnecessarily.

The island of Anguar was not defended nearly as stoutly as Peleliu and was taken by an army division in three days (September 17–20) at a cost of 540 dead and 2,735 wounded. The Japanese garrison of 2,600 fought, as usual, to the death with only a handful of PRISONERS being taken. Peleliu (see also, PELELIU, BATTLE OF) proved much tougher.

Perhaps most importantly, as part of the Palau Campaign the unoccupied atoll of ULITHI was taken over as a fleet base to support future operations.

Palawan, Philippines

A local port, with a good anchorage but limited facilities, Palawan also had potential as an air base, given that it fronted on both the South China Sea and the Sulu Sea, as well as northern Borneo. Palawan was overrun by the Japanese in early 1942, and retaken by the United States three years later.

Palembang, Battle of, Sumatra, Netherlands East Indies

In early 1942 Palembang was a small upland city, the administrative center of much of Sumatra. It was the site of some recently discovered oil deposits, which were just being exploited. That made it a prime target for the Japanese.

The Japanese attacked Palembang in mid-February 1942. The Dutch garrison had two months warning that the Japanese were on the way, but did not destroy the oil facilities in time because they wanted to keep pumping oil for the revenue it would bring in for the cash-strapped Dutch government-in-exile.

The Japanese were aware that the Dutch had not yet destroyed the oil facilities and sought to capture them intact. They did this with an airborne assault, dropping in a battalion of SNLF paratroopers on February 14. A tough fight ensued, in which the Dutch got the upper hand. However, the airdrop so disrupted the defense that the Dutch were unable to effect demolition before substantial Japanese reinforcements arrived by sea, on the 15th. By the 16th the Japanese had secured the city and the substantially intact oil fields.

It was the speed of the assault that was the key to this battle, a classic example of airborne assault as a way to achieve surprise and a quick victory. The battle was over in two days.

Allied naval forces were still active in the area, but Japanese air and naval forces were too strong for these Allied efforts to have any effect on the campaign in the NETHERLANDS EAST INDIES.

Palmyra Island

One of the LINE ISLANDS. Like a number of other normally deserted places, Palmyra, a thousand miles south of HAWAII, had very great potential as an air base, helping to control extensive areas of the central Pacific, in which role it served as a US base throughout the war.

Panama Canal

Connecting the Atlantic Ocean with the Pacific, the Panama Canal was possibly the most important strategic place in the world in early 1942. So critical to US strategic thinking was the canal that until the Second World War all US warships were designed to pass through the canal, so that the Atlantic Fleet could quickly reinforce the Pacific, and vice versa. As a result, until 1940 no US warship was designed with a beam greater than the width of the canal locks (110 feet). The first vessels that exceeded that beam were the MONTANA CLASS battleships, authorized in 1940 but never laid down. The first ships to exceed the width of the

locks were several units of the MARYLAND and CALIFORNIA CLASSES, which emerged from their post-PEARL HARBOR refits in 1943–44 with a beam of some 114 feet. The first ships deliberately designed and built wider than the locks were the three units of the MIDWAY CLASS, which entered service after the war.

The US Navy had given considerable thought to the defense of the canal, and as early as 1929 (in Fleet Problem 9) had postulated a surprise carrier aviation attack to disable it. With this in mind, the canal was heavily fortified. Although the navy dismissed the possibility that the Japanese would attempt a carrier raid on the canal—with considerable reason, given limited Japanese logistical resources—there remained the constant fear that Japanese or other Axis saboteurs might try to disable it. The simplest way of doing this would have been to sink a merchant ship in one of the "cuts" or blow up one of the sets of locks. Although these scenarios were so obvious that they actually turned up in movies, the Japanese never attempted either.

During the war, recognizing that ships were going to become wider, construction began on a new, wider set of locks, but the project was abandoned after the war. Another Panama construction project, which did see completion, was that of an oil pipeline to run parallel to the canal. Originally planned as a single 20-inch line, even before completion a second pipeline began being laid. Completed in 1945, daily capacity on the 46-mile-long line was reportedly over 300,000 barrels.

Without the Panama Canal the war in the Pacific would certainly have dragged on into 1946, if not longer.

Panay Incident

The USS *Panay* (PR-5) was a small (450-ton) gunboat built in the 1920s for service on the Yangtze River in China. On Sunday, 12 December 1937, she was escorting three US flag tankers downriver to the sea from above Nanking. At about 1330 hours, *Panay* and the tankers were anchored near

Hoshein, upstream from Nanking. It was a clear, calm day. Although plainly marked as an American vessel, *Panay* was attacked by Japanese dive bombers, which sank her and machine-gunned the wreck. Two of the tankers were also hit but managed to survive. The attack took over 20 minutes and was conducted by three waves of aircraft. Two American sailors were killed, as well as an Italian journalist, and 11 others were wounded.

After a protest from the United States, the Japanese government issued an apology for the "accident" and paid some $2.2 million in compensation. The officer responsible for the attack, Col. Kingona Hashimoto, was reassigned. After PEARL HARBOR Hashimoto received a decoration for the sinking of *Panay*, which subsequent investigation has determined was a deliberate act, apparently inspired by orders from higher commanders.

See: TUTUILA, US RIVER GUNBOAT; WARSHIPS, US, CAPTURED.

Ref: Perry, *The Panay Incident*.

Paramushiro, Kuriles, Japan

Through perseverance and sacrifice the Japanese had developed a modest naval base and a surprisingly extensive air base at desolate Paramushiro, with an eye on operations toward Siberia and the ALEUTIANS. It was several times subject to US air raids from the Aleutians and was taken by the Russians in August 1945.

Patch, Alexander McC., III (1889–1945)

Alexander McCarrell Patch, an army brat, graduated from West Point in 1913. Commissioned in the infantry, he saw active service on the Mexican border and in combat as commander of a machine gun battalion during World War I. He afterward held various posts, attended several army schools, and rose slowly through the ranks. One of the officers who developed the "triangular" infantry division table of organization in 1936, PEARL HARBOR found him in a training command, from which he was sent in January of 1942 to prepare the defense of NEW CALEDONIA. Organizing the Americal Division from odd units he found in the South Pacific, Patch took the division to support the Marines on GUADALCANAL in October of 1942. Succeeding to command on Guadalcanal later that year, he oversaw the final reduction of the Japanese forces. In February of 1943 Patch was ordered home to the United States, where he assumed command of a corps. In March of 1944 he was given command of the Seventh Army for the invasion of Southern France, which he executed flawlessly. He led his army until the end of the war, which found his troops in Bavaria. During Patch's operations in Lorraine his son, Captain Alexander McCarrell Patch IV, was killed in action. After the war assigned to head a study of how best to organize the army for the postwar world, Patch died suddenly in late 1945.

PB2Y Coronado, US Flying Boat

The PB2Y Coronado was a four-engine US flying boat designed two years after the two-engine PBY. The PB2Y was a much larger aircraft, weighing 30 tons fully loaded. It was also faster than the PBY, with a max speed of 224 MPH and a cruise speed of 141 MPH. The PB2Y was so large, in fact, that it was used primarily as a transport, getting men and supplies to front-line bases quickly. Only 210 PB2Ys were built, and one was the personal plane of Admiral NIMITZ, enabling him to move across the vast Pacific comfortably, and to work with his staff while doing so.

See also AIRCRAFT TYPES, DEVELOPMENT; RECONNAISSANCE, NAVAL.

PBM Mariner, US Flying Boat

The US PBM Mariner was a follow on for the PBY Catalina. Although the Mariner was a generally better aircraft, it wasn't superior enough to cause cessation of PBY PRODUCTION. The Catalina was cheaper and easier to build and it did its job well. So the PBY did most of the naval reconnaissance during the war, with PBMs being added as they were available.

See also AIRCRAFT TYPES, DEVELOPMENT; RECONNAISSANCE, NAVAL.

PBY Catalina, US Flying Boat

The PBY Catalina was the most common US flying boat of the war, mainly because it was the first to enter service, in 1936. This aircraft served several purposes. Reconnaissance was the PBY's main job. But that could be done more effectively by B-17s and B-24s. What made the PBY unique was its ability to "land" on the water. This allowed PBYs to be stationed in places where there were no airfields, or where the local airfields were crammed with conventional bombers and fighters. Seaplane tenders (ships with fuel, repair facilities, and ground crews) would anchor in the same bays and inlets that the PBYs operated from. The ability to float

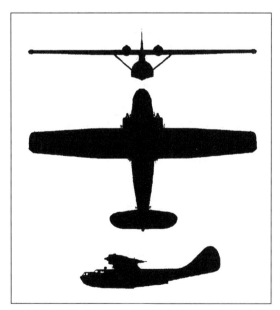

Although a mid-1930s design, the PBY Catalina was the most successful American flying boat of the war.

also made PBYs invaluable (and quite popular) for picking up the crews of downed aircraft. Thousands of airmen owed their lives to the timely arrival of a PBY. Unfortunately, the PBY was too slow (175 MPH top speed) to make an effective bomber. But it was effective against SUBMARINES, as they were less likely to shoot back and were more vulnerable to any damage. Nearly 3,300 PBYs were built during the war, about 40% of them being "amphibian" (with wheels allowing them to land on an airfield if available). Some 20% were given to allies. Although the PBY was slow (cruising speed of 110–115 MPH), it was well armed. Up to 4,000 pounds of bombs or depth charges could be carried, and the average PBY was equipped with five machine guns facing in various directions. PBY range was over 2,000 miles and the maximum weight was 16 tons. Normal patrols were 8 to 10 hours long. All in all, not too shabby for an ugly two-engine aircraft that could float.

See also AIRCRAFT TYPES, DEVELOPMENT; RECONNAISSANCE, NAVAL.

Peace Feelers, Japanese with Russia

By the late spring of 1945 the Japanese government was attempting to get the Soviets to use their good offices with the United States to bring about an end to the war. Somehow the message never got to the appropriate authorities. By the time the Japanese realized what the Russians were up to (stonewalling) and attempted to reach the United States through Sweden, it was too late to avoid the final horrors of HIROSHIMA and NAGASAKI. The extent to which Stalin deliberately impeded the peace process has never been established, although this may come out now that the old Soviet archives are opening up.

Pearl Harbor, The Campaign

Japan opened the war with three major attacks and several minor ones. The first strike (by a number of hours) was at Pearl Harbor. The objective was to cripple the only force (the US Pacific fleet, and particularly its battleships) in the Pacific that could interfere with the other two Japanese attacks (on the Philippines and MALAYA). Surprise was essential to the Pearl Harbor attack. This was so not only because surprise put the defender at a disadvantage, but also because attacking a major naval base with carrier aircraft in broad daylight had never been done before and no one was sure how successful it would be. On paper it appeared it would work, and the British had been rather successful in a night-time carrier air raid on the Italian fleet in Taranto Harbor on 11–12 November 1940. The experienced and history-savvy officers of the Japanese fleet knew that the first time anything is tried, particularly something risky, the unexpected can be expected.

The Pearl Harbor operation was the brainchild of Admiral Isoroku YAMAMOTO, who first suggested the idea in a conversation with another admiral in February 1941. That spring he ordered his staff to gather information about the proposal. Formal planning began in the summer, and was completed in November of 1941. The basic concept was to injure American military power in the Pacific to the extent that Japan would be able to overrun a territory so vast that the United States would ultimately decide on a negotiated peace rather than a protracted war. Japan could not grab a lot of territory in the Pacific if a large enemy fleet were in the same waters. America had the only other large fleet, and most of it was based at Pearl Harbor in the Hawaiian Islands. Cripple that fleet, and Japan could do whatever it wanted in the Pacific.

The Pearl Harbor Striking Force (six carriers, two fast battleships, two heavy cruisers, a light cruiser, nine destroyers, and three SUBMARINES, supported by eight tankers and supply ships) was concentrated in great secrecy at TANKAN BAY, a secure anchorage in the KURILE ISLANDS north of Japan. As part of the undertaking, another group of submarines was assigned to ferry five two-man midget subs tasked with penetrating Pearl Harbor from the sea at the same time the airmen attacked.

On 26 November 1941, the strike force sailed, under the command of VAdm Chuichi NAGUMO.

Maintaining total radio silence, the Strike Force took a route through the North Pacific, which had proven wholly devoid of shipping under normal circumstances. The progress of the strike force across the Pacific was relatively fast, despite the necessity of having to refuel by the inefficient tow method.

Although American and Allied intelligence were aware that war was increasingly imminent, the much less secretive concentration of Japanese forces for their offensive southward into the "Southern Resources Area" (Malaya, the NETHERLANDS EAST INDIES, the Philippines, and so on) attracted Allied attention. War warnings to Pacific Theater commanders only confirmed their expectations that something would soon happen in that quarter.

In December of 1941 the naval and air base at Pearl Harbor and other installations on Oahu, in the central Hawaiian Islands, represented the greatest concentration of American military power in the world. In normal circumstances the island was the home of nine or ten battleships, three carriers (with over 250 aircraft), a score or more cruisers, and literally dozens of destroyers, submarines, mine warfare vessels, and support ships, plus about 500 land-based aircraft and two understrength infantry divisions. On the morning of 7 December 1941, there were eight battleships, two heavy cruisers, six light cruisers, 29 destroyers, five submarines, one gunboat, nine minelayers, and 10 minesweepers, and 24 auxiliaries plus several ancient hulks being used for various purposes (including a cruiser so old she had fought at Manila Bay in 1898). In addition to combat forces, Oahu had elaborate maintenance and repair facilities, extensive warehouses, and a large fuel dump. Command of these forces was divided between Admiral Husband KIMMEL and LG Walter C. SHORT. Typical of the haphazard command structure that prevailed in the US armed forces before (and to some extent during) World War II, neither officer was in overall command. Short was responsible for the defense of HAWAII from attack, including air attack and the protection of the fleet when in port. Kimmel was responsible for all naval forces and for the direction of naval operations. Although the two socialized occasionally, and even played golf together, there was little professional communication between them, and they did not consult with each other very often on matters respecting their commands and missions.

As early as February of 1941, Short, newly arrived in Hawaii, had dismissed the possibility of a carrier air raid on the place, despite the fact that the navy had several times practiced such a strike against the PANAMA CANAL, SAN DIEGO, and Pearl Harbor itself. These practice raids had demonstrated that such operations were not all that difficult. Although air raid drills were held periodically—there was one at 0200 on December 6—Short's principal concern was the perceived threat of sabotage by members of Hawaii's large resident-Japanese and Japanese-American population.

The Japanese Strike Force arrived at a point some 230 miles north of Pearl Harbor late on 6 December. At 0600 the next morning Admiral Nagumo launched his first strike, of 49 high-level bombers, 40 torpedo bombers, and 51 dive bombers, escorted by 42 fighters. As these flew southward, they split up into different sections, each with its particular objective.

Two US Army enlisted men manning an experimental radar system spotted the incoming aircraft and called air defense headquarters twice. However, the duty officer at air defense headquarters

To cries of "Banzai!" from the ship's company, Japanese aircraft begin taking off from their carrier for the attack on Pearl Harbor at approximately 0600 hours, December 7, 1941.

As Hickam Field burns in the background, Japanese aircraft begin the attack on Battleship Row, off Ford Island, in Pearl Harbor. In the lower left is the battleship Nevada *(BB-36), with some lighters alongside. To her right in the picture is* Arizona *(BB-39), with the minelayer* Vestal *alongside. To her right are* West Virginia *(BB-48), which has just taken a torpedo, and* Tennessee *(BB-43). Foreward of them are* Maryland *(BB-46) and* Oklahoma *(BB-37). The large vessel foreward of them is the oiler* Neosho; *barely visible foreward of her is* California *(BB-44).*

—a very junior lieutenant without much military experience—twice dismissed the bogie, suggesting that it was a flight of B-17s due in from California.

At about the same time, a destroyer exercising outside the harbor entrance spotted a submarine periscope, made a vigorous attack, and confirmed a kill (getting one of the five Japanese midget subs that were trying to enter the harbor), but no one took the destroyer skipper's frantic messages seriously. As a result, the air raid achieved complete surprise, the first bombs falling at 0753. Air bases were hit first, to ensure no interference from American aircraft. Then the bombers went after the

fleet, anchored neatly in the shallow and narrow waters of Pearl Harbor. Although it was a Sunday morning, and many of the ships' companies were understrength, having sent men ashore on weekend passes, fleet antiaircraft guns came into action quite quickly. The first strike worked the ships over heavily. The principal objective was the battleships, of which seven were tied up along "Battleship Row" and an eighth was in dry dock. These took an enormous pounding, notably the ships moored outboard of Ford Island. Within a half-hour, all eight battleships were damaged or sunk, as were 10 other warships. The strike ended at

UNITED STATES CASUALTIES AT PEARL HARBOR		
Service	Killed	Wounded
Army	233	364
Navy	1,998	710
Marines	109	69
Civilians	48	35

Note that the casualty figures are found with minor variations in different official sources.

0825. A second strike almost as strong as the first (36 high-level bombers, 78 dive bombers, and 54 fighters) came over at 0840, Nagumo having launched it at 0700. Hampered by dense smoke from the damage inflicted by the first strike, and by an increasingly voluminous antiaircraft fire, the second strike inflicted relatively little damage. It flew home at 0945.

Even as the second strike flew back to its carriers, a critical argument was going on aboard the Japanese flagship. Impressed by the success of their first strike, air-minded officers like Minoru GENDA and Mitsuo FUCHIDA tried to convince Nagumo to undertake a third strike, this time against the harbor installations, repair facilities, warehouses, and fuel dumps. Nagumo demurred, concerned over the whereabouts of the American carriers, which had not yet been located. As a result, as soon as the second strike had been recovered, the strike force turned back for Japan. No Japanese naval task force ever again penetrated so far eastward.

USS Shaw (DD-373), a Mahan-class ship, blows up in her floating dock. Despite extensive damage, the ship was repaired and returned to service.

USS Arizona (BB-39), burning after the Japanese attack, during which she suffered a magazine explosion and lost about 1,177 of her 1,512 crewmen.

Pearl Harbor was a devastating defeat for the United States. A total of 21 vessels were sunk or heavily damaged, including two battleships that were total losses, *Arizona* and *Oklahoma*. In addition, nearly 200 aircraft had been destroyed, virtually all on the ground. CASUALTIES were 2,388 killed and 1,178 wounded.

Japanese losses were five midget submarines and about 29 aircraft, for a total of 55 airmen and nine submarine crew members. Arguably, the defeat could have been worse. The three Pacific Fleet carriers escaped the debacle, the carriers were spared. (*Saratoga* was undergoing a refit at San Diego, while LEXINGTON and *Enterprise* were at sea, returning from delivering aircraft to Wake and other island garrisons).

A case can be made that Nagumo's decision not to undertake a third strike was in error, for it would have destroyed the fuel dumps, thereby crippling the remnants of the fleet, and so seriously damaged the harbor facilities that not even minor repairs would be practical—in effect, forcing the United States back to the West Coast. While such a possibility existed, it is important to note that Nagumo's second strike had been relatively ineffective in fact, most of the Japanese aircraft losses occurred during the second strike. Moreover, since his own pilots had just demonstrated the devastating effectiveness of carrier aviation, his concern over the location of the US carriers was by no means unreasonable.

See also DECEPTION.

Ref: Goldstein and Dillon, *The Pearl Harbor Papers: Inside the Japanese Plans*; Prange, Goldstein, and Dillon, *At Dawn We Slept* and *Pearl Harbor: The Verdict of History*.

Pearl Harbor, The Doomed Survivors

In the aftermath of the Japanese attack on Pearl Harbor, much was made of the heroic efforts to release men trapped in the hulls of the sunken ships. Nothing was said at the time, nor for some 25 years afterward, about the men who survived for days, and in some cases even weeks, trapped deep in the bowels of capsized battlewagons, beyond hope of rescue, who died of their injuries or slowly suffocated or starved to death. In virtually every case the identities of these men are known but have never been revealed, out of consideration for their families. Similarly, the navy has never revealed the number of Pearl Harbor survivors who were eventually classified as psychological CASUALTIES, some of whom remained in institutions for the rest of their lives.

Pearl Harbor, Oahu, Hawaii

The principal American naval and naval air base in the Pacific, Pearl Harbor had extensive repair and maintenance facilities, including large dry docks, enormous workshops, great ammunition magazines, and a very large oil tank farm, not to mention vast airfields. However, it had a very

Damage control parties coping with fires aboard USS West Virginia (BB-48), burning after taking six or seven torpedoes and two bombs, as well as damage from the debris of Arizona (BB-39), which blew up astern.

Although a devastating defeat, Pearl Harbor ultimately sealed the fate of the Japanese Empire, by dragging a hitherto isolationist America into World War II.

narrow and not easily navigated entrance, and was cramped, with barely three square miles of surface area. The biggest problem, in 1941, was that its defense was based on an assumption of army-navy cooperation, which was not always forthcoming.

Despite the devastating Japanese attack of 7 December 1941, the base facilities at Pearl Harbor were little harmed, and it almost immediately resumed its role as the main fleet base in the Pacific, a role that it never lost.

Pearl Harbor, The Plot

The most enduring World War II conspiracy theory contends that President ROOSEVELT and sundry other national political and military leaders "knew" that the Japanese were about to attack Pearl Harbor, and, indeed, even provoked the attack. There are numerous variations on the theme. For example, one suggests that Winston CHUR-

CHILL "knew" but refused to tell, so that the United States would be able to come to Britain's rescue against Germany. These theories are all based on "evidence," often "new" evidence that has "just come to light." Unfortunately, when all this evidence is examined, including the "new" evidence (which always turns out to be information of little value or relevance and long available to the public if it cared to inquire), the most charitable thing that can be said is "not proven."

Consider, for example, the statement of the US ambassador to Japan, Joseph C. Grew. Grew claimed that in January 1941 he forwarded to the State Department information from a "reliable source" to the effect that the Japanese were planning an attack on Pearl Harbor. There are two things wrong with this statement. To begin with, Grew was constantly forwarding rumors and tips from allegedly reliable sources. More importantly, however, in January 1941 there was no Japanese plan to attack Pearl Harbor, as it was not until February of that year that YAMAMOTO came up with the idea, having digested Minoru GENDA's report about the British attack on the Italian Fleet in Taranto Harbor on 11 November 1940, and serious planning did not begin until the summer.

Some of the "theories" about the attack are completely fantastical, including one contention that the attack was actually carried out by British aircraft based on one of the outlying islands of the Hawaiian group!

In fact, the disaster at Pearl Harbor was the result of a lot of audacity and luck on the part of the Japanese and numerous blunders by many American political and military leaders, with no particular person being criminally responsible. As historian Gordon Prange said, "There's enough blame for everyone."

See also KIMMEL, HUSBAND; LANIKAI, US SCHOONER; SHORT, WALTER C.

See also DECEPTION.

Ref: Goldstein and Dillon, *The Pearl Harbor Papers: Inside the Japanese Plans*; Prange, Goldstein, and Dillon, *At Dawn We Slept* and *Pearl Harbor: The Verdict of History*.

Pedang, Sumatra, Netherlands East Indies —

A small coastal port, with a good harbor but limited resources, Pedang (or Padang) was potentially of value due to its location, on the western—mostly harborless—side of Sumatra, fronting on the Indian Ocean.

Peking, China

The capital of China, long in Japanese hands, Peking had some value as an industrial center and as a critical rail junction.

Peleliu, Battle of

One of the PALAU ISLANDS, Peleliu was in an excellent strategic location, about 500 miles east of the Philippines and a similar distance west of Japanese bases in the CAROLINES. A thick coat of jungle concealed the unusually rugged nature of this island. It had a small population, and neither port nor air facilities.

Peleliu was the setting of one of the toughest and perhaps least necessary battles of the Pacific War. It was suspected at the time, and confirmed shortly thereafter, that an invasion of Peleliu was not necessary. Other bases in the area were being captured more easily, and the Japanese lacked the airpower and shipping to keep Peleliu active as an air base.

What made the conquest of Peleliu such a bloody endeavor was it was where the Japanese first used their new tactic of defending off the beach. This was a technique later used effectively on IWO JIMA and OKINAWA. The Japanese had examined earlier American island assaults and decided that it was a wasteful proposition to resist on the beach. American ships were able to bombard beach defenses at point-blank range, and US aircraft had a simple run in over the water to beach-front targets. The Japanese knew how to build CAMOUFLAGED fortifications anywhere, and on larger islands, like Peleliu, there were plenty of places off the beach

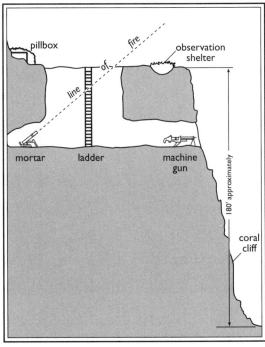

A "typical" Japanese defensive bunker in the latter period of the Pacific War, such as were found on Peleliu and numerous other islands. From MacArthur's New Guinea Campaign by Nathan Prefer (Conshohocken, Pa.: 1995); used with permission.

where defending troops could dig in, hide, and wait for the Americans to come after them. Thus it was on Peleliu. The First Marine Division lost 1,252 killed and 5,274 wounded before the 11,000-man Japanese garrison was wiped out. The fighting went on from September 15 to October 13, 1944, about three weeks longer than the original expectation.

Ref: Hallas, The Devil's Anvil.

Penang, Battle of

Late on May 15, 1945, the Japanese NACHI CLASS heavy cruiser Haguro and destroyer Kamikaze were returning from a voyage to supply Japanese troops in Burma when they were spotted in the Malacca Straits, between MALAYA and SUMATRA by carrier reconnaissance aircraft from a British task force.

Two Marines, PFC Gerald Churchby and PFC Douglas Lightheart, take a cigarette break on Peleliu, September 14, 1944. Note the Amphtrak in the background, and Lightheart's .30 caliber machine gun.

Fleet Air Arm aircraft succeeded in damaging *Haguro*, but lost her as darkness fell. A task group built around the French battleship RICHELIEU was not too far from the Japanese ships. Stripping away the battleship's escorting destroyers, which could make 36 knots to her 30, the task force commander sent them after the Japanese vessels. The destroyers, HMS SAUMAREZ and her near-sisterships *Venus, Verula, Virago,* and *Vigilant,* caught up with the Japanese ships northwest of Penang shortly after midnight on 15 May. A running fight ensued, as the Japanese ships tried to escape. The British destroyers gradually gained on them. At about 0150 hours the British executed a classic destroyer attack, and put eight TORPEDOES into *Haguro.* She sank shortly afterward with considerable loss of life. The destroyer KAMIKAZE managed to escape. *Saumarez* was the only British ship damaged, when she took a shell from the Japanese cruiser, but CASUALTIES were light. This was the last surface action of the Pacific War.

Penang, Malaya

On an island off the west coast of Malaya, Penang had a good harbor, with good facilities and a small airport. It was overrun by Japanese forces in early

USS Pennsylvania (BB-38) steams into Lingayen Gulf in January 1945, followed by a battlewagon of the Colorado class and three heavy cruisers. Some of the ship's numerous antiaircraft guns can readily be seen.

1942, and served thereafter as a local military and naval base.

Pennsylvania Class, US Battleships

A good design, the Pennsylvanias were a derivative of the preceding NEVADA CLASS. They were among the strongest battleships in World War I, and both saw service with the ROYAL NAVY, although they were never in combat. Extensively reconstructed during the 1930s, they emerged with improved underwater protection and modernized engines, while modifications to their 14-inch turrets made for improvements in gunnery range.

Pennsylvania, BB-38 (1913–1915–1916), was flagship of the Pacific Fleet at the time of PEARL HARBOR. In dry dock during the attack, she was only lightly damaged and returned to service within a few days. With the transfer of the NEW MEXICO CLASS ships from the Atlantic in early 1942, she was sent to the West Coast for some modernization, but this was less than the extensive rebuilding the more heavily damaged battlewagons received. Back in service in August 1942, she served to the end of the war, providing fire support for amphibious landings. Present at SURIGAO STRAIT, she did not fire. One of the first American warships to be damaged by enemy action in the war, she was also the last, taking a Japanese aerial TORPEDO on August 12, 1945 while lying off OKINAWA. Since the war was at an end, she was not fully repaired. *Pennsylvania* was in the target fleet at the Bikini ATOMIC BOMB tests, and was finally sunk in naval gunnery tests in 1948.

Arizona, BB-39 (1914–1915–1916), was the most seriously hit ship at Pearl Harbor, blowing up apparently as a result of a magazine explosion caused by a Japanese bomb. Over a thousand men went down with *Arizona*. Her wreck is preserved as a war memorial.

Pensacola Class, US Heavy Cruisers

The first American "Treaty Cruisers," the Pensacolas were provided with a powerful offensive armament but were lightly protected. Their main batteries had an unusual arrangement, with two triple 8–inch gun turrets mounted above two double ones. The turrets were actually very lightly built, hardly armored at all, and the guns in each were mounted on a single sleeve, so that they had to be elevated together. "Wet" ships, taking a lot of water when under way, they rolled badly in heavy weather. They cost about $11 million each. Like all US heavy cruisers, they had their TORPEDO tubes removed before the war, a loss that would be felt during the numerous surface actions of the Pacific War.

Pensacola, CA-24 (1926–1929–1930), was escorting the PENSACOLA CONVOY to the Philippines when the Japanese attacked PEARL HARBOR. She took her charges to Australia, then joined the fleet, serving mostly in the southwest Pacific, fighting at TASSAFARONGA, where she took a torpedo, and in many other actions. She was sunk as a target in 1948.

Salt Lake City, CA-25 (1926–1929–1929), was nicknamed "Swayback Maru" and had a busy war. She began it at Pearl Harbor, where she got away to sea and took part in the abortive attempt to relieve WAKE ISLAND. She then joined the fast CARRIER raids on Japanese territories, shooting up

WOTJE and Wake in February 1942, took part in the DOOLITTLE Raid that April, supported the GUADALCANAL landings that August, and did in the Japanese heavy cruiser FURUTAKA at the battle of CAPE ESPERANCE (11 October 1942). As she took three hits in that action, she returned to the states for repairs and modernization, and in March 1943 headed north for the ALEUTIANS, where she served as the American flagship in the Battle of the KOMANDORSKI ISLANDS. Thereafter her life was less hectic, but she served through to the end, to be expended as a target in 1948.

Pensacola Convoy, The

The Pensacola Convoy, several transports carrying reinforcements to the Philippines, escorted by the heavy cruiser *Pensacola*, was transporting several thousand troops; in addition to the B-25s of the 27th Bombardment Group (the crews were already in the Philippines), the ships carried two battalions of 105mm howitzers (the 2nd/131st and one from the 147th Field Artillery), plus large supplies of ammunition.

The convoy was between HAWAII and Australia when the Japanese attack on PEARL HARBOR occurred. It was immediately ordered to Australia. None of the troops, equipment, or supplies ever reached the Philippines, but the 2nd/131st did get into action on JAVA, where it was captured by the Japanese.

See also FUJITA, FRANK, JR.

Percival, A. E. (1887–1966)

A British career army officer with limited service in World War I, Percival began World War II as chief of staff to the British I Corps, with which he saw service in France. After Dunkirk he served for a time as a division commander, and in July of 1941, by then a lieutenant general, he was sent to command in MALAYA and vicinity. There were many things wrong with Percival's command. His ground troops, mostly Indians and Australians, were mostly of less than the finest quality, poorly trained and very unseasoned, the best units of both nations being in the Middle East. His air force was composed primarily of obsolescent aircraft. However, when the Japanese did attack, in December, although they had some material superiority, notably in the air, they were otherwise greatly outnumbered by the defenders (about 60,000—later rising to 100,000—to 130,000). The Japanese didn't even realize they were outnumbered until the campaign was almost over, but had been operating on a shoestring even without that knowledge. Ultimately, Percival never developed an adequate plan of campaign, so that the Japanese retained the initiative throughout, repeatedly outflanking his many attempts to form defensive lines, until he was forced onto SINGAPORE Island, where he surrendered the remnants of his command, some 73,000 troops, to greatly inferior Japanese forces within 70 days of the beginning of the war. Percival spent the balance of the war in a Japanese prison camp, from which he was liberated in time to attend the surrender of Japan aboard USS *Missouri*. Although admittedly entrusted with a very flawed command, Percival certainly did not act with skill or determination. An inept, unlucky commander.

Perth Class, Australian Light Cruisers

Australia's Perth class was typical of British-designed light cruisers. Although lightly protected, they were rather resilient.

Sydney (1933–1934–1935, ex-HMS *Phaeton*) saw considerable service in the Mediterranean, where she sank the Italian light cruiser *Bartolomeo Colleoni*, 19 July 1940. On 19 November 1941 she engaged the German surface raider *Kormoran* in the Indian Ocean, northwest of Australia. After taking at least one TORPEDO and numerous 5.9-inch rounds she drifted away, burning and sinking, and was never seen again, but had meanwhile so heavily damaged *Kormoran* that the raider had to be abandoned.

Perth (1933–1934–1936, ex-HMS *Amphion*) served with the ABDA squadron at the beginning

of the war, fighting in the JAVA SEA and the Sunda Strait February 28–March 1, 1942), where after a long fight in company with USS *Houston* she succumbed to three Japanese torpedoes and several 8-inch rounds.

Hobart (1933–1934–1936, ex-HMS *Apollo*) spent most of the war in the southwest Pacific, fighting in the Battle of the CORAL SEA and in the GUADALCANAL, SOLOMONS, and New Guinea Campaigns, and during the liberation of the southern Philippines. She was scrapped in 1962.

See also GERMANY IN THE PACIFIC WAR; JAPAN, ATTITUDE TOWARD THE ENEMY.

Philippine Army

The Tydings-McDuffie Act of 1934 established an autonomous government for the Commonwealth of the Philippines, with the intention of granting full independence on July 4, 1946. Among the measures the new Philippine government adopted upon taking office was to hire the retired US Army chief of staff, General Douglas MACARTHUR, promote him to field marshal, and put him in charge of organizing a national military force.

Recognizing the financial and industrial limitations of the infant nation, MacArthur's staff, headed by Dwight D. EISENHOWER, developed a plan that by 1946 would have given the Philippines a Regular Army of about a thousand officers and 10,000 enlisted men, plus a large Reserve Army of some 400,000 men, supported by a coast defense navy of about 50 motor torpedo boats and an air force of some 250 airplanes, mostly fighters and light bombers. This force was to be built up gradually. An annual contingent of 35,000–40,000 20-year-old men was to be drafted in two batches for about 24 weeks of training, with short annual refresher courses thereafter. Once the system was properly established a new reserve division would be created in each of the 10 military districts every three years, toward a projected goal of one million men organized in 100 small divisions by 1966, plus the naval and air contingents.

There were many obstacles to creating armed forces for the Philippine Commonwealth. Money was an obvious one, and budgets remained very tight. Optimally about $24 million was needed annually, but the Commonwealth could afford only about $1 million. Both to save money and stimulate the local economy, an attempt was made to rely on locally manufactured substitutes for many items of equipment. For example, a fairly effective HELMET could be made from coconut fiber, while shoes and web gear were made from other native fibers. At one point a surprising problem arose in terms of relations with the War Department, which proved unwilling to sell surplus Springfield '03 rifles at a discount rate to the Philippines for fear they might be used in an insurrection!

By mid-1941 much had been accomplished. A small Regular Army had been established, totaling about 510 officers and 3,650 enlisted personnel, who could be supplemented by the Philippine Constabulary, with 350 officers and 4,500 men. Some equipment had been accumulated and 140,000 men had actually been called up and had received some basic training.

Providing officers for the new army was difficult. Since 1908 at least one Filipino had been admitted to West Point every year, and several others had gone to Annapolis. Some of these men were on duty with the PHILIPPINE SCOUTS, but a number had transferred over to the Philippine Army. The new Philippine Military Academy, modeled on West Point, had graduated a few hundred young officers, and ROTC programs at various colleges in the archipelago had produced a few thousand more. In addition, some senior NCOs from the Philippine Scouts had accepted commissions in the Philippine Army, as had some officers from the Constabulary. The most experienced officers had served either in the US Army or as reserve officers in the Philippine National Guard Division during World War I. (Authorized by the Philippine Territorial Legislature, this was raised in late 1918 and numbered about 14,000 men. Most of the junior officers were Filipino, as was one of the field grade officers, Vicente Lim, USMA 1912. It served for three

months, one of US expense and two at that of the Philippines. Although some Filipinos wished to maintain the division in the NATIONAL GUARD, there was little interest in doing so either in Manila or in Washington.) Nearly 6,000 men held regular or reserve commissions in the Philippine Army, which was not enough, particularly since most of these officers were quite junior. As a result, many of the senior positions in the Philippine Army were held by American officers.

With the threat of war rising, in late 1941 President ROOSEVELT federalized the entire Philippine Army, from Field Marshal MacArthur on down to the greenest private. In August 1941 the Philippine Army began mobilizing, a process only partially completed when the Japanese invaded in December.

Everything was in desperately short supply. In practice, most divisions were woefully lacking in everything, including rifles. There was also supposed to be a small contingent of army troops, including the Philippine Army Air Force, engineers (the equivalent of 18 battalions), heavy artillery (several regiments of 105mm howitzers and 155mm guns), and the like, to support the front-line troops, but they were short of everything as well. The PAAF, for example, had only 16 obsolete P-26 fighters, 12 equally obsolete B-10 bombers, and a handful of other aircraft, with only 500 men. Nevertheless, despite their lack of equipment and training, and ultimately the debilitating effects of hunger and disease, the hardy and brave Filipino troops did extremely well during the defense of BATAAN. Many of those who eluded capture by the Japanese later joined the resistance, where they proved particularly effective. The Filipinos were much encouraged in their war efforts by the prewar declaration that they would have their independence in 1946. This American decision was not made under any wartime duress, but in recognition of the desires of the Filipino people (and the desire to avoid another insurrection like the one at the turn of the century). America also had pretty good relations with Filipinos, and these emotional ties were further strengthened by the subsequent shared wartime experiences.

Had the outbreak of the war been delayed, MacArthur's mobilization timetable provided that by April of 1942 there would have been about 150,000 troops in the Philippine Army, and some 180,000 by mid-year, with each man having received at least three months of training. Moreover, by then there would have been more equipment, albeit still not enough to properly outfit all the divisions. And American troop strength in the archipelago would have reached some 50,000 men, nearly half in the Philippine Scouts. So, had the Japanese delayed their offensive into the spring, they would have found the Philippines a far tougher nut to crack than was actually the case. As it was, the Philippines took longer to conquer than any other of Japan's southeast Asian or Pacific targets. A better prepared Philippine Army could have made for a much more interesting first year of war.

The Philippine Army did not die with WAINWRIGHT's formal surrender in May 1942. In some areas only 25% of the Philippine Army troops turned themselves in to the Japanese. While in the Philippines the survivors of the Philippine Army organized GUERRILLA bands to fight the Japanese, the government of the Philippines in exile, under President Manuel Quezon, created a new Philippine Army. Working with a cadre of officers and men who had escaped the Japanese invasion or who were abroad at the time, the Commonwealth government reestablished the administrative core, of the army creating essential elements such as a military government branch, and managed to raise some combat troops among Filipinos living in the United states.

See also UNITED STATES ARMY, OTHER NOTABLE UNITS.

Ref: Baclagon, *Military History of the Philippines*; Salazar, Reyes, and Nuval, *Defense, Defeat, and Defiance*; Trota, *The Philippine Army*; Whittam, *Bataan*.

Philippine Army, Divisions and Other Major Formations

Under Douglas MACARTHUR's plan for the development of the Philippine Army, by independence in 1946 there were to have been 40 small (8,200-man) divisions, in an armed force of some 400,000. On paper each Philippine division was supposed to have 420 officers, 7,881 enlisted men, and about 40 US advisers, in three infantry regiments, plus an artillery regiment of 36 pieces (24 2.95–inch mountain guns of 1898–1903 vintage and 12 75mm Model 1917 field guns), a 500–man engineer battalion, and small reconnaissance, service, and medical contingents. By December of 1941 10 divisions had been formed, and several more were organized in the opening weeks of the war. However, none of these had completed training nor possessed their proper allocations of equipment. These divisions were all destroyed during the Japanese invasion.

Despite the general surrender of US and Philippine forces in May 1942, many men and some small units managed to escape into the mountains and jungles, to begin a GUERRILLA war against the invaders. The guerrillas soon began to reestablish the Philippine Army. A number of divisions were formed to oversee operations and prepare for the day that MacArthur would return.

First Division. Composed of most of the prewar regulars of the infant Philippine Army, reinforced by many new recruits, on paper the division was supposed to number about 10,000 men. However, the division never served as a unit, since some elements were rather widely dispersed (the Second Regiment was on Mindanao, the rest of the division on Luzon), and it had no artillery. Activated after the Japanese attack, the rump division entered combat on BATAAN in early January, as part of I Corps. It performed well, undertaking several successful counterattacks, but was eventually destroyed in the final Japanese offensive. The Second Regiment performed well in fighting on Mindanao, but surrendered upon receipt of WAINWRIGHT's instructions of 7 May 1942, although many of the men fled to the hills, where they shortly began a guerrilla campaign against the Japanese occupiers. The division was reactivated in mid–1945.

Second Division. Hastily organized in December 1941–January 1942, the division was formed around the First and Second Regiments of the Philippine Constabulary, to which were added new recruits, for a total of about 6,000 men. It proved an excellent unit, although its lack of artillery was only partially compensated for by the presence of an antitank battalion, the only one in the Philippine Army. The division actually entered combat even before it was formed, when the First and Second Regiments were grouped into the 51st Provisional Brigade, and opposed the Japanese invaders in southeastern Luzon with the South Luzon Force. It joined the retirement to Bataan, where it performed well in numerous actions until the final disaster. The division was reactivated in August 1945.

Fifth Division. Activated in April 1945, the Fifth Division was organized from the best of the guerrilla forces and the cadre of regular Filipino troops that was maintained throughout the war. Intended as the Philippines' contribution to the invasion of JAPAN, its officers and men were undergoing intensive training when the war ended.

11th Division. Activated in October 1941, the division formed part of the North Luzon Force. It was one of the best PA divisions, performing well during the staged retreat from LINGAYEN Gulf and in several counterattacks on Bataan.

21st Division. Activated in October 1941, the division formed part of the North Luzon Force, and anchored the left of the line during the retreat from Lingayen Gulf to Bataan. Well trained, by Philippine Army standards, albeit possessed of only 24 artillery pieces, the division served in reserve in II Corps, being committed to several counterattacks until overwhelmed during the final Japanese offensive.

31st Division. Activated in October 1941 in North Luzon Force, the division saw little fighting until after the retreat to Bataan, where it was committed to the line in II Corps and was eventually overwhelmed.

41st Division. Recruited from southwestern Luzon and activated in October 1941, the 41st was the best of the PA reserve divisions. Not only was it larger than most PA divisions, with some 8,000 men, but it also had a greater than average number of troops who had completed their prewar training, and most of its allotment of equipment, including, eventually, all of its artillery. Its commander was BG Vicente Lim (1889–1944), the first Filipino to attend West Point (Class of 1912), who had served as a temporary lieutenant colonel in the 1918 Philippine National Guard Division, and retired from the US Regular Army as a lieutenant colonel in the 1930s. Although reputed to be touchy, Lim was tough, and a good organizer. The division formed part of South Luzon Force, and defended the area southwest of Manila during the initial phases of the Japanese invasion. It entered the lines on Bataan as part of II Corps, and was thereafter continuously on the front until smashed by the Japanese Fourth Division and 65th Brigades on 3 April, the opening day of Japan's final offensive. (Lim was captured on Bataan. Subsequently released by the Japanese, he joined the guerrillas, was recaptured, and was executed in late 1944.)

51st Division. Activated in October 1941, the division contested the Japanese advance northwestward up the Bicol Peninsula, thereby covering the retirement of the rest of the South Luzon Force to Bataan, which it reached on 7 January. The division was seriously injured in the Japanese assault on II Corps of January 10–25, and thereafter passed into reserve and was not again committed to serious combat until the final days of the defense.

61st Division. Activated on Panay in October 1941, after the fighting began the division was forced to send two infantry regiments and its artillery to support operations on Mindanao, but managed to recruit some manpower locally. Left alone by the Japanese for several months, it eventually numbered some 7,000 men, who, although ill-equipped, were surprisingly well-trained. Upon the Japanese invasion of Panay, April 16, 1942, the division undertook a fighting withdrawal into the interior, where a base of sorts had been established and supplies stockpiled. Under COL Albert F. Christie it began a guerrilla campaign against the invaders. When MG Jonathan Wainwright issued his orders for all US forces in the Philippines to surrender, Christie initially refused, doing so only on 20 May, by which time some 90% of his men had deserted, fleeing to the hills. The division was reorganized as a guerrilla force under LTC (later BG) Macario Peralta Jr. in mid-1942. By late 1944 it had liberated most of the interior of Panay, the Japanese managing to hold only the principal coastal towns.

71st Division. Activated in October 1941, in the central islands, the division was transferred to Luzon before hostilities began, leaving behind one infantry regiment. On Luzon it formed part of the North Luzon Force, and was committed to action against the Japanese landings at Lingayen Gulf. Elements were badly mauled during the retreat to Bataan, and the division was effectively broken up, its combat elements going to strengthen the 91st Division.

72nd Division. Organized on Negros Island in late 1942 and engaged in guerilla operations against the Japanese, particularly in 1944–45.

81st Division. Activated on CEBU and Bohol, in the central islands, in October 1941, the division was committed to action on Mindanao in April and May of 1942. It surrendered to the Japanese after confirmation of Wainwright's 7 May order to do so. Many of the troops slipped away, to eventually fight as guerrillas.

82nd Division. A guerrilla command organized on Bohol in late 1942.

83rd Division. A guerrilla command organized on Cebu in late 1942.

91st Division. Activated in the central islands in October 1941, the division was shortly transferred to Luzon, leaving behind one infantry regiment. With the US Army's Philippine Division, it formed MacArthur's principal reserve. The division was committed to combat on December 23, on the right of the US-Philippine defensive line confronting the Japanese beachhead at Lingayen Gulf. It anchored the right of the line during the staged withdrawal toward Bataan with considerable success, but was severely handled by the Japanese. Once inside the Bataan lines, the division, greatly depleted and suffering from poor morale, was reinforced with the combat elements of the 71st Division and was for a time held in the rear. It eventually recovered sufficiently to occupy the lines in I Corps, but was destroyed in the last days of the campaign.

92nd Division. A guerrilla force of about 3,000 raised on Leyte in late 1942, which performed very well during the liberation of the island late in 1944 and early 1945.

101st Division. Activated on Mindanao in October 1941, the division benefited from the protracted Japanese inactivity in the south to recruit additional manpower and train all hands. As a result, when the Japanese finally undertook serious operations on Mindanao, in April and May, the division, reinforced by the 81st Division and the Philippine Regular Army's Second Infantry Regiment, offered rather stiff resistance, despite a shortage of equipment. The division surrendered upon receipt of Wainwright's order of 7 May.

102nd Division. Formed in northeastern Mindanao from miscellaneous units and raw recruits in January 1942, the division was heavily attacked by Japanese forces on May 2, 1942, and virtually destroyed within a week.

105th–110th Divisions. Guerrilla formations created on Mindanao from December 1942 through June 1943. The 105th, with about 4,300 men, was on the long, narrow western part of the island around ZAMBOANGA, while the other units, totaling 25,000 men were on the larger eastern part of the island. They made an important contribution to the liberation of Mindanao in early 1945.

First Filipino Regiment. Technically a unit of the United States Army, the regiment was activated in California in July 1942 from Filipinos who had escaped from the Philippines or were residents of the United States. It was intended as the cadre about which the Philippine Army would form a new division, to fight for the liberation of its homeland. The regiment shipped out to the South Pacific in early 1944. Meanwhile a Second Filipino Regiment had been raised in the United States. However, it proved difficult to recruit sufficient manpower to form a full division. As a result, it was never formed. The Second Regiment never left the United States, serving essentially as a training formation for the first. The First Filipino Regiment saw considerable action, fighting in New Guinea in mid-1944, on Leyte from October through May 1945, and then on Samar until the end of the war, shortly after which it was inactivated.

Ref: Baclagon, *Military History of the Philippines*; Salazar, Reyes, and Nuval, *Defense, Defeat, and Defiance*.

Philippine Constabulary

The Philippine Constabulary was a paramilitary national police force similar to Italy's Carabinieri or Spain's Guardia Civil. It had its origins in the early period of US rule in the Philippines. By the 1930s the Constabulary was entirely staffed by Filipino personnel, many of the enlisted men being retired PHILIPPINE SCOUTS.

Members of the Constabulary were the first troops in the Philippines to fight the Japanese invaders, when a patrol of the Fourth Regiment went into action against them near Vigon, in northern Luzon, shortly after 0200 hours on 10 December.

Throughout the Philippine Campaign of 1941–42, the Philippine Constabulary fought alongside US and Philippine troops, and two regiments were used to form the Second Division. After the Japanese conquest of the islands many of the men joined the GUERRILLAS.

See also PHILIPPINES, CAMPAIGN FOR, 1941–42.

Philippine Division

See PHILIPPINE SCOUTS.

Philippine Islands

An archipelago of over 7,000 islands, mostly of volcanic origin and most quite small (the 11 largest constitute over 90% of the land area), the Philippines encompass some 115,000 square miles (about the same as Britain or Italy). Although they spoke scores of different—albeit somewhat related—languages, the approximately 16 million inhabitants, for the most part Christian were more or less Westernized, though there were some Moslems in the southern areas. Long a Spanish colony, the islands came under US control in 1898. By 1941 they were internally self-governing and were slated for independence in 1946, which helps explain why the inhabitants put up the stiffest resistance of any colonial people to Japanese aggression. Although chiefly agricultural, there was some mining and manufacturing in the islands, as well as a number of excellent harbors, including Manila, which was a major world port.

Philippine Scouts (PS)

The Philippine Scouts had their origin in the numerous Filipinos who supported the United States during the Philippine Insurrection (1899–1902), when the primarily Tagalog-speaking anti-Spanish Philippine insurgents under Emilio Aguinaldo attempted to form an independent "Philippine Republic." Recruited initially from among the scores of non-Tagalog ethnic groups in the islands, with Aguinaldo's acceptance of US authority in 1901 the force was opened to all Filipinos. Authorized at a strength of 5,000 in 1902, the officers of the Philippine Scouts were at first entirely American, while the rank and file were Filipino. Many later prominent American officers, such as John J. Pershing, served in the Scouts during the ongoing Moro insurgency, a rebellion among the Moslem tribes of the southern islands, who had few ties to Aguinaldo's earlier movement.

Although initially companies were recruited on the basis of linguistic unity, in 1908, when battalions were authorized, this policy was abandoned, and Tagalog tended to become the common language of the Scouts. By the end of World War I there were five provisional regiments of Scouts, who had come to comprise the bulk of the US garrison in the islands. In 1920–21 the Scouts were formally incorporated into the Regular Army, forming several infantry regiments (43rd, 45th, and 57th), the 26th Cavalry Regiment, the 23rd and 24th Field Artillery Regiments, the 91st and 92nd Coast Artillery Regiments, the 14th Engineers, and various ancillary units. The infantry, field artillery, engineers, and signals formed the bulk of the Philippine Division, with the 31st Infantry, an American unit. The division had only about 10,000 men, mostly Filipinos, with American officers. It was the primary combat force in the islands.

When the Japanese came in 1941, the Philippine Scouts, numbering about 12,000 seasoned men, formed the backbone of the American-Filipino defense of the islands. During the desperate fighting that followed, Scout personnel won three MEDALS OF HONOR (Sgt. Jose Calugas, 6 January 1942; 2Lt Alexander R. Nininger, January 12, 1942, posthumously; and 1Lt Willibald Bianchi, 3 February 1942), some 40 Distinguished Service Crosses, and over 200 Silver Stars. The few detachments of the Scouts not involved in the surrender on BATAAN in April 1942, mostly surrendered in May, on orders from General WAINWRIGHT, but some men took to the hills to join GUERRILLA bands.

In late 1944 Douglas MACARTHUR and others began urging that the Philippine Scouts be reactivated. Tradition aside, it was hoped that the revived Scouts would be available for service during the invasion and subsequent occupation of Japan. The process was a lengthy one, and not until after the surrender of Japan was legislation enacted to permit the Scouts to be reactivated. By June 1946 there were some 25,000 men in the Scouts, which had been expanded from three infantry regiments to six, as well as CAVALRY, artillery, and service troops. Although the Philippines became independent a few weeks later, the Philippine Scouts continued in US service under a special agreement with the new republic. For a time it was planned to raise three divisions of Scouts (the reactivated Philippine Division, redesignated the 12th Infantry Division, plus the 14th and 16th Infantry Divisions), and strength reached over 30,000 officers and men by June 1947. At that point it was decided that the continued existence of the Philippine Scouts violated American sensibilities concerning mercenary forces. The Philippine Scouts were officially disbanded as of 30 September 1949. All surviving prewar Scouts were offered comparable rank in the Regular Army, an offer that many took. Other personnel were discharged. Although its existence was relatively short, and it fought in only two wars in its 50 years of service, the Philippine Scouts proved one of the premier fighting forces in history.

See also FRIENDLY FIRE, ALLIED PRISONER OF WAR DEATHS BY.

Ref: Stanton, *Order of Battle*.

Philippine Sea, Battle of

The greatest (and last) carrier battle of the war, at least in terms of the number of carriers and aircraft involved, the Battle of the Philippine Sea resulted from an effort by the Japanese Navy to reverse the fortunes of war in the Pacific. The Japanese plan was rather simpler than previous ones, a tribute to the direction and clear thinking of VAdm Jisaburo OZAWA.

Ozawa had assumed command of the First Mobile Fleet, comprising most of Japan's surface warships, in late 1943. Ordered by the chief of naval operations, Admiral Soemu TOYODA, to annihilate the American Fifth Fleet, Ozawa concentrated five battleships, nine carriers (with 430 aircraft), 11 heavy cruisers, two light cruisers, 34 destroyers, and several auxiliaries at TAWI TAWI, a small island group at the southeastern end of the Philippines, with a fine but rather open anchorage and great proximity to the Borneo oil fields, which produced a crude oil so light it could be burned by ships' boilers without refining.

While this fleet was concentrating, hundreds of aircraft were being ferried into the MARIANAS and CAROLINES, as also were 25 SUBMARINES, all intended as part a trap that Ozawa would spring on Raymond SPRUANCE's Fifth Fleet.

Ozawa's plan was simple. When word came that the Americans were hitting the Marianas, their next logical target for an amphibious landing, he would sortie from Tawi Tawi and head directly to intercept the attackers, deployed in such a fashion that three of his light carriers would act as "bait" about a hundred miles in advance of the main body, which was deployed in two task forces. Considering the circumstances, Ozawa's plan was probably the best he could do, and a lot better than most previous Japanese carrier battle plans.

Raymond Spruance, commanding Fifth Fleet, had enormous resources at hand for the Marianas operation. In addition to the fast carriers (Task Force 58, 15 carriers with over 890 aircraft embarked, plus seven battleships, eight heavy cruisers, 13 light cruisers, and 69 destroyers) assigned to defend the landings from interference by the Imperial Navy, he had available nearly a dozen escort carriers and numerous older battleships, cruisers, and destroyers assigned to actually support the landings. So Spruance was overwhelmingly superior to Ozawa.

On 15 June, learning that the Americans had landed on SAIPAN, Admiral Toyoda ordered Ozawa to implement "Operation A." For three days Ozawa steamed slowly northeastward. One reason

for the lack of speed was that Ozawa had summoned the "Kon Force," a battleship-cruiser task force assigned to relieve BIAK, and it needed time to rejoin the main fleet

Spruance, apprised of Ozawa's coming by submarine reconnaissance, calmly laid his plans. One task group was dispatched on a scheduled raid to the BONIN ISLANDS, where it took out numerous aircraft assigned to assist Ozawa in the destruction of the Fifth Fleet. Meanwhile, Spruance borrowed a few additional ships from the invasion force to further bolster his defensive screen, and ordered the fleet to rendezvous about 140 miles west of TINIAN at 1800 hours on 15 June.

Marc MITSCHER, the actual Task Force 58 commander, formed his task groups into a "T" with its base pointing toward the enemy. Three task groups formed the cross bar, supported by another, forward and to their right, with the pointing base of the "T" formed by his fast battleship task group, closest to the enemy. Despite his great superiority, Spruance moved with caution, as Japanese aircraft were longer legged than American ones. This was a wise decision, as Ozawa knew where Spruance was, while Spruance did not know where Ozawa was.

On the morning of June 19, Task Force 58 made some air strikes at Japanese air bases on GUAM, usefully destroying aircraft intended to support Ozawa. Meanwhile, at about 0800 Ozawa launched 69 aircraft from his three "bait" light carriers against the American carriers. Spotted on radar at 0959, the strike was quickly intercepted and only about 16 of the attackers got through the swarm of F6F HELLCATS that met them, inflicting insignificant damage on the US fleet. Only 24 of the 69 Japanese aircraft made it back to their carriers.

Ozawa's second strike, 130 aircraft dispatched from the main body at about 0900, did even worse than the first, 98 falling after having inflicted only minor damage. Worse, even as this strike was getting off, a US submarine put a TORPEDO into Ozawa's newest and largest carrier, TAIHO, which shortly succumbed to a series of massive internal explosions.

Ozawa launched a third strike at 1000 hours, 47 aircraft, all but seven of which returned safely because they completely failed to intercept the American ships, the others falling to roving patrols of F6F Hellcats.

At 1100 hours Ozawa launched 82 aircraft from *Zuikaku*, RYUHO, and JUNYO. Although these also failed to intercept, the strike commander led them further and they managed to attack Task Group 58.2, but they inflicted no damage and only 28 made it back to the carriers, most badly shot up. Meanwhile Ozawa lost yet another carrier, SHOKAKU, to an American submarine. By now night was falling. So far the battle had been one of Japanese air strikes on American ships, Mitscher having difficulties locating the enemy carriers.

During the night of June 19–20, Mitscher kept feeling for the enemy, while Ozawa maneuvered to keep within range, yet undetected. Not until 1540 on 20 June was Mitscher able to get a fix on the enemy, when Ozawa was about 275 miles southwest of Task Force 58. At 1620 Mitscher launched 216 planes from 10 carriers.

These reached Ozawa at about 1840. With darkness closing in, the aircraft attacked, sinking carrier *Hiyo*, damaging *Zuikaku* and some other ships, and disabling two fleet oilers. In this action Ozawa lost 65 more aircraft, while the United States lost only 20.

With night falling, the American aircraft hastened back to their carriers, and several were damaged or lost making night landings, despite the fact that Mitscher gallantly ordered the carriers to light up their flight decks (thus making it easy for potentially lurking Japanese subs to find targets).

The final count of Japanese losses on June 19–20, was three carriers sunk plus damage to another, and two oilers so badly damaged they had to be scuttled. The Japanese lost about 410 aircraft, and nearly 200 land-based planes, not to mention hundreds of men. All of this was done at the cost of 130 US aircraft lost, plus some slight damage to a few ships. Only 76 Americans had been killed.

During the night of June 20–21, Ozawa tried to put as much distance as possible between himself and Spruance. The latter undertook a pursuit, but then broke it off to rescue downed aircrewmen (59 of whom were fished out of the sea). The lopsided massacre of Japanese carrier aviation was promptly dubbed the GREAT MARIANAS TURKEY SHOOT. In the aftermath of the battle it seems clear that Spruance should have pursued Ozawa more vigorously, so that he might have inflicted a decisive defeat on the 21st. But Spruance had two missions, one to defeat the Imperial Navy and one to support the landings on Saipan.

See also CARRIER TASK FORCES, TACTICAL FORMATIONS, JAPANESE; CARRIER TASK FORCES, TACTICAL FORMATIONS, US.

Philippines, Campaign for, 1941–42

The Philippines had the grim distinction of suffering two major invasions during World War II.

While General Douglas MACARTHUR is generally considered one of the most capable military leaders America ever produced, he had his failures. One of the most devastating was his defense of the Philippines. In late 1941, the Philippines were defended by 25,000 US and Philippine regular troops and over 100,000 poorly trained Filipino reservists and conscripts. Using airbases on FORMOSA and some carrier forces, the Japanese first established air superiority over the Philippines, then their navy established maritime supremacy around the islands. The Japanese Army then invaded with 50,000 troops and, after five months of hard fighting, conquered the islands.

Despite ample warning of a Japanese attack, nearly a half-day after PEARL HARBOR MacArthur allowed his air force to be largely destroyed on the ground. Although the Japanese air bases were only 500 miles away, MacArthur did not order his aircraft dispersed nor did he take pains to resist the Japanese air attacks effectively. Similar errors were made with the ground forces. Although MacArthur had been in the Philippines for several years, he failed to take into account the low training levels of his Philippine troops when reacting to the actual Japanese invasion. Most of the PHILIPPINE

ARMY's troops had less than a month's training on December 7, 1941 (December 8 in the Philippines, Japan, and other places west of the International Date Line).

When the Japanese invaded, MacArthur, rather than implement the long-standing operational plan, which called for an immediate withdrawal to the rugged BATAAN Peninsula, decided to try to halt the Japanese in mobile operations on the North Luzon Plain, which has no significant natural obstacles aside from two small rivers. The results were disastrous. The American and Philippine troops fought bravely, if not skillfully, and actually managed to slow the Japanese advance. But on the whole the Japanese were almost always able to overwhelm the defenders with their more skillful manpower and leadership, and their material superiority. In the process many of the few experienced men and much of the best equipment of the Philippine Army was lost. Meanwhile, troop and supply movements were bungled before and during the land battles with the Japanese invasion force. As a result, 4.5 million tons of rice, about five months' rations, plus about 6 million gallons of gasoline and 500,000 artillery shells, were abandoned or destroyed. When the surviving US and Philippine troops finally did retreat to the Bataan Peninsula, they did so short of ammunition, food, and spare parts, all of which were available, but had not been ordered moved in time. Part of this was due to the usual bureaucratic sloth, but politics and incompetence played a part in it also. Overall, MacArthur performed in a decidedly lackluster manner, especially compared to his later accomplishments.

What prevented "MacArthur's Disaster" from becoming "The End of MacArthur's Career" was largely MacArthur's reputation, his skill at public relations, and the need for a presentable hero in the dark days of early 1942. MacArthur was one of the most famous American officers of the post–World War I period. A genuine hero of World War I, he had been the head of the US Army during the early 1930s and had accepted the job of leading the infant Philippine Army (which brought with it the title "field marshal") partially because the Japanese threat was recognized and everyone felt safer with someone of his caliber in charge. Although many military leaders in the United States could see that MacArthur was making significant mistakes in December of 1941, the political leaders looked at the bright side. While British and Dutch forces were collapsing in weeks all over the Pacific, MacArthur's forces were still holding out through the spring of 1942. Although the American situation was hopeless in the Philippines, MacArthur was declared a hero, and evacuated just before his army had to surrender and march off to four years of Japanese captivity. This gave MacArthur a chance for a rematch, with better results later. But the veterans of the campaign always remembered that "Dugout Doug" spent most of his time in a bunker (a "dugout") and then fled.

The 1942 Philippines campaign was not an unmitigated disaster for America. The Japanese had expected to conquer the Philippines by January 1942. The stout resistance of the American and Filipino troops kept additional Japanese troops engaged until May 1942. This had a serious impact on later fighting in New Guinea and GUADALCANAL. If one or two of the divisions tied down in the Philippines through the first week of May had been available for use in New Guinea earlier, the Japanese would have had more success against the Australian troops defending PORT MORESBY. An Allied defeat in New Guinea may well have hastened the assault on Guadalcanal. Such a result would have had serious consequences, for once the Japanese airfield there became operational, an invasion would have required more carriers than the United States had available in 1942. Seen in that light, MacArthur's defense of the Philippines was not so unsuccessful after all.

Nevertheless, the loss of the Philippines rankled. For the rest of the war Douglas MacArthur's headquarters bore the code designation "Bataan" as did his personal B-17. And on 19 August 1945 when a Japanese delegation arrived at Manila to negotiate the details of the surrender their aircraft had to broadcast "Bataan" as a recognition sign.

Ref: Beck, *MacArthur and Wainwright*; Whittam, *Bataan*.

Philippines, Campaign for, 1944–45

The Japanese put a lot more into defending the Philippines in late 1944 than the United States had in 1941. America had about 130,000 mostly untrained troops defending the islands in 1941. Japan had 350,000 troops as a garrison in 1944. The Japanese troops were also better trained, motivated, and equipped. Japan also had a larger air force and fleet to defend the islands. In turn, the United States went after the Philippines with far larger forces than Japan had used in 1941. During the 1941 invasion, the Japanese actually had fewer troops than the defending Americans. The Japanese went straight for the main island of Luzon (containing the capital, Manila), while in 1944 the United States first landed on Leyte, in the east-central part of the Philippines. In both cases, the area first invaded was dictated by the presence of friendly air bases. The 1941 Japanese invasion was staged out of Taiwan, which was a few hundred miles north of Luzon. In 1944, the Allies came from the south because they had just established air bases on recently captured islands northwest of New Guinea. In 1944 the Japanese were under far more pressure than the Americans had been in 1941. For Japan, the Philippines was the Allied staging area for an invasion of the Japanese Home Islands. This brought out the Japanese air and naval forces in large numbers, which the United States proceeded to destroy. After that, a series of amphibious landing extending into mid-1945 led to the liberation of all the Philippine islands. By early March of 1945, Manila was again in US hands. Although fighting continued in remote areas until Japan surrendered, the Philippines were effectively liberated. MacArthur had kept his promise to the Philippine people and "returned."

Philippines, Commonwealth of the

The "Territory of the Philippines" became the "Commonwealth of the Philippines" under the terms of the Tydings-McDuffie Act of 1934, which created it as an internally self-governing entity in preparation for independence. The president of the Commonwealth was Manuel Quezon y Molina (1878–1944). Quezon had been elected the first president of the Commonwealth in 1935, defeating the famous Philippine Insurrection leader, Emilio Aguinaldo. Reelected in November 1941, Quezon's inauguration took place in Manila on December 30, as the Japanese were closing in on the city. Initially somewhat inclined to try to make terms with the Japanese, at the "urging" of MacArthur, he fled with his cabinet, to the security of Bataan, and then CORREGIDOR. From there, he escaped by submarine to the United States. In the United States he represented Philippine interests as best he could, establishing a government-in-exile, which was financed by Philippine gold and silver reserves (20 tons), which had been brought out of the islands by submarine, and by a special reserve fund established under the terms of Tydings-McDuffie, into which duties on Philippine goods brought into the United States were deposited. President Quezon's health failed, and he died on 1 August 1944. Vice President Segismondo Osmeña (1878–1961) assumed the presidency. As the liberation of the Philippines proceeded in 1944–45 the Commonwealth government was prepared to reestablish itself, but a decision by MACARTHUR (who knew that Osmeña disliked him intensely) put the initial civil administration of liberated areas under US Army Civil Affairs personnel, a matter that rankled with the Philippine political leadership. Not until after the surrender of Japan was most of the Philippines returned to civil administration.

Philippines, Republic of the

On October 14, 1943 the Japanese declared the Philippines "independent," with José Laurel, a prominent politician and former official of the Commonwealth government, as president. The new government had limited power and served primarily as a means by which the Japanese occupa-

Work details unloading two LSTs on the beach at Leyte, October 1944.

tion forces could better control the populace. Laurel and the other officials of the government were by no means abject puppets of the Japanese, and clashed with the occupiers on numerous occasions. After the war most of the officials, including Laurel, were let off lightly by the Commonwealth of the Philippines.

Philippines, Resistance to the Japanese

Of all their early campaigns, the Japanese had the hardest time in the Philippines. It took six months to defeat the regular American and Filipino forces, far longer than any of their other early conquests. Most of the troops were Filipino and few had more than rudimentary training. While most of the fight-

ing was concentrated northwest of Manila, on the BATAAN Peninsula, there were thousands of American and Filipino troops elsewhere on the many islands that comprise the Philippines. Not all of these troops surrendered, and many simply took their weapons into the hills, there to continue the resistance. Because of the generally good relations between Americans and Filipinos (aided by the prewar promise to grant the islands their independence in 1946), the Japanese encountered a hostile population.

Bolstered by popular support, the first Philippine GUERRILLAS were able to recruit more fighters and withstand strenuous Japanese attempts to eradicate them. While there were some American officers and troops among these partisans, many of the units were led by patriotic Filipinos. Guerrilla operations actually began long before the formal surrender of regular US and Filipino troops in April and May 1942. By late December 1941 some troops on Luzon who had been unable to join the retreat to Bataan were already operating as guerrillas, and in one instance managed to kill a Japanese general in an ambush.

At first there was little the guerrilla bands could do but survive. Some of them did this badly, preying on local villagers who eventually turned them in to the Japanese. Other bands, with better leadership, formed more effective ties to local villagers. Gradually the many small bands coalesced into a few larger ones, not always peacefully.

Unfortunately, before the Americans came back, the guerrillas were isolated for two years deep inside Japanese-controlled territory. Until 1944, when physical contact with the outside world was reestablished, the guerrillas were pretty much on their own. Despite the regular radio contact with some of the guerrillas, Washington was rather surprised at the vigor and size of the anti-Japanese guerrilla movement. As early as February 1943, however, MACARTHUR was making efforts to strengthen the resistance movement. Operation Baus Au (Tagalog for "Get it back") was instituted, to send supplies, equipment, and even personnel in by submarine (62 missions) and aircraft. MacArthur also granted formal recognition and rank to guerrilla leaders, assigning them territorial commands on the basis of the 10 prewar military districts in the islands, and involving them in planning. Nevertheless, fearing that premature large-scale operations would lead to the destruction

Heavily laden with US Army assault troops, Coast Guard-manned LCVPs head into the beach at Lingayen Gulf, Luzon, shortly before 0930 on January 9, 1945.

of the guerrillas, MacArthur urged them to "lie low" until the day of liberation was at hand.

Constantly harassing the Japanese and supplying valuable information to the Allies, the guerrillas waited for the day when MacArthur would return. Meanwhile, the Japanese built up their forces in the Philippines in anticipation of a late 1944 American attack. The larger number of Japanese troops led to increased anti-guerrilla activity, simply because there were now more targets. The clumsy and brutal Japanese anti-guerrilla tactics served to increase the number of guerrillas and the desire for revenge by the much abused Filipinos.

Hardened by over two years of living and fighting in the jungles, the guerrillas became a substantial force. By the time MacArthur and his troops returned to the Philippines in late 1944, there were tens of thousands of organized guerrillas (estimates vary from 100,000 to 180,000) waiting to act as scouts and fighters. The arriving American troops were surprised at the quantity, and quality, of the guerrilla troops. Although later official accounts of the Philippines fighting played down the contributions of the guerrillas, at the time American units were glad to have these local troops available.

The guerrillas served the US forces in many ways. They provided valuable pre-invasion intelligence, conducted sabotage and harassment raids against the Japanese, made diversionary attacks, served as scouts, helped rescue downed pilots, performed security duties to prevent Japanese infiltration, and undertook mopping up operations. On more than one occasion, when a US unit had outrun its supplies, the guerrillas provided food and sometimes ammunition from their own stocks. Just about the only thing the guerrillas were not very good at was serving on the front lines in conventional combat, having neither the training nor the equipment for the role; they occasionally performed that function too, but not always successfully, a matter that became the basis for official denigration of their prowess.

There were a number of notable guerrilla leaders.

LTC Martin Moses and LTC Arthur Noble, formerly advisers to the Philippine 11th Division, had escaped to northern Luzon in early 1942 and were shortly in command of some 6,000 guerrilla fighters. Prone to daring, even foolhardy undertakings, they were eventually captured by the Japanese, tortured, and murdered. Their replacement, LTC R. W. Volkman, proved less rash and was probably a better administrator. By late 1944 Volkman's North Luzon Force had expanded to some 25,000 men, organized into five infantry regiments, an artillery battalion, and various support and service elements. The North Luzon Force proved a valuable asset to MacArthur in the early months of 1945.

On Leyte LTC Ruperto Kangelon organized about 3,000 guerrillas into the 92nd Division, which, supported by part-time guerrillas, proved highly effective. According to a Japanese account there were 561 clashes with Kangelon's men during the first eight months of 1944. Although the 92nd Division's support of the Leyte landings was immensely valuable, perhaps its most impressive achievement was the clandestine evacuation of thousands of villagers from the invasion area on the eve of the American landings.

On Panay, LTC Macario Peralta Jr. organized the 61st Division in mid-1942. A very effective administrator, Peralta had his division up to about 15,000 men and women by mid-1943, and over 21,000 by September 1944, albeit that only about a third of the troops were properly armed. The division suffered about 1,100 killed in action, died of wounds, or murdered by the Japanese, in the process of inflicting thousands of CASUALTIES on the enemy. So effective was Peralta as a commander, that when the Philippine Army created the Fifth Division in April 1945, he was given command of one of its regiments. Peralta served as deputy chief of staff of the Philippine Army from late 1945 until shortly after independence.

On Mindanao COL Wendell Fertig had some 30,000 regular guerrillas, forming six divisions, the 105th through 110th, plus perhaps 15,000 or more part-time guerrillas. By the time US troops landed in early 1945, Fertig's men had effectively liberated about 90% of the island, although the Japanese still held most of the major population centers.

In central Luzon, Luis Tarluc, a communist sympathizer, created the Hukbalahap (or Huk) movement. The name is an acronym for the Tagalog phrase *Hukbu Ng Bayan Laban Sa Hapones*, which may more or less be translated as "Patriotic Army for Killing the Japanese." The Huks appear to have mobilized some 10,000 to 15,000 guerrillas by late 1944, taking advantage of widespread peasant dissatisfaction with traditional landowning policies. The Huks were organized into regiments, military districts, and squadrons. The success of the Huks in fighting the Japanese is difficult to assess. They themselves claim to have killed more than 5,000 Japanese and some 10,000 Filipino collaborators, figures that cannot be reconciled with Japanese records. After the war the Huks refused to demobilize, went underground, and in 1948 emerged to begin an "armed struggle" to establish a communist regime in the Philippines, which was put down with some difficulty by the early 1950s.

Because many of the Japanese subsequently fled to the hills to fight on in early 1945, the Filipino guerrillas proved invaluable in hunting the Japanese down and limiting the damage the enemy irregulars could cause. There was a certain amount of payback involved here, as the Japanese had indulged in savage reprisals when confronted with the generally pro-American attitude of the Filipinos.

Ref: Baclagon, *Military History of the Philippines*; Manikan, *Guerrilla Warfare on Panay*; Salazar, Reyes, and Nuval, *Defense, Defeat, and Defiance*.

Philipps, Thomas (1891–1941)

Tom Philipps, the son of a colonel and an admiral's daughter, entered the ROYAL NAVY in 1904. During World War I he saw action in cruisers, notably at the Dardanelles and in the Atlantic. Between the wars he rose steadily, and on the outbreak of World War II was vice chief of the Naval Staff. He was still in this post in late 1941, when he was promoted two ranks and sent to command Force Z, the Royal Navy's squadron in the Far East. Philipps was wholly unsuited to his command, having spent most of his career as a staff officer. Although it is unlikely that any British admiral could have avoided defeat at the hands of the Japanese off MALAYA in December of 1941, Philipps' lack of understanding of the influence of air power turned defeat into disaster. A very short man, he was nicknamed "Tom Thumb."

Phoenix Islands

Eight uninhabited Pacific islands totaling 11 square miles, the Phoenix Islands are just south of the equator. Administered jointly by the United States and Britain (which considered them part of the GILBERT ISLANDS), on the eve of World War II several of the islands, (CANTON, Enderbury) had small air bases established to help guard the supply lines from the US West Coast to the South Pacific.

Pidgin

A language common among the peoples throughout much of the South Pacific, either as their primary tongue or as a second language. Its vocabulary derives mostly from English, so that, for example, World War II in some forms of Pidgin is referred to as *taemfaet* ("time-fight"), while woman is usually *mary* and man is *fella*. However, the grammatical structure is essentially Melanesian, so, for example, plurals are formed by repetition: *mary-mary* means "women." The prevalence of Pidgin (sometimes written as Pijin) made communication between Allied troops and the native peoples relatively easy.

Pilots, Quality and Quantity

On the eve of the Pacific War the Japanese Navy may have had the best pilots in the world, carefully selected men, intensively trained to extraordinarily

US Navy carrier pilots being briefed prior to a raid on Tokyo on February 17, 1945. American training produced such prodigious numbers of pilots that by mid-1944 the number of men in flight training was actually reduced.

exacting standards. However, an inability to maintain these standards in wartime was deleterious and ultimately disastrous to the Japanese war effort.

The Imperial Navy had about 1,500 pilots in late 1941, including men who had graduated flight school but not yet completed all their training. In fact, in December of 1941 there were not enough qualified pilots to man all available aircraft, which included about 550 on active carriers, plus another 100 or so on a new escort carrier and two light carriers still working up, plus some hundreds of floatplanes on battleships, cruisers, and seaplane carriers and tenders, as well as about 500 land-based aircraft, for a total of about 2,210 aircraft. In contrast, the US Navy had about 3,500 regular pi-

lots, plus a pool of nearly 3,500 reservists, more than sufficient to man all available aircraft—about 600 on fleet carriers, 40 on escort carriers, about 150–200 floatplanes on battleships and cruisers, plus hundreds of flying boats and land-based aircraft, for a total of about 8,500 aircraft. The US Navy originally had a pilot training program almost as rigorous as that of the Japanese. But in the mid–1930s it was restructured to produce more pilots, albeit less spectacularly qualified ones than their older comrades.

On the eve of the war a man needed a minimum of 700 hours of flight time to qualify as a full-fledged pilot in the Imperial Navy, while his American counterpart needed only 305 hours. About half of the active duty pilots in the US Navy in late 1941 had between 300 and 600 hours flying experience, a quarter between 600 and 1,000 hours, and the balance more than 1,000 hours. So at the beginning of the war nearly 75% of the US Navy's pilots had fewer flying hours than did the least qualified of the Japanese Navy's pilots. And that was just in terms of flying hours: Many of the Imperial Navy's pilots had seen combat against the Chinese and the Russians, experiences that most US Navy pilots lacked.

However, the Japanese pilot training program was so rigorous that only about 100 men a year were being qualified, in a program that required 50 to 64 months to complete, depending upon

education completed on entry (high school graduates vs. elementary school graduate). In January of 1940 some prescient officers had proposed reorganizing the Imperial Navy's pilot training program to make it shorter, less rigorous, and more productive, in order to build up the pool of available pilots to about 15,000. This was rejected as visionary.

As a result, as soon as the war began, the Imperial Navy started losing pilots faster than they could be replaced. For example, the 29 pilots lost at Pearl Harbor represented more than a quarter of the annual crop. Then came the losses at the Battles of the CORAL SEA and MIDWAY, and during the GUADALCANAL and SOLOMONS Campaigns—lit-

"Back to the barn": Fighter pilots aboard the second USS Lexington (CV-16) celebrate shooting down 17 of 20 Japanese aircraft intent on attacking the Tarawa beachhead in November 1943. The airplane is an F6F Hellcat.

erally hundreds of superb pilots. In a desperate attempt to replace the lost airmen, the Japanese began cutting corners on their pilot training programs. Initially the ground component of pilot training was cut from 14 or 28 months (high school/elementary school grads) to three, then to one, and then virtually eliminated. Soon afterward the flight, operational, and carrier training portions of the program were cut as well, from 12 months each to four, then three, then one month each. By 1945 men were being certified fit for combat duty with less than four months training. In contrast, the US Navy was actually increasing its flight time, while keeping pilot training programs to about 18 months.

Unlike the Japanese, the US Navy applied mass production techniques to pilot training, with the result that by mid-1944 it was qualifying about 8,000 pilots a month, at which point pilot training programs actually began to be cut. Altogether, the US Navy seems to have peaked at about 60,000 pilots. Total Japanese pilot strength may actually have approached this figure, albeit with men trained to decreasingly rigorous standards.

Aside from the Imperial Navy's initially overly exacting pilot training program, there were several other factors that contributed to the decline in the quality of Japanese naval pilots.

Lack of Rotation. Pilots were kept with line units until killed or wounded. This had two negative effects. One, veteran pilots were not normally available to lend a hand with training, which deprived novice pilots of their valuable advice and experience. Two, experienced men soon became over-experienced, tired, and careless from excessive and continuous exposure to combat. The US Navy regularly rotated men from line to training units and back again, and pulled combat-weary units out of action for regular rests. This maintained skills and morale, and helped trainees learn the ropes from the best qualified instructors.

"Beaching" of Carrier Aircraft. On several occasions, notably during the Solomons Campaign, the Imperial Navy transferred entire carrier AIR

FLYING HOURS TO QUALIFY FOR COMBAT		
Year	USN	IJN
1941	305	700
1942	305	700
1943	500	500
1944	525	275
1945	525	90

GROUPS to land bases to provide air support for ground operations. Carrier operations require constant training, and once committed to ongoing operations from a land base, carrier pilots quickly begin to lose the skills necessary to operate safely from carriers. The US Navy occasionally committed carrier pilots to land-based operations, but with great reluctance.

Lack of Search-and-Rescue. As the war went on, the US Navy developed an elaborate search and rescue system, which used SUBMARINES, flying boats, and surface vessels to locate and rescue downed flyers. As a result, on average about 50% of US airmen who crash-landed or parachuted into the sea were rescued (among them George BUSH), a figure that was rising to 75% by the end of the war. The Japanese had no such system, which cost them the services of many valuable men.

Ill-trained pilots were not simply less effective against more experienced pilots, they were also a greater danger to themselves. Throughout the war, a quarter of the aircraft lost were due to accidents, most of them "pilot errors." More experienced pilots made fewer errors. When operating over the open ocean, things could get particularly complicated. Navigation skills were crucial when flying over open water, and the weather was different. In the northern Pacific, the weather and operating conditions in general were particularly horrendous. In this region, nearly 90% of American aircraft losses were due to noncombat causes. The Japanese had a similar experience. Experience was a valuable resource, and the Japanese learned the hard way how easy it is to lose and how difficult it is to regain. New pilots, of any nation, are most at risk, and if there are few experienced pilots to help the inexperienced pilots, the survival rate will remain dismal. American pilots had a 7% chance of getting shot down on their first mission. This went down to under 1% after about 10 missions.

Only 5% of pilots shot down five aircraft and became ACES. But most managed to keep going and survive. American pilots knew the importance of helping the new guys along to even the odds in combat. The Japanese had such a low ratio of experienced to inexperienced pilots by 1944 that they were slaughtered in lopsided battles with their American counterparts. After 1943, few Japanese pilots survived long enough to become aces. From 1944 on, American pilots had more to fear from mechanical problems or bad luck than from the skill of Japanese pilots. Meanwhile, the Japanese saw their aircraft losses from poor flying skills skyrocket. This was made worse by the increasing shortage of key raw materials for Japanese industry. Certain alloys were not available and this led to less than ideal substitutes when building aircraft engines. The Japanese aircraft engine industry was never top of the line in the best of times, and by 1944 their pilots had to be ever watchful of sudden engine problems. Inexperienced pilots were less able to coax a cranky engine into performing long enough to allow the aircraft to be landed and this produced ever more "noncombat" losses. It saved Allied pilots some work and not a little risk.

Poison Gas

While chemical weapons were not used in combat during World War II, they were used in other ways. Lieutenant General Suri Hasimoto ordered his First Army to use poison gas against civilians in China (Shansi Province) during 1939. The Germans and Japanese used PRISONERS to test the effects of existing and experimental chemicals. All nations used chemical weapons in tests (on volunteers) of their protective masks and clothing. While the Germans and Japanese caused thousands of deaths with their "experiments," there were also

hundreds of injuries and some fatalities in the more humane Allied tests as well. And then there were the accidents.

Thousands of tons of various chemical agents were produced and shipped to the front, by all nations. While no one wanted to use chemicals, no one wanted to be caught unprepared if the enemy decided to "go chemical." One of the worst of these accidents occurred in 1943, when a German air raid on the Italian port of Bari managed to hit an Allied cargo ship carrying mustard gas. Few people in the harbor knew what the ship was carrying. Mustard gas is basically an oily substance that, when it hits the skin (or lungs, if inhaled), begins to burn through the flesh. The poison got into the water of the harbor and floated to the surface along with oil from the fuel tanks of sunken ships. The survivors were hauled out of the water and wrapped in blankets, but were still covered with oil and mustard gas. Hours later, many of these victims began to die in agony. It took a while before the medical personnel could figure out what was going on. But even more quickly, the security people made sure that everyone was sworn to secrecy. This incident did not become generally know until many years after the war.

Beyond accidents, there were also the methods by which the thousands of tons of German chemical weapons, (including nerve gas, which the Nazis invented) were disposed of after the war. Most were dumped in the Baltic Sea, or deep lakes, or left in bunkers and deep mountain tunnels, and soon no one was around who knew where the substances were. Fish are still dying and occasionally people are seriously injured. In an incident during the mid-1980s a large number of Danish fishermen became ill after accidentally trawling up a number of gas canisters in their nets. In some parts of Germany, one is cautioned to be careful nosing around in the many World War II-era tunnels that still exist. Similarly, Japanese chemical weapons were dumped into the Sea of Japan, where some remain.

On at least three occasions during the Pacific War US military leaders seriously considered the possibility of using poison gas. The tenacity of the Japanese defense of BIAK, in June 1944, caused LG Robert L. EICHELBERGER to suggest the use of captured Japanese stocks of poison gas to kill Japanese troops ensconced in deep caves. The staff demurred, one officer observing that not only would it result in Eichelberger's removal from command within 24 hours, but it would also probably cost more in time and CASUALTIES than conventional methods.

During the preparations for the invasion of IWO JIMA, where it was known that there were no civilians, the subject again came up. On consideration, it was decided that the possible saving of American lives was not worth the bad press that was sure to result.

Planners for the invasion of JAPAN—operations Olympic and Coronet—also considered the use of poison gas, because of the extreme fanaticism that it was believed would characterize Japanese resistance. Although the proposal was formally rejected, it is likely that the matter would have arisen again had the invasion been undertaken.

There was one occasion during the New Guinea Campaign where poison gas was detected in the atmosphere, although it caused no significant harm. Initially attributed to the deliberate Japanese use of chemical weapons, upon investigation it was concluded that the incident was an accident, and no retaliation in kind was made. This was the only occasion on which poison gas was released in the Pacific War. However, the Japanese did use poison

American sailors stacking 6-inch shells at the Naval Ammunition Depot, Espiritu Santo, in the New Hebrides, thousands of miles from the disaster at Port Chicago, but only a second's misstep from a similar catastrophe.

gas many times during their war with China, including one reported incident on March 28, 1942, near Toungoo in Burma. The Japanese were also the only nation to use biological weapons in World War II, or in any war in this century. They made several such attacks in China before and after Pearl Harbor and were still developing such weapons at the end of the war.

See also BIOLOGICAL WARFARE.

Ponape, Caroline Islands

A large, high island with a fairly good lagoon, Ponape, in the eastern CAROLINES, had limited port facilities. The island had seen much Japanese investment before the war, and the Ponapans were relatively prosperous and moderately devoted to the empire.

In the late 1930s the Japanese began to fortify the island, installing some coast defense guns, establishing a seaplane base, and finally constructing two air fields.

During the Pacific War the Japanese recruited hundreds of workers on Ponape, many of whom served on distant islands. In May 1942 the Japanese drafted 20 men, five from each of the island's four tribes, for combat service. The men were sent to Japanese units at RABAUL and later took part in the BUNA-GONA CAMPAIGN in New Guinea. Only three of them survived.

Ponape figured in US war plans on several occasions, and was marked for invasion at least twice. But as American confidence in "island hopping" grew, the island was bypassed. Although it was bombed an estimate of 250 times from February 1944 to the end of the war, and subject to a naval bombardment in April of 1944, it remained in Japanese hands until their surrender.

Ref: White and Lindstrom, *The Pacific Theater*.

Port Arthur, Manchuria/Manchukuo, China

A major port, with important docking and service facilities, Port Arthur was also a major Japanese naval base, although one of limited strategic value.

Port Blair, Andaman Islands

The principal port of the ANDAMAN ISLANDS, a small miserable place with no particular facilities but some potential as an air or naval base, since it could be used to project power over a wide area of the Indian Ocean and Bay of Bengal. The Japanese occupied it in early 1942. Although they attempted to turn Port Blair into a base, this proved impossible in view of the increasingly effective presence of the British Far Eastern Fleet. Although the British contemplated recapturing the Andamans–and nearby NICOBAR–from the Japanese, in the end they were satisfied with neutralizing them. Over 40,000 Japanese troops were effectively isolated in the two island groups until the end of the war.

See also ROYAL NAVY.

Port Chicago Mutiny

On July 17, 1944, an explosion occurred at the ammunition depot at Port Chicago, California, on the Sacramento River about 40 miles northwest of SAN FRANCISCO. The resulting blast—estimated at five kilotons—killed 323 people and destroyed five ships, an entire train, and numerous buildings, in addition to causing considerable damage in a wide area surrounding the town.

Shortly after the explosion, one of the US Navy ammunition handling companies, which had lost about 200 men in the explosion, was ordered to load ammunition aboard a ship. Most of the men, virtually all of whom were BLACK AMERICANS, refused. Although the navy convinced a majority of the protesters to return to work soon afterward, about 50 flatly refused to do so. Subject to courts-martial for mutiny, most were sentenced to 15 years hard labor and a dishonorable discharge. Shortly after the war the sentences and discharges were revoked and the men issued honorable discharges. The question of whether there actually was a "mutiny" or whether racism was the principle reason for the prosecutions remains controversial.

The Port Chicago disaster was one of several noncombat-related ammunition explosions that have occurred in the United States or to US forces in the Pacific War. Some other notable incidents were:

April 14, 1944. The steamer *Fort Strikene*, a merchant ship carrying 1,300 tons of TNT, exploded in Bombay Harbor. This touched off another ammunition ship nearby. A total of 21 ships were destroyed and nearly a thousand people were killed, with hundreds of others injured.

May 21, 1944. LST-553, loaded with ammunition in preparation for operations in the MARIANAS, blew up in the West Loch at PEARL HARBOR. Five other LSTs were destroyed or sunk in the blast ((LSTs-43, 69, 179, 353, and 480) and hundreds of men were killed, including 207 from the Fourth Marine Division, with hundreds more injured. The blast delayed the departure of the Fourth Marine Division for the Marianas by one day. Salvage operations on the sunken vessels resulted in the only noncombat-related award of the MEDAL OF HONOR during World War II, to US Navy diver Owen F. P. Hammerberg, who died on 17 February 1945 as a result of injuries sustained in rescuing two other divers who had been trapped by collapsing wreckage.

Port Moresby, New Guinea

A modest-sized town, with limited use as a port, although possessing a valuable, if small, airfield. As a potential base, Port Moresby would give anyone holding it easy entrée into either New Guinea or the CORAL SEA.

With the approach of the Japanese, in February 1942 all white civilians, government officials included, were evacuated from Port Moresby. This touched off a major disorder on the part of some green Australian troops stationed there, who rioted and looted until steadier troops were brought in.

Port Moresby was soon built up as the principal Allied base in New Guinea, serving as MacArthur's headquarters for much of the war.

Porter Class, US Destroyers

Designed to serve as flotilla leaders (i.e., flagships to squadrons of destroyers) the eight US Porters, built 1934–37, were large, benefiting from modifications to the naval DISARMAMENT TREATIES in this regard. However, they were badly armed, having only surface-capable main guns, rather the dual-purpose ones of the preceding FARRAGUT CLASS, albeit eight to the latter's five. They were rather cramped, but seaworthy, and saw considerable service in the war, during which they were several times modified and in which only *Porter* was lost in action. After the war several of the surviving units were retained for various experiments.

Portland Class, US Heavy Cruisers

Designed as follow-ons to the NORTHAMPTON CLASS, the Portlands were somewhat better protected. They cost about $13 million each but were still not very satisfactory, sharing the lightly protected turrets and sleeve-mounted 8–inch guns of earlier designs. They were fitted as flagships but designed without TORPEDOES, a flaw they shared with all US heavy cruisers.

Portland, CA-33 (1930–1932–1933), nicknamed "Sweet P," accompanied the fast carriers on numerous raids in early 1942, and fought to the end of the war, including such famous actions as the CORAL SEA, SANTA CRUZ, the First Naval Battle of GUADALCANAL and SURIGAO STRAIT. She was broken up in 1959.

Indianapolis, CA-35 (1930–1931–1932), accumulated 11 battle stars in 36 months of war, serving for a long time as SPRUANCE's flagship for the Fifth Fleet. She took a KAMIKAZE off OKINAWA in April 1945 and returned to the West Coast for repairs. Upon completion of these in July she was selected to carry the ATOMIC BOMBS from the West Coast to TINIAN. She then made a short voyage to GUAM to pick up ammunition, and left unescorted for LEYTE GULF where she was to engage in gunnery exercises. Shortly after midnight on 30 July 1945, while running at medium speed on a straight course across the PHILIPPINE SEA, she was torpedoed by the Japanese submarine *I-58*, skippered by Cdr. Mochitasura Hashimoto. The ship sank within 15 minutes. Remarkably, about 880 of the 1,197 men aboard survived the sinking and managed to cling to rafts and wreckage. Unfortunately, the ship had not gotten off a distress call. As no one at either Leyte or Guam bothered to notice that the vessel had not arrived (orders having been given that no communications should be made regarding the routine arrival of ships), the crewmen remained adrift four and a half days before a PBY on routine patrol chanced by. Only 317 of the ship's company survived, the rest succumbing to thirst, salt water poisoning, exposure, wounds, or shark attacks. She was the last major warship lost by the United States in the Pacific.

In December 1945 the ship's skipper, Capt. Charles B. McVay III, the son of an admiral, was subject to a court-martial, on the grounds that his failure to zigzag put the vessel at unnecessary risk. On 13 December McVay's defense counsel produced Cdr. Hashimoto as a witness, who testified that whether the cruiser had been zigzagging or not made no difference to his shot. This was the only time in US military history that a foreign enemy officer testified at a court-martial, and there is a possibility that Hashimoto lied when he said the Kaiten Weapon (see p. 622) was not used in the attack.

McVay later committed suicide

See TORPEDOES

Ref: Hashimoto, *Sunk*.

Pound, Alfred Dudley (1877–1943)

Alfred Pound entered the ROYAL NAVY as a very young boy in the late 1880s and rose steadily, if slowly, thereafter. During World War I he served as a staff officer, being present at Jutland. After the war he held a variety of posts and commanded the Mediterranean Fleet in the late 1930s, a trying time during which Italian SUBMARINES were illegally active against Spanish Republican shipping. In 1939 he was promoted Admiral of the Fleet and made First Sea Lord, chief of staff of the Royal Navy. Pound had an enormous capacity for administrative work, and was totally devoted to his duties (even having a cot placed in his office so that he could sleep there rather than return home). Unfortunately, he tended to over-concentrate control of operations in his own hands, which often led to unfortunate results. By 1942 he was aware that he had a terminal brain tumor, but remained on active duty until almost the last.

Prisoners of War

While Japanese violations of the rights of prisoners of war under the terms of the GENEVA CONVENTION never reached the scale of the mutual violations of those rights by the Germans and Russians during World War II, they were nevertheless very serious.

In addition to brutal treatment, as in the BATAAN DEATH MARCH, the Japanese generally failed to provide medical supplies to prisoners of war, used them in medical, chemical, and biological experiments, employed them in prohibited occupations (prisoners of war may not be employed in direct war work; they can, for example, be used as agricultural workers, but not in munitions factories, shipyards, or to dig trenches), and denied them pay for their work. Prisoners of the Japanese generally suffered from malnutrition, but this was a more difficult problem, not addressed by the Geneva Convention.

The rules of war prevailing at the time merely required the capturing power to feed prisoners of war a ration equal to that it normally provided its own personnel. This failed to take into account physical and cultural differences between various peoples regarding food, so that even in cases where the Japanese fed Allied prisoners strictly according to the Geneva Convention, the prisoners were likely to slowly starve to death. The Geneva Convention of 1949 adjusted the provisions governing prisoners of war to require the capturing power to take into account the normal diet of prisoners.

American prisoners of war holding a secret Independence Day party in the Japanese POW camp at Casisange, Malaybalay, Mindanao, the Philippines, 4 July 1942.

Excluding members of the PHILIPPINE ARMY, approximately 130,000 Americans were taken prisoner during World War II; about 22,000 fell into Japanese hands, some 80% in the Philippines. About a third of the American prisoners held by the Japanese—7,000 men—died. The number of dead was approximately the same as that among the nearly 110,000 American POWs held by the Germans and Italians, but the death rate among those troops was only about 15%.

The total number of western POWs held by Japan seems to have been about 170,000, of whom about 130,000 were British or Commonwealth troops, mostly Indian, 22,000 were Dutch, and 22,000 American. The Japanese rarely took Chinese prisoners, and no figures are available.

Until the collapse of Japanese resistance, only about 11,600 Japanese military personnel were held by the Western Allies. This was rooted mostly in the Japanese penchant to die rather than surrender. Moreover, Allied troops tended to be wary of taking Japanese prisoners. For one thing, a Japanese soldier who appeared to be surrendering often did so only to pull out a grenade or other weapon in order to go out gloriously, while "taking one with him," a practice in which even wounded Japanese often indulged. This was one reason why pictures of Japanese prisoners often show the men wearing only their loin cloths: Their captors were ensuring that the men were not carrying any concealed weapons. In addition, in war brutality breeds brutality. Very early it became clear that the Japanese tended to mistreat and even murder prisoners. As early as December of 1941 Filipino troops making local counterattacks during the retreat from Lingayen to Bataan often found comrades who had fallen into Japanese hands bound and murdered, often after being subject to torture and other ATROCITIES. These sorts of behavior quickly inclined all Allied troops against taking Japanese prisoners.

The Russians took over 600,000 Japanese prisoners in MANCHURIA, but most of these were taken after the Japanese surrender. Many were held in Siberian labor camps for over a decade. Many did not return.

The Japanese also captured many Western civilians. The fate of these people was hard. Those

Two Marines escort a Japanese prisoner off a US submarine, May 1945.

Gaunt Allied prisoners welcoming their liberators at the Aomori POW Camp, Honshu, 29 August 1945. Note the Dutch, American, and British flags.

who were not murdered outright (and after the war several Japanese officers and soldiers were punished for killing European civilians, including children, rather than be burdened by them), were treated as prisoners of war, not as internees, as prescribed by the Geneva Convention. For example, of some 1,100 civilian construction workers captured on Wake Island in December 1941, 400 did not survive the war: 47 were killed during the fighting, 98 were executed in October 1943 in "retaliation" for an American air raid on the island, and the rest died of disease, malnutrition, and casual brutality in labor camps and MINES in Japan, Manchuria, and China. Some Dutch women captured by the Japanese in the NETHERLANDS EAST INDIES were forced to become COMFORT WOMEN.

See also FRIENDLY FIRE, ALLIED PRISONER OF WAR DEATHS BY; FUJITA, FRANK, JR.; TOKYO WAR CRIMES TRIBUNAL.

Ref: Daws, *Prisoners of the Japanese*; Dower, *War without Mercy*; Fujita, *Foo*; Kerry, *Surrender and Survival*.

ARMAMENTS SPENDING, 1935–1945 (BILLIONS OF 1994 DOLLARS)							
Nation	**1935–38**	**1939**	**1940**	**1941**	**1942**	**1943**	**1944**
United States	13.5	5.4	13.5	40.5	180.0	342.0	378.0
Canada	?	?	?	4.5	9.0	13.5	13.5
Britain	22.5	9.0	31.5	58.5	81.0	99.0	100.0
USSR	72.0	30.0	45.0	76.0	104.0	125.0	144.0
Germany	108.0	31.0	54.0	54.0	77.0	124.0	153.0
Japan	18.0	4.5	9.0	18.0	27.0	42.0	54.0

Production, Spending

The war was won with courage and determination, and the help of those nations who possessed sufficient resources to arm and supply their troops. National economies and wealth were at the base of

BUY WAR BONDS

A war bond poster, early 1942. American ability to mobilize enormous sums of money was a major factor in helping to win the production war.

each nation's military strength. Consider the money spent on armaments by each nation each year (left).

One explanation for Germany's initial success in the war can be found in the figures for 1935–38, when HITLER spent nearly as much as all the other powers indicated combined, and certainly outspent Britain, France, and Poland, his principal opponents in the first nine months of the war.

What kind of armaments were purchased and how efficiently money was spent were also important. American arms were more "expensive" than German arms because the United States paid its workers good wages while the Germans used millions of slave laborers—Jews, Poles, Czechs, Russians, Italians, and so forth—who didn't get paid at all. Russia paid its workers, but didn't give them much to buy, thus making the wages nearly worthless (to the workers). The US "bang for the buck" tended to get better as the war went on, due to increased efficiency, greater skill, and economies of scale. By 1945 a dollar spent on defense procurement was buying about 25% more than one spent in 1940, and that despite some wartime inflation.

Nations concentrated on different things. America spent over $300 billion (1996 value) on aircraft between 1941 and 1944. In that same period the United States also spent nearly as much on ships, but only half as much on vehicles and only about $80 billion on guns and artillery. Russia spent little on ships, not nearly as much on aircraft, and a lot more on artillery and TANKS. Even so, American production dwarfed all others, no matter how much the workers were paid. America came very close to matching its peak World War II defense spending in the late 1980s, and the Soviet Union began regularly exceeding its peak World War II spending in the 1970s.

Production, US

Enormous amounts of weapons and equipment were built during World War II. America was the most prodigious producer.

In addition, America contributed enormous (and significant) amounts of industrial material to its allies (particularly Britain and Russia). This aid ranged from raw materials (ores, fuel, etc.) to industrial machinery. Substantial supplies of food and medicines were also shipped. America provided the guns and the butter throughout the war, primarily through LEND-LEASE.

By the end of the war the United States was accounting for approximately 50% of the gross world product. At the beginning of the war, America was already the major industrial power in world, accounting for nearly 30% of world product, despite the Great Depression. By 1945, every other major industrial power (including Britain) had some, or most, of its industries wrecked. The dominant economic position of the United States from 1945 until the 1970s, while profitable for Americans, was not sustainable. Once the other industrial nations rebuilt their factories and infrastructures, America's share of gross world product fell back to a more "normal" 20–25%. This is still huge, for a nation containing less than 6% of the world's population.

PT-Boats, US Motor Torpedo Boats

The American version of motor torpedo boats, PT-boats were small, fast, combatant vessels whose primary weapon was supposed to be the TORPEDO, but they were eventually loaded down with all sorts of other weapons as well, usually heavy machine guns, light cannon, and depth charges, as the crews "customized" their boats. In fact, PT-boats used guns far more often than they used torpedoes.

Their hulls were made of shaped marine plywood, and they had four very powerful gasoline engines, with a very clumsy gearshift system (basically the skipper shouted commands down to two sailors in the engine compartment, each of whom was responsible for two of the four propeller shafts, using manual clutches and stick shifts). Most PT-boats served in the Pacific.

The distribution of PT-boats in the Pacific was dictated by the nature of the operations in which the three commands indicated engaged. The Third/Fifth Fleet operated primarily on the broad reaches of the Central Pacific, and its PT-boats were used mostly to patrol advanced bases and keep Japanese forces on bypassed islands entertained. The Seventh Fleet operated in the SOLOMONS, the BISMARCKS, NEW GUINEA, and the Philippines, where the numerous islands made the use of large numbers of small patrol craft necessary. The Hawaiian Sea Frontier used its PT-boats to patrol the small atolls and islets, which stretched northwest from the main islands, lest the Japanese use them as anchorages for SUBMARINES capable of launching floatplanes or refueling flying boats for airstrikes against HAWAII, as had been done once early in the war.

Most PT-boats listed under "All other commands" were in the Mediterranean.

Altogether, 70 PT-boats were lost during the war, all but six in the Pacific. A majority of the losses (39) were due to accidents, such as groundings, collisions, fires, and explosions; one was sunk by a KAMIKAZE.

See also HIGGINS, ANDREW JACKSON; KENNEDY, JOHN F.

Item	Worldwide	By U.S.	% U.S.
Aircraft	542,000	283,000	52%
Guns (all types)	49,300,000	17,500,000	36%
Vehicles	5,100,000	2,470,000	48%
Ships (tons)	79,000,000	54,000,000	68%

PT-BOATS ON HAND, 1 JAN. 1945	
Third/Fifth Fleets	75
Seventh Fleet	221
Hawaiian Sea Frontier	10
Total Pacific Commands	306
All Other Commands	165
Total Available	471

PT-boats on patrol off New Guinea, mid-1943. Although originally conceived as cheap weapons to use against major warships in narrow waters, PT-boats came into their own operating against Japanese coastal shipping that was attempting to supply isolated garrisons.

Publicity, False Reports

In modern war the demands of "propaganda" or "public information" to keep the folks back home happy have often led to rather extraordinary claims of success on the part of one's armed forces. Some apparently fraudulent claims are perfectly innocent of propagandistic intent, merely being made on the basis of honest mistakes. For example, on 20 October 1942 the Japanese submarine *I-175* claimed to have sunk a "battleship of the Texas Class" southeast of GUADALCANAL. In fact, the submarine had put a TORPEDO into the heavy cruiser *Chester*, damaging but not sinking her.

During the Pacific War a number of vessels achieved the distinction of having been claimed as sunk numerous times. The US submarine *Tang* (SS-306) seems to hold a world's record, being reported as sunk by Japanese forces no less than 25 times before she succumbed to a torpedo malfunction in October of 1944. The most frequently sunk American surface ship was "The Big E," the carrier *Enterprise*, claimed no less than six times, a record apparently matched by US claims of having sunk the Japanese battleship *Haruna*, including the one that really counted, when US carrier aircraft finally did her in at KURE on 28 July 1945.

The record for exaggerated claims of success is held by the Japanese. In early October 1944 the Third Fleet raided FORMOSA, the Philippines, and OKINAWA. This provoked an enormous air-sea battle, with the Japanese committing as many as a thousand aircraft, hundreds of which were shot down. On 10 October the Japanese claimed to have sunk 11 aircraft carriers, two battleships, three heavy cruisers, and one destroyer or light cruiser, as well as inflicting varying degrees of damage on 40 other vessels (including eight carriers and two battlewagons). Actually, although a number of ships in the Third Fleet were hit, only two suffered serious damage, heavy cruiser AUSTRALIA and light cruiser HOUSTON, both of which survived.

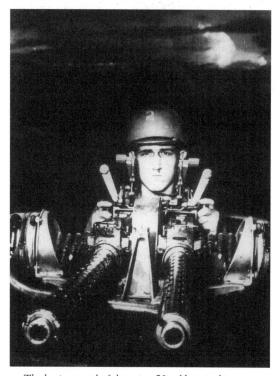

The business end of the twin .50 caliber machine-gun mount on a US PT-boat, somewhere off New Guinea, in July 1943. Although their primary weapon was supposed to be the torpedo, PT-boats did most of their work with machine guns and light cannon.

There was at least one occasion when the United States claimed to have sunk a non-existent ship. Because of different possible readings of Japanese characters, when the light carrier *Shoho* was sunk, during the Battle of the CORAL SEA in May 1942, the navy claimed to have sunk a carrier named *Ryukaku*.

Puller, Lewis B. (1898–1971)

Lewis "Chesty" Puller enlisted in the US Marines in mid-1918, after a brief stay at VMI. Although he secured a commission, he was shortly discharged in the post–World War I reorganization of the Corps. He reenlisted as a private. Puller's service was typical of a Marine of his generation, including tours in Haiti, Nicaragua, and China, and aboard ship, between which he attended various schools, was recommissioned, and was repeatedly decorated. On the eve of World War II he was a battalion commander in the Seventh Marines, with which he went to GUADALCANAL in August of 1942. Puller greatly distinguished himself on Guadalcanal, earning his third Navy Cross and sundry other decorations. He went on to command in several other operations, culminating in command of the First Marine Regiment on PELELIU, meanwhile earning a fourth Navy Cross. The end of the war found him in a training assignment at Camp Lejeune.

In the postwar years Puller held various assignments, and then in 1950 was once more given the First Marines, which he led with great élan during the Inchon landings and in the battle for Seoul, winning another Navy Cross.

Returning stateside, he rose to division command and assistant commandant before retiring for reasons of health in 1957. A short, tough, profane man, Puller, the most decorated Marine in history, was an ideal tactical commander.

Purple

The principal Japanese diplomatic code, purple was introduced in 1937. By 1941 the United States had broken the code through the efforts of the navy's

Laurence Stafford and the army's William Friedman. This enabled American intelligence to read Japanese diplomatic communications throughout the war. The Japanese never realized that the code had been broken, and continued to use it for the most sensitive messages between the Foreign Ministry and Japanese diplomatic officials overseas even after the surrender of Japan.

See also MAGIC.

PV-1 Ventura, US Patrol Bomber

The PV-1 Ventura was originally built by an American firm in response to a 1940 British order. After going into action in late 1942, it was found that the PV-1 (called the Vega 36 at the time) was not a very effective bomber. The US Army didn't want them and most of the 1,600 built (plus 535 improved PV-2s) were used by the US Navy for ocean reconnaissance. In this role, the PV-1 was quite good.

See also RECONNAISSANCE, NAVAL.

Pyle, Ernest T. (1900–1945)

The most respected American correspondent in the war, Ernie Pyle began his wartime career in London in 1941, and covered operations in North Africa, Sicily, Italy, and France before going to the Pacific, where he reported from IWO JIMA and OKINAWA. Unlike a great many war correspondents, Pyle spent most of his time up front with the troops, reporting on the common soldier's war. Rather than discuss grand matters of command and STRATEGY, he focused on the daily routine of the soldier's life, the stress of combat, the simple pleasures and pains. Although like all correspondents he left much of the misery and horror unsaid, it was clearly evident from the sensitivity expressed in his writings, for which he won a Pulitzer in 1943. Pyle was killed by a Japanese machine gunner on IE SHIMA, 18 April 1945. On the site was erected a simple monument, originally just of wood and paint but later replaced in stone: "On this spot the 77th Division Lost a Buddy, Ernie Pyle."

Q

Queen Elizabeth Class, British Battleships

The "QEs" were the finest battleships of their generation, the most powerful and speediest of World War I, and the decade after as well. They were the first capital ships to burn oil fuel exclusively. Well protected, heavily armed, and relatively speedy (25 knots), they had excellent sea-keeping qualities. Though old by World War II, they were still of considerable value, not only for shore bombardment, but also in ship-to-ship action, as proven in several surface actions with German and Italian warships. Several saw service with the British Far Eastern Fleet, primarily as escorts for convoys and on bombardment duty.

Queen Elizabeth (1912–1913–1915) served in the Far East, 1944–45.

Malaya (1913–1915–1916) saw no service in the Far East.

Warspite (1912–1913–1915) served in the Far East, 1944–45.

Valiant (1913–1914–1916) served in the Far East, 1944–45.

One unit, *Barham* (1913–1915–1916), was sunk in the Mediterranean. The survivors were disposed of 1946–48.

See also ROYAL NAVY.

Queen Mary and *Queen Elizabeth*, RMSs

Two of the three largest and fastest ocean liners ever built, the third being the French NORMANDIE.

Queen Mary (80,000 GRT) entered transatlantic service in the spring of 1936, for a time holding the Blue Ribband for the fastest crossing. She was converted into a troop transport shortly after the German invasion of Poland in 1939.

Queen Elizabeth (83,000 GRT, later increased) was still under construction when the European War began. She made her maiden voyage in great secrecy in 1940, laying up for a time in New York (with *Queen Mary* and *Normandie*, the only occasion on which all three superliners were together). Although there was some discussion about converting her into an aircraft carrier, she entered service as a troop transport.

As both ships were fast, 28–29 knots, they could make high-speed crossings with minimal escorts, since SUBMARINES were much too slow to intercept them: On one such voyage *Queen Elizabeth* rammed and sank a light cruiser. As each could carry as many as 15,000 men at one time (50% more than any other ship, and more than three times the capacity of the average liner), they were the mainstay of Allied troop movements throughout the war, turning up in all theaters. By one calculation about 24% of US troops in Europe reached there aboard one of the Queens, which made a total of 37 Atlantic crossings.

At the time of the PEARL HARBOR attack they were engaged in transporting the Sixth and Seventh Australian Divisions home from the Middle East.

Unlike the United States, which took merchant ships into the navy or the army for use as transports, Britain permitted the ships to be run by their owners, a move that proved more economical than the American approach. Not only did the owners take better care of the ships, but they also operated them with sailors who were not necessarily fit for

With the Manhattan skyline behind her, RMS Queen Mary steams up the North River, crowded with over 10,000 homebound American troops, June 20, 1945.

military service, an important consideration given Britain's strained manpower resources.

After the war both were engaged in repatriating troops and were then overhauled for commercial service. Both plied the North Atlantic into the early 1960s when they were sold. *Queen Elizabeth* was destroyed by a fire in HONG KONG Harbor, while undergoing conversion into a floating university, and *Queen Mary* is preserved as a tourist attraction and movie set at LONG BEACH, California.

R

Rabaul, New Britain, Bismarck Archipelago

Rabaul, a modest settlement at the northern end of NEW BRITAIN, had a wonderful natural harbor, although very limited facilities for servicing and maintaining ships. Well suited for a naval or air base, being within easy reach of New Guinea and the SOLOMONS, in January 1942 the garrison of Rabaul was only some 1,500 Australians, comprising an infantry battalion and a few old coast defense guns, plus some Hudson reconnaissance aircraft. The Japanese undertook air strikes against Rabaul on 20 January, then landed troops. Australian resistance was stiff, but the situation was clearly hopeless. On 23–24 January the Australians fell back into the jungle.

The Japanese built Rabaul up into their largest base south of TRUK, concentrating very large ground, air, and naval forces there. When they arrived they found two dirt airstrips, to which they added three more, paving four of the five, which were capable of housing over 500 aircraft. It was from Rabaul that all Japanese operations in the Solomons were supported. Although initial Allied plans called for the capture of Rabaul (code named CARTWHEEL) some time in 1943, these were later changed. Subsequent operations against Rabaul were primarily intended to bypass it and let it "wither on the vine." This subjected well over 100,000 Japanese troops to increasing isolation and increasing ineffectiveness for the rest of the war.

See also JAPAN, FORCES ABROAD AT THE SURRENDER.

Range, Aircraft

The radius of air patrol shows the greatest extent to which aircraft at a land base are likely to spot ships or aircraft. No matter how many aircraft are stationed at a base, the chances of spotting something always decrease with distance. This is a matter of simple geometry; the farther away from the base, the more area there is to cover. Reconnaissance reaches out farther than air attacks because the recon aircraft do not have to carry large-weapons loads or conserve fuel for high-speed combat.

See also RECONNAISSANCE, NAVAL.

Ranger, US Aircraft Carrier

An unsuccessful ship, *Ranger* (1931–1933–1934) was America's first carrier designed as such from the keel up. However, this occurred before much experience had been gained in operating the LEXINGTONS. As a result, far too much was attempted on a limited hull. Her wartime career was confined to the Atlantic, where she rendered valuable service in support of the North African landings and in air strikes on German installations in Norway. She was eventually relegated to service as a training carrier, and scrapped in 1947.

Rangoon, Burma

A river port of some pretensions, but only limited facilities, albeit the nerve center of British power in Burma, with an important air base and other military installations. Captured by the Japanese in March 1942, it was liberated in June 1945.

RANKS, OFFICERS, ARMY, AIR FORCE, AND MARINE, COMPARATIVE TABLE

| United States | China | British Commonwealth | | | Japan |
		Army	Air Force		
General of the Army	Chi Shang-Chiang	Field Marshal	Marshal of the RAF		Cen-Sui
General	Erh Chi Shang-Chiang	General	Air Chief Marshal		—
Lieutenant General	—	Lieutenant General	Air Marshal		Tai-Sho-gen +
Major General	Chun-Chiang +	Major General	Air Vice-Marshal		Chun-jo +
Brigadier General	Shao-Chiang +	Brigadier	Air Commodore		Sho-sho +
Colonel	Shang-hsiao	Colonel	Group Captain		Tai-sa
Lieutenant Colonel	Chung-hsiao	Lieutenant Colonel	Wing Commander		Chu-sa
Major	Shao-hsiao	Major	Squadron Leader		Sho-sa
Captain	Shang-wei	Captain	Flight Lieutenant		Tai-i
First Lieutenant	Chung-wei	Lieutenant	Flying Officer		Chu-i
Second Lieutenant	Shao-wei	Second Lieutenant	Pilot Officer		Sho-i

A British brigadier is not a general officer. The PHILIPPINE ARMY and the PHILIPPINE CONSTABULARY, which used US ranks, also had "third lieutenants," who ranked just below second lieutenants. As generalissimo of the Chinese armed forces, CHIANG KAI-SHEK appears to have borne the title T'e Chih Shang Chiang. The crossed (+) Chinese and Japanese ranks are usually translated into English at the next highest equivalent. In the Japanese Army field marshal was essentially an honorary distinction, rather than a rank. The comparison is easier to understand by looking at the normal commands held by the ranks in question, using US terminology.

NORMAL RANK OF MAJOR UNIT COMMANDERS

Unit	China	Japan	United States
Army Group	I Chi Sang-Chiang	Gen-Sui/Tai Sho-gen	General/Lieutenant General
Army	I Chi Sang-Chiang	Tai Sho-gen	General/Lieutenant General
Corps	Erh Chi Shang-Chiang	Tai Sho-gen/Chun-jo	Major General/Lieutenant General
Division	Chun-Chiang	Chun-jo	Major General
Brigade	Shao-Chiang	Sho-sho	Brigadier General
Regiment	Shang-hsiao	Tai-sa	Colonel

See also ORGANIZATION, HIGHER ARMY COMMANDS, COMPARATIVE.

Reagan, Ronald Wilson (1911–   )

Despite very poor eyesight, Reagan, already a moderately prominent actor, was a prewar reserve officer in the CAVALRY. In April 1942 he went on active service as a second lieutenant. Reagan was initially assigned to the SAN FRANCISCO Port of Embarkation, where he helped oversee the loading of troopships and transports. He was subsequently transferred to the Army Air Force First Motion Picture Unit, with which he made numerous training films. He was discharged in July 1945 as a captain. After the war he returned to acting, entered politics, and served as governor of California, 1967–75, and as president, 1981–89.

Rearmament, US, 1930s

US rearmament for the Second World War began in a modest way as a result of the ROOSEVELT administration's attempt to fight the Great Depression through economic pump priming. The preceding three Republican administrations had been rather tightfisted, and the Hoover administration's reaction to the onset of the Depression was to make severe cuts in already modest defense spending, and very deep reductions in manpower.

RANKS, OFFICERS, NAVY, COMPARATIVE TABLE

British Commonwealth	Japan	United States
Admiral of the Fleet		Fleet Admiral
Admiral	Taisho	Admiral
Vice Admiral	Chujo	Vice Admiral
Rear Admiral	Shosho	Rear Admiral (Upper Half)
Commodore		Rear Admiral (Lower Half)
Captain+	Taisa	Captain+
Commander	Chusa	Commander
Lieutenant Commander	Shosa	Lieutenant Commander
Lieutenant	Tai-i	Lieutenant
Sub-Lieutenant	Chu-i	Lieutenant, j.g. [junior grade]
Midshipman++	Sho-i	Ensign

+A captain commanding a flotilla or the senior captain in a flotilla usually bore the courtesy title commodore. In the US Navy, commodore was also given to a small number of selected officers, such as the chief of naval history, who needed to outrank most other people but did not really need to be an admiral.

++Actually there is no rank equivalent to ensign in the Royal Navy, since the Royal Navy's midshipmen serve afloat while functionally filling the same role as ensigns.

Between 1921 and 1933 not a single destroyer had been added to the US Navy, and only three aircraft carriers, 15 heavy cruisers, and seven SUBMARINES had been built or ordered. In contrast, during Roosevelt's famous "Hundred Days" two aircraft carriers, four light cruisers, 20 destroyers, and six other vessels were ordered, in a package worth $238 million, a bit of economic "pump priming" that had beneficial effects in terms of modernizing the navy. Although the president had to cope with charges of warmongering, he was ably assisted by naval enthusiasts in Congress such as Carl Vinson, and by the time the European War broke out in September of 1939, the navy had four battleships, three carriers, two heavy, and nine light cruisers, 70 destroyers, and 27 submarines, newly built or under construction. It was the war in Europe that really sparked US rearmament, albeit that resistance to even modest measures intensified.

On 8 September 1939, with the war underway, the president proclaimed a "limited national emergency" and ordered an increase in the enlisted strength of the armed forces, permitting the addition of 130,000 men to the army (to about 280,000), some 35,000 more to the navy (to about 145,000), and about 7,000 more to the Marines (to 25,000), in addition authorizing the recall of retired personnel to active duty, while also authorizing a modest increase in the strength of the NATIONAL GUARD. This was possible because existing legislation authorized much larger forces than were actually in uniform.

In May 1940, the president requested military spending be increased to $1.1 billion, and declared that the nation's aircraft industry must be prepared to produce 50,000 new aircraft a year. The program was quickly approved in Congress, but not without acrimony. In mid-June, with the Germans having occupied Paris, the president signed "An Act to Expand the Navy by 11 Percent," which added 167,000 tons of combat ships and 75,000 tons of auxiliaries. This was followed by a bill expanding naval aviation, and a request by the chief of naval operations, Admiral H. R. Stark, for the creation of a "Two Ocean Navy," at a cost of $4 billion. Between 12 June and 1 July 1940 the navy awarded contracts for the construction of 66 new ships.

In July, in the face of fierce resistance by isolationists and pacifists of all political pursuasions (from right-wing "America Firsters" to left-wing communists), Congress passed what became known as the "Two Ocean Navy" bill, part of a package of emergency defense measures that appropriated about $12 billion between June and October of 1940. Included in the Two Ocean Navy bill was $4 billion (nearly $43 billion in 1996 terms) for new ships: seven battleships, 18 aircraft carriers, 27 cruisers, 115 destroyers, and 43 submarines, plus many auxiliary vessels, this represented an increase in the fleet of 70%, with 1,325,000 tons of combat ships, 100,000 of auxiliary vessels, and 15,000 new aircraft. By early September the navy had awarded contracts for seven new battleships, a dozen new carriers, and nearly 200 other ships.

Much of the attention in American rearmament had hitherto been focused on the navy, although the strength of the army had been increased and it had been authorized 20,000 new aircraft. This was largely due to the fact that it requires years to build a fleet, while to some extent armies can be improvised in a much shorter time. However, by mid–1940 it was becoming clear that the expansion of the army could no longer be deferred. On 27 August Congress authorized the federalization of the National Guard, and three weeks later, on 19 September, passed the Selective Service Act.

This set the tempo for the military build-up over the next 14 months, until PEARL HARBOR, when even greater measures were undertaken.

It must not be forgotten that without the naval building begun in 1939 and 1940, America would not have been ready for a counteroffensive against the Japanese until 1944. Had the Japanese carrier fleet not been lost at MIDWAY in June 1942, the delay could have been another year. The prewar rearmament made more of a difference in the way the war was fought than any of the battles later fought.

See also CONSCRIPTION; LINDBERGH, CHARLES; NEUTRALITY ACTS; PRODUCTION, SPENDING.

Ref: Abbazia, *Mr. Roosevelt's Navy.*

Reconnaissance, Naval

The very first, and perhaps most important, role that aircraft had in warfare was that of reconnaissance—information gathering. Aircraft especially designed for reconnaissance were introduced in the decade before World War II. By the outbreak of the war there were essentially two types of reconnaissance aircraft, long-range and short-range.

Navies were particularly interested in long-range reconnaissance aircraft because of the need to patrol vast expanses of ocean and to escort convoys. Multi-engine aircraft were the norm, and flying boats were very popular, since they could operate with a minimum of basing facilities.

The ideal long-range reconnaissance airplane was not particularly fast but had a very high endurance, giving it a long "loiter" time, and was capable of attaining considerable altitude, to keep it safe from enemy fighters. Such aircraft usually had one or two machine guns for self-defense, and were often equipped to carry some small bombs or depth charges, to enable them to attack targets of opportunity. Bombers, particularly obsolete types, were often pressed into the role of maritime patrol, a duty for which they were generally satisfactory.

Short-range reconnaissance aircraft were designed to engage in tactical reconnaissance. Both armies and navies needed information on the enemy's local resources, information that could be obtained by relatively fast, small aircraft. During World War I navies began experimenting with catapult-launched seaplanes on major warships, and by World War II virtually all cruisers and battleships were equipped with such. Their duties were to help the ships' gunners find their targets. They proved valuable in this role, but by the end of the war were increasingly being dispensed with. There were two reasons for this. The increasing availability of carrier aircraft to support shore bombardment was an important factor, but perhaps even more significant was the extreme danger that the aircraft and their highly volatile fuel posed on the ships. Not a few battleships and cruisers suffered serious damage when their recon planes or the fuel for them caught fire, occasionally due to the blast effects of their own guns.

The US Navy developed a third type of reconnaissance aircraft, the blimp. The blimp was a "non-rigid" airship, essentially a collection of helium gas bags loosely held together by an aluminum frame. Blimps were very slow, 80–90 knots being their maximum speed. But they had enormous range and a wonderful ability to loiter in an area for hours on end. Armed with depth charges, they proved immensely useful in convoy defense in the Atlantic, but saw little service in the Pacific.

While ships have always conducted searches for other ships and landward obstacles, aircraft were the premier search methods in World War II. Nevertheless, aircraft could not do it all. At night and in bad weather, ships still had to rely on their own onboard resources.

Search by ships was, and still is, performed by sailors "on watch." While most sailors on watch are doing vital jobs like manning the engines, steering the ship, and monitoring the radio, others are lookouts. The Japanese in particular carefully trained their lookouts and equipped them with excellent optical devices (binoculars and telescopes). Drilled at night and in bad weather, Japanese lookouts often outperformed the crude radar that US ships had (and Japanese ships lacked) early in the war.

American radar soon improved and by the end of 1942, the Japanese had lost their lookout advantage. Radar was first used on ships in the late 1930s and saw rapid development during the first few years of World War II.

By 1943, it was increasingly common for large aircraft to carry radar. This was particularly important for naval reconnaissance. For army units on land radar was useless because of the "clutter" created by hills, forests and buildings, but ships at sea could be spotted clearly by airborne radar. The bigger the ship, the farther away it could be spotted. Since most warships traveled in groups, a spotter merely had to locate the largest ship in order to find the entire group.

SUBMARINES were another matter, as they are the smallest ships that operate on the high seas and are small enough to be hard to spot by ship's radar. But subs could still be spotted by airborne radar, and it was this vulnerability that eventually doomed the German U-boat threat in the Atlantic and made Japanese submarines much less lethal in the Pacific.

The Allies had the edge in radar development and in the number of long-range aircraft built during World War II, and this provided them with a considerable advantage. However, effective radar and abundant search aircraft did not give the Allies perfect knowledge of what was afloat on the vast Pacific since there were never enough aircraft to cover all the ocean areas simultaneously. It was never possible to equip all recon aircraft with radar and darkness and bad weather often made recon flights futile. What was possible was to increase the probability of spotting enemy ships depending on how many aircraft were at a particular base, or on a task force's carriers. Moreover, spotting was also

RANGES OF SEARCH METHODS

Method	Range in km.	
	Low	High
Lookout	12	22
Aircraft	30	40

The low range is for smaller ships (lower lookouts) and aircraft (fewer crew to keep a sharp lookout). These are clear weather ranges and don't show the lesser probability of spotting something that is farther away. Weather is also a factor, mist and fog severely limiting range. Night spotting is highly dependent on available moonlight, and even under the best of conditions is less than half the range of daylight.

more likely the closer you got to the base or carriers that the aircraft were flying from. As recon aircraft flew out from their own base, the area to be covered increased. Recon aircraft customarily flew a course that resembled a slice of pie. Often they would fly back and forth across an area in much the same way a lawnmower would cover an area of grass to be cut. Thus the range of the aircraft was critical not so much for the distance it traveled from its base as it was for the amount of sea area it could cover before it had to land. The farther from the aircraft's base, the less likely aircraft were to spot what was out there, since the area to be covered increased.

The sharp-eyed lookout is an old naval tradition. There are many dangers at sea that can be seen before you encounter them (including enemy ships), and there are always alert lookouts standing watch on ships. The 20th century brought with it a new vantage point for naval lookouts, the floatplane, an airplane with pontoons instead of wheels, to enable it to operate from water.

About the same time aircraft carriers came into use, battleships and cruisers began to carry floatplanes for reconnaissance purposes. The Japanese were quite fond of floatplanes, but they were popular with all nations possessing cruisers (which carried one or two aircraft each) or battleships (which carried two or more).

The Japanese relied heavily on their floatplanes for reconnaissance instead of their carrier aircraft. After 1942, the Japanese had little choice because most of their carriers were sunk. But in addition to floatplanes on warships, Japan formed floatplane units that operated from the coves and bays of Pacific islands.

The Japanese built special supply ships that could repair and maintain these floatplanes wherever their island base might be. Some of these support ships looked like carriers and could launch amphibious (with wheels and floats) planes from their decks. The Allies had sufficient engineering units to quickly build landing strips on islands. Moreover, the Allies also had thousands of larger (two- or four-engined) floatplanes that had larger range than the normally single-engine Japanese floatplane.

Radar gave a spotting range a bit farther than lookouts, but with greater probability of spotting something and considerable immunity from atmospheric and night effects. Radar early in the war was erratic, and it wasn't until late 1943 that Allied ship radar became routinely reliable. The Japanese were still struggling with radar technology when the war ended. A persistent problem with radar was the difficulty in using it close to land. It was very difficult to separate distant ships from islands and other landforms.

Renown Class, British Battlecruisers

As ships, the Renowns were speedy, maneuverable, and good sea boats. They had been hastily built during World War I, and saw considerable service against the German High Seas Fleet. Modernized between the wars, they—and the even larger and more famous *Hood*, which was lost to the German *Bismarck* in May 1941—were the only old big-gun ships able to keep up with modern battleships and aircraft carriers, and they saw extensive service during the war. However, they suffered from all the handicaps common to battlecruisers; they were virtually unprotected and rather lightly armed.

Repulse (1916–1916–1916) saw considerable service in the European War, before being sent with HMS *Prince of Wales* to the Far East, where they were both sunk by Japanese air attack on 10 December 1941. Her maneuverability helped *Repulse* survive for about an hour, but she could not escape and succumbed to five TORPEDOES. There were few survivors, among them the ship's chaplain, the Reverend J. T. Bezzent, who later returned to the war as fleet chaplain to the British Pacific Fleet.

Renown (1915–1916–1916) saw extensive service in the European War, and then in the Indian Ocean from 1944, where she supported offensive operations in Burma. She was retired in early 1945.

See also ROYAL NAVY.

Repatriation of Civilians and Diplomatic Personnel

Early in the war, acting in accordance with well established custom and international law, the United States, Japan, and other belligerents began negotiations to arrange for the repatriation of diplomatic and other personnel caught in each others' country. These negotiations were conducted through the good offices of the respective "protecting powers," neutrals who had assumed responsibility for overseeing the interests of the belligerents in each other's country. Eventually arrangements were made to transfer thousands of people. Among them were the Japanese ambassadors to the United States, with their staffs and families, US Ambassador to Japan Joseph C. Grew, with his staff and their families, and many civilians, including a number of Japanese residents in the United States. Among both the Japanese and American personnel repatriated were military officers who returned to active duty upon reaching their homelands, which was perfectly legitimate under the terms of the GENEVA CONVENTION.

The actual number of persons repatriated in this fashion is unknown. In addition to transporting personnel to be repatriated, the ships involved carried relief supplies and mail for PRISONERS OF WAR.

The process of repatriation was extremely difficult. Not only did ships have to be procured (the United States chartered the Swedish liner GRIPSHOLM, while the Japanese used two of their precious merchantships, AWA MARU and *Asama Maru*), but safe conducts had to be arranged, special markings agreed upon, and notification made to military forces. The ships involved in such transactions usually sailed to neutral ports. This was one reason why the United States continued to maintain friendly relations with Vichy France, since Madagascar was the most conveniently "neutral" place for such exchanges.

By 1945 there still remained large numbers of people not yet repatriated. Those in Japanese hands were by this time suffering considerable privation. The process of repatriation broke down following the sinking of the Japanese transport *Awa Maru*, by a US submarine in March 1945.

Ref: Corbett, *Quiet Passages*.

Richelieu Class, French Battleships

The Richelieus were large vessels, of unusual design, carrying their main armament forward in two quadruple turrets. They were built in dry dock, rather than on a shipway, and took a long time to build due to technical problems, design changes, and the strains that France was undergoing in attempting to mobilize rapidly during the late 1930s. The Richelieus were very well protected. Like all World War II battleships except American and British ones, they had large-caliber secondary armament (nine 6" guns), which were of no use for antiaircraft purposes.

Richelieu (1935–1939–1940) while still only partially completed fled France in June 1940 to avoid being captured by the Germans, taking refuge in Dakar, West Africa. Under Vichy control at Dakar from 1940 to 1942, she took some damage in action against British and Free French forces on two occasions, one of which involved a clash with ROYAL NAVY battleships. In early 1943, now with the Free French, she was completed at the Brooklyn Navy Yard and served with the Royal Navy in the North Sea and Arctic Ocean from mid-1943 to early 1944. She then joined the British Far Eastern Fleet, serving with it until the end of the war, protecting carrier task forces and shelling Japanese installations, and just missing the last surface action of the war, when her escorting Royal Navy destroyers sank HIJMS *Haguro* in May 1945. She saw some postwar service and was scrapped in 1968.

Jean Bart (1936–1940–1950) was very incomplete at the time of the fall of France to the Nazis. Heavily escorted, she was taken to Casablanca, where from her dockside in November of 1942 she traded shots with the USS *Massachusetts*, much to her loss. She saw no further service in the war. Finally completed in 1950, she was the last battleship ever built. Scrapped in 1970.

A sistership was broken incomplete on the ways.

Roosevelt, Franklin D. (1882–1945)

The scion of a very prosperous family, which had been prominent in New York society for generations, FDR was a Harvard man (he earned a "gentleman's C") and a graduate of Columbia Law School. Roosevelt had no formal military experience, although not for want of trying. The Spanish-American War broke out when he was a 16-year-old student in a posh boarding school. With another boy, he plotted to run away and join the navy, only to have their plans frustrated by an outbreak of scarlet fever, which imposed a quarantine on the school. After Columbia he worked at law for a time, and became involved in Democratic Party politics, earning him an appointment as assistant secretary of the navy in the Wilson administration When the United States entered World War I, he offered his resignation in the hope of securing a commission in the navy, but was prohibited from doing so by the president. Despite this, he did get to the front on several occasions, visiting the Marines while in France, once narrowly missing death in a German shelling. He ran unsuccessfully for vice president in 1920. Shortly afterward he contracted polio and spent several years in rehabilitation. Elected governor of New York in 1928 and again in 1930, in 1932 he was elected president.

Like his distant cousin Theodore Roosevelt, FDR was a close student of history, and particularly naval history. An able shiphandler himself (on several occasions he took the helm of destroyers, once bringing that of Lieutenant William HALSEY into port; the nervous young officer realized the assistant secretary knew his business when he saw Roosevelt glancing back to see if the ship's stern was clear), he identified so closely with the navy that he probably visited every major warship in the fleet during the 1930s (his particular favorite was the heavy cruiser *Augusta*). In conversation he often referred to the navy as "us" and to the army as "them," until George C. MARSHALL asked him to stop.

President Franklin D. Roosevelt signs the declaration of war against Japan, December 8, 1941. The strain of events can readily be seen in the president's face. The black armband was a sign of mourning due to a death in the family.

Roosevelt's pro-navy attitude was fortunate in many ways, for just at the moment when the Nation was fighting its most important sea war, it was led by a man who had a more intimate knowledge of the navy than any other chief executive ever.

Roosevelt took an active part in running the war. Not only did he involve himself in strategic decision making, but he was also instrumental in the introduction of the escort carrier and the light aircraft carrier. As he knew most of the senior officers in the navy and Marine Corps, some for as long as 30 years, and many of those in the army as well, he selected personnel for most senior positions personally, and it speaks well of his judgment that very few of his appointees proved wanting. His principal flaw as commander-in-chief was that he thought he'd be around to see the end.

Ref: Larrabee, *Commander in Chief.*

Roosevelt Family at War

The living male offspring of the two presidents Roosevelt (Theodore Roosevelt's son Quentin having been killed in action in France in World War I, in which his daughter Edith Roosevelt Derby served as a nurse) all served in World War II, mostly in the Pacific.

Theodore Roosevelt's sons were:

Theodore Roosevelt Jr. (1887–1944), who entered the army via the Plattsburg program in World War I, during which he was wounded. He returned to civilian life after the war, entering politics unsuccessfully. On the eve of the US entry into World War II he was recalled to active duty as a brigadier general. He fought in North Africa and Sicily, before earning a MEDAL OF HONOR for his work on Utah Beach on D-day. The only general to land in the first wave, upon discovering that he had been deposited on the wrong beach, Roosevelt signaled the troop ships to land the follow-up waves there anyway, saying "We'll start the war from here." He died in his sleep of a heart attack several weeks later. During his military career he earned every American decoration for ground combat.

Kermit Roosevelt (1889–1943) joined the British Army prior to American entry into World War I, later transferring to the US Army; he again joined the British Army in World War II, serving in Norway (Military Cross) and North Africa. Transferring to the US Army after PEARL HARBOR, he died of natural causes in Alaska in 1943, a lieutenant colonel.

Archibald Roosevelt (1894–1979) served as a captain in World War I, during which he was wounded and decorated (Croix de Guerre). He rejoined the army for World War II, winning a Silver Star while commanding a battalion on NEW GUINEA. Apparently the oldest battalion commander in the infantry, he was badly wounded on BIAK, and later discharged as disabled.

Presidential grandson Quentin Roosevelt (1918–1948) served as a captain in the army during the war, and was present on D-day in Normandy.

Franklin D. Roosevelt's sons were:

James Roosevelt (1907–1991), who served in the Marines, rising from captain to colonel. He won a Silver Star for his part in the Second Marine Raider Battalion (Carlson's Raiders) raid on MAKIN ISLAND in August 1942, and later commanded the Fourth Marine Raider Battalion, rose to colonel, and won a Navy Cross.

Elliott Roosevelt (1910–1990), who served in the Army Air Corps in Europe, rising from captain to brigadier general. A licensed pilot, though not a military flying officer, he was decorated for taking the controls of a damaged B-24 after both the pilot and copilot had been wounded, and landing the aircraft safely.

FDR Jr. (1914–1988), who served in the navy, distinguishing himself during the North African invasion, and later rising to command of the USS *Ulvert H. Moore* (DE-442) in the Pacific, aboard which he endured radar picket duty off OKINAWA. He ended the war as a commander, with a Silver Star and Purple Heart.

John Aspinwall Roosevelt (1916–1981), who served as a logistics officer, mostly aboard the second carrier WASP, being discharged as a lieutenant commander.

Royal Navy

Rich in tradition and experience, in 1941 the Royal Navy was still the largest in the world, although the US Navy was shortly to overtake it. Overstretched by the demands of the European War, the threat of war with Japan found the RN with only limited resources to commit to the Indian Ocean.

Force Z, a task force consisting of the battleship *Prince of Wales* and battlecruiser *Repulse* plus some destroyers, was scraped together and sent east in late 1941 (carrier INDOMITABLE was supposed to accompany them, but ran aground on her way to the Pacific and could not make it in time). Under Admiral Thomas PHILIPPS, these sortied from Singapore on the first day of the war, and were sunk by Japanese aircraft off MALAYA on 10 December. British fortunes in the Far East were long in recovering from the disaster.

By early 1942 a modest task force of old battleships, carriers, a few cruisers, and destroyers had been formed into the British Far Eastern Fleet under Admiral James SOMERVILLE. Apprised of Japanese movements through ULTRA, Somerville kept his fleet away from the Japanese First Air Fleet (the PEARL HARBOR strike force) when it sortied into the INDIAN OCEAN in March and April of 1942. Although he lost a few ships, including the old carrier HERMES, he preserved his fleet. Somerville remained in the Indian Ocean until mid-1944, conducting raids on Japanese shore installations in Burma and the Netherlands Indies, blockading the Japanese garrisons in the ANDAMAN and NICOBAR ISLANDS, lending a hand in the capture of Madagascar, supporting amphibious operations against Burma, and even conducting some diversionary attacks in support of US operations in the Pacific. His Far Eastern Fleet was always a scratch force, made up of what could be scraped together by the Royal Navy, mostly older ships, plus some French vessels, including the battleship RICHELIEU, an occasional Dutch or Polish ship, and even, for a time, the US carrier *Saratoga*.

In 1944, as the strategic situation in Europe became increasingly favorable, the Royal Navy began transferring more modern vessels to the Far Eastern Fleet. Meanwhile CHURCHILL and First Sea Lord Sir Andrew CUNNINGHAM won from a reluctant US Navy consent to send a fleet to support operations against Japan. In November 1944 the British Pacific Fleet was created out of the enlarged Far Eastern Fleet, and placed under the administrative command of Admiral Bruce FRASER. Early in 1945, even as the Far Eastern Fleet continued operations in the Indian Ocean, the British Pacific Fleet joined the US Third/Fifth Fleet for operations against Japan.

Forming a distinct task group within TF 38/58, the British Pacific Fleet, under the immediate command of Sir Philip VIAN, operated against Okinawa, the Mandates, and the Japanese Home Islands until the end of the war, by which time battleships of the KING GEORGE V CLASS were joining their American counterparts in raiding Japanese coastal installations. A contingent of the British Pacific Fleet was present in Tokyo Bay for the surrender of Japan, while other elements accepted the surrender of Japanese forces in various British colonies, including HONG KONG.

In addition to providing task forces in the Indian Ocean and Pacific, the Royal Navy supplied many officers and technicians to the Commonwealth Navies, including most of the senior personnel.

See also AIRCRAFT CARRIERS; AUSTRALIAN NAVY, ROYAL; CARRIERS, DESIGNING AIRCRAFT FOR; CRUTCHLEY, V.A.C.; NEW ZEALAND NAVY, ROYAL.

Ref: Barnett, *Engage the Enemy More Closely*; Marder, *Old Friends, New Enemies*; Roskill, *White Ensign* and *The United Kingdom Military Series: The War at Sea*.

Royal Sovereign Class, British Battleships

Apparently having expended all their ideas on the QUEEN ELIZABETH CLASS, the ROYAL NAVY's designers produced a very inferior battleship in the succeeding Royal Sovereign Class. They were poorly conceived and poorly designed, and, in a moment of panic over fuel oil supplies, were designed to burn coal. Although converted to oil during construction, they never matched the older class either in performance or sea keeping. Unlike the older "QEs," they were not extensively reconstructed between the wars. Their principal role in World War II was convoy escort. Many were sent to the Indian Ocean in early 1942, there being nothing else to spare. It is unlikely that they would have withstood the Imperial Japanese Navy had it taken a more aggressive role in the Indian Ocean in early 1942. The four ships in the class, *Royal Sovereign* (1914–1915–1916), *Revenge* (1913–1915–1916), *Resolution* (1913–1915–1916), and *Ramilles* (1913–1916–1917), were all scrapped in 1948–49. A fifth unit, *Royal Oak* (1914–1914–1916), had been sunk by a German submarine in 1939.

Rudderow/Butler Classes, US Destroyer Escorts

Derived from the BUCKLEY CLASS destroyer escorts, the Rudderows (the "TEV" Class) were about the same size (roughly comparable to the old FARRAGUT CLASS destroyers) and dimensions, but mounted two 5"/38 dual-purpose guns rather than three 3"/50 dual-purpose guns, with heavier antiaircraft and TORPEDO allotments as well (three tubes rather than two). This made the 22 Rudderows, as well as the 24 virtually identical John C. Butlers ("WGT"), the most successful American destroyer escorts in the war. "TEV" referred to turbo-electric drive DEs with 5-inch (hence the "V") guns, "WGT" to geared turbine engines using small gears.

Russia, Battles with Japan Before Pearl Harbor

In 1939 the Soviets and Japanese fought a series of battles in Mongolia, the most notable of which were at Khalkin-Gol (or Nomonhan). The Japanese got the worst of it, and this had a major impact on later battles in World War II. In this border dispute, the Japanese tested their army against the Russian forces. The Japanese failed the test, and as a result decided to leave the Russians alone during World War II. This had a considerable effect on the Russian battles with the Germans far to the west. In 1941, Russia had nearly 40 divisions facing a dozen Japanese divisions in MANCHURIA, and most of these Russian units were quickly shipped west when the Germans invaded in June. The Japanese, Germans, and Italians had signed a military alliance in 1936 (the "Axis"), but the terms were vague. The Germans hoped that the Japanese would attack Russian forces in Siberia if the Germans invaded Russia from the west. The outcome of Khalkin-Gol caused the Japanese to leave the Russians alone throughout World War II.

In the mid-1930s, Japan felt that it was militarily superior to the Russians. Having defeated the Russians on land and at sea in the 1904–05 war, they believed they still held a military edge. Then came the series of border clashes. The Japanese were defeated in a division-sized battle in eastern Manchuria in 1938. They rationalized this defeat and spoiled for another round with the Russians. While the Japanese had some success in smaller border skirmishes, they had yet to defeat the Russians in a deliberate battle. They sought to test their imagined advantage in May 1939 by forcibly redrawing the border between Japanese-held Manchuria and Russian-controlled Mongolia. A Japanese division advanced to the Khalkin-Gol (or Halha) River, and a reinforced Russian division threw it back. Undeterred, the Japanese planned a larger attack in July. This battle involved two major changes. The Japanese reinforced the division they had used in May by adding two tank regiments (70 TANKS) and a new infantry regiment. The Russians brought in General Georgy Zhukov (later to be the architect of the Russian defeat of the Germans) and a larger force (about three divisions, mostly motorized). Because the battlefield was 500 miles from the nearest railroad, the Japanese

thought the Russians incapable of reinforcing their forces so quickly and heavily. Despite their transportation problems, the Russians massed over 300 tanks against the Japanese. In the air, both sides were more evenly matched.

The July battles were another disaster for the Japanese. Their initial attack on July 3rd made some progress, but then the Russians attacked and forced the Japanese back. By July 14th, both sides halted. At this point, the Japanese decided that artillery was the key, and brought in heavy guns. The artillery duels during the last week of July went against the Japanese. The Russians were able to fire three times as many shells, and had generally heavier guns. In August, the Russians planned their own attack, an armored offensive that would settle this border dispute once and for all. Bringing up four divisions and 500 tanks (as well as 24,000 tons of ammunition), the Russians moved forward against the two Japanese divisions on August 20th. This was, in effect, the first real armored offensive of the 20th century and was a smashing success. Within four days, the Japanese had been pushed back to what the Russians considered the real border. There the Russians halted, although they could have kept chasing the shattered Japanese. Events back in Europe (Germany was about to invade Poland) made further involvement in Manchuria inadvisable. In September a cease-fire agreement was signed, thus ending the fighting.

As World War II battles go, the Khalkin-Gol fights were not big ones. The Japanese committed two divisions, plus replacements, and suffered 18,000 CASUALTIES (out of 40,000 troops involved). The Russians suffered 14,000 casualties, out of 70,000 troops sent in. Altogether, some hundred tanks were lost and nearly 200 aircraft.

The Japanese drew the correct conclusions from this three-month clash. They acknowledged that the Russians were superior, and discarded their pre Khalkin-Gol plan for assembling 45 divisions in 1943 in order to drive the Russians back to the Ural Mountains. At the same time the battle was ending, the Nazi-Soviet treaty was announced. This caused the Japanese to renounce their 1936 treaty with the Germans. These diplomatic and battlefield defeats hurt Germany the most, as the lack of an active ally in the Far East enabled the Russians to concentrate their full strength against the Germans. Many of the best Russian troops facing the Japanese were sent west to defend Moscow in late 1941. These divisions made a big difference, especially to the German troops who got close enough to Moscow in late 1941 that they could see the spires of the Kremlin. It was as close as the Germans ever got.

One of the most curious things about Khalkin-Gol is that the rest of the world knew virtually nothing about it, or any of the other smaller Russo-Japanese clashes, until several years afterward. The Japanese naturally were not inclined to spread the word about their unpleasant experience and the Russians were obsessed with secrecy. The Germans remained blissfully unaware of Japanese reluctance to take on the Russians, and attacked the Soviet Union with the idea that the Japanese could eventually get involved. Had the word got out about Khalkin-Gol, the course of World War II might have been rather different.

Russia, Relations with China

Soviet Russia had aligned itself politically with the Chinese Nationalists for a time in the 1920s and 1930s, much to the chagrin of the Chinese communists. This was a purely realpolitik arrangement, as the Soviets had territorial and political designs on China. Nevertheless, the arrangement greatly benefited the Chinese. Chinese military officers (including CHIANG KAI-SHEK), for a short time studied in Russia, while Russian military advisers helped train Chinese troops. Meanwhile, the Soviets urged a "popular front" behind Chiang Kai-shek against the Japanese. Although viewed by the Nationalists with suspicion, the proposal appears to have been made in the belief that Chiang was the man mostly likely to be able to sustain a united resistance against the Japanese. Certainly the Chinese communists were not particularly happy about it. When the CHINA INCIDENT broke out in 1937,

the Soviet Union sent "volunteer" aviation units to support the Nationalist war effort, although these were withdrawn by 1939.

During World War II the Soviets supplied some arms and equipment to the Chinese, mostly to the Nationalists. They also attempted to help themselves to some Chinese real estate. For example, in May 1943 the Russians engineered local uprisings in northwestern Sinkiang, which permitted them and their Mongolian surrogates to occupy two areas of the vast province (the "Altai Incident" and the "Eli Incident"). Not until the final year of the war did the Soviets more or less begin to support the Chinese communists, turning over to them vast amounts of Japanese military equipment captured when they overran Manchuria in August and September of 1945.

Russian attitudes toward China changed drastically once the Russo-Japanese neutrality treaty was signed in April 1941. When the Germans invaded Russia two months later, the Soviets were eager not to provide Japan with any incentives to break their truce. This meant that any assistance given to the Chinese had to be very discrete. As a result, there was little aid of any significance. Diplomatically, however, the Russians took a keen interest in the Chinese situation. As the Russian war with Germany reached its conclusion, it was obvious to the Russians that they could pick up some real estate in the Far East and play a large role in postwar Chinese affairs. With this in mind, Russia attacked Japanese forces in MANCHURIA and northern China with the intention of beefing up the strength of the Chinese communists. After 1941, the Chinese communists had remained away from the Chinese coast and Japanese troops. Rebuilding their military and political forces, the Chinese communists had, by 1945, created a core of support that controlled 65 million Chinese, 250,000 square miles of territory, and a disciplined army of half a million troops. Russia constantly pressured the United States to provide weapons and diplomatic support for the Chinese communists, and at the same time played down reports (substantially correct) that the Chinese communists had arranged truces with the Japanese, a situation that allowed Japanese forces to spend more time attacking Chinese Nationalist troops. Russia also encouraged the idea that the Chinese communists were not really communists at all, but rather social reformers who had been unfairly tagged as communists. While the Russian and Chinese communists had their doctrinal differences, there was no doubt that the Chinese communists were indeed Marxists, and arguably more doctrinaire ones than the Russian version. America did not catch on to this subterfuge until 1947, even though many Americans on the spot had long insisted that the Chinese communists were indeed communists and cut from the same ideological cloth as their Soviet counterparts.

The Russians, in particular Stalin, told American officials outright that the Soviet Union would support American policy in China after the war. In other words, the Russians said they would back the Chinese Nationalists after World War II. Despite reports that the conquering Russian armies in Manchuria were handing over captured Japanese weapons to the Chinese communists, America did not make any moves to counter this Russian support for the communist faction in the ongoing Chinese civil war. As a result of the shrewd Soviet diplomacy in China during World War II, America supported the Chinese Nationalists against the Japanese, while the Russians saw to it that the Chinese communists stayed out of most of the fighting, received most of the surrendered Japanese weapons and equipment, and were in a good position to quickly defeat the battered Chinese Nationalists when the Chinese civil war resumed in earnest after the Japanese surrender. The Russians followed the same STRATEGY in Korea when they occupied the northern part of that country during their Manchurian offensive in 1945. Korean communists were promptly installed in North Korea, a government that went on to outlast the Soviet Union itself.

Ryuho, Japanese Light Aircraft Carrier

The submarine tender *Taigei* (1933–1933–1935) was built to a plan that permitted her to be converted rather quickly into an aircraft carrier. In 1941 she was taken in hand for conversion. Reengined and partially reconstructed, she emerged as a light carrier in late 1942. *Ryuho* was not as successful a vessel as *Zuiho,* being slow and poorly constructed. She served mostly as a training carrier. Severely damaged at KURE by a carrier air raid on 17 March 1945, she was not repaired and was scrapped in 1946.

Ryujo, Japanese Aircraft Carrier

Ryujo (1929–1931–1933) was a poor vessel, lightly constructed, unstable, and top-heavy, designed to squeeze the last few tons out of Japan's carrier quota under the terms of the naval DISARMAMENT TREATIES. Subjected to a virtual reconstruction in 1934–37, the ship emerged only little improved. She took part in a number of operations in the war against China, and began World War II by making some of the first attacks on the Philippines on 8 December 1941, before going on to support operations in the NETHERLANDS EAST INDIES and serve with the Combined Fleet. She was sunk by four bombs and a TORPEDO from US carrier aircraft in the Battle of the EASTERN SOLOMONS.

Ryukyu Islands, Japan

Stretch roughly southwestward for about 650 miles between Kyushu, the southernmost of the Japanese Home Islands, and Taiwan. Although the 143 islands total about 1,700 square miles, more than a third of the land area comprises OKINAWA.

S

Sabang, Sumatra

The westernmost important port in the NETHER-LANDS EAST INDIES, Sabang, on Sumatra, had a good harbor but only limited resources. If properly developed, however, Sabang could have been used to project power into the Indian Ocean, an undertaking beyond the capacity of the Japanese, who occupied the place early in 1942 and remained in possession until their surrender. It served as the principal base for Italian and German submarine operations in the Far East.

See also GERMANY IN THE PACIFIC WAR; ITALY IN THE PACIFIC WAR.

SACO

See SINO-AMERICAN COOPERATIVE ORGANIZATION.

Saguenay Class, Canadian Destroyers

Canada's Saguenay Class destroyers, built 1929–31, were sisters to the British Acasta class. They saw considerable service in the northeast Pacific.

Saigon, Indo-China

A major city, with a good river port, Saigon had only limited facilities to service ships. There were important French military installations there in 1940. It was several times bombed by US aircraft in the closing months of the war.

Sailors, Homemade Alcohol

Sailors and strong drink have been an inseparable combination since time immemorial. Unfortunately for Uncle Sam's bluejackets, potable alcohol has been prohibited on US Navy ships since tee-totaling Secretary of the Navy Josephus Daniels banned it in 1914. The last night of legal booze found the fleet lying off Vera Cruz, with parties of officers rowing from ship to ship heroically trying to drink up every last drop before the midnight deadline. So the hardest stuff officially available on American ships was coffee, of which endless gallons were consumed. Indeed, British officers often complained of caffeine overdoses after staff conferences on American warships. This was one reason why such conferences tended to be on the foreign ships when US vessels were operating in conjunction with British or other Allied vessels. The Allies avoided caffeine jags and the Americans could be treated to some alcohol (in exchange, since the British were on tight rations for the entire war, the Americans always brought a few hams or some other items to donate to the officers' mess).

Improvisations were commonplace in the US Navy throughout the war. Given some rice and raisins, the seamen would brew up a rather powerful homemade whiskey called "tuba" (after an Asian plant used to make alcoholic drinks). This was potent stuff, usually concocted by shipfitters, cooks, or other below-deck types with access to the tools and supplies needed for assembling, operating, and hiding a still.

Alcohol content varied, but was usually high and unpredictable—"smoothness" varied from harsh on up. Other improvisations were common. For example, the advent of alcohol-fueled TORPE-DOES was shortly followed by the discovery that "torpedo juice" was drinkable, if strained through stale bread or some other dense material, which improved the taste. A few sailors are said to have rigged up stills to improve the character of torpedo juice, which was already 160 proof, and were reportedly able to boost it to 190 proof.

Some captains were more fanatical about eliminating tuba (and other such improvisations) than others. A few captains and even senior officers (like William HALSEY) winked at minor violations of the ban. Some officers even went out of their way to circumvent it, procuring hard liquor for "medicinal" purposes and issuing it to their men on special occasions. There was also quite a lot of beer shipped to the fleet, which was periodically issued for consumption "off the ship." The sailors would literally take one of the ship's boats a few hundred yards from their vessel, consume their two cans of brew, and then come back so the next batch of men could do the same.

On the whole, let's just say that a sailor was in a lot more trouble if he left his ship drunk than if he returned to it in that state.

Saipan, Battle of

A critical stage in the CENTRAL PACIFIC CAMPAIGN, the battle for Saipan began on 15 June 1944, when the US Second and Fourth Marine

Troops of the 27th Infantry Division land on Saipan from LSTs beached offshore, June–July 1944.

A Marine discovers a Japanese woman with four children and a dog, hiding in a cave on Saipan, June 21, 1944. This family was lucky. Thousands of Japanese civilians on Saipan committed suicide—willingly or otherwise—rather than fall prisoner to the Americans.

Divisions began what was the largest of the invasions in the MARIANAS Islands. Saipan had been controlled by the Japanese for 30 years, and they had garrisoned it with 30,000 troops (43rd Division, 47th Brigade, two separate infantry battalions, and a naval infantry brigade). The Japanese were determined to win. To this end, over a hundred TANKS were assembled on the island. On the second and third days of the battle the Japanese used these tanks to spearhead attacks on the Marines. These armored operations failed, as American tanks (M-4 Shermans) and antitank weapons were far more capable. The Japanese tanks were

annihilated in short order, as was the accompanying infantry. Nevertheless, these were the largest tank battles in the Pacific outside of China.

The aggressive Japanese tactics on Saipan made life exciting for the Marines, and led to more Japanese troops getting killed a lot sooner. But American firepower and infantry prevailed, and by early July the Japanese defenses were in tatters. On July 7, many of the surviving Japanese (about 3,000 troops) made a suicidal charge on American lines. The attack was stopped and after that there was only mopping up until the island was declared secure on 9 July. In the final stages of the fighting thousands of Japanese and Saipanese civilians committed suicide, voluntarily or under duress from Japanese troops.

In addition to the two Marine divisions, the army's 27th Infantry Division came ashore to help finish the job. This led to the "Battle of the SMITHS" as General Smith (USMC), commanding all forces on Saipan, relieved General Smith, commanding the army division. The dispute is still argued among army and Marine officers to this day and spotlights the differences in operating procedures between the two services. Nevertheless, the CASUALTIES were heavy on the American side. The Second Marine Division had 1,256 dead and 6,170 wounded. The Fourth Marine Division had 1,107 dead and 6,612 wounded (including the uncle of one of the authors), while the 27th Division suffered 1,034 dead and 3,566 wounded. While most of the Japanese garrison fought to the death, for the first time in the Pacific several hundred PRISONERS were taken. Not all of the Japanese prisoners were captured unconscious or while wounded. Many laid down their arms and gave up.

Saipan, Marianas

Long in Japanese hands, this island located about a thousand miles south of Tokyo had a large Japanese population, with an extensive system of air bases under construction in 1941. There were only limited port facilities, however.

Saipan Class, US Light Carriers

Inspired by the success of the INDEPENDENCE CLASS, CVL-48 *Saipan* (1944–1945–1946) and CVL-49 *Wright* (1944–1945–1947) were intended as light carriers based on the BALTIMORE CLASS heavy cruiser design. Unlike the Independence class, they were built from the keel up as carriers. Had the war continued into 1946 they would certainly have seen service. Two additional vessels were never laid down, and both ships saw only limited service before being relegated to the reserve. They were scrapped in the 1970s.

Sakai, Saburo (1916–   )

A Japanese Navy enlisted fighter pilot, Sakai was the highest scoring Japanese naval ACE to survive the war (4th, with 64 victories). Educated in an American mission school, Sakai enlisted in the Imperial Navy in the 1930s and became a fighter pilot. He first saw combat during the CHINA INCIDENT, and was heavily engaged from then until he was wounded during the GUADALCANAL Campaign, losing an eye after he managed to fly the thousand miles to RABAUL, he was sent home to Japan to recuperate, and later became a flying instructor, his injuries presumably disqualifying him from further combat. However, late in the war he flew several interceptor missions against B-29s.

See also KELLY, COLIN.

Sakakida, Richard (1921–1996)

A Japanese American from HAWAII, Sakakida was drafted in early 1941. An honor graduate of high school ROTC, he skipped basic training and was trained as an intelligence agent. With another young Japanese American, he was sent to the Philippines to spy on resident Japanese. Disguised as merchant seamen who had jumped ship, Sakakida and his associate arrived in the Philippines in April 1941. They soon made contact with the local Japanese community, convincing them that they were unhappy with America. Information they provided proved useful in rounding up Japanese agents and freezing Japanese assets after PEARL HARBOR. Both men served on BATAAN and CORREGIDOR, as uniformed members of the army, interrogating prisoners of war, translating documents, and helping decrypt Japanese messages. Sakakida's associate was among those evacuated in the closing weeks of the first Philippine campaign (ending up on MacArthur's staff in Australia). However, Sakakida gave up his place on the aircraft to a married man and remained behind.

Captured by the Japanese, he managed to resume his "cover," even convincing them that his services as a translator and interrogator had been forced through torture. Although some Japanese officers were unconvinced, by mid–1943 he had been released, to become a civilian employee at Japanese headquarters in Manila. From this position he was able to supply information to Filipino GUERRILLAS, who passed it on to MACARTHUR's headquarters. In addition to supplying information that proved essential to the Allied victory in the Battle of the BISMARCK SEA, he once engineered the release of a large number of guerrillas by disguising himself as a Japanese officer. When Japanese headquarters withdrew from Manila into northern Luzon in early 1945, Sakakida went with them. Shortly after the surrender of Japan he made contact with American troops. Save for the period when he was on active duty on Bataan and Corregidor he had been undercover for over 1,600 days.

After the war Sakakida served as a prosecution witness in the trial of General YAMASHITA, and during the court-martial of at least one American collaborator. He remained in the army, retiring in 1975 as a heavily decorated lieutenant colonel.

Aside from Frank FUJITA, he was the only Japanese-American prisoner of the Japanese during the war.

Ref: Crost, *Honor by Fire*; Harrington, *Yankee Samurai*.

Samar, Battle off

One of the more dramatic naval battles of the war occurred during the Leyte Campaign in late 1944. On October 25, after several days of cat and mouse searching and fighting among the many small Philippine islands, a Japanese task force of four battleships, six cruisers, and 10 destroyers sneaked through the San Bernardino Strait at night and in the predawn hours appeared off the coast of Leyte,

and prepared to attack U.S. amphibious shipping in Leyte Gulf. The only American warships present were an escort carrier task force with the radio call sign "Taffy 3" (six escort carriers, three destroyers, and four destroyer escorts). There were 10 other escort carriers within flying distance (a hundred miles or so), and these sixteen carriers had available 235 fighters and 143 TBF AVENGER bombers. Although some of these aircraft were already on their way to attack land targets when the Japanese were discovered at dawn, all aircraft were soon turned against the Japanese ships. What followed was one of the wildest shootouts of the war. The Japanese could hardly believe their good fortune and immediately attacked what they believed were the American fleet carriers, beyond which presumably lay the scores of American transports and troopships standing off the Leyte shore. But after two and a half hours of combat, the combination of hundreds of American aircraft and desperate attacks by the handful of US destroyers convinced the Japanese that they were up against a strong opposition. The Japanese withdrew, still under attack by US aircraft. American losses were one carrier, two destroyers, and one destroyer escort. Some 1,130 US sailors were killed and 913 wounded. The Japanese lost three cruisers in the battle, and most of their remaining ships were damaged.

See also LEYTE GULF, BATTLE OF.

Samoa

An archipelago of 15 islands totaling c. 1,150 square miles in central Polynesia, Samoa was controlled mostly by Britain, but six of the easternmost islands, smaller, (c. 77 square miles) including the fine harbor at Tutuila, were in US hands. Until the late 1930s the islands were virtually bereft of military facilities, but with war raging in Europe, by 1940 the United States was developing air and naval stations there. Samoa formed a link in the chain of bases between the United States, Australia and New Zealand. Not attacked by the Japanese, the islands were on their list of "Far South

Pacific" objectives had they won the Battle of MID-WAY.

In their part of Samoa (eight major islands, c. 1,080 square miles), the British recruited many labor troops and raised a local defense force, which did not see combat.

American Samoa was under the administrative control of the navy from its acquisition in the late 1800s until after World War II. For local security, the navy raised the Fitafita Guards, composed of Samoan men under naval officers. Initially a mostly police and ceremonial force, the Fitafitas, who wore lavalavas, were reorganized as light infantry on the eve of the Pacific War, while the Marines recruited the First Samoan Battalion, USMC Reserve. During the war many Samoans also joined the navy. Well over a thousand men served in uniform, and many other people, women as well as men, in labor detachments.

Ref: White and Lindstrom, eds., *The Pacific Theater*.

San Diego, California, United States

With nearby Coronado, the second most important American naval base in the Pacific (after PEARL HARBOR), with enormous resources, extensively supported by several major air bases, and easy access by rail to the rest of the United States.

San Francisco, California, United States

Including not only the city of San Francisco, but also the extensive port facilities surrounding San Francisco Bay, one of the premier harbors of the world, with valuable naval and air bases at Alameda and Treasure Island, considerable industrial resources, and access by rail to the rest of the United States.

See also PORT CHICAGO MUTINY.

Sandakan, Borneo

A very small port, with limited capacity and no facilities, of some value as a local base for domi-

nating the Sulu Sea and northern BORNEO. Japanese forces occupied it early in 1942, and remained there until the end of the war.

Sangamon Class, US Escort Carriers

These four ships were converted from incomplete tanker versions of the standard Maritime Commission C3 hull. The Sangamons (all 1939–1939–1942) were much superior to LONG ISLAND or BOGUE, being larger (23,800 tons full load), somewhat faster (18 knots), with slightly more aircraft (31), better defensive armament, and more internal space, making servicing the aircraft much easier. As an added bonus, they retained an enormous fuel capacity (over 12,000 tons), being, in effect, self-escorting tankers. They were among the best escort carriers, and reached the Pacific in early 1943, supporting operations in the SOLOMONS and helping to compensate for the desperate shortage of fleet carriers. They saw considerable service, and inspired the design of the COMMENCEMENT BAY CLASS.

The four, *Sangamon*, CVE-26; *Suwannee*, CVE-27; *Chenango*, CVE-28; and *Santee*, CVE-29 were all scrapped in 1960–62.

Sansapor, New Guinea

A good harbor, with no facilities, on the northwesternmost part of NEW GUINEA, with the possibility of being used as a base to dominate portions of the Philippine Sea, the entire "Vulture's Head" region of New Guinea, and surrounding regions.

Santa Cruz Islands

A small volcanic group about 400 miles north of ESPIRITU SANTO, in the NEW HEBRIDES. Under Australian control before the war, the small number of Europeans were evacuated in mid-1942, and the islands virtually ignored thereafter. Some recruiting for labor service occurred in 1943. Although well suited for an advanced base, only NDENI figured in the war, and then only marginally.

Santa Cruz Islands, Battle of

The late October 1942 Battle of the Santa Cruz Islands was the result of a Japanese effort to undertake a major ground offensive on GUADALCANAL supported by carrier aircraft. Unable to secure command of the sea through a naval engagement, the Japanese now decided to do so by capturing Henderson Field, through a combination of ground attack and naval air assault.

As YAMAMOTO was willing to commit a fleet of four battleships, five carriers (with 267 aircraft), eight heavy cruisers, three light cruisers, plus 38 destroyers, a dozen SUBMARINES, and a number of auxiliary vessels, as well as considerable land-based air power, this might have worked if the Japanese Army had not taken too long to "soften up" the Marines. The fleet was supposed to intervene in the ground action on October 22, but the army stretched out the softening up process until the 26th. This gave newly appointed Allied theater commander VAdm William F. HALSEY time to strengthen his forces, calling up the *Enterprise* Task Force, which was at NOUMEA, on the 22nd (thus giving him two carriers with 169 aircraft, plus one battleship, six cruisers, and 14 destroyers), while sending all available troops and aircraft to bolster Guadalcanal.

So while Halsey grew stronger during the protracted ground fighting for Henderson Field, Yamamoto grew weaker, as his ships kept to sea for days on end, consuming precious fuel, developing engine trouble (which forced one carrier back to TRUK), and exhausting their crews. The Japanese Army, of course, lost the battle for Henderson, which for a time was so desperate that US Army infantrymen were fed into the front-line Marine units. Had Yamamoto known this, there would never have been a Battle of the Santa Cruz Islands. But at 0126 on 25 October an Imperial Navy liaison officer with the troops on Guadalcanal signaled that the airfield was now in Japanese hands. So Yamamoto ordered the fleet south.

American PBYs spotted VAdm Chuichi NAGUMO's carriers, SHOKAKU and *Zuikaku*, at about noon on 25 October. RAdm Thomas KINKAID, commanding the *Enterprise* Task Force, attempted a strike that afternoon but failed to locate the enemy. Although each side groped for the other, neither was successful. During the night of 25–26 October Kinkaid maintained a steady course northwestward, toward the probable location of the Japanese. Before dawn he launched several scouts, and these soon apprised him of the location of the enemy carriers. Passing the word back to Halsey in Noumea, he received the order, "ATTACK—REPEAT—ATTACK!" Kinkaid was ahead of him, having already dispatched a scouting group, and at 0740 several dive bombers inflicted severe damage on the light carrier ZUIHO, knocking her out of the battle.

However, Japanese fleet commander Nobutake KONDO's scouts had by this time spotted *Hornet* and ordered a major strike. Shortly afterward, *Hornet* and *Enterprise* both dispatched major strikes (by some accounts the two hostile air groups passed each other en route to their respective targets; it is unclear as to whether this actually occurred).

Kinkaid adopted the then-standard defensive formation, with his carriers each surrounded by a ring of escorts (later in the war it was found better to concentrate all carriers within a single ring of escorts), with a healthy CAP overhead. *Enterprise* was about 10 miles from *Hornet* when the Japanese struck, at just about 0900. A fortuitous rain squall sprang up, shielding "The Big E" from the enemy, who promptly concentrated on *Hornet*. The latter took several bombs, two suicidal crash dives, and two TORPEDOES, knocking her completely out of action, before the Japanese broke off the attack on her to work over *Enterprise* as she emerged from the rain squall. Superb ship handling, and voluminous fire from the battleship SOUTH DAKOTA and anti-aircraft cruiser *San Juan*, kept *Enterprise* from serious harm. At just about the time *Hornet* was being battered, the American air strikes hit Nagumo's carriers, quickly inflicting damage on SHOKAKU, knocking her out of action and heavily damaging a cruiser as well. But the Japanese had more carriers than the Americans. Kondo ordered strikes from his two undamaged carriers, *Zuikaku* and JUNYO. Kondo's strike hit at 1101. Although *Enterprise*'s escorts took some damage, she escaped unscathed. Not so the already severely battered *Hornet*, which took three more hits. She would later have to be abandoned after an unsuccessful attempt to sink her; Japanese destroyers sank her with torpedoes the next day. As Kondo's strike winged its way home, Kinkaid decided to break off the action and began steaming southward. Surprisingly, Kondo did not pursue. He might have essayed another air strike, still having two intact carriers and lots of pilots. Apparently unaware of the extent of the damage he had inflicted on the US Navy, Kondo believed that the action would be renewed the next day. It was not.

Santa Cruz was a tactical victory for the Japanese, for they inflicted greater losses than they suffered; indeed, it left them with the only undamaged carriers in the Pacific. But they had suffered about 100 pilots lost, and pilot replacement was becoming an increasingly serious problem. Strategically the battle was an American success, for the Japanese once again failed to crush the numerically inferior US Navy, thereby failing to secure control of the seas, thereby failing to retake Guadalcanal.

Sapwahfik (Ngatik), Caroline Islands

A small atoll southwest of PONAPE, in the CAROLINE ISLANDS. Although under Japanese control from World War I, Sapwahfik was little affected by Japanese rule, and preserved a unique cultural heritage. During the 1830s the entire male population of the atoll was massacred by British and American sailors, aided by some warriors from Ponape, who then settled down with the local women. Sapwahfik developed its own form of PIDGIN and became Christian, traits that survived Spanish, German, and finally Japanese rule, all of which touched the atoll only lightly, mostly in the form of increased trade and the recruitment of men for work on Ponape.

During the war, many men and women from Sapwahfik were recruited for work on Ponape, but the island was otherwise unaffected. It was, in fact, one of the few inhabited islands in the Carolines that was never bombed or subject to surface bombardment. The islanders attributed their good fortune to messages traced on beach sands in English saying things like "No Japanese on this Island" and "Help this island," and claims that US pilots dropped food, tobacco, and other valuable gifts, and that American flying boats and floatplanes occasionally landed in the lagoon bearing gifts. While the accuracy of these claims cannot be established beyond oral tradition, it is known that US seaplane and flying boat pilots made informal visits to other islands.

Ref: White and Lindstrom, eds., *The Pacific Theater*.

Sasakawa, Ryoicho (1899–1995)

Right-wing Japanese politician, industrialist, expansionist, and militarist, Sasakawa, a former army officer, formed the Patriotic Masses Party in 1931 to promote his ideas. He made an enormous fortune from investments in MANCHURIA during the Japanese occupation. Wealthy enough to maintain his own "air force" of some 20 bombers, in 1939 he flew one to Rome, where he met with Mussolini. During World War II he served in the Diet. After the war he was arrested, tried as a war criminal, and served four years in prison. He later recouped his wealth through a variety of schemes—including motorboat racing and gambling—and became a noted philanthropist, anticommunist, and ultranationalist. He was the last surviving prominent Japanese war criminal.

Sasebo, Honshu, Japan

A major port, with important naval and air installations, Sasebo was one of the four principal bases of the Imperial Navy. It specialized in the construction of destroyers and lighter warships, and was the headquarters of one of the four SNLF commands.

Saumarez Class, British Destroyers

A further evolution of Britain's TRIBAL CLASS, the Saumarez class—or S-class—destroyers were laid down 1941–1942, launched in 1942–1943, and entered service 1943–1944. Including the very similar T, U, V, and W classes, the ROYAL NAVY had some 80 ships of this design in service by the end of the war. Several were active with the British Far Eastern and Pacific Fleet in the latter part of the war. HMS *Saumarez* herself was one of the destroyers that took part in the last surface action of the war, the Battle of PENANG, during which they sank the heavy cruiser *Haguro*.

Savo Island, Battle of

On the night of 9 August 1942, a Japanese squadron steamed undetected into the waters north of GUADALCANAL and within a few minutes inflicted the most serious and most one-sided reverse ever suffered by the US Navy in a surface action, sinking four heavy cruisers (one of them Australian) and a destroyer, killing 1,270 men and wounding 709 others, all in about 30 minutes, with virtually no loss to themselves. These CASUALTIES amounted to about two-thirds the number of the US ground troops killed during the entire Guadalcanal campaign, which lasted from August of 1942 into February of 1943.

Savo Island is a small, conical island at the north end of the sound between Guadalcanal and Florida Island, which later became known as IRON BOTTOM SOUND.

The course of the battle may be told simply. The Japanese military headquarters in RABAUL was alarmed when it received word that its base on Guadalcanal had been invaded by US troops on 8 August 1942. Knowing that there would be American ships in the area for a while, a number of warships were sent south. An Allied reconnaissance plane actually detected the approaching squadron, but its report was misrouted. After 0100 hours on 9 August, a Japanese squadron of five heavy cruisers, two light cruisers, and a destroyer under Admiral MIKAWA slipped into Iron Bottom Sound to the south of Savo, evading a pair of US destroyers clumsily patrolling the western approaches to the sound. There were three Allied squadrons in the sound. One was posted at the eastern end of the southern channel around Savo, another at the eastern end of the northern channel around Savo, and the third much farther back, protecting the transports unloading supplies for the Marines. The battle took little more than a half hour. Superior Japanese night fighting training counted heavily in their favor. They spotted the southern group of Allied cruisers and destroyers at 0136, and fired TORPEDOES four minutes later, sinking a cruiser and a destroyer, and heavily damaging one more of each within minutes. Then the Japanese squadron turned north, splitting into two columns, with the heavy cruisers on the right, and passed on both sides of the Allied northern squadron, opening fire between 0150 and 0156. Despite the fact that they should have been alerted to the presence of the enemy by the fate of the southern force, the US cruisers were caught unprepared and were badly shot up; three were sunk, one of which did land some hits on the Japanese flagship, the only damage inflicted on the Japanese. At this point Mikawa ought to have pressed eastward, to shoot up the transports and their protective screen. However, at about 0200 he changed course to the northwest, and the Japanese drew off. Their victory had been won at the cost of fewer than 50 casualties, with no serious damage to any of their ships. Japanese reluctance to push on and go after the American transports denied them a decisive victory. The Japanese commander did not know how many warships the Allies had off Guadalcanal and did not want to risk running into a larger, and now fully alerted, enemy force.

The disastrous outcome of the Battle of Savo Island had several causes. The Japanese were clearly superior in night combat, for which they had trained intensively. Indeed, their lookouts spotted the Allied ships even before Allied radar detected the Japanese squadron. The pattern maintained by the US destroyers supposedly patrolling the channels around Savo Island left approaches to Iron Bottom Sound uncovered for long periods. The patrol sectors and deployment of the two squadrons near Savo Island were very poorly thought out. In addition, the Allies were overconfident, believing that they were definitely superior to the Japanese, and were excessively enamored of the abilities of radar, which most of the senior officers did not understand at all. Communications between the three squadrons were not well coordinated. There was also a disrupted chain of command; since the senior officer, Britain's Admiral CRUTCHLEY, was at a conference with his superior, Admiral Richmond Kelly TURNER (USN), it was unclear who was in overall command of the ships. Finally, the US and Australian sailors had been on full alert for several days, standing by their guns, even eating and sleeping by them, so that they were literally exhausted at their posts. Alert procedures were shortly modified to permit a less intense state of readiness.

Savo Island, the Cover-up

The commander of the Allied squadron defeated in the Battle of Savo Island, Britain's RAdm V. A. C. CRUTCHLEY, was not present during the engagement, having gone off to a staff conference with the overall local commander, RAdm Richmond Kelly TURNER (USN), taking his flagship, heavy cruiser HMAS *Australia*, with him. After the battle both Crutchley and Turner continued in command. As the 20th anniversary of the battle approached, a prominent conservative monthly advanced the theory that the ROOSEVELT administration had promoted a massive cover-up of Crutchley's incompetence in order to preserve good relations with the British.

In fact, aside from the general excellence of the Japanese at night naval combat, the disaster that befell the Australian and American ships off Savo Island was due more to failures of prewar doctrine and training, a continuing peacetime mindset, a surprisingly durable contempt for the enemy, and excessive confidence in the as-yet inadequate ra-

dar, than to command failures by Crutchley and Turner. If Crutchley had been present at the battle, the Japanese would probably have killed him and sunk his flagship as well.

SB2A Buccaneer, US Carrier Dive Bomber

The SB2A Buccaneer was an unsuccessful American dive bomber design. It first flew in June 1941, and 750 aircraft were produced in 1942 and 1943. None were used in combat, serving instead as trainers and target tugs.

See also AIRCRAFT TYPES, DEVELOPMENT; CARRIERS, DESIGNING AIRCRAFT FOR.

SB2C Helldiver, US Carrier Dive Bomber

The US SB2C Helldiver was a replacement for the SBD DAUNTLESS dive bomber. Unfortunately, the SB2C took so long to enter PRODUCTION that, by the time it arrived in 1943, the TBF AVENGER had already taken over many of its missions. The SB2C was a major improvement over the SBD Dauntless, but dedicated aircraft types for dive bombing and TORPEDO bombing were increasingly seen as unnecessary. It was obvious that carriers needed more fighters and, by 1944, many fighters were being equipped to carry bombs. The age of "multipurpose" aircraft was dawning, and the Helldiver simply arrived at the wrong time. Although some 5,000 were produced, they were not one of the favorite carrier aircraft.

See also AIRCRAFT TYPES, DEVELOPMENT; CARRIERS, DESIGNING AIRCRAFT FOR.

SBD Dauntless, US Carrier Dive Bomber

The US SBD Dauntless dive bomber entered service in 1941 and was considered obsolete even then. The prewar experts were wrong, as the SBD proved one of the most effective carrier bombers of the war. Its long range (1,200 miles for bombing, 20% more for scouting) and reliable operation enabled the SBD to rack up a credible war record. SBDs sunk 300,000 tons of enemy shipping, as well as 18 warships of all sizes, including six carriers. It could defend itself, shooting down 138 Japanese aircraft, while losing only 80 to enemy fighters. Nearly 6,000 were delivered, including 1,000 for the US Army as the A-24. Despite its excellent record, a replacement, the Helldiver, was already in the works when the war broke out. Moreover, the TBF AVENGER, the replacement for the hapless TBD1 DEVASTATOR torpedo bomber, proved to be a capable dive bomber also. TORPEDO bombing declined in importance as the war went on, and the TBF Avenger was used, quite successfully, as a regular bomber most of the time. What kept the SBD in service throughout the war was its versatility and delays in getting the Helldiver into service. Even

so, SBDs went from half of all carrier aircraft in mid-1942 to about 6% by mid-1944. Many SBDs were transferred to the Marines for land-based operations. A testimony of the SBD's worth can be seen in its use into the 1950s by many foreign air forces. The French used SBDs during the early stages of their war in Vietnam.

See also AIRCRAFT TYPES, DEVELOPMENT; CARRIERS, DESIGNING AIRCRAFT FOR.

SC Seahawk, US Reconnaissance Floatplane

The SC Seahawk was an American floatplane used on cruisers and battleships for scouting. It was a new design, to replace the 1930s models in use through most of the war. The first SC flew in early 1944, and only nine were built (out of 500 ordered) before the war ended. The SC had a top speed of 312 MPH and a range of 625 miles. Armament consisted of two .50 caliber machine guns and up to 500 pounds of bombs or depth charges.

See also AIRCRAFT TYPES, DEVELOPMENT; CARRIERS, DESIGNING AIRCRAFT FOR; RECONNAISSANCE, NAVAL.

Scott, Norman (1889–1942)

Norman Scott graduated from Annapolis in 1911 and served in destroyers during World War I, being decorated for heroic action when his ship was sunk by a U-boat in the Atlantic. Between the wars he served as a presidential aide, attended several navy schools, and held various staff and line assignments, including the heavy cruiser PENSACOLA. By 1941 he was on the staff of the chief of naval operations. From this post in June of 1942 he was promoted to temporary rear admiral and given command of various task forces in the South Pacific. A tough but very well liked commander, Scott drove his men hard, training them in night tactics to meet the Japanese, hitherto masters of the art. As a result, Scott neatly dished up an enemy squadron in the Battle of CAPE ESPERANCE (October 11–12 1942), for which he was named a

Navy ordnancemen loading belted .30 caliber machine-gun ammunition on an SBD Dauntless dive bomber, Norfolk Naval Air Station, Virginia, September 1942.

permanent rear admiral. Scott might have gone on to greater things, but navy regulations intervened. In early November he was superseded in command by Dan CALLAGHAN, whose commission as a regular rear admiral antedated Scott's by a few days, despite the fact that Callaghan had been skippering a desk for most of the war. Scott was killed in the Japanese ambush of Callaghan's squadron during the night action off GUADALCANAL on November 12–13, 1942, a few minutes before Callaghan himself perished. Both men were awarded the MEDAL OF HONOR

Seabees, US Navy Construction Battalions

The impetus for the organization of the famous "Seabees" was the need for the navy to quickly prepare forward areas for use as bases. Prewar experience with contracted construction workers on outlying islands such as Wake and MIDWAY had demonstrated their probable unreliability in time of war. Not only did they insist on strict adherence to the terms of their union contracts, but they were also ineligible to serve in combat, not only for lack of training but also because of their civilian status. This problem was demonstrated most clearly during the Battle for WAKE ISLAND in December 1941, when the nearly 1,150 construction workers on the island proved more of a hindrance to the defense than a help, an impression reinforced by difficulties with construction workers on Midway in June of 1942.

Fortunately, RAdm Ben Moreell, chief of the Bureau of Yards and Docks, had devoted some thought to this problem before the war, and came up with the idea of creating a combat engineer corps for the navy, men organized, trained, equipped, and disciplined to serve as construction workers capable of defending themselves.

The first Seabee battalions—the name Seabee derived from the initials CB, for Construction Battalion—were organized in March of 1942. They were raised from construction workers, mostly men otherwise unsuited for normal combat duty by rea-

son of age, thereby economizing on manpower. In fact, many enlisted Seabees were World War I veterans. The average age of the enlisted men in the Seabees was 31, about five years older than the average for the armed forces as a whole. Enlisted men were recruited from professional specialists in virtually every civilian construction trade, with considerable cooperation from industry and unions. Their officers were recruited from the navy's Civil Engineering Corps, which normally builds docks and barracks, and from reservists with construction industry backgrounds. Such reservists made the best officers, since Seabees were notoriously careless about military propriety. As one admiral put it, "They're a rough, tough bunch of men who don't give a damn about anything but getting the job done, the war won, and going home."

About 350,000 men served in the Seabees, who were organized into battalions and regiments, and occasionally brigades.

The first Seabee unit to enter combat was the Sixth CB Battalion, which landed on GUADALCANAL on 1 September 1942. Using a lot of captured Japanese construction equipment, they completed Henderson Field under trying conditions, suffering attacks by Japanese air and naval units, and having to defend themselves against enemy snipers as well. Thereafter Seabees were active in every theater of the war, but were of particular importance in the Pacific, usually getting to work even before the troops were off the beaches. Seabees often developed enormously creative solutions to construction problems, frequently inventing new techniques that were subsequently applied to civilian construction.

Their motto was "Can Do!" and their mascot was a bee, wearing a sailor's cap and armed with a Tommy gun and various tools.

Seafire, British Carrier Fighter

The Seafire was a navalized version of Britain's SPITFIRE fighter. Some 2,000 were built. As the Spitfire went through its many wartime versions, the Seafires were produced to the same plans with the addition of folding wings and other modifications needed for carrier operation. The Seafire was an effective carrier aircraft, but had a weak undercarriage, so that the airframe tended to shake apart after too many carrier landings. PRODUCTION continued after the war.

See also AIRCRAFT TYPES, DEVELOPMENTS; CARRIERS, DESIGNING AIRCRAFT FOR.

Seaplane Tenders and Carriers

The enormous distances between land in the Pacific led both Japan and the United States to make considerable use of seaplanes and floatplanes for reconnaissance, since they could land on and take off from water. Smaller floatplanes could be carried on cruisers and battleships, but large seaplanes, which had much greater range, required special vessels to serve as home bases.

The US Navy had 74 seaplane tenders during the war, in 10 classes. Of these, 24 were prewar conversions from other types: the former carrier *Langley*, 14 old "four stacker" destroyers, and nine old minesweepers. The remaining classes were built 1940–45.

Seaplane tenders, most of which could make only about 20 knots, could support their charges from any convenient moderately sheltered waters, and it was not unusual for them to be more or less permanently stationed in an area.

In contrast to American practice, Japan did not have seaplane tenders. Instead, the Imperial Navy built seaplane carriers, a category of warship unknown to most navies. Seaplane tenders supported multi-engine aircraft, that took off from and landed on water. Japan's seaplane carriers were capable of launching small seaplanes from catapults. The Imperial Navy was keen on using non-carrier aircraft for reconnaissance purposes, thereby reserving all aircraft in an air group for combat missions. This was one reason for the existence of the TONE CLASS heavy cruisers, with their large complement of floatplanes, and also for the use of seaplane carriers, the idea being that they could accompany the fleet and conduct reconnaissance.

Secrecy

More than a half-century after its end there are still a surprising number of things about the Second

US SEAPLANE TENDERS						
Class	Launched	Displ.	Speed	Avgas	Number	Note
Langley (AV–3)	1912	11,000	15	30.0	1	A
"Bird" (AVP–1)	1917–19	950	13.5	40.0	9	
Clemson (AVD–4)	1918–21	1,200	24	50.0	14	B
Curtiss (AV–4)	1940	12,053	18	269.6	2	
Currituck (AV–7)	1943–44	15,000	19.2	278.0	4	
Barnegat (AVP–10)	1941–45	2,040	20	80.0	38	C
Tangier (AV–8)	1943	11,760	16	312.0	1	
Pocomoke (AV–9)	1943	11,760	17	291.0	1	
Chandeleur (AV–10)	1944	11,760	16	300.0	1	
Whiting (AV–14)	1944–45	12,000	16	312.0	4	D

Key: Class, name ship of the type; Launched, year of launching; Displ., standard displacement; Speed, in knots; Avgas, aviation fuel carried, in thousands of gallons; Number, units completed; Note, as below:

A. Sunk off Java, 27 February 1942, while ferrying aircraft.

B. Former Clemson Class destroyers, converted 1939–40. Many of them were converted to other uses beginning in 1943, as the Barnegat Class AVPs became available.

C. After the war they were turned over to the Coast Guard.

D. Properly the Kenneth Whiting Class, converted from standard C–3 merchant hulls requisitioned while still on the ways. Several additional units were canceled.

JAPANESE SEAPLANE CARRIERS AND TENDERS

Class	Launched	Displ.	Speed	A/C	Avgas	Number	Note
Notoro	1920	14,050	12	10	??	1	A
Kamoi	1922	17,000	15	22	??	1	B
Chitose	1936–37	11,000	29	24	??	2	C
Mizuho	1938	10,929	22	24	??	1	D
Nisshin	1939	11,217	28	20	??	1	E
Akitsushima	1941	4,650	19	1	??	1	F
Maru Types	??	6,000 to 9,000	10–14	8	??	9	G

Key: As previous table; A/C, number of aircraft carried; Note, as below:

A. Converted from a tanker in 1924; reconverted to a tanker in 1942.

B. Converted from a tanker 1932–33 and reverted to same 1943. Sunk in Hong Kong Harbor by US carrier aircraft, April 5, 1945.

C. Built purposely to be converted to light carriers, which was done 1942–43.

D. A modified *Chitose*, she could carry midget submarines in lieu of some aircraft. Sunk 2 May 1942 by a US submarine, which probably prevented her from being converted into an escort carrier.

E. An improved *Mizuho*, able to carry 700 mines, in lieu of some aircraft, or midget submarines. Sunk by American aircraft in the southwest Pacific, July 22, 1943. Two somewhat larger sisters were projected but never begun.

F. Actually a seaplane tender, able to service one large flying boat. Sunk by US carrier aircraft on September 24, 1944. Several proposed sister ships were never begun.

G. Converted from merchant ships 1937–42, these ships were apparently not commissioned into the Imperial Navy, as they retained their "maru" names. The figure under Displacement is GRT. They varied greatly in size and speed but were outfitted and armed identically. One was lost 28 May 1943, in the South Pacific. Most of the rest reverted to transports during the war. See also RECONNAISSANCE, NAVAL.

World War that remain secret, or are at best only partially known. Some of these unrevealed items deal with minor matters, but others are of considerable importance. For a variety of reasons, most are unlikely to be revealed for many years to come, if ever. Some British documents dating back to the Armada (1588) allegedly have never been made public.

There are many reasons for this secrecy. Bureaucratic inertia is one. At other times, such policies are designed to protect the lives, or at least the reputations, of certain people, politicians, or officers who found themselves entrapped in enemy espionage, or foreign officials, even enemy politicians and officers, who collaborated in the defeat of their own nations. And some things really ought to remain classified. For example, revealing where the remains of Hermann Göring and other Nazi leaders were disposed of could turn the site into a Nazi shrine, grounds enough for perpetual secrecy. Many times it's politically expedient to keep certain things secret, rather than open the proverbial can of worms.

Human nature and modern media being what they are, it's not surprising that people have a tendency to come up with theories about conspiracies, treachery, cover-ups, and other nefarious Machiavellian plottings, particularly in cases where they learn of unpleasant things that occurred and were classified. In fact, most of the secrets of World War II were declassified long ago. But the volume of materials is enormous, so interesting or important stories sometimes do not come before the public eye until someone stumbles across them and begins hurling charges about a "cover-up."

Security Breaches, Critical

For a variety of reasons, on several occasions during the war serious breaches of security occurred. Some of the most notable were as follows.

In December 1941, days before PEARL HARBOR, several newspapers published details of the War Department's "Germany First" plans. The information was presented as an example of conspiratorial war planning on the part of the ROOSEVELT administration. The leak may have had some influence on HITLER'S decision to declare war on the United States shortly after Pearl Harbor. The leak was later traced to an isolationist captain in the War Department, but there were suggestions that other officers of isolationist bent may have been involved, including Albert WEDEMEYER, then a lieutenant colonel serving under EISENHOWER in the Office of War Plans.

As part of its coverage of the Battle of MIDWAY, in June 1942 the *Chicago Tribune* casually revealed that one reason for the American victory was that the United States was able to read Japanese naval codes—in effect, revealing MAGIC. By good fortune the Japanese never learned of it. President Roosevelt, General MARSHALL, and senior officials chose to ignore the breach, rather than act against the paper and thereby draw attention to the incident. The source of the leak has never been determined. The *Chicago Tribune* was a notoriously anti-Roosevelt paper, and it is possible that an anti-Roosevelt officer or official in the War Department or the Navy Department passed along the information.

At a press conference in May 1943 Representative Andrew Jackson May, a member of the House Military Affairs Committee, announced that the Japanese were setting their depth charges to detonate too shallowly, thereby saving many US SUBMARINES from destruction. The Japanese apparently caught on to this leak and began increasing the settings on their depth charges. VAdm Charles Lockwood, chief of Pacific submarines, later stated that at least 10 US submarines had been lost as a result of May's indiscretion. May appears to have been taken to the woodshed by the Speaker of the House.

At a diplomatic reception in Moscow in October 1944 the Soviet foreign minister "casually" mentioned to the Japanese ambassador that US heavy bombers based in China were about to undertake operations against the Philippines, alerting the Japanese as to the next US objective in the Pacific.

In February 1945, *Amerasia*, a semi-monthly journal of Asian affairs, published portions of a top secret report on China's internal political situation that had been prepared by the OSS. The leak was traced to a Foreign Service officer who believed that the United States should not support CHIANG KAI-SHEK as leader of China, and who had been passing secret documents to *Amerasia*'s publisher, a Soviet sympathizer. Surprisingly, although indictments were issued against several of the participants, the case dragged on into the early 1950s and eventually disappeared in a series of cover-ups. It had little effect on Chinese-American relations.

See also SOVIET UNION.

Ref: Klehr and Radosh, *The Amerasia Spy Case.*

Sendai Class, Japanese Light Cruisers

The best of the older Japanese cruisers, the Sendais served as flotilla leaders during the war. Although lightly built ships, they took a surprising amount of punishment.

Sendai (1922–1925–1925) served as a flotilla leader during operations in the Philippines and East Indies, and was later in the SOLOMONS, fighting in the Second Battle of GUADALCANAL, before being sunk November 2, 1943 at EMPRESS AUGUSTA BAY, having taken numerous 6-inch hits.

Jintsu (1922–1923–1925) led a destroyer flotilla during the conquest of the Philippines and East Indies, fighting in the JAVA SEA, and later at the EASTERN SOLOMONS and KOLOMBANGARA, where she was sunk July 13, 1943, having been repeatedly hit by 6-inch and 5-inch shells.

Naka (1922–1925–1925) led a destroyer flotilla during operations in the Philippines and East Indies, and then with the Combined Fleet until she was sunk at TRUK by carrier aircraft on 17 February 1944.

Shakishima Islands, Ryukyu Islands

The southernmost group of the RYUKYU chain, the Shakishima Islands contained an important Japanese naval and air station during World War II. Since aircraft there could threaten Allied forces operating against Okinawa, in the spring of 1945 the group received a thorough going over by the British Pacific Fleet.

See also ROYAL NAVY.

Shanghai, China

Before the outbreak of the Sino-Japanese War Shanghai was the most important city in China, the center of business, industry, and banking. It was also the largest port in China, with considerable resources to build and service all but the largest vessels. The Japanese occupied most of Shanghai in 1937, after a hard fight with the Chinese. The part they did not occupy was the so-called International Sector, a district with considerable extraterritoriality, ruled by a commission of representatives from the Great Powers, including Japan. This was occupied in December 1941. The city subsequently served as an important rear-area base for Japanese forces in China and as a port of embarkation for Japanese units being transferred to other areas.

Sherman, Forrest P. (1896–1951)

Forrest P. Sherman attended MIT for a time before entering Annapolis in 1914. He graduated second in the three-year class of 1917, and served aboard ship in European waters during World War I. After the war he took flight training, served variously in fighter squadrons, in training assignments, including a tour as an instructor at Annapolis, on various staffs, and attended the Naval War College. In December 1941 he was on the staff of the chief of naval operations. In May 1942 he was named captain of the carrier WASP. When *Wasp* was sunk that September, he was assigned as chief of staff to Admiral John TOWERS, the principal aviation officer

in the Pacific Fleet, and in November 1943 became deputy chief of staff to NIMITZ, in which post he helped plan operations from the CAROLINES to OKINAWA. Present at the surrender of Japan, after the war he had a very distinguished career, working to strengthen the navy's influence in the defense reorganization of 1947, and tirelessly struggling to increase, the fleet's carrier forces, a victory that he had won at the time of his death, which occurred while he was still on active duty, as chief of naval operations.

Sherman, Frederick C. (1888–1957)

Nicknamed "Ted," Frederick C. Sherman graduated from the Naval Academy in 1910, and served for several years in battleships and armored cruisers, before transferring to SUBMARINES in 1914. He commanded several submarines during World War I, and after the war transferred to Naval Aviation. In the 1920s and 1930s he held various line, staff, and training assignments, attended the Naval War College, and in June 1940 became captain of the carrier LEXINGTON. He commanded *Lexington* in all her operations from PEARL HARBOR to CORAL SEA, when she was lost. He was the last man to leave the ship. Promoted to rear admiral, he served for a time as assistant chief of staff to Admiral King, before returning to the Pacific in October 1942, to command various carrier divisions through March 1944, meanwhile taking part in operations in the SOLOMONS, against RABAUL and BOUGAINVILLE, and during the TARAWA invasion. For a time in 1944 he commanded all naval aviation on the West Coast but returned to sea as a task force commander, fighting from Leyte through OKINAWA and in operations off the Japanese coast. In July 1945 he was named a vice admiral and commander of the First Fast Carrier Task Force, in which post he ended the war. His service in the postwar period was cut short by his participation in the so-called "Revolt of the Admirals," a group of senior naval officers who fought to preserve the navy's air arm in the face of threats from the air force after the "unification" of the armed forces in 1947.

Shimakaze, Japanese Destroyer

Shimakaze (1941–1942–1943) was intended to be the prototype of a large class (18 ships) of a radically new destroyer design. She was very large (nearly 2,600 tons standard), very fast (over 40 knots on trials), and very well armed (six 5-inch guns, numerous AA guns, and 15 TORPEDO tubes). However, wartime strains on shipbuilding (she took from August 1941 to May 1943 to build) limited the class to the one ship. Shimakaze saw only limited service before she was sunk by U.S. naval aircraft in the Philippines in mid-November 1944. During her 17 months of operational life, she was rearmed twice, each time enhancing antiaircraft capabilities at the expense of her surface combat weaponry.

Shinano, Japanese Aircraft Carrier

Arguably the most poorly designed carrier built during the war, Shinano (1940–1944–1944) was laid down as a battleship of the YAMATO CLASS, and ordered converted while still on the building ways, when about 50% complete. She retained much of her battleship armor. As redesigned she was not intended to serve as a fleet carrier, but rather as a support carrier, providing aircraft repair facilities and replacement aircraft for other carriers, an idea adopted by the British with more success in HMS UNICORN. As a result, Shinano could store

about 50% more aircraft than she could operate. She was sunk when Archerfish (SS-311) put four TORPEDOES into her on 29 November 1944, just 10 days after she had been completed and just a few hours into her maiden voyage. She required seven hours to sink, testimony to her excellent protection. The largest ship ever sunk by a submarine, Shinano was the largest aircraft carrier built until the nuclear-powered Enterprise was commissioned in 1960.

Shinyo, Japanese Escort Carrier

The German passenger liner Scharnhorst (1932–1934–1936) found refuge in Japan when the European War broke out in 1939. In early 1942 the Imperial Navy bought her for conversion into an escort carrier. Shinyo entered service at the end of 1943. The shortage of aircraft and trained airmen confined her to serving as an aircraft transport and training ship. She was TORPEDOED by Spadefish (SS-411) on 17 July 1944 off the coast of China (see table below).

Ship Sinkings, Accidental

The Soviet SUBMARINE sunk by I-25 was in the mid-Pacific, en route from VLADIVOSTOK to Panama. As she went down with all hands, it was not until after the war that her correct identity was known. I-19 may also have sunk two Soviet vessels.

The Soviet ships sunk by Sawfish (SS-276) and Sandlance (SS-381) were proceeding with lights

Flag	Vessel	Type	Date	Sinker	Locale
USSR	L–16	submarine	11 Oct. '42	HIJMS I–25	Mid-Pacific
USSR	Ilmen	merchantship	17 Feb. '43	USS Sawfish	Honshu
USSR	Kola	merchantship	17 Feb. '43	USS Sawfish	Tsushima Strait
USSR	Belorussia	merchantship	3 May '43	USS Sandlance	Tsushima Strait
USSR	Seiner No. 20	trawler	4 Jul. '43	USS Permit	North Pacific
US	Seawolf	submarine	4 Oct. '44	USS Rowell	Philippines
US	Extractor	salvor	3 Jan. '45	USS Guardfish	Marianas
Jap.	Awa Maru	transport	28 Mar. '45	USS Queenfish	China Seas
USSR	Transbalt	merchantship	13 Jun. '45	USS Spadefish	Sea of Japan

and neutrality markings, but were torpedoed because they were using Tsushima Strait, between Korea and Japan, rather than the more northern La Perouse Strait, between Japan and the Kuriles, having been rerouted due to severe icing. The United States acknowledged responsibility and paid an indemnity. The captain of the trawler sunk by *Permit* (SS-178) notified his government that the vessels had been damaged by Japanese attack, and that *Permit* had come to its rescue, thereby avoiding an international incident. In August 1944 *Tambor* (SS-198) fired upon but missed an unidentified Soviet vessel in the Sea of Japan.

The skipper of *Richard M. Rowell* (DE-403), LtCdr Harry A. Barnard Jr., was found at fault for having ignored recognition signals from *Seawolf* (SS-197) and also the safety zone in which she was operating (she was carrying supplies and personnel to Filipino GUERRILLAS. This was probably an unjust decision on the part of the navy. *Rowell* had been alerted to the presence of the submarine by naval aircraft off the escort carrier *Midway* (later renamed), and *Seawolf* was operating in an area in which a Japanese submarine had torpedoed a US ship only the day before. The loss of *Seawolf* seems, to have been the only occasion in the war of an American submarine being sunk by friendly fire.

A board of inquiry into the sinking of *Extractor* by *Guardfish* (SS-217) concluded that the skippers of both vessels were at fault. H. M. Babcock, of *Extractor*, was censured because he had not requested a repeat of a garbled transmission, which turned out to be a warning that *Guardfish* was in the area and he was to return to port immediately. Douglas Hammon, of *Guardfish*, was admonished for failing to properly identify his target, which he claimed looked like a Japanese submarine. The incident was the only one in the war in which a US submarine sank an American vessel. However, two US submarines are known to have been sunk by their own torpedoes, which malfunctioned: *Tuillbee* (SS-284) on 26 March 1944 and *Tang* (SS-306) on 24 October 1944, survivors living to tell the tale.

The AWA MARU incident is treated in a separate entry.

Shipbuilding, American Plans

During the 1930s the navy attempted to calculate its needs in the event of a future major war. Prewar construction programs were based on these estimates, as were the emergency programs that were adopted in 1940 and 1941. But the war came rather sooner than planned and was somewhat different than anticipated. As a result, the actual navy was quite different from the planned wartime strength of the navy.

The table gives a fair notion of the difference between the war that was expected and that which occurred. Clearly in the 1930s the navy's brass still believed the battleship would play a major role in the next war, and they planned to have an almost completely new battleline for the occasion. However, the exigencies of war resulted in fewer new

	Planned	Actual	Percent	Inc.	Canc.
Battleships: New	17	10	58.8	2	2
Old	5	15	300.0		
Carriers: Fleet	15	28	186.7	11	2
Light	0	9	—	2	0
Escort	5	85	1,700.0	11	4
A/C	1,600	4,500	281.3	1,920	310
Cruisers: Large	6	2	33.3	1	1
Heavy	26	38	146.2	14	0
Light	49	51	104.1	17	6
Destroyers: Fleet	450	620	133.8	65	5
Escort	0	337	—	0	0
Submarines	200	350	175.0	39	24

Key: "A/C" is the number of aircraft slots on the carriers, not the number of aircraft available; "Planned" is the number of ships that the navy expected to have available by the outbreak of war, sometime around 1944; "Actual" is the number of ships in commission during the Second World War (note that figures for destroyers and SUBMARINES have been rounded); "Percent" is the number of ships actually in commission as a proportion of the planned figures; "Inc." (incomplete) covers ships laid down but still not in commission by the summer of 1945, when the war was effectively over; "Canc." shows how many of these were canceled, the balance being completed postwar.

battleships being built, and all (except two demolished at Pearl Harbor) the older ones being upgraded and put to work. Note, too, that the navy certainly did not dismiss the aircraft carrier as a useful weapon, and planned to have about as many flattops as battlewagons. But it certainly greatly underestimated the need for carriers.

Of particular interest are the figures for escort carriers, which ultimately included about a quarter of all carrier-borne aircraft (listed under "A/C"). In fact, the escort carrier was an idea more or less foisted upon the navy by President ROOSEVELT. His enthusiasm was well rewarded, for their role in antisubmarine and amphibious operations was one of the more interesting developments of the war.

Figures for cruisers are also rather interesting. The so-called "large" cruisers were really light battleships, often erroneously called "battlecruisers," which were built on the erroneous assumption that the Japanese were building similar vessels. They turned out to be fine ships, but had even less of a role than did proper battleships. In contrast, the predicted need for heavy cruisers was rather lower than the demand, while that for light cruisers was pretty much on target.

It is interesting to note that despite the experience of World War I, the navy underestimated the need for destroyers to curb the submarine menace. Indeed, the average monthly completion rate for destroyers rose enormously during the war: 1.33 per month in 1941, 6.75 in 1942, and peaking at 10.83 in 1944. The shortage of destroyers was a critical factor in the creation of the destroyer escort, a sort of "second class" destroyer designed primarily for antisubmarine operations, rather than general fleet operations. In addition, considering that the navy's prewar plans were predicated upon a submarine campaign against Japanese shipping, the prewar estimate of the need for submarines was extremely low.

A great many ships that had been ordered were never laid down, including five battleships, three MIDWAY CLASS carriers, and three large cruisers. By mid–1944 the navy had begun to cancel orders for

ships that it considered no longer necessary for the war effort, including many already under construction.

Another area in which prewar estimates fell short was in terms of auxiliary and amphibious warfare vessels. The navy actually ordered very few of these before hostilities broke out, but by war's end they formed the greatest proportion of the navy's approximately 75,000 vessels, counting everything from battlewagons and aircraft carriers to lighters and "honey bucket" barges.

See also GIBBS, WILLIAM F.; REARMAMENT, US, 1930s.

Ref: Abbazia, *Mr. Roosevelt's Navy.*

Shipbuilding, Japanese Plans

The Imperial Navy projected its needs in the 1930s and adopted what it considered a realistic program for expansion. Between 1931 and the attack on PEARL HARBOR a large number of warships were ordered to be built, or converted from other types of vessels. When war came, additional orders were made, and changes authorized in existing orders, leading to a quite different fleet.

Shipbuilding, Warships, Japan vs. United States

From the mid–1930s both the United States and Japan began building warships at a rather prodigious rate, a pace that, at least in the case of the United States, did not slacken until the war was virtually over. Note particularly the sudden jump in United States launchings in 1942, a consequence of the "Two Ocean Navy" bill of 1940. In the end, Japan lost the war in the shipyards as much as on the high seas.

During the war both powers greatly reduced the time required to build ships.

Each navy required about 12 months to convert a ship to a light carrier, the United States using partially complete light cruiser hulls for this purpose, and the Japanese prewar seaplane carriers and

JAPAN: WARSHIPS ORDERED

	Older	1930s	1941–45	Total	Compl.	Fleet	Canc.	Inc.
Battleships:	10	4	0	4	2	12	1	0
Aircraft Carriers								
Fleet:	2	9	13	22	11	11	0	3
Light:	2	3	3	6	5	7	0	1
Escort:	0	3	4	7	5	5	0	0
A/C	200	800	960	1,760	970	1,170	0	200
Cruisers	25	17	8	25	14	39	1	0
Destroyers								
Fleet:	58	89	38	127	77	135	0	2
Escort:	0	0	113	113	32	32	0	9
Submarines:	53	90	642	732	151	204	1	18

Key: "Older" indicates pre-1930s vessels that were available for first-line service at the outbreak of the Pacific War. All completion figures include conversions from other types: one battleship was converted to an aircraft carrier; cruisers include six ordered as light cruisers in the 1930s and converted to heavy cruises, plus one ordered as a heavy cruiser during the war, and then taken in hand for conversion to a light carrier. "Warships Ordered" includes vessels not laid down; "Compl." covers only ships that entered service; "Fleet" is the total available to the Imperial Navy of each type during the war; "Canc." covers ships that were laid down but canceled during construction; "Inc." includes ships laid down but not completed by the end of the war. Escort carrier figures omit the so-called Japanese Army escort carriers; aircraft figures are approximate; cruisers omits two captured from the Chinese; submarine figures omit midget, suicide, and transport boats.

MAJOR WARSHIP LAUNCHINGS, 1937–45

Year		CV	CVE	BB	CA/CL	DD	DE	SS
1937–1940	Jap.	3	0	2	4	27	0	21
	U.S.	2	1	3	7	47	0	28
1941	Jap.	2	1	0	2	8	0	10
	U.S.	0	2	3	6	27	0	15
1942	Jap.	0	1	0	3	11	0	22
	U.S.	6	14	2	10	120	25	37
1943	Jap.	5	2	0	0	9	0	39
	U.S.	12	25	3	11	92	205	66
1944	Jap.	6	0	0	1	5	24	31
	U.S.	8	35	1	19	64	101	78
1945	Jap.	0	0	0	0	0	12	30
	U.S.	11	9	1	10	73	0	22
Total	Jap.	16	4	2	10	60	36	153
	U.S.	39	76	13	63	315	331	246

Figures for carriers (CV) include light carriers and, as with escort carriers (CVE), include conversions. Escort carrier figures exclude aircraft transports (the Japanese Army built several of these, which looked like carriers but could not operate combat aircraft). US battleship figures include three "large cruisers." Japanese submarine figures exclude numerous midgets and 28 cargo boats built by the Imperial Army. Note that not all vessels launched were actually completed, particularly in the case of the United States, which canceled numerous partially completed hulls.

AVERAGE CONSTRUCTION TIME IN MONTHS

	Prewar		Wartime	
Type	U.S.	Jap.	U.S.	Jap.
BB	35–42	53–61	32	—
CV	32–34	36–44	15–20	22–24
CVE	—	—	8	12
CA	32–38	40–50	24–30	—
CL	32–38	40–50	20–30	19–24
DD	13–14	24–30	5	12
SS	14–15	24–36	7	15
Liberty	12–14	20–30	1	18–24

other vessels especially built to be converted in an emergency. The US figure for escort carriers (CVE) is for new construction, but conversions took about the same time; the Japanese figure is for conversion.

LIBERTY SHIPS, the standard mass-produced US general purpose cargo vessels of the war, were based on a prewar Maritime Commission design. Although they were larger than the average prewar merchantmen (10,000–14,000 GRT vs. about 6,000), they are useful as a basis of comparison. The

Japanese, of course, did not build Liberty ships, but did produce some large marus (the Japanese word for merchantman) of similar concept, albeit smaller.

There were a number of factors that contributed to the considerable reduction in building times. Economies of scale were obviously one factor, since wartime orders were made in large numbers. The extensive use of welding and prefabrication were of great importance. The operation of shipyards on a 24-hour, seven-days-a-week, no-holidays basis also contributed. In the case of the United States modularization was a major factor: A lot of the equipment on US ships was interchangeable, regardless of type of vessel. The best example of this was the twin 5"/38 dual-purpose gun mount, which

Submarines under construction for the US Navy at Groton, Connecticut, in August 1943. These appear to be Balao-class boats, of which Groton produced 48 during the war.

appeared on battleships, carriers, cruisers, and destroyers, even being "retrofitted" on vessels undergoing refits.

It is interesting to note that even before the war the Japanese took much longer to build ships than the Americans, and that, although they improved considerably, it was not proportional to the reductions in time effected by US yards. In fact, US construction time figures for cruisers might actually have been lower but completion of many vessels was deliberately delayed in order to give priority to more desperately needed carriers, destroyers, and destroyer escorts.

See also GIBBS, WILLIAM F.

Shipping, War Against Japanese

While the Germans got most of the publicity for their spectacular U-boat (submarine) success in the Atlantic, less is said about America's successful campaign against Japanese shipping in the Pacific. US SUBMARINES accounted for over half of Japanese merchant shipping and were able to prowl every corner of Japan's maritime empire. Complementing this effort was the increasing reach and dominance of American carrier and land-based aviation at the front lines. Japanese shipping had to run an obstacle course from the time it left port (and promptly encountered waiting American subs) until it reached front-line bases and was pummeled by US bombers.

In 1945, US subs and B-29s began planting thousands of MINES in Japanese coastal waters. In addition to the shipping sunk, these mines virtually shut down Japanese ports. The mines worked day and night and in any weather. With the mines, Japanese ships had neither bad weather nor darkness as protection from enemy subs and aircraft.

Although the Allied anti-shipping campaign wiped out the Japanese merchant marine by the end of the war, the campaign had already severely crippled the latter by the end of 1943. This meant that Japan had less ability to meet the multiple Allied offensives during 1944. Japan began the war

The launching of the Gato Class submarine USS Robalo (SS-273), May 9, 1943, at Manitowoc, Wisconsin. The unusual sideways launch was one of many innovative construction techniques introduced during the war, in this case permitting vessels to be built on rivers and bays too narrow for normal launching. Robalo, skippered by Manning Kimmel, son of Admiral Husband Kimmel, was lost in mid-1944.

with about six and a half million tons of shipping. That amount steadily declined throughout the war, despite some captures and new construction.

Japan fought a poor man's fight for the entire war, using much less ammunition and fewer weapons. This lowered its combat capability and increased its CASUALTIES. The Japanese had little choice in the matter, as they were simply unable to move much over the water because they never had enough shipping.

The Japanese shipping crisis was made worse by the policies of their army and navy. At the begin-

ning of the war, each service appropriated large amounts of shipping (1.8 million tons for the navy, 2.1 million for the army) to support its offensive operations. This left the civilian economy about a million tons short of its minimum needs. Since the arms factories depended on imports for most of their raw materials, PRODUCTION took a beating from the beginning. To make matters worse, the army and navy would not cooperate with each other or with industry in the use of shipping. The army would send a supply ship to JAVA and, instead of coming back with raw materials, it would come

JAPANESE SHIPPING SUNK
(THOUSANDS OF GRT)

Sunk by	Total Lost	% lost in				Total
		1942	1943	1944	1945	
Submarines	5,880	69%	83%	69%	23%	62%
Naval Air	1,740	11%	2%	23%	28%	18%
Land Air	825	9%	11%	6%	12%	9%
Mines	600	0%	0%	0%	28%	6%
Misc.	450	11%	3%	2%	8%	5%
Total	9,495	875	2,175	4,330	2,115	
		9%	23%	46%	22%	

Note that these figures are not necessarily as authoritative as they may appear. Most statistics on shipping losses were compiled shortly after the war. Those compiling the figures were often not privy to certain secret information, notably Ultra and Magic. In recent years a number of additional sinkings of Japanese ships—about 120—have been credited to various submarines.

Misc. includes accidents at sea (storms, breakdowns, etc.) as well as losses to enemy surface warships. Naval air is primarily carrier-based aircraft but also includes land-based Navy planes.

back empty because moving raw materials was not an army responsibility. This situation was not rectified until 1944, when it was too late.

It got worse. Japan never developed an effective convoy system or antisubmarine techniques. But underlying all of this was the fact that Japan was still a minor industrial power. It was during the 1930s that Japan began to industrialize in a serious way. Even so, by 1940 Japan was producing only half a million tons of shipping a year. This was less than a tenth of US capability. Even with a massive effort, Japan was never able to produce more than

JAPANESE MERCHANT SHIPPING
(MILLIONS OF GRT)

Date	Available	Loss to Date
Dec. '41	6.4	0
Jan. '43	5.9	.9
Jan. '44	4.8	3.1
Jan. '45	2.4	7.4
Aug. '45	1.5	9.3

1.7 million tons of shipping a year. That was in 1944, the year that American subs and aircraft sunk 2.7 million tons.

Japan did have one item in its favor. For the first 18 months of the war American submarines were equipped with defective TORPEDOES. It wasn't until September 1943 that this problem was completely resolved, although by the end of 1942 many submarine crews had developed ways to get some use out of their torpedoes. Nevertheless, this gave the Japanese merchant marine something of a free ride through the middle of 1943. After that, Japanese shipping disappeared beneath the waves with great rapidity.

Oddly enough, Japanese submarines were never a menace to Allied shipping. The Japanese felt that the only proper target for their submarines was enemy warships. It was considered a waste of good torpedoes to shoot at merchant ships. However, the Japanese subs did have some success against Allied warships. Two carriers were sunk (one an escort carrier) as were two cruisers. Several other major warships (carriers and battleships) were put out of action for months by Japanese submarine torpedoes.

The Americans also went after Japanese warships, when there were merchant ships handy. Arguably, the US submariners were better at it than their Japanese counterparts.

American subs spent 31,671 days on patrol, about three weeks per patrol. Many patrols were cut short by mechanical problems and some were in support of fleet operations. These fleet patrols were much shorter. To attack 4,112 Japanese merchant ships, 14,748 torpedoes were used. This was 3.6 torpedoes per attack and indicates how the typical attack involved firing a "spread" of torpedoes to maximize the chances of hitting something. Even at that, only about a third of these attacks succeeded in sinking anything. Because of defective torpedoes, the odds were under 20% from 1941 to late 1943, but rose to over 50% thereafter. For the entire war, some 350 tons of enemy shipping was sunk for every torpedo fired.

US SUBMARINE ACTIVITY IN THE PACIFIC

	1941–42	1943	1944	1945	Total
Warships sunk	2	22	104	60	188
Merchantmen sunk	180	325	603	186	1,294
War Patrols	350	350	520	330	1,450
US Subs Lost	7	15	19	8	49

Note that a "war patrol" is one submarine going out looking for the enemy for up to two months, or until damaged or out of torpedoes. Not counted are enemy warships and merchantmen damaged by submarine attacks. These amounted to a smaller number than those sunk, mainly because warships attacked tended to be small escort types and Japanese shipping was, on average, rather smaller than Western ships. These smaller ships were much less likely to survive a torpedo hit. Not all of these ships sank from torpedo hits. When the opportunity presented itself (no enemy warships around), the sub would surface and use its deck gun, usually a 76mm–127mm piece (3-inch to 5-inch) to sink smaller ships. This would save torpedoes, as only about 24 to 30 were carried by an American sub.

Of 52 US submarines lost in World War II from all causes, 49 were lost in the Pacific War. The Japanese lost 130 subs during the war, most of them to aircraft attacks, while the Germans lost 11 in the Pacific Theater. The British also lost three subs and the Dutch five in the Pacific or Indian Oceans. Allied subs accounted for about 2% of the Japanese shipping sunk.

At the beginning of the war, Japan was the premier submarine user in the Pacific, with 67 boats. The United States had 56 in the Pacific, more in the Atlantic, and the ability to outproduce Japan in this area. This is precisely what America did, building over 200 new subs. Japan was able to build only 120.

Unrestricted submarine warfare was prohibited by the London Naval DISARMAMENT TREATY of 1930, of which both the United States and Japan were signatories. Unrestricted submarine warfare is the policy of deliberately attacking non-warships without warning. The traditional law of the sea, embodied in the GENEVA CONVENTION, required that regardless of flag, merchant vessels could not be attacked in wartime without giving them the opportunity to heave to and permit inspection and possible seizure. Although the initiation of unrestricted submarine warfare in the Pacific is generally attributed to the US Navy, it was in fact first employed by the Imperial Navy. Japanese attacks on merchant shipping began soon after the attack on PEARL HARBOR. On 7 December 1941, the USAT *Cynthia Olsen* was torpedoed and sunk by the Japanese submarine I-26, about a 700 miles northeast of Oahu. Before the end of December three other merchant ships were sunk by Japanese submarines between Hawaii and California, while five others were attacked unsuccessfully in the same area.

Had the Japanese Navy committed itself more vigorously to unrestricted submarine warfare it would have made the war longer and far more difficult for the United States, since considerable resources would have been committed to antisubmarine patrol. However, Japanese naval doctrine eschewed attacks on merchant shipping. The Japanese Navy viewed submarines as auxiliaries to the battlefleet. Their task was to scout for the battlewagons, to locate the enemy and perhaps whittle his strength down by successful torpedo attacks, rather than waste time with less honorable objectives such as merchant ships. Precisely why the attacks on US shipping in the eastern Pacific occurred is unclear. In their aftermath the US Navy began to organized a convoy system. However, once it became evident that there was not going to be an antisubmarine "Battle of the Pacific" similar to the Battle of the Atlantic, the US Navy began permitting merchant ships to proceed from the West Coast without escort. It was not long before US and allied merchant ships in rear areas were proceeding individually, without escort. By the end of 1942 the only shipping that moved in heavily escorted convoys in rear areas was troop movements.

But what principally defanged Japanese subs was American airpower and warships using effective antisubmarine weapons and tactics. Thousands of American patrol aircraft constantly crisscrossed the Pacific, making life decidedly uncomfortable for Japanese subs. America also produced over 600 destroyers and destroyer escorts. While over half of these initially went to the Atlantic (to confront German U-boats), plenty were left for the Pacific.

Japan produced fewer than a hundred destroyers and smaller antisubmarine ships during the war and used them much less efficiently.

Another serious Japanese shortcoming was many long and exposed sea routes. Many of these were outside the range of friendly aircraft, and the Japanese had far fewer long-range patrol aircraft anyway. Roundtrips for merchantmen from Japan to outlying bases took from 30 to 90 days. This was particularly true of bases in the central Pacific. By the end of the war, many of these bases could no longer be reached anyway because American forces had seized nearby islands and installed air bases. Japanese troops on these bypassed islands often starved before the war ended, though not before resorting to cannibalism. Even some shot down American pilots ended up in the stew pot.

As successful as they were, American sub crews still took high losses, with 22% of the US submariners being killed during the course of the war. This was the highest percentage loss of any arm of the US service.

Ref: Alden, *U.S. Submarine Attacks during World War II*; Blair, *Silent Victory*; Boyd and Yoshia, *The Japanese Submarine Force in World War II*; Friedman, *Submarine Design and Development*; Parillo, *The Japanese Merchant Marine in World War II*; Roscoe, *United States Submarine Operations in World War II*.

Ships, Classes

Warships are usually built in groups called "classes," with each vessel in the class being more or less identical to all the others. This saves money on design and during construction and repair, and makes it easier to create homogeneous squadrons. Some classes numbered in the hundreds, while others included only two or three ships.

Warships are occasionally built to unique designs for a variety of reasons. Parsimony is one. A navy without much money may be able to afford only one new ship of a particular type every few years. So it tries to build the most up-to-date one it can, each time it does so. Another reason for building a ship to a unique design is experimentation. When a new design incorporates a number of innovative, or perhaps revolutionary, ideas, it's best to build a single ship, rather than invest money in a fleet of potential lemons. A good case in point is the US heavy cruiser WICHITA, based on the BROOKLYN CLASS light cruiser design, the experience with which led to the creation of the more successful BALTIMORE CLASS. The naval DISARMAMENT TREATIES of 1922–30 provided yet a third reason for building a ship to an individual design. The treaties very clearly defined the total tonnage of the navies of the signatory powers. As a result, a number of navies discovered that if they built one ship, to a unique design, they could use up those last few thousand tons of their quota. In this way the US Navy acquired the carrier WASP and the Japanese Navy its RYUJO, both squeezing the last few tons out of their national quotas, and both rather unsatisfactory as a result.

Note, by the way, that even when built in classes, ships will differ from each other in numerous ways. These differences are usually minor. For example, only two of the four battleships of the IOWA CLASS had the same hull length, 887 feet 3 inches, *Iowa* being 887 feet 2.75 inches and *New Jersey* 887 feet 6.626 inches long, while the British DIDO CLASS antiaircraft cruisers differed so much among themselves that they are sometimes listed as five separate classes. The differences are caused by many factors: variations in the quality of materials, differing skills, modifications during construction, wartime shortages, unanticipated technical problems, and even weather (which affects the coefficient of expansion).

Ships, Naming Conventions

Most nations adopted systems for naming their warships.

The US Navy named battleships after states. Aircraft carriers were mostly named after famous ships of the "Old Navy" or famous battles, with a handful named after individuals (*Langley* and *Franklin D. Roosevelt*). Escort carriers were produced in such numbers that they were mostly named after bays or rivers, although as the war went on some were renamed after battles. Large cruisers were named after US territories, while heavy and light cruisers were named after large cities. Destroyers and destroyer escorts were mostly named after naval heroes or persons who made important contributions to the navy, including, in one case, a woman. This was the USS *Higbee* (DD-806) a GEARING CLASS ship named after Lenah Higbee, who had been the chief of the Navy Nurse Corps during World War I. The only other ships named after real women were the Coast Guard cutters *Harriet Lane*, a traditional name in the Coast Guard, after the daughter of a mid-19th-century secretary of the treasury, and *Spars*, after the Coast Guard's women's reserve. SUBMARINES received the names of "denizens of the deep," both real and mythical. There were also conventions for naming various types of smaller warships. Gunboats, for example, were named after small cities or islands. Hospital ships, were given "soothing" names, such as *Solace* or *Bountiful*, while ammunition ships were appropriately named after volcanoes.

The Imperial Navy named battleships after ancient provinces of Japan, or, in the case of the KONGO CLASS, which were converted from battlecruisers, after famous mountains. Aircraft carriers mostly were given picturesque names related to flying, to flying creatures, or to the sea, but this system was not always adhered to. Several carriers were converted from another type of ship, or for other reasons had different types of names. For example, KAGA and SHINANO were originally intended to be battleships, AKAGI a battlecruiser, IBUKI a heavy cruiser, and CHITOSE and *Chiyoda* seaplane carriers. In addition, several of the ships of the Unyu Class were named after famous cruisers of the Imperial Navy.

A complete list of Japanese carrier names: *Akagi*, "Red Castle," a mountain near Tokyo; *Amagi*, "Castle in the sky"; *Aso*, a volcano on Kyushu; *Chitose*, "A Thousand Years!"; *Chiyoda*, "A Thousand Generations!"; *Chuyo*, "Middle Sea"; *Hiryu*, "Flying Dragon"; *Hiyo*, "Bright Sea"; HOSHO, "Flying

Bird" (see *Shoho*); *Ibuki*, a volcano on Kyushu; *Ikoma*, a mountain near Osaka; JUNYO, "Deep Sea"; *Kaga*, "Increased Joy," a former region around Ishikawa Prefecture; *Kasagi*, a mountain near Osaka; *Katsuragi*, a mountain; KAIYO, "Eternal Sea"; RYUHO, a mythological bird; RYUJO, "Sacred Dragon"; *Shinano*, ancient region of Honshu, as well as Japan's longest river; SHINYO, "Holy Sea"; *Shoho*, "Flying Bird" (see *Hosho*); SHOKAKU, "Flying Crane"; SORYU, "Blue Dragon"; TAIHO, a mythological bird; TAIYO, "Spirit of the Ocean"; UNRYU, "Cloud Dragon"; *Unyo*, "See of Clouds"; ZUIHO, "Auspicious Bird"; *Zuikaku*, "Auspicious Crane."

Battle cruisers and heavy cruisers were named after mountains, while light cruisers were named after rivers. Seaplane carriers were given inspiring names, which also happened to be the names of places, thus *Nisshin*, "Ever Advancing!" Destroyers received names related to meteorological or physical phenomena, for example: KAMIKAZE, "Divine Wind"; *Tanikaze*, "Valley Wind"; *Kasumi*, "Mist of Flowers"; *Shiranui*, "Phosphorescent Foam"; *Yagumo*, "Mountain Cloud"; *Asagumo*, "Morning Cloud"; *Murakumo*, "Gathering Clouds"; *Natsugumo*, "Summer Cloud"; *Akizuki*, "Autumn Moon"; *Shirayuki*, "White Snow"; FUBUKI, "Snowstorm"; *Katsuyki*, "First Snowfall"; *Nenoni*, "New Years' Day"; *Katuharu*, "First Days of Spring"; *Wakaba*, "Fresh Green of Springtime"; *Hatusimo*, "First Frost"; *Akebono*, "Daybreak"; *Usugumo*, "Fleecy Clouds"; *Oboro*, "Moonlight Through Haze"; *Usio*, "Ocean Tide"; *Hibiki*, "Echo"; *Inazuma*, "Lightning"; *Ikazuchi*, "Thunder"; *Nozake*, "Wind in the Sails"; *Shiokaze*, "Wind Rising from the Turn of the Tide."

The ROYAL NAVY had a complex system for naming ships. In general, the names of famous old warships were used for battleships, battlecruisers, and aircraft carriers, but battleships were also given royal names or titles, and the names of famous commanders as well. Cruisers built after World War I were usually named after towns, counties, or colonies, but mythological and traditional names, including those of naval heroes, were also common.

There was little system to the name of smaller warships, which were sometimes named in bunches, after flowers, tribes, naval heroes, jewels, and so forth, there being so many of them.

Shiratsuyu Class, Japanese Destroyers

Built 1933–37, the Shiratsuyus were similar to the preceding HATSUHARU CLASS, but had a heavier TORPEDO armament. During the war they lost one of their 5-inch dual-purpose guns in order to accommodate additional antiaircraft armament. All 10 units became war losses: one in a collision, one by air attack, three in surface actions in the SOLOMONS, and five by submarine attack.

The most notable unit in the class was *Shigure* (1933–1935–1936). *Shigure*, which means "Drizzling Autumn Rain," was undoubtedly the luckiest ship in the Imperial Navy. Although repeatedly "in harm's way" from the start of the war, she led a charmed life. *Shigure*'s battle honors read like a record of the principal actions of the war. Escort for the battleships covering operations in the Philippines and East Indies early in the war, she later fought in Battle of the CORAL SEA without a scratch. Thereafter based at RABAUL, she fought through the GUADALCANAL Campaign, bombarding the beachhead on the night of 14–15 October 1942 without injury, taking part in the chaotic Second Battle of Guadalcanal, November 14–15, with no damage, then VELLA GULF (August 6–7, 1943), where she was the only one of the four Japanese destroyers involved to survive, and did so without any damage. Ten days later she joined with several other destroyers to successfully land reinforcements on VELLA LAVELLA despite a skirmish with American destroyers. At the Battle of Vella Lavella (October 6–7 1943) she was part of a squadron of nine destroyers and a number of lighter vessels assigned to evacuate Japanese troops, but apparently took no damage when six American destroyers attempted to intercept, coming off the worse for it. The "apparently" turned into an "almost" when, a few months later, it was discovered that a US torpedo had hit one of *Shigure*'s rudders,

but not detonated, leaving instead a rather neat 21-inch hole. During the Battle of EMPRESS AUGUSTA BAY (November 2, 1943) she was one of four cruisers and six destroyers that came off second best in an action with four American cruisers and eight destroyers while trying to disrupt the Allied landings at Cape Torokina on BOUGAINVILLE, but once again suffered not at all. During the Battle of BIAK (June 7, 1944), *Shigure*, one of several Japanese ships engaged in a long-range stern chase by some US destroyers, was near-missed five times, with no significant damage. In the Battle of the PHILIPPINE SEA (June 19–21, 1944) she was one of the escorts for Carrier Task Force B, but came away from the battle with no damage. During the Leyte Campaign she fought at SURIGAO STRAIT (October 25, 1944), being the only ship in her squadron to survive, with only slight damage from an 8-inch dud, despite tangling with a nest of US PT-BOATS and some cruisers in the midst of the biggest shoot-'em-up of the Pacific War.

Shigure's luck ran out on January 24, 1945, when she took a torpedo from the US submarine *Blackfin* (SS-322) while escorting a small convoy about 150 miles north of SINGAPORE. She sank with great loss of life. *Shigure*'s skipper—and perhaps her luck—for most of the war was Cdr. Tameichi Hara, who was promoted to captain in mid-1944 and given command of the new light cruiser *Yahagi*, of the AGANO CLASS.

Ref: Hara, Saito, and Pineau, *Japanese Destroyer Captain*.

Shokaku Class, Japanese Aircraft Carriers

The Shokakus were Japan's best prewar carriers, and the first Japanese carriers to be sisterships, all eight previous carriers having been single-ship designs. *Shokaku* and *Zuikaku* entered service only a few months before PEARL HARBOR (August and September 1941, respectively), and, indeed, the details of the attack were planned so that they could complete training. Much larger versions of HIRYU, they were better protected and had a greater avgas capacity, but could operate only about the same number of aircraft. They formed Carrier Division Five and were at Pearl Harbor, helped support Japanese operations in New Guinea in January 1942, then accompanied the First Air Fleet into the Indian Ocean. They went on to fight at CORAL SEA, where damage to *Shokaku* and losses among their air groups resulted in their missing MIDWAY. They were also together at EASTERN SOLOMONS, SANTA CRUZ, and the PHILIPPINE SEA.

Shokaku (1937–1939–1941) was so seriously damaged at the Coral Sea that she almost sank on the return voyage to Japan, but her aircraft had mortally wounded LEXINGTON. She took two bombs in the Battle of the Eastern Solomons and survived six during the Battle of the Santa Cruz Islands. She was sunk by three TORPEDOES from the submarine *Cavalla* (SS-244) on June 19, 1944 during the Battle of the Philippine Sea.

Zuikaku (1938–1939–1941) led a charmed life, apparently taking no injury despite being in numerous actions until the Battle of the Philippine Sea, when she was heavily damaged. She returned to service in time for the Battle of LEYTE GULF in October 1944, in which she took seven torpedoes and six or seven bombs from US naval aircraft before sinking off Cape Engaño. As the ship was going down, her crew stood to attention on her increasingly sloping flight deck to give several cries of "Banzai!" for the glory of the emperor. She was the last of the Pearl Harbor carriers to be sunk.

Short, Walter C. (1880–1949)

Short graduated from the University of Illinois in 1901 and accepted a direct commission in the US Army in 1902. He served in various garrisons, in the Philippines, and on the Pershing Expedition, before going to France in 1917. During World War I his service was entirely in staff and training posts, and he ended the war as chief of staff of the Third Army, on occupation duty in the Rhineland. From 1920 to 1940 he held various staff and line positions, attended several army schools, and rose to brigadier general. Short commanded a corps in the

maneuvers of 1940, and was promoted major general. Early in 1941 he was given command of the Hawaiian Department and promoted to temporary lieutenant general. He was in command at the time of the Pearl Harbor attack. Relieved about two weeks after the attack, Short was soon forcibly retired in his permanent rank of major general. He began hurling accusations as to responsibility for the attack. A congressional investigation in 1942 concluded that he—and his naval counterpart, Admiral Husband KIMMEL—had been derelict in his duty and had committed errors of judgment. A second investigation, in 1946, cleared him of charges of dereliction of duty, but confirmed that he had committed errors of judgment. He spent the rest of his life attempting to clear his name.

While some controversy still clings to the investigative conclusions concerning Short's responsibility (much of it motivated by anti-Roosevelt sentiments in some political circles), in fact at the very least he had committed serious errors of judgment. Like most army officers he believed that the main event in any future war would be with Germany, and viewed his posting to HAWAII as likely to keep him out of it, ending his chances for further advancement. He seems to have had little understanding of the capabilities of air power. In a memorandum available at the National Archives, dated in February of 1941, shortly after he assumed command in Hawaii, he dismissed the possibility of a serious Japanese carrier raid on the islands. Upon receiving the famous November 27, 1941 message from General MARSHALL that concluded with the line "This is to be considered a war warning," Short's initial reaction was to make preparations to cope with possible sabotage by Japanese Americans, but he instituted few changes in the daily routine or procedures of the troops under his command.

Shoup, David M. (1904–1983)

One of the controversial officers the Marines seem to produce from time to time, Shoup graduated from DePauw University in 1926 and was commissioned a second lieutenant in the Corps. He served afloat and in China, attended various schools, and at the outbreak of the Pacific War was commanding a battalion of the Sixth Marines in Iceland. In mid-1942 he was assigned to the staff of the Second Marine Division, and served in the New Georgia operation. Promoted to colonel, he commanded the Marines who assaulted Betio, the principal island comprising TARAWA Atoll, being awarded the MEDAL OF HONOR for refusing to be evacuated despite serious wounds. Later he was chief of staff of the Second Marine Division, serving during the Marianas Campaign in mid-1944 and until the end of the war, when he was assigned to an administrative command in Washington. After the war Shoup held various increasingly important posts, ending his career as commandant of the Corps in 1963. Afterward an outspoken critic of intervention in Vietnam, Shoup found himself vilified and ostracized by many formerly close associates.

Siam (Thailand)

A large kingdom in Southeast Asia, between Burma and French INDO-CHINA, Siam's population was mostly Buddhist. Its economy was primarily agricultural, with some export of timber and raw materials.

Siam had maintained a precarious independence during the Age of Imperialism. By the outbreak of the war in Europe, the Thais were ruled by a military dictatorship. The Fall of France led them into a brief, unsuccessful border war with the Vichyite forces in French Indo-China (see SIAMESE ARMED FORCES).

Despite some admiration for Japan, as an Asian nation that had modernized itself and risen to the status of a great power, the Thais decidedly wanted to remain neutral in the war.

Siam was in a most bizarre situation during World War II. The only independent nation in Southeast Asia, it had maintained its independence by deft diplomacy. Even before PEARL HARBOR, the Japanese made it known that they might call upon Siamese "cooperation." When a Japanese army showed up on its border, demanding passage through Siam to Burma, the Siamese did what they had learned to do in order to survive. After a token resistance, they concluded an armistice and let the Japanese march through. But the Japanese wanted more "cooperation" than that and soon had Siam under what amounted to military occupation. This did not make the Japanese popular with the Siamese people, or the government. So by late 1942 there was a typically Siamese "resistance movement." This was not a typical guerrilla resistance movement, although there were some armed people in the jungles and a few acts of sabotage during the war. The Siamese resistance had strong ties to the government. It maintained contact with the Allies and provided a steady stream of reliable information on Japanese activities in Siam. As a result, the Allies never declared Siam "hostile" and simply treated it as another victim of Japanese aggression after the war.

The name of the country was changed from Siam to Thailand in June 1939, back to Siam in September 1945, and then to Thailand once more in the late 1940s.

Siamese Armed Forces

Siam had a small, relatively well equipped military establishment, but it was not particularly efficient. The Siamese Army had four modestly equipped divisions. It performed rather well in the brief 1940–41 border war with French INDO-CHINA, but found itself hopelessly outclassed when the Japanese occupied the country in December 1941. An armistice was soon arranged. Although Siam subsequently formally allied herself with Japan, the Siamese Army saw little action. Had the Siamese gotten into more serious action, indications are that they would not have done well against first-line Allied or Japanese troops. Peak wartime strength was 127,000 troops, plus about 25,000 more in paramilitary forces.

The Siamese Air Force had about 150 aircraft in 1941, mostly older models, many of them more or less obsolete. It saw some action against the even weaker French Air Force during the Franco-Siamese Border War. In addition, it put up a token resistance against the Japanese for a few hours after the invasion on 8 December 1941. For most of the war, the Siamese Air Force remained largely inactive.

The Siamese Navy was a small force, consisting mostly of obsolete vessels until the early 1930s, when an ambitious expansion program was undertaken. This added two coast defense ships of 2,265 tons (with four 8-inch guns), two sloops, and two gunboats, plus torpedo boats and many smaller coastal craft by the late 1930s, by which time there were also two light cruisers on order from Italian shipyards, completion of which was prevented by the outbreak of the war in Europe. The Siamese Navy saw limited action in World War II, and that only against Vichy French forces during the brief Siamese-French War of 1941.

In a bid to grab some territory, the Siamese invaded French Indo-China in November 1940. The result was a war that lasted less than three months (November 1940–January 1941). Siamese land forces made some gains against Vichyite French forces on the Cambodian-Siamese frontier, and as a result the French Far Eastern Squadron sortied into the Gulf of Siam. This resulted in the principal action of the war, the Battle of the Gulf of Siam or Koh-Chang (16–17 January 1941), when the French light cruiser LAMOTTE-PICQUET and four gunboats had a running night action of about 105 minutes with a Siamese squadron, which included the coast defense ships *Sri Ayuthia* and *Dhonburi* and three torpedo boats, in the Koh-Chang Islands off the southwest coast of Cambodia. Both Siamese coast defense ships were heavily damaged and sank in shallow water, as did the three torpedo boats, with little loss to the French. Siam signed an armistice on 29 January 1941. Despite their victory, the Vichy French were forced by the Japanese to cede several provinces from Cambodia to the Siamese.

Sims Class, US Destroyers

The dozen destroyers of the Sims Class, built 1937–40, were intended to be a major evolutionary development over preceding designs, which had been restricted to 1,500 tons by the various DISARMAMENT TREATIES. As completed they turned out unsuccessfully, displacing much more than expected, and they had to be extensively redesigned and refitted before entering service. Redesigned, they proved rather successful, despite the loss of some armament, and they became the prototypes for the succeeding two classes. They saw considerable service. Five were lost in action. The surviving vessels were broken up or expended as targets in the late 1940s.

Singapore, Malaya

A major port, and the principal British naval and air base in the Far East. Although well appointed, Singapore was ill-suited to its role as the bastion of British power in Southeast Asia. It was a small island, bereft of industrial resources, very close to the Malayan mainland, and with no really open sea around it. Despite this, between the wars the British invested heavily in developing it as a major base. Not only was a first-class naval dockyard constructed, but there were also several airfields and an elaborate system of fortifications. Altogether some 60 million pounds sterling was spent (over $3 billion in money of 1997). Unfortunately, it was poorly spent. The installations at Singapore were all badly planned. The naval base, for example, was on the landward side of the island, approachable only through the narrow Straits of Johore, and within artillery range of the Malay Peninsula. Similarly, the coast defense facilities, which included five 15-inch naval guns (not 18-inch, as is often claimed), capable of firing upon targets on the landward side of the island fortress (claims to the contrary notwithstanding), and a half-dozen 9.2-inchers, were supplied only with armor-piercing ammunition that was of dubious value against infantrymen in jungles.

In the years before World War II the British buildup of Singapore as their principal military base in the Far East led to the place assuming considerable psychological importance. It was a formidable place, but by no means as impregnable as it was touted in the press. All the propagandizing about the fortifications was a little ploy to keep the colonials happy. Thus, when the fortress fell to the Japanese with very little fuss early in 1942, British prestige plummeted throughout Asia.

In reality, Singapore was virtually indefensible unless one commanded the skies and seas around it, and in 1941–42 the ROYAL NAVY did not have the ships nor the RAF the aircraft to secure such control. Moreover, the city was on an island and its water supply came from the mainland. Should a hostile force control the mainland water (as the Japanese did when they invaded), this tropical city and its thirsty population would quickly capitulate. This was precisely what happened to the British.

What might have saved Singapore was the Japanese supply situation, which provided for only a week's worth of food. The average Japanese infantryman had but a hundred bullets with him, to last the entire campaign. Moreover, the Japanese commander thought the British garrison comprised only 30,000 troops, not the nearly 90,000 that were there. The Japanese had to storm the island of Singapore and could not wait for the British to run out of water (there was a small reservoir on the island). The British didn't know of the precarious Japanese supply situation, not that it would have done much good. British leadership was so inept that they were unable to prevent the outnumbered and ill-supplied Japanese from getting across the water, onto the island, and into the city. The fall of Singapore unleashed a host of rumors and tall tales. There were numerous stories of treachery (always a reliable crutch when one doesn't want to admit to ineptitude or carelessness). Incompetence in high places was also a good target.

Despite their inability to hold Singapore, the British really had built it up into an extraordinary fortress. As a result, it turned into a valuable resource for the Japanese. They very quickly began to use bits and pieces of equipment captured at Singapore to bolster their defenses elsewhere. One result of this was that US Marines assaulting TARAWA found themselves being fired upon by 8-inch coast defense guns from Singapore, firing some of His Majesty's best munitions.

Sino-American Cooperative Organization (SACO)

Pronounced "Socko," SACO was formed on April 15, 1943 and was a collaborative effort between Chinese intelligence and the US Naval Group, China (NGC), a navy-Marine Corps-Coast Guard mission to China. Commanded by RAdm Milton E. Miles, the NGC was formed in mid-1942, initially to collect weather information and provide technical support and training to the Chinese armed forces. The NGC eventually comprised about 2,500 volunteers from the navy, Coast Guard, and Marine Corps. With Chinese auxiliaries, these men were organized into eight GUERRILLA training detachments, 27 medical teams, and numerous weather detachments.

Although their headquarters near CHUNGKING was designated Weather Central (and codenamed Happy Valley), NGC personnel actually performed a variety of duties in addition to operating weather stations. They trained Chinese guerrillas, conducted long-range reconnaissance, rescued downed fliers, mined Chinese rivers and coastal waters, and undertook special warfare missions against the Japanese.

SACO coastwatchers regularly communicated the movements of Japanese ships to US SUBMARINES in the China Seas and to American aircraft operating out of the Philippines in the last months of the war. By the armistice, SACO controlled about 200 miles of the Chinese coast.

SACO operated a dozen training camps for guerrillas, medical personnel, radio operators, and other technical specialties. An estimated 80,000 Chinese troops were trained in these camps, although only about 30,000 could be properly armed. By its own estimates, SACO guerrillas rescued 76 Allied airmen who had bailed out over Japanese-held territory, and destroyed 141 ships and other vessels, 209 bridges, 84 locomotives, and 97 Japanese depots, ammunition dumps, and arms warehouses, while killing nearly 24,000 Japanese, wounding about 10,000 more, and taking nearly 300 PRISONERS. SACO losses were reported as about 8,000 men killed, including a small number of Americans. Three Americans were also captured by the Japanese and subsequently put to death.

Nor was the NGC's official mission, weather reporting, neglected. By October 1944 there were some 150 American and 700 Chinese personnel operating more than a dozen weather stations all over China, which provided invaluable meteorological data for the Pacific Fleet. This mission took naval personnel to the most exotic locales, from the jungles of Yunan to the sands of Inner Mongolia.

The NGC had a number of truly unique achievements.

On 18 January 1944, the NGC established what will undoubtedly remain the most unusual naval station in history, when it set up shop in Suiyan, in the Gobi Desert of Mongolia, literally hundreds of miles from the sea. Under the command of Marine Maj. Victor R. Bisceglia, a dozen Americans and about 80 Chinese operated the station until the end of the war. To provide protection from Japanese patrols, Maj. Bisceglia organized about 600 local Mongol tribesmen into a mounted security detail, to whom he had the navy issue CAVALRY saddles. With these troops, he occasionally attacked Japanese installations, and once defeated a Japanese motorized column of about 500 men.

The NGC also conducted the last naval action of World War II, on August 20, 1945, nearly a week after the emperor's announcement that Japan would surrender. A SACO detail was patrolling in a sailing junk off Wenchow, on the Chinese coast, when it was attacked by several Japanese motorized junks, which the personnel proceeded to board and capture with pistol and cutlass in hand.

The NGC's operations were tinged with some controversy. It conducted a running feud with the OSS, which was constantly trying to assert control over its activities. In addition, SACO's ties with Chinese intelligence were quite controversial. Admiral Miles' Chinese contact was General Tai Li, chief of the Investigation and Statistics Bureau, which has been variously described as "China's FBI" or "China's Gestapo," depending upon one's political perspective. The truth is probably somewhere between the two. Tai did a lot of CHIANG's dirty work, but no one in China had particularly clean hands, and the fact that he made a tidy profit through corruption was hardly surprising in a Chinese official. He was a highly effective intelligence chief, and helped hold Chiang's fragile coalition together in China's most desperate hours.

Ref: Stratton, SACO.

Skull Island

Off the southwest coast of New Guinea, Skull Island was of little strategic value and only occasionally visited. The island lacked even the most rudimentary anchorage, was incapable of supporting airfields, was possessed of a hostile population, and was plagued by numerous dangerous and unpleasant animals.

Slim, William J. (1891–1970)

Of working-class background, William Slim enlisted in Britain's Indian Army during World War I, and by its end had earned a regular commission in the Gurkhas. By the outbreak of World War II he commanded a brigade, which he led with considerable distinction in East Africa in 1940–41, where he was wounded. During the Iraqi Revolt and the Syrian Campaign (spring 1941) he again proved himself. Promoted to lieutenant general in early 1942, he was sent by Sir Archibald WAVELL

(C-in-C India) to try to stem the Japanese invasion of Burma, commanding the I Burma Corps. With troops mostly of mediocre quality, Slim, ably supported by his superior, Sir Harold ALEXANDER, performed wonders. Although an attempted counteroffensive failed, Slim was able to effect a remarkably arduous retreat of some 900 miles back to India. Given command of XV Corps, he subjected it to an intensive regimen of physical toughening, jungle training, and irregular tactics. Appointed to command 14th Army in October of 1943, Slim directed the defense of India ably, and then went over to the offensive in late 1944. By the spring of 1945 Slim had liberated most of central Burma, having inflicted over 350,000 CASUALTIES on the Japanese Army. Shortly afterward appointed to command all Allied ground forces in Southeast Asia, at the end of the war he was poised to liberate MALAYA. After the war Slim served in several prominent military and civil posts. A simple man, Slim was a no-nonsense soldier with enormous regard for the welfare of his men. A meticulous planner, he was not averse to unconventional methods, employing irregular forces and air supply to a degree unprecedented in the war. One of the most successful, and least famous, of all World War II commanders.

Small Arms

The Pacific War was an infantry war, and the infantryman's personal weapons counted for more than in Europe. Most of the Pacific fighting was done in jungles and mountains, in general under conditions where the infantryman had to depend more on his personal weapons than in other theaters.

Most of the troops fighting in the Pacific used a combination of older (World War I-era) and newer weapons.

The Japanese used a bolt-action rifle that was literally a World War I weapon, being a 1905 design. This was not as surprising as it may seem, since most World War II armies used relatively older rifles, including the German Army. In 1941,

INFANTRY RIFLES OF THE PACIFIC WAR					
	Name	Caliber	Weight	Action	Magazine
Chinese	Mauser 98	7.9mm	9.0 lbs.	bolt	5
Commonwealth	No. 14	7.7mm	9.4 lbs.	bolt	5
Japanese	Model 38	6.5mm	9.4 lbs.	bolt	5
	Model 99	7.7mm	8.8 lbs.	bolt	5
United States	M–1	7.62mm	9.5 lbs.	semi-auto	8
	M–1903	7.62mm	8.6 lbs.	bolt	5

Magazine: the number of bullets the weapon carried.

most Japanese troops were equipped with the original 6.5mm 1905 design rifle. Most other armies had long since upgraded to 7.5mm–8mm weapons, which had longer range, greater stopping power, and superior accuracy. Gradually throughout the war, Japanese infantry were reequipped with a newer, 7.7mm version of the 1905 "Arisaka" rifle, the model 99 of 1939

The Chinese Army actually used a great variety of infantry rifles, but the standard was the reliable old German Mauser, the *Infanterie Gewehr '98*, introduced in the late 19th century. A limited number of units eventually received the US M-1 Garand rifle.

British and other Commonwealth troops mostly fought using the No. 14 rifle. Although designed after 1919, it was essentially a World War I weapon. As time went by, however, light automatic weapons, such as Sten guns, came into wide usage.

US troops were much better off. While the troops who went into combat on WAKE ISLAND, GUAM and in the Philippines in late 1941 and early 1942 were still equipped mostly with the 1903 bolt-action (7.62mm/.30 caliber) Springfield rifle, the semi-automatic M-1 Garand (also 7.62mm) rapidly replaced the Springfield.

The semi-automatic M-1 could deliver about 30–36 aimed shots per minute, about twice as many as a bolt-action rifle. This was because the M-1 would fire as quickly as you pulled the trigger, while the bolt-action rifle required you to pull the bolt back to extract the shell casing and then move the

Two men of the First Marine Division in action against Japanese positions near Wana, Okinawa, May 1945. The Marine on the left wields a Thompson submachine gun, uncharacteristically taking aim with a weapon better suited for short bursts while advancing. His comrade carries an M-1 Garand semi-automatic rifle, the standard American infantry weapon of World War II. As this man is more elaborately equipped than the first, the two were probably working as a team.

bolt forward to load another round. In combat most fire was aimed in only a general sense. Thus the higher rate of fire of the M-1 (about 50 rounds per minute to about 20) gave it an edge. In a tight spot, which was normal for infantry combat, the ability to get off eight shots in a few seconds was decisive.

For well aimed fire, both sides had sniper versions of their rifles. The Japanese used Model 38 and 99 rifles manufactured to higher production standards and equipped with telescopic sights. The United States used special M-1903 "Springfield" bolt-action rifles equipped with telescopes. For well aimed fire, a bolt-action weapon had an intrinsic advantage over a semiautomatic one, although a good sniper was lethal with either type.

Japanese pistols came in a wide variety of types, both revolvers and automatics, most of which were 9mm. The principal US pistol was the .45 caliber (11.4mm), which was originally designed for close-in jungle combat in the Philippines at the turn of the century.

The Japanese had no submachine guns, while the United States had three. The most popular was the .30 caliber (7.62mm) M-2 carbine. This was actually a small rifle (weighing 5.3 pounds) firing a pistol-type cartridge. It came with a 20- or 30-

round magazine. The M-3 (or "grease gun") was .45 caliber (11.4mm), weighed six pounds, and had a 30-round magazine. US troops, particularly Marines, and SEABEES, also made use of the Thompson .45 submachine gun. None of these weapons was accurate beyond 100 meters. But at night, in the jungle, the action was commonly a lot closer than that. The carbine was comfortable to carry, but distrusted by combat troops for the low stopping power of its lightweight pistol cartridge. Japanese infantry attacks were carried out with much vigor, and a large bullet was often needed to stop the hard-charging Japanese troops. For that reason, the grease gun was preferred. But the M-3 was heavy and awkward to carry. It was also, because of its short barrel and pistol cartridge, accurate only at very short ranges. The carbine, because of its longer barrel, had greater accuracy when aimed and fired one shot short at a time at longer ranges. The "Tommy" gun was less accurate, but easier to carry. British and Commonwealth troops used the Sten M3, a cheaply produced, light (6.5 pounds) weapon firing 9mm pistol ammunition. The normal clip was 20 rounds, but it was physically impossible to manually load a clip beyond 18. It lacked a safety and was highly inaccurate.

Smith, Holland M. (1882–1967)

Holland "Howlin' Mad" Smith was a lawyer in Alabama when he received a commission in the US Marines in 1905. He served in the Philippines, PANAMA, and the Dominican Republic before going to France in 1917 as a machine gunner and later a staff officer, fighting in virtually all of the AEF's operations, Aisne-Marne, the Oise, St.-Mihiel, and the Meuse-Argonne. After occupation duty in Germany, he went through a series of staff and command assignments, helped develop the Corps' amphibious doctrine, and on the eve of the Pacific War was a major general in command of the newly formed First Marine Division. Smith trained not only the Marine Corps' amphibious forces, but also the army's, and was responsible for

training both the First and Third Infantry Divisions in amphibious operations. Promoted to command what would become the V Marine Amphibious Corps, and later commander of Fleet Marine Force, Pacific. Smith directed the assaults on TARAWA, ENIWETOK, SAIPAN, TINIAN, GUAM, IWO JIMA, and OKINAWA, several times personally leading the assault forces. Smith retired shortly after the war, in the rank of general. A non-nonsense commander, Smith's nickname came from his occasional bursts of temper. One of his most famous acts was the so-called "War of the SMITHS," in which he relieved an army division commander also named Smith during the Marianas Campaign.

Smith, Oliver P. (1893–1977)

Oliver Prince Smith graduated from Berkeley in 1916 and was commissioned in the US Marines the following year. He saw no action in World War I, being in the Pacific. His interwar service was typical of a Marine of the time, serving on shipboard, in Haiti, on various staffs, and attending several schools, including the army's Infantry School. In May of 1941 he took his Sixth Marine Regiment to Iceland, where the outbreak of the Pacific War found him. In March of 1942 he was transferred to Marine Corps headquarters. In January of 1944 he got into action, receiving command of the Fifth Marines, which he led on NEW BRITAIN. Shortly made brigadier general, he served on PELELIU as assistant commander of the First Marine Division and on OKINAWA as Marine deputy chief of staff to Simon B. BUCKNER's 10th Army. After Okinawa he returned stateside to command the Marine schools at Quantico, in which post peace found him. After the war he was assistant commandant for a time, and in 1950 was made commander of the newly reactivated First Marine Division, which he led at Inchon, in the fighting for Seoul, at the Chosin Reservoir, and in the retreat to the coast, one of the most distinguished episodes in the history of American arms. Smith afterward rose to lieutenant general and retired in 1955.

Smiths, War of the

Arguably the most long-enduring interservice wrangle of World War II, the "War of the Smiths" broke out when MG Holland M. Smith (USMC) relieved MG Ralph Smith (USA) on SAIPAN in June 1944.

Ralph Smith commanded the 27th Infantry Division, of the New York NATIONAL GUARD. He and his division had served under Holland Smith's V Amphibious Corps during operations against MAKIN in the GILBERT ISLANDS in late 1943 and on Saipan in the MARIANAS in mid–1944.

The 27th Division had come in for some criticism during the Makin operation, the Marines considering that it had taken too long to overcome what seemed to be relatively light Japanese opposition. (There were 6,500 US troops involved, against about 700 Japanese, including several hundred Korean laborers; CASUALTIES were 64 Americans killed, and virtually all of the Japanese.) When questioned about the matter, Ralph Smith appeared to have agreed that his division had not acted energetically on Makin. However, Makin was the division's baptism of fire. Moreover, the island had been designated the division's objective only a few weeks earlier, prior to which the division had been preparing for an invasion of NAURU. In addition, the landing had taken place after the division had spent 18 months on garrison duty in HAWAII. Some senior officers believed that it was stale from overtraining and inactivity, and considered the matter of little importance. Then, on Saipan, the division was assigned a sector between two Marine divisions. To the Marines, the division took much too long to get into position (some units were up to three hours late in reaching their assigned lines of departure) and then it attacked piecemeal. During the action, it appeared to be lagging behind the adjacent Marine units, creating a potentially dangerous situation as the flanks of these Marine units were exposed to the enemy. "Howling Mad" Smith took the matter up with Ralph Smith, with whom he was on fairly good personal terms. Ralph Smith seemed to agree that

the division was not progressing as fast as it might, and H. M. Smith ordered him to take care of the matter and get his front-line abreast of the Marine divisions. However, the performance of the division did not apparently improve. After consulting with MG Sandeford Jarman (USA), who was to become the commander of Saipan once it was secured, H. M. Smith took the matter up with VAdm Raymond SPRUANCE, his superior, requesting that Ralph Smith be relieved. After considering the matter, Spruance authorized H. M. Smith to effect the relief.

The relief of Ralph Smith was officially the result of poor performance on the part of his division. However, the problem was as much one of training, perception, and pride as it was of operational inefficiency. Ralph Smith was a likable, easygoing man, not a hard-driving, strong commander. Nor was he an effective communicator. He totally failed to apprise H. M. Smith of the nature of the opposition that his troops were facing. In fact, they had encountered the principal Japanese positions on the island, much stronger than those confronting the two Marine divisions. Indeed, the casualties borne by the 27th Division bear this out: Although the overall losses of each of the two Marine divisions were greater, the ratio of killed-to-wounded in the 27th Division was higher.

CASUALTIES ON SAIPAN			
Division	Killed	Total	Ratio
2nd Marine	1,256	6,170	1:4.9
4th Marine	1,107	6,612	1:5.9
27th Infantry	1,034	3,566	1:3.4

Further complicating the situation were differences in mindset between the army and the Marine Corps. Despite operating on islands, army commanders tended to think in continental terms. If you encounter difficult opposition, go around it. Unfortunately, on an island there is no room to go around. The only way to make progress is to go forward, using infiltration if possible, but in any case being prepared to take the losses. In addition, the Marine perception is essentially a naval one. The uppermost issue is the safety of the fleet. The quicker an island can be secured, the quicker the enormous concentration of ships lying off it to support the operation can disperse. Although unsaid at the time of Ralph Smith's relief, both H. M. Smith and Spruance believed that the delay in securing Makin in November 1943 was at least peripherally connected with the loss of the escort carrier *Liscome Bay*, TORPEDOED off the island on 24 November, with heavy loss of life.

The relief of an army general by a Marine struck a nerve in the army's high command, although some of the brass had also been critical of the 27th Division's performance. A number of senior army commanders in the Pacific undertook an investigation, bypassing the chain of command, which ran through Spruance and H. M. Smith. They concluded that there were no grounds for the relief, arguing that the operations of the 27th Infantry Division were conducted properly and with regard for conserving soldiers' lives, implying that the Marine Corps was not particularly concerned about that commodity. The relief of Ralph Smith still echoes in the US Army, specifically in the 27th Division, New York National Guard, where it remains a matter of "fighting words."

However, it seems reasonable to conclude that there would have been little furor if Ralph Smith had been relieved by an army officer. Four other army division commanders were relieved during the Pacific War. Little controversy, attended three of these reliefs, all effected by army superiors. The fourth case stirred up trouble because an admiral relieved the commander of the Seventh Infantry Division on Attu. In at least one case a relief by an Army officer was unjustified, that of MG Edward Herring of the 32nd Division. Herring was sacked by MACARTHUR for not taking BUNA quickly enough, despite the fact that he had no artillery, little air support, only half his manpower, few supplies, and a green division. No controversy resulted.

See also TARAWA, BATTLE OF.

Smoke

It has long been noted that fog, mist, and clouds can produce militarily useful concealment. Some parts of the world commonly have morning fog or mist, and the local troops have to learn to deal with it. Until artificial smoke devices were invented in this century, fog and the like would usually be a danger to defending troops, as they would allow attackers to get close without being exposed to missile fire (spears, arrows, muskets, cannon, etc.). Defenders derived some benefit from these natural obscurants because the attackers had to find their way partially blinded. One could always hope that the attacking troops would get lost, and this sometimes happened. But a well trained attacker knew how to find his way in the fog and usually didn't cover much more than a few hundred meters under these conditions anyway. Sometimes fires would be set to provide a smokescreen, but this was rather obvious, the enemy would thus be alerted, and was never commonly used. With the coming of gunpowder weapons in the past 500 years, battlefields often became obscured by the smoke of thousands of muskets and cannon being fired. Since these primitive weapons weren't all that accurate, and were fired in the general direction of the enemy, this black powder smoke screen was rarely a major factor for either side.

In this century, right about the time smokeless gunpowder appeared and cleared the battlefield somewhat, it was discovered that smoke grenades, smoke shells, and smoke pots could provide copious amounts of smoke on demand. This led to a new form of DECEPTION—blowing smoke. Rather than wait for nature to provide a convenient fog, artificial smoke could be used as needed. While a strong wind would rapidly disperse artificial smoke, average weather conditions were, quite naturally, the norm and no problem. Artificial smoke is delivered by three means: smoke grenades, smoke shells, and smoke pots. Smoke grenades are thrown like regular grenades. Smoke shells are like high-explosive shells, but contain smoke producing material instead of high explosive. Smoke pots are containers of various size that contain smoke producing material. The characteristics of these various items are as follows.

	Grenade	Shell	Pot
Weight (lbs.)	1–2	5–100	5–100
Time to Form (sec.)	10–20	1–3	10–30
Max. Length of Cloud (m.)	20–40	20–100	50–200
Duration of Smoke (sec.)	60–120	40–160	300–900

The variation in weight of the item results from different national designs as well as a variety of different sizes available for most items. Time to form reflects how long it takes to achieve a useful amount of smoke; the maximum length of cloud is in meters. The smoke is designed to stay close to the ground, so most smoke clouds are less than 10 meters high. Duration of smoke is the average time that the smoke cloud will last before dissipating into uselessness. In most cases, more than one of these items is used at once. Several grenades are tossed out to make sure there is sufficient smoke created. Smoke shells are fired in volleys, the number of shells depending on whether it's a battery volley (four to six guns) or a battalion volley (12–24 guns). The shells land in a line, quickly putting up a wall of smoke. Volleys may then be fired again and again to maintain the concealment provided by the smoke. Smoke pots have to be placed and ignited by hand, although in some rare cases the pots can be ignited by remote control. The normal use of artificial smoke is to hide troops from observation. If the enemy couldn't see troops, he couldn't accurately fire at them. While smoke did not stop bullets and shells, it made them much less accurate.

Infantry are very fond of smoke grenades, as they often find themselves in need of concealment, fast. But the infantry are also fond of using smoke as a pure deception. A knowledgeable enemy will expect something to be happening behind the cloud created by a few smoke grenades and will often fire into the cloud. For the smoke-using infantry, that enemy fire means the other guys are preoccupied with smoke, thus allowing for other maneuvers by the troops that tossed the grenades. In Vietnam, smoke grenades of various colors were used to mark targets for air strikes. Desperate troops could hurl colored smoke at the enemy even if there wasn't any friendly aircraft around. The enemy, not knowing about the absence of aircraft, but seeing the colored smoke that usually preceded the appearance of bombs and rockets, would take cover. The US troops could then make their escape.

Armored vehicles also use smoke. Most TANKS now have smoke-grenade launchers mounted on the turret. One or more of these grenades can be launched by the crew, putting an obscuring cloud of smoke to the front, thus ruining the aim of enemy gunners. Tank battles are often rather like chess games, with individual tanks moving to and fro trying to get a favorable firing position against any enemy tanks that might become visible. Smoke thus becomes a key tool in hiding tanks and their location or direction of movement. Smoke is so important that many older tanks had the ability to automatically pour oil over the hot engine manifold and create an impromptu smoke cloud that a tank could back up and retreat through. Along the same lines, some nations issue smoke grenades that put out black smoke. These are used to make a vehicle look like it's been hit by enemy fire. This usually fools pilots, and often ground troops as well. The most common use of black smoke grenades is to make a fake tank parking lot (full of inflated rubber tanks) look like the real thing after the bombs hit. But this trick is even used on the battlefield. The enemy will usually stop shooting at a target once it appears to be hit. A clever tank crew can stop their tank, pop a black smoke grenade out the hatch and then wait for the enemy artillery or antitank fire to shift.

Although SUBMARINES have little need for smoke grenades, they used a similar deception during World War II when they would release some oil (and perhaps debris from the torpedo tubes) when under attack. The destroyers topside would conclude that the sub had sunk and stop their attack. Unless, of course, the destroyer commander wasn't fooled. As always, a deception is only as good as its believability.

Smoke pots are most often used to hide rear area targets from observation or attack. Protecting a vital target like a bridge from air attack often involved the use of smoke pots. When it is known that enemy aircraft are in the area, the pots are ignited and the bridge covered with smoke. This will not stop the attack, but it will spoil the pilot's aim. Pots were also used to support major attacks. Crossing a river under enemy fire, for example, would often require the use of hundreds of smoke pots to hide the troops going across the water in assault boats. Most smoke pots can float, and can be released to flow with the current while emitting their protective cloud. Any attack across open ground benefits from smoke, and smoke pots are the best way to do it, given the time, and opportunity, to get the pots up front and ignited.

In the combat zone, smoke shells are the more common form of delivering large quantities of smoke. Everything from mortars to heavy artillery fire smoke shells. A particular favorite smoke shell type for Americans is White Phosphorus (WP, or "Willie Peter"). In addition to emitting a large quantity of shell, the phosphorus burns intensely, is difficult to extinguish, and provides a very unpleasant way to die. A little Willie Peter not only blinds the enemy, but also does a number on his morale as well.

Destroyers were also commonly equipped to make smoke, and both US and Japanese destroyes men made frequent use of it during the war.

SNLF

See MARINES, JAPANESE (NAVY GROUND FORCES).

SO3C Seamew, US Reconnaissance Floatplane

The SO3C Seamew was a US Navy floatplane used by cruisers and battleships for scouting. Although 800 SO3Cs were built between 1942 and 1944, it was an unsuccessful design that was withdrawn from service in 1944.

See also AIRCRAFT TYPES DEVELOPMENT; RECONNAISSANCE, NAVAL.

SOC Seagull, US Reconnaissance Floatplane

The SOC Seagull was a US Navy 1930s era biplane floatplane used for scouting by cruisers and battleships. It was a very successful design. The models entered service in 1935 and over 200 were built. The SOC continued in service until the end of the war.

See also AIRCRAFT TYPES DEVELOPMENT; RECONNAISSANCE.

Society Islands

Including Tahiti, these form the principal part of French Polynesia. Although they were too far to the east to experience any fighting, the islands were useful for air and naval bases. The Japanese never attacked the Society Islands, but they were on their list of objectives to be pursued after the expected victory at MIDWAY. In early 1942 the United States established a modest base at Bora Bora.

Soerabaya, Java, Netherlands East Indies

The principal Dutch naval base in the East Indies, Soerabaya had good, if limited facilities to service warships, even a decent dry dock, and was an important air base. Despite Allied efforts to sabotage the base, and the ships in it, the Japanese were able to put it, and them, into service. Soerabaya was several times bombed by carrier aircraft from the British Far Eastern Fleet, but remained in Japanese hands until the end of the war.

See also ROYAL NAVY.

Solomon Islands

The Solomon Islands comprise seven large and many small islands forming two chains that stretch about 900 miles southeastward from the BISMARCK ARCHIPELAGO in the southwest Pacific, totaling about 60,000 square miles. Very wet, the jungle-covered, mountainous islands were poor but supplied various tropical products to the world market (copra-dried coconut meat, for the soap trade, for example). In 1941 the islands had a thin population consisting mostly of Melanesians (c. 100,000) with a few Australians and Britons (c. 650), mostly managers of the copra plantations and colonial officials. Most of the Europeans were evacuated before the Japanese invaders arrived in early and mid-1942.

Solomon Islands, Campaign for

This was the longest campaign of the Pacific War and was still going on when the war ended. Japanese troops kept fighting in the Solomons until mid-1945, and for some years after that. The portion of the Solomon Islands campaign that is most often remembered is the initial battle for Guadalcanal. This American landing in August of 1942 led to three months of furious land, air, and naval battles that resulted in a Japanese decision to withdraw from the island by early 1943. But the Japanese were not giving up on the Solomons, but rather pulling back toward their major base to the north, at RABAUL.

Throughout 1943, two American divisions (one army and one Marine) moved up the Solomons from island to island. Hundreds of bombers and fighters supported these amphibious operations. Japanese warships in the area would give battle from time to time, usually in support of moving troops from an island or bringing in supplies. Having lost control of the air to the Allies, the Japanese could only resist the enemy advance, not stop it.

The Japanese ground forces involved were the Sixth Infantry Division, based on BOUGAINVILLE Island (the northernmost of the Solomons), and the equivalent of another division in various smaller army and navy infantry units. Because the Japanese were defending a lot of island, or trying to, their units were spread out, allowing the Amer-

icans to concentrate on one smaller Japanese garrison at a time. During the summer of 1943, American amphibious and air attacks destroyed Japanese defenders in the central Solomon islands. New Georgia and the surrounding islands were taken by September, although fight-to-the-death Japanese tactics kept the attacking American units occupied through the rest of 1943. In October of 1943, the NEW ZEALAND Third Infantry Division and the US Third Marine Division joined the operation for the assault on Bougainville. The fighting here died down by the end of 1943. But the shooting never stopped. The Allies built airfields on Guadalcanal, and sent troops to defend them. The aircraft then bombed Japanese bases on Bougainville and surrounding islands, while keeping Japanese ships from supplying their island garrisons. The Japanese were still fighting when the war ended. But because of American air superiority, Japanese troops never had sufficient ammunition or other supplies to launch serious attacks. After the war, the remaining Japanese troops were often hunted with tracking dogs. After a few years, all the remaining and defiant Japanese were either dead of natural causes or hunted down.

Considering the remaining Japanese resistance, the Solomons Campaign continued until after the war ended. But for all practical purposes, Japanese forces in the Solomons were no longer a threat by early 1944. It had taken the Allies some 20 months to retake the Solomons, once the campaign got under way in August 1942. New Zealand and Australian troops, for the most part, remained behind to harry the Japanese. The American units continued north for the invasion of the Philippines in late 1944.

Solomon Islands Defence Force

In 1939 the British colonial authorities in the Solomon Islands raised the small Solomon Islands Defence Force, composed of local enlisted men under British and Australian officers, using PIDGIN as the language of command. When the Japanese came, most of these troops took refuge in the rugged, jun-

Freshly landed troops of the 43rd Infantry Division take shelter among the trees on Rendova, June 30, 1943. The invasion of Rendova, in the central Solomons, was a further step toward the isolation of Rabaul. The landings occurred at daybreak in a rainstorm, and this may have contributed to light Japanese resistance to the initial assault

gle-covered interiors of the islands. Although it never numbered more than about 400 men, the Solomon Islands Defence Force proved invaluable to the Allies. Not only did its men collect information, rescue downed pilots, and act as guides for US and Commonwealth troops, but they also regularly ambushed Japanese troops and provided essential protection for COASTWATCHERS.

The most famous SIDF soldier was Sergeant Major Jacob Vouza. A former chief of police in the local constabulary and a native of GUADALCANAL, Vouza, a Christian, served with Coastwatcher Martin Clement. He had many heroic adventures during the war. For example, on the eve of the Japanese attack across the Tenaru River, on Guad-

alcanal, he was scouting behind Japanese lines when he was captured. Finding a small American flag on his person, the Japanese tied him to a tree, then beat him and bayoneted him several times. They then left, leaving him to die. Vouza managed to get loose from his bonds and crawl three miles through the jungle to warn the Marines of the impending attack. He later guided the MARINE Raiders on their month-long (4 November–4 December 1942) foray behind Japanese lines. For his efforts he received a Silver Star from the United States and a knighthood from Britain. So impressed by his courage were the Marines that they presented him with a sword of honor and made him an honorary sergeant major in the Corps. A national hero in the SOLOMONS, Vouza wore his Marine uniform on ceremonial occasions for the rest of his life, and was ever willing to talk over old times with old comrades.

In addition to the SIDF there was also a Solomon Islands Labour Corps, which had a peak strength of some 3,700 men who performed a variety of tasks, from unloading supplies to clearing brush, often under fire.

See also KENNEDY'S ARMY.

Ref: Ready, *Forgotten Allies*; White and Lindstrom, eds., *The Pacific Theater*.

Somers Class, US Destroyers

Designed as flotilla leaders, the five destroyers of the Somers class, built 1936–39, were about 10% larger and mounted 50% more TORPEDO tubes than the PORTERS, completed two or three years earlier. As their hull dimensions were virtually the same as that of the Porters, the Somers were rather top heavy. A disappointment in service, in order to increase their antiaircraft capability they had to lose four torpedo tubes and two 5-inch guns to retain their stability. One became a war loss.

Somerville, James (1882–1949)

James E. Somerville joined the ROYAL NAVY in 1897. After serving in gunboats on the Nile in the Sudan he became one of the Royal Navy's first radio specialists. During World War I he held various posts as a wireless officer, notably distinguishing himself during the Dardanelles Campaign. He rose through the ranks between the wars, and actually retired from the service for reasons of health shortly before World War II broke out.

Somerville remained inactive until Dunkirk, when he voluntarily offered his services to Admiral Bertram Ramsay, for whom he performed yeoman service in coordinating the movements of the numerous ships involved in the evacuation. He soon found himself back on active duty (his health problems meanwhile having been cleared up), assigned to command Force H, at Gibraltar, from June 1940

through March of 1942, one of the most demanding posts in the Royal Navy, during which period he commanded the attack on the French Fleet at Mirs-el-Kebir, and attempted with considerable success to keep the sea lanes open to Malta. In March of 1942, with the Japanese overrunning much of Southeast Asia, Somerville was transferred to command the hastily assembled British Far Eastern Fleet. Although his performance in this post was successful, Somerville was also quite lucky and he made the most of ULTRA information, so that in March and April of 1942, when the Japanese First Air Fleet (i.e., the PEARL HARBOR Strike Force, of six carriers) did considerable damage to shipping and port facilities in the Bay of Bengal (racking up a light carrier, two heavy cruisers, and much else besides), he was able to avoid a direct confrontation with the enemy.

In 1944 Somerville was sent as head of the British Naval Mission to the United States, in which capacity he ended the war, having meanwhile been promoted to admiral of the fleet. A good officer, Somerville was also lucky.

Sorge, Richard (1895–1944)

A German journalist, the Tokyo correspondent for the *Frankfurter Zeitung* from 1933, and a member of the Nazi Party, Sorge was actually a Russian agent, having been recruited by Soviet intelligence in the 1920s. An apparent admirer of Japanese culture, and married to a Japanese woman, Sorge had several links into the Japanese high command. One of his closest friends was Ozaki Hozumi, a closet communist sympathizer who was an aide to Prince Konoye, a kinsman of the emperor. Sorge also cultivated the German ambassador to Japan, General Eugene Ott. He provided Stalin with the critical information that the Japanese were going to attack the United States and Britain in December of 1941, not Russia. This enabled Stalin to safely shift troops from the Far East to undertake the Moscow counteroffensive the day after Pearl Harbor.

Sorge was arrested by the Japanese in October 1941 and hanged in 1944.

Ref: Prange, Goldstein, and Dillon, *Target Tokyo.*

Soryu, Japanese Aircraft Carrier

Soryu (1934–1935–1937) was a well-designed ship, lightly built and fast, with an aircraft operational capacity equal to that of AKAGI or KAGA, both of which were about twice her displacement. She took part in operations against China, 1937–39, and then, paired with HIRYU, which was sometimes classed as her sister, Soryu formed Carrier Division Two and served with the First Air Fleet from Pearl Harbor to MIDWAY, where she took three bombs, burst into flames, and blew up.

South Dakota Class, US Battleships

Although displacing slightly more than the NORTH CAROLINA CLASS battleships, the South Dakotas were shorter by about 50 feet and narrower by about 2 feet. They were also built with several innovative ideas in mind, none of which had been adequately tested, and not all of which proved satisfactory. As a result, they were not only rather cramped and uncomfortable, but were also slightly slower, less stable, and less maneuverable than were their predecessors. On the other hand, they were probably somewhat better protected.

South Dakota, BB-57 (1939–1941–1942), fitted as a flagship with four fewer 5"/38 dual-purpose guns than her sisters, was the only unit seriously engaged in the Pacific. Entering the Pacific in August of 1942, she provided antiaircraft protection for the carrier *Enterprise* at SANTA CRUZ ISLAND (26 October), repeatedly beating off Japanese air attacks. In one action she was attacked by 29 dive bombers, only one of which was able to plant a bomb on her, which caused one death, about 50 other injuries, and some serious damage to one 16-inch gun. She was more heavily damaged by Japanese shell fire on the night of 14–15 November 1942, taking 26 hits by 5-inch to 8-inch shells, plus one 14-inch, the only confirmed enemy battleship hit on an American battlewagon ever, suffering 38

killed and about 60 wounded. Repair, in Brooklyn, required 62 days of round-the-clock work. Upon being repaired she served with the ROYAL NAVY in Europe in 1943, before returning to the Pacific to support fast carrier operations and amphibious landings. Although the ship was scrapped in 1962, certain relics were preserved for display in South Dakota.

Indiana, BB-58 (1939–1941–1942), began active service off GUADALCANAL in early November 1942, but missed the ferocious night battles there on 12–15 November. Her career in the war was rather pedestrian, firing on shore targets (Guadalcanal, TARAWA, HOLLANDIA, TRUK, the MARIANAS, IWO JIMA, OKINAWA, and the Home Islands) and providing antiaircraft protection to the fleet. Her only damage due to enemy action (she suffered severely in a collision with the battleship *Washington* in 1944 and less so in the typhoon of 5 June 1945) occurred on 19 June 1944, during the Battle of the PHILIPPINE SEA, when a Japanese plane crashed into her, wounding several men but causing only a barely perceptible dent in her armor. Scrapped in 1964.

Massachusetts, BB-59 (1939–1941–1942), nicknamed "Big Mamie," first went into action at Casablanca on November 8, 1942, where 786 of her 16-inch and 221 of her 5-inch rounds put a partially completed French battleship (see RICHELIEU CLASS, FRENCH BATTLESHIP) out of action, helped sink two destroyers, and damaged another destroyer and a light cruiser, as well as various shore installations, while taking several hits in return, albeit without serious damage or any CASUALTIES. She entered the Pacific in early 1943, helping to bombard enemy-held islands and to protect the fleet from air attack. During the war she was in action against enemy forces 35 times, sinking or damaging five ships by gunfire and downing 18 Japanese aircraft, all while never losing a man to enemy action. In 1965 she became a war memorial at Fore River, Massachusetts.

Alabama, BB-60 (1940–1942–1942), served with the Royal Navy March–July 1943, helping to cover Arctic convoys to Russia. She began operations in the Pacific at Tarawa in November of 1943, and from then to the end of the war provided shore bombardment and antiaircraft defense to the fleet. She was never damaged by enemy action. In 1964 she became a war memorial at Mobile, Alabama.

Soviet Union

In 1941 the Soviet Union was the third most populous nation on the planet. With 199 million people, it was eclipsed only by India (controlled by Britain) and China. When Japan attacked in the Pacific, the Soviet Union was already six months into its war with Germany. The Nazis were within sight of Moscow and were about to be tossed back by the first successful Soviet counterattack. Germany expected Japan to attack Russia shortly after it conquered its objectives in the Pacific. But Japan refused to do so, and for good reason. Throughout the war, the Soviets always maintained at least a million troops in their Far East.

Despite the need to maintain enormous forces against the Germans, and in the face of over 10 million combat deaths, the Russians managed to maintain formidable combat forces facing the Japanese in northern China. In the chart (below), the "Military Situation" shows that, despite the fact that the German invasion in June 1941 was a major catastrophe for the Russians, their forces in the Far

East were nearly doubled in the following six months. The Russians did not discount the possibility that the Japanese might attack them, and this shows as the Soviets increased their Far East manpower through the summer of 1942. Two things happened that summer. First, the Japanese lost their naval advantage when four of their carriers were sunk at the Battle of MIDWAY. Then, in the fall, the German summer offensive stalled and the stage was set for the Battle of Stalingrad in late 1942. This battle became the first major decisive defeat for the Germans. At this point, any alliance of Japan with Germany seemed less likely, as did a Japanese attack on the Russian Far East. So Soviet troops strength declined in the Far East.

Although the number of Russian troops was large, the quality of these Far Eastern forces was not the same as those facing the Germans. Many of the Russian troops were lower quality local reservists. As long as they could move and hold a weapon, the Russians put them in uniform. The equipment, by and large, was not first rate. Second-line TANKS and aircraft could be safely sent to the Far East. While the Japanese had a lot of good aircraft in MANCHURIA, they were always outnumbered by Russian equipment. Moreover, the Japanese never developed world-class tanks, so even the older Russian models were superior.

Despite 30 million dead by early 1945, the Soviet Union still managed to have 11 million troops in the field by the time the Germans surrendered in May of that year. Millions of tons of weapons, equipment, and raw materials from the Western Allies (mainly the United States) kept the Russians going. The Germans had, by the fall of 1942, occupied areas containing 40% of Russia's population and over a third of its industry. This was not enough to knock the Soviet Union out of the war, nor tempt Japan to attack in the Far East.

The battles Russia and Japan fought on their borders in 1939 had left an impression on the Japanese Army. There was no desire to take on the Russians again unless the situation looked very favorable. Indeed, the Japanese went out of their way to maintain cordial relations with the Russians

SOVIET MILITARY FORCES IN THE FAR EAST

Date	Troops (x1000)	Armored Vehicles	Combat Aircraft	Military Situation
1941 June	703	3,100	4,100	German Invasion
1941 December	1,343	2,100	3,100	Battle of Moscow
1942 July	1,446	2,500	3,100	German Summer Offensive
1942 November	1,296	2,500	3,300	Battle of Stalingrad
1943 July	1,156	2,300	3,900	Battle of Kursk
1944 January	1,162	2,000	4,000	Russian Winter Offensive
1945 May	1,185	2,300	4,300	Germany Surrenders
1945 August	1,577	5,500	5,400	Attack on Japan

throughout the war. In April 1941, the Japanese signed a five-year non-aggression pact with the Soviet Union and were careful to avoid any incidents that might threaten this treaty. Thus Russian pilots were able to freely fly thousands of American LEND-LEASE aircraft from Alaska to airfields in the Soviet Far East throughout the war. In addition, Russian ships regularly carried American aid from US ports to Vladivostok throughout the war. The Japanese never molested these ships or aircraft.

The Soviets also made contributions to these good relations. In 1939, the Russians cut off their aid to the Nationalist Chinese. This was not insubstantial, as thousands of Russian military advisers, including combat pilots, worked with the Chinese. Aid continued to the communist Chinese, but this was not substantial and was done discreetly. On at least one occasion during the war, the Soviets deliberately leaked critical information about US war plans to the Japanese. Early in October 1944 the Japanese were still uncertain as to whether the next major US objective in the Pacific would be the Philippines, FORMOSA, or possibly even OKINAWA. At a diplomatic cocktail party, the Soviet foreign minister "casually" mentioned to the Japanese ambassador that US heavy bombers based in China were about to undertake operations against the Philippines, a matter that the ambassador dutifully communicated to his government. Soviet motivation for this leak is unclear, but may have represented a desire to ensure that the Pacific War lasted long enough for Russia to get involved.

The Japanese believed, once it was obvious that the Americans would keep on coming to Japan itself, that a deal could be made with the Russians. In early 1945, Japan offered to form a coalition with Russia and "rule Asia." The Russians strung the Japanese along, not letting on that the Soviet Union had promised Britain and America that Russian armies would invade Manchuria, "within three months of Germany surrendering." Germany gave up on 8 May and Russia attacked Japan on 8 August. Not only that, but the Russians began their invasion of Japanese-held Sakhalin Island on 16 August, a day after Japan surrendered. America protested, but did nothing to interfere with the Soviet conquest of Sakhalin and the KURILE ISLANDS throughout late August.

Millions of Japanese colonists lived and worked in Korea and Manchuria. Moreover, most of the Japanese Army was still in Manchuria and China. The Japanese leadership expected to fall back on these mainland resources even if Japan itself was invaded. The only thing that could spoil this grand plan was the entry of Russia into the war. The Soviets, with advance knowledge of the American ATOMIC BOMB project, saw no reason whatsoever to ally themselves with the Japanese. Yet the senior people in Tokyo continued to believe a deal with Russia was possible until the Soviet Union invaded Manchuria on August 8, 1945.

See also ANTI-COMINTERN TREATY.

Ref: Glantz, *August Storm*.

Soviet Union, Internment of US Airmen

Although allied with the United States in the European War, the Soviet Union was formally neutral in the Pacific. As a result, US pilots who landed in Soviet territory after missions over Japan were interned.

The first internees were the crew of one of the B-25s that participated in the DOOLITTLE Raid, in April 1942. They were eventually joined by 242 US Army and Navy airmen who participated in missions from the ALEUTIANS to the KURILES and were forced to make emergency landings on Soviet territory. Still others became lost during air raids over Japan and were interned after landing B-29s.

US airmen interned in the USSR were treated according to the provisions of the GENEVA CONVENTION. Their aircraft were generally impounded by the Russians and used for experimentation and, in the case of B-29s, became the basis for the PRODUCTION of a line of Soviet postwar bombers. In a number of cases interned American airmen somehow managed to "escape" from Soviet internment, make their way to Iran, and turn themselves in to US occupation authorities. Of those not previously spirited out of the country, all known US internees in the Soviet Union were released beginning August 24, 1945.

Spitfire, British Fighter

The Spitfire, the principal British fighter throughout the war, went through continuous upgrades and modifications to keep it competitive with new enemy aircraft. This resulted in many Spitfire types, each having substantially different performance. The first (1938) Spitfire, the Mark 1, had a speed of 360 MPH and four .30 caliber machine guns. The last wartime version, the Mark 18, had a top speed of 448 MPH and was armed with two 20mm cannon and two .50 caliber machine guns. Loaded weight went from 2.6 tons to 4.6 tons. Ceiling, rate of climb, maneuverability, range, and bomb load all improved with the many different versions. Some 20,000 were produced during the war and several hundred more into the late 1940s. By 1943, the Spitfire was a common foe for Japanese aircraft over Burma. For service with the ROYAL NAVY there was a "navalized" version, the SEAFIRE.

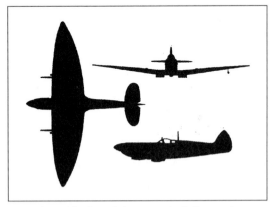

One of the finest fighter aircraft of all time, the Supermarine Spitfire was in continuous production from 1936 through 1947, 22 distinct models being produced, as well as eight models of the Seafire.

Spruance, Raymond (1886–1969)

One of the most successful American admirals of the war, Raymond Spruance graduated from Annapolis in 1906, made the Great White Fleet's world cruise, commanded a destroyer, and helped complete and commission the new battleship PENNSYLVANIA, all by 1916. During World War I he commanded the destroyer *Aaron Ward* in the Atlantic. After the war he held various command and staff positions, taught in several navy schools, and attended the Naval War College. Shortly after PEARL HARBOR he was given command of Cruiser Division 5, which served with Task Force 16 on the DOOLITTLE Raid. Due to William HALSEY's illness, Spruance was in temporary command of TF 16 at MIDWAY, and performed so well in this role that despite not being aviation qualified, he continued thereafter to command carrier task forces, being provided with a staff consisting mostly of aviators. For a time chief of staff to NIMITZ, Spruance was shortly put in command of what would become the Fifth Fleet (an assignment he rotated with Halsey, under whom it was called the Third Fleet). With Fifth Fleet Spruance commanded in the TARAWA Operation, at ENIWETOK, in the MARIANAS (during which he won the Battle of the PHILIPPINE SEA), IWO JIMA, and OKINAWA.

At the end of the war Spruance became president of the Naval War College. He retired in 1948, and served for a time as ambassador to the Philippines. Spruance proved surprisingly effective as a carrier commander. However, although he did everything right at Midway, his actions during the Philippine Sea were less effective. Failing to realize that he had the Japanese carriers at his mercy, he defeated but did not destroy them, despite the urging of several members of his staff. This was a failure without much penalty, as the Japanese force had been basically ruined during the battle, if not completely destroyed. But in other circumstances, such a lack of follow-through on Spruance's part might have had serious aftereffects. However, considering Halsey's more disastrous failure during the

Battle of LEYTE GULF, which led to the Japanese battleship attack on the escort carriers off SAMAR, it seems strange that Halsey was promoted to fleet admiral and Spruance was not.

Stilwell, Joseph W. (1883–1946)

One of the most controversial American officers of the war, Joseph "Vinegar Joe" Stilwell graduated from West Point in 1904 and soon afterward was in action against the Moro tribesmen in the Philippines. Over the next few years he rose through the ranks. The outbreak of World War I found him as an instructor at West Point, from which post he was sent to France to serve first as a liaison officer with the Allied armies and later as staff officer with the AEF. After the war he was an intelligence officer in China, attended various army schools, commanded the 15th Infantry in China, once again served on various staffs and as an instructor, was military attaché to China, and at the time of PEARL HARBOR was commanding the III Corps in California. Early in 1942 he was promoted to lieutenant general and sent to command all US forces in the CBI, while simultaneously serving as chief of staff to the Chinese Nationalist Army. Although reinforced by several Chinese divisions, the Allied position in Burma collapsed, and Stilwell led a remarkably arduous retreat to the security of India. In India he reorganized US forces, while training Chinese divisions that were then flown home over the Himalayas. Although he did well in these assignments, even when made deputy commander to Lord MOUNTBATTEN, Stilwell's personality was abrasive. A "tell it like it is" sort, Stilwell tended to irritate CHIANG. Although President ROOSEVELT attempted to get Chiang to place Stilwell in overall command of Chinese forces, in the end he had to recall the general. For a time chief of Army Ground Forces, in the spring of 1945 Stilwell was put in command of the 10th Army on OKINAWA. After the war he held an administrative command until his death, from stomach cancer. He was a brilliant officer, with excellent ideas that would probably have worked, but without much chance of getting them into practice due to Chinese resistance.

Strategic Planning, Average Speeds

Since different types of ships had different speeds, coordinating the movements of large forces for offensive undertakings was no easy task. Consider the difficulties a fleet commander would have if he was trying to effect an amphibious landing on a hostile shore, supported by appropriate naval forces.

The Landing Force probably could sustain 12 knots, which was very likely its maximum speed as well, because LSTS could make no more than that, albeit they could do so for over 3,500 miles without refueling.

The Bombardment Group, old battleships assigned to "soften up" the landing beaches, could sustain 15 knots, and in a pinch make 20 or so for a while.

The Escort Group, "jeep" carriers providing close air support to the assault force, could sustain about 15 knots for short periods, but 12 was more practical for extended voyages.

The Support Group, the cargo ships, tankers, hospital ships, repair vessels, and so forth, could sustain 15 knots, albeit not for very long periods, 12 being more practical.

The Carrier Task Forces supporting the landings could cruise at 15 to 25 knots for extended periods, and could maintain as much as 30 for days on end as well.

Now, making allowances for maneuvering, replenishment and the like, the Carrier Task Force could cover 300 to 500 miles a day, and the Bombardment and Escort Groups could probably manage 300, while the Landing Force and Support Group would be lucky to make 250. In addition, it was common to have SUBMARINES support operations, as a scouting screen and to pick up downed flyers, and these could cover only 200 to 250 miles a day. Note that on land, the average speed of a mechanized unit (when not fighting) was rarely more than a hundred miles a day.

So the admiral in command had to juggle his task groups. This was one factor that made life on the fast carriers a grueling experience. While the slower ships maintained relatively steady courses, the fast carriers ended up making frequent, irregular course changes, moving back and forth in irregular patterns, so as to provide cover for the slower moving ships. And in order to confuse the enemy as to location of the landings, the carriers would probably undertake air strikes at everything within range.

A knot is a unit of time and distance. Saying that a particular force "proceeded at 20 knots" is the equivalent of saying it "proceeded at 20 nautical miles an hour," which is the same as "23 miles per hour" in landlubberese, or "37 kilometers an hour" in metric.

Strategic Planning, Japanese Wishful Thinking

Military planners tend to be an optimistic lot. After all, there are so many things that can go wrong in war that one has to have a pretty positive outlook in order to have any faith whatsoever in success. But optimism can be taken to extremes. And perhaps never in military history has wishful thinking come to substitute for solid planning as much as in the Imperial Japanese Navy during World War II.

For example, during staff wargames (simulated operations on paper, using elaborate rules), it was not uncommon for umpires to allow "operations" to proceed despite an absence of supplies. They often permitted units to "refuel" from tankers the fleet did not possess, without any loss of time, so that the planned operations could proceed as scheduled.

But there were worse cases of cheating at wargames than the refueling gambit. The Japanese naval general staff held a major wargame as part of the planning for the MIDWAY Operation. Early in the game the American player managed to "sink" several of the attacking carriers, a matter that so upset the umpires that they restored the carriers to

play. Even the subsequent disaster at Midway did not prove a salutary lesson.

Aware of the shortcomings of these earlier wargames, a new approach was decided on. Shortly after Midway, there was another wargame with even more interesting results, and some unusual players, namely Japanese diplomats just returned from the United States. During the early part of the war all the belligerents, including the United States and Japan, arranged for the REPATRIATION of diplomatic personnel (including military attachés) who had found themselves trapped in enemy countries by the outbreak of hostilities. As a result, a number of senior and middle-ranking Japanese naval personnel actually spent much of the first eight or nine months of the Pacific War living in relatively comfortable circumstances in the United States.

When the last batch of these officers returned to Japan, shortly after Midway, they were deliberately not briefed on the status of the war as understood by the Imperial Navy, and were then organized into a team to play the American side in a simulation game, which was to cover the next two years of the war. The idea was sound, as these officers, one of whom was a rear admiral had full access to the American press while awaiting repatriation, and might be expected to have a useful perspective on American notions of how the war should be fought.

The game was conducted around the time the Marines landed on GUADALCANAL. Despite rules that were generally favorable to the Japanese (such as reduced US industrial productivity), by October 1944 the "Americans" were landing in the Philippines, a matter that was extremely upsetting to the naval staff. The results of these games so shocked the Japanese High Command that no official notice of the game was circulated, all documentation was destroyed, and the officers who had taken the part of the Americans were scattered to various obscure posts, and told "Keep your mouth shut." This despite the fact the game could easily have been used to help develop more realistic industrial PRODUCTION and strategic plans.

The initial US landings in the Philippines occurred approximately three weeks later than those in the wargame.

Strategy, Multiple and the Japanese

An ancient bit of military wisdom is that it is unwise to fight a "two front" war. Japan went into World War II struggling to deal with five fronts.

Two of these are familiar to Americans, with General MACARTHUR's offensive in the southwest Pacific, from the SOLOMONS and NEW GUINEA and northwestward toward the Philippines, and Admiral NIMITZ's series of island assaults across the central Pacific.

A third campaign is rather less familiar to Americans—Burma and the Indian frontier—where sizable Japanese armies struggled with British and Indian soldiers for three years.

The fourth front was where most of the Japanese Army (which ultimately comprised 10% of Japan's adult population) was occupied, the war in China. Here, millions died during the war, mostly Chinese.

And finally, there was that potential fifth front, as tensions had existed between the Soviet Union and Japan for a long time. In 1939 the Japanese initiated several battles with Soviet forces on the Manchurian border. The Japanese lost, and decided to defer their plans to run the Soviets out of eastern Siberia. Japan had to maintain large forces in MANCHURIA to guard against an attack by the Soviet Union, an attack which did not come until literally the last week of the war.

Because Japan is an island, all these battlefronts had to be supplied by ship. Japan began the war with a shipping shortage and this only got worse. Japan's prospects of success on any of these fronts were dim. Indeed, even if Japan had had but one front, her shipping problems would have been enormously difficult. America opened two widely separated fronts in the Pacific because US industry was able to produce enough ships and aircraft to support two separate assaults on Japan.

The war in China had been dragging on since the early 1930s, with slim prospects for eventual Japanese success. The occupation of Burma and subsequent invasion of India was largely based on the assumption that if the Japanese got into India proper, the Indians would rise up and drive the British out. The British took the precaution of promising the Indians independence when the war was over; the Indians believed the British and most of the "British" fighting the Japanese were actually Indian.

Japan had long seen Russia, and later the Soviet Union, as its major enemy in Asia. The war with America and her allies was something Japan wanted to avoid, and believed she could avoid. But the Soviet Union bordered the Japanese colony of Manchuria. Through most of the war, there were at least 30 Soviet divisions in what the Russians called "the Far East" (Siberia is the region to the north and west). Japan had only a dozen divisions in Manchuria, but the Japanese believed they could eventually increase this force and successfully attack the Russians.

The Japanese kept the peace on their border with the Soviet Union from then on and assumed that all would be forgotten. Especially when the Japanese did not take advantage of Soviet weakness when most Russian divisions were sent west against the Germans in late 1941. In 1942, the Japanese made plans to rebuild their Manchurian forces. But defeats in the Pacific soon undercut these aspirations.

The Soviets did not forget, and in August 1945 the Soviets opened a fifth front with a massive invasion of Japanese-controlled Manchuria. Japan surrendered to the Allies on August 15 1945.

Strategy, US, FDR vs. MacArthur

Douglas MACARTHUR and his numerous sycophants often claimed that his command was starved of men and resources during the war because high-ranking military and political leaders feared that if he proved too successful against the Japanese, he would almost certainly win the presidency in 1944, unseating the jealous Franklin ROOSEVELT.

Actually, MacArthur's command was hardly "starved." Particularly in 1942, far more men and equipment were sent to him than to Europe. Both FDR and George C. MARSHALL, the army chief of staff, although committed to the "Germany first" strategy, recognized the desperate nature of the situation in the southwest Pacific. An examination of available figures on troop and materiel movements bears this out. Six of the first 10 divisions to ship out during the war went to the Pacific, where there were already two US divisions, not counting the forces in the Philippines.

What did give MacArthur some cause for concern was that, although massive amounts of shipping, troops, and supplies were sent to the Pacific, much was diverted to the ALEUTIANS. The Japanese occupation of several islands in the Aleutians during June 1942 caused consternation on the west coasts of Canada and the United States. It became politically imperative to get the Japanese out of there as soon as possible. But this took enormous amounts of materiel, and to this day it is little known that, for months at a time, over a third of the materiel sent to the Pacific went north to Alaska rather than west to New Guinea and the SOLOMONS. By spring of 1943, the Aleutians were cleared of Japanese and all supply efforts again went west.

See also NATIONAL GUARD.

Ref: Larrabee, *Commander in Chief*.

Strategy, US and Japanese

Strategy is the overall plan a nation has for winning a campaign or war. The United States and Japan had quite different strategies for winning in the Pacific.

The original, 1920s-era US plan for a war with Japan ("WAR PLAN ORANGE") was to advance across the central Pacific to the Philippines (whether those islands were under attack or not). Most of the central Pacific islands were under Japanese control and many were known to be heavily fortified. The principal weapon would be the battleship, with the aircraft carriers used for scouting and support. Once the enemy battleships were found, the decisive battle would be fought, the United States would win, and it would all be over within about six months or so. Not much attention was paid to Japanese aircraft that might be on their central Pacific islands, as aircraft had not yet demonstrated that they could demolish a large battle fleet.

By the late 1930s prescient naval officers were beginning to realize that War Plan Orange was unworkable, but it was not really formally replaced because other officers continued to argue that the plan would work. The pessimists were right, of course. The problem now was that all those Japanese-held islands had airfields, and an increasing number of naval officers were accepting the fact that warships on the high seas would be very vulnerable to enemy bombers. The optimists were not yet convinced, although they would be during December 1941. When the war came the Philippines were lost, along with nearly everything else west of HAWAII, and the battleships that were not sunk at PEARL HARBOR were now acknowledged to be quite vulnerable to carrier aircraft.

Forced to use Australia as the main forward base in the Pacific, the primary American advance initially was from the south, through New Guinea and on to the Philippines, which were reached after nearly three years of war. All this was supported by some carrier, but mostly land-based, aircraft.

The US Navy had built so many carriers and support ships by late 1943, that a second advance through the central Pacific was proposed. This was accomplished with massive carrier air power, huge amphibious operations, and admirals determined not to let the army run the show by itself.

This brings up another important point about Pacific war STRATEGY, the ongoing conflict between army and navy commanders. This was a problem in both Japan and America. It was worse for the Japanese, where there was no one like President ROOSEVELT or Admiral KING and General MARSHALL (the senior US officers) to resolve, or at least defuse, the disputes. It's ironic that the Japanese are now known for their devotion to consensus, for they were anything but during World War II. It was the Americans who managed to work out their different approaches to strategy during the war.

In both nations, the army and navy had long been quite separate worlds. But there were some unique aspects to the army-navy situation in America.

The United States was, and is, a maritime power. Normally, it does not need much of an army because there are no threatening armies on its land borders. But from its beginnings, America depended on overseas trade, and the protection of its shipping, in order to provide a livelihood for many of its people. In the century before Pearl Harbor:

The army and navy rarely operated together. The one major exception was the Civil War. But that was seen as a unique situation and no lasting wisdom was obtained from the experience.

The army had always seen itself as the senior service when it came to planning and directing military operations. Of course, this began to change with the Spanish-American War, where the navy had to go first, defeat the Spanish fleets, and then the army followed. The army was not happy about this new state of affairs, but it was obvious that any future war would see the army traveling by sea, under navy protection, to future battlefields.

While the president was commander in chief, nothing was done to create any organization to coordinate planning and operations by the army and navy. Early in World War II, something was cobbled together, but it was improvisation all through the war.

The Japanese army-navy situation was also characterized by some uniquely Japanese conditions:

The army was heavily involved in domestic, and foreign, politics. The navy was relatively apolitical and, as a result, kept its distance from army commanders.

Japan was, like America, a maritime power and even more dependent on overseas trade to sustain its people. Protecting sea lanes was, of course, a navy responsibility. But until the war began, the most crucial routes were short (between Japan and Korea and China) and could, in theory, be secured by army land-based air power. As a result, the army didn't pay as much attention to working with the navy as it should have. In effect, the army acted like it was doing the navy a favor by letting the navy help out in the China war.

When the Pacific war began, the army and navy had to improvise all their cooperation. In many cases, like the central Pacific, the navy often did everything with its own resources, including naval infantry (SNLF) to seize islands.

Keep in mind, that, relative to the squabbling between American generals and admirals, that between their Japanese counterparts was infinitely worse. Prominent examples of the damage done by Japanese army-navy rivalry were:

The refusal (until too late in the war) to coordinate the use of shipping. The Japanese had a shipping shortage from the beginning of the war, and the situation got worse as the war went on. The army and navy insisted on maintaining their own separate merchant fleets and not cooperating with each other or Japanese commercial interests. In other words, if an army cargo ship was leaving Japan for JAVA half-full, and the navy needed to get supplies to Java at the same time, the army would not allow the navy cargo in the empty space on its outgoing ship. Moreover, when these ships returned from places like Java, they would not carry commercial cargo back to Japan, they would come back empty. It was an absurd policy, but persisted for most of the war.

The army and navy would not consult with each other when they were planning operations in the same area. Part of this was the navy's fault, because what joint planning that did occur took place in Tokyo, where the army had the last word, since it ran the government. So the navy just went ahead and did what it thought best and hoped the army didn't find out until it was too late. The army-navy rivalry in Japan was a considerable asset for the Allied war effort. And it made similar army-navy conflicts in the American camp look trivial by comparison.

It's difficult to discern a coherent positive strategy on the part of the Japanese. In effect, their strategy was to seize as many islands as possible and fortify enough of them with so many ground troops and aircraft that the Allies would not be able to get through to Japan. This was the whole point behind Pearl Harbor, which was designed to gain as much time as possible for the Imperial Army and Navy to grab real estate that the United States would presumably eventually want to take back. If enough territory was seized, and if it was held with sufficient tenacity, the Japanese thinking went, the United States might eventually decide that the cost of recovering it wasn't acceptable, whereupon Japan would emerge with more than what it had at the start of the war. It didn't work. The keystone of Japanese strategy, however, was not so much grabbing real estate as it was gaining economic resources. The Japanese Home Islands had few natural resources, and nearly all the raw material for Japanese industry had to be imported. While China and Korea provided sufficient ores and food, the oil had to come from fields in INDONESIA. It was to obtain access to this oil that Japan went to war with America, the British Empire, and Holland. Japan's strategy was one of desperation, as it turned out that the Indonesian oil fields could not produce sufficient oil for Japanese needs. More to the point, Japan could not produce sufficient tankers to get the oil from Indonesia to Japan. Allied SUBMARINES kept sinking Japanese tankers, and shipping in general. Many senior Japanese military leaders recognized the futility of the war, but they carried out their orders anyway. Loyal unto death was more than just a catchphrase in the Japanese military.

Submarines

Historically, the submarine is a rather recent development. Submarines first became practical in the late 19th century. They were the first "stealth" weapons, being essentially torpedo boats with the capacity to operate underwater for limited periods,

albeit with a considerable loss of speed and endurance. Submarines proved of considerable value during World War I, when Germany almost succeeded in severing Britain's maritime lifeline through an aggressive submarine campaign. This campaign ultimately failed, but attracted considerable attention. As a result, between the wars many navies invested rather heavily in submarines. By World War II there were essentially two types of submarine.

The "coastal" submarine, built in considerable numbers by many navies, was of modest dimensions, less than 800 tons surface displacement. It generally had a relatively low surface speed, 18 knots being at the high end. Coastal submarines usually carried four to six torpedo tubes, plus a deck gun and one or two antiaircraft machine guns. Despite their name, they were designed to roam the oceans and snipe at enemy shipping, or linger along the coast and ambush enemy warships.

Then there was the "fleet" submarine, to use its American name. The fleet submarine was large, 1,000 tons or more, and usually had a relatively high surface speed, 20 knots, from which came the term "fleet submarine," since it was able to keep up with the battlefleet. Being larger, the fleet submarine was better armed, usually with six to ten torpedo tubes, plus the usual deck armament, usually one gun of 3-inch to 5.5-inch caliber, plus one or two antiaircraft guns or machine guns. Fleet submarines also had more endurance than coastal submarines, since they could carry more diesel fuel and more batteries. When submerged there was little difference in speed between the two types, 8 knots being more or less the norm. The only other important technical difference was that the fleet submarine was slightly more habitable.

Most navies had a mix of coastal and fleet submarines, the idea being that the coastal types were supposed to raid enemy commerce, while the fleet types were supposed to serve as supports for the battlefleet, scouting for the enemy, harassing him before battle, mopping up fleeing enemy vessels after a victory, or covering the retreat of friendly vessels after a reverse. For various reasons, however,

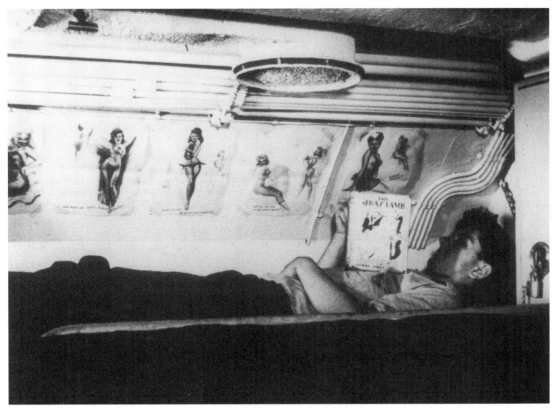

Although American submarines were roomier than most, they were still very cramped. Here a sailor aboard USS Capelin *(SS-289) reads in his bunk, which he probably shares with another sailor who is on duty.*

the United States built only fleet submarines, since it intended to meet any enemy—specifically the Japanese—in a decisive surface clash as soon as possible. This proved of considerable benefit once the war began, because the main use of US subs was to attack Japanese merchant ships at great distances from American bases.

See also SHIPPING, WAR AGAINST JAPANESE.

Ref: Alden, *The Fleet Submarine in the U.S. Navy*;———, *U.S. Submarine Attacks during World War II*; Blair, *Silent Victory*; Boyd and Yoshida, *The Japanese Submarine Force*; Carpenter and Polmar, *Submarines of the Imperial Japanese Navy*; Friedman, *Submarine Design and Development*; Hezlet, *Submarines and Sea Power*; Roscoe, *United States Submarine Operations*.

Submarines, Appendectomies Aboard

A staple of several submarine films, the emergency appendectomy performed by a navy medic with improvised tools was by no means the figment of some scriptwriter's imagination. During the war three such operations are known to have been performed, all successfully.

Boat	Corpsman	Patient
Seadragon (SS–194)	Wheeler B. Lipes	Darnell Rector
Grayback (SS–208)	Harry B. Roby	W.R. Jones
Silversides (SS–236)	Thomas Moore	George Platter

ALLIED SUBMARINES OF THE PACIFIC WAR								
Fleet	Class	Launched	Displ.	Speed	TT	Number	Lost	Note
British	Porpoise	1932	2,500/2,053	15.5/8.8	6	1	1	
British	S	1941–43	715/990	14.8/9	7	22	9	
British	T	1940–45	1,090/1,570	15.3/9	11	53	17	A
Neth.	K-VII	1922–23	573/712	15/8	4	3	1	B
Neth.	K-XI	1924	670/815	15/8	6	3	1	
Neth.	K-XIV	1932–33	771/1,008	17/9	8	5	3	
Neth.	0–16	1936	869/1,170	18/9	8	1	1	
Neth.	0–19	1938–39	998/1,536	19.3/9	8	2	2	

Key: Class, the official designation of the type; Launched, years in which the boats were launched; Displ., displacement, in tons, with standard followed by submerged; Speed, in knots, with surface and then submerged; TT, torpedo tubes carried; Number, units available during the war; Lost, units lost during the war, including losses in all theaters; Note, as indicated below:

A. The class comprised five slightly differing groups, ordered prewar, 1939, 1940, 1941, and 1942.

B. Laid down during World War I, the two surviving units were scrapped in Australia in 1942.

Submarines, British and Dutch

Although US submarines dominated the Pacific, British and Dutch boats did a great deal of work in the Indian Ocean and in East Indian waters.

The ROYAL NAVY lost *Porpoise*, two S Class boats, and one T Class to the Japanese, while all Royal Netherlands Navy losses shown were in the East Indies. One Dutch boat, *K-XVIII*, was scuttled while under repair in Soerabaya, to prevent her capture. She was partially salvaged by the Japanese, who used her hull as a picket boat until a British submarine sank her in July 1945. Surviving Dutch boats operated with the Royal Navy in the Indian Ocean and the East Indies until the end of the war. The Royal Navy also employed a number of midget submarines in the Pacific.

See also NACHI CLASS.

Ref: Alden, *U.S. Submarine Attacks during World War II*; Friedman, *Submarine Design and Development*; Hezlet, *Submarines and Sea Power*.

Submarines, Japanese

Japan had some of the finest submarines in the world. They were broadly classified into three groups:

JAPANESE SUBMARINE TYPES			
Class	Designation	Surface Displacement	Completed
1st	I	1,000 tons or more	112
2nd	RO	500–1,000 tons	47
3rd	HA	under 500 tons	20

These designations had less to do with the missions the boats were designed to perform than with their size. So although I boats were supposed to be "first class" submarines, there were some that were designed to carry cargoes, others equipped to transport landing parties, and some to carry seaplanes for attacks on distant targets such as the PANAMA CANAL. While RO boats were "second class" submarines, they usually had enormous range, and were used for fleet operations interchangeably with I boats. Even the little "third class" HA boats had more than one mission: coast defense and the supply of isolated garrisons.

There were also some submarines designated "Yu," of which 14 were built of 200 proposed. Unlike I, RO, and HA boats, the two classes of Yu boats belonged to the Imperial Army. Quite small (273 and 392 tons surface displacement), slow, and lightly armed, they were intended to carry cargo to isolated garrisons

JAPANESE NAVY SUBMARINES

Class (Lead Boat)	Launched	Displ.	Speed	TT	Number	Lost	Note
L3 (RO-57)	1922–23	897/1,195	10/4	4	3	0	A
KT (RO-30)	1923–24	665/1,000	10/4	4	3	0	A
KD2 (I-52)	1922	1,390/2,500	22/10	8	1	0	A
L4 (RO-60)	1922–26	988/1,322	16.5/9	6	9	5	
J1 (I-1)	1924–28	1,970–1,791	18/8	6	4	4	B
KD3a (I-53)	1925–26	1,635/2,300	20/8	8	4	0	
KRS (I-21)	1926–27	1,142/1,768	14.5/7	4	4	3	C
KD3b (I-56)	1927–28	1,635/2,300	20/8	8	4	0	
KD4 (I-61)	1927–29	1,635/2,300	20/8.5	6	3	1	
J1M (I–5)	1931	2,080/2,921	18/8	6	1	1	C
KD5 (I-65)	1931	1,575/2,330	20.5/8.2	6	2	2	
KD6a (I–68)	1933–35	1,400/2,440	23/8.2	6	6	6	
J2 (I-6)	1934	1,900/3,061	20/7.5	6	1	1	
K5 (RO-33)	1934–35	700/1,200	19/8.3	4	2	2	
J3 (I-7)	1935–36	2,231/3,538	23/8	6	2	2	C
KD6b (I-74)	1936–37	1,420/2,564	23/8	6	2	2	
C1 (I-16)	1938–39	2,184/3,561	23.6/8	6	5	5	
A1 (I-9)	1939–41	2,434/4,149	23.5/8	6	3	3	C
B1 (I–15)	1939–42	2,198/3,654	23.6/8	6	20	20	C
KD7 (I-76)	1941–43	1,630/2,602	23/8	6	10	10	
KS (RO-100)	1941–43	525/782	14.2/8	4	18	18	
B2 (I-40)	1942–43	2,230/3,700	23.5/8	6	6	6	C
K6 (RO-35)	1942–44	960/1,447	19.7/8	4	18	17	
A2 (I-12)	1943	2,390/4,172	17.7/6.2	6	1	1	C
B3 (I-54)	1943–44	2,140/3,688	17.7/6.5	6	3	2	C
C2 (I-46)	1943	2,184/3,564	23.5/8	8	3	2	
C3 (I-52)	1943	2,095/3,644	17.7/6.5	6	3	2	
D1 (I-361)	1943–44	1,440/2,215	13/6.5	0	12	9	D
D2 (I-373)	1944	1,660/2,240	13/16.5	0	1	1	E
AM (I-13)	1944	2,620/4,762	16.7/5.5	6	2	1	F
ST (I-201)	1944	1,070/1,450	15.8/19	4	3	0	G
SH (I-351)	1944	2,650/4,290	15.8/6.3	4	1	1	
SS (HA-101)	1944–45	370/493	10/5	0	10	0	H
STO (I-400)	1944	3,530/6,560	18.7/6.5	8	3	0	I
STS (HA-201)	1944–45	320/440	10.5/13	2	10	0	J

Key: Class, the official designation of the type; Launched, years in which the boats were launched; Displ., displacement, in tons, with standard followed by submerged; Speed, in knots, with surface and then submerged; TT, torpedo tubes carried; Number, units available during the war; Lost, units lost during the war, including losses in all theaters; Note, as indicated below:

A. Assigned to training duties.

B. Carried a floatplane and had two 5.5-inch deck guns.

C. Carried a floatplane.

D. Transport submarines, able to carry 82 tons of cargo and 110 passengers.

E. High-speed transport submarine, able to carry 150 tons of fuel and 110 of other cargo.

F. Carried two floatplanes.

G. Experimental high-speed boats.

H. Transport submarines, able to carry 60 tons of cargo.

I. Designed to attack the Panama Canal, they had a surface range of 30,000 nautical miles at 16 knots, and carried three aircraft.

J. High-speed coast defense submarines.

Ref: Boyd and Yoshida, *The Japanese Submarine Force*; Carpenter and Polmar, *Submarines of the Imperial Japanese Navy*; Friedman, *Submarine Design and Development*; Hezlet, *Submarines and Sea Power*.

Submarines, US

The US Navy had over 20 different submarine designs during the war, several of which were represented by only a single unit, while some numbered scores of boats. Save for some old O, R, and S Class boats and two experimental units, all US submarines were large "fleet" boats, displacing more than a thousand tons on the surface. They were designed to keep up with the battle fleet, which they were intended to support as scouts, and had great range and a relatively high surface speed.

US SUBMARINES								
Class	(Lead Boat)	Launched	Displ.	Speed	TT	Number	Lost	Note
O-1	(SS-62)	1917–18	521/629	14/10.5	4	7	0	A
R-1	(SS-78)	1917–19	569/680	13.5/10.5	4	18	1	B
S-1	(SS-105)	1918–22	854/1,062	14/11	4	23	3	B
S-3	(SS-107)	1919–21	876/1,092	15/11	4	7	0	B
S-42	(SS-153)	1923–24	906/1,126	14.5/11	4	6	1	B
S-48	(SS-159)	1921	903/1,230	14.5/11	5	1	0	
Barracuda	(SS-163)	1923–25	2,119/2,506	18.7/9	6	3	0	
Argonaut	(SS-166)	1927	2,878/4,045	13.5/7.4	4	1	1	C
Narwal	(SS-167)	1927–30	2,987/3,960	17.5/8	6	2	0	C
Dolphin	(SS-169)	1932	1,688/2,215	17/8	6	1	0	
Cachalot	(SS-170)	1933	1,120/1,650	17/8	6	2	0	
Porpoise	(SS-172)	1935	1,316/1,934	19/10	6	2	0	
Shark	(SS-174)	1935	1,315/1,968	19.5/9	6	2	2	
Perch	(SS-176)	1936–37	1,330/1,997	19.3/8	6	6	3	
Salmon	(SS-182)	1937–38	1,449/2,210	21/9	8	6	0	
Sargo	(SS-188)	1938–39	1,450/2,350	20/8.5	8	6	2	
Seadragon	(SS-193)	1939	1,450/2,350	20/8.5	8	4	2	D
Tambor	(SS-198)	1939–40	1,475/2,370	20/8.5	10	6	2	
Gar	(SS–206)	1940–41	1,475/2,370	20/8.5	10	6	5	
Mackerel	(SS-204)	1940	825/1,190	16.2/11	6	1	0	E
Marlin	(SS-205)	1941	800/1,165	16.5/11	6	1	0	E
Gato	(SS-212)	1941–43	1,526/2,410	20/8.5	10	73	20	
Balao	(SS-285)	1942–45	1,525/2,415	20/8.5	10	116	13	
Tench	(SS-417)	1944	1,570/2,415	20/8.5	10	24	0	

Key: Class, the official designation of the type; Launched, years in which the boats were launched; Displ., displacement, in tons, with standard followed by submerged; Speed, in knots, with surface and then submerged; TT, torpedo tubes carried; Number, units available during the war; Lost, units lost during the war, including losses in all theaters; Note, as indicated below:

Notes:

A. Relegated to training duties.

B. Several transferred to the Royal Navy.

C. Large boats, designed as submarine cruisers, with two 6-inch guns. *Argonaut* (which was also equipped as a minelayer) and *Nautilus* (SS–168) carried 200 Marines for the Makin Raid.

D. *Squalus* (SS–192) of this class was sunk in a prewar accident. When salvaged, she was recommissioned as *Sailfish*, under the same number.

E. Experimental boats.

The most successful US submarines were those of the Gato Class and the closely related Balao and Tench Classes, which altogether totaled nearly 200 units completed during the war, and a number after it. Most saw extensive service against Japanese shipping. Of the 12 US submarines accredited with the highest amount of enemy tonnage sunk, eight were Gato Class boats and three others were Balao Class. Many of these boats were built inland, on rivers like the Ohio, using innovative techniques, including sideways launching. Submarines of these three classes formed the backbone of the US underwater fleet well into the 1950s, and many served in other navies long after that. Most were broken up for scrap in the 1960s, but four Gatos and eight

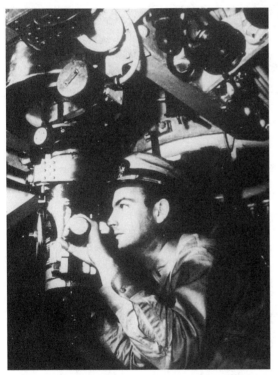

An American submariner at his periscope, sometime in 1942. Relatively ineffective in 1942, due to poor tactics, defective torpedoes, and a certain lack of aggressiveness on the part of older skippers, US submarines became more efficient with the introduction of better tactics, better torpedoes, and younger skippers.

Balaos are preserved as war memorials in various places.

Ref: Alden, *The Fleet Submarine in the U.S. Navy*; Blair, *Silent Victory*; Friedman, *Submarine Design and Development*; Roscoe, *United States Submarine Operations in World War II*.

Submarines, US, Highest Scoring

In terms of patrol scores, on her fifth patrol *Archerfish* (SS-311) attained the highest score for a single patrol, and for a single target, when she sank the Japanese carrier SHINANO, at 59,000 tons, the largest ship ever sunk by a submarine. While on her third patrol, *Tang* (SS-306) sank 10 ships, the maximum number ever, for a total of 39,100 tons. It is interesting to note that only one boat listed was commissioned before PEARL HARBOR—*Tautog*.

Ref: Alden, *U.S. Submarine Attacks During World War II*; Blair, *Silent Victory*; Roscoe, *United States Submarine Operations in World War II*.

SUBMARINES, US, HIGHEST SCORING				
Rank	Boat	Tonnage	Ships Sunk	Class
1.	*Flasher* (SS-249)	100.2	21	Gato
2.	*Rasher* (SS-269)	99.9	18	Gato
3.	*Barb* (SS-220)	96.6	17	Gato
4.	*Tang* (SS-306)	93.8	26	Balao
5.	*Silversides* (SS-236)	90.1	23	Gato
6.	*Spadefish* (SS-411)	88.1	21	Balao
7.	*Trigger* (SS-237)	86.5	18	Gato
8.	*Drum* (SS-228)	80.5	15	Gato
9.	*Jack* (SS-259)	76.7	15	Gato
10.	*Snook* (SS-279)	75.5	17	Gato
11.	*Tautog* (SS-199)	72.6	26	Tambor
12.	*Seahorse* (SS-304)	72.5	20	Balao

Tonnage is in thousands

Subversion, Japanese in America

In the years before Pearl Harbor the Japanese government is known to have provided covert financial assistance to a number of organizations in the United States. Most of this money went to Japa-

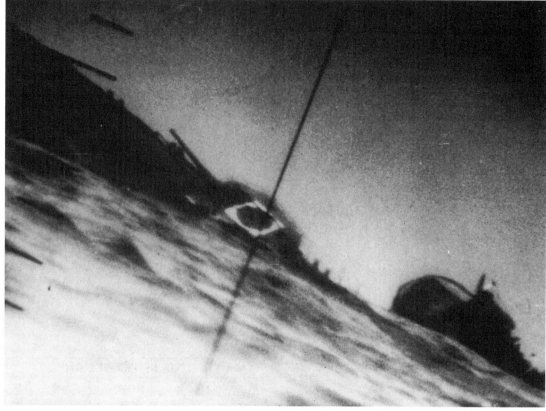

The Japanese destroyer Yamakaze *goes down, in a photograph taken through the periscope of the USS* Nautilus *(SS-168), June 25, 1942.*

nese-American social and cultural organizations, or to groups like the Society of the Black Dragon, ostensibly composed of veterans of the Russo-Japanese War, but actually a cover for Japanese nationalist activities in the United States. Some went to dissident American movements, such as certain radical black organizations including one religious group which has since gained considerable prominence. While the US government has never revealed the extent of such aid, nor even formally acknowledged that it existed, the National Archives contain a good deal of material on the subject, as some of the secret Japanese radio messages American codebreakers read related to such dealings.

See also AMERICAN CITIZENS, RELOCATION OF; JAPANESE AMERICANS, IMPERIAL ARMED FORCES.

Ref: Harries and Harries, *Soldiers of the Sun*; Stephan, *Hawaii under the Rising Sun*.

Sugiyama, Gen (1896–1945)

Gen Sugiyama joined the Japanese Army in 1911, commanded forces in China during the 1930s, and was promoted to full general in 1936. An enthusiastic supporter of Japanese expansion in China and the Pacific, he became chief of staff of the army in 1940 and presided over the planning for army operations in the Pacific during the initial expansion. Became field marshal in 1943 and lost chief of staff post to TOJO in 1944. Became commander of army forces in Eastern Japan until the end of the war. Committed suicide when Japan surrendered.

Suicide, US Officers

While the Japanese penchant for self-destruction is well known, a number of Americans also took their own lives during or after the war.

Capt. Howard Bode, former skipper of the USS *Chicago*, eventually killed himself, apparently because he believed he had commanded the ship badly at the Battle of SAVO ISLAND.

Capt. Charles B. McVay III, former skipper of the USS *Indianapolis*, killed himself several years after the war, apparently plagued by doubts concerning his performance in command at the time of the ship's loss.

LG George Moore, who commanded the CORREGIDOR garrison under Jonathan WAINWRIGHT, and had spent three years as a Japanese POW, killed himself shortly after the war.

See also KAMIKAZE; KELLY, COLIN.

Sullivan Brothers, The

The sons of Thomas Sullivan, an Irish-American railroad worker from Waterloo, Iowa, and his wife Alleta, who served and died together aboard the antiaircraft cruiser USS *Juneau*. Shortly after PEARL HARBOR, George (b. 1913) and Francis ("Frank," b. 1915), who had both served an enlistment in the navy 1937–41, as well as Joseph ("Red," b. 1918), Madison ("Matt," b. 1919), and Albert ("Al," b. 1921), volunteered for the navy. When told that they would not be allowed to serve together, they requested special permission to do so. This was granted, as well as a waiver of Al's exemption, he being the only one of the five who was married. Amid considerable publicity they were assigned to the newly commissioned *Juneau* at the Brooklyn Navy Yard in February 1942, after abbreviated boot camp at Great Lakes Naval Training Station. The ship's company was shortly augmented by another set of brothers, Patrick ("Pat,"

b. 1917) and Joseph ("Joey," b. 1920), both semipro boxers who had already served a year each in the army, plus Louis ("Louie," b. 1921) and James ("Jimmy," b. 1924) Rogers, of Italian and Irish descent (their father, had changed his name to Thomas Rogers), from Bridgeport, Connecticut, who had also received special permission to serve together, again with considerable publicity.

Shortly after arriving in the South Pacific, the ship acquired another set of brothers. When the survivors of the carrier WASP, sunk 15 September 1942, were brought into NOUMEA for reassignment, *Juneau*'s skipper, Capt. Lyman K. Swensen, agreed to the request Boatswain's Mate Russell Coombs that his brother Charles be signed on. The Sullivan, Rogers, and Coombs brothers served aboard *Juneau* in the Battle of SANTA CRUZ (26 October 1942), during which *Juneau* proved enormously effective in helping to beat off Japanese air attacks. Shortly afterward the navy had second thoughts about brothers serving together, and refused to permit siblings to do so in the future. While not ordering those brothers already serving together to be separated, the navy urged them to transfer voluntarily to other ships. The inherent wisdom of this suggestion, plus the opportunity to engage in amateur boxing, caused two of the Rogers brothers, Joey and Jimmy, to transfer to another ship, a move that they urged upon the Sullivans, who deferred a decision.

Soon afterward *Juneau* took part in the First Naval Battle of GUADALCANAL (12–13 November 1942), a ferocious night surface action in which three cruisers, including her sister ATLANTA, were sunk. *Juneau* survived, although with heavy damage to her hull. Early the next morning she was TORPEDOED by the Japanese submarine I-26. The torpedo struck her in a previously damaged part of the hull, and she blew up almost instantly. The Coombs brothers, Louie and Pat Rogers, and Frank, Matt, Red, and Al Sullivan all appear to have been killed instantly. George Sullivan was one of 140 to 150 men who escaped on rafts and floating debris, to watch the remnants of the US squadron steaming away, Capt. Gilbert Hoover of

USS *Helena*, the senior surviving officer, having decided that it was too risky to attempt to rescue the survivors. He was subsequently relieved of duty, perhaps unjustly, given that there were army aircraft overhead and that he attempted to signal the survivors' location and did have the safety of the remnants of the squadron to worry about. Due to failures in command, communications, and staff procedures the survivors were "lost" by the navy. AAF recon planes that spotted the survivors failed to make timely reports. Over the next few days their location was reported to higher headquarters several times, by recon aircraft and even by Capt. Hoover. However, a junior staff officer placed a low priority on the messages. He too was subsequently relieved of duty, with more justification than in the case of Capt. Hoover. Over the next week most of the survivors died of thirst, drowning, wounds, or shark attacks. Among them was George Sullivan, who was killed in a shark attack, a fact not revealed for more than 40 years. Only 10 of the scores of *Juneau*'s men who had taken to the water on the morning of November 13 were picked up on the 20th. Of nearly 700 men in the ship's company, 676 had perished.

Shortly after the loss of *Juneau*, the navy forcibly separated other siblings who had been serving together.

The last surviving Sullivan child, sister Genevieve, subsequently joined the Waves.

On April 4, 1943 the FLETCHER CLASS destroyer USS *The Sullivans* (DD-537) was christened by Alleta Sullivan. The ship had a distinguished career in the Pacific War, and served for many years after it. In 1974 she was designated a war memorial. A new USS *The Sullivans* has since joined the fleet.

Ref: Kurzman, *Left to Die.*

Sunglasses

World War II aviators, particularly fighter pilots, were a dashing bunch. "Aviator glasses" (sunglasses) certainly added to the slick appearance. But the sunglasses weren't there just to sustain a striking image. For fighter pilots in particular, sun-

glasses were often a matter of life and death. Aircraft usually fought above the clouds, and a pilot who turned into the sun could be temporarily blinded. In the tropical Pacific the sunlight was particularly intense. Early in the war, more or less through the end of the GUADALCANAL Campaign, Allied pilots (at least those who didn't already know) learned the advantage of sunglasses. The aviator glasses were considered as important as a parachute, because having shades made it less likely a pilot would need his 'chute.

Surigao Strait, Battle of (24–25 October 1944)

During the Battle of LEYTE GULF, a US squadron including the refurbished old battleships *Mississippi*, MARYLAND, *West Virginia*, *Tennessee*, CALIFORNIA, and PENNSYLVANIA (all but the first, veterans of PEARL HARBOR), supported by numerous smaller warships, ambushed a Japanese force including the old battleships FUSO and *Yamashiro*, which were annihilated in an action so one-sided the *Pennsylvania* never got to fire. This was the last time battleships ever fired on each other. Considering that both the Imperial Navy and the US Navy had put so much emphasis on battleships in their prewar plans, it is worth noting that only two of the nine battleship slug-outs during World War II occurred in the Pacific.

See also BATTLESHIPS, ENCOUNTERS.

Surprise Attacks, Japanese

Imperial Japan's major foreign wars were all begun by surprise attacks without benefit of a declaration of war.

Sino-Japanese War (1894–95). By midsummer of 1894 relations between China and Japan had been deteriorating for some time, due to Japanese pressures on Korea, which China considered a dependency, but the possibility of war did not seem imminent. However, Japanese troops in Korea had engaged in some ATROCITIES, and even attacked the king's palace in Seoul. As a result, the Chinese had dispatched several shiploads of troops to Korea. At about 0600 on 25 July, two Chinese warships escorting a chartered British transport carrying about 1,200 troops in the Gulf of Korea, were approached by a Japanese squadron of considerably greater strength. Quite suddenly the Japanese opened fire (they, of course, charged that the Chinese made "threatening" moves). The Chinese warships were severely damaged, and the merchantship sunk, despite her British flag. Over 700 Chinese troops died in the water, many of them by machine-gun fire. This touched off the Sino-Japanese War (and almost caused Britain to break relations with Japan).

Russo-Japanese War (1904–05). Tensions between Japan and Russia had been rising for some time, over the status of MANCHURIA and Korea. On 6 February 1904 Japan recalled her ambassador, effectively breaking relations. Three days later, a Japanese squadron jumped two Russian warships lying off CHEMULPO (Inchon) in Korea without warning, both of which were scuttled in order to avoid capture. That same night the Japanese fleet conducted a surprise attack on the Russian fleet, at anchor outside of PORT ARTHUR, torpedo boats sinking a cruiser and a gunboat, and severely damaging two battleships and another cruiser. This gave the Japanese the initiative in the war, which they maintained through a series of bloody battles on both land and sea, until peace was concluded on highly favorable terms in 1905.

World War II (1941–45). Even as the First Air Fleet was steaming across the Pacific for Pearl Harbor, two Japanese officials with ambassadorial rank were in negotiations with the president and secretary of state concerning the possibility of cooling things off in the Far East; the surprise attack was so secret that the ambassadors themselves did not know it was imminent.

Suva, Fiji

An important harbor, with limited resources but a fine location, about 1,200 miles north of New Zealand. During the war Suva served as a staging area for US divisions being committed to the South Pacific, as an important link in the chain of air bases between the United States and the South Pacific, and as a naval base.

Suzuki, Sasaki (1893–1945)

Sasaki Suzuki joined the Japanese Army in 1912 and spent much of his early career as a staff officer and military attaché. This marked him for greater things in the future. He received troop commands in the 1930s and was chief of staff of the 25th Army during the invasion of MALAYA, then went back to a series of key staff jobs after that. In July 1944, given command of the 35th Army in the Philippines and told to prepare to defend against expected American invasion, he led his troops in a resourceful resistance, successfully moving troops to other islands. Suzuki was killed by US aircraft in June 1945, while moving by boat to another island.

Swordfish, British Carrier Torpedo Bomber

The Swordfish was the most successful biplane of the war. An early 1930s British design, with nearly 2,400 eventually built, the Swordfish was a torpedo bomber and had considerable success in that role in the European Theater. In the Pacific they were more commonly used as reconnaissance aircraft (often as floatplanes), but a few conducted combat missions in the Indian Ocean as late as 1944, attacking Japanese shipping. The Swordfish prototype flew in 1934 and PRODUCTION began shortly thereafter. The Swordfish was slow (top speed 139 MPH), but had a long range (about 1,000 miles) and could carry 1,500 pounds (a TORPEDO, or MINES, rockets, and bombs). The aircraft was very steady and maneuverable, and quite rugged. Its admirable qualities were the primary reason it survived the entire war. The Swordfish would have had a harder time if it had been involved in the 1942 Pacific carrier battles. Its slow speed would have been fatal in the face of carrier antiaircraft fire and Japanese fighters. Later in the war, at least the enemy fighter threat could be smothered. By then it was common to plaster Japanese ships with heavily escorted dive bombers and then bring in the torpedo bombers to finish off the stricken vessels. At this, the Swordfish would still be effective.

See also RECONNAISSANCE, NAVAL.

Sydney, Australia

One of the roomiest harbors in the world, with considerable port facilities, extensive industrial resources, a modest naval base, and several air bases, Sydney was the most important Allied base between Pearl Harbor and SINGAPORE.

Sydney was attacked once during the war. On the afternoon of 31 May 1942 a floatplane from a Japanese submarine reconnoitered Sydney Harbor. That night, Japanese SUBMARINES *I-12, I-22, I-24, I-27,* and *I-29* stood off the entrance to Sydney Harbor and each launched a midget submarine. At least two of the five midget subs managed to penetrate the harbor and fired several TORPEDOES. These caused little damage, missing entirely several transports, an American heavy cruiser, and several destroyers, but they did sink an old accommodation ship, killing several sailors who were sleeping aboard. In response to the attacks, shore batteries opened fire and antiaircraft guns began tearing up the sky, causing some CASUALTIES among civilians. Meanwhile, the warships present in the harbor got underway and attempted to hunt down the attackers. Although the Allied warships were completely unsuccessful in detecting them, none of the Japanese midget submarines survived the operation. Two were actually found inside the harbor, with no apparent damage, and it is believed that the crews scuttled them as a way of committing suicide.

Six nights later, on 7 June, another Japanese submarine surfaced off Sydney and fired several rounds into the city, with little effect, before getting completely away.

See also I-26

T

Tachibana Class, Japanese Destroyer Escorts

A follow-on to Japan's MATSU CLASS destroyer escorts, the Tachibanas were designed almost simultaneously with the former. They were larger and somewhat better armed, but easier to build, taking only about five or six months each. Only 23 of nearly 40 ordered were actually laid down, in late 1944–45, of which only 14 were completed between January and June of 1945, while four others were still fitting out when the war ended. Three of the ships became war losses. After the war most of the survivors were transferred to various Allied powers for disposal.

Taclaban, Leyte, Philippines

A fishing village with limited port facilities but a fine harbor. Occupied by the Japanese in early 1942, it was retaken by US forces in October 1944, and served as a major forward base during further operations in the Philippines.

Taiho, Japanese Aircraft Carrier

Taiho (1941–1943–1944) was arguably the culmination of Japanese carrier design. A large, fast, well protected ship, like all Japanese carriers, she suffered from a limited aircraft operating capacity. In *Taiho*'s case, however, the limitation was due to the installation of a 3-inch armored flight deck, the first in Japanese service. Displacing about 10% more than the American ESSEX, *Taiho* was rated at only about 75–85 aircraft, as against 100 on *Essex*.

Despite this impressive number of aircraft, she was actually apparently able to operate only about 50 to 60 airplanes, due to poorly designed facilities. Supposed to be the lead ship of a batch of seven carriers more or less on the same design, she was the only one ever laid down. *Taiho* was sunk just weeks after completing her training, on 29 June 1944, during the Battle of the PHILIPPINE SEA. The US submarine *Albacore* (SS-218) put a single torpedo into her. This caused an avgas leak, a leak with which inept damage control failed to cope, leading to the accumulation of volatile fumes in confined spaces, resulting in a fatal explosion.

Tainan, Formosa

A major port on the southwestern edge of FORMOSA, with good facilities to service and repair ships, Tainan had been developed by the Japanese as their principal base against the Philippines, only a few hundred miles to the south, and it was an important air base during the initial Japanese operations against Luzon in 1941. During the war it was subject to heavy attacks by carrier-based aircraft, and, after the liberation of Luzon, by land-based airplanes as well.

Taiyo Class, Japanese Escort Carriers

The Taiyo Class were converted 1941–42 from ocean liners under construction at the start of the war. They were much larger than comparable Allied escort carriers. Due to a shortage of aircraft and trained pilots, their primary service was not as escorts, but rather as aircraft transports and training ships. In this role they were quite busy.

Taiyo (?–1940–1941) (ex-*Kasuga Maru*) was TORPEDOED by USS *Trout* (SS-202) near TRUK on 28 August 1942, but did not sink. On 18 November 1944 she was sunk by USS *Rasher* (SS-269) in the Central Pacific.

Unyo (?–1939–1942) (ex-*Yawata Maru*) was sunk 16 September 1944 by USS *Barb* (SS-220) off the Coast of China.

Chuyo (?–1939–1942) (ex-*Nitta Maru*) was sunk by USS *Sailfish* (SS-192) off Honshu on 2 December 1943.

Takagi, Takeo (1892–1944)

A 1912 naval academy graduate, Takagi specialized in TORPEDO warfare and SUBMARINES, but also commanded various surface ships and served on a number of staffs over the following two decades. Late in 1941 he was given command of the Fifth Fleet as a rear admiral. He commanded the carrier strike force during the Battle of the CORAL SEA and assumed command of Sixth Fleet (submarines) in late 1943 as a vice admiral. Takagi was killed on Saipan in July 1944 during the American invasion.

Takao Class, Japanese Heavy Cruisers

An improvement on the NACHI CLASS heavy cruisers, the Takaos were bigger and better protected. All had extensive war service, *Atago* as a flagship. All became war losses, taking considerable punishment before succumbing. They formed the Fourth Cruiser Squadron and saw service in the NETHERLANDS EAST INDIES, during the GUADALCANAL Campaign, and with carrier task forces on several occasions. All four were hit, and three sunk, during the Battle of LEYTE GULF.

Takao (1927–1930–1932) accompanied *Atago* during early operations in the Philippines and Netherlands East Indies, but otherwise had a relatively quiet war. She was hit, but not sunk, by two TORPEDOES from *Darter* (SS-227) on 23 October 1944, during the preliminary phases of the Battle

of Leyte Gulf. This sent her back to SINGAPORE, where she remained until the British midget submarine *XE3* sank her in the harbor on 31 July 1945.

Atago (1927–1930–1932) was Admiral KONDO's favorite flagship, serving him in this capacity from the initial operations in the Philippines and Netherlands East Indies right on through the fighting off Guadalcanal, and later serving as such for Admiral KURITA, in which capacity she was sunk by two torpedoes from *Darter* (SS-227) October 23, 1944, on the eve of the Battle of Leyte Gulf.

Maya (1928–1932–1932) served with *Chokai* in the Netherlands East Indies and the Solomons, fought at the KOMANDORSKI ISLANDS. Severely damaged by US aircraft at RABAUL in November 1943, she lost her "C" turret, leaving her with only eight 8-inch guns. She was sunk by several torpedoes from the USS *Dace* (SS-247) on October 23, 1944 on the eve of the Battle of Leyte Gulf.

Chokai (1928–1931–1923) took part in operations against the Netherlands East Indies and in the SOLOMONS (SAVO ISLAND and the Tokyo Express), and attacked the US escort carriers off SAMAR on October 25, 1944, during which she was sunk by dive bombers and destroyer gunfire.

Tana, New Hebrides

A small port, with limited facilities, overshadowed as a potential base by ESPIRITU SANTO, a hundred miles or so to the north. The United States developed a modest base there during the SOLOMONS CAMPAIGN.

Tanaka, Raizo (1892–1969)

Raizo Tanaka graduated from the Japanese naval academy in 1913 and specialized in destroyers and TORPEDO warfare. He rose steadily, commanding a series of ships culminating with the battleship KONGO in 1939. Promoted to rear admiral in 1941, Tanaka led destroyer units on escort duties during the Dutch East Indies invasion and later during the MIDWAY operation. His main fame came when he organized and led the TOKYO EXPRESS that used de-

TANKS OF THE PACIFIC WAR

Country	Model	Weight	Gun	MG	Armor	Crew	Speed	Year
Britain	Mk VI Light	5.2	—	1	15	3	35.0	'39
	Matilda	26.5	40	1	78	4	15.6	'39
	Valentine	17.0	40	1	65	3	15.6	'41
Japan	Type 95 Light	4.7	—	1	16	2	25.0	'37
	Type 97 Medium	15.0	57	2	25	4	23.5	'37
United States	M3 Medium (Grant)	29.5	75	1	76	6	20.0	'40
	M3 Light (Stuart)	12.5	37	2	44	4	36.3	'41
	M4 Medium (Sherman)	30.0	75	2	76	5	25.0	'42
	LVT A Amtrak	16.0	75	2–4	76	6	17.0	'44

Key: Model is a simplified form of the tank's official designation; some of these were quite intricate, such as M4A2, indicating the second variant of the A version of the Sherman. Weight, in tons, is that of the tank, loaded but unmanned. Gun is given in millimeters, for the principal cannon carried; MG, the number of machine guns carried. Armor is the thickest carried, in millimeters. Crew, the normal complement. Speed, in miles per hour on roads; cross-country would be much less. Year is that of introduction.

stroyers to supply and reinforce the Japanese troops on GUADALCANAL during 1942, his doggedness causing the Americans to bestow on him the nickname "Tenacious Tanaka." By the end of the year he was removed from command for his outspoken criticism of how the Guadalcanal operation was being run, and spent the rest of the war commanding naval bases in Burma. Promoted to vice admiral before the end of the war, Tanaka didn't get around to surrendering until January 1946. Tanaka was one of the most able Japanese commanders, a resourceful and wily tactician. He didn't get more important posts because he saw the situation as it was, not as many of his overly optimistic commanders wanted to see it.

Tanaka, Shimishi

Shimishi (or Shinichi) Tanaka graduated from the military academy in 1913. He held a variety of posts, primarily as a staff officer, and was one of those who believed Japan should take over all of China and attack the Soviet Union. The head of the army's Operations Division at the outbreak of the Pacific War, in 1942 he was sent as chief of staff to the Southern Area Army, which supervised operations in INDONESIA and Southeast Asia. In March of 1943 he received a division in Burma,

leading it with great ability in tenacious rearguard actions. In September 1944, he became chief of staff, and virtual commander, of the Burma Area Army headquarters and from there constantly urged defense of Burmese positions to the last man.

Tankan Bay, Kuriles, Japan

Plagued by subarctic weather, and with only limited facilities, Tankan Bay was roomy and isolated. It was the base from which the PEARL HARBOR Strike Force sortied in late November of 1941. Otherwise it played little role in the war.

Tanks in the Pacific War

Although ground combat in the Pacific Theater was very much an infantry show, tanks often played an important role in the fighting. Tanks, both Japanese and Allied, fought in virtually every land campaign, usually in an infantry support role but occasionally in tank-to-tank clashes.

By British or American standards, Japanese tanks and antitank weapons were not particularly good. Even the best Japanese tank, the Type 97 medium tank, was vulnerable to a 37mm antitank gun, while the British Matildas and Valentines were virtually impregnable to Japanese A/T weaponry, and the Sherman nearly so. As a result Allied tanks that were essentially obsolete in the European Theater were still useful in the Pacific. However, Japanese tanks proved effective and useful against infantry, or lighter Allied tanks, such as they encountered in Malaya, the Philippines, Burma, and the NETHERLANDS EAST INDIES in 1941–42

Although Australia organized two armored divisions in 1941–42 (to use Stuarts, Matildas, and Grants which were in short supply), these saw no active service and were eventually disbanded. The largest Allied armored units used in the Pacific War were several brigades employed by the British in India and Burma, where the Sino-American First Tank Group also operated. For the most part Allied tank operations were conducted by separate battalions and even companies. The Japanese usually deployed their tanks in small regiments (about 40 medium tanks and a dozen lights, about the allotment of an American tank battalion), but did organize four tank divisions in MANCHURIA. The Third Tank Division conducted offensive operations in China as part of ICHI GO, and the Second Tank Division fought on Luzon in 1944–45, where any possibility of its use as a massed formation was lost when it was dispersed in small detachments to help hold back the advance of US forces while the

An M-4 Sherman medium tank supporting troops engaged in "mopping up" Japanese stragglers and infiltrators on Bougainville, March 1944. Note that the infantrymen have fixed bayonets, not normally used in combat but useful during mopping up. Tankers in the South Pacific suffered greatly from heat and dehydration, but had the comfort of knowing that Japanese antitank equipment was relatively ineffective.

An M-4 Sherman in action on Bougainville, 1944, accompanied by troops of the 25th Infantry Regiment.

bulk of the Japanese troops on the island retired to the mountains. The other two tank divisions were brought to Japan in 1944 as part of preparations for the expected Allied invasion.

The largest tank battle of the Pacific War occurred on SAIPAN, where three companies of the Japanese Ninth Tank Regiment, equipped with the 1943 version of the Type 97 medium tank, supported by a company of SNLF Type 95 light tanks, conducted two major tank attacks. At dawn on 16 June 1944, the Fourth Company of the regiment, and the SNLF company, took part in a major attack against the Marine beachhead, and were virtually wiped out by the Shermans of the Marines' Second and Fourth Tank Battalions. At 0200 the next morning, about 44 Japanese tanks from the Ninth Tank Regiment and SNLF undertook an at-

tack on the Marine lines carrying infantry, to be met by a storm of antitank fire, and then hit with an attack by Marine tanks and tank destroyers, with very heavy losses. This was the biggest Japanese tank attack of the war outside of China.

Had the war lasted until the spring of 1946, the United States would have committed two armored division to the invasion of Honshu, an endeavor that would almost certainly have led to a major clash with the Japanese First and Fourth Tank Divisions, deployed to defend Tokyo.

Note that in 1940 an upgraded version of the Japanese Type 97 medium tank was designed, with a superior model 47mm gun, but this did not enter large-scale PRODUCTION until 1943. The US M3 Grant tank carried its 75mm gun in a sponson on the right front of the hull, and also had a 37mm in a turret. These were employed in the Pacific on only one occasion, during the capture of Makin. Beginning in 1944 the M4 Sherman was equipped with a superior 76.2mm high-velocity gun. US forces also used the M5 light tank, a development of the Stuart. The LVT (A), or "Assault Amphtrak," was strictly speaking not a tank; some early models had a 37mm antitank gun, but the later LVT A4 had a Sherman turret. The principal Allied tanks were the Sherman and Stuart, although the British and Australians made considerable use of the Matilda. While the obsolete Japanese Type 89 medium tank (introduced in 1929) saw considerable service in China, their principal battle tanks against the Allies were the Type 97 medium and Type 95 light.

In addition to the tanks shown, about 50 obsolete Vickers Carden-Lloyd and Marmon Herrington light tanks served with Dutch forces in the Netherlands East Indies in 1941–42, and Chinese forces used a number of older Soviet models brought in during the late 1930s.

See also AMPHIBIOUS VEHICLES; Malaya Campaign in

Tarakan, Borneo

An oil port, with limited facilities to service ships, but with a refinery of some value. Tarakan was strategically of some value for its location on the east coast of BORNEO, about halfway between BALIKPAPAN and Sandikar.

Tarawa, Battle of

Although its atoll could protect a considerable number of ships, Tarawa had the barest port installations and no facilities to service or repair shipping. Despite its very limited land area, Tarawa was of great value as an air base, having the potential to dominate the GILBERTS.

In November 1943 Tarawa—and nearby MAKIN—became the object of the first US amphibious attack against heavily fortified Pacific atolls. Planning for this operation began in the summer of

1943, although such amphibious assaults had been discussed long before that. The GILBERT ISLANDS, particularly Tarawa and Makin atolls, were selected. These would be taken from their Japanese defenders and turned into air bases for the support of future island invasions to the west. Makin was easy, the garrison was only 800 troops, of which only 300 were combat troops. Still, it took a reinforced regiment of the army's 27th Infantry Division four days to take the place. The US Army lost 64 dead, the Japanese nearly 800. Meanwhile, the Japanese brought up submarines and sank a US CVE, *Liscombe Bay*, killing 644 sailors. Had the army troops hustled, the carriers would have been gone by the time the Japanese subs showed up.

Tarawa would also be costly, especially to the Marines assaulting the principal island, Betio. The Japanese garrison was 4,836 troops. These had spent the last year fortifying an area only 3.7 kilometers long and about half a kilometer wide, smaller than New York's Central Park. The US Second Marine Division would do the invading. Since this was the first assault of its type, lots of things went wrong. The amount of pre-invasion shelling and bombing necessary was underestimated. The Japanese had bombproof shelters for all of their troops, and it would have taken extraordinary shelling and bombing to get at them. Most of the Japanese troops were unharmed by the shelling. Next, the CORAL reefs that comprise Tarawa atoll were of a typically complex nature, and this in combination with the tides made it difficult to predict when the landing craft could get across the reefs and right up to the beach on Betio Island, the "mainland" of sprawling Tarawa Atoll. Not knowing the exact layout of the reefs, nor the precise schedule of the local tides proved disastrous. On the first day, thousands of the troops had to wade through 400 to 500 meters of waist-high water. Of the 5,000 Marines landed that day, some 1,500 were killed or wounded. TANKS that tried to land stalled in water that flooded their engines before they could get ashore. On the second day, the reefs were located and the tides sorted out. The US landing craft were now able to get right onto the

Marines heavily engaged on Tarawa, amid the devastation wrought by the preliminary bombardment, November 1943.

beaches with more troops, equipment, and supplies, including tanks. At the end of day two there were enough Marines ashore to put the Japanese on the defensive. By day four, all but 146 of the Japanese garrison were dead. The Marines had 900 killed, and 3,300 wounded. Less than a hundred sailors were killed.

This was not the bloodiest of the Central Pacific assaults, nor the longest. But as far as intense fighting in a short time, Tarawa was the worst. There were also many, many mistakes made, and they were pretty obvious to all concerned. But this provided opportunities to fix things and this was done quickly. Tarawa was also the first of the modern island assaults, using the new landing craft designs. Much had to be learned in a short time and Tarawa

was the live test. Thus the next series of assaults in the MARSHALL ISLANDS went much more smoothly. Yet because Tarawa was the first of the Marine assaults, and a bloody one at that, it will always hold a special place in Marine history.

See also SHOUP, DAVID; SMITHS, WAR OF THE.

Task Force, Task Group, Task Unit

Task force is a US Navy term for squadron of ships given special mission. A task group is a substantial portion of a task force given a separate ancillary mission, while a task unit is a subdivision of a task group. During the war, task forces tended to get larger and larger. A carrier task force in 1942 was likely to include only one carrier, plus escorts, whereas by 1945 it might include a dozen carriers with their escorts, organized into several task groups. Task forces were usually named after the fleet under which they operated, thus TF 38 or TF 58. A task group was numbered as a fraction of its parent task force, thus TF 38.1, and a task unit similarly, TU 38.1.1. The US Fleets operating in the Pacific were: First (originally the whole Pacific Fleet, but later confined to the West Coast); Third/ Fifth, in the Central Pacific; and Seventh, in the Southwest Pacific. Occasional task forces were given numbers outside the system, such as TF 44, which operated during the CORAL SEA Campaign.

Tassafaronga, Battle of

This naval action between US and Japanese ships on November 30, 1942, was fought off the north coast of GUADALCANAL, near Tassafaronga Point). During the battle for Guadalcanal, the Japanese kept their troops on the island supplied via fast transports (disarmed destroyers) escorted by destroyers running down the "Slot" (the north-south channel between the major islands). After the fierce naval battles off Guadalcanal in the first half of November, the Japanese seemed to be reeling. They were, but they still had plenty of fight in them. Admiral TANAKA, who ably led the "Tokyo Express" down the Slot throughout the Guadalcanal Campaign, was leading eight destroyers down the slot on the night of November 30. He was intercepted by a larger US force of five cruisers and seven destroyers. The battle was over quickly, as Tanaka's force promptly turned, launched TORPEDOES, and sank one cruiser and damaged three others. Some 400 Americans were killed. The Japanese were unhurt.

Tawi Tawi, Philippines

A roomy but exposed anchorage in the southern Philippines (virtually the southernmost place in the Philippines), Tawi Tawi—or Tawitawi—lacked even the most rudimentary facilities to service ships, but was convenient to the oil producing areas of Borneo and had potential as a base for projecting naval power in a broad arc eastward, and that was how the Japanese used it, in preparation for the Battle of the PHILIPPINE SEA.

Tawi Tawi was reoccupied by US forces on 1 July 1945, in an operation sometimes called the "last amphibious landing of World War II," a distinction more correctly belonging to the Australian landings at Balikpapan.

TBD-1 Devastator, US Carrier Torpedo Bomber

The TBD-1 Devastator was the standard US Navy torpedo bomber at the start of World War II and was markedly ill-equipped for that role. The fatal flaw for the TBD was its slow speed and the low height from which it had to drop its TORPEDO. These characteristics caused TBDs to take very heavy losses from Japanese flak and interceptors. At MIDWAY, nearly all the attacking TBDs were shot down without scoring any hits. Because the TBF AVENGER was just entering service in 1942, it wasn't until early 1944 that all the TBD-1s could be withdrawn from combat units.

See also AIRCRAFT TYPES, DEVELOPMENT; CARRIERS, DESIGNING AIRCRAFT FOR.

TBF Avenger, US Carrier Bomber

The US TBF Avenger was originally designed as a new torpedo bomber, but proved so successful that it became the only bomber aircraft carriers needed. Nearly 10,000 TBFs were built from 1942 to 1945. Half a dozen participated in the Battle of MIDWAY, and by the end of 1943 the TBF was the most common bomber on carriers. The TBF was much better than the TBD-1 DEVASTATOR, with 50% more speed, nearly as much additional range, twice the bombload (2,000 pounds), and was more heavily armed. While outclassed in most categories by the new Helldiver, the TBF still had twice the bombload, which in the later stages of the war was most

Avenger TBM variants from USS Essex *(CV-9) in a bombing raid on Kokadate, late July 1945. The aircraft in the left background are SB2C Helldivers.*

important. Equally important was the ease with which the TBF could be equipped with radar, making it an optimal scout aircraft. The TBF was supplied to allies, particularly Britain, where it served well during the battle against German U-boats in the Atlantic. TBF Avengers served with foreign air forces into the 1960s. There were many variants, including a transport version.

See also AIRCRAFT TYPES, DEVELOPMENT; CARRIERS, DESIGNING AIRCRAFT FOR.

Tempest, British Fighter Bomber

The Tempest was Britain's second-generation fighter bomber (after the Typhoon). Entering serv-

ice in the summer of 1943, it was fast (427 MPH) and heavily armed (four 20mm cannon and 2,000 pounds of bombs and rockets). It was also heavy (6.1 tons loaded) and not as nimble as fighters like the SPITFIRE. Nevertheless, it was a terror to Japanese ground troops in Burma. Nearly 1,000 were produced.

See also AIRCRAFT TYPES, DEVELOPMENT.

Tenryu Class, Japanese Light Cruisers

Japan's oldest light cruisers, the Tenryus were designed during World War I to serve as squadron leaders for destroyer flotillas. They were very small by World War II standards, indeed not much bigger than some destroyers, and no better armed. Beyond the addition of some antiaircraft armament, they were not modernized between the wars.

Tenryu (1917–1918–1919) served as a flotilla leader in the South Pacific, at the CORAL SEA and in the SOLOMONS, fighting at SAVO ISLAND. She was sunk by *Albacore* (SS-218) on 18 December 1942, in the BISMARCK SEA.

Tatsuta (1917–1918–1919) served as a flotilla leader in the South Pacific, including the Coral Sea. She was sunk by *Sundance* (SS-381) off Honshu on 13 March 1944.

Terauchi, Hisaichi (1879–1946)

Count Hisaichi Terauchi, the son of Field Marshal Count Masakata Terauchi (who started his military career as a samurai, rose to army command during the Russo-Japanese War, and later held important government posts), graduated from the military academy in 1899. He fought in the Russo-Japanese War, attended various schools, and spent several years as an attaché and student in Germany and Austria before World War I. Between 1914 and 1936 he rose to general and war minister, in which role he crushed the last vestiges of parliamentary authority over the military. In 1937 he commanded the forces that invaded China from MANCHURIA, and in 1941 was given the Southern Area Army, which controlled all army operations in Southeast Asia and the South Pacific. Made a field marshal in June 1943, Terauchi suffered a mild stroke in April 1945, but remained in command until the end of the war because his staff did not report his ill-health to Tokyo. That he did not stand trial for war crimes was due to his illness, which proved terminal. Surprisingly, he was looked after by Lord MOUNTBATTEN once the war was over. Terauchi was a soldier of the old school and did not agree with all the army involvement in politics. His noble rank and personal ability allowed him to retain his command despite these attitudes. Despite this, he gave orders that all PRISONERS OF WAR in his command were to be executed if Allied forces landed in Japan.

Tientsin, China

The port of PEKING, Tientsin had limited, but adequate facilities to fulfill its primary function. It was held by the Japanese for the entire war. In 1945 it was for a time occupied by the US Marines.

Timor

An island in the East Indies, Timor was divided between the Dutch, on the western side, and the Portuguese, on the east, which included Dili, the largest town and principal port of the island. On the outbreak of the Pacific War, Dutch and Australian troops occupied Portuguese Timor. Allied GUERRILLA forces, mostly Australian but with some

Five TBF Avengers on a training flight near Norfolk, Virginia, in September 1942. Introduced in early 1942 and intended as a torpedo bomber, the Avenger soon proved itself an immensely versatile airplane, and quickly became the navy's primary carrier-based bomber.

Dutch troops, were active on Timor from December 1941 through February 1943, when they were withdrawn due to increasing enemy pressure.

Ref: *Australia in the Second World War*, series I, vol. 5.

Tinian, Marianas

Shortly before the war began the Japanese had started to develop Tinian as a major base, despite the fact that it lacked a proper port. Strategically, Tinian, one of the MARIANAS, shared with SAIPAN and GUAM an excellent location that could act either as an outlying bastion of Japan or an offensive base against Japan (with Tokyo only a bit more than a thousand miles to the north). It figured prominently in the CENTRAL PACIFIC CAMPAIGN.

Tinker, Clarence L. (1887–1942)

Clarence L. Tinker entered the US armed forces as a third lieutenant in the PHILIPPINE CONSTABULARY before World War I. Later transferring to the Regular Army, he took flight training in 1921. Over the next 20 years he performed a variety of line and staff duties in the Air Corps, attended various army schools, rose to brigadier general, and managed to acquire an army life saving medal as well. Promoted to major general shortly after PEARL HARBOR, in March 1942 he was sent to HAWAII to command the Seventh Air Force, which controlled all Army Air Corps units in the central Pacific. Tinker directed Army Air Corps operations during the Battle of MIDWAY, from Midway Island. Late on June 6, 1942, he took part in a very-long-range raid intended to bomb WAKE ISLAND using four specially-prepared B-24 LIBERATORS. Sometime during the night his aircraft developed engine trouble and disappeared at sea. He was the first Regular Army general killed in the war. He was also probably the highest ranking person of American Indian descent killed in the war, being one-eighth Osage.

Tjilatjap, Java

A small port on the south coast of JAVA, of some value as a base for projecting power into the eastern Indian Ocean. It served the allies as a base until overrun by the Japanese in early 1942. They made some use of it for naval and air operations in the Indian Ocean.

Tojo, Hideki (1884–1948)

General Hideki Tojo was not a field commander during World War II, but he was the most important Japanese army commander because he ran the government for most of the war and was generally considered the one man most responsible for getting Japan into a war that many senior Japanese military officers knew Japan could not win. He graduated from the military academy in 1905. Most of his early career was spent in staff assignments and at the war college. From 1919 through 1922 he served with the Japanese Embassy in Berlin. Considered bright, but not among the brightest, Tojo made up for this with a workaholic dedication to whatever he was doing and an intense nationalism and ambition. Tojo was posted to the Kwantung (Manchurian) Army in the summer of 1934, as the head of the army military police. The Kwantung Army was a hotbed of army enthusiasm for Japanese expansion, and Tojo was caught up in what was, to him, a very congenial cause. In 1937 he became chief of staff of the Kwantung Army. He actively participated in operations against Chinese troops and, in 1938, went back to Japan to become vice minister of war. He offended so many senior officials with his ultra-nationalist attitudes that he was removed to the more obscure post of inspector of army aviation at the end of 1938.

By hard work and much politicking, he worked himself into the job of minister of war by the summer of 1940. By late 1941 he had gotten the post of prime minister and, in effect, control of the government. He retained his rank in the army. While Japan never became a military dictatorship in the classic sense, by the end of October 1941 the army was calling the shots. (Tojo was also both the minister of home affairs and minister of war.) The decision to go to war was already made when Tojo took over, and he heartily supported it. Through 1942 and 1943, he became the head of more ministries (foreign affairs, education, commerce and industry, munitions). By late 1943 he capped all this by becoming the chief of staff (commander) of both the army and the navy. For the first six months of 1944, Tojo was a one-man government. But he was not a complete dictator. In July 1944, the Privy Council (composed of older, semi-retired senior officials) agreed that he should go and forced him to retire. The main reason for this vote of no-confidence was that Japan was losing the war and Tojo refused to face reality. Although Tojo was then given a place on the Privy Council, he spent the rest of the war writing and (literally) tending his garden.

At the end of the war, he attempted suicide, but an American doctor was able to save his life. During his incarceration pending trial as a war criminal, a US Army dentist is alleged to have engraved the Morse Code for "Remember Pearl Harbor" on his teeth. Tried by the TOKYO WAR CRIMES TRIBUNAL, he was condemned and hanged. Although Tojo's body was burned and the ashes secretly buried by the Allies, Japanese crematorium workers stole some of the ashes and turned them over to the government after the occupation had ended. In 1960 an impressive tomb was constructed at the YASUKUNI SHRINE to contain these ashes (mixed in with six other war criminals). The monument is inscribed, "The Tomb of the Seven Martyrs."

Ref: Butow, *Tojo and the Coming of the War*.

Tokyo, Honshu, Japan

Including the nearby cities of Yokohama and Yokosuka, in 1940 there were more than 10 million people in the Tokyo area, concentrated around an extensive bay on the east coast of Honshu.

Tokyo was a major industrial and commercial center, as well as the seat of the Japanese government and armed forces. Tokyo was also the site of the Imperial Navy's Paymasters' Academy, which trained officers for the administrative branches of the service; other officer candidates went to Eta Jima, at KURE, or MAIZURU.

Nearby Yokohama was a major industrial city and port, with extensive shipbuilding facilities, suitable for merchantships and cruisers. Yokosuka was one of the four main bases of the Imperial Navy, with facilities to build any kind of warship. It was the headquarters of the Yokosuka SNLF.

Tokyo Express

In October 1942 the Japanese established a standing force of destroyers converted to carry troops and cargo. These high-speed transports were intended to take troops and supplies to GUADALCANAL, an island American troops had taken from the Japanese the previous August. The United States had promptly established an airfield and the bombers stationed there would spot Japanese transports during daylight and attack the ships before nightfall provided any protection. The faster destroyer transports could wait until nightfall and then move into range of US aircraft, land their cargo on Guadalcanal, and be back out of range of American aircraft before the sun came up. For the second half of 1942, as the battle for Guadalcanal raged, this Japanese force was called the "Cactus Express" ("Cactus" was the US code word for Japanese forces on Guadalcanal).

But even after the Japanese were forced out of Guadalcanal in early 1943, the Japanese fast transports continued to supply Japanese garrisons in the adjacent islands. At that point, these fast transports came to be known as the "Tokyo Express," and continued to operate in 1944 from bases like RABAUL. The original organizer of the Tokyo Express, Raizo TANAKA, was an able destroyerman and an outspoken naval officer. By early 1943 he had been transferred elsewhere for being too outspoken on how Japanese commanders were mismanaging the war effort. In the summer of 1943 the Tokyo Express took such a hammering in a series of losing battles with American ships that its operations were greatly reduced. Japan was running out of destroyers. There were several dozen available for the Tokyo Express in late 1942, but after a year, nearly two-thirds of these were sunk or under repair. Few replacements were forthcoming, and the destroyer component of the Tokyo Express eventually faded away because of attrition.

There were, however, other types of transport running the same routes. While traditional merchant ships proved too slow and vulnerable, slow-moving barges and smaller ships found ways to survive. They did this by running up on a beach before dawn and camouflaging themselves so Allied aircraft could not spot them. Some were spotted anyway, but most made it down to Japanese garrisons, unloaded their cargo at night, and returned north time and again. For special missions the Japanese would also use submarines and parachute drops. By late 1944, Rabaul, the northern terminus for the Tokyo Express, was itself cut off from Japan. With nothing to send south, the dogged supply service faded away in early 1945.

Tokyo Rose

The name given to several women who made English-language broadcasts for the Japanese in an effort to weaken US morale. The troops often listened because, between propaganda pitches, it was common to play American popular music. Senior US officers wisely did nothing to prevent their troops from listening, and there were no noticeable morale problems due to these broadcasts.

The only "Tokyo Rose" who was an American citizen was Iva Toguri (1916–   ). Pearl Harbor found her visiting Japan, where she secured employment as a disc jockey with an English-language radio station. Although she apparently did not broadcast propaganda, after the war she was arrested by the US Army and tried on treason charges. She received a 10–year sentence and a $10,000 fine. After her release she worked for many years to clear her name, meanwhile marrying and

"Tokyo Rose," Iva Toguri, being interviewed by war correspondents in Tokyo, September 1945.

becoming Iva d'Aquino. In January 1977 President Gerald FORD issued her a full pardon.

Ref: Duus, *Tokyo Rose.*

Tokyo War Crimes Tribunal

The International Military Tribunal for the Far East convened in 1946 to try the highest-ranking Japanese officials charged with war crimes. The court consisted of representatives from the various Allied powers. The trials lasted from 3 May 1946 to 12 November 1948, and were held in the former Japanese War Ministry building. The charges were various, including both general and specific counts of conspiracy to make war, violations of international law, and countenancing ATROCITIES. In deference to the claim that while Japan had signed the 1929 GENEVA CONVENTION it had never ratified the signature and was thus not bound by it, the charges were brought under the terms of the 1899 Hague Convention, which Japan had signed and ratified.

Altogether 28 men were tried. Two of them died during the trial. Seven were sentenced to death, 16 to life, one to 20 years in prison, and one to seven years in prison. One was found mentally unfit to stand trial and was relegated to an insane asylum. By one reckoning the Tokyo trial cost $9 million and used 100 tons of paper.

Those sentenced to death were:

Gen. Kenji DOHIHARA

Koki Hirota, prime minister during the CHINA IN-CIDENT

Gen. Seishiro ITAGAKI, former war minister

Gen. Heitaro KIMURA

Gen. Iwane Matsui, commander of the Japanese forces during the "Rape of Nanking"

Gen. Akira Muto, chief of staff of the occupation forces in the Philippines

Gen. Hideki TOJO, head of the Japanese government for much of the war

This trial dealt with the principal war criminals. Other trials took up the cases involving persons of lesser importance, such as those involving generals HOMMA and YAMASHITA.

Only a handful of Japanese war criminals were ever tried. Most of those sentenced had their sentences reduced and few served for very long, and even those who had been sentenced to death had their sentences commuted to life. By the mid-1950s there were no Japanese war criminals still in jail.

Tomozuru Class, Japanese Torpedo Boats

Like several nations, Japan continued to build so-called "ocean-going" or fleet TORPEDO boats, basically very small destroyers specialized for torpedo attack. They were poorly designed, being unstable (*Tomozuru* once capsized in a storm, later to be salvaged and returned to service) and unsuited to their original purpose—coordinated high-speed torpedo attacks in fleet actions. They were pressed into service as convoy escorts after extensive modifications to their armament, a role in which they proved surprisingly effective, as they could carry 48 depth charges each, far more than most fleet destroyers. Three were lost in action.

Tone Class, Japanese Heavy Cruisers

The two Tones were designed as light cruisers with a dozen 6–inch guns, in four turrets all forward, but converted to four 8-inch guns while still building. Grouping the main armament forward gave the cruisers an odd appearance, but permitted them to carry a very large complement of floatplanes. As a result, the Tones were the best Japanese heavy

---

RESULTS OF WAR CRIMES TRIALS IN THE FAR EAST

	Australia	Britain	Nation Holding Trial France	Netherlands	United States	Total
Cases	296	306	39	448	474	1,563
Defendants	924	920	230	1,038	1,409	4,521
Convictions	644	811	198	969	1,229	3,851
Acquittals	280	106	31	55	180	652
Prison Terms	369	532	134	719	1,066	2,820
Death Sentences	148	279	63	236	163	889
Executed	148	265	26	226	92	757
Commuted	0	14	37	10	71	132
Other	0	3	1	14	0	18

Trials by China and Russia unknown. "Other" includes persons who died during trial or who were found unfit to stand trial for reasons of mental or physical health.

cruisers, combining high speed, heavy armament, extensive protections, good sea-keeping qualities, excellent maneuverability, and all those floatplanes that enhanced their role as fleet scouts. Although rated at six aircraft, they apparently never carried more than five.

The two ships served together for virtually the entire war, helping escort the First Air Fleet to PEARL HARBOR, and serving with it in the Indian Ocean and at MIDWAY (where one of *Tone*'s scout planes located the US carriers). They were with the Japanese carriers from then to the PHILIPPINE SEA, fighting in virtually all of the carrier battles. During the Battle of LEYTE GULF they took part in the attack on the US escort carriers off SAMAR on 25 October 1944.

Tone (1934–1937–1938) was damaged during Leyte Gulf, and retired to Japan for repairs, which were never fully effected. She was sunk in shallow water by US carrier aircraft in KURE Harbor on 24 July 1945, and broken up postwar.

Chikuma (1935–1938–1939) was sunk by US carrier aircraft bombs and a TORPEDO off Samar on October 25, 1944.

Tonga

A Polynesian kingdom in the South Pacific, under British protection, Tonga provided useful naval and air basing sites. In addition, the kingdom raised a small brigade group, composed of two infantry battalions, with a small artillery and engineer element, plus support troops, which was supplemented by a NEW ZEALAND infantry battalion. Although most of the Tongan Brigade did not see action, a special infantry platoon did.

Usually attached to Fijian forces, the Tongan contingent occasionally served independently. Attached to US forces during the New Georgia landings in mid-1943, the Tongans performed so well that one was awarded a Silver Star.

Ref: Gillespie, *Official History of New Zealand in the Second World War, 1939–1945, The Pacific*; Ready, *Forgotten Allies*.

Torpedoes

World War II was the golden age of torpedo warfare. This was the only conflict in which torpedoes were used extensively by SUBMARINES, aircraft, and surface ships. The Japanese had a significant advantage in torpedo warfare for the first two years of the war. This was because their principal surface ship torpedo was larger and more capable than anyone else's and because the prinicipal US submarine torpedo was defective. The Japanese aerial torpedo was also superior during this period, giving the Japanese an advantage in every torpedo category. This was a particularly decided edge for the Japanese during the first year of the war.

In the early part of the war Japanese surface ships used their so-called "Long Lance" torpedoes to destroy far more Allied ships than their opponents could using the same technique. US carrier aircraft caused less damage with their less capable torpedoes, and US submarines were practically disarmed because of their defective torpedoes. The entries below shows the torpedo situation in detail.

Torpedo Types Range and speed are given, when needed, as the two extreme settings for the torpedo, with range in kilometers and speed in knots (1 knot = 1 nautical mile or 1.9 kilometers per hour).

The Japanese Type 8 was a 24-inch surface weapon that weighed 5,207 pounds and had a 761-pound warhead. The range (kilometers) and speed (knots) were from 10 and 38 to 15 and 32. The Type 8 was a 1920s design that was still being used by older destroyers and light cruisers early in the war. An effective torpedo similar to the US Mark 15.

The Japanese Type 89 was a 21-inch submarine weapon that weighed 3,677 pounds and had a 661-pound warhead. The range (kilometers) and speed (knots) were from 5.5 and 45 to 10 and 35. The Type 89 was a 1920s design for SUBMARINES and was widely used during the first year of the war. During that period, it was much more effective than the newer US Mark 14.

Torpedoes

The Japanese Type 90 was a 21-inch submarine weapon that weighed 5,743 pounds and had an 827-pound warhead. The range (kilometers) and speed (knots) were from 7 and 46 to 15 and 35. The Type 90 was a 1930s design for cruisers. Used extensively early in the war.

The Japanese Type 93 (nicknamed Long Lance by the Allies) was a 24-inch surface weapon that weighed 5,952 pounds and had a warhead of 1,080 pounds. The range (kilometers) and speed (knots) were from 20 and 49 to 40 and 36. The Japanese were way ahead of everyone else with this 24-inch surface ship torpedo. Very reliable, fast, and deadly. Widely used throughout the war, especially in the first year.

The Japanese Type 95 was a 21-inch submarine weapon that weighed 3,671 pounds and had an 893–pound warhead. The range (kilometers) and speed (knots) were from 9 and 50 to 12 and 46. The Type 95 was a smaller, submarine version of the Type 93 Long Lance and was quite effective. There was also a Type 92 electric torpedo that was produced from 1942 on in small quantities (650) to supplement the more widely used Type 95.

The Japanese Type 97 was a 17.7-inch submarine weapon weighing 2,094 pounds with a 772-pound warhead. The range (kilometers) and speed (knots) were 5.5 and 45. The Type 97 was an even smaller version of the Long Lance, for use in midget submarines. Only 100 Type 97s were built, and it was used only by the midget subs at PEARL HARBOR, where recent evidence suggests one may actually have struck a battleship. The Type 97 was not very reliable in any event.

The Japanese Type 91-1 was a 17.7-inch aircraft weapon weighing 1,728 pounds and having a 331-pound warhead. The range (kilometers) and speed (knots) were two and 42. The Type 91-1 was the standard aircraft torpedo in the first year of the war. This was an early 1930s design and was being replaced by the Type 91-2 in 1941. All Type 91s could be launched at over 200 knots (twice the launch speed of early US airborne torpedoes) early in the war and 350 knots by 1944. Launch altitude

was, for tactical reasons, rarely more than a few hundred feet.

The Japanese Type 91-2 was a 17.7-inch aircraft weapon weighing 1,841 pounds with a 452-pound warhead. The range (kilometers) and speed (knots) were two and 42. The Type 91-2 replaced the 91-1 in 1942.

The Japanese Type 91-3 was a 17.7-inch aircraft weapon weighing 1,872 pounds with a 529-pound warhead. The range (kilometers) and speed (knots) was two and 42. The Type 91-3 replaced the 91-2 in 1943.

The Japanese Type 04 was a 17.7-inch aircraft weapon that weighed 2,169 pounds and had a 670-pound warhead. The range (kilometers) and speed (knots) were 1.5 and 42. The Type 04 was a further development of the Type 91 that could be launched at speeds over 400 knots. In service by late 1944.

The Japanese Kaiten was a 39.4-inch submarine weapon that weighed 18,300 pounds and had a 3,420-pound warhead. The range (kilometers) and speed (knots) varied from 23 and 30 to 78 and 12. The Kaiten was a manned suicide torpedo. Although 330 were put into service, only one US ship (fleet oil tanker *Mississinewa* at ULITHI Atoll in the CAROLINE ISLANDS, in November 1944) is known for certain to have been sunk by one, although it has been suggested that the heavy cruiser *Indianapolis* was actually sunk by a Kaiten and not a torpedo, as *I-58* skipper C. Mochitasura Hashimoto stated at the court-martial of Capt. Charles B. McVay III and in his memoirs.

The US Mark 10 was a 21-inch submarine weapon weighing 2,215 pounds with a 497-pound warhead. The range (kilometers) and speed (knots) were 3.2 and 36. The Mark 10 was a World War I torpedo still in use on "S" class US submarines early in World War II.

The U.S. Mark 15 was a 21–inch surface weapon weighing 3,841 pounds with an 825-pound warhead. The range (kilometers) and speed (knots) varied from 5.5 and 45 to 13.7 and 26. The Mark 15 was the standard destroyer torpedo throughout the war. Compared to the Japanese Type 93 Long

Lance, the Mark 15 was decidedly inferior. But the Type 93 was arguably the most effective torpedo used by any navy during the entire war. The Mark 15 was reliable and effective, even though it was slower and had a 20% smaller warhead than the Type 93.

The US Mark 14 was a 21-inch submarine weapon weighing 3,280 pounds and with a 643-pound warhead. The range (kilometers) and speed (knots) varied from 4.1 and 46 to 8.2 and 31. The Mark 14 was the 1930s replacement for the Mark 10 and got off to a rocky start. It was designed to explode under its target using a magnetic field-detecting detonator. In this way it would do maximum damage ("breaking the ship's back," or generally breaking up the internal structure of the ship). It worked during tests in the Atlantic Ocean. But the conditions in the Pacific turned out to be different enough to make the Mark 14 almost useless. It seems that the magnetic field of ships, because of the Earth's own magnetic influence, took a different shape nearer to the equator. In effect, the magnetic field of metal ships flattened out and extended farther from the ship when near the equator. Thus the magnetic detonator caused the torpedo to explode prematurely. Moreover, the depth-setting mechanism reacted differently to the different water conditions in the Pacific to the extent that the torpedo ran 10 or more feet deeper than it was supposed to. It took nearly a year for submarine captains to convince the navy's torpedo establishment that there was a problem. A new detonator of more conventional design was then put on the Mark 14, but this one also turned out to be unreliable, the "firing pins" being made of relatively cheap metal, which bent at the critical moment. It wasn't until the middle of 1943 that the Mark 14 finally became a reliable torpedo. With more modifications, Mark 14s continued in use until the late 1970s.

The US Mark 13 was a 17.7-inch aircraft weapon that weighed 2,216 pounds and had a 600-pound warhead. The range (kilometers) and speed (knots) were 6.7 and 33. The Mark 13 was the standard US airborne torpedo for most of the war.

While not a bad design, it suffered from the need for low and slow launching speed (50 feet and 110 knots). This caused many lost aircraft, as at that altitude and speed the torpedo bombers were perfect targets for enemy fighters or ships' antiaircraft guns. At MIDWAY, an entire squadron of torpedo bombers carrying Mark 13s was shot down while approaching their targets. In early 1944, some simple modifications were made to the Mark 13 that allowed it to be dropped at a thousand feet and speeds of over 200 knots. By the end of the war, the configuration of the Mark 13 had been tweaked to the point that it could be dropped at 2,400 feet while traveling at over 400 knots. Aside from the height and speed problems, the Mark turned out to be an effective weapon, with 40% of those launched actually hitting a target. The Mark 13 was also used successfully on PT BOATS.

The US Mark 18 was a 21-inch submarine weapon weighing 3,154 pounds and having a 575-pound warhead. The range (kilometers) and speed (knots) were 3.6 and 29. The Mark 18 was an unsuccessful copy of the more effective German G7e submarine torpedo. This model did not leave a track and was a lot cheaper to build than the Mark 14. But while the design could be copied, the reliability of the German original could not. Many Mark 18s were fired late in the war, but submarine captains tended to prefer the older Mark 14.

The US Mark 24 was a 19-inch aircraft weapon weighing 680 pounds and with a 92-pound warhead. The range (kilometers) and speed (knots) were 3.6 and 12. The Mark 24 was the first effective homing torpedo. Four sensors steered it toward the noise of a diving or snorkeling (running on diesel engines via a periscope-type air vent) submarine. The Mark 24 was quite effective, with 346 used and 101 obtaining hits (two-thirds resulting in destroyed subs, the others were badly damaged). Only about 10% of subs attacked with air-dropped depth charges would be sunk or damaged. The Mark 24 was first used in the summer of 1943 against German subs in the Atlantic.

The US Mark 27 was a 19-inch submarine weapon weighing 720 pounds and having a 95–

pound warhead. The range (kilometers) and speed (knots) were 4.5 and 12. The Mark 27 was a submarine version of the Mark 24. Rails were added so that it would fit the submarine's 21–inch torpedo tubes. The Mark 27 was used only against Japanese escorts. It was quite effective, with 106 fired to obtain 33 hits (73% of which were fatal to the surface ship, usually something smaller than a destroyer). First used in mid-1944.

One reason that the flaws in several US torpedo designs were not detected earlier was that they were not fully tested before the war under wartime conditions. This was a way to cut costs, as it saved $8,000–$10,000 for each torpedo not expended, but it would have been money well spent.

As good as tested torpedoes were they all had a "wander" problem. "Wander" is the maximum distance a torpedo will "wander" off course at different ranges. The "wander" of the Japanese Type 93 was typical of all torpedoes. At 15 kilometers, a Type 93 would wander off a straight-line course as much as 500 meters right or left. At 25 kilometers wander was 700 meters and at 30 kilometers it was 1,000 meters. Even at range of a few kilometers, wander could be as much as 100 meters. For this reason, you usually launched a "spread" of torpedoes. Because of "wander" and the fact that they carried only one weapon per aircraft, which had very short ranges, torpedo bombers were a risky proposition.

Ref: Hashimoto, *Sunk.*

Torpedoes, Malfunctions

On at least two occasions US SUBMARINES were sunk by their own torpedoes, which malfunctioned and ran in a circular pattern.

Date	Boat	Area
March 3, 1944	USS *Tulibee* (SS–284)	Palau
October 24, 1944	USS *Tang* (SS–306)	Philippines

Towers, John H. (1885–1955)

Among the most important molders of the US Navy's carrier forces in World War II, John Henry Towers is one of the most unsung heroes of the Pacific War, a man so forgotten that he is often overlooked in most standard works on naval history: He is mentioned barely a dozen times in Samuel Eliot MORISON's 15–volume *History of U.S. Naval Operations in World War II*. A 1906 graduate of the naval Academy, Towers was taught to fly by Glenn Curtis in 1911 and was thereafter closely involved with the development of naval air power, among other feats, taking part in the navy's 1919 transatlantic flight as pilot of *NC-3*. From the early 1920s until 1939 he served as assistant director of naval aviation, as assistant chief of the Bureau of Aeronautics, and as skipper of the carrier *Saratoga*; during breaks he served as an aviation adviser for the London Naval DISARMAMENT Conference Treaty. Chief of the Bureau of Aeronautics from 1939 to 1942, from early 1942 until the end of the war, Towers was the principal naval air officer in the Pacific, serving first as commanding officer, Air Forces, Pacific Fleet, later as deputy commander in chief, Pacific, and once again as chief of the Bureau of Aeronautics. Instrumental in the development of the fast carrier task force, the evolution of AIR GROUP composition, the coordination of carriers with escorts, and the assignment of flying officers as chiefs of staff to non-flying commanders (and vice-versa), Towers' enormous intellectual and administrative powers kept him from active command until virtually the end of the war, when, in August of 1945, he was named commanding officer of the newly formed Second Fast Carrier Force, and later CINCPAC after the surrender of Japan.

Townsville, Australia

Although possessed of only a modest port, Townsville had the distinction of being one of the principal air transport centers in Australia, making it an important air base, of considerable strategic value, as it lay on the northeastern coast of the country.

Toyoda, Soemu (1885–1957)

Soemu Toyoda graduated from the naval academy in 1905. A naval gunnery specialist, his career was impressive, including numerous special assignments and duty as an admiral's aide, along with the usual run of ship and staff posts. In the late 1930s, as a vice admiral, he commanded naval forces during the heavy fighting in China. Opposed to the idea of war with America, Toyoda had little respect for the militant army officers running the government. He spent the early part of the Pacific War commanding naval bases in Japan. In early 1944 he became commander of the Combined Fleet and was ordered to gather his forces for a "decisive battle" against the approaching American naval might. Despite his earlier attitudes toward war with America, he proposed that Japan fight on even after most of the Japanese fleet was destroyed by early 1945. Nevertheless, he accepted the emperor's surrender order. Arrested as a war criminal, he was cleared of culpability for war crimes committed by naval personnel. He had given his sword to Admiral NIMITZ at the end of the war, but Nimitz returned it as a gesture of goodwill in 1952.

Tradition

Tradition is one of the mainstays of a military service. Some customs practiced during the Second World War go back centuries. For example, as late as World War II it was common for old chiefs (chief petty officers, the most senior enlisted men) to say that upon retirement they were going to put an anchor over their shoulder and begin walking inland. When someone asked "Where'd you get the funny fishhook?" they planned to settle down to raise chickens, as far from blue water as physically possible. This is a seaman's joke so old that it is virtually identical to one Homer told in *The Odyssey* nearly 3,000 years ago.

Several other old customs were (and are) still common in the navy. For example, by early 1945 an astute observer aboard a US Navy ship might have gotten a good sense of how soon the war was going to end by noticing that many of the sailors were working on "homecoming" pennants. These are long multicolored streamers that are flown from the mainmast as ships return victorious from a war. It's an ancient tradition, maintained by the old salts since time immemorial. By early 1945, with the fleet operating off Japan, sailors on many ships began sewing homecoming pennants. Most ships had one by the time Japan surrendered in August of 1945, and they can be seen streaming astern from the mainmasts in pictures of ships returning home after the war. By tradition, a homecoming pennant is one foot long for every man aboard who had been away from home a year or more. The longest belonged to "The Big E," the carrier *Enterprise*, which, upon her return to the United States in late 1945, had been continuously away from the 48 states for well over 500 days. Her streamer was so long, in fact, that helium balloons were needed to keep it aloft.

The submarine service preserved another very old maritime tradition. Boats returning from successful war patrols customarily wore a broom at the top of their mainmast. This custom dates back to the 17th century, when the Dutch seadog Michael DeRuyter tied a broom to his mainmast to let everyone know that he had "swept" the seas of enemy ships.

One tradition common to all navies was continued during the war, whenever practical. This was the initiation of pollywogs into Neptune's Kingdom. During these ceremonies, in which men who had never crossed the equator (Pollywogs) were made loyal subjects of King Neptune (the senior enlisted men on the ship), many a fuzz-cheecked seaman and ensign found himself far more worried about the shave that the Shellbacks (old salts) were preparing for him than anything that the enemy was likely to throw his way. Among those so initiated during the war was Secretary of the Navy

Frank Knox. FDR had been initiated during the 1930s.

The Japanese Armed Forces had one interesting custom. When a man was killed in action he was automatically promoted two grades. This, as well as traditional obligations to honor the dead, is one reason why the families of missing Japanese servicemen have often traveled to distant islands in an effort to find the remains of their loved ones. If they prove the guy died in action they receive a better pension.

There was one hoary naval tradition that was not practiced in the US Navy, the awarding of prize money, upon the successful conclusion of a war. Originally a way to organize the division of loot, prize had passed out of fashion in the US Navy shortly after the Spanish-American War. It was a wonderful custom, about which the Civil War Union admiral, David Dixon Porter, who greatly profited from prize, remarked, "Armies loot, Navies take prize." Prize was, however, still awarded in the ROYAL NAVY, and shortly after the end of World War II His Majesty's tars and jollies (sailors and marines) received a rather nice little bonus, amounting to several hundred dollars each for the common seamen, and proportionately more as one went up the ranks.

Tribal Class, British Destroyers

The Tribal Class (named after the great native tribes of the British Empire) marked a significant increase in British destroyer size, being about 30% larger than the previous classes, and set the model for subsequent British destroyer construction. The initial run of 16 ships was built 1936–39. A repeat run of 11 more for Australia and Canada were ordered in 1939, but not all were completed before the end of the war. Several of the Canadian ships and the three Australian ones saw extensive service in the Pacific.

Trincomalee, Ceylon

The principal British naval and air base in the eastern Indian Ocean, in 1942 Trincomalee lacked ex-

tensive facilities, making it of only limited utility. It was raided by the Japanese during their Indian Ocean foray, March–April 1942. The British later expended its facilities.

Trobriand Islands

A small island group off the east coast of NEW GUINEA, the Trobriands (of which Kiriwana is the largest) were noted before the war chiefly for the interesting sexual practices of the natives, made known to the world by various anthropologists. Militarily, their position provided potentially useful sites for air bases from which to dominate the BISMARCKS, and eastern Papua-New Guinea. The Japanese occupied them briefly in mid-1942, but withdrew in September. The Allies ignored them until June of 1943, when they were occupied by the US 158th Regimental Combat Team.

Truk, Carolines

A fine natural harbor in a roomy atoll, with the surrounding islands and islets suitable for several airfields, by late 1941 Truk was well on its way toward becoming one of the most important military bases in the Pacific, being roughly equidistant from New Guinea, GUADALCANAL, and the GILBERT ISLANDS. It was the principal Japanese military base in the South Pacific. Truk was raided repeatedly by US naval aircraft and surface vessels during the course of the war. Although there were initially plans to take the place, these were dropped in favor of neutralizing it, and it remained in Japanese hands throughout the war, though increasingly on starvation rations. Today it possesses one of the most extensive collections of sunken ships in the world.

Truman, Harry S (1884–1972)

Harry S Truman came from a modest background in his native Missouri. Entering retail trade, he sub-

President Harry S Truman makes the formal announcement of the Japanese surrender, Washington, D.C., August 14, 1945.

sequently joined the NATIONAL GUARD in order to improve his business connections. Activated during World War I, Truman proved a very able artillery captain, reputedly the best mule skinner in the war, and, after acquiring that skill, among the best "cussers" in the AEF. After the war he remained in trade and in the National Guard, and entered politics. He did well in the latter two (his partner managed the business quite successfully, however), and by 1939 was a National Guard colonel and a senator. Although he volunteered for active service when the Missouri National Guard was federalized, General George C. MARSHALL urged him to remain in the Senate, where he was a staunch supporter of REARMAMENT. Truman's

chairmanship of one of the numerous congressional committees investigating the war brought him to the attention of President ROOSEVELT, with the result that he was elected vice president in 1944. Although not a member of FDR's inner circle, when Roosevelt died in April of 1945, Truman very quickly assumed control, proving an effective president in the final months of the war.

Truman's decision to use the ATOMIC BOMB is considered in some circles highly controversial, although among military historians it is generally regarded as a logical response to the strategic situation confronting the nation at the time.

Truman's nephew, Louis W. Truman, was a Regular Army officer, and served in the ETO.

Tsuji, Masanohu (1901–1961?)

Probably the most notorious Pacific War criminal to escape justice, Tsuji was a military academy graduate, and one of the most belligerent and nationalistic officers in the emperor's service. A distinguished intelligence officer, he served as a fixer and troubleshooter on numerous fronts: Before the war he helped engineer the takeover of MANCHURIA in 1931, was deeply involved in the CHINA INCIDENT in the mid- and late 1930s, and helped provoke the clash with Russia at Nomonhan in 1939. In anticipation of a general war, he conducted extensive intelligence missions in Southeast Asia and Burma. His meticulous intelligence work and planning were critically important to the Japanese victory in MALAYA. He later served on GUADALCANAL and in Burma.

At the time Japan surrendered he was in Siam, where he joined a Japanese monastery under an assumed name, and later reportedly worked as an adviser to CHIANG KAI-SHEK during the Chinese Civil War. In the late 1940s he returned to Japan, where he managed to avoid trial for, among other things, the murder of an American PILOT in Burma. He subsequently became involved in various nationalist and veterans organizations, and wrote a memoir, *Underground Escape* (1952). In 1961 he took a still unexplained trip to North Vietnam and was never heard from again. He was declared legally dead in 1968.

Tulagi, Solomons

A modest island group off the much larger Florida Island, just a few miles north of GUADALCANAL, Tulagi was the administrative center of the Solomon Islands. It had a fine anchorage, but otherwise had only very rudimentary port facilities. It was the scene of some bitter fighting on 7 August 1942, when the Marines landed there preparatory to their landing on Guadalcanal.

Turner, Richmond Kelly (1885–1961)

The unquestioned master of amphibious warfare during the Second World War, Richmond Kelly Turner graduated from the US Naval Academy in 1908. His early career was typical of that of a junior naval officer of his generation, including sea duty, some staff time, and some schooltime. During World War I he served in battleships, but did not get overseas. After the war he continued in the peacetime routine of the navy until he took flight training in the late 1920s. Thereupon his career began to blossom. He commanded several aviation squadrons, was involved in planning the future of naval aviation, was an adviser to the US delegation at the Geneva Disarmament Conference of 1932, saw some more sea time and staff duty, and in October of 1940 was named director of war plans. In this post he was deeply involved not only in planning the navy's war, but also in developing amphibious doctrine in cooperation with Marines such as Alexander A. VANDEGRIFT. As a result, in mid-1942 he was ordered to the South Pacific to assume command of the task force that landed Vandegrift's First Marine Division on GUADALCANAL. Despite SAVO ISLAND and other setbacks, Turner's tenacity and determination helped keep the Marines on Guadalcanal and they kept Henderson Field in American hands. Thereafter Turner directed numerous amphibious operations with increasing skill and success. In April of 1945 he was named commander, Amphibious Forces, Pacific, comprising the III and V Marine Amphibious Corps, in anticipation of the invasion of Japan, which he would have directed. When peace came he briefly held some minor diplomatic posts, retiring in 1947.

Ref: Dyer, *The Amphibians Came to Conquer.*

Tutuila, U.S. River Gunboat

A small (150-ton) US gunboat on the Yangtze in China, *Tutuila* (PR-4) was caught well up the river when the Japanese invaded China in 1937. In violation of the treaties governing foreign gunboats in Chinese waters, the Japanese refused to permit her to pass through their lines, and she remained upriver thereafter. In air raids on Chungking on July 6–7, 1939 she was almost struck by several Japanese bombs. The same air raids had resulted in the bombing of an American mission church. Despite a Japanese apology, President ROOSEVELT used these two incidents as a pretext not to renew the 1911 United States-Japan commercial treaty, which meant that after January 26, 1940 Japan had to negotiate every transaction with the US government separately.

The ship was again struck by Japanese bombs at Chungking on July 30, 1941. The Japanese government apologized the next day.

Tutuila was eventually turned over to the Chinese Navy as part of LEND-LEASE.

See also PANAY INCIDENT; WARSHIPS U.S., CAPTURED.

Typhoon, British Fighter Bomber

The Typhoon was Britain's first-generation fighter bomber. It entered service in the summer of 1941. Teething problems limited its effectiveness for about a year, but by 1943 the Typhoon was the terror of any enemy ground forces within range. Initially armed with eight .50 caliber machine guns and 1,000 pounds of bombs, this was soon changed to four 20mm cannon and 2,000 pounds of bombs and rockets. Top speed was 410 MPH, and loaded weight was six tons. Typhoons eventually went to the Far East, where they were found to be particularly effective against Japanese shipping. Some 3,300 were produced.

See also AIRCRAFT TYPES, DEVELOPMENT.

Typhoons and Tropical Storms

As if the normal hazards of war were not enough, war at sea adds a few extra. One enemy encountered often during the Pacific War were the ty-phoons ("cyclonic storms," or hurricanes) that regularly sweep across the ocean.

The Pacific Fleet was hit by several typhoons of unusual force during 1944–45.

October 10–18, 1944. The Third Fleet was operating in the western Pacific, conducting raids on FORMOSA and OKINAWA, when a typhoon passed through the central CAROLINES, battering ULITHI Atoll. Although damage to the fleet was slight, since the eye of the storm passed to its east, heavy seas made some operations difficult, and almost resulted in the abandonment of the light cruiser *Houston* and heavy cruiser AUSTRALIA, both of which were under tow, having just been heavily damaged by enemy action.

December 17–18, 1944. A small, fast-moving (9 knot) storm blindsided Task Force 38 off the Philippines on December 17, 1944. Over 800 sailors were killed, three destroyers were sunk, and 20 other ships severely damaged, while many aircraft were damaged or destroyed. One reason for the seriousness of this incident may be that Admiral HALSEY—though a "brown shoe" (i.e., flying) admiral—used a battlewagon for his flagship, which was very stable in foul weather, and it has been charged that he underestimated the danger of this storm, because the seas didn't seem so rough to him as he stood on the bridge of his battleship. In addition, the three destroyers lost appear to have been riding high, having pumped out ballast in anticipation of refueling. Another complicating factor may have been that many skippers were relatively young, and had not had years of experience in coping with heavy seas.

January 8–10, 1945. A typhoon passing nearby in the western Pacific interfered with Task Force 38 air operations against Formosa, the Pescadores, and the RYUKYU ISLANDS.

June 4–5, 1945. Task Group 38.1 was hit square by a typhoon northeast of the Philippines, and had to lie to until the eye passed over it. Two carriers (*Hornet* and *Bennington*), three cruisers, and several smaller ships were damaged, while 76 aircraft were destroyed and 16 damaged, but only six men lost (swept overboard) and four injured. Having had ample warning, all ships were riding deep, with full ballast.

September 9–10, 1945.   Occurring after the surrender of Japan, this was probably the worst of the major storms to hit the fleet, Typhoon Louisa passed 15 miles east of Okinawa. It sank 12 small ships and landing craft, beaching 222 more, and damaging a further 32. Loss of life was considerable. Of the beached and damaged vessels, 52 were considered not worth repairing. Over the next few days, as the storm passed east of Japan and gradually lost force, a number of ships of the Third Fleet were damaged, none seriously. The vessels destroyed had originally been earmarked for Operation Olympic, but were now engaged in preparing to transport troops from Okinawa to Japan for occupation duties. Had the war lasted just a few more days, losses might readily have been far greater.

The "nursery" for Pacific typhoons north of the equator is between 155 and 165 degrees east longitude, and from the equator to about 20 degrees north, at least for most of the year. From January through March it's between 145 and 155 degrees east. Further complicating matters, some ferocious storms form west of Japan in the Sea of Japan and a few even farther north, over land in northeast Siberia, and then gain typhoon-strength as they move out over the water. Most of these "northern" typhoons don't get beyond storm strength (over 34 knots wind), but some do. For every typhoon, there are several storms of (somewhat) lesser ferocity, which can be almost as disruptive as a typhoon, as carrier operations were not possible during most storms, and this made it easier for enemy SUBMARINES to get close to the carriers. All of this storm activity happens smack in the middle of the Central Pacific Theater of Operations. Interestingly, the Great White Fleet had a rough time with a typhoon in about the same area during its around-the-world voyage in 1908, but the navy seems not to have remembered this, despite the fact that some later senior admirals had been on that cruise as junior officers.

Making life even more difficult was the fact that since the Japanese held so many of the central Pacific islands, there was often insufficient meteorological information on the formation of new storms or the paths of existing ones. For this reason the US Navy regularly used submarines to report the weather, and maintained weather stations in China, including several in the Gobi Desert in Inner Mongolia, probably about as far from blue water—perhaps from open water—as the navy has ever operated, until the Apollo Program. The Japanese were not the only enemy ready to hit you while you weren't looking.

U

UDT (Underwater Demolition Team)

Many technological advances in the 1920s and '30s led to unique new weapons systems in World War II. Perhaps the most curious was scuba-diving gear. The use of an air tank and mask allowed a swimmer to stay underwater for an hour or more. This led to two "special weapons": underwater COMMANDOS and manned TORPEDOES. The underwater commandos' primary function was gathering information on beaches to be invaded and clearing some obstacles. This latter task was achieved by having the swimmers attach explosives to man-made obstacles and blow them up. This was particularly useful for obstacles lying on the bottom, but not protruding above the surface. These obstacles were designed to rip the bottoms off landing craft. The UDTs first had to find these (although many were visible at low tide) and then destroy them. The UDTs also went ashore at night to check the condition of the beach, sometimes taking sand samples (which, after analysis, would show what types of vehicles could safely traverse the beach).

Being able to stay underwater for long periods gave these intruders an enormous advantage. With the primitive radars available during World War II, it was possible for small boats or SUBMARINES to get close to heavily defended areas. Naval minefields could be crossed by rubber boats before the divers made their final approach underwater. So the UDTs played an important role in the amphibious war. Realizing, of course, that the Germans and Japanese would take the presence of UDTs as portending an American landing, the US

Navy began using them as part of DECEPTION plans. Special UDTs ("Beach Jumpers") were deliberately sent to explore beaches that no one had any intention of hitting, so that the enemy would believe a landing was imminent. On several occasions the UDTs were particularly successful in diverting enemy attention and resources from a genuine objective.

It was the Italian Navy that first made extensive use of underwater commandos. Transported off an enemy port by submarine or small craft, the divers would swim inside, place MINES on ships' bottoms, and then make their getaway. This technique was particularly successful at Gibraltar, for the Italians were able to turn a merchant ship, interned at a Spanish dock across the Bay of Algeciras, and a nearby villa into secret underwater assault team bases. Divers would enter the water through a secret airlock cut into the ship's bottom, swim across to the British side of the bay, and plant mines on the bottoms of various ships. By timing the mines so that they went off when the ships were far out at sea, the Italians were able to confuse the British as to the causes of various sinkings. The secret base was never detected, and closed down only when Italy joined the Allies.

The US Navy did not get into the UDT business until quite late. Its UDT force was largely the creation of LtCdr Draper L. Kaufman. The first teams were organized in early 1943. They were first used in action in Sicily that July. But it was TA-RAWA that convinced the navy of the need for UDT. No UDTs served at Tarawa, but it was clear that had they been used to conduct pre-invasion reconnaissance, the Marines would have had a much easier time getting ashore.

UDTs were organized in platoons of three officers and 15 men, with four platoons plus a headquarters platoon (four officers and 20 men) forming a company totaling 96 officers and enlisted men.

The other development that made use of scuba gear was the so-called "human torpedo." These came in two varieties, but both were essentially miniature submarines. One type might best be called an "underwater motorcycle," able to carry two men astride. The Italian Navy developed these shortly before the war, as a vehicle for its UDT teams. Called *Maielli* ("Pigs"), they were used with considerable success to damage British warships in heavily defended ports, the most notable being when two battleships were sunk at their moorings in Alexandria harbor. These devices were so effective that the ROYAL NAVY began its own experiments with "human torpedoes," giving them the more dignified name "Chariots." These were used with some success to sink several ships in Axis-controlled ports in the Mediterranean later in the war. The Japanese also developed a manned torpedo, in the literal sense, a one-man suicide submarine called the "Kaiten Weapon." Over 300 of these were sent to sea to take on Allied shipping. However, they were very inefficient and not particularly useful on the high seas, so that only one Allied ship was sunk. On the other hand, some hundreds of kaiten were available to attack the invasion fleet if the United States had undertaken Operation Olympic, the invasion of Japan. Supporting them would have been thousands of suicide swimmers, men equipped with a simple breathing apparatus who were supposed to walk along the sea floor and hit the bottom of landing craft with bomb-tipped poles. The direct descendant of these World War II scuba warriors is the US Navy SEAL force, and similar commando units in many nations. The adventure continues.

See also TORPEDOES.

Ref: Dwyer, *Seaborne Deception*; Hashimoto, *Sunk*.

Uganda Class, British Light Cruisers

The three Ugandas, sometimes referred to as the "Second Group" of the "Colony Class," were a rather successful attempt by the ROYAL NAVY to improve the stability of the FIJI CLASS light cruisers by reducing the number of 6-inch guns from 12 to nine to save weight. They were actually all laid down in 1939, as part of the original order. Launched in 1941–42, their completion was delayed due to the pressures of war. As a result, the stability problems of the original eight Fijis having become evident, they were redesigned and completed in 1943. All accompanied the Royal Navy's carrier task force in the Pacific during 1945. *Uganda* (1939–1941–1943) and *Newfoundland* (1939–1941–1943) accompanied the British Pacific Fleet in 1945, the former manned by a Canadian crew. *Uganda* was scrapped in 1961, *Newfoundland* and *Ceylon* (1939–1942–1943) were sold to Peru in 1959, and later scrapped 1979–80.

The Swiftsure Class, built 1941–45, was quite similar, being a few hundred tons heavier and a foot wider, to improve stability still further. HMS *Swiftsure* (1941–1943–1944) served with the British Pacific Fleet in 1945. She was scrapped in 1962.

Ujeland, Carolines

One of many atolls in the CAROLINES with a roomy anchorage, but otherwise unprovided with port facilities. The war passed it by.

Ulithi, Carolines

A large atoll, providing an enormous protected anchorage for ships and some land for support facilities and air bases, Ulithi had been wholly neglected by the Japanese, who had owned it for over 25 years. It had, however, come to the notice of US Navy planners as a potential advanced base for even more years than that. Ulithi became the major forward fleet base for the final US advance against Japan.

Underage Soldiers, Sailors, and Marines

It is estimated that several hundred boys under the age of 17 managed to enlist during World War II using false documents. The youngest combatant in the armed forces during World War II (and probably the youngest since the Spanish-American War, if not the Civil War) was Calvin Graham (1930–1992) of Fort Worth, Texas. Early in 1942 12–year-old Graham forged his mother's name to enlistment papers, and joined the navy. He served in the battleship SOUTH DAKOTA during the GUADALCANAL Campaign, in which he was wounded and decorated. His correct age having meanwhile been established to the satisfaction of the ship's skipper, Capt. T. L. Gatch, when *South Dakota* returned to the United States for repairs, Graham was given a one-way pass to his original recruiting station, which didn't know what to do with him. Meanwhile, Gatch having been transferred from the ship, when Graham failed to return, he was classed as a deserter, arrested, and jailed. Released after he finally managed to convince the navy that he was only 13, Graham was promptly stripped of his decorations and campaign ribbons, given a dishonorable discharge, and denied medical benefits because he had enlisted under false premises. Graham, who later reenlisted for a time in the navy after attaining the proper age, was eventually the beneficiary of special legislation in May 1978, which restored pay, decorations, and benefits lost upon his original discharge. By a curious twist of fate, Graham's division officer while aboard *South Dakota* was Sargent Shriver, who was later President John F. Kennedy's brother-in-law, while another of his shipmates was a future English teacher of one of the authors of this work, serving as a steersman.

The shabby treatment accorded Graham by the navy stands in contrast to that accorded Jimmy Baker (1931–). At 12 Baker enlisted in the Marine Corps. He served eight months, fortunately not in combat, before being discovered, and was promptly issued an honorable discharge. Another Marine, PFC Jacklyn H. Lucas (1928–) had en-listed when just 16, and was only six days over 17 when he won the MEDAL OF HONOR on IWO JIMA.

The actual number of underaged American boys who served in the war will never be known, as many of them were never detected. Nor can the number killed in action be determined.

Unicorn, British Light Aircraft Carrier

Although they built her as an aircraft maintenance and depot ship, intended to support fleet carriers by servicing and supplying aircraft, the British soon found that *Unicorn* (1939–1941–1943) was eminently suitable as a light, if slow, carrier. Lacking the extensive protection preferred by British carrier designers, her aircraft capacity was equal to that of the ILLUSTRIOUS CLASS fleet carriers. She began her wartime service during the Salerno landings in September 1943, later served as a convoy escort in the Atlantic, and then went to the Pacific in early 1945, where she supported the OKINAWA landings and operations against the Japanese Home Islands. Scrapped in 1959.

Uniforms, Sailors

Anyone who has read the book or seen the film *Mister Roberts* will recall that one of the captain's hobbyhorses was that all men had to wear their shirts at all times, even when working in the ship's stifling hold. This was not a figment of the author's imagination. One of the numerous petty naval regulations during the Pacific War was the mandatory wearing of shirts, with sleeves rolled down at all times. US sailors were also prohibited from wearing short pants, unlike their Commonwealth comrades. As a result, while Australian and New Zealand sailors generally sported terrific tans, being practically naked while on duty and most of the rest of the time as well, American bluejackets tended to be rather pale. This may seem to have been a manifestation of militaristic authoritarian bureaucraticism, but it was actually a very intelligent and reasonable measure.

Quite early in the war some prescient US Navy medical personnel noted that there were significant differences in the severity of burns suffered by men who had been wearing shirts and those who had not, despite the fact that they had come through the same infernos. A little experimentation soon determined that the navy's standard blue cotton denim work shirts and jeans actually offered considerable protection from burns, especially "flash" burns from onboard explosions. If flames touched a man's bare skin, it quickly began to burn, but if they licked at his shirt, that burned first, and the additional few seconds were often enough to save a man's life, not to mention a good deal of his skin. Also, the shirt offered some protection against short but intense bursts of high, searing heat. So the orders went out and American sailors sweated through the rest of the war. Hotter and paler than their Commonwealth counterparts, they also tended to get burned less often.

By the way, the flash protection works only with cotton. Polyester burns hotter and faster, and in the process adheres to human flesh, causing extremely serious burns. But then, during World War II the navy issued only cotton uniforms.

The one common exception to these dress regulations was on board destroyers. The "tin can sailors" tended to dress any way they pleased, at least when not in immediate danger of engaging the enemy (at which point the long pants and long-sleeve shirts went on). Their workaday "uniforms" consisted of regulation dungarees cut down to shorts, homemade sandals, and sundry improvised headgear. Earrings and pigtails were often quite popular, as were beards. Since senior officers rarely visited destroyers, the bohemian lifestyle was maintained until the ships returned to port, at which point a certain amount of dress discipline was restored. For a time a similar regime prevailed under Captain T. L. Gatch on the battleship SOUTH DAKOTA. Gatch, a wonderfully eccentric fellow (he used to read the lesson at divine services every Sunday), was allowed to get away with this because his "wild men" proved the best shots in the fleet, even if they happened to be virtually—and sometimes

literally—naked at times. But after he was promoted upstairs a less understanding skipper came aboard and the men had to tidy up.

See also UNDERAGE SOLDIERS, SAILORS, AND MARINES.

United States Army

Although the main event for the US Army was the war against Germany, nearly a quarter of the army's total divisional strength (21 of 89) ended up in the Pacific. Army units served in all parts of the Pacific Theater, some even getting into action in Burma and the NETHERLANDS EAST INDIES. The army conducted 17 division-sized assault landings, plus many others on a smaller scale (the Eighth Army alone conducted 58 amphibious landings), so that the army actually "hit the beach" more often than the Marine Corps.

Initially, army units were not well prepared for the unique kind of fighting they encountered in the Pacific. The army had been focused on affairs in Europe for a long time, and unit organization, doctrine, equipment, and training were not always well suited to the terrain most typical in the Pacific (jungle and swamp), nor to Japanese tactics. In addition, several of the first units to go into action were from the NATIONAL GUARD, and these sometimes experienced leadership, manpower, and training problems, some of them caused by the character of the Guard itself, but many by the Regulars' lack of confidence in the Guardsmen. The army's attitude toward infantry also created difficulties, as it was assumed that the infantry had the least need for quality manpower.

In time, many of these problems were ironed out (albeit that the manpower procurement and replacement problem was never properly resolved), and army units generally did well. Special training programs were set up in the Pacific, to get new troops in shape for the unique kind of fighting encountered in the tropics. Although the Pacific is generally regarded as a maritime theater, an awful lot of ground fighting went on. Aside from China, which tied up more Japanese troops than all the other areas of the theater combined, there was considerable ground combat in Burma and on many of the islands, from the Philippines in 1941–42 to OKINAWA in 1945.

Ref: Perret, *There's a War to Be Won; United States Army in World War II.*

United States Army, Divisions

Some prewar estimates by military planners placed the maximum possible mobilization effort of the United States at 334 divisions. In September 1941 less optimistic army planners projected that the nation would be able to mobilize 215 divisions, exclusive of the Marine Corps. As late as October 1943 they were estimating as many as 105. In fact, the maximum number of divisions in the army was 90, a figure attained in January 1944, which dropped to 89 when the Second Cavalry Division was disbanded a few months later. Even after including the six Marine divisions, in relative terms this was a very low number. With nearly 140 million people by the end of the war, the US Army and Marines managed to create 95 divisions at peak strength, while Australia, with 7.2 million people (5% of the United States), for a time maintained 10 divisions (10.4% of the US division total).

There were several reasons why the number of divisions raised by the United States was relatively low. Unlike most countries, the United States maintained not only a very large army (c. eight million men), but also a large air force (c. three million), and very large sea services (c. three million—navy, Coast Guard, and Marines taken together). In addition, the US Army put a lot of manpower into non-divisional formations. There were, for example, about 50 independent infantry regiments, 20 separate tank groups, 16 cavalry reconnaissance groups, and two separate cavalry regiments, not to mention numerous independent battalions of all arms. Altogether, in mid-1944 there were nearly 1,300 non-divisional combat battalions of infantry, armor, cavalry, and artillery, which, if organized into proper divisions, would have almost doubled the number available. In fact,

about 45% of US combat forces were in non-divisional formations, a figure that greatly exceeded that of other armies (the Soviets maintained about 20% of their combat strength in independent units, and the Germans only about 10%) but was more or less matched by the Marine Corps. Another factor in reducing the number of American divisions available, was the insistence by the army that all divisions be maintained at full strength. In most other armies, particularly those of the totalitarian states (Germany, Russia, and Japan), divisions fought until they had exhausted their manpower, whereupon they were disbanded or rebuilt. US divisions received a continuous flow of "replacements," which kept them at relatively full strength even in the most serious circumstances.

In any case, the 89 divisions the US Army did field gave a good account of themselves. The following descriptions cover those that served in the Pacific. Note that the divisional CASUALTIES can be better appreciated if you keep in mind that most of them were incurred by a division's nine infantry battalions, each of which contained only about 500 to 600 actual infantrymen (or other specialists always at the front). Divide the casualties by ten to get a rough idea of how many losses the infantry in each of these infantry battalions took. Infantry divisions took over two-thirds of all US casualties in World War II. Many troops were wounded more than once. In the course of the war, some battalions had to replace nearly all their infantry at least once because of incapacitating wounds and deaths.

First Cavalry Division. Active as a mounted outfit in the Regular Army since 1921, the division was dismounted in 1942 and reorganized as an infantry division on a special T/O&E (two brigades, each of two dismounted cavalry regiments, totaling 12 infantry battalions, plus four battalions of 105mm howitzers, a medium tank battalion, a reconnaissance troop, an engineer battalion, and sundry service and support units). It was the "lightest" infantry division in the army, with only about 11,000 men. Reaching Australia in July of 1943, the division fought in NEW GUINEA, the BIS-

MARCKS, and the Philippines, before going to Japan on occupation duty, where it remained after the war. Casualties totaled 4,055, including 970 (23.9%) combat fatalities. Two men from the division won the MEDAL OF HONOR.

Sixth Infantry Division. Activated in the Regular Army in October 1939, the division arrived in HAWAII in July 1943. From January 1944 it saw action in New Guinea and the Philippines, and afterward served on occupation duty in Korea, where it was inactivated in 1949. Casualties were 2,370, including 514 (21.7%) dead. Two men earned the Medal of Honor.

Seventh Infantry Division. Activated in July 1940 from Regular Army personnel, to whom were added a regiment of National Guardsmen from California. The division undertook the first opposed US Army amphibious landing of the Pacific War when it took Attu from the Japanese, May 11–29, 1943. Subsequently served in the Marshall Islands, the Philippines, and OKINAWA, ending the war on occupation duty in Japan and Korea, where it remained. Combat casualties were 9,212, of whom 2,334 (25.3%) were killed in action or mortally wounded. It had the highest losses of any army division in the Pacific, but more than 20 divisions in the ETO had higher losses. Three men won the Medal of Honor.

11th Airborne Division. The only one of five US airborne divisions to serve in the Pacific, the division was activated in February 1943 from volunteers. It shipped out for the South Pacific in May 1944, and served in New Guinea and the Philippines, where it earned the unique distinction of being the only airborne division to undertake an amphibious assault, landing at Nasugubu, Luzon, the Philippines, on 31 January 1945. Although individual battalions and regiments made a number of combat jumps, it never made a division-sized jump. It incurred 2,431 casualties, of whom 614 (25.3%) were killed or died of wounds. The division remained on active duty for many years after the war. Two men won the Medal of Honor.

12th Infantry Division. A postwar redesignation of the old "Philippine Division" (See PHILIPPINE SCOUTS). Two other Scout divisions were planned postwar, to have been designated the 14th and 16th Infantry Divisions.

23rd Infantry Division. A postwar redesignation of the "Americal Division" (see page 629).

24th Infantry Division. A Regular Army unit organized as the garrison of Hawaii in 1921, the division was known as the Hawaiian Division until "triangularized" and redesignated as the 24th Infantry Division in the summer of 1941, surplus personnel going to form the 25th Infantry Division. The division lost some personnel in the Japanese attack on PEARL HARBOR. It remained on garrison duty in Hawaii until transferred to Australia, arriving in September 1943. The division saw action in New Guinea, the Caroline Islands, and the Philippines, before going to Japan on occupation duty, where it remained after the war. Casualties totaled 7,012, including 1,689 (24.1%) deaths by combat. Three men won the Medal of Honor.

25th Infantry Division. Activated in Hawaii in July 1940, from elements of the old Regular Army Hawaiian Division (the balance becoming the 24th Infantry Division), to which a NATIONAL GUARD regiment from the state of Washington was added. Headquartered at Schofield Barracks, the division incurred some casualties during the Japanese attack on Pearl Harbor. It served as part of the garrison of Hawaii until December 1942, when it went to GUADALCANAL, subsequently seeing action in the Northern SOLOMONS and the Philippines, suffering 5,432 casualties, 1,497 (27.6%) of them battle deaths. The division remained in Japan on occupation duty after the war. Six men won the Medal of Honor.

27th Infantry Division. National Guardsmen from New York, federalized in October 1940, this division was the first to ship out for the Pacific Theater, arriving in Hawaii from the West Coast in March 1942, while still based on a "square" T/O&E. It was the last in the army to retain a "square" T/O&E, not being triangularized until September 1942. When the division invaded MAKIN ISLAND in the GILBERTS in late 1943, some Marine officers suggested that its performance was not optimal. The division subsequently took part in the capture of SAIPAN in June 1944, and fought on Okinawa the following spring. On Saipan the division became the focus of the "War of the SMITHS," when MG Holland "Howling Mad" SMITH (SMC), in overall command of the landing force, relieved division commander MG Ralph Smith. The division suffered 6,533 battle casualties, of whom 1,844 (28.2%) were deaths from combat. The division was inactivated at the end of 1945. Three men won the Medal of Honor.

31st Infantry Division. A National Guard unit (Alabama, Florida, Louisiana, and Mississippi) federalized in November 1940, the division saw action in New Guinea and the Philippines, incurring 1,733 casualties, of whom 414 (23.9%) were killed or mortally wounded, before being inactivated at the end of 1945.

32nd Infantry Division. A National Guard division (Michigan and Wisconsin), the 32nd arrived in Australia in May 1942, and served in New Guinea, the Philippines, and Japan, incurring 7,268 casualties, of whom 1,985 (27.3%) were combat deaths. Inactivated in Japan at the end of 1945.

The 32nd Division, called into federal service in October 1940, was the first army division to enter combat in the Pacific, after the surrender in the Philippines, during the BUNA-GONA CAMPAIGN in New Guinea in late 1942. The division's performance was denigrated by many senior personnel, but considering the state of its training, the failure of American supply service, the unwillingness of higher headquarters (i.e., Douglas MACARTHUR) to understand the character of the terrain or the nature of Japanese resistance, and the excessive optimism about American martial skills, it appears that the division performed about as well as any could have in the circumstances. The division went on to be one of the best fighting divisions in the Pacific. Japanese LG Tomoyuki YAMASHITA, "The Tiger of Malaya," probably Japan's best field commander, who commanded the Japanese defense of Luzon in 1945, rated it as the best American division in that campaign. This outfit took a beating. Eleven of its men won the Medal of Honor.

33rd Infantry Division. National Guardsmen from Illinois, the division was federalized in March 1941. It reached Hawaii in July 1943 and went on to the South Pacific in May 1944, seeing action in New Guinea and the Philippines. It suffered 2,426 casualties, including 497 (20.5%) deaths. Inactivated in Japan in February 1946. Three men earned the Medal of Honor.

37th Infantry Division. National Guardsmen from Ohio, federalized in October 1940. Arrived in FIJI, then considered a possible Japanese objective, in June 1942, thereafter seeing combat in the Northern Solomons and the Philippines. The division suffered 5,960 casualties, of whom 1,344 (22.6%) were battle deaths. Inactivated at the end of 1945. Seven men were awarded the Medal of Honor.

38th Infantry Division. A National Guard organization (Indiana, Kentucky, and West Virginia) federalized in January 1941, the division saw action in New Guinea and the Philippines, suffering 3,464 battle casualties, including 784 (22.6%) deaths, before being released from federal service in November 1945. One man won the Medal of Honor.

40th Infantry Division. Composed of California National Guardsmen called into federal service in March 1941, the 40th Infantry Division deployed to Hawaii in September 1942. In April 1944 it went into action on NEW BRITAIN, in the Bismarcks, fighting thereafter in the Philippines. Combat casualties were 3,052, of whom 748 (24.7%) were killed in action or mortally wounded. Inactivated in April of 1946. One man won the Medal of Honor.

41st Infantry Division. A National Guard unit (Washington, Montana, Oregon, and Idaho), federalized in September 1940. In the summer of 1941 Gen. MARSHALL considered this division sufficiently well trained for overseas deployment and offered it to Gen. MacArthur, in the Philippines. The latter rejected the offer, although it would have more than doubled the number of active troops under his command. This saved the division from defeat and captivity, and probably would not have slowed the Japanese down that much, as US troops defending the Philippines were brought down more by supply problems than anything else. The division deployed to Australia in April 1942. It served in New Guinea and the Philippines, and helped occupy Japan, suffering 4,260 casualties, 960 (22.5%) of them combat fatalities. Inactivated in Japan at the end of 1945. Two men won the Medal of Honor.

43rd Infantry Division. National Guardsmen from New England (Maine, Vermont, Rhode Island, and Connecticut), the division was federalized in February 1941. It reached NEW ZEALAND in October 1942, and fought thereafter in New Guinea, the Solomons, where it was granted the army's first "Assault Arrowhead" (awarded to units making amphibious or airborne assault), for its landing on Rendova, 30 June 1943, and the Philippines. Casualties were 6,026, of whom 1,406 (23.3%) were combat-related fatalities. Inactivated in October 1945. Two men won the Medal of Honor.

77th Infantry Division. Activated from New York State reservists and draftees in March 1942, the division was shipped to newly liberated GUAM in July 1944, and thereafter saw combat in the Philippines and Okinawa. Casualties were 7,461, of whom 1,850 (24.8%) were battle-related deaths. The division performed occupation duties in Japan until it was inactivated in March 1946. Six men won the Medal of Honor.

81st Infantry Division. Activated in June 1942 from draftees, the division reached the central Pacific in September 1944, fighting in the PALAU ISLANDS and the Philippines. It incurred 2,314 casualties, of whom 515 (22.3%) were killed in action or died of wounds.

86th Infantry Division. Activated from draftees in December 1942, the Battle of the Bulge caused the army to cancel plans to ship the division to the Pacific virtually as it was ready to board the transports in SAN FRANCISCO. It arrived in Europe in March 1945, the last US infantry division to reach the ETO, and saw action during the final drive into Germany. Upon the surrender of Germany, the division was shipped back to the United States, given 30 days leave, and then sent to the Pacific. The troops learned of Japan's surrender aboard their transports. The division landed in the Philippines in early September 1945, and it remained there until inactivated at the end of 1945. Casualties in Europe had been 785, of whom 161 (20.5%) had been killed in action or mortally wounded. With the 97th Infantry Division, this was the only US division to serve in both theaters of war.

93rd Infantry Division. Activated in May 1942, mostly from black draftees but including the Regular Army's 25th Infantry Regiment. The division arrived in the South Pacific in February 1944 and saw some action in New Guinea and the Northern Solomons, mostly in "mopping up" operations. At no time did the division serve as a unit. Combat casualties were 135 officers and men, including 17 (12.6%) killed in action (12) or died of wounds (5), the smallest loss of any US division committed to combat. The division was inactivated in February 1946.

96th Infantry Division. Activated from draftees in August 1942, the division reached the Pacific in mid–1944 and saw action in the Philippines and Okinawa. Casualties totaled 8,812, including 2,036 (23.1%) deaths. It was inactivated in February 1946. Five men won the Medal of Honor.

97th Infantry Division. Activated from draftees in February 1943, in December 1944 the Battle of the Bulge caused the army to cancel plans to ship the division to the Pacific. Sent to Europe in February 1945, it saw action in the final offensive into

Germany. Upon the surrender of Germany, the division was shipped back to the United States, given 30 days leave, and then shipped to the Pacific, arriving in Japan for occupation duty in late September 1945, where it remained until inactivated at the end of March 1946. Casualties in Europe had been 979, of whom 217 (22.2%) had been killed in action or mortally wounded. With the 86th Infantry Division, this was the only US division to serve in both theaters of war.

98th Infantry Division.   Activated from draftees in September 1942, the division shipped to the Pacific in mid–1944 but remained on garrison duty in Hawaii thereafter, one of only three US divisions that did not see combat in the war (the others were the Second Cavalry Division, disbanded in North Africa in 1944, and the 13th Airborne Division, in Europe). In August of 1945 the division went to Japan on occupation duty, and was inactivated there in February 1946.

Americal Division.   Activated in NEW CALEDONIA during May 1942 from elements of Task Force 6814, a conglomeration of mostly miscellaneous National Guard units (primarily from Illinois, Massachusetts, and North Dakota), under MG Alexander PATCH. Taking its name from "America" and "New Caledonia," it was the only American division not activated on US soil. Saw action on Guadalcanal, in the Northern Solomons, and the Philippines, suffering 4,050 casualties, of whom 1,157 (28.7%) were killed in action or died of wounds. Inactivated in late 1945, the division was subsequently given the numerical designation "23rd Infantry Division" and assigned to the Regular Army. One man won the Medal of Honor.

CAM (Combined Army-Marine) Division.   A provisional division-sized task force created in January 1943 to facilitate the pursuit of the Japanese in the final weeks of the Guadalcanal Campaign. It incorporated the army's 147th Infantry Regiment (Separate) and 182nd Infantry (Americal Division), plus the Sixth Marine Regiment (Second Marine Division), with the artillery of the Amer-

ical Division, under the control of the headquarters of the Second Marine Division. The CAM Division was disbanded in February 1943.

Hawaiian Division.   See 24th Infantry Division, page 626.

Philippine Division.   See PHILIPPINE SCOUTS, separate entry.

Ref: Stanton, *Order of Battle*.

United States Army, Army Air Forces, Numbered Air Forces

A numbered air force was the administrative equivalent of a numbered army, usually operating directly under an army group or theater commander. The USAAF organized 16 numbered air forces in the war (the First through 15th, plus the 20th), 10 of which had some connection to the Pacific Theater.

Air Force	Operational Area
Second	Washington, Oregon, Northern California
Fourth	Central and Southern California
Fifth	Southwest Pacific, under MacArthur
Sixth	Panama Canal Zone
Seventh	Central Pacific, under Nimitz
Tenth	India and Burma
Eleventh	Alaska and the Aleutians
Thirteenth	Southeast Pacific, under MacArthur
Fourteenth	China
Twentieth	Marianas and Japan (B–29s)

Ref: Craven and Cate, eds., *The Army Air Forces in World War II*.

United States Army, Engineer Special Brigades

Engineer Special Brigades, initially designated Engineer Amphibious Brigades, were very large formations (initially about 7,350 men, later reduced to some 7,100) designed to facilitate landings on enemy-held beaches. Each brigade was capable of supporting the landing of one or more divisions. Their particular utility was in a shore-to-shore landing, where troops could be loaded into landing craft on a beach, escorted a short distance, and then landed on a hostile beach. The US Army raised seven Engineer Special Brigades during World War II, including a provisional one for the Normandy Invasion. One of the brigades served in both the ETO and the Pacific, three others operated only in the Pacific, while the other two regular ones served in the ETO and were en route to the Pacific when Japan surrendered.

An Engineer Special Brigade consisted of three Engineer Boat and Shore Regiments, which had two battalions, one a "boat" battalion, operating landing craft to get troops and equipment ashore, and the other a "shore" battalion, which organized the beach. In addition, each brigade had an artillery battery (for self-defense), two ordnance companies (to repair weapons), a maintenance battalion (to repair other equipment), a quartermaster battalion (to organize and move supplies), and an Amphtrac company (to facilitate the movement of supplies from transports offshore or from one point on the beach to another). During an operation it was not at all unusual for an ESB to be reinforced with as many as four or five independent Boat and Shore regiments or individual battalions. Each brigade had 540 landing craft, 32 command boats, and 72 miscellaneous craft, such as patrol boats, fire support boats, salvage boats, floating workshops, and so forth. Those serving in the Pacific were:

The First Engineer Special Brigade. Activated in Massachusetts in January 1942, the brigade served in North Africa, December 1942–July 1943, supported the landings in Sicily and at Salerno, June-September 1943, and then those at Utah Beach, Normandy, from D-day through September 1944. The brigade was then transferred to the Pacific via the United States from December 1944 to February 1945 (the troops being given 30 days leave during the movement), and supported the landings on OKINAWA in the spring of 1945. Preparing to support the invasion of Japan when the war ended, the brigade served for a time as part of the occupation force in Japan before being inacti-

vated there in February 1946. No other ESB saw such extensive service.

Second Engineer Special Brigade. Formed in June 1942 in Massachusetts, the brigade arrived in Australia in April 1943, and supported the landings at Oro Bay, New Guinea, October 1943, and on Leyte, October 1944. Preparing for the invasion of Japan when the war ended, it facilitated the occupation of Japan, and was inactivated in California in late 1946.

Third Engineer Special Brigade. Organized in Massachusetts in August 1942, the brigade deployed to the South Pacific in June 1944, and supported landings in New Guinea, July 1944, BIAK, September 1944, and in the southern Philippines in early 1945, where it ended the war. It was inactivated in Oregon in December 1945.

Fourth Engineer Special Brigade. Activated in February 1943 in Massachusetts, the brigade deployed to New Guinea in May 1944, and supported the landings on Morotai, in September 1944, and at Lingayen Gulf, Luzon, in January 1945. Preparing to support the invasion of Japan when the war ended, it took part in the occupation of Japan, where it was inactivated in April 1946.

See also AMPHIBIOUS OPERATIONS, LOGISTICAL ARRANGEMENTS; UNITED STATES ARMY, FORCES IN TRANSIT, 12 AUGUST 1945.

Ref: Stanton, *Order of Battle.*

United States Army, Forces in Transit, August 12, 1945

At the time Japan surrendered the United States was in the midst of redeploying large forces from the European Theater to the Pacific, for use in the second phase of the projected invasion of Japan. Two divisions that had served in the ETO, the 86th and 97th Infantry, were already in the Pacific at the time of the surrender, although neither had seen active service.

Army Headquarters. First Army headquarters, staff, and service elements were reorganizing to

Some of the happiest people at the news of the surrender of Japan were US troops in Europe and America scheduled to ship to the Pacific for the invasion of Japan. In Paris, soldiers at the "Rainbow Corner Red Cross Club" celebrate.

take part in Operation Coronet. Fifth and Ninth Army headquarters, staff, and service elements were preparing for redeployment to China, where they were to command mostly Chinese forces against the Japanese.

Armored Divisions. The 13th and 20th, which been only lightly engaged in the ETO, were training in California.

Engineer Special Brigades. The Fifth and Sixth, which had taken part in several invasions, including Normandy, were training in Florida when Japan surrendered.

Infantry Divisions. The Second, Fourth, Fifth, Eighth, 44th, 87th, 95th, and 104th Infantry Divisions were all training in the United States.

Mountain Division. The 10th Mountain Division was on trains bound from Virginia to Colorado, where it was to train for operations on Honshu.

Ref: Stanton, *Order of Battle*.

United States Army, Other Notable Units

In addition to divisions, the US Army raised a large number of non-divisional and specialized units for various duties. Some of the more notable were:

First Provisional Tank Group. Organized in the Philippines in November 1941; supported US and Philippine troops in the defense of Luzon, during the retreat to BATAAN, and in the defense of Bataan, until the surrender in April 1942. The group comprised two tank battalions and an ordnance company. The 192nd Light Tank Battalion consisted of four companies, and had been activated in the United States in December 1940 from NATIONAL GUARD light tank companies from Wisconsin, Illinois, Ohio, and Kentucky. The 194th Light Tank Battalion, of three companies, was activated in the United States in March 1941, from National Guard tank companies from Minnesota, Missouri, and California (a fourth company was created, but did not ship out with the battalion). Both battalions reached the Philippines in late September 1941. They had a total of 108 Stuart M-3 TANKS. The group repeatedly engaged the Japanese during the retreat to Bataan, and was virtually destroyed in combat.

First Special Reconnaissance Battalion. Organized as the 5217th Recon Battalion in October 1943, from Filipino personnel in Australia. Initially based in NEW GUINEA, and later on Leyte, the battalion sent special reconnaissance details into the Philippines by air and submarine. It was disbanded in Manila in August 1945.

First Special Service Force. Organized in 1942, from American and Canadian personnel, the 1st SSF was essentially a stripped-down division of three specialized regiments, with very small contingents of artillery, combat support, and service forces, totaling about 7,000 men. It was trained to fight in deep winter, in jungles, mountains, and swamps, in amphibious and airborne operations, and as COMMANDOS. Committed to action in the unopposed KISKA landings in mid–1943, later that year the First SFF was shipped to Europe, where it took part in the Anzio operation, turning in an heroic performance securing the right flank during the protracted struggle for the beachhead. After the Anzio breakout, however, both US and Canadian brass concluded that the First SFF consumed too much quality manpower, which might otherwise serve to boost the performance of regular formations, and it was broken up. The battle honors of the First SSF were later assigned to the 474th Infantry Regiment.

Sixth Ranger Battalion. Organized at HOLLANDIA, New Guinea, from the 98th Field Artillery Battalion in September 1944, the battalion saw action in New Guinea and in the liberation of Leyte and Luzon. It was inactivated in late 1945.

24th Infantry Regiment. A non-divisional regiment, the regiment was one of the army's four regiments of "Colored" regulars organized after the Civil War. Forming the core of the 24th RCT, the regiment was sent to the Pacific in early 1944. It performed mopping up and occupation duties on BOUGAINVILLE in March-May 1944, on SAIPAN and TINIAN from December 1944 to March 1945, and on OKINAWA in July-August 1945, seeing some action against Japanese holdouts. The regiment returned to the United States from Okinawa in 1946.

112th Cavalry Regiment. A Texas National Guard unit, the regiment was federalized in November 1940 and deployed without its HORSES to NEW CALEDONIA in August 1942. The regiment performed garrison duties as horse CAVALRY, using livestock procured in Australia, which the men had to train themselves. Dismounted and converted to infantry in Australia May–June 1943. With the 148th Field Artillery Battalion attached, the 112th Cavalry RCT occupied Woodlark Island and fought elsewhere in the northern SOLOMONS and on New Guinea, before being attached to the First Cavalry Division, with which it remained through the Philippine Campaign. Because the regiment consisted of dismounted cavalry, it had only some 1,500 men, about half that of an infantry regiment, a matter that commanders sometimes forgot, leading them to give it tasks for which it was too weak. It was inactivated in Japan in January 1946. Two of its men won the MEDAL OF HONOR.

124th Cavalry Regiment. Part of the Texas National Guard, the regiment was federalized in November 1940 and deployed to India as an infantry unit in mid–1942. Attached to Task Force Mars in mid–1944, it was flown into Myitkyina, Burma, in

October of that year and served with TF Mars until inactivated in southern China in July 1945. At times during the campaign elements served mounted. One of its men won the Medal of Honor.

147th Infantry Regiment. A unit of the Ohio National Guard, the regiment was activated in October 1940 as part of the 37th Infantry Division, becoming a separate infantry regiment when the division was "triangularized"; deployed to FIJI in May 1942. It entered combat for the first time on Guadalcanal in November 1942, literally shoulder-to-shoulder with the Marines (the situation being so critical that the Guardsmen were sent into the Marine ranks), and fought to the end of the campaign. Thereafter the regiment served entirely as a garrison or mopping-up force on various islands, including IWO JIMA and Okinawa. It was inactivated in Washington State in December 1945.

158th Infantry Regiment. A unit of the Arizona National Guard, the regiment was federalized along with the rest of the 45th Infantry Division in the "First Increment," September 1940. When the division was triangularized, the regiment became a non-divisional one. There were an unusual number of Native Americans in the regiment, and Company F was reputedly composed mostly of Pueblo Indians. Shipped to the PANAMA CANAL for jungle training in December 1941. Shipped to the South Pacific in early 1943, the regiment formed the core of the 158th RCT (with the 147th Field Artillery Battalion), occupied the TROBRIAND ISLANDS and fought on NEW BRITAIN in 1943, and on New Guinea from May through July 1944, before going on to fight in the Philippines, where it ended the war. Nicknamed the "Bushmasters," it was inactivated in Japan in January 1946.

475th Infantry Regiment. See 5307th Composite Unit, Provisional, below.

503rd Parachute Infantry Regiment. A separate regiment, the 503rd Infantry was organized in February 1942 from two independent parachute battalions raised earlier. It arrived in Australia in November 1942 and was shipped to New Guinea in August 1943, where it served for over a year, and later fought in the Philippines. It made three operational air drops, at Nadzab, New Guinea, in September 1943, and at Noemfoor, a small island north of New Guinea, in July 1944—both of which were unopposed—and on CORREGIDOR, in Manila Bay, the Philippines, in February 1945, against stout resistance. This was the only US combat jump of the Pacific War. The regiment was inactivated in California at the end of 1945. Two men won the Medal of Honor.

5332nd Brigade. See Task Force Mars, below.

5307th Composite Unit, Provisional. Better known as Galahad Force or "MERRILL'S MARAUDERS," the 5307th CUP was organized in India in October 1943. Configured for special operations, it had three long-range penetration battalions, which operated more or less on the model of Orde WINGATE's CHINDITS. Merrill's Marauders—a name bestowed by the press, and not used by the troops—served in Burma from February 1944. In May 1944 the unit captured the airport at Myitkyina, in central Burma, which paved the way for the eventual capture of the town itself by the Marauders and STILWELL's Chinese forces in early August 1944. By then the troops had been in continuous action for six months, under the most trying conditions. Pushed beyond their physical and spiritual limits, the men were having serious morale and discipline problems, particularly after their commander, BG Frank D. Merrill (1903–1955), was evacuated for medical reasons (he had suffered several heart attacks during the grueling campaign, and was ill with malaria as well). Shortly afterward the 5307th CUP was withdrawn to Ledo, India, where it was disbanded, and the troops reorganized as the 475th Infantry. The 475th joined Task Force Mars in October 1944, and served with it until inactivated in China in July 1945. In the early 1960s the battle honors of the 475th were granted to the newly raised 75th Infantry, the Special Forces.

Alamo Scouts. Ten long-range reconnaissance teams organized from Sixth Army personnel beginning in December 1943. From then until the end of the war, the Alamo Scouts conducted over 60 special, deep-penetration intelligence, reconnaissance, and combat missions in New Guinea and the Philippines.

Kachin Rangers. Organized in 1944 from among Kachin tribesmen in northern Burma by the OSS, with the help of Dr. Gordon Seagraves, a US medical missionary in northern Burma, who was serving on Stilwell's staff. The Kachin Rangers specialized in long-range reconnaissance and raiding operations, and were particularly useful during the liberation of northern and central Burma.

Mars, Task Force. Organized in Burma in July 1944, and officially known as the 5332nd Brigade, TF Mars initially comprised the partially mounted 124th Cavalry plus two US field artillery battalions and the Chinese First Separate Regiment, to which was added the 475th Infantry in October 1944. TF Mars took part in operations to clear the BURMA ROAD in January–February 1945. In April 1945 it was transferred by air to south China, where it was inactivated in June 1945.

Merrill's Marauders. See 5307th Composite Unit, Provisional, above.

See also PHILIPPINE ARMY; PHILIPPINE SCOUTS.
Ref: Stanton, *Order of Battle.*

United States Strategic Bombing Survey

Interservice squabbling over the effectiveness of strategic bombing led to the creation of the Strategic Bombing Survey. The USSBS was staffed by military personnel and civilian specialists (such as economist John Galbraith), assisted, after the war ended, by former enemy officers as technical advisers. They were charged with investigating the consequences of strategic bombing. The USSBS began to work during the war, and several staffers were actually killed by enemy action. Preliminary studies revealed that this job would mean investi-

gating just about every aspect of the war. With the help of former Japanese and German military personnel the USSBS produced an enormous series of reports on everything from battle analyses to the production of soft coal in Japan. These were published in over 300 volumes.

Not surprisingly, the USSBS confirmed that air power had played a vital role in the war. However, this role was not necessarily the one that prewar air enthusiasts had predicted. For example, the USSBS concluded that one of the most important consequences of the strategic bombing of Germany was not so much that it had a negative impact on German war PRODUCTION as that it forced the Luftwaffe to concentrate resources for the defense of Germany, thereby rendering it less able to support ground forces, particularly on the Eastern Front. Likewise, it concluded that bombing from high altitude was unprofitable.

Unfortunately, the USSBS is like Holy Writ—in that what it says can be subject to misquotation and interpretation. The air power mavens argued—and continue to argue—that the USSBS vindicated their prewar position that strategic bombing could win the war.

Unryu Class, Japanese Aircraft Carriers

Essentially a modified version of HIJMS HIRYU, *Unryu* and her half-sisters were built quickly (22 to 24 months from keel to completion). The initial order, placed in 1941, was for two ships, *Unryu* and an identical sister. However, the sistership was canceled before being laid down, since Japanese naval architects had convinced the brass that a modification to the original design would be superior. Eight ships were ordered to this slightly different design, of which only five were laid down. In practice, all the ships differed considerably in design detail. Only two actually were commissioned. Good ships, they saw little service, the Imperial Navy being unable to provide AIR GROUPS for them.

Unryu (1942–1943–1944) actually went to sea with a small air group, and was sunk by two TOR-

PEDOES from the US submarine *Reldfin* (SS-272) in the South China Sea off SHANGHAI on December 19, 1944.

Amagi (1942–1943–1944) never saw active service. She capsized in sheltered waters near KURE on July 24, 1945 after being pounded by US naval aircraft, and was later scraped in situ.

Katsuragi (1942–1944–1944) never saw active service. Damaged in US carrier air strikes against Kure in July 1945, after the surrender of Japan she was found sufficiently reparable to be used as a transport, and served to repatriate Japanese troops before being scrapped in 1947.

Three other units were begun—*Kasagi* (1943–1944–   ), *Aso* (1943–1944–   ), and *Ikoma* (1943–1944–   )—but were never completed and were all scrapped in 1947.

Ushijima, Mitsuru (1887–1945)

Mitsuru Ushijima graduated from the military academy in 1908. A regimental officer during World War I, in 1918–19 he was on the staff of the Siberian Expedition. His later career included staff, line, and school duty, and in 1939 he was given command of a division, which he led in Burma with some distinction in early 1942. There followed a tour as commandant of the military academy, from which post he was sent in mid-1943 to command the Thirty-second Army on OKINAWA, an island considered part of Japan proper and populated by Japanese. With nearly two years to organize the defenses, Ushijima put up a tenacious and bloody resistance to the American invasion in April 1945. About 100,000 Japanese troops were killed or captured (10,755, an unusually high number) in this battle. Many Okinawan civilians also died, with estimates ranging from 40,000 to 110,000. The battle saw the highest American losses for any single operation in the Pacific, between the ferocity of the resistance and the dedication of the KAMIKAZE. It was these high losses that convinced American commanders and troops that resistance on the Japanese Home Islands would be equally fanatic and costly. After leading the stubborn defense, Ushijima committed suicide on 21 June when he saw that further resistance was futile.

V

Van Ghent and Van Galen Classes, Netherlands Destroyers

These two closely related classes formed the Royal Netherlands Navy's destroyer force in the East Indies at the outbreak of the Pacific War. The four Van Ghents were built 1924–28 in Dutch shipyards, to a British design with British technical assistance, while the three surviving Van Galens (one having been sunk by the Luftwaffe in 1940) were built 1927–31 on the basis of experience gained from the construction and operation of their predecessors. The principal differences between the two classes were subtle. Although identical in displacement, dimensions, and appearance, the Van Galens carried slightly different antiaircraft armament (one 75mm AA gun and two 40mm guns, rather than two 75s). Both classes were obsolescent by 1941. All seven ships were lost in the last two weeks of February 1942. *Van Ghent* was wrecked on the 15th in Banka Strait, *Piet Hein* was sunk by the destroyers *Oshio* and *Asashio* in the Bandung Strait on the 19th, *Kortenaer* by destroyer TORPEDOES in the Battle of the JAVA SEA on the 27th, and *Evertsen*, set afire in a clash with Japanese cruisers and destroyers on the 28th, had to be abandoned the next day. Of the Van Galens, *Van Ness* was sunk by Japanese air attack in Banka Strait on the 17th, *Banckert* was scuttled in a dry dock at Soerabaya on 2 March, while under repair for bomb damage received earlier, and *Witte de With* had to be scuttled after being bombed at Soerabaya on 2 March. *Banckert* was partially salvaged by the Japanese, as *Patrol Boat Number 106*. Never fully op-

erational, she returned to Dutch control in 1945 and was sunk as a target in 1949.

Vancouver, British Columbia, Canada

A major port, Vancouver had extensive facilities to service and maintain ships, but was of limited value as a naval base.

Vandegrift, Alexander A. (1887–1973)

The first US Marine to rise to four-star rank while on active duty, Alexander A. Vandegrift enlisted in the Marine Corps in 1908 rather than complete college. Commissioned the following year, he had an active career before World War I, serving in Cuba, Nicaragua, PANAMA, MEXICO, and Haiti by 1915, where, with some minor interruptions, he remained until 1923. After teaching or attending several advanced courses, he was in China for a time, and then on staff assignments at Marine headquarters. In the mid- and late 1930s he was again in China, later becoming secretary to the commandant of the Corps. When the Pacific War broke out he was assistant commander of the First Marine Division, assuming command in April of 1942. On August 7, 1942, Vandegrift undertook the first American amphibious operation of the war, landing his division on GUADALCANAL, beginning an arduous campaign that ended six months later, by which time his division had been relieved. Awarded a MEDAL OF HONOR, promoted to lieutenant general, and given command of I Marine Amphibious Corps in the spring of 1943, Vandegrift undertook the landings on BOUGAINVILLE in later 1943. He was shortly afterward named commandant of the Marine Corps. Promoted to full general in March of 1945, Vandegrift retired in 1949.

Vanguard, British Battleship

Britain's last battleship, Vanguard (1941–1944–1946) was not ready for sea until after the war. Although equal in size and protection to contemporary foreign battlewagons, Vanguard's main battery dated from World War I, her turrets and guns being those removed from the "large light cruisers" Glorious and Courageous when they were converted to aircraft carriers during World War I. The decision to complete her was a tremendous waste of resources, given Britain's strained situation during the war.

Vella Gulf, Battle of

Naval battle fought on the night of 6–7 August 1943, in the SOLOMONS, between the islands of VELLA LAVELLA and KOLOMBANGARA. During the battle for the Solomons, the Japanese kept their troops on the islands supplied via fast transports (converted from old destroyers) escorted by destroyers running down the "Slot" (the northwest-southeast channel between the major islands). At first, the United States responded with cruiser and destroyer task forces. But many American naval commanders felt that the cruisers got in the way and that pure destroyer forces would be more effective. In the summer of 1943, it was decided to try the "destroyers only" approach. After all, the Japanese had been successful with this method. The first test came in Vella Gulf 6–7 August, when a force of six American destroyers caught four Japanese destroyers and sank three of them without loss to themselves. The American commander, Commander Rodger Moosbugger, was a genuine ace as a destroyer commander, and he managed to surprise the Japanese as well as deploy his own ships handily. This battle threw the TOKYO EXPRESS off track for a while, if only because the Japanese were starting to run out of destroyers.

Vella Lavella, Battle of

Naval battle in the SOLOMONS off Vella Lavella Island on the night of October, 6–7, 1943. The battle was brought about by a Japanese attempt to evacuate the survivors of their garrison on Vella Lavella. After three weeks of fighting against American and NEW ZEALAND troops, there were only about 600 Japanese troops left. A force of nine destroyers and a dozen smaller ships were sent to get these soldiers away from certain destruction at the hands of the Allied troops. Six American destroyers were sent in when the Japanese evacuation effort was detected. In the ensuing battle, one Japanese and two American destroyers were sunk, and other American ships were damaged. The Japanese evacuated their troops.

This was the last Japanese naval success in the Solomons and was the last battle fought for the central Solomons. In three months of naval battles, the United States had lost six warships and the Japanese 17. The Americans could afford these losses, the Japanese could not.

Venereal Disease

Venereal disease has long been recognized as a major cause of non-battle-related military non-effectiveness in wartime. Through World War II the problem was of significant, but declining, importance. During World War I the VD rate for men

VD CASES PER 1,000 MEN PER YEAR		
War	Rate	Ratio
World War I	87	100.0%
World War II	49	56.3
Korea	146	171.3
Vietnam	325	373.6

Ratio compares the World World II, Korea, and Vietnam rates as a percent of that for World War I

in the US Army was quite high, about 87 cases per 1,000 men per year, higher than that prevailing in the French Army. During World War II the VD rate in the US Army decreased markedly, to about 56% of that of the earlier war, due largely to an intensive educational program to alert the troops to the dangers of venereal infections, plus the introduction of penicillin, and, not incidentally, to the fact that many troops campaigned in areas where there were few opportunities to contract VD (e.g., the ALEUTIANS, NEW GUINEA, most atolls, etc.). Despite this, VD cases still accounted for over a third of all infectious and parasitical disease cases among US Army personnel in World War II. It is interesting to note that in American military operations since World War II (with the exception of the 1990–91 Gulf War) the VD non-effectiveness rate has actually increased. In fact, while the World War I rate was considered disastrous, that for the Korean War was much worse, and that for Vietnam worse still. The rate for the Gulf War was a fraction of the World War I incidence. There were strong religious and social prohibitions against extramarital sex in Saudi Arabia. There was VD among US troops in the Gulf, but the exact data was kept confidential for diplomatic reasons.

Veterans, Pacific War

An enormous number of people served in uniform during World War II, by one estimate over 100 million. What follows is a random sample of some of those who served in the Pacific who were, or later became, famous for reasons other than being warriors.

Eddie Albert (1908–), the actor, served as an officer aboard an amphibious transport in the navy, and commanded a casualty evacuation landing craft at TARAWA.

Idi Amin (1925–), repressive dictator of Uganda for many years during the 1960s and 1970s, served as a sergeant in the King's African Rifles during the Burma Campaign of 1944–45, during which he was actually disciplined for mistreating enemy prisoners, a rare event considering the general brutality of the campaign.

Howard Baker (1925–), later a senator and White House chief of staff under RONALD REAGAN, was a PT-BOAT skipper in the South Pacific.

Hank Bauer (1922–), major league baseball player, served as a platoon sergeant in the Marines, winning two Bronze Stars, two Purple Hearts, and 11 battle stars.

Arthur A. Benline (1903–1995), a distinguished architect and public official in New York, served in the SEABEES during the war, rising to captain in the navy and battalion commander. Wounded at OKINAWA, he was awarded the Bronze Star.

Richard Boone (1917–1981), the actor ("Have Gun, Will Travel," etc.), was a tail gunner on TBF AVENGERS in the Pacific.

Vincent L. Broderick (1921–1995), for several years police commissioner of New York, and later a highly regarded federal judge, served in the army's Amphibious Engineers in New Guinea and the Philippines during the war, and on occupation duty after it, rising to captain.

Art Buchwald (1925–), the humorist and columnist, joined the Marines while UNDERAGE, at 16, and served with an aviation unit in the CAROLINE ISLANDS.

Johnny Carson (1925–), the noted television personality, served in the US Navy, managing to survive a TORPEDO that severely damaged his ship off Okinawa in 1945.

John Connally (1917–1994), Navy secretary and Texas governor who was riding with President Kennedy when he was assassinated, served in the navy during the war, initially as a member of EISENHOWER's staff in Europe, and later aboard carriers in the Pacific, earning a Bronze Star and Legion of Merit.

Jackie Coogan (1914–), the actor, was an army glider pilot in Burma, and landed the first glider at Myitkyina during the March 1944 invasion of Burma.

Tony Curtis (1925–), the actor, was a submariner from 1943 to the end of the war.

Jack Dempsey (1895–1983), former heavyweight champion of the world, served in the Coast Guard, taking part in the Okinawa invasion.

Joseph B. DiMaggio (1914–), Yankee baseball star, served as a USAAF physical training instructor in HAWAII for a time during the war, despite persistent ill-health.

Kirk Douglas (1916–), the actor, served in the navy in the Pacific, until discharged due to injuries incurred in the service.

Melvyn Douglas (1901–1981), already a well-known actor and over-age to boot, joined the army in 1942 and eventually served in the CBI.

Paul H. Douglas (1892–1976), although a politician of some note, and a pacifist, joined the Marines at age 50, made it through boot camp, and served in the First Marine Division on Peleliu and Okinawa, being so severely wounded that he spent 18 months in hospitals before being discharged as a lieutenant colonel.

Eddy Duchin (1909–1951), the band leader, served in the navy, taking part in the IWO JIMA and Okinawa invasions as a antisubmarine warfare officer.

Buddy Ebsen (1908–), the actor, served as a junior officer in the Coast Guard, in the ALEUTIANS.

Henry Fonda (1905–1982), already a noted actor, enlisted in the navy in mid-1942, was later commissioned, and served as an intelligence officer in the central Pacific.

George MacDonald Fraser (1925–), the novelist (*Flashman*) and critic, served as an enlisted man in the British Army during the Burma Campaign.

John Glenn (1921–), the astronaut and senator, was a Marine pilot during the war, flying F4U CORSAIRS in the MARSHALL ISLANDS. Between World War II and Korea he had a total of 149 combat missions, accumulating four DFCs and 18 Air Medals.

John Gorton (1911–), for several years prime minister of Australia, served as a fighter pilot in the RAAF from 1940 to 1944, when he was discharged as a result of injuries received in combat.

Alex Haley (1921–1992), author of *Roots,* served as a messman in the Coast Guard in the southwest Pacific.

Mark Hatfield (1922–), for many years a prominent Republican senator from Oregon, several times suggested for the presidency in the 1960s and 1970s, served in the navy in the Pacific and was present during the Okinawa Campaign.

Charlton Heston (1924–), the actor, served in the AAF 1942–45, mostly as a radioman on medium bombers in the Aleutians.

Gil Hodges (1924–1972), the famous baseball player, served as a sergeant in the Marines, in antiaircraft units in the central Pacific.

Edmund Hillary (1919–), who with Tenzing Norgay became the first man to climb Mt. Everest in 1953, was wounded serving in the RNZAF in the South Pacific.

Jim Lee Howell (1915–1995), coach of the football Giants for their 1954–60 winning streak, served as a company commander in the Marine Corps for three years in the South Pacific.

William Kunstler (1919–1995), the famous attorney and champion of leftist causes, served as an army officer during the war, for a time in the Pacific, where he received a Bronze Star, and was later at the Battle of the Bulge, rising to major.

Norman Mailer (1923–), American novelist, served as an enlisted man in the army's intelligence service on Luzon in 1945.

William Manchester (1922–), noted historian and author, served as a Marine rifleman on Okinawa.

Lee Marvin (1924–1987), the actor, joined the Marines at 17 and served in the Fourth Marine Division in the Marshalls and MARIANAS, until severely wounded on SAIPAN, requiring 13 months to recuperate. He is buried in Arlington National Cemetery, next to Joe Louis, who served in the Army.

Ed McMahon (1923–), the television and sweepstakes personality, served as a Marine fighter pilot for most of the war.

Raymond Meek (1897–1995), noted pioneer eye surgeon, served in the US Navy Medical Corps during the war, including a tour aboard the hospital ship *Bountiful,* off Okinawa.

Joseph Papp (1921–1991), noted theatrical producer, staged his first play while a sailor aboard the escort carrier USS *Solomons Sea* in the Pacific.

Philip, H. R. H. the Duke of Edinburgh (1921–), a career officer in the ROYAL NAVY, served on a destroyer in the Pacific from late 1944 to the end of the war, and was present aboard the USS *Missouri* when the Japanese surrendered.

Jason Robards Jr. (1922–), the distinguished actor, served in the navy during the war, from PEARL HARBOR, where as a radioman he received the famous message, "Air Raid Pearl Harbor, This is no drill," to V-J Day, during which he survived the loss of two cruisers and won a Navy Cross.

George Lincoln Rockwell (1918–1967), founder and leader of the American Nazi Party (1958–67), served as a fighter pilot in the navy.

Barney Ross (1909–1967), world middleweight boxing champion in the 1930s, served as a Marine, winning a DSC and Silver Star on GUADALCANAL.

Sabu (1924–1963), star of the *The Elephant Boy* and *Jungle Book* (his full name was Sabu Dastagir), served in the Army Air Forces in the Pacific, flying 42 missions as a B-29 tail gunner, and winning the Distinguished Flying Cross and four Air Medals, in a squadron that earned the Presidential Unit Citation.

Rod Serling (1925–1975), author and television producer ("The Twilight Zone"), served in the 11th Airborne Division, in the Philippines, where he was wounded during the Battle for Manila.

Sargent Shriver (1915–) the first head of the Peace Corps, and a brother-in-law to President John F. Kennedy, was a gunnery officer aboard the battleship SOUTH DAKOTA in the South Pacific during the great naval battles of late 1942.

George Stafford (1915–1995), chairman of the Interstate Commerce Commission from 1970 to 1977, was an infantryman in the southwest Pacific, rising to captain and earning a Bronze Star and Purple Heart.

Harold Stassen (1907–), perennial Republican presidential candidate in the 1950s and 1960s, was governor of Wisconsin when the war broke out, whereupon he resigned the state house to serve as a staff officer with the navy in the Pacific for the entire war. After the emperor's surrender proclamation, Stassen parachuted into Japan, virtually the first US officer to land there. He was also present at the founding meeting of the United Nations.

Leon Uris (1924–1980), the novelist, served in the Marine Corps on Guadalcanal and Tarawa, but was later discharged due to malaria.

Gore Vidal (1925–), author and critic, served as a warrant officer on an army transport in the Aleutians.

Mike Wallace (1918–), the television journalist, served as a navy communications officer in the Pacific.

James Whitmore (1921–), the actor, enlisted in the Marines in 1942 and took part in several amphibious landings, winning a commission.

Ted Williams (1918–), the baseball star, joined the Marines in 1942, took flight training (George BUSH was in the same class), and became a fighter pilot, logging over a thousand hours in the air before the end of the war.

Veterans, Warships, in the War

A number of the warships in service during the Pacific War were already seasoned veterans.

USS *Baltimore* (C-3), a cruiser so old she had fought at Manila Bay in 1898, was present as a storage hulk during the Japanese attack on Pearl Harbor. By 1944 the ship was in such bad shape that the navy towed her out to sea and scuttled her.

USS *Rochester* (CA-2), which as the armored cruiser *New York* had fought at the Battle of Santiago in 1898, was a station ship (a floating office and workship) at OLONGAPO in the Philippines when the war began. She was scuttled on Christmas Eve of 1941, to prevent her from falling into Japanese hands.

USS *IX-25*, the erstwhile Spanish unprotected cruiser *Reina Mercedes*, built for the Royal Spanish Navy in the 1880s and captured in 1898, served throughout the war as a receiving ship at the Naval Academy. She was scrapped in 1957.

USS *Oregon* (BB-3), the battlewagon famous for her voyage around South America during the Spanish-American War, had entered service in the mid-1890s. Preserved as a relic since the 1920s, she was to have gone to the scrap yard in a recycling drive when the navy converted her into an ammunition barge. Towed to the MARIANAS, she supplied the newer battlewagons. *Oregon* remained there after the war. On one occasion she was wrested from her anchorage by a typhoon and not found until several days later—some 500 miles away. Towed back to GUAM, in 1956 she was scrapped in Japan.

USS *Kearsarge* (BB-5), the only American battleship not named for a state, had been completed under Theodore Roosevelt. Demilitarized in the 1920s, she was converted to a "crane ship," equipped with an extremely heavy lift crane. The most powerful crane afloat at the time, it could lift a 16-inch gun. She served in various navy yards throughout the war, helping to build and repair warships of all types. She was disposed of in the 1950s.

USS *Arkansas* (BB-31), commissioned in 1912, served more or less continuously for over 33 years, until decommissioned after the war and later expended as a target at Bikini. She had the longest active life of any major modern American warship until the 1970s, when she was surpassed by the carrier *Midway*.

The old Japanese battleship *Asashi*, which had fought at the Battle of Tsushima Strait in May 1905, was serving as a submarine tender when she was sunk by USS *Salmon* (SS-182) in Vietnamese waters on May 25, 1942. Her sistership *Shikishima* served as an accommodation ship at Sasebo until scrapped after the war. Another old battlewagon that had been at Tsushima, *Fuji*, served as an accommodation ship at Yokosuka. The flagship of the Japanese fleet at Tsushima, *Mikasa*, was preserved as an historical relic. Damaged by US aircraft, she survived the war and was restored in the 1960s, primarily by donations from Americans.

The old armored cruisers *Asama*, *Tokiwa*, *Idzumo*, *Iwate*, *Yakumo*, *Adzuma*, and *Kasuga*, which had all served in the Russo-Japanese War (1904–05), were re-rated as "coast defense ships" in the early 1920s. In this guise, they continued in service, some seeing action supporting Japanese operations in China in the 1930s and during World War II. *Iwate* and *Idsumo* were sunk in KURE Harbor by carrier aircraft on 28 July 1945, *Tokiwa* was sunk by carrier aircraft on 9 August 1945, and the others were scrapped 1945–47. The old light cruiser *Yahagi*, completed in 1912, served as a training ship at the Eta Jima Naval Academy during the war.

The oldest warship to have a role in the war was undoubtedly the wooden ship of the line HMS *Victory*, Nelson's flagship at Trafalgar, which, although preserved as an historic relic in Portsmouth Harbor, was used for staff conferences by senior

ROYAL NAVY officers from time to time, apparently in the hope that Nelson's ghost might provide some inspiration.

Veterans, Warships, of the War

Many of the ships that served in the war continued to do so for many years afterward. From 1945 until well into the 1970s, the huge US World War II fleet provided the bulk of the secondhand warships for thrifty fleets around the world. Some of these ships will still be in service into the 21st century.

Several units of the BROOKLYN CLASS were transferred to various Latin American navies in the 1950s, including *Brooklyn* herself, which became the Chilean *O'Higgins*. The only one to see any action was *Phoenix*, which, as the Argentine *General Belgrano*, was TORPEDOED by HMS *Conqueror* on 2 May 1982, during the Argentine-British War, thereby gaining the dubious distinction of being the first, and so far only, ship ever to have been sunk in action by a nuclear submarine.

The Indian Navy acquired HMS *Achilles*, a veteran of the Royal New Zealand Navy, which had fought in the Battle of the River Plate and in several of the most heated actions in the SOLOMONS. As INS *Delhi* she saw some action during the brief Indian-Portuguese War of 1961. She was scrapped in 1978.

The Circle Line, which conducts boat rides around New York's Manhattan Island, does so in former LCIs, which performed yeoman service at numerous amphibious landings throughout the Pacific. *Circle Line X* was originally *LCI-758*, which made five combat landings in the Philippines, shot down two Japanese aircraft, and was under fire many more times. *LCI-758*'s adventures did not end on V-J Day. In September 1945, the ship survived a typhoon off OKINAWA, the same typhoon that was featured so prominently in the book and movie *The Caine Mutiny*. In October 1945, *LCI-758* was sent to China to take part in US operations on the Yangtze River. During two years of war service, *LCI-758* received three battle stars. After 1945, *LCI-758* was retired from military serv-

ice and purchased as war surplus by Circle Lines. Rebuilt and reengined, *LCI-758* became *Circle Line X*. In a fitting retirement for a warship, the former *LCI-758* now spends its time running in circles around Manhattan Island, still within the sound of gunfire and aircraft (and at least one blimp) falling from the skies.

USS *Prairie*, the last of the prewar US Navy ships that fought in World War II, was decommissioned on March 27, 1993. A destroyer tender, providing maintenance and support for destroyers while far from base, *Prairie* was built in Camden, New Jersey, and entered service in late 1939. She was for a time the flagship for the Atlantic Fleet support forces, but during the war the ship was assigned to the Pacific, and stayed there afterward. Over 10,000 sailors served on *Prairie* including, since 1982, many women. Traditionally, the oldest serving ship flies the "Don't Tread on Me" pennant. Upon *Prairie*'s retirement this was transferred to USS *Orion*, another tender that entered service during the war, in 1944.

The last major combatant ship in continuous commission in the US Navy to have seen action in World War II was USS *Lexington* (CV-16), an ESSEX CLASS carrier that served as a training ship into the late 1980s, before becoming a war memorial at Corpus Christi, Texas.

The last World War II ship to serve in the Japanese Maritime Self-Defense Force was the TACHIBANA CLASS DE *Nashii*. Sunk by air attack at KURE on 28 July 1945, in 1955 she was raised, refurbished, and put into service as one of the first ships in the new Japanese Maritime Self-Defense Force. The revived *Nashi* was taken out of service in the 1960s, after more than half a century of service above, and below, the waves.

Vian, Philip (1894–1968)

Sir Philip Vian entered the ROYAL NAVY as an officer cadet shortly before World War I. During the war he served in destroyers, mostly in the Mediterranean. By World War II he was skipper of HMS *Cossack*, which he took into neutral Norwegian waters on the night of 16 February 1940, to liberate British PRISONERS OF WAR held in the German ship *Altmarck*. During the hunt for the German *Bismarck* he commanded a destroyer flotilla, and may have put several TORPEDOES into the battle-wagon on the night of 26–27 May 1940. He commanded a cruiser squadron in the Mediterranean in 1941–42, several times running supplies into Malta, for which he was knighted. Although a non-flyer, he was given command of a carrier task force in 1943 and helped cover the Salerno landings. The following year he commanded the Eastern Task Force during the Normandy invasion. In late 1944 he was given tactical command of the British Pacific Fleet, under Adm Bruce FRASER, leading it until V-J Day. After the war he held several high military and civil posts until his retirement.

Victoria, Australia

A major city, with a major port, possessed of important facilities to service and repair ships, though by no means a major naval base.

Vietnam, Resistance to the Japanese

There was already GUERRILLA activity in Vietnam before World War II. In this case it was against the French, who had controlled Vietnam (and neighboring Cambodia and Laos) since late in the 19th century. The Japanese relationship with Vietnam proved to be a curious one. As a French colony, Vietnam had to answer to the pro-German Vichy French government established after the Germans defeated France in June of 1940. This technically made Vietnam an "ally" of Japan (because Japan and Germany were tied by treaties). Britain and America protested when the French, under Japanese pressure, shut down Allied supply routes to China through Vietnam in late 1940. In July 1941, the local Vichy officials gave into Japanese demands for access to Vietnamese ports and airfields and the right to station an unlimited number of troops in Vietnam. The local resistance then shifted its operations to oppose the Japanese, and

because of this received Allied aid. The Vietnamese resistance, dominated by communists, did not get help in keeping the French out after the war and this led to prolonged fighting that eventually dragged in the United States in the 1960s. The guerrillas were quite bitter about their treatment by the Allies. Immediately after the war, British troops moved in and rearmed Japanese soldiers to fight the communist guerrillas for few months.

Vildebeeste, British Torpedo Bomber

The Vildebeeste was an early 1930s British torpedo bomber that was quickly superseded by the SWORD-FISH. Only 200 Vildebeestes were built, and only 30 aircraft—owned by New Zealand—were in the Pacific during the first year of the war. The aircraft had about the same speed, range, and bombload as the Swordfish.

Vladivostok, Soviet Union

The largest and most important Russian military and naval base in the Pacific, with extensive industrial facilities, ample repair and maintenance establishments, and a number of air bases in support. It was one of the ports through which American Lend-Lease aid reached Russia from West Coast ports and carried in Soviet-flag vessels, which were themselves often supplied by the United States.

Volcano Islands

The Volcano Islands are a chain of actively volcanic islands, islets, and reefs lying about 650 miles south of Tokyo, and about the same distance north of SAIPAN. Total land area is about 11 square miles, most of them barren. The principal ones, Chichi Jima and IWO JIMA, were important Japanese outposts in the final defenses of the Home Islands.

Interestingly, the few inhabitants were of mixed American, Hawaiian, and Japanese descent. In 1830 two Americans, one Italian, and about 25 Hawaiians set up a trading post on Chichi Jima, then uninhabited. Other Americans later settled there, mostly whalers jumping ship and survivors of ships, including several African Americans. After his visit to Japan in 1853, Commodore Peary urged the United States to annex the islands, but to no avail. The Japanese occupied them in 1861, and moved some settlers in about 25 years later. By the 1940s the population was rather mixed. During 1944 the civilian inhabitants were evacuated.

W

Wadke, New Guinea

Aside from a roomy harbor, and its location on the north side of New Guinea between HOLLANDIA and BIAK, Wadke had little to recommend it in 1941. Later, the Japanese turned it into a base, which was expanded considerably when taken by the Americans.

Wainwright, Jonathan M., IV (1883–1953)

Jonathan M. Wainwright came from a family with a long military tradition: His father and grandfather both died while on active service, the latter in action during the Civil War. He graduated from West Point in 1906 and was commissioned in the CAVALRY. Aside from serving on a number of famous old posts in the West and Southwest, he saw action in the Philippines against the Moros, some staff time, and some school time. On the eve of World War I he was an instructor at the Plattsburg Officer's Training Camp, where he remained until early 1918, when he went to France. In France, Wainwright served as a division chief of staff during the St. Mihiel and Meuse-Argonne Offensives, and later on occupation duty in Germany, not returning to the United States until 1920. His peacetime service was a mixture of troop duty, staff time, and school time. In late 1940 he was promoted to major general and sent to command the Philippine Division, a Regular Army outfit composed primarily of Philippine troops (see PHILIPPINE SCOUTS). Upon the Japanese invasion of the Philippines, Wainwright's command formed the backbone of the defense. Given command of a corps by MACARTHUR, he did well on BATAAN. When MacArthur was ordered to Australia in February of 1942, Wainwright assumed command of US forces in the Philippines. Following the surrender of Bataan he withdrew to CORREGIDOR, which in turn surrendered on May 6, 1942. Wainwright spent the rest of the war in various Japanese prisoner of war camps, ending up in a Manchurian camp reserved for senior Allied officers. Convinced that he would be court-martialed upon his release, Wainwright was surprised to learn that he had been awarded a MEDAL OF HONOR and promoted to general for the tenacity with which he had held on in the Philippines. He retired in 1947.

Wake Island, Battle for

Wake Island, some 2,000 miles west of PEARL HARBOR, is actually a small atoll (three square miles of land on three islets) with limited port facilities and no particular value, except as a base for reconnaissance aircraft, being some 2,300 miles west by southwest from Pearl Harbor. The island has no ground water and is covered by scrub, which often grows to 10 feet despite infrequent rain. In 1941 it was a stopover on the Pan American Clipper route to the Far East, and a small naval air station was under construction.

In December 1941 the Wake garrison consisted of elements of the First Marine Defense Battalion (449 men under Maj. James P. Devereaux, later a senator), who manned various coast defense installations and supported a dozen old-model F4F WILDCAT fighters. There were also some sailors

(68) and soldiers (5), plus 70 employees of Pan American and 1,146 construction workers.

The Japanese occupation of Wake Island was a subsidiary aspect of the Pearl Harbor operation. The island first came under attack by Japanese surface ships and aircraft operating out of the MANDATES on 8 December. These severely punished the garrison, destroying many of the handful of fighters available. Three days later a detachment of the Special Naval Landing Force (the SNLF or "Imperial Marines") essayed a landing, only to be beaten off with considerable loss, the defenders sinking two destroyers in the process, *Kisaragi* by air attack and *Hayate* by coast defense gunnery, an almost unique occurrence in the war, while inflicting serious damage to several other ships. At least 500 Japanese personnel were killed, but only one American.

Carriers SORYU and HIRYU, returning from the Pearl Harbor Operation, were detached from the Pearl Harbor strike force and called in to work over the island's defenses by air attacks. These carriers lingered in the vicinity of Wake for most of three days, December 21–23, on the last of which the Japanese attempted another landing, which was successful in putting about 1,200 SNLF troops ashore. Shortly afterward the garrison surrendered. US losses in the two attacks were 49 Marines, three sailors, and about 70 civilians killed. Japanese losses were at least 820 killed. Historically, that was the end of the struggle for Wake.

But there might have been more.

As the US Navy began picking up the pieces from the Pearl Harbor disaster, Admiral Husband KIMMEL, still commanding the Pacific Fleet, decided to strike back at the Japanese, and ordered the three carriers in the Pacific to the support of Wake. One, *Saratoga*, under RAdm Frank Jack FLETCHER, was in position to intercept the Japanese carriers before the island fell. At dawn on 23 December *Saratoga* was about 425 miles northeast of the island, and about the same distance due east of the Japanese carriers. Moreover, at that moment the LEXINGTON and her escorts were less than 750 miles southeast of Wake and the *Enterprise* group

a little more than a thousand miles east of the island. In the event, the attempted relief of Wake was called off by VAdm W. S. Pye, who had just replaced Kimmel in an acting capacity pending the arrival of Chester W. NIMITZ. Had Pye not called off the operation, it is perfectly possible that the first carrier battle of the war would have taken place off Wake. And the outcome of that engagement would certainly have dramatically altered the entire course of the Pacific War.

Had the US carriers succeeded in sinking both Japanese carriers at Wake, the sudden loss of a third of their first-line carriers might have seriously injured Japanese morale, provoking a major offensive against HAWAII early in 1942, rather than the MIDWAY operation in June of that year. The resulting battle for Hawaii might have been fought on even better terms for the United States than was historically the case, with perhaps five first-line US carriers against four Japanese.

But it is also possible that the Japanese could have won the battle of Wake. One US carrier air group was still equipped with Brewster F2A BUFFALOS, an older aircraft even more outclassed by the Zeros than were the F4F Wildcats on the other two flattops. A Japanese victory at Wake, with the attendant loss of one or maybe two carriers, would have seriously crippled the US war effort in the Pacific. Such a victory might also have brought on a much earlier Japanese offensive against the Hawaiian Islands than was actually the case, at a time when American resources would have been much slenderer than they were at Midway.

After they seized Wake, the Japanese renamed it Otori Shima, "Bird Island," and developed it as a modest base. Although the US Navy several times struck the island with air raids or surface attack, it made no serious plans to recapture Wake, a possibility that gave the Japanese some concern.

Ref: Cressman, "*A Magnificent Fight.*"

War Plans, US, Color Plans

In peacetime, armies and navies are supposed to consider possible threats and make plans accordingly. Of course such matters have to be kept secret, lest a journalistic leak lead to embarrassment or even an international incident. As a result, from quite early in the 20th century the US Armed Forces began referring to potential opponents, allies, locations, and objectives by various colors. Thus, while discussing a hypothetical operation, the brass could refer to "War Plan Indigo," knowing that it was the plan for the occupation of Iceland in the event that Denmark fell under the control of an unfriendly power. Similarly, they could discuss our options if we had to assist "Lemon" in the event that it was attacked by "Olive," or were allied with "Red" against "Black," all the while confident that outsiders would be thoroughly confused by the "cover names" for the countries involved. This was the origin of the famous "War Plan Orange," the scheme (actually a successive series of blueprints developed over nearly 40 years) for war with Japan, designated "Orange." Altogether there were more than 20 color plans. The accompanying list indicates the countries and other places represented by the various colors, so far as is known today.

The origin of the colors is unclear. In some cases there is an obvious link, such as Britain and red (and variations of red for the Commonwealth), perhaps deriving from the reddish tint traditionally used to indicate British territories on maps. Gray for the Azores probably comes from an old poem about Columbus, which includes the line "Behind him lay the gray Azores." And "Yellow" for China seems rooted in blatant racism. But others are more obscure. Orange, for example, might refer to the color of the Japanese flag, and olive might refer to one of the principal products of Spain, but what was the connection of purple to Russia or indigo to Iceland?

Although the first version of War Plan Orange was developed quite early in the century, all versions envisioned a systematic island-hopping advance across the Pacific, so that the plan remained the principal guide for the conduct of the war in the Pacific.

Color	Country
Black	Germany
Blue	USA (foreign involvement)
Brown	Netherlands East Indies; also used for local plans to cope with insurgencies in the Philippines and other US colonies
Citron	Brazil
Crimson	Canada
Emerald	Ireland
Garnet	New Zealand
Gold	France
Gray	The Azores
Green	Mexico
Indigo	Iceland
Lemon	Portugal
Olive	Spain
Orange	Japan
Purple	Russia
Red	Britain
Ruby	India
Scarlet	Australia
Silver	Italy
Tan	Cuba
Violet	China (internal problems)
White	USA (domestic disorders, e.g., race war, communist putsch, etc.)
Yellow	China (international conflict)

Beginning in 1939 the army and navy began to develop a new series of war plans, the "Rainbow" plans, based on the assumption that the United States would participate in a war against the Axis. There were five different Rainbow plans.

Rainbow 1: A US defense of the Americas north of 10 degrees south latitude, without any European allies.

Rainbow 2: The United States allied with Britain and France, with American power free to be used primarily in the Pacific.

Rainbow 3: A United States-Japan war, without European involvement.

Rainbow 4: A US defense of all of the Americas, without European allies.

Rainbow 5: The United States allied with Britain and France, in a "Germany First" situation.

In view of the changing international situation, in mid–1941 versions 2 and 3 were explicitly rejected as they no longer reflected likely possibilities. "Rainbow Five" became the basis of US STRATEGY after PEARL HARBOR. Although it incorporated the final version of War Plan Orange, its basic assumption was the "Germany first" strategy, that is, that in the event of war with both Germany and Japan, the Allies would concentrate their efforts on defeating Germany first, as the more dangerous of the two.

Ref: Miller, *War Plan Orange.*

Warships, Fuel Consumption

Warships are notorious fuel hogs. A "typical" 1944–45 US carrier task force of three fleet carriers, a light carrier, a couple of heavy cruisers, several light cruisers, and a dozen destroyers would consume nearly 50 tons of fuel oil an hour at 15 knots, or 1,200 tons a day. Even at this very economical speed, the task force would require a tanker loaded with fuel about every eight days. And at full speed, around 30 knots, consumption would more than triple. Some figures based on US and Japanese ships are of interest.

Aside from the battleships NAGATO, TENNESSEE, and YAMATO, and the escort carrier CASABLANCA all of the ships on this table could do 30 knots or better at full speed, at the cost of skyrocketing fuel consumption. At full steam an American destroyer's fuel consumption roughly quadrupled. This was the main reason destroyers always seemed to be refueling: At 30 knots they ran out of fuel in about four days.

Being short of fuel not only put a ship at an operational disadvantage, but also created safety problems, particularly in a smaller vessel, since it affected stability. At full load (c. 2,900 tons), fuel constituted about 17% of the displacement of a FLETCHER CLASS destroyer. The three destroyers lost in the typhoon of 17 December 1944 all appear to have been low on fuel, and unballasted with sea water in anticipation of refueling.

The most "fuel efficient" ship on the list is the battleship IOWA, burning only 6.5 tons of fuel an hour to move some 57,000 tons of warship, or about one ton of fuel for each 8,800 displacement

Type	Year	Displacement	Fuel	Usage	Efficiency
Battleships					
Nagato	1919	42,750	5,600	8.4	5.8
Tennessee	1919	40,345	4,700	5.8	7.0
Yamato	1940	69,990	6,300	9.5	7.3
Iowa	1942	57,540	6,250	6.5	8.9
Alaska	1943	34,250	4,619	4.5	7.6
Aircraft Carriers					
Lexington	1925	43,055	3,600	4.9	8.8
Ranger	1933	17,577	2,350	3.1	5.7
Soryu	1935	19,800	3,670	5.5	3.6
Shokaku	1939	32,100	4,100	6.2	5.2
Essex	1942	34,881	6,330	6.2	5.6
Independence	1942	14,751	2,600	3.0	4.9
Taiho	1943	37,700	5,700	8.6	4.4
Casablanca	1943	10,902	2,200	3.2	3.4
Cruisers					
Aoba	1926	10,650	1,800	3.0	3.0
Mogami	1934	10,990	2,163	3.2	3.4
Brooklyn	1936	12,200	1,800	2.7	4.5
Atlanta	1941	8,350	1,360	2.4	3.5
Agano	1941	8,535	1,400	2.1	4.1
Baltimore	1942	17,030	2,000	3.0	5.7
Destroyers					
Fubuki	1927	2,057	500	0.8	2.6
Somers	1937	2,765	400	0.8	3.5
Akitsuki	1941	3,700	1,097	1.6	2.3
Fletcher	1942	2,925	492	1.1	2.7

Ships are grouped by type (with the "Large Cruiser" *Alaska* placed among the battleships due to her size) and according to year of launching, which more or less puts together vessels of comparable age and levels of engine technology. Displacement is full load, in standard tons. Fuel is full load capacity, in tons. Usage is hourly consumption in tons at 15 knots, a quite common speed for long voyages, even by ships capable of much better. Efficiency is the number of tons of displacement (in thousands) each ton of fuel can move at 15 knots, so the higher the figure the more efficient the ship.

tons, followed by the carrier LEXINGTON, burning only 4.9 tons of oil an hour to move some 43,000 tons of warship, or little more than one ton of fuel per hour for each 8,700 tons of displacement—extraordinarily economical vessels. In general, larger ships were more fuel efficient than smaller ones, longer ones more than shorter ones (speed in a ship is partially a factor of hull length), and newer ones more than older ones. The prime exception to the last point, about age, was *Lexington*. Although she had been commissioned in 1927, she possessed unusually powerful engines (180,000 shp) and an experimental electric drive. Other factors influencing fuel consumption were type of engines (reciprocating vs. turbine), time between engine overhauls, condition of the hull (clean or foul), weather, and crew training, not to mention basic design. Note also that US ships were consistently more fuel efficient than Japanese ones, a matter of superior technology.

Warships, Small

In addition to the major warship types there were numerous classes of "small boys."

Gunboats (PGs), a catchall designation that included vessels that ranged in size from 100 to 2,000 tons, were highly specialized vessels designed to impress the various "natives" in peacetime. The smaller ones were mostly used on rivers, especially in China. Larger ones were usually oceangoing, designed to patrol distant colonial outposts.

Frigates (PFs) were essentially cut-rate destroyer escorts of about 500 to 1,000 tons; in some navies called sloops.

TORPEDO boats (TBs) were speedy vessels much smaller than destroyers (600–800 tons) and designed primarily to deliver torpedo attacks against surface vessels.

Motor torpedo boats (MTBs) were very small (50–60 tons), high-speed motor boats (35–40 knots) armed with a small number of torpedoes; called PT-BOATS in the US Navy.

Mine warfare vessels (AMs) were small ships specializing in the planting and clearing of MINES.

Corvettes and submarine chasers (PCs) were very small (300–800 tons), very uncomfortable, slow vessels, which could be produced cheaply in great numbers and sent out to escort convoys.

Mine warfare vessels aside, most of the "small boys" were of only marginal value and were at best expedients.

Although some navies continued to build torpedo boats, by World War II they had long been supplanted by destroyers. Gunboats, frigates, sloops, torpedo boats, and the like were all pressed into service as antisubmarine escort vessels when the war came, to be quickly joined by submarine chasers and corvettes, and anything else that could be adapted to the role. Motor torpedo boats had some value for coastal operations, but on balance they were probably not worth the money, resources, and manpower invested in them.

Several navies, including the Japanese and US, converted obsolescent warships for use as minor combatants, such as old destroyers to minelayers (DMs) and sweepers (DMSs), patrol boats, and the like. This was an economical use of available resources in a wartime emergency.

Warships, US, Captured

Since the War of 1812, only one US warship has ever struck its colors, the river gunboat USS *Wake* (PR-3). A sister to the equally ill-fortuned TUTUILA, *Wake* surrendered without firing a shot at SHANGHAI on 8 December 1941, being then in a hopeless situation, tied up at a dock and surrounded by Japanese troops. *Wake* saw service with the Imperial Army and was eventually turned over to the Chinese. Note that in December 1968 the US Navy electronic intelligence gathering ship *Pueblo* surrendered to North Korean warships off the coast of North Korea. *Pueblo* was not a warship, possessed minimal armament, and was not trained or intended to fight. However, some consider this a "warship surrender."

The Imperial Navy also acquired a US destroyer, albeit not by surrender. USS *Stewart* (DD-224), an old CLEMSON CLASS four-stacker, had been damaged during the fighting in the NETHER-LANDS EAST INDIES early in 1942. She was put into a dry dock at Soerabaya, in JAVA, but was still undergoing repairs when the Japanese overran the island. Although demolition charges were set, these only slightly damaged the ship, and she was captured by Japanese troops on 2 March 1942. Repaired, *Stewart* was commissioned as an escort in the Imperial Navy, and occasionally caused the radio waves to heat up when spotted by American or Allied long-range reconnaissance aircraft. After a relatively uneventful career in the emperor's service, *Stewart* was returned to American control in 1945 and expended as a target during the nuclear weapons trials at Bikini in 1946.

Wasp, US Aircraft Carrier

Wasp, CV-7 (1936–1939–1940), was designed so that the navy could use the last 15,000 tons remaining from America's carrier allocation under the terms of the naval DISARMAMENT TREATIES, which became a dead letter even before she was launched. A greatly improved RANGER, with better protection and stability, she was still too small to be considered a fully useful fleet carrier. In the Atlantic early in the war, she made two trips to bring British fighter aircraft to Malta through the Axis siege. Entering the Pacific in mid-June of 1942, she took part in the operations against GUADAL-CANAL, but was refueling during the Battle of the EASTERN SOLOMONS. On 15 September 1942, while escorting a troop convoy from ESPIRITU SANTO to Guadalcanal, she was hit by three TOR-PEDOES from the Japanese submarine *I-19*, which also torpedoed the battleship NORTH CAROLINA and a destroyer. These started fires that proved uncontrollable, probably due to design flaws, and she was sunk by torpedoes from the destroyer *Lansdowne* (DD-486).

Wavell, Archibald (1883–1950)

One of the few British officers to hold important commands throughout the war, Wavell joined the British Army in time to see service in the South African War (1898–1902). He ended World War I as a brigade commander, and rose slowly to high command between the wars. Appointed commander in chief, Middle East, shortly before World War II broke out, he oversaw operations on as many as four fronts simultaneously: East Africa, the Western Desert, Greece, and Iraq/Syria. This disparate array of responsibilities was a critical factor in explaining the general success of Rommel's spring offensive in 1941 and the failure of British counteroffensives in the desert, for which Wavell nevertheless bore the blame. Transferred as commander in chief in India in late 1941, Wavell shortly found himself Allied supreme commander of the ABDA Theater in the Far East, when the Japanese launched the Pacific War. In this capacity he oversaw a succession of Allied disasters: Malaya, SINGAPORE, the NETHERLANDS EAST INDIES, and Burma. By the time the situation had stabilized, Wavell's troops were confronting the Japanese along the Indo-Burmese frontier. Although he attempted an offensive on the Arakan front in late 1942, Wavell was convinced that the Allies had little hope of recovering Burma by a ground offensive, considering the manpower and logistic difficulties, not to mention the political ones (i.e., India was restive, Nationalist China unreliable, and the United States uncooperative). At American urging, CHURCHILL jumped Wavell up to viceroy of India, in which post he exercised no control over military operations. After the war Wavell almost immediately passed into retirement. A good officer, with considerable administrative abilities, Wavell, who had only one eye as a result of an old wound, had the bad luck to always be given hopeless tasks. A man of great intellectual power, he was the author of nearly a dozen books, including *Generals and Generalship*, which Rommel found interesting, and an anthology of poems, *Other Men's Flowers*.

Wedemeyer, Albert C. (1897–1990)

A 1918 West Point graduate, Wedemeyer saw no combat service in World War I. In the 1920s he served in troop units, on various staffs, and attended several army schools. From 1930 to 1932 he was assigned to the 15th Infantry, at Tientsin, China, where he learned the language. After various other assignments, from 1936 to 1938, Wedemeyer, a German American, attended the German Kriegsakademie as an exchange student, during the Nazi regime. He later held several school and command posts in the United States. Wedemeyer served on the War Department general staff as an expert on war plans from 1941 to 1943. An isolationist, he is thought by some scholars to have been involved in several "leaks" of preliminary war plans to the press in the period before PEARL HARBOR, and in his memoirs charged that such contingency planning "proved" the ROOSEVELT administration was "plotting" to bring the United States into the war. For a time in 1943 he served as an observer in the ETO. In August 1943, as a major general, he was appointed as deputy chief of staff of Allied forces in Southeast Asia, under Lord Mountbatten. In October 1944 he was sent to replace General STILWELL as CHIANG KAI-SHEK's chief of staff. This appointment signaled President Roosevelt's displeasure with Chiang's handling of the situation in China. Wedemeyer continued in this post until May 1946, rising to (temporary) lieutenant general in the process. He afterward held various administrative posts until retiring in 1951.

Wellington, New Zealand

The capital of New Zealand, Wellington was an important city and port, though with only limited facilities to service vessels. It served as an important supply port during the war.

Wewak, New Guinea

A good harbor, with no facilities but a good location on the north coast of NEW GUINEA, east of AITAPE.

Whampoa Military Academy

Created by Sun Yat-sen in the spring of 1924, at Whampoa, near CANTON, to train junior officers for the KUOMINTANG army. The academy's first president was CHIANG KAI-SHEK, and the faculty included a number of Soviet military advisers, as well as many Chinese officers who had formal military training at foreign military academies, including Chou En-lai, the later Chinese communist defense minister.

The academy was created on a Soviet model. It provided a six-month course for secondary school graduates. The program was based on the principles of ideological purity, rigid discipline, practical knowledge, flexibility of thought, thoroughness of training, and individual responsibility. The curriculum included not only modern Western military theory, but also some innovative Soviet notions, particularly as introduced by Leon Trotsky to the Red Army's officer training programs, and the Chinese military classics, which were edited and annotated by Chiang himself.

The academy trained officers not only for the army, but also for the air force, the navy, and the national police. All candidates took basic training together, and then passed on to specialized programs. In addition to the six-month course at Whampoa, there was a series of post-graduate courses in various specialities, which were attended by many of the graduates.

The course was as much practical as academic. The first class, in May 1924, numbered 960 young cadets in a single training regiment. They alternated among classroom, drill field, and battlefield. By November 1925 the cadet corps was serving as part of the cadre of a training corps of some 30,000 men, learning as they led troops in battle against warlord armies. The communists were ousted from the academy staff in 1926. The academy rapidly became the source of the best officers in the Chinese Army. By 1929 there were already some 5,000 graduates, of whom about 2,600 were serving in the Northern Expedition. The number of graduates rose to about 3,000 a year, where it remained through 1945.

When the capital of Republican China was established at Nanking, the academy was moved there and renamed the Central Military Academy. When the capital moved to Chungking, the academy followed.

See also CHINA, ARMIES.

Ref: Liu, *A Military History of Modern China.*

Wichita, US Heavy Cruiser

An experimental design, *Wichita* (1935–1937–1939) was essentially a heavy cruiser version of the light cruiser BROOKLYN. As ships of that class were by no means wholly successful, neither was she, being a bit top-heavy. She was however, much better protected than earlier American heavy cruisers and had an improved 8-inch turret. Experience gained from *Wichita* proved enormously valuable in the design of the BALTIMORE CLASS. She saw considerable service during the war but was rarely in heavy action. Scrapped in 1959.

Wingate, Orde C. (1903–1944)

One of the most unconventional soldiers of the 20th century, Orde Wingate entered the British Army between the wars. Assigned to the Palestine garrison during the Arab Revolt in the mid–1930s, he developed a passion for the Zionist cause, and soon went beyond his authority to train Jewish settlers for self-defense. Shortly after Italy's entry into World War II, Wingate was sent to East Africa, where he commanded Gideon Force, a GUERRILLA column that had enormous success in disrupting Italian defenses in Ethiopia in 1940–41.

Sent to the Far East shortly after the Japanese overran Burma, Wingate organized and led numerous guerrilla raids into the Japanese rear, dis-

rupting the enemy at a time when regular British Empire forces were in desperate shape. A pioneer in the use of air supply, Wingate's basic strategy was to use air supply to support raids by his specially trained troops (the CHINDITS). He would parachute troops into inaccessible areas behind Japanese lines, where they would hack out an airstrip, be joined by additional troops and supplies brought in by air, and then cut their way back toward British lines. His two most successful operations (February '43 and March '44) were very deep penetrations, literally hundreds of miles into the enemy rear. Although enormously disruptive of Japanese logistics and communications, and although they tied down considerable Japanese forces at a critical juncture, the cost of the operations in manpower was extraordinary. Despite retaining influence with CHURCHILL and other unorthodox thinkers, Wingate would probably have been replaced had he not died in an aircraft accident. As the airplane was an American one, and none of the recovered bodies could be positively identified, Wingate lies in a group grave in Arlington National Cemetery. (He is one of only two foreign soldiers buried at Arlington, the other being Sir John Dill, British representative to the Combined Chiefs of Staff, who died in Washington in 1944.) Like many other successful commanders, Wingate was an eccentric, fond of quoting the Old Testament, eating raw onions, and the like, and was certainly mentally unstable (he attempted suicide after the East African Campaign)—never by itself a disqualification for military genius.

Wirraway, Australian Trainer/Fighter

The Wirraway was an American design built under license in Australia. Originally intended as a two-seat trainer, the aircraft was also used as a fighter (with disastrous results) and as a light bomber (a few hundred pounds of bombs, at most) in the early days of the war. Some 750 were built between 1939 and 1946.

Women, American, In the Pacific War

On the eve of World War II there were very few American women in uniform, and all of them were in either the Army Nurse Corps or the Navy Nurse Corps, old institutions founded in the early years of the century. Down to only a few hundred women each by the early 1930s, these had begun recruiting again during the gradual buildup of US forces that preceded PEARL HARBOR.

When the war actually broke out the armed forces did not at first express any interest in putting women in uniform, save for nurses. However, as manpower became increasingly scarce, the idea of enrolling large numbers of women became increasingly attractive. In 1942 the enlistment of women began in earnest, under the slogan "Free a man to fight." By the end of the war some 350,000 American women had served in uniform.

Army. Over 210,000 women served, including about 4,000 black women, who served in segregated units. There were three distinct ways in which women could serve.

Army Nurse Corps. Some 60,000 women served as officer nurses in all theaters, more than a 50-fold increase in numbers over those of 1939.

Women's Army Auxiliary Corps (WAAC). About 150,000 women were enrolled in a new separate emergency branch of the army. These women served in numerous ways, such as truck driver, hospital orderly, and aviation mechanic, and in all theaters. Before the war ended this became the Women's Army Corps (WAC), a part of the regular establishment.

Women Air Service Pilots (WASPS). Under the leadership of famed aviatrix Jacqueline Cochrane, who had earlier served as a ferry pilot for the RAF, about a thousand women were enrolled as pilots, ferrying aircraft of all types (including B-17s) throughout the United States and occasionally overseas as well.

Navy. About 115,000 women served in the navy during the war.

A 1944 poster by artist Steele Savage, urging women to enlist. From left to right, the WAACs, WAVES, Women Marines, and SPARS.

Navy Nurse Corps. Some 14,000 women served, a substantial increase over the 442 who had been on duty in 1939.

Women Accepted for Volunteer Emergency Service (WAVES). About 100,000 women served in a variety of duties, much as did their sisters in the WAAC. Several women served as air navigators, and as such became the first women permitted to serve in airplane crews on what were theoretically combat missions, in patrols off both coasts. At the war's end, by which time the "Emergency" had been dropped from their title, WAVES comprised 55% of the personnel at Headquarters, Department of the Navy.

Marine Corps. The Marines were the last service to enlist women, creating the Women's Reserve, which had no "cute" acronym, in 1943. About 23,000 women served. Although women Marines endured a more difficult regimen than their sisters in the other services ("They *will* be Marines," as the Corps put it), their duties differed little.

Coast Guard. The SPARS (from the motto of the Coast Guard, "Semper Paratus," Latin for "Always Prepared") enrolled a total of 12,000 women in the course of the war. They performed what was perhaps the broadest range of duties of any of the women in uniform, from radar operators to carpenter's mates, with some even serving afloat. So pleased was the Coast Guard brass with its women that they honored them by naming a cutter *Spars*.

While a large proportion of the women in the two nurse corps served outside the continental United States, relatively few of the other women in uniform got overseas. For example, only 4,000 WAVES served outside the United States, all in the Pacific and most of them in HAWAII, and only 450 SPARS in Hawaii and Alaska. A handful of women Marines also served in Hawaii. About 8,000 WACs served in Europe, and about 5,500 in the Pacific, with small numbers in the CBI. Douglas MACARTHUR was probably the most enthusiastic supporter of women in uniform, and openly sought to increase the number of women troops in his command. By the end of the war there were more American women serving in his theater than in any other.

Figures on CASUALTIES among American military women are indeterminate. An estimated 300 died in the service, counting all theaters and including deaths from disease and accident, as well as a number by enemy action. The Army Nurse Corps had 16 women killed in action, five others missing in action, and 26 wounded. At least five navy nurses were killed in action when a KAMIKAZE hit the hospital ship *Comfort* on 25 April 1945. The number of women killed in action in the other branches is not clear. A number of American military women became PRISONERS OF WAR, 68 in the Philippines (and one other in the ETO). Although mistreated, they were not subjected to the mass rape and murder that was inflicted on the Canadian nurses captured at HONG KONG or the British nurses captured at SINGAPORE.

Ref: Larsen, " *'Till I Come Marching Home.'* "

Women's Voluntary Service Corps

A Japanese organization that conscripted women age 16 and above for service as factory workers, clerical employees, and nurses, depending upon their education. Service was under quasi-military conditions, with the women having little say in their assignments, which could take them considerable distances. Pay was minimal. In Korea the WVSC served as an agency for the recruitment of COMFORT WOMEN.

Worcester Class, US Light Cruisers

Designed with wartime experience in mind, *Worcester* (1945–1947–1948) and *Roanoke* (1945–1947–1948) were very large light cruisers equipped with a new double turret that permitted their 6-inch guns to be used in both an antiship and an antiaircraft role. These, and their 24 new-pattern 3-inch secondary dual-purpose guns, made them the most powerful antiaircraft cruisers ever built, but they were never used in their designed role. They were scrapped in the 1970s.

Wotje, Caroline Islands

Although potentially useful as both a naval or air base, Wotje had facilities for neither in 1941. During the war the Japanese developed it in a modest way, even using it as a base for flying boat raids on Pearl Harbor, via FRENCH FRIGATE SHOAL. It was repeatedly raided by carrier aircraft during the war, but remained in Japanese hands throughout.

Y

Yamada, Otozo (1881–1965)

Otozo Yamada graduated from the military academy in 1903 and entered the CAVALRY. Surprisingly, Yamada appears to have seen no service during the Russo-Japanese War. Over the years he passed through a variety of command, staff, and school assignments, all of which demonstrated his considerable abilities. In 1938 he was appointed to a senior command in China. At the start of the Pacific War he was a full general commanding the General Defense Command in Japan. He served on the Supreme War Council for most of the war, and was given command of the Kwantung Army in mid–1944, which was crushed by the Soviets in August 1945. Tried for war crimes by the Russians and sentenced to 25 years in labor camps, he was released in 1956 (he was 75 years old and in ill health) and sent back to Japan.

See also TOKYO WAR CRIMES TRIBUNAL.

Yamaguchi, Tamon (1892–1942)

One of Japan's most talented carrier admirals, Tamon Yamaguchi graduated from the naval academy in 1912. Over the years he held various posts, studied at Princeton (1921–23), served on the naval general staff, was a delegate to the London disarmament conference, and naval attaché in Washington (1934–37). Although a non-flyer, in 1940 he was promoted rear admiral and given the Second Carrier Division, HIRYU and SORYU. With his command he participated in the PEARL HARBOR operation, the subsequent operations in the Dutch East Indies and, finally, MIDWAY. There he committed suicide by going down with his flagship, *Hiryu*. Yamaguchi was known to criticize his superiors for their narrow-minded handling of carriers. He would have been a formidable opponent had he survived Midway.

Yamamoto, Isoruku (1884–1943)

Isoruku (or Isoroku) Yamamoto—born Takano—was among the outstanding admirals of World War II. He graduated from the Japanese Naval Academy in 1904 and saw action during the Russo-Japanese War, losing several fingers while commanding a TORPEDO boat in the Battle of Tsushima Strait in 1905 (his principal opponent in the Pacific War, Chester W. NIMITZ, was also missing a finger). During World War I he served as a staff lieutenant commander, but saw no action. He later attended Harvard for two years, and then Yale as a graduate student in the 1920s, where he became well acquainted with the military and industrial potential of the United States. It was this experience that caused him to constantly counsel against war with America.

The commander of the Japanese Combined Fleet since 1939, Yamamoto was recognized by Americans and Japanese alike as the most capable Japanese commander, architect of the spectacular success that attended Japanese efforts early in 1942. Yamamoto's undoing was the American success at breaking the Japanese naval codes. His staff suspected that their secret communication codes had been broken, but Yamamoto never believed it to be the case, at least he didn't believe it sufficiently to do much about it. As a result, American P-38 fighters ambushed Yamamoto's aircraft and its seven escorts on April 18, 1943, killing Yamamoto in the process.

Beyond being an excellent leader and combat admiral, Yamamoto spoke English. He was quite an independent thinker and, by Japanese standards, something of an eccentric. For example, Yamamoto had a Bible with him wherever he traveled and regularly consulted it, even though he was not a Christian. What made Yamamoto dangerous to America was his pragmatism. He knew that Japan could not defeat America, but he had the skill and rank to cause maximum CASUALTIES to American troops. The Midway operation was a workable plan, if only Yamamoto had known that his codes were compromised and been able to change the codes (thus keeping the enemy in the dark for at least a few months). The Pearl Harbor attack was his doing, and he had many other bold plans to make the American advance across the Pacific as costly as possible.

The other obstacle Yamamoto faced was the Japanese Army, which saw him as a dangerous freethinker. If Yamamoto had had his way, Japan would never have gotten involved in World War II in the first place. As early as 1940 he had told senior Japanese officials that war with America would be futile and disastrous for Japan. But Yamamoto was still very Japanese. He allowed himself to be adopted into the Yamamoto clan when he was 32 years old and already a distinguished naval officer because the higher status Yamamotos would help him overcome the stigma of his original family's lower social status (and because the Yamamotos wanted someone already famous like Isoruku Takano to be the leader of their clan). Yamamoto also believed in the emperor, whom he was obliged to serve as a sailor unto death. Yamamoto was typical of the many (but not nearly all) Japanese admirals who saw the army's policy in China (and eventual takeover of the government) as not in Japan's best interests. But because the army managed to get the emperor to agree (or at least remain silent) to their plans, there was nothing other Japanese could do but follow "the Emperor's wishes."

Yamashita, Tomoyuki (1888–1946)

Tomoyuki Yamashita joined the Japanese Army in 1906. In 1914 he saw action during the capture of the German colony of Kai-chow, China. Noted as an able officer, he spent most of the 1920s and 1930s in staff and school positions, rising rapidly in rank. By 1941 he was a lieutenant general and in command of the Twenty-fifth Army. His task was to invade MALAYA and take SINGAPORE. This he did in a stunning operation. In the summer of 1942 he moved to a command in MANCHURIA and in the summer of 1944 was put in charge of all the forces defending the Philippines. He commanded his forces on Luzon until ordered to surrender on August 19, 1945. He still had 50,000 troops left, even though completely cut off from outside assistance. After the war he was tried for ATROCITIES in Singapore and Manila, convicted, and hanged in 1946. Yamashita was considered the most able of all Japanese generals, and his final campaign in the Philippines bears this out. However, he did not get along with other Japanese leaders and was paranoid, among other things believing that TOJO was trying to have him killed. Tojo was jealous and afraid of Yamashita, but there is no evidence to support Yamashita's assassination fears.

Yamato Class, Japanese Battleships

The largest battleships ever built, and the largest warships ever until the commissioning of the nuclear-powered carrier USS *Enterprise* in 1960, *Yamato* and *Musashi* were enormous yet graceful looking behemoths, mounting the heaviest guns afloat and impressively protected. Nevertheless, they were probably a bad investment. Neither ship saw much service in the war. They were rather slow by World War II standards, lacked maneuverability, and were probably no better than an even match for US battleships of the IOWA CLASS. They were also expensive, and their construction limited the expansion of the Japanese Navy in terms of other, more vital types of vessels, such as aircraft carriers or destroyers. Construction of this class entailed construction of a special 13,000–ton GRT ship to transport their guns to the shipyards and several enormous floating cranes to help mount the guns. For the same investment in time, money, steel, shipyard facilities, and manpower, two or three SHOKAKU CLASS carriers (including aircraft) might have been built for each *Yamato* completed, and the carriers would have been available in considerably less time. The Japanese appear to have recognized this, for the third ship in the class was converted to a carrier while still on the ways and the fourth was canceled.

Yamato (1937–1940–1941) became the flagship of Combined Fleet in February of 1942, but her first war mission occurred during the MIDWAY Campaign, in which she saw no combat. On August 29 she led Combined Fleet into TRUK Lagoon, which was to serve as the main base for operations in the South Pacific. Save for one day when she changed her location, she spent the next 253 days swinging at anchor in the lagoon. On May 9, 1943 she departed for KURE, where she was refitted, returning to Truk Lagoon in mid-August, to once again swing at anchor, this time until mid-October, when US carrier raids on WAKE prompted an abortive sortie of Combined Fleet in the belief that a landing on the island was imminent. Sent to Japan to escort troop convoys to the South Pacific, in December 1943 she was TORPEDOED by USS *Skate* (SS-305), which revealed serious flaws in her construction. She did not return to Combined Fleet until April 1944. She took part in the Battle of the PHILIPPINE SEA and during the Battle of LEYTE GULF, absorbing some bomb damage in the Sibuyan Sea on October 24 1944; the next day she fired her 18.11–inch guns for the only time in anger, when she attacked the US escort carriers off SAMAR. Returning to Japan for repairs, she was damaged in the 19 March 1945, Task Force 58 carrier air strikes on Japanese ports, but was soon repaired. In April she was sent to attack American shipping off OKINAWA, and on April 7, 1945 was sunk by carrier aircraft, after absorbing about a baker's dozen torpedoes and at least eight bombs.

Musashi (1938–1940–1942) had an even less distinguished career than her sistership. Her first war mission was in early 1943, when she relieved *Yamato* as flagship of Combined Fleet at Truk. She brought Admiral YAMAMOTO's ashes back to Japan in May 1943, and then returned to Truk as Admiral Koga's flagship on August 5, not leaving the anchorage again until November, when she conducted a patrol east of the CAROLINES, before returning to stay at anchor until early February 1944, when she was withdrawn to Japan out of fear of US naval airpower (a prescient decision, given that Truk was subjected to a devastating air and surface raid in mid-February). In March 1944 she was torpedoed by *Tunny* (SS-282), with the resulting damage paralleling that to *Yamato* the previous December. She later took part in the Battle of the Philippine Sea, and was sunk in the Sibuyan Sea on October 24, 1944, during the early phases of the Battle of Leyte Gulf: She absorbed an estimated 20 torpedoes and 17 bombs, plus 18 near-misses before sinking. She had never fired her main battery at an enemy vessel.

SHINANO, the third ship of the class, was completed as an aircraft carrier. The fourth vessel, designated *Number 111*, was laid down in 1940 but broken up on the ways when about 30% completed. A fifth vessel was proposed in 1942, but never begun, as were two similar ships with six 20-inch guns in lieu of the 18.11-inchers.

Yap, Carolines

Although of limited potential as a naval base, Yap, one of the large, "high" islands of the CAROLINES, was well located for an air base, which the Japanese proceeded to construct. By mid-1944 US strategic plans envisioned capturing the island in October. In a reassessment of US plans, the operation was canceled several weeks before it was to have taken place, and the forces assigned to it was committed to the Leyte landings. The island remained in Japanese hands until the end of the war.

Yasukuni Shrine

A Shinto temple in Tokyo where the 2.46 million Japanese who died in battle—though not those killed in air raids—during the Japanese Empire's wars from the 1850s through 1945 are worshiped as *kami*, demi-gods. World War II accounts for the bulk of those memorialized, some 2.3 million, including virtually all of the 56,000 female nurses and auxiliaries commemorated. The shrine, which occupies 24 acres, includes numerous war memorials, such as the tomb of the "Seven Martyrs," the principal Japanese war criminals executed by the Allies at the end of World War II, and a museum dedicated to the KAMIKAZE. In 1965 a small memorial, named Chinreisha, was added to commemorate the war dead of all nations.

Once closely identified with the Imperial Government, since World War II the shrine has been maintained by private contributions. Informal ties to government, however, are strong; Japanese premiers and cabinet members regularly make formal pilgrimages.

Yorktown Class, US Aircraft Carriers

Arguably the most successful class of warship ever built, and certainly one of the most decorated, the Yorktowns were the model for all future US carrier designs. Relatively large, fast, very seaworthy vessels with excellent protection and large aircraft complements, they played an enormous part in the Pacific War, garnering great distinction in the process.

Yorktown, CV-5 (1934–1936–1937), was in the Atlantic when PEARL HARBOR was bombed, and was shortly transferred to the Pacific. She took part in several raids, and then fought in the Battle of the CORAL SEA, where she was severely damaged. Rushing to Pearl Harbor, she was partially repaired in order to get her into action in time for the Battle of MIDWAY. At Midway she took several bombs and two TORPEDOES on 4 June and was temporarily abandoned. Still afloat the next day, she was taken in tow. On 6 June the Japanese submarine *I-168*

put two more torpedoes into her and she finally went down.

Enterprise, CV-6 (1934–1936–1938), was flagship of the HALSEY Task Force at the time of Pearl Harbor, delivering reinforcements to WAKE ISLAND. She took part in the early raids on Japanese islands, escorted *Hornet* on the DOOLITTLE Raid, fought at Midway, EASTERN SOLOMONS, and the SANTA CRUZ ISLANDS, covered numerous landings throughout 1942–44, and fought on through to the end of the war, suffering frequent damage in action. By the end of the war she was the most decorated ship in American history. Despite a campaign to preserve her as a war memorial, "The Big E" was scrapped in 1958.

Hornet, CV-8 (1939–1940–1941), was laid down after the final collapse of naval limitations. Rather than wait for a new and better design, the navy decided to repeat the successful *Yorktown* design. Shaking down in the Atlantic when the war began, she shortly passed into the Pacific. Her first wartime mission was transporting Jimmy Doolittle's B-25s to within bombing range of Japan, in April 1942. She subsequently took part in several raids, fought at the Battle of Midway, the Eastern Solomons, and the Santa Cruz Islands, where on 24 October 1942 she took four Japanese bombs and three aerial torpedoes plus two suicide crashes by damaged Japanese aircraft, which caused considerable damage and engine failure. Since her hull remained sound, she was taken in tow, only to absorb three more Japanese bombs the following morning. As Japanese surface units were known to be closing in, it was decided to scuttle the ship. Despite about 300 rounds of 5-inch shells and nine torpedoes from US destroyers (not all of which detonated), she refused to sink. Abandoned, her burned out hulk was later found still afloat by Japanese surface forces, who finished her off with four 24-inch "Long Lance" torpedoes.

Yubari, Japanese Light Cruiser

An experimental vessel, the smallest cruiser in the war, *Yubari* (1922–1923–1923) was perhaps the most graceful looking vessel in the Japanese Navy, a service noted for some particularly graceful ships. On the whole, however, the ship was a failure. She was quite overloaded and unstable. On a hull designed to displace about 2,900 tons she mounted virtually the same armament as the 5,900-ton SENDAI. The principal difference was six rather than seven 5.5-inch guns and four rather than eight 24-inch torpedo tubes, but in compensation she carried three reload sets of TORPEDOES, where most ships carried two. She had a busy war as a flotilla leader, mostly in the southwest Pacific. She fought at the CORAL SEA and SAVO ISLAND, among other actions. Near PALAU on 27 April 1944 she was hit by a torpedo from *Bluegill* (SS-242) and sank the next day.

Yugumo Class, Japanese Destroyers

Japan ordered 36 Yugumo Class destroyers between 1939 and 1942, of which only 20 were completed, the last not until May of 1941. Closely resembling the KAGERO CLASS, they were better designed and their main armament had a superior elevation, on virtually the same displacement and with the same speed. Extensively modified during the war, they saw considerable service. All were lost in action, one to MINES, four to surface ships, one in a surface and air attack, nine to aircraft, and five to SUBMARINES.

Z

Zamboanga, Philippines

A small port, with limited resources and an airstrip occasionally frequented by the USAAF before the war. During the war it served as Japanese HQ for eastern Mindanao.

Zuiho Class, Japanese Light Aircraft Carriers

These two ships were designed as submarine tenders readily convertible into aircraft carriers, in a covert effort to expand Japan's carrier tonnage beyond that allowed by the naval DISARMAMENT TREATIES. *Tsurugisaki* actually entered service in that role in early 1939, while the second, *Takasaki*, was completed as a carrier while still building. Rather successful ships, fast and with a reasonable aircraft operating capacity, they were surprisingly tough.

Shoho (1934–1935–1942, ex-*Tsurugisaki*) was converted from a submarine tender 1941–42. Commissioned in February 1942, her only war mission ended in the CORAL SEA on 7 May 1942, when she was hit by aircraft from USS YORKTOWN, absorbing 11 bombs and about seven TORPEDOES in a few minutes, which turned her into a burning wreck that soon plunged to the bottom. She was the first Japanese carrier lost in the war.

Zuiho (1935–1936–1940, ex-*Takasaki*) helped support operations in the East Indies in early 1942, was damaged in the Battle of the SANTA CRUZ ISLANDS in October of that year, supported several attempts to run supplies into GUADALCANAL in December, served in the central Pacific in 1943, formed the core of one of the "bait" task forces in the PHILIPPINE SEA in mid-1944, and went down off Cape Engaño on October 25, 1944, having taken numerous bombs and torpedoes.

CHRONOLOGY

This Chronology is designed to give a sense of the day-to-day flow of events during the Pacific War. It outlines the principal developments in the Pacific Theater for each month of the war, with an occasional reference to critical events in the European War. Each month is treated separately. There is a brief summary of the general trend of the action that month, followed by daily detail. Of course, not everything that occurred each day can be summarized. Moreover, for all its vast size and scope, even the Pacific War tended to have long periods during which nothing spectacular happened. When there was action, there was a lot of it. But at other times there was little of note going on. Of course, there was always the tedium of patrolling, maintaining equipment, moving supplies, and getting ready for the next operation. For most of the soldiers, sailors, airmen, and Marines this was how they spent most of their time.

In addition to the material on the great events, this Chronology also covers the key dates in the military career of one of the millions of people who participated in the Pacific War.

Bill Howell (b. 1920) was a civilian on December 7, 1941. He soon volunteered for the navy and went to war. Howell survived the war and went on to live a normal life indistinguishable from that of the other 16 million Americans who had served in World War II. Like most of them, he hasn't gotten any mention in the history books, until now. But it should be remembered that without the Bill Howells, there would be no history to write about. It's easy to overlook the details of history, but it is in the details that the real work is done. So consider well the experiences of Bill Howell. You are more likely to find yourself in his situation than in that of Douglas MACARTHUR or Bill HALSEY.

Note: The dating of events in the Pacific War is somewhat confused by the presence of the International Date Line, running roughly through the middle of the Pacific Ocean. For example, the Japanese attack on PEARL HARBOR occurred on the morning of December 7, 1941 in HAWAII, while the Japanese attacks in the Philippines and MALAYA later that same morning are dated 8 December.

Outline History of World War II. While putting this together, it occurred to us that the history of World War II could be aptly summed up in three short quotations:

September 1, 1939: Adolf HITLER orders his troops to "Close your hearts to pity," as he sends them into Poland and starts World War II.

December 7, 1941: Mitsuo FUCHIDA cries *Tora! Tora! Tora!* from the cockpit of his aircraft over Pearl Harbor. His radio carries the message— "Tiger! Tiger! Tiger!"—back to the Japanese carriers, to let them know the sneak attack was a success.

September 2, 1945: The Japanese surrender documents having been signed on the US battleship *Missouri*, Douglas MacArthur says "These proceedings are closed," bringing World War II to an end after 2,193 days.

November 1941

The Pacific War began before the bombs fell on Pearl Harbor on December 7, 1941. For China the war began in 1931, when the Japanese seized Manchuria, or perhaps in 1932, when the Japanese briefly seized Shanghai, or maybe 1933, when they grabbed Jehol Province. Certainly for China the war was in progress by 1937, when the Japanese began a sustained campaign to conquer the entire country, the CHINA INCIDENT. But, however many Americans may have sympathized with the sufferings of the Chinese people, they did not think of China's war as an American war. For Americans the war began at Pearl Harbor. But even that date is erroneous.

Military operations actually began on November 26, 1941, when the Japanese First Air Fleet sailed from the KURILE ISLANDS for HAWAII unbeknownst to anyone, except a few Japanese. All anyone else noted that November was the frantic diplomatic activity between Japan and America.

If it is necessary to pick a date for the start of the Pacific War, it's either November 26, when the Japanese fleet set off for Pearl Harbor, or a few days before the attack, when the Japanese committed to the bombing raid no matter what their diplomats in Washington worked out with the Americans.

So, on November 26 the Japanese First Air Fleet sorties from TANKAN BAY in the Kurile Islands at a cruising speed suitable for a long voyage, destination—Pearl Harbor. The next day, the 27th, an official communiqué from the US Army chief of staff, issued with the concurrence of the chief of naval operations, goes out to all major US headquarters in the Pacific, concluding "this is to be considered a war warning." That same day HMAS *Parramatta*, a patrol vessel, is sunk by an unknown agent off Australia. On the 28th, the US chief of naval operations informs Adm Husband KIMMEL, at Pearl Harbor, "Hostile action is possible at any moment..." Carrier *Enterprise* sails from Pearl Harbor with aircraft for Wake; RAdm William HALSEY, the task force commander, orders the crew to full wartime alert, a measure also adopted by Adm Thomas HART, commanding the Asiatic Fleet, and LG John L. DEWITT, commanding US Army forces on the West Coast. But LG Walter SHORT, commanding in Hawaii, takes less vigorous measures, as does Adm Kimmel. On the 29th, Hi-

deki TOJO, a general and prime minister of Japan, announces that "Nothing can be allowed to interfere in Japan's sphere of influence in the Pacific, because it has been decreed by Divine Providence." By the 30th it appears that Japanese diplomatic efforts with the Americans are going nowhere, but both sides keep trying, the Japanese diplomats in Washington being unaware of the imminent attack on Pearl Harbor.

December 1941

December began with Japanese warships and troopships scurrying all over the Pacific. This activity did not go unnoticed, and Allied headquarters were alerted that something was up. It was obvious that the Japanese had decided upon war. Not until 7 December did it become obvious how bold their planning was. The rest of the month saw Japanese forces running amok all over the Pacific. The Japanese appeared unstoppable and, in December of 1941, they were.

The coming of war was not a complete surprise to many American military men. On the first of the month, the US SUBMARINES *Argonaut* and *Trout* take station off MIDWAY, *Triton* and *Tambor* off WAKE, as a defensive measure against any approaching Japanese vessels. On the 2nd, President ROOSEVELT asks Japan to clarify its intents with regard to French INDO-CHINA, where the Japanese show signs of taking over the entire region. That same day the British declare a state of emergency in MALAYA, where "Force Z" (battleship *Prince of Wales*, battlecruiser *Repulse*, and four destroyers) has just arrived at SINGAPORE. Reconnaissance aircraft on HAWAII are ordered to search out as far as 400 miles, in an arc from the northwest to the south. At 43 degrees north latitudes, 158 degrees 30 minutes east longitude, about 3,200 miles northwest of Pearl Harbor, the Japanese First Air Fleet alters course due east. To thunderous cheers, the officers and crewmen of the First Air Fleet are informed that their objective is Pearl Harbor. On the 3rd, reconnaissance aircraft on Hawaii are ordered to search out to 400 miles in an arc from the northwest to the south. Meanwhile, the First Air Fleet refuels, 45 degrees north latitude, 170 degrees east longitude, about 2,400 miles northwest of Pearl Harbor. Upon completion of the refueling, the tankers return to Japan and the fleet resumes its eastward course, increasing speed. It crosses the International Date Line during the night, so the next day for the First Air Fleet is the 5th. The Japanese carrier fleet is now committed to the attack, no matter what. On the 4th, heavily escorted Japanese invasion forces begin to sail for their objectives in Southeast Asia. At the same time, US carrier *Enterprise* flies off reinforcements for Wake Island. Reconnaissance aircraft on Hawaii are ordered to search up to 400 miles from the northwestward to the south. On the 5th, additional Japanese invasion forces sail from CAM RANH BAY and SAIGON. Carrier LEXINGTON steams from Pearl Harbor to deliver aircraft to Midway. At 45 degrees north latitude, 178 degrees west longitude, about 1,200 miles northwest of Pearl Harbor, the Japanese First Air Fleet alters course from due east to southeast. On the 6th, President Roosevelt makes a personal appeal to Emperor HIROHITO asking him to use his influence to help preserve peace in the Pacific. Reconnaissance aircraft on Hawaii are ordered to concentrate their efforts to the west and south. At 2100 hours the Japanese First Air Fleet arrives at 31 degrees north latitude, 158 degrees east longitude, about 500 miles north of Pearl Harbor. On the 7th, the First Air Fleet attacks the US Pacific Fleet at its anchorage in Pearl Harbor, inflicting heavy damage at little loss to itself. Japanese destroyers shell Midway Island. Later that same day, west of the International Date Line, and therefore officially the 8th, Japanese aircraft destroy US air power in the Philippines in a massive raid on Clark and Iba airfields on Luzon. Japanese destroyers attack Wake. Japanese troops begin landing in Malaya, attack HONG KONG, occupy the International Settlement in SHANGHAI, and invade Siam. The United States and Britain declare war on Japan, and British "Force Z" sails from Singapore. An Australian independent infantry company lands on western TIMOR, in the

NETHERLANDS EAST INDIES. A Dutch submarine sinks the Japanese destroyer *Isonami* off Celebes, the first Japanese warship to be sunk in the war. Japanese troops land on GUAM. Bill Howell, age 21, a resident of New City, in New York's Hudson Valley, is having a beer with friends at the local Knights of Columbus hall when the Pearl Harbor attack is announced. Bill works 40 miles south in New York City. At a time when as many people graduated from high school as today finish college, Bill had used his high school diploma to get a job with McCann-Erickson, a major advertising agency. The Great Depression was still going on and for a 21-year-old to snag a job like that, even if it was mainly because of skill at the typewriter, was quite an accomplishment. Bill knew how to type and take stenography, skills that he would find very useful during the war. And on hearing about Pearl Harbor, it was obvious that America was now in the war. Bill Howell's life, and the lives of millions of other young men, would never be the same. On the 9th, Japanese troops from KWAJALEIN occupy TARAWA in the GILBERTS. SIAM agrees to a cease-fire with Japan. Japanese bomb Nichols Field in the Philippines. Japanese capture KHOTA BARU airfield in northern Malaya. China declares war on Japan, after four years of "unofficial" warfare. On the 10th, Japanese aircraft sink *Prince of Wales* and *Repulse* in the South China Sea. Guam surrenders to a Japanese landing force after a two-day battle. Japanese troops begin landings in northern Luzon. Japanese naval aircraft bomb the CAVITE Navy Yard, Manila Bay. On the 11th, Marines on Wake Island beat off a Japanese landing, sinking destroyers *Hayate* and *Kisaragi*. This was rare during World War II, in which nearly all amphibious assaults succeeded. US submarines commence war patrols against Japanese shipping. Germany and Italy declare war on the United States. On the 12th, Japanese troops land at Legaspi, southeastern Luzon. In northern Luzon, Japanese troops advancing from Vigan and Aparri capture two airstrips. Japanese troops complete the occupation of southern Thailand, crossing the Burmese frontier. The British decide to abandon northern Malaya. Bill Howell acts on a decision he—and many other Americans—made on 7 December, and enlists in the navy. Because so many young men enlisted right after the Pearl Harbor attack, the day on which these new recruits are to report is set for a later date. Bill is ordered to report to the Brooklyn Navy Yard (40 miles down the Hudson River, in New York City) on 26 December. On the 13th, British and Canadian troops abandon the mainland portions of Hong Kong. The Japanese temporarily abandon the attempt to capture Wake, returning to base but continuing to subject the island to air attacks from the MANDATES. On the 14th, Japanese forces in Malaya occupy Kroh, and Japanese air units begin repairing northern Luzon airfields for their own use. On the 15th, Congress votes an additional $10.1 billion (some $60 billion in 1997 dollars) for the war effort. The surviving B-17s in the Philippines are ordered to Australia. Japanese forces in Malaya occupy Gurun. On the 16th Japanese troops land at Miri, in Sarawak, on BORNEO. Carriers HIRYU and SORYU, with escorts, separate from the homeward bound First Air Fleet to attack Wake Island. In Malaya Japanese forces land at PENANG. A carrier task force sails from PEARL HARBOR to relieve Wake Island. On the 17th, Adm Husband KIMMEL is relieved of command of the Pacific Fleet. VAdm W. S. Pye is in temporary command until Adm Chester W. NIMITZ arrives. LG Walter C. Short, commanding the Hawaiian Department, is also relieved. Japanese troops land in British North Borneo. On the 18th the Japanese 38th Division lands on Hong Kong Island. Japanese aircraft begin operating from strips in northern Luzon. Japanese destroyer *Shinonome* mined and sunk off Borneo. In Malaya the British reorganize forces and prepare for further withdrawal. British and Dutch troops occupy Portuguese Timor. On the 19th, Japanese attack Del Monte Field, Mindanao. In Malaya the Japanese occupy Penang Island, while the British continue withdrawal. Congress authorizes the president to draft men up to 44 years of age. On the 20th, Adm Ernest J. KING is named commander-in-chief, US Fleet. The American Volunteer

Group (FLYING TIGERS) goes into action for the first time, shooting down six Japanese bombers over Kunming, China. On the 21st, heavily reinforced and supported by carriers *Hiryu* and *Soryu*, the Japanese renew their attempt to capture Wake Island. Japanese land on Mindanao, rapidly occupy DAVAO. Siam allies itself with Japan. On the 22nd, Japanese task forces arrives off Wake, begin intensive bombardment. Japanese troops begin a major landing on Luzon, at Lingayen Gulf in the northwest. B-17s based in Australia attack Japanese shipping off Mindanao. The PENSACOLA CONVOY lands the first US troops in Australia. On the 23rd, Japanese begin air raids on RANGOON, Burma. Japanese troops land on Wake, which surrenders. US carriers speeding to support Wake Island are recalled when 400 miles east of the island. Heavy fighting on Luzon as US and Philippine troops attempt to hold the Japanese to their beachhead. Gen. Douglas MACARTHUR decides to withdraw to BATAAN. On the 24th, Japanese troops land at KUCHING, Sarawak. Japanese troops land at Lamon Bay, in east-central Luzon, and on Jolo, in the southern Philippines. Manila is bombed severely by Japanese aircraft. At the Arcadia Conference, in Washington, Roosevelt, CHURCHILL, and their principal advisers plan Allied STRATEGY. The Italian BLOCKADE RUNNER *Orseolo* departs KOBE for Bordeaux. On the 25th, Hong Kong surrenders to the Japanese 38th Division. On Luzon the Japanese dislocate a US-Philippine temporary defense line, while the South Luzon Force begins withdrawing northward. Manila is heavily bombed by Japanese aircraft. British attempt to stabilize their lines in Malaya north of Johore. On the 26th the Japanese continue to press the defenders on Luzon, the Philippines, from the north and the southeast. Manila is declared an open city. Japanese columns advancing down the west coast of Malaya merge near Taiping. The day after Christmas, Bill Howell reports for basic training at 52nd Street and First Avenue, the Brooklyn Navy Yard's Bay Ridge annex. He is told that because of the need to train sailors quickly he will receive an abbreviated three weeks of training, rather than the usual eight. It is cold and the accelerated training goes by as a blur. On the 27th, under heavy Japanese pressure US/Philippine troops occupy a temporary line running through Gerona and San Jose on Luzon. On the 28th, Japanese forces in Malaya capture Ipoh, having advanced about 150 miles since landing, with 200 more to Singapore. On Luzon, US/Philippine troops fall back to the Tarlac-Cabanatuan phase line. The US Navy authorizes the raising of special construction battalions (the SEABEES). On the 29th, Japanese troops eject US/Philippine troops from the Tarlac-Cabanatuan line on Luzon. First Japanese air raid on CORREGIDOR. On the 30th, Japanese troops occupy Kuantan, on the east coast of Malaya. On Luzon, US/Philippine troops occupy the Bambam-Gapan line, but the Japanese unhinge the line's right flank by capturing Gapan as the Philippine 91st Division collapses. On the 31st in the Philippines, by denying his right flank, Major General Jonathan Wainwright manages to preserve portions of the old Tarlac-Gapan line, hanging his right on Mt. Arayat while other forces cover the Paridel and Calumpit positions, vital for the withdrawal of the South Luzon Force to Bataan. In Malaya, British forces maintain a relatively stable line.

January 1942

If December 1941 was bad for the Allies, January 1942 was worse. At the beginning of 1942, the Allies still possessed considerable military forces in the Western Pacific, but the Japanese appeared more and more irresistible. The year opened with the Japanese advancing everywhere. Fighting continued in MALAYA and the Philippines, but it was clear that the Japanese would eventually prevail. The Japanese also moved into the NETHERLANDS EAST INDIES, the islands northwest of Australia, and Burma. Things looked grim. Yet there was some hope, the United Nations Pact was signed, as representatives of 26 nations meeting in Washington adopted the principles of the Atlantic Charter and declared that none of them would make a separate peace.

On the 1st, PHILIPPINE ARMY units begin holding the Borac-Guagua line, to cover the final withdrawal into BATAAN. Japan is temporarily halted in Malaya. On the 2nd, on Luzon, the Japanese Army occupies MANILA and CAVITE from the south, but the Borac-Guagua line, farther north, holds. Japanese forces in Malaya occupy Kampar. On the 3rd, the ABDA Command is formed to unite Allied efforts in Southeast Asia and the Netherlands East Indies, under the overall command of Sir Archibald WAVELL. The Borac-Guagua line holds on Luzon. British once again withdraw under pressure in Malaya. On the 4th US aircraft attack Japanese shipping in DAVAO harbor, damaging the cruiser *Myoko*. The Philippine Army abandons the Borac-Guagua line, and the withdrawal to Bataan is nearly completed: Japanese troops continue to advance in Malaya. On the 5th, the Japanese 48th Division begins withdrawing from the Philippines for duty on JAVA. US/Philippine troops begin consolidating the defenses of Bataan. Japanese troops continue to advance in Malaya. First British reinforcements (elements of 17th Indian Division) arrive in Burma. On the 6th, Philippine Army units hold the Dinalupihan-Orani line, last defensive position before Bataan. In Malaya the British manage to hold the Japanese north of Kuala Lumpur. On the 7th, US and Philippine troops complete occupation of the Bataan position: 15,000 US and 65,000 Philippine troops are immediately put on half-rations. In Malaya the Japanese turn the British defenses north of Kuala Lumpur. On the 8th, British troops in Malaya are ordered to fall back on the "Johore Line," about 50 miles north of SINGAPORE. On Bataan, US/Philippine troops continue to organize their defenses as Japanese units close with them. On the 9th, Japanese SUBMARINES begin operating in the Indian Ocean. First Japanese offensive against the Bataan defenses. In Malaya the Japanese make an amphibious "end run" around the British left and occupy Port Settenham on the Strait of Malacca. On the 10th Japanese troops continue pressure on Bataan, begin landing at Tarakan Bay, BORNEO. Sir Archibald Wavell arrives at Bandung, near BATAVIA, to take over the ABDA Command. On the 11th Japanese Navy airborne troops land on Celebes, in coordination with an amphibious attack. US carrier *Saratoga* is TORPEDOED south of HAWAII. Heavy fighting on Bataan. In Malaya the Japanese capture Kuala Lumpur. A Japanese submarine shells Pago Pago, in American SAMOA. On the 12th the Japanese in Malaya begin to advance on Malacca. Dutch coast-defense battery sinks two Japanese minesweepers off Tarakan, Borneo. Heavy fighting on Bataan. On the 13th heavy fighting continues on Bataan, as Philippine troops counterattack. Elements of British 18th Division reach Singapore, as forces in Malaya complete withdrawal to the Johore line. On the 14th, the Japanese capture Malacca in Malaya. Heavy fighting on Bataan. Arcadia Conference ends. On the 15th, Chinese troops halt a Japanese offensive near CHANGSHA in Hunan Province. The Japanese Southern Army invades Burma from the Isthmus of Kra in Thailand. In Malaya the Japanese make several small "end run" amphibious landings to dislocate the British left. On Bataan, Japanese troops penetrate US/Philippine defenses. As Bill Howell's navy basic training comes to an end, he is told that he will be kept at the training center to help out with the processing of new recruits: His typing and stenographic skills are proving more useful than he had anticipated. On the 16th the British in Malaya attempt to hold the line of the Muar River against Japanese forces advancing down the west coast. Heavy fighting on Bataan. Rio Conference begins, as 21 American republics discuss hemispheric defense. On the 17th the British are under heavy pressure on the Muar River line in Malaya. Heavy fighting on Bataan continues. On the 18th British troops in Malaya heavily engaged on the Muar River Line. Heavy fighting continues on Bataan, as attempts to restore original lines fail. On the 19th US/Philippine troops continue to try to restore lines, under increasing Japanese pressure. In Malaya British troops abandon the Muar River

line; all forces are now within the Johore line. On the 20th Japanese aircraft carriers raid RABAUL and KAVIENG, in the BISMARCKS. The Japanese 55th Division invades Burma from central Thailand. On the 21st a British task force built around the carrier INDOMITABLE arrives at ADDU ATOLL, in the Indian Ocean southwest of India. Heavy fighting continues on Bataan. Rabaul and Kavieng again raided by Japanese aircraft. In Malaya, the Japanese begin to dislocate the Johore line. On the 22nd, Japanese troops begin landings on New Ireland and NEW BRITAIN. Japanese air strikes on LAE and Salamaua, in NEW GUINEA. CHIANG KAI-SHEK agrees to let USLG Joseph STILWELL serve as his chief of staff, authorizes movement of Chinese troops into Burma. Heavy fighting on the Johore line in Malaya. US Army Task Force 6814 (later the Americal Division) sails from New York for the South Pacific. On the 23rd, US destroyers and a Dutch submarine attack Japanese shipping off BALIKPAPAN, Borneo. Heavy fighting on Bataan, and US/Philippine troops begin to fall back to secondary defensive positions, while Japanese troops land at Quinauan and Longoskayan Points in the American rear but are contained. In Burma the Japanese capture the Sittang River bridge, in the British rear, causing the collapse of the understrength and green 17th Indian Division. In Malaya the Johore line crumbles. British reinforce Singapore with an additional new Indian brigade. On the 24th, Australian resistance at Rabaul ends. Japanese begin landings at Balikpapan, Borneo, and Keita, BOUGAINVILLE. In Malaya, British plan for withdrawal to Singapore. On the 25th, US task forces built around carriers *Enterprise* and YORKTOWN rendezvous off Samoa and proceed on raid into the MANDATES. In the Philippines, the American/Filipino troops complete their withdrawal to secondary positions. On the 26th, US and Philippine troops consolidate the Bagac-Orion line on Bataan; Japanese troops land at Canas Point, and other headlands, in their rear but are contained. In Malaya the Japanese make major inroads into the Johore line position. On the 27th, HMS *Indomitable* flies off 48 aircraft to reinforce the defense of Java. *En-*

terprise and YORKTOWN task forces raid the MARSHALL ISLANDS. US submarines begin supply runs to CORREGIDOR. On the 28th the Japanese attack the new US/Philippine line on Bataan. Under heavy pressure, the British forces in Malaya begin to withdraw toward Singapore. On the 29th Japanese pressure continues on Bataan, but the lines hold. The first US troops arrive on FIJI. An additional brigade of the British 18th Division reaches Singapore from India, as British troops in Malaya continue withdrawing into the island city. On the 30th, Japanese undertake a surprise attack on Moulmein, Burma. On Bataan, US/Philippine troops begin clearing Japanese pockets along the coast. Japanese attack AMBOINA, in the Netherlands East Indies. On the 31st, the British abandon Moulmein, Burma, and retire across the Salween River. British troops in Malaya are withdrawn to Singapore Island. Japanese pressure on Bataan eases.

February 1942

February saw the situation beginning to turn around for the Allies, or at least become less grim. American forces continued to hold off the Japanese in the Philippines and the British were still holding out against the Japanese in Burma. U.S. carrier groups began raiding Japanese island bases and interfering with Japanese invasion operations. Otherwise, the Japanese advance kept moving forward. February demonstrated that the Japanese could be slowed down, but not that they could be stopped.

On the 1st, US carriers *Enterprise* and *Hornet* raid Japanese bases in the GILBERT and MARSHALL ISLANDS. On the 2nd, the British carrier INDOMITABLE arrives at TRINCOMALEE, on CEYLON. US and Philippine troops counterattack in BATAAN. On the 3rd, US and Philippine troops successfully restore the Bagac-Orion line on Bataan, despite Japanese counterattacks. On the 4th, Japanese aircraft catch the ABDA cruiser-destroyer squadron in Madoera Strait, north of Bali, inflicting heavy damage on US cruisers *Marblehead* and *Houston*. The last Allied (Australian) troops on AMBOINA

surrender. On the 5th, Japanese artillery begins bombarding Singapore from across the Strait of Johore, while the final elements of the British 18th Division arrive by sea. On the 6th, Japanese make local attacks on Bataan but are beaten off. On the 7th, US/Philippine troops begin clearing Japanese pockets and beachheads on Bataan. On the 8th, Japanese troops begin crossing the Strait of Johore, to land on Singapore Island. Japanese land at MAKASSAR, Celebes. Philippine troops eliminate Japanese troops holding Quinauan Point. On the 9th, Japanese troops effect a second beachhead on Singapore Island, which is subject to a heavy air raid. Japanese troops on Bataan suspend offensive operations and begin a long period of rest and reorganization; for the first time since the Pacific War began in early December the Japanese have been stopped cold. On the 10th, Gen. WAVELL visits Singapore, orders continued resistance, despite Japanese presence on the island. On the 11th Japanese overrun elements of the Indian 46th Brigade as it retreats from the Salween River. Japanese demand surrender of Singapore. On the 12th, US/Philippine troops on Bataan mop up isolated Japanese pockets in their rear. On the 13th, US and Philippine troops eliminate Japanese forces at Canas Point beachhead on Bataan, eliminating the last Japanese pockets in their rear. Japanese light surface forces sink the British gunboat *Scorpion* in Banka Strait, prompting the ABDA cruiser-destroyer force to sortie from BATAVIA. United States and Canada agree to construct the ALCAN HIGHWAY. That night the Japanese submarine *I-17* shells an oil depot at Goleta, California, with little serious effect. On the 14th, Japanese Navy paratroopers land near PALEMBANG. Attempting to intercept a convoy proceeding through Banka Strait, ABDA cruisers and destroyers are attacked by Japanese aircraft and break off the effort. On the 15th, Singapore surrenders to the Japanese, depriving the Allies of the major British naval base in Asia. Japanese amphibious troops land at Palembang, where there is heavy fighting. Dutch destroyer VAN GHENT runs aground in Banka Strait and must be abandoned. The Japanese First Air

Fleet departs PALAU for the Dutch East Indies. On the 16th, Japanese secure Palembang. An Australian and American convoy attempting to reach TIMOR is turned back by Japanese air attack. On the 17th, the Dutch destroyer *Van Ness* is sunk by Japanese aircraft in Banka Strait. On the 18th, the Dutch coast defense ship *Soerabaya* and a submarine are destroyed by air attack on Soerabaya Naval Base. On the 19th, Japanese naval- and land-based aircraft raid the port at DARWIN, northwestern Australia, inflicting heavy damage. Japanese troops begin landing on Bali. Later that night the ABDA cruiser-destroyer force engages Japanese shipping, losing Dutch destroyer *Piet Hein* and suffering a cruiser and two destroyers damaged while damaging two Japanese destroyers (Battle of Lombok Strait). On the 20th, the USS LEXINGTON beats off a Japanese air attack some 300 miles east-northeast of RABAUL, but is forced to abandon a planned raid on that place. In a combined amphibious and airborne attack, Japanese troops land on Timor. On the 21st, on Timor, Dutch and Australian troops begin GUERRILLA resistance. British Seventh Armoured Brigade reaches RANGOON, in Burma, while the 17th Indian Division begins defending the Sittang River bridgehead. On the 22nd, the Japanese 48th Division arrives at BALIKPAPAN from the Philippines. President ROOSEVELT orders MACARTHUR to leave the Philippines for Australia to assume command of all Allied forces in the southwest Pacific. On the 23rd, Japanese submarine *I-17* shells Elwood, California. B-17s from Australia raid Rabaul. On the 24th, USS *Enterprise* raids WAKE ISLAND. Heavy fighting for the Sittang River bridgehead in Burma. On the 25th the ABDA Command is formally dissolved; US, British, and Commonwealth forces pass under Dutch control in the NETHERLANDS EAST INDIES. In Burma the Japanese threaten to flank the 17th Indian Division, penetrating between it and the First Burma Division. On the 26th the aircraft transport USS *Langley* is sunk off Java with 32 aircraft aboard. Heavy fighting by the 17th Indian Division in Burma. On the 27th, the Battle of the JAVA SEA: Under VAdm Karel DOORMAN, an Al-

lied cruiser-destroyer force attempts to intercept a Java-bound Japanese invasion force, only to be intercepted by a superior Japanese squadron, losing two light cruisers and three destroyers, with heavy damage to other ships. On the 28th, the Battle of Sunda Strait: After nightfall, as Japanese troops begin landing on Java, USS *Houston* and HMAS *Perth* attempt to escape from the Java Sea by way of Sunda Strait. En route they encounter a Japanese convoy and attempt to attack it, only to be sunk, along with three of the accompanying destroyers, by overwhelming Japanese naval forces.

March 1942

Allied resistance began to stiffen in places like Burma and New Guinea, but Japanese forces continued to advance everywhere. Allied prospects were still in free fall, and the bottom wasn't even in sight.

On the 1st, Japanese troops continue landing on Java. Battle off Soerabaya: HMS EXETER and an American and a British destroyer are intercepted and sunk by Japanese naval and air forces while trying to escape eastward from Java. Japanese battleship *Hiei*, supported by cruisers and destroyers, sinks two US destroyers south of Java. Chinese troops reach the front in Burma, where Japanese pressure remains steady. On the 2nd, Japanese troops occupy ZAMBOANGA, on Mindanao in the Philippines. Japanese encounter heavy fighting on Java. On the 3rd, heavy fighting on Java, while Japanese cruisers and destroyers sink destroyer HMS *Stronghold*, several smaller warships, and a merchant ship south of Java. Japanese aircraft raid Broome, Australia, inflicting heavy damage. On the 4th, the USS *Enterprise* raids MARCUS ISLAND. In the Netherlands East Indies, heavy fighting continues on Java, while three damaged Allied destroyers and other vessels in the SOERABAYA navy yard are scuttled. Refueling from a submarine at FRENCH FRIGATE SHOAL, two Japanese flying boats raid Pearl Harbor, inflicting no damage. On the 5th, the Japanese First Air Fleet raids TJILATJAP, sinking several vessels. Japanese troops land at Salamaua, in northeastern New Guinea. General Harold ALEXANDER is appointed British commander in Burma. On the 6th, Dutch resistance on Java becomes fragmented; the Dutch Navy begins scuttling its last vessels in Javan ports. In Burma, after an unsuccessful counterattack, Gen. Alexander orders RANGOON evacuated. On the 7th, Japanese surface units shell CHRISTMAS ISLAND (Indian Ocean), sinking one ship. Having only recently arrived, the US Americal Division sails from MELBOURNE, Australia, for NOUMEA. Japanese troops land at Lae and Salamaua, in northeastern New Guinea. Japanese naval units reconnoiter Buka, north of BOUGAINVILLE. Japanese troops depart SINGAPORE for northern Sumatra. On the 8th, Japanese troops occupy Rangoon. On the 9th, Allied forces on Java (c. 20,000) surrender. Adm Ernest J. KING, commander-in-chief, U.S. Fleet, is also named chief of naval operations, replacing Adm Harold Stark. British withdrawal in Burma proceeds smoothly. On the 10th, Adm Wilson BROWN's carriers LEXINGTON and YORKTOWN make a daring raid over the OWEN STANLEYS in New Guinea, to hit Japanese shipping at Lae and Salamaua, sinking an auxiliary cruiser and two merchant ships, and damaging four warships and several merchantmen. MacArthur appoints MG Johnathan WAINWRIGHT commander of forces on Luzon. US 27th Infantry Division sails from SAN FRANCISCO for HAWAII. On the 11th, over two weeks after receiving orders to proceed to Australia, MACARTHUR leaves CORREGIDOR on a PT-BOAT bound for Mindanao. In Burma British and newly arrived Chinese forces prepare to defend the central region of the country. On the 12th, the US Americal Division lands at Noumea. Japanese troops land at SABANG, in northern Sumatra. General Joseph STILWELL arrives in Burma to assist Sir Harold Alexander as combined US and Chinese commander. On the 13th, Japanese troops land at Buka, north of Bougainville, and begin building an airfield. British Commonwealth and Chinese troops establish the Prome-Toungoo line in Burma. On the 14th, the Japanese forces in Burma halt in order to rest and reorganize, as the British and Chi-

nese hold on the Prome-Toungoo line. The Joint Chiefs of Staff reaffirms the "Germany first" policy. MacArthur arrives on Mindanao. On the 15th, the US 27th Infantry Division arrives in Hawaii. In the Philippines, the Japanese begin an intensive bombardment of the island forts guarding Manila Bay. On the 16th, a small task force from the US Americal Division sails from Noumea bound for Efate, in the NEW HEBRIDES. On the 17th, MacArthur leaves Mindanao by B-17, and arrives in Australia. On the 18th, a task force from the Americal Division occupies Efate, in the New Hebrides. On the 19th, British LG William SLIM takes command of the British Burma Corps. In central Burma the Japanese attack the Chinese 200th Division. US 41st Infantry Division sails from San Francisco for Australia. On the 20th, elements of the Japanese 18th Division sail from PENANG, MALAYA, for the ANDAMAN ISLANDS. On the 21st, in Burma, a massive Japanese air raid on Magwe seriously damages airfield facilities and aircraft, as the Japanese prepare a new offensive to break the Prome-Toungoo line. On the 22nd, the Japanese complete the destruction of the Magwe air base, forcing British and American aircraft to withdraw to fields closer to India and China. The British Fifth Division departs from Britain bound for Madagascar. On the 23rd, troops of the Japanese 18th Division occupy PORT BLAIR, in the Andamans, without opposition (the small British garrison withdrew on the 12th). On the 24th, the US-British Combined Chiefs of Staff declares the Pacific Theater a US responsibility. Japanese forces begin an intensive air and artillery bombardment of BATAAN. Japanese troops conduct "mopping up" operations throughout the Netherlands East Indies, landing troops at numerous small ports bypassed during the invasion. In Burma the Japanese open an offensive up the Sittang, Irrawaddy, and Chindwin Rivers. On the 25th, US Task Force 39 (carrier WASP, a fast battleship, two heavy cruisers, and eight destroyers) steams from the East Coast bound for Scapa Flow, northern Scotland, where it will relieve British forces earmarked for operations in the Indian Ocean. US troops (162nd Infantry, 41st Division) occupy Bora

Bora, in the SOCIETY ISLANDS. On the 26th, the Japanese First Air Fleet departs the Celebes bound for the Indian Ocean. Heavy Japanese pressure against Chinese forces near Toungoo, in central Burma. On the 27th, British Adm James SOMERVILLE assumes command of the British Far Eastern Fleet (three carriers, five battleships, seven cruisers, including one Dutch, and 14 British, Dutch, and Australian destroyers, divided into a "fast" division able to make 24 knots, and a "slow" one able to make 18), based on CEYLON. A Japanese submarine flotilla (six boats) departs Penang for the Indian Ocean. Chinese 200th Division beats off Japanese attacks on Toungoo, Burma. On the 28th, in preparation for a major offensive, the Japanese undertake a probe against US lines on Bataan. On the 29th, the British Burma Corps attacks to support Chinese troops at Toungoo. After reconnaissance reports the presence of the Japanese First Air Fleet in the Indian Ocean, Admiral Somerville concludes it will attack his bases in Ceylon and orders his ships to deploy so as to ambush them. On the 30th, the Joint Chiefs of Staff issues directives dividing the Pacific Theater into the Southwest Pacific Area, under MacArthur, and the Pacific Ocean Areas, under Adm Chester W. NIMITZ, further dividing the latter's command into North, Central, and South Pacific areas. In Burma Japanese pressure forces the Chinese 200th Division to withdraw from Toungoo, as the Burma Corps falls back as well. On the 31st, Japanese troops in Burma occupy Toungoo, thus unhinging the Prome-Toungoo line.

April 1942

The Allied situation hits rock bottom, although this wouldn't be clear until the following month. At the beginning of the month, American troops in the Philippines were barely hanging on, the British were falling back toward the Indian frontier in Burma, and a Japanese carrier fleet was raiding into the Indian Ocean. By month's end, BATAAN had fallen, the British had virtually abandoned Burma, and the Japanese seemed everywhere triumphant.

But American bombers, flying off a carrier, had bombed Tokyo.

On the 1st, US/Philippine troops on Bataan go on quarter-rations because of the inability to get supplies through the Japanese naval blockade. The British Far Eastern Fleet continues to search for the Japanese First Air Fleet south and east of CEYLON. The First Air Fleet refuels south of JAVA. A Japanese cruiser-destroyer force departs Megui for operations in the Bay of Bengal. On the 2nd, the US carrier *Hornet*, carrying 16 Army B-25 medium bombers, sails from SAN FRANCISCO. Low on fuel, the British Far Eastern Fleet is ordered to retire to ADDU ATOLL in the Maldive Islands, as the whereabouts of the Japanese First Air Fleet is still unknown, making Ceylon too dangerous. The Japanese 18th Division sails from SINGAPORE for RANGOON. US bombers operating from India attack Japanese shipping in the ANDAMAN ISLANDS. In Burma, the British abandon Prome. On the 3rd, heavily reinforced with fresh troops, heavy artillery, and lots of ammunition, the Japanese launch a major offensive on Bataan. In Burma, as the British withdraw from Prome, STILWELL orders the Chinese to make a stand at Pyinamana. On the 4th, the Japanese succeed in dislocating the front on Bataan, and US and Philippine troops fall back to a reserve line. The British detect the Japanese First Air Fleet south of Ceylon, where all operational ships are ordered to put to sea. Japanese carrier aircraft sink the British heavy cruisers *Cornwall* and *Dorsetshire*, at sea off Ceylon, as well as several other vessels. On the 5th, the British Far Eastern Fleet hastily sorties from Addu Atoll in an attempt to intercept the Japanese First Air Fleet. Japanese aircraft from the First Air Fleet strike COLOMBO, Ceylon, sinking a destroyer, an auxiliary cruiser, and another minor warship as well as many auxiliaries and merchant ships, downing 27 British aircraft, while losing only seven airplanes. The British and Japanese fleets in the Indian Ocean fail to spot each other, although coming within 200 miles of each other. On Bataan, Japanese troops capture Mt. Samat, unhinging the defenses. When a counterattack by US/Philippine troops fails to throw them back, a withdrawal is ordered. On the 6th, elements of the Japanese First Air Fleet begin a raid into the Bay of Bengal. CHIANG KAI-SHEK agrees to provide additional forces for Burma, as Stilwell's Chinese forces prepare to defend Pyinamana. On the 7th, US/Philippine troops fail to form a new defensive line, as the Japanese advance continues. Japanese troops land on BOUGAINVILLE, in the Solomon Islands. The Japanese 18th Division lands at Rangoon. In the Indian Ocean the British Far Eastern Fleet is ordered to return to Addu Atoll. On the 8th, as US/Philippine resistance on Bataan begins disintegrating, the decision to surrender is made. US carrier *Enterprise* and her escorts, under RAdm William F. HALSEY, sail from PEARL HARBOR. On the 9th, aircraft from the Japanese First Air Fleet sink nine merchant ships off the coast of India, while cruisers raid commerce in the Bay of Bengal, accounting for three more ships, for a total of about 92,000 tons. Japanese carrier aircraft raid Trincomalee, inflicting little damage save to defending aircraft, but sink carrier HERMES, two smaller warships, and two tankers in nearby waters. US/Philippine forces on Bataan (c. 75,000) surrender to the Japanese, ending the desperate resistance of the "Battling Bastards of Bataan." US troops still hold CORREGIDOR, which lies in the entrance to Manila Bay. On the 10th, the British Far Eastern Fleet (mostly older battleships and cruisers, plus carriers INDOMITABLE and *Formidable*) retires to Bombay and East Africa. Japanese troops land on CEBU, in the central Philippines. Japanese renew their offensive in Burma. In the Philippines the Japanese begin bombardment of Corregidor and the smaller island forts in Manila Bay. On the 11th the Japanese begin a major offensive against the British in Burma. The Japanese rapidly overrun the settled portions of Cebu. On the 12th US/Philippine forces on Cebu retire to the interior to begin GUERRILLA warfare. Japanese heavy bombardment of Corregidor and the Manila harbor forts continues. In Burma the British Burma Corps requires support from Chinese troops to hold off Japanese attacks. Bill Howell achieves the rank of petty officer third class, as a yeoman. Because of his clerical skills and hard work, it was decided earlier that he would "strike" for the navy rating of yeoman (clerk, handling the paperwork). This means that he underwent on-the-job-training in navy administrative procedures. Successful completion of that training resulted in the rank yeoman third class. On the 13th VAdm Robert L. GHORMLEY is designated commander, South Pacific Area. In Burma the front of the Burma Corps breaks. On the 14th in Burma the Yenangyaung oil field is ordered destroyed. Australia approves the appointment of MACARTHUR as commander, Southwest Pacific. On the 15th, Japanese troops threaten to encircle the British Burma Division. On the 16th, Japanese troops land on Panay, in the southern Philippines, as the defenders retire to the interior to begin guerrilla warfare. Japanese troops occupy Magwe, in central Burma. On the 17th, British, Indian, and Chinese forces are unable to hold the Japanese advance; Stilwell abandons plans to make a stand at Pyinamana. On the 18th, the DOOLITTLE Raid: From little more than 650 miles east of Honshu, carrier *Hornet* launches 16 B-25 medium bombers against Tokyo and other targets, which comes as quite a shock to the Japanese, even though the damage is slight. In Burma, despite some local success by Allied forces, the Chinese 55th Division collapses under Japanese pressure, breaking the Allied front and uncovering the road to Lashio, in northern Burma. On the 19th, the British abandon the Yenangyaung oil fields in Burma, despite a partially successful Chinese counterattack. On the 20th British forces in Burma begin a general withdrawal. On the 21st the Japanese close up on the retiring Allied forces in Burma. On the 22nd, the US 32nd Infantry Division sails from San Francisco for Australia. In Burma Stilwell attempts to reorganize Chinese forces to better hold the Japanese. On the 23rd, uncovered by the British withdrawal to their west, Chinese troops in central Burma begin to pull out northward to avoid being outflanked by the Japanese. On the 24th, Japanese troops advance on all fronts in Burma. On the 25th, ALEXANDER orders Allied forces to retire to the north bank of the Irrawaddy River, as Chinese counterattacks fail to halt Japanese advance toward Lashio. Task Force 16 returns to Pearl Harbor; its mission (the Tokyo Raid) remains a closely guarded secret for months. Japanese reaction to the raid is to recall some fighter groups from the front, while Adm Isoroku YAMAMOTO is inspired to propose a plan to expand Japan's defensive perimeter to the ALEUTIANS and MIDWAY. On the 26th, Alexander decides that Burma is lost, and all efforts must be concentrated on the defense of India. On the 27th Stilwell proposes to CHIANG that a new Chinese army be organized and trained in India. On the 28th Stilwell orders the Chinese 28th Division to defend Lashio, which the Japanese are rapidly approaching. On the 29th, Japanese troops begin a systematic campaign to clear Mindanao of US and Philippine forces. In Burma, the Japanese capture Lashio, arriving before the Chinese 28th Division. China is now completely isolated from overland contact with the outside world. On the 30th, British troops evacuate MANDALAY in Burma, retiring to the north side of the Irrawaddy, abandoning all central Burma to the Japanese. On Mindanao the Japanese continue pressing the defenders back, while on Luzon the bombardment of Corregidor and the harbor forts continues.

May 1942

The Allies finally began to slow down the Japanese advance. Although the British and Chinese continued to fall back in Burma, and organized resistance in the Philippines ceased with the surrender of CORREGIDOR, the Japanese were stopped in New Guinea and suffered their first naval reverse in the Battle of the CORAL SEA. Moreover, the scene was set for the climactic Battle of Midway in June.

On the 1st, Japanese troops occupy MANDALAY, Burma, and press on toward India, while on Mindanao Japanese troops press their advance and the bombardment of CORREGIDOR continues. On the 2nd, US submarine *Drum* TORPEDOES the Japanese seaplane carrier *Mizuho* off Honshu. On Mindanao, Philippine troops make a stand in the north, briefly holding the Japanese. The small Australian garrison at TULAGI near GUADALCANAL in the eastern SOLOMONS, is withdrawn. On the 3rd, Japanese troops land on Tulagi, near Guadalcanal. Japanese troops land at Cagayan, Mindanao, last important town in the Philippines still in US hands. Despite fierce resistance US/Philippine troops on Mindanao fall back. A US submarine evacuates a few key personnel from Corregidor as the Japanese continue to bombard the island. On the 4th, the US carrier YORKTOWN attacks Japanese at Tulagi, seriously damaging a destroyer, which has to be beached and abandoned. Corregidor subject to an intense artillery and aerial bombardment. US and Philippine troops on Mindanao regroup as Japanese pressure lets up. On the 5th, Japanese carriers *Zuikaku* and SHOKAKU enter the Solomons Sea from the north, intent upon supporting operations against the eastern Solomons and PORT MORESBY, while the *Yorktown* and LEXINGTON task forces rendezvous in the Coral Sea. Japanese troops land on Corregidor, in the Philippines. British troops land at Diego Suarez, a Vichy-held naval base in northern Madagascar. British forces evacuate Akyab in Burma. Japanese Imperial General Headquarters orders the Combined Fleet to prepare for an attack on Midway and the ALEUTIANS. On the 6th, on Corregidor, LG Johnathan WAINWRIGHT surrenders all US and Philippine forces in the Philippines. Japanese resume their advance on Mindanao. Chinese forces in northern Burma are ordered to retire to China. In the Coral Sea, US and Japanese carrier task forces search for each other. On the 7th, Battle of the Coral Sea begins: US carrier aircraft sink carrier *Shoho*, while Japanese carrier aircraft sink a US oiler and destroyer. Japanese submarine-borne aircraft reconnoiter Aden. The British capture Diego Suarez, Madagascar, from the Vichy French. On the 8th, the Battle of the Coral Sea continues: US and Japanese carrier task forces trade blows, the United States losing *Lexington* while the Japanese suffer heavy damage to *Shokaku* and severe aircraft loss. This is the first setback for the Japanese Navy since the war began. Japanese SUBMARINES begin reconnaissance operations off East Africa. In Burma, Japanese troops close on Myitkyina, in the far north, held by the Chinese. MACARTHUR urges the Joint Chiefs of Staff to authorize an offensive in the Solomons, under his command, to stop the Japanese from advancing any farther. On the 9th the Japanese abandon the Port Moresby operation, the first time since the war began that Allied resistance has forced them to cancel their plans. US troops arrive on TONGA and the Galapagos. On the 10th, US troops on Mindanao surrender to the Japanese, ending formal resistance, but some flee to the interior to conduct GUERRILLA operations. In Burma the Japanese attack the British rear guard near Shwegyin. On the 11th, US submarine *S-42* sinks Japanese merchant cruiser *Okinoshima* in St. George's Channel, NEW BRITAIN. On the 12th, in revenge for the DOOLITTLE Raid on Tokyo, and Chinese assistance in getting the American airmen safely away, the Japanese launch a punitive expedition in China, eventually killing thousands of Chinese. In Burma Japanese troops cross the Salween River. On the 13th, other US forces relieve New Zealand troops holding FIJI. On the 14th, US troops in the mountains of north Luzon surrender to the Japanese, but some resort to guerrilla warfare. In Burma the Japanese reach the foothills of the Arakan Mountains near Shwegyin, leaving the British in control of only small areas of the country along the Indian frontier, the Burma Army having been completely shattered, although small groups (including STILWELL and his staff) make their way out of Japanese-held territory in the following months. The US 32nd Infantry Division arrives in Australia. On the 15th, the US 41st Infantry Division completes its movement to Australia. British headquarters for the Burma front is established at Imphal, in the mountainous eastern portion of Assam, in the extreme northeast of India. Australian troops in Papua begin fortifying Port Moresby. On the 16th, the first US service troops arrive in India, to be greeted with hostile demonstrations by Indian nationalists. On the 17th, US submarines sink two of their Japanese counterparts, *I-28* by *Tautog* (SS-199) off TRUK, in the CAROLINES, and *I-164* by *Triton* (SS-201) southeast of Kyushu. On the

18th, US/Philippine troops on Panay surrender to the Japanese, ending formal resistance in the Philippines, but some desert and form guerrilla bands that fight on until MacArthur returns in 30 months. US intelligence begins detecting evidence of an imminent Japanese attack on MIDWAY. On the 19th, in accordance with orders from NIMITZ, as of 20 May all air forces in the South Pacific are to be under the command of RAdm John S. McCain. On the 20th, the United States begins sending reinforcements to Midway and Alaska. Japanese submarine-borne aircraft reconnoiter Durban, in South Africa. The last organized British forces retire from Burma, as Japanese troops assume a defensive posture along the Indo-Burmese frontier, but some Chinese forces are still in retreat toward China, and the Japanese never overrun the rugged northern parts of the country, where Kachin tribesmen engage in a guerrilla war against them. The Burma Campaign has cost the Japanese only about 7,000 CASUALTIES, while British Empire forces have suffered 18,000–20,000 and the Chinese almost as many, with losses among the civilian population undetermined. On the 21st Japanese troops occupy SAMAR and Leyte, in the eastern Philippines. US RAdm Robert Theobold assumes command of all US and Canadian forces in Alaska, in anticipation of a Japanese offensive. On the 22nd, US aircraft begin airlifting small contingents of troops to Wau, in northeastern New Guinea, to support the local Australian forces. On the 23rd US fighter aircraft use a new airfield at Unmak, in the Aleutians, for the first time. On the 24th, Japanese submarine-borne reconnaissance aircraft scout Kodiak Island, south of Alaska. On the 25th Japanese submarine-borne reconnaissance aircraft scout KISKA, in the Aleutians. Japanese carriers sortie from Onimato, Hokkaido, for the Aleutians. On the 26th, Japanese submarine-borne reconnaissance aircraft again scout Kiska. U.S. Task Force 16 (*Enterprise* and *Hornet*) arrives at PEARL HARBOR. The Japanese First Air Fleet sorties from the INLAND SEA, bound for Midway, while the Midway occupation force sails from SAIPAN and GUAM. The US 37th Infantry Division sails from

SAN FRANCISCO for the Fiji Islands. In North Africa, Rommel attacks the Gazala Line. On the 27th, USS *Yorktown* arrives at Pearl Harbor and immediately goes into dry dock for emergency repairs. Japanese troop convoy and escorts leave Onimato bound for the Aleutians. On the 28th, the Main Body of the Japanese Combined Fleet sorties from the Inland Sea for Midway. US Task Force 16 puts to sea from Pearl Harbor, followed later in the day by TF 17, with *Yorktown* still under repair. US Army and Navy personnel from Efate begin to establish a base on ESPIRITU SANTO. On the 29th, a Japanese submarine-borne reconnaissance plane scouts Diego Suarez, in northern Madagascar. Japanese and US naval forces begin converging on Midway. On the 30th, a Japanese midget submarine torpedoes the British battleship *Ramilles* and a tanker at Diego Suarez. First US troops reach New Zealand. Last elements of Chinese New 38th Division cross the Chindwin River, into India. On the 31st, a squadron of old US battleships sorties from San Francisco to support the carriers in the Central Pacific. Japanese and US fleets converge on Midway. That night Japanese midget submarines penetrate SYDNEY harbor, sinking one old vessel and causing considerable panic.

June 1942

This was the month that the tide turned in favor of the Allies. The US victory at Midway crippled the Japanese carrier fleet. Meanwhile, planning went ahead for the first Allied amphibious operation, the attack on GUADALCANAL in the SOLOMON ISLANDS.

On the 1st, Japanese SUBMARINES begin taking station off Midway and the Hawaiian Islands. On the 2nd, US TFs 16 and 17 unite 350 miles northeast of MIDWAY. The Japanese Main Body nears Midway from the west and south. The Japanese ALEUTIANS task force is about 400 miles south of KISKA. On the 3rd, Japanese carriers RYUJO and JUNYO raid DUTCH HARBOR in the Aleutians. Battle of Midway begins: Japanese invasion force is attacked southeast of Midway by B-17s and PBY CA-

TALINAS, the latter sinking a tanker. TFs 16 and 17 keep station northeast of Midway as the Japanese Main Body approaches. On the 4th, the Battle of Midway: Japanese aircraft raid Midway, sparking a daylong action that costs Japan four carriers sunk and one US carrier, YORKTOWN, so badly damaged as to have to be towed. Japanese carrier aircraft bomb Dutch Harbor in the Aleutians. On the 5th, the Battle of Midway: B-17s attack damaged Japanese cruisers retiring from Midway with no effect. Damaged carrier *Yorktown* remains afloat and under tow. Admiral Isoroku YAMAMOTO orders the Combined Fleet to retire. Japanese submarines operating in Mozambique Strait. On the 6th, the Battle of Midway: US carrier aircraft attack damaged Japanese cruisers retiring from Midway, sinking *Mikuma* and severely damaging MOGAMI; USS *Yorktown*, still under tow, is TORPEDOED by Japanese submarine *I-168*, along with an escorting destroyer, which sinks. Japanese troops land on Kiska in the Aleutians. On the 7th, the Battle of Midway: *Yorktown* sinks, other US carriers retire from Midway. Japanese fleet retires from Midway. Japanese troops land on Attu in the Aleutians. In China, the Japanese continue their offensive in Chenkiang. On the 8th MACARTHUR again urges the Joint Chiefs of Staff to undertake an offensive in the Solomon Islands. On the 9th there is consternation in Imperial Navy circles at Tokyo as the scale of the Midway disaster becomes clear: While an attempt is make to keep it secret, details are soon circulating throughout the navy's officer corps, although the army is not informed until much later. On the 10th, as damaged US ships from Midway begin reaching PEARL HARBOR, major reinforcements to the US fleet enter the Pacific via the PANAMA CANAL (carrier WASP, a fast battleship, a heavy cruiser, and eight destroyers). Lead elements of the US 37th Infantry Division reach FIJI. Chinese fall back in Chenkiang. On the 11th, Japanese ships from the Midway operation begin returning to bases in the MARIANAS. US and Canadian aircraft begin attacks on Kiska. On the 12th, Japanese submarines withdraw from Mozambique Strait. MacArthur authorizes construction of air bases at MILNE BAY, New Guinea. On the 13th, nothing much happened. On the 14th, German merchant cruiser *Thor* begins operating in the Indian Ocean. Headquarters and first echelon of the First Marine Division debark in New Zealand. On the 15th, US and Australian Pacific Fleets reorganized into TF 1 (battleships) at SAN FRANCISCO, TF 8 (cruisers and destroyers) in the Aleutians, TF 11 (*Saratoga* and escorts), TF 16 (*Enterprise* group), and TF 17 (*Hornet* group) at Pearl Harbor, and TF 18 (*Wasp* group) temporarily at SAN DIEGO, plus TF 44 (cruisers and destroyers) in Australian waters. On the 16th, Japanese submarine-borne airplane reconnoiters Mauritius in the Indian Ocean. On the 17th, the Japanese deploy six submarines in the Aleutians. On the 18th Prime Minister CHURCHILL arrives in Washington for consultations with President ROOSEVELT. On the 19th, US submarine *S-27* is lost by grounding in the Aleutians. On the 20th, Japanese submarine I-26 shells Port Estevan, near VANCOUVER. On the 21st, Allied intelligence estimates Japanese land-based air forces in the Solomons, BISMARCKS, and northeastern New Guinea at 126 combat and reconnaissance aircraft, with a further 33 two-engined bombers at TIMOR believed capable of intervening in operations around the Solomon Sea. On the 22nd, the Japanese are estimated by Allied intelligence as having about two brigades at RABAUL, two companies on New Ireland, a battalion in the Admiralties, a regiment at TULAGI, and a few companies on BOUGAINVILLE, plus air base and service personnel. An estimated 1,000 SNLF troops are believed at LAE and Salamaua. MG Robert L. EICHELBERGER assigned to command the US I Corps in Australia. On the 23rd, Rommel's success in breaking the Gazala line leads to a drive on Egypt, disrupting Allied plans: 24 B-17s crossing Africa bound for China and some Air Corps officers in India are ordered to Egypt. On the 24th, Japanese submarine *I-25* shells Port Stevens, Oregon. Chief of Naval Operations KING suggests to the army's Chief of Staff MARSHALL that an amphibious offensive be undertaken in the Solomon Islands on 1 August, to be under navy control. On the 25th, in New Guinea

the Australians activate Maroubra Force (most of the Australian 39th Battalion, plus the Papua Light Infantry) to defend the KOKODA TRAIL across the OWEN STANLEYS. A small Australian force reaches Milne Bay, eastern Papua. US submarine *Nautilus* (SS-168) sinks the Japanese destroyer *Yamakaze* about 50 miles southeast of Tokyo Bay. On the 26th, Germans begin unrestricted submarine warfare off the east coast of the United States (limited attacks had begun earlier); the resulting carnage puts a further strain on US naval resources and makes it more difficult to divert ships to the Pacific. On the 27th, reactions to Japanese shellings by submarine of US and Canadian coastal installations in the past week bring calls for more naval resources to guard the west coast of North America. On the 28th, MacArthur unfolds his plans for undertaking an offensive in the New Guinea-Bismarcks-Solomons area. On the 29th, CNO KING suggests MacArthur control offensive operations in New Guinea and GHORMLEY in the Solomons, a compromise that is shortly adopted. US airfield construction engineers arrive at Milne Bay and begin work. On the 30th, Congress votes $42 billion (over $400 billion in 1997 dollars) for defense for the next fiscal year. Australian Kanga Force, in northeastern New Guinea, raids Salamaua.

July 1942

Not much combat took place in July, but there was a lot of activity. The Japanese were busy taking control of the vast areas they had conquered in the last six months. But there was vicious fighting in New Guinea, and some action in China. Meanwhile, the British were still hanging on by the Burma-India border and the Americans were massing forces for their invasion of GUADALCANAL in the SOLOMON ISLANDS.

On the 1st, Task Force 18 (WASP group) sorties from SAN DIEGO, bound for the South Pacific and escorting the Second Marines, to complete the First Marine Division already at New Zealand. On the 2nd, the US Joint Chiefs of Staff finally adopts a compromise plan to begin driving back the Japanese in the South Pacific: the navy to drive up the Solomon Islands while MACARTHUR recovers northeastern New Guinea and then drives on RABAUL. The JCS authorize "Operation Watchtower," the seizure of Guadalcanal. CHIANG names STILWELL commander of Chinese forces in India. On the 3rd, Japanese troops land on Guadalcanal from TULAGI and begin constructing an airfield (expecting to complete it by 15 August). On the 4th, Australian COASTWATCHERS report Japanese airfield construction on Guadalcanal. Japanese destroyer *Nehoni* is sunk in the ALEUTIANS by US submarine *Triton* (SS-201). The AVG (FLYING TIGERS) is inducted into the US Army Air Force, passing from the Chinese payroll to the American. On the 5th, aerial reconnaissance confirms Japanese airfield construction on Guadalcanal. US submarine *Growler* (SS-215) sinks Japanese destroyer *Arare* in the Aleutians, near KISKA. On the 6th, based on reconnaissance information, CNO KING orders "Operation Watchtower" (the capture of Guadalcanal) implemented immediately. On the 7th, US Task Forces 11 (*Saratoga*) and 16 (*Enterprise*) sortie from PEARL HARBOR to support the Guadalcanal operation. In Papua, Maroubra Force begins its march to Kokoda. On the 8th VAdm GHORMLEY and General MacArthur confer in MELBOURNE over details of "Operation Watchtower." On the 9th, the general plans for "Watchtower" take shape, as the First Marine Division practices amphibious landings in New Zealand, between which it helps load and unload ships due to local labor union problems. Advanced elements of the Australian Seventh Brigade sail from TOWNSVILLE for MILNE BAY. On the 10th, USAAF agrees to increase the allocation of aircraft to the Pacific Theater, thereby slowing its planned buildup in Britain. Allied aircraft land a small party near BUNA, northeastern Papua, to reconnoiter airfield sites. On the 11th, Japanese Imperial General Headquarters acknowledges the results of the Battle of MIDWAY (the destruction of Japanese carrier superiority) and cancels its orders of 5 May to capture Midway and other outlying islands. Second echelon of the First Marine Division debarks in New Zealand. On the 12th, the US Joint Chiefs of Staff proposes that, following the completion of an offensive up the Solomons to Rabaul, the logical course of action would be to proceed northward along the axis Truk-Guam-Saipan "and/or" through the Dutch East Indies to the Philippines. The first elements of the Australian Maroubra Force reach Kokoda, in central New Guinea, pressing on toward the north coast. On the 13th, Allied ground combat forces potentially available for offensive operations in the Pacific total more than four divisions: US 37th Infantry Division, in the FIJI ISLANDS; US Americal Division, on NEW CALEDONIA; Australian Seventh Division, in Australia; US First Marine Division (understrength), in New Zealand; Fourth New Zealand Brigade, in the Fijis; US Seventh Marine Regiment (of the First Marine Division), SAMOA; 147th Infantry Regiment, Tongatabu. Additional US and Australian divisions are available in Australia, but are either committed to the defense of the western and northern portions of the country or not yet trained. On the 14th, Japan's Admiral YAMAMOTO reorganizes the Combined Fleet as a consequence of Midway, among other things creating the Eighth Fleet, at Rabaul under VAdm Gunichi MIKAWA, to oversee operations in the Solomons and New Guinea. On the 15th, US submarine *Grunion* (SS-216) sinks three Japanese submarine chasers and a large merchant ship (c. 8,600 tons) in the Aleutians, beginning the interdiction of Japanese forces in the Aleutians. On the 16th, the Allies postpone the target date for the Guadalcanal operation from August 1 to August 7, as the convoy transporting the Seventh Marines is delayed. The Japanese push preparations for operations in New Guinea. On the 17th, massive amounts of manpower are committed to building up military strength in Alaska, and the west coast of North America in general, putting a considerable drain on resources for the Pacific Theater and slowing offensive operations farther west. MacArthur issues orders to occupy Buna, northeastern Papua. The Amphibious Force, South

Pacific Area, is established under RAdm Richmond Kelly TURNER. On the 18th, US planners see reconquest of Japanese bases in the Aleutians in 1943, it being politically impractical (due to public fears) to simply cut off the Japanese and leave them there. On the 19th, US naval forces available to support "Operation Watchtower" total three aircraft carriers, one fast battleship, nine heavy cruisers, two antiaircraft cruisers, 31 destroyers, six SUBMARINES, and numerous smaller vessels. Australian naval forces total two heavy cruisers and a light cruiser. At Rabaul, escorted by cruisers and destroyers, 1,800 Japanese troops take ship for GONA, to capture nearby Buna. On the 20th, all but one of six Japanese submarines in the Aleutians are withdrawn, having sunk only one ship in 34 days of patrolling. The German merchant cruiser *Thor* sinks a British freighter in the Indian Ocean. On the 21st, Japanese troops land at Gona, northeastern Papua, despite Allied air attacks, while Japanese warships shell Buna, and several nearby villages. On the 22nd, Japanese troops at Gona advance on Buna and Giruwa, and begin to move up the KOKODA TRAIL toward PORT MORESBY on the southern coast. Allied aircraft attack Japanese shipping off Buna and Gona, inflicting some damage. The First Marine Division sails from AUCKLAND, New Zealand, for the Fiji Islands. In North Africa, the British halt Rommel on the Alamein line. On the 23rd, Japanese ships at Buna and Gona depart for Rabaul. Japanese troops advancing up the Kokoda Trail clash with elements of the Australian Maroubra Force at Awala, which falls back. On the 24th, US submarines being operating in the KURILE ISLANDS. US carrier aircraft available to support "Operation Watchtower" total 230 (99 fighters, 102 dive bombers, and 39 torpedo bombers) aboard carriers *Saratoga, Enterprise,* and *Wasp.* This is the bulk of US carrier assets in the Pacific. In Papua, the outnumbered Australian Maroubra Force is again forced back by the Japanese. On the 25th the Japanese outflank the Maroubra Force in Papua, to come within six miles of Kokoda. On the 26th Japanese reinforcements land at Buna. Desperate

fighting near Kokoda in Papua; Australians fall back to Deniki. The First Marine Division arrives at Fiji for amphibious landing rehearsal; virtually all navy and Marine elements involved in "Operation Watchtower" are now concentrated. Allied land-based or amphibian combat and reconnaissance aircraft concentrated for "Watchtower" total 321 (196 US Navy or Marine, 95 US Army, and 30 Royal New Zealand Air Force), organized into TF 63 and deployed mostly in the NEW HEBRIDES and on New Caledonia. In addition, about 175 aircraft (c. 120 USAAF, 30 RAF, 20 RAAF) based in Australia and New Guinea are capable of supporting operations at Guadalcanal by air attacks on Rabaul and on surrounding Japanese-held areas. On the 27th Australian forces continue to hold Deniki, south of Kokoda in Papua. The First Marine Division continues amphibious exercises at Fiji. On the 28th, US RAdm Frank Jack FLETCHER, overall commander of the landing forces and covering forces in "Operation Watchtower," issues his operational orders, detailing the courses and duties of all forces for the invasion of Guadalcanal. US forces continue amphibious assault rehearsals at Fiji. In Papua, the Australians retake Kokoda in a counterattack. On the 29th, some Japanese reinforcements land at Buna, despite the loss of one of two transports to Allied air attack. In Papua the Japanese retake Kokoda from the Australians, who again fall back on Deniki. On the 30th, US submarine *Grunion* (SS-216) declared "over due" from a patrol in the Aleutians, probably lost to hazards of the sea. VAdm Gunichi Mikawa arrives at Rabaul to assume command of the Eighth Fleet. An additional Australian company reaches Deniki. On the 31st, TF 62 (the First Marine Division) sails from Fiji toward Guadalcanal, escorted by TF 61 (TFs 16, 17, and 18). Fast division of the British Far Eastern Fleet returns to COLOMBO from East Africa. US aircraft carrier ESSEX is launched at Newport News, Virginia, the first of an order of 26 to the same design. A Japanese convoy bound for Buna (New Guinea) with reinforcements is forced to return to Rabaul by intensive Allied air attack, although no vessels are lost. Another company reinforces the Australians at Deniki.

August 1942

The Allies begin their counterattack as US Marines land on Japanese-held GUADALCANAL Island in the Solomons. This begins a six-month campaign that will see heavy use of air, naval, and ground forces. Fighting continues in Burma and NEW GUINEA, but attention is focused on Guadalcanal.

On the 1st, Allied fleet units are moved around to mask the Guadalcanal operation: The US Pacific Fleet battleline (seven old battleships, 10 destroyers) is transferred from SAN FRANCISCO to PEARL HARBOR, while the British "Force A" (two carriers, one battleship, several cruisers and destroyers) sorties from COLOMBO toward the ANDAMANS. On the 2nd, the new US battleship SOUTH DAKOTA begins operating in the Pacific. On the 3rd, the Japanese Army begins the formation of three tank divisions in Manchuria. On the 4th, MG George C. KENNEY assumes command of Allied air forces in the southwest Pacific, under MACARTHUR. US destroyer *Tucker* is mined at ESPIRITU SANTO. On the 5th, blockade-running Japanese submarine *I-30* arrives at Lorient, France. Japanese superbattleship *Musashi* is commissioned. A Japanese convoy leaves Rabaul with reinforcements for BUNA. On the 6th, MacArthur brings all forces on New Guinea under control of the New Guinea Force, unifying command under Australian General Thomas BLAMEY. On the 7th, Watchtower begins as the First Marine Division is landed on Guadalcanal, TULAGI, and some smaller islands by TF 62, finding spotty resistance. A Japanese convoy bound for Buna with reinforcements from Rabaul is recalled. US warships bombard KISKA for the first time. On the 8th, Marines on Guadalcanal advance westward from their landing beaches, capture the unfinished Japanese airstrip. The first Japanese air raids on Guadalcanal occur. On the 9th, the Battle of SAVO ISLAND: Shortly after midnight seven Japanese cruisers and one destroyer smash an Allied squadron in the waters north of Guadalcanal, sinking four heavy cruisers (one Australian) and one destroyer with minor loss to themselves, the worst defeat in a surface naval action in US history. The Marines on Guadalcanal consolidate their hold on Henderson Field and occupy several small islands near Tulagi. Chinese forces defeat a Japanese offensive in Kiangsi Province. On the 10th, TF 62 pulls out of Guadalcanal waters. A US submarine sinks the Japanese heavy cruiser *Kako* as she retires from the Battle of Savo Island. Marines on Guadalcanal are put on two-thirds rations because many of the supply ships withdrew before they could be unloaded. The British Far Eastern Fleet returns to COLOMBO from its diversionary mission near the Andaman Islands. Maroubra Force (c. 500 men) counterattacks along the KOKODA TRAIL in Papua. On the 11th, the Japanese Combined Fleet begins to move from the ISLAND SEA to TRUK, in order to support operations at Guadalcanal. On the 12th, Japanese convoys land reinforcements at Buna, in northwestern New Guinea. US destroyer-transports land supplies on Guadalcanal. First US airplane lands at Henderson Field, Guadalcanal. Japanese troops reach Kokoda, the principal pass across the OWEN STANLEY MOUNTAINS on New Guinea. On the 13th, the Japanese seize the main pass in the Owen Stanley Mountains, on the Buna-Kokoda Trail in New Guinea, as the Australians fall back on Isurava. On the 14th, the Japanese complete the landing of 3,000 construction troops near GONA, in New Guinea. On the 15th, US transports land supplies at Guadalcanal, but Marine rations remain cut to conserve supplies. The last Japanese submarine in the ALEUTIANS, *I-6*, is withdrawn. On the 16th, heavily escorted, the Ichiki Detachment (c. 1,000 infantry) sails from Truk for Guadalcanal. Japanese convoys land reinforcements at Buna, in northwestern New Guinea. On the 17th, the Marine Second Raider Battalion, landed from SUBMARINES, begins two-day raid on MAKIN ISLAND in the GILBERTS: An unfortunate aftereffect of this raid is that the Japanese decide to heavily fortify the many small islands they occupy in the central Pacific, which comes back to haunt the Marines when they storm TARAWA in the following year. After nightfall the Japanese land the Ichiki Detachment on Guadalcanal, at Taivu and Kokumbona. On the 18th, Japanese troops land unnoticed at Basabura, New Guinea. On the 19th, Japanese convoys land reinforcements at Buna, in northwestern New Guinea. On Guadalcanal the Fifth Marines conducts a sweep eastward from the beachhead, skirmishing with the Ichiki Detachment. Japanese dispatch 1,500 troops from RABAUL in a convoy bound for Guadalcanal. Australian 21st Brigade (Seventh Division) arrives at PORT MORESBY by air, immediately begins marching to support the Maroubra Force. On the 20th, Henderson Field on Guadalcanal is completed; 31 Marine Corps fighters are landed from CVE LONG ISLAND. Japanese order landing of 1,500 troops at MILNE BAY, southeastern Papua. On the 21st, before dawn the Japanese Ichiki Detachment attacks the eastern face of the Guadalcanal beachhead, and is crushed by the defenders, who envelop their rear (Battle of the Tenaru River). US destroyers and fast transports deliver supplies to Guadalcanal, at the cost of one escorting destroyer. On New Guinea the Japanese land reinforcements at Basabura, while the Australian 18th Brigade reinforces Milne Bay. On the 22nd, Marines continue to consolidate their hold on Guadalcanal and Tulagi. US Army fighters begin landing at Henderson Field (five P-400s from NEW CALEDONIA. Off Savo Island, Japanese destroyer *Kawakaze* TORPEDOES US destroyer *Blue*, which is towed to Tulagi. On the 23rd, Japanese cruisers and destroyers shell NAURU. US recon aircraft spot a Japanese force intent on reinforcing Guadalcanal. That night Japanese destroyers shell the Marines on Guadalcanal. US destroyer *Blue* (damaged on the 22nd) is scuttled at Tulagi. The US 40th Infantry Division begins leaving San Francisco for HAWAII. On the 24th, the Battle of the EASTERN SOLOMONS: Aircraft from carrier *Saratoga* sink Japanese carrier RYUJO, while Japanese carrier aircraft damage *Enterprise*. Before she retires for repairs, *Enterprise* lands 11 dive bombers at Henderson Field. That night Japanese destroyers

shell Henderson Field, while Japanese SNLF troops land on the Goodenough Islands, off northeastern New Guinea. On the 25th, Marine and navy aircraft attack Japanese reinforcing squadrons near Guadalcanal. Japanese SNLF troops land at Milne Bay, in southeastern New Guinea, but are contained by Australian defenders. North of the Solomons, army B-17s sink the Japanese destroyer MUTSUKI with high-altitude bombing, the first and only time this tactic works against an underway warship. On the 26th, Japanese troops occupy Nauru Island against no resistance. Australian troops at Milne Bay stoutly resist the Japanese landing force. At Ramgarh, in India, the US Army opens a training center for Chinese troops. On the 27th, Japanese reinforcements are landed at Milne Bay, where Australian and US troops put up heavy resistance. On Guadalcanal, elements of the Fifth Marines make an overland and amphibious raid against Kokumbona On the 28th, Australian and American troops at Milne Bay beat off determined but ill-planned Japanese attacks. Off Guadalcanal, several Japanese destroyer transports are intercepted by US aircraft and sunk or damaged, but others manage to land reinforcements later that night. Battleship *Washington* and several destroyers enter the Pacific via the PANAMA CANAL. On the 29th, initial elements of the Japanese Kawaguchi Detachment are landed on Guadalcanal from destroyers and high-speed transports. A Japanese cruiser squadron attempts to support SNLF troops at Milne Bay with little success, but reinforcements are landed. The Australian 21st Brigade relieves the Maroubra Force confronting the Japanese on the Kokoda Trail in the Owen Stanley Mountains. Japanese battleship YAMATO arrives at TRUK as flagship to Adm YAMAMOTO; save for one day, when she changes her mooring, she will swing at anchor for the next seven months. On the 30th, Japanese aircraft sink a US destroyer transport attempting to reinforce Guadalcanal. US troops land on unoccupied Adak Island, in the Aleutians. Japanese make another attack on Milne Bay and press forward along the Kokoda Trail. On the 31st, US carrier *Saratoga* is torpedoed by Japanese submarine

I-26 west of the SANTA CRUZ ISLANDS. US destroyers and fast transports land reinforcements on Guadalcanal. The Japanese decide to abandon their landing at Milne Bay. In Egypt, Rommel begins the Battle of Alam Halfa.

September 1942

Most of the action was in the SOLOMON ISLANDS, particularly on, around, and above GUADALCANAL. American and Japanese forces struggled for control of the island, with the Allied troops getting the upper hand, as was also the case on NEW GUINEA. But more hard fighting was to come as the Japanese sent more ground, naval, and air forces into action.

On the 1st, "Tokyo Express" destroyers en route to resupply Guadalcanal are slightly damaged by US B-17s. US fast transports run supplies and reinforcements into Guadalcanal. Japanese press on along the KOKODA TRAIL in Papua. On the 2nd, Marines on Guadalcanal consolidate beachfront defenses, deploying the Third Defense Battalion. Japanese land reinforcements at Basabura, New Guinea, and press on along the Kokoda Trail. On the 3rd, the US Fifth Air Force is given responsibility for operations over the SOLOMONS and New Guinea. On the 4th, the "TOKYO EXPRESS" lands the last elements of the Kawaguchi Detachment on Guadalcanal. Off Lunga Point Japanese destroyers sink two US destroyer transports. Japanese aircraft also threaten US daytime supply efforts. Marine First Raider Battalion scouts SAVO ISLAND, which is free of Japanese. On the 5th, Japanese troops withdraw by sea from MILNE BAY, in eastern Papua-New Guinea. On the 6th, Japanese troops on New Guinea occupy Efogi on the Kokoda Trail, about 50 miles north of PORT MORESBY. On the 7th, US transports land supplies on Guadalcanal. In Egypt the Battle of Alam Halfa ends; Rommel's attempt to reach the Nile is frustrated. In Russia, the German Stalingrad offensive is virtually halted. On the 8th, on Guadalcanal, some 700 Raiders and Paramarines effect a landing at Tasimboko, in the rear of the Kawaguchi Detachment, disrupting Japanese preparations for an offensive, and then withdraw. Japanese air raids on Guadalcanal. That night a Japanese destroyer squadron shells TULAGI. In Papua, five Japanese battalions open a fresh attack on the Australians at Efogi on the Kokoda Trail, driving back or encircling the three defending battalions. On the 9th, major elements of the Japanese Combined Fleet sortie from TRUK to cover reinforcements to Guadalcanal from Rabaul and support an offensive planned for the 12th. That night Japanese Navy pilot Nobuo Fujita, in an airplane from the submarine I-25, drops incendiary bombs on a wooded area of Mt. Emily, Oregon, with little effect. The Australian 25th Brigade is rushed up the Kokoda Trail to support troops engaged near Efogi. On the 10th, British troops effect a landing on the west coast of Vichy French-controlled Madagascar. On the 11th, having failed to secure a lodgment at Milne Bay, the Japanese also withdraw from the nearby TROBRIAND ISLANDS. Australian forces disengage at Efogi, on the Kokoda Trail, and fall back to a position near Oribawiba. On the 12th, an Australian ship steams from DARWIN to reinforce GUERRILLAS on TIMOR. On Guadalcanal, the Battle of BLOODY RIDGE: The Kawaguchi Detachment attacks the southeastern face of the beachhead with heavy losses; on the 13th, after the Kawaguchi Detachment is beaten off, Raiders and Paramarines attempt to probe the Japanese positions but are driven back. On the 14th, the Japanese retire from Bloody Ridge on Guadalcanal, but make small attacks at other points on the Marine perimeter. The WASP and *Hornet* task forces join south of the Solomons to support a convoy carrying the Seventh Marines to Guadalcanal from ESPIRITU SANTO. KISKA is bombed for the first time, by US aircraft based on Adak. In Papua, despite reinforcements, the Australians fall back along the Kokoda Trail, taking up positions on the Imita Ridge, just 32 miles north of Port Moresby. On the 15th, US carrier *Wasp*, battleship NORTH CAROLINA, and destroyer *O'Brien* are TORPEDOED south of the Solomons ("Torpedo Alley"), the carrier sinking. US reinforcements reach Guadalcanal, where the

Marines extend their perimeter. Elements of the 126th Infantry (32nd Division). Are flown into Port Moresby, the first US infantry to arrive on New Guinea. On the 16th, the Third Marine Division is activated at SAN DIEGO. On New Guinea the Australians hold along Imita Ridge, which marks the high point of the Japanese offensive over the OWEN STANLEY MOUNTAINS. On the 17th, US reconnaissance parties in Papua begin looking for sites for airfields and possible trails around Japanese positions. An Australian ship lands reinforcements on TIMOR. On the 18th, the Seventh Marine Regiment is landed on Guadalcanal with a large quantity of ammunition, fuel, and other supplies. British troops land at Tamatave, on the east coast of Madagascar. On the 19th, Marine lines on Guadalcanal are reorganized and consolidated, while full rations are restored because of the improved supply situation. On the 20th, the Japanese Combined Fleet is ordered back to Truk. Japanese intelligence estimates that there are only 7,500 US troops on Guadalcanal; the actual figure is over 19,000. On the 21st, British Commonwealth forces undertake an offensive on the Arakan coast of Burma. On the 22nd, confronted by advancing British and Free French forces, Vichy French troops on Madagascar abandon the capital, Tananarive, and withdraw south. On the 23rd, British troops occupy Tananarive, capital of Madagascar. On Guadalcanal, the First Battalion, Seventh Marines (LTC Lewis "Chesty" PULLER), infiltrates through the Japanese lines and advances on Mt. Austen, deep in the interior. On the 24th, Puller's battalion engages Japanese troops on Mt. Austen. On the 25th, Marines on Guadalcanal are heavily engaged on Mt. Austen and in the Matanikau-Kokumbona area. Australian troops open an offensive along the Kokoda Trail. While attempting to run supplies to Dutch and Australian guerrillas on Timor, the Australian destroyer *Voyager* goes aground, to be scuttled when she is attacked by Japanese aircraft. On the 26th, Marines press limited offensives on Guadalcanal. Stealthily entering SINGAPORE harbor in three canoes, British raiders manage to sink or damage about 40,000 tons of shipping. On the

27th, frustrated in an attempt to attack across the Matanikau River on Guadalcanal, one attacking Marine battalion is sealifted to Point Cruz, where it is hoped this will enable the other two battalions to break across the Matanikau, but the Japanese counterattack in a double envelopment, pocketing the battalion, which nevertheless manages to cut its way back to the coast. Japanese aircraft bomb Guadalcanal. Japanese fall back from Oribawiba on the Kokoda Trail. On the 28th, the last regiment of the US 32nd Division arrives at Port Moresby. On the 29th, South African troops land at Tulear, in southwestern Madagascar. US troop strength on Guadalcanal is slightly over 19,000, with nearly 3,300 more on Tulagi; Japanese troop strength is about 12,000. On the 30th, the Japanese make their first air strike against Adak, in the ALEUTIANS.

October 1942

Again, most action in the Pacific was in the SOLOMONS, particularly at GUADALCANAL. In America and Japan, it was obvious that this was a crucial battle. The outcome was in doubt. A victory for Japan would prolong the war, an Allied victory would demonstrate to all that Japanese arms were no longer triumphant and that Japanese defeat was at hand.

On the 1st, US and Australian forces prepare a three-pronged offensive to throw the Japanese out of Papua. In Russia, the Germans are virtually halted in heavy fighting at Stalingrad. The Italian BLOCKADE RUNNER *Orseolo* departs Bordeaux for KOBE. On the 2nd, a US air raid on RABAUL damages the Japanese cruiser YUBARI and other shipping. Marines occupy Funafuti, in the ELLICE ISLANDS, southeast of the Japanese-held GILBERTS. On the 3rd, US troops occupy the Andreanof Islands, in the Aleutians. On the 4th, a US submarine sinks the Japanese merchantman *Setsuyo Maru* (c. 4,150 GRT) just east of Tokyo: Since the war began Japan has lost 156 merchant ships for a total of over 700,000 tons of shipping, a loss of about 11% of her prewar merchant tonnage. On the 5th,

US Navy and Marine aircraft raid Japanese shipping in the Shortland Islands (north end of Solomons chain). On the 6th, despite being urged to concentrate all available efforts on securing Guadalcanal, Admiral GHORMLEY orders the 147th Infantry to occupy NDENI in the SANTA CRUZ ISLANDS. On the 7th, the First Marine Division begins a new offensive on Guadalcanal to clear Japanese troops from within artillery range of Henderson Field, the Fifth Marines advancing westward along the coast against some resistance from the Japanese Fourth Infantry, while elements of the Second and the Seventh Marines advance across country farther inland against little opposition. On the 8th, heavy rains impede the Marine offensive on Guadalcanal, but some gains are made, and Japanese counterattack plans are captured. On the 9th, Japanese destroyers land elements of their Second Division on Guadalcanal. As the Fifth Marines hold Japanese attention on the Matanikau River, the Second and Seventh Marines advance westward and then northward, trapping the Japanese Fourth Infantry and inflicting heavy CASUALTIES before falling back eastward across the Matanikau in the afternoon. On the 10th, the Marines on Guadalcanal prepare to meet the expected Japanese counteroffensive. On the 11th, the Battle of CAPE ESPERANCE: US cruisers and destroyers ambush the "Tokyo Express" off Guadalcanal, sinking a heavy cruiser and destroyer, while losing one destroyer, in the first surface action in which US ships defeat their Japanese counterparts. On the 12th, US aircraft sink two Japanese destroyers, one near SAVO ISLAND and the other nearly 90 miles to the northwest. Japanese submarine begin operations in the Gulf of Oman, threatening Allied oil being shipped from the Persian Gulf. On the 13th, US destroyers shell Japanese positions on Guadalcanal during the day, while Japanese aircraft and artillery join battleships and other naval forces to shell Marine positions on Guadalcanal after dark. The 164th Infantry (Americal Division) lands on Guadalcanal, raising the garrison to over 23,000. On the 14th, Japanese cruisers shell Marine positions on Guadalcanal, temporarily knocking Henderson Field out of action, while covering the landing of reinforcements. Australians advancing along the KOKODA TRAIL encounter stiff Japanese resistance near Templeton's Crossing. On the 15th, before dawn, four Japanese transports have to beach on Guadalcanal under US air attack, but about 3,000 to 4,000 troops and tons of supplies are landed. That night Japanese cruisers again shell Henderson Field. US destroyer *Meredith* sunk by *Zuikaku* aircraft off San Cristobal. On the 16th, USAAF sink a Japanese destroyer near KISKA, off Alaska. US destroyer *O'Brien* (damaged by a TORPEDO on the 15th) founders off SAMOA, en route to PEARL HARBOR. Japanese submarines, ignoring plentiful Allied supply ships, concentrate on attacking warships (as was their custom) to increasing effect, and the area south of Guadalcanal is nicknamed "Torpedo Alley" because of all the Japanese subs lurking there. On the 17th, there is heavy fighting on the Kokoda Trail, at Eorea Creek in Papua. On the 18th, VAdm Ghormley is replaced by HALSEY as Allied commander in the South Pacific; Halsey immediately cancels ancillary operations, including the movement of the 147th Infantry to Santa Cruz, to concentrate all forces for the battle for Guadalcanal. A US submarine damages a Japanese "Tokyo Express" light cruiser off Guadalcanal. Heavy fighting continues at Eorea Creek, Papua. On the 19th, US aircraft damage a Japanese destroyer off Guadalcanal. On the 20th, the Australian 16th Brigade relieves the 25th in the fighting at Eorea Creek. Troops are flown over "the HUMP" to strengthen Chinese divisions training at Ramgarh, India. On the 21st, US destroyers land supplies on Guadalcanal, where the Marines beat off a limited Japanese tank attack across the Matanikau. On the 22nd, Australian troops land on Goodenough Island to find only about 300 Japanese troops. On the 23rd, Battle of Edson's Ridge begins: A fierce Japanese assault against the southern face of the Guadalcanal beachhead is stopped, while the Marines beat off an attack across the Matanikau. The US 43rd Infantry Division begins arriving in New Zealand. In North Africa, the Battle of El Alamein begins. On the 24th, US carriers *Enterprise* and *Hornet* rendezvous northeast of ESPIRITU SANTO to block a move by a Japanese carrier force known to be to the northwest. On Guadalcanal, the Battle of Edson's Ridge ends, as fierce Japanese attacks are thrown back. Japanese destroyers evacuate the 250 surviving troops on Goodenough Island. On the 25th, Battle of Lunga Point, Guadalcanal: Japanese cruisers and destroyers engaged in daylight bombardment of Henderson Field, chase two US destroyers and sink two small US harbor craft, before being attacked by Marine and army aircraft, suffering one destroyer lost and damage to other vessels. Battle of the Santa Cruz Islands: US and Japanese carriers search for each other northeast of the Solomons. After nightfall a Japanese attempt to flank the Marine Matanikau line is defeated. On the 26th, Battle of the Santa Cruz Islands: USS *Hornet* is put out of action, eventually to be sunk by Japanese destroyers, while Japanese carriers are heavily damaged, in an action that frustrates a Japanese attempt to use carrier aviation to support efforts on Guadalcanal. Elements of the US 43rd Infantry Division arrive at Espiritu Santo. On Guadalcanal the Marines begin preparing for a new offensive westward toward Kokumbona. At Espiritu Santo the liner *President Coolidge* sinks after hitting a mine: Only two of the thousands of troops aboard are killed, but all their equipment is lost. On the 27th, Britain's General WAVELL and American-Chinese commander STILWELL agree that US and Chinese troops will begin an offensive in northern Burma shortly in order to reopen the BURMA ROAD, which will be linked to a new "Ledo Road." On the 28th, Japanese "Tokyo Express" uses its destroyer transports to land troops on Guadalcanal from Kokumbona to Cape Esperance. On the 29th, the ALCAN HIGHWAY is opened, the only motor road to Alaska, freeing shipping for service in the Western Pacific. On Guadalcanal the Japanese withdraw toward Koli Point and Kokumbona, disengaging from the Marines' front. On the 30th, the Marines on Guadalcanal prepare to assume the offensive. On the 31st, America announces that 800,000 US troops are now serving overseas. After nightfall, the Marines on Guadalcanal begin establishing outposts west of the Matanikau River.

November 1942

The campaign for GUADALCANAL reached a climax, with the Japanese getting the worst of it. A stalemate on New Guinea favored the Allies. Germany suffered major setbacks in Russia (Stalingrad) and Africa (Alamein), which demoralized the Japanese, who were expecting the Germans to keep advancing east to link up with Japanese forces in India. From this point on, the War in the Pacific was all downhill for the Japanese.

On the 1st, on Guadalcanal, supported by heavy naval, air, and artillery bombardments, the Marines attack across the Matanikau River. On the 2nd, the Australian 25th Brigade captures Kokoda and its airfield from the Japanese. On Guadalcanal, the Marine offensive gains ground against heavy resistance, while after nightfall the "Tokyo Express" lands about 1,500 troops and supplies at Tetere, about 15 miles east of the main beachhead on Guadalcanal. On the 3rd, Marines on Guadalcanal clear Point Cruz of Japanese troops. In North Africa, Rommel begins pulling out of the Alamein line, conceding victory to the British. On the 4th, additional Marines arrive on Guadalcanal, where the offensive is halted to regroup and consolidate gains. In Papua, the 16th Australian Brigade begins an attack on Oivi, on the KOKODA TRAIL. On the 5th, the 164th Infantry makes a limited attack on Guadalcanal to support the Seventh Marines, threatened by a Japanese concentration on their flank. In Papua, Australian troops on the Kokoda Trail continue their attack on Oivi, while also moving against Gorari. Vichy French troops on Madagascar surrender to the British at Fort Dauphin in southeastern Madagascar. On the 6th, the Seventh Marines resumes the offensive, supported by the 164th Infantry. MacArthur establishes his headquarters at PORT MORESBY. Heavy fighting on the Kokoda Trail. On the 7th, while the Japanese land reinforcements on Guadalcanal, Marines and army troops press them back from Koli Point. On the 8th, the Japanese land reinforcements on Guadalcanal, but east of Koli Point the Marines and army troops make an amphibious "end run" around them, pocketing them at the mouth of Gavaga Creek. A large US reinforcement convoy sails from NOUMEA for Guadalcanal, supported by a heavy escort (*Enterprise*, two battleships, eight cruisers, 23 destroyers). Operation Torch begins as US and British forces land in northwestern Africa, an operation that has caused the Pacific to be somewhat starved of amphibious shipping and, to a lesser extent, warships. On the 9th, the Japanese Second Fleet sorties from TRUK to support a planned major naval offensive at Guadalcanal on November 12–13. On Guadalcanal, the Marines and army troops encircle some Japanese forces. On the 10th, the Japanese land reinforcements on Guadalcanal, where US troops begin reduction of the Gavaga pocket. On the Kokoda Trial, in Papua, the Australians eject the Japanese from Oivi. On the 11th, United States lands reinforcements on Guadalcanal, but halts offensive moves in anticipation of a Japanese assault. Japanese aircraft raid Henderson Field. West of Australia, Royal Indian Navy minesweeper *Bengal*, escorting a tanker, beats off an attack by two Japanese auxiliary cruisers, sinking one. In Papua, elements of the US 32nd Division are firmly established at Pongani, having flown in over the last few days. On the 12th, the Australians take Gorari, on the Kokoda Trail in Papua, while the US 32nd Division begins moving overland toward the BUNA-GONA area. US reinforcements land on Guadalcanal, where Marines and army troops eliminate the Gavaga pocket. Japanese aircraft raid Henderson Field. Protracted Naval Battle of Guadalcanal begins: Shortly before midnight Japanese cruisers and destroyers inflict a severe defeat on US Navy, which loses several cruisers and destroyers, plus several more damaged, at a cost to the Japanese of one destroyer sunk, plus severe damage to battleship *Hiei* and several destroyers. On the 13th, Naval Battle of Guadalcanal continues: US aircraft further damage Japanese battleship *Hiei*, which has to be scuttled, while a US cruiser sinks a disabled Jap-

anese destroyer and a Japanese submarine sinks CLAA *Juneau*, on which the five SULLIVAN BROTHERS perish. In Papua, the Australians drive the Japanese across the Kumusi River. On the 14th, Naval Battle of Guadalcanal continues. In "The Slot" *Enterprise* and Marine aircraft from Henderson Field batter Japanese ships, sinking a cruiser and two transports, and damaging several others. Japanese transports beach on Guadalcanal in order to land reinforcements. During the night, large Japanese forces (one battleship, two heavy cruisers, two light cruisers, and eight destroyers) try to bombard Henderson Field, to be ambushed around midnight by US battleships *Washington* and SOUTH DAKOTA with four destroyers. *South Dakota* is badly damaged, but the Japanese lose a destroyer and battleship *Kirishima* is reduced to a burning wreck, in the first fleet action by US battleships against enemy warships since the Spanish-American War (1898). On the 15th, unable to provide air cover for a tow, the Japanese scuttle *Kirishima* off Guadalcanal. On the 16th, in Papua, the US 32nd and Australian Seventh Divisions close on Buna Gona, and Sanananda, against increasing resistance. On the 17th, the Japanese commit aircraft and land reinforcement to support their troops at Buna and Gona, in Papua. On the 18th, an army infantry battalion advances west of the Matanikau River, on Guadalcanal; although resistance is slight, the troops make slow progress, being green and unacclimated. In Papua, US and Australian troops begin encountering Japanese outposts around Buna and Gona. On the 19th, on Guadalcanal the drive westward is strengthened with seasoned troops, but resistance remains slight; during the night Japanese troops move up. At Buna and Gona, US and Australian troops come up against the Japanese main line of resistance and are soon bogged down. The Soviet Stalingrad offensive begins, heralding a major turning point of the war in Russia, and comes as a blow to Japanese morale, as they had expected eventual assistance from the Germans once the Nazis had conquered southern Russia and driven on into the Persian Gulf area. On the 20th, on Guadalcanal the Japanese launch a surprise attack at the two battalions west of the Matanikau River, but US troops hold with air and artillery support, as reinforcements begin moving toward them. On the 21st, on Guadalcanal, US Army troops of the 164th and 182nd Infantry Regiments make some gains against the Japanese but are held by skillfully constructed defenses. In Papua, US and Australian troops make unsuccessful attacks on Japanese positions at Sanananda, near Buna, which is holding back an attack by the US 32nd Division. On the 22nd, army troops again make small gains against the Japanese on Guadalcanal, while the Eighth Marines prepares to attack through their lines. In Papua, the Japanese hold US and Australian troops before Buna and Gona, making skillful counterattacks. On the 23rd, the Eighth Marines attempts to attack through the 164th Infantry, on Guadalcanal, but meets with no success; offensive operations are called off. In Papua, US and Australian troops make no gains against the Japanese at Buna-Gona, suffering heavy losses. On the 24th, US aircraft sink a Japanese destroyer attempting to reinforce Guadalcanal. Allied troops continue unsuccessful attacks at Buna-Gona in Papua. On the 25th, the fighting at Buna-Gona eases, as both sides exchange artillery fire and engage in patrolling. On the 26th, cruisers HNMS JACOB VAN HEEMSKERCK and HMAS ADELAIDE intercept a German BLOCKADE RUNNER bound for France from the NETHERLANDS EAST INDIES. In Papua, Allied troops make some gains at Buna-Gona. On the 27th, US and Australian troops cease offensive efforts at Buna-Gona, to regroup. US troops on Guadalcanal also regroup, giving the Japanese some respite. On the 28th, Teheran Conference begins, as FDR, Prime Minister CHURCHILL, and General Secretary Stalin discuss policy and STRATEGY for three days, while celebrating their victories at Stalingrad, El Alamein, Northwest Africa, and Guadalcanal: After years of Axis success, the tide has turned. On the 29th, Japanese troop strength on Guadalcanal peaks, 30,000 men (about equal to US strength), then rapidly declines to about 20,000 in the next two months due to lack of food and medicine,

while US strength rises to 40,000 well-supplied troops in December. Allied aircraft prevent four Japanese destroyers from landing reinforcements at Gona. On the 30th, Battle of Tassafaronga: In a night action, eight Japanese destroyers attempting to reinforce Guadalcanal get the better of five U.S. cruisers and six destroyers trying to stop them, sinking one heavy cruiser and damaging three others while losing one destroyer, but are forced to break off their mission. German merchant cruiser *Thor* destroyed in a fire while docked at Yokohama. At Teheran, the "Big Three" reach tentative agreements on strategy. In Papua, Australian and US troops resume the offensive at Buna and Gona, making small gains.

December 1942

Fighting continued on GUADALCANAL, NEW GUINEA, and in Burma. Superior Allied resources had began to make their presence felt on the battlefield. Japan began adopting a defensive posture, falling back from one defeat after another, a trend that will continue until the end of the war.

On the 1st, LG EICHELBERGER is put in command of the BUNA-GONA operation in Papua, where the Australians capture GONA village. On Guadalcanal, staff officers from the US Americal Division assume control of supply functions from Marine Corps personnel. In Burma, having completed a long refit of their forces, the Japanese begin moving into offensive positions. On the 2nd, in Papua, despite Allied air interference, the Japanese land reinforcements about 12 miles behind their forces in the BUNA area, and beat off another American attack. Eichelberger relieves the commanders of the 32nd Division and several of its subordinate units. The Italian BLOCKADE RUNNER *Orseolo* arrives at KOBE from Bordeaux. On the 3rd, Japanese destroyers land reinforcements on Guadalcanal, where the First Marine Division is preparing to be withdrawn. US aerial reconnaissance discovers that the Japanese are building an airstrip on MUNDA, in the central Solomons. On the 4th, Carlson's Marine Raiders complete a month-long raid through Japanese-controlled portions of Guadalcanal, having killed 400 of the enemy, for the loss of only 17 dead. In Papua, Eichelberger reorganizes US forces before Buna. On the 5th, Australian troops at Gona put pressure on Japanese troops at nearby Gona Mission, while other Australian troops move westward to prevent the arrival of reinforcements, and US troops make a major attack against Buna, which, although only partially successful, does isolate the village. On the 6th, US aircraft bomb Munda to slow Japanese work on a new airbase. In Papua, US forces employ "time on target" artillery tactics for the first time, against Buna. On the 7th, Japanese destroyers attempting to land reinforcements on Guadalcanal are beaten off by a combination of aircraft and PT-BOATS, among them *PT-109*, skippered by John F. KENNEDY. On the 8th, the 132nd Infantry (Americal Division) lands on Guadalcanal, where the division assumes full control of all staff duties. US aircraft turn back a Japanese attempt to land more troops to support the Buna area, in northeastern Papua, while Japanese troops withdrawing from Gona sustain heavy losses. On the 9th, in Papua, Australian troops complete capture of the Gona area in hand-to-hand fighting. On Guadalcanal, MG Alexander A. VANDEGRIFT and the First Marine Division are officially relieved and MG Alexander PATCH (USA) assumes command. The Fifth Marines boards transports and sails away that afternoon, with the balance of the division to follow over the next few days: Guadalcanal was the first major Marine operation of the Pacific War and one of the longest, lasting four months. British prepare an offensive from India into Arakan, the westernmost coastal province of Burma. On the 10th, Australian troops land at Oro Bay, New Guinea, near Buna, into which Japanese aircraft manage to airdrop supplies. US aircraft bomb Munda. British offensive into Arakan gets underway, moving between the sea and the mountains. On the 11th, Japanese destroyers land reinforcements on Guadalcanal, but lose one of their number to PT-boat attacks. US aircraft bomb Munda. The overstrength 14th Indian Division advances slowly in

Arakan region of Burma. On the 12th, Japanese destroyer *Teruzuki* is sunk by US *PT-45* northeast of KOLOMBANGARA. On Guadalcanal, Japanese infiltrators destroy a P-39 and a fuel truck, while the Second Marine Division begins taking up positions west of the Matanikau. On the 13th, Australian troops prepare to make an "end run" around Buna, which is subjected to a heavy artillery barrage: That night the surviving Japanese defenders (c. 100 men) evacuate the village and escape across the Giruwa River. US aircraft bomb Munda. The British advance cautiously in Arakan region of Burma. On the 14th, Australian reinforcements land at Oro Bay, near Buna. Japanese destroyers land 800 troops at the Mambare River, near Buna, which Allied troops occupy after discovering it has been abandoned by the enemy. The British advance cautiously in Arakan region of Burma; rather than resist, weaker Japanese forces begin to retire. On the 15th, on Guadalcanal, US reconnaissance patrols scout Mt. Austen. US aircraft bomb Munda. The British advance cautiously in Arakan region of Burma, even though the Japanese are beginning to fall back. On the 16th, the British offensive on the Arakan coast takes Maungdaw only to discover that it has been abandoned by the Japanese. In Papua, Eichelberger takes direct command of the 32nd Division, after two commanders in succession have been wounded in action. On the 17th, US Americal Division attacks toward Mt. Austen on Guadalcanal. Elements of US 25th Division land on Guadalcanal. US aircraft bomb Munda. On the 18th, Japanese cruiser TENRYU is sunk by US submarine *Albacore* (SS-218) near the BISMARCKS. In Papua, US and Australian troops begin a major assault on Sanananda, while elsewhere Allied forces make limited but important gains. On the 19th, the CASUALTY rate from malaria among US troops on Guadalcanal reaches a statistical rate of 972 cases in every thousand men per year, and it is even worse for the Japanese, who have lost most of their troops on the island to disease and malnutrition. The British advance in Arakan, Burma, but the outnumbered Japanese begin to develop a major defensive position in front of Akyab, more than a hundred miles to their rear, giving themselves time to bring up reinforcements. In Papua, the Allied assault on Sanananda moves forward. On the 20th, the new US policy of using SUBMARINES to mine the waters off major Japanese ports finds its first victim, as an 8,000-ton Japanese transport goes down off Tokyo. In Papua, Allied forces make important gains in the Sanananda area. On the 21st, Australians make major gains in the Sanananda area. On Guadalcanal, the Americal Division's attack on Mt. Austen falters. US aircraft bomb MUNDA. On the 22nd, Australian and American troops overcome the last Japanese resistance in the Buna area, in northeastern Papua, but are brought to a halt on the Sanananda Front. On Guadalcanal the Americal Division's Mt. Austen offensive continues to run into problems. On the 23rd, the US 41st Infantry Division ships out from Australia for New Guinea. On Guadalcanal, the Americal Division's attack on Mt. Austen is temporarily halted. On the 24th, on Guadalcanal, the Americal Division encounters the main Japanese defenses, the "Gifu," in the Mt. Austen area. On the 25th, US aircraft continue their incessant bombing of Munda Island, slowing Japanese efforts to build a base there. On Guadalcanal the Americal Division can make no gains against the Gifu position. On the 26th, the Japanese 20th Division movement from Korea to New Guinea is underway. The Americal Division makes limited gains against the Gifu on Guadalcanal. On the 27th, lead elements of the US 41st Infantry Division land at PORT MORESBY, Papua-New Guinea, while to the northeast Allied forces continue to make gains in the Buna area but are held before Sanananda. Heavy fighting around the Gifu, on Guadalcanal. On the 28th despite constant US bombing, Japanese begin using new airstrip on Munda, in the Central Solomons. In Papua, Japanese forces in the Buna area begin withdrawing to Giruwa. On the 29th, the US destroyer-minesweeper *Wasmuth* sinks off the ALEUTIANS, after a gale causes two of her depth charges to detonate, causing extensive damage. In Papua, Japanese forces near Buna Mission are cut off by US troops. On the 30th, on Guadalcanal,

the Americal Division rotates fresh units into the line and prepares for a renewed attack on the Gifu. On the 31st, Japan's Prime Minister TOJO decides to abandon Guadalcanal. US aircraft carrier ESSEX is commissioned.

January 1943

Fighting entered its final phase on GUADALCANAL, as the United States set out to clear the island of Japanese forces. As a foretaste of things to come, the Japanese put up a desperate resistance, fighting to the death. Even so, the Japanese high command had already decided to abandon Guadalcanal. The aircraft and ship losses were too great to support ground combat that far south in the SOLOMONS. Allied ground forces also succeeded in clearing out Japanese forces in eastern Papua, New Guinea. In Burma, the British offensive stalled.

On the 1st, Japanese destroyers run supplies into Guadalcanal, despite attempts by US aircraft and PT-BOATS to interfere. Additional elements of the US 25th Infantry Division land on Guadalcanal, where the Americal Division resumes its assault on Mt. Austen. In Papua, US and Australian forces make steady if slow gains in the BUNA Mission area. On the 2nd, the US I Corps captures Buna Mission in Papua: Fighting for Buna has cost the Japanese about 1,400 troops, mostly killed, and the Australians and Americans 2,817 CASUALTIES, 620 of whom were killed. US forces on Guadalcanal (Second Marine, Americal, and 25th Infantry Divisions) are reorganized as XIV Corps under MG PATCH. The British continue their advance in the Arakan region of Burma, but Japanese resistance stiffens. On the 3rd, the Americal Division succeeds in partially surrounding the Japanese Gifu position on Mt. Austen, Guadalcanal. US and Australian forces mop up in the Buna area of Papua. On the 4th, Japanese Imperial General Headquarters issues orders for the evacuation of forces from Guadalcanal to New Georgia. Additional elements of the Second Marine Division and the last echelon of the 25th Infantry Division land on Guadalcanal. A US-Australian cruiser-destroyer force shells MUNDA, suffering slight damage in a Japanese air attack, during which the USS *Helena* introduces the use of proximity-fuzed antiaircraft ammunition for the first time in the Pacific. On the 5th, on Guadalcanal, US Army engineers complete a truck bridge across the Matanikau River, greatly easing supply problems. In Arakan, Burma, a stalemate begins to develop, as the Japanese hold the British before Akyab. On the 6th, on Guadalcanal, General Patch lays plans for a major offensive that will drive the Japanese from the island. In Papua, American and Australian troops mass for a final assault on Sanananda. On the 7th, US strength on Guadalcanal reaches 50,000 men (Marine, army, and navy); Japanese strength is less than 25,000. On Guadalcanal, small detachments of soldiers and Marines begin to be sealifted to strategic locations along the coast in the rear of the Japanese, to establish "block" positions should the enemy attempt to retreat. A stalemate develops in Arakan, Burma, where the British will take heavy losses in several major attacks over the next weeks. On the 8th, British occupation forces turn control of Madagascar over to the Free French. Allied aircraft attack Japanese transports landing 4,000 troops at LAE, in northeastern NEW GUINEA. In Papua, US troops make limited attacks to prepare for a major assault on Sanananda. On the 9th, an Australian brigade is airlifted to a jungle airstrip at Wau, near Salamaua in northeastern New Guinea, where it begins to build a major base. On the 10th, Japanese destroyers bringing supplies to Guadalcanal are ambushed by US PT-boats, which sink two of the Japanese ships with slight damage to themselves. US forces on Guadalcanal begin a general offensive to eliminate Japanese forces. Henderson Field now usable in all weather due to a paved runway. Limited Allied attacks continue in the Sanananda area of Papua. On the 11th, the US 35th Infantry succeeds in encircling the Gifu, but Japanese resistance remains fierce. In northeastern New Guinea, the Australian Kanga Force undertakes a three-day raid against Japanese-held Mubo, inflicting considerable damage. On the 12th, losing the destroyer *Worden* to the hazards of the sea, US

troops land on unoccupied Amchitka in the ALEUTIANS and commence building an airstrip. On Guadalcanal US forces encounter heavy fighting at the Gifu and Galloping Horse positions. On the 13th, US submarine *Guardfish* TORPEDOES a Japanese patrol vessel off New Ireland. On Guadalcanal, the US 25th Division, in a daring attack, breaks Japanese resistance and occupies the Galloping Horse area, clearing the entire western flank of the American beachhead, while the Second Marine Division attacks westward along the coast. On the 14th, Japanese destroyers bringing about 600 men and supplies to Guadalcanal are attacked by US aircraft and PT-boats with little effect, while on the island the US offensive is temporarily held to limited gains. Casablanca Conference opens, as President ROOSEVELT and Prime Minister CHURCHILL begin 10 days of meetings, enunciating the "unconditional surrender" policy and outlining future Allied global STRATEGY, with Chinese leader CHIANG present. On the 15th, Japanese superbattleship *Musashi* arrives at TRUK. On Guadalcanal and in the Sanananda area of Papua, Allied forces make only limited gains. On the 16th, the Second Marine Division cautiously clears Japanese troops out of "the Ravine" on Guadalcanal, while other US forces make only limited gains. Near Sanananda, US and Australian forces clear outlying areas of Japanese holdouts. On the 17th, XIV Corps on Guadalcanal forms the CAM (Combined Army-Marine) Division, which attacks westward along the coast. In Papua, Allied forces begin a major offensive against Sanananda. On the 18th, a US cruiser-destroyer force bombards Japanese-held Attu, in the Aleutians. On Guadalcanal, having gained only 1,500 yards in five days of fighting, the Second Marine Division halts its offensive against the last Japanese stronghold in the interior, while the CAM Division offensive gains ground. On the northeast coast of Papua, Sanananda, falls to Allied troops, who press the Japanese westward. On the 19th, US destroyers shell Japanese positions on Guadalcanal, while the CAM Division presses westward. Fierce Japanese resistance on the Sanananda front, in Papua. In Burma, the British attempt a renewed attack at Japanese forces before Akyab, with little success. On the 20th, on Guadalcanal, the US 25th Infantry Division tightens its hold on the Gifu, as Japanese resistance weakens all along the front. In Papua, Japanese resistance on the Sanananda front collapses. On the 21st, US troops on Guadalcanal pause to resupply. In Papua, Allied troops mop up Japanese remnants in the Sanananda area. On the 22nd on Guadalcanal, the US 25th Infantry Division tightens its hold on the Gifu, despite a Japanese BANZAI attack after nightfall, while the CAM Division renews its offensive westward along the coast, making surprising gains. In Papua the last organized Japanese resistance ends in the Buna-Gona-Sanananda area: Of 16,000 Japanese troops committed to the area at least 7,000 have been killed or died of disease (the Allies buried that many) and many others wounded or seriously ill, while Allied casualties (about two-thirds Australian) are 8,500, with some 2,000 dead from all causes. On the 23rd, US cruisers and destroyers, supported by aircraft from the carrier *Saratoga*, bombard Japanese positions on Guadalcanal, in support of the CAM Division, which overruns Kokumbona. Casablanca Conference of Allied leaders agrees on strong offensive in Burma, a "dual" approach to the Philippines, from the central and southwest Pacific, and "unconditional surrender" for Axis. On the 24th, the Japanese on Attu begin a series of air raids against Amchitka, in the Aleutians. The US offensive on Guadalcanal continues to gain ground. On the 25th, the Japanese are in full retreat on Guadalcanal, closely pursued by US forces. In Papua the US 41st Division relieves the 32nd and the Seventh Australian Divisions. The Italian BLOCKADE RUNNER *Orseolo* departs KOBE for Bordeaux. On the 26th, the 25th Infantry Division is pulled out of the line on Guadalcanal, as the CAM Division sweeps the Japanese westward. On the 27th, a US submarine sinks the Japanese merchantman *Shoan Maru* (c. 5,600 GRT) : Since PEARL HARBOR Japan has lost 273 merchant ships, for a total of about 1.3 million GRT, roughly 20% of her prewar merchant tonnage. On the 28th, the Japanese make a final at-

tempt to reach PORT MORESBY by an overland offensive, attacking the Australian Kanga Force at Wau, northeastern New Guinea. On Guadalcanal, the CAM Division advances across the Nueha River. On the 29th, Japanese submarine *I-1* is sunk off Cape Esperance by two New Zealand corvettes, which salvage important cryptographic equipment, greatly assisting American experts who have been cracking Japanese codes since before the war began. At Wau in northeastern New Guinea the Australian Kanga Force holds the Japanese to limited gains. On the 30th, the United States lands reinforcements and supplies on Guadalcanal. Air-Sea Battle of the Rennell Islands: Japanese aircraft sink heavy cruiser *Chicago*. In northeastern New Guinea, the Australian Kanga Force, reinforced by air with the Australian 17th Brigade, decisively defeats attacking Japanese forces. On the 31st, the CAM Division on Guadalcanal advances to the Bonegi River, against light resistance. The Japanese 20th Division completes its concentration at WEWAK in New Guinea. At Wau, in northeast New Guinea, Australian troops mop up Japanese forces.

February 1943

The Japanese abandoned GUADALCANAL, successfully evacuating almost 13,000 troops by sea. American troops took the Russell Islands and both sides continued to reinforce their positions in NEW GUINEA. Stalemate developed in Burma. Most of 1943 will see low-level activity in the SOLOMONS and New Guinea, as both sides rebuild their forces for larger campaigns in 1944.

On the 1st, US Marine regiment lands on the west coast of Guadalcanal, in an attempt to outflank the defending Japanese. Twenty Japanese destroyers sortie from RABAUL to evacuate remaining troops on Guadalcanal, and are virtually uninjured in a running fight with US aircraft and PT-BOATS, but lose one of their number to a mine, while sinking three PT-boats. On the 2nd, 19 Japanese destroyers evacuate thousands of Japanese troops from Guadalcanal before dawn, while the US

CAM Division captures Cape Tassafaronga. In the NETHERLANDS EAST INDIES the last Australian GUERRILLAS on TIMOR (operating there since 8 December 1941) are withdrawn by sea. On the 3rd, US battleship *Massachusetts* begins operating in the Pacific. Heavy skirmishing between Allied and Japanese troops along the Indo-Burmese frontier. In northeastern New Guinea, the Australian Kanga Force counterattacks from Wau, driving the Japanese back on Mubo. On the 4th, the United States lands reinforcements and supplies on Guadalcanal. Japanese light cruiser *Isuzu* and 22 destroyers sortie from Rabaul to evacuate troops from Guadalcanal, suffering serious damage from US aircraft. Heavily escorted, the battle-hardened Australian Ninth Division sails home from Suez after two years of service in North Africa. On the 5th, Japanese light cruiser *Isuzu* and escorts evacuate thousands of Japanese troops from Guadalcanal, where the US CAM Division continues to advance along the northern coast. On the 6th, additional US reinforcements arrive on Guadalcanal, while the CAM Division reaches the Umasani River. In northeastern New Guinea, the Japanese lose 24 aircraft in an attack on the Wau airfield, while no Allied aircraft are lost. On the 7th, 18 Japanese destroyers sortie from Rabaul to evacuate troops from Guadalcanal, suffering some damage from US air attacks. On Guadalcanal, US troops advance on both the northern and the northwestern coasts. Admiral HALSEY authorizes "Operation Cleanslate," the occupation of the Russell Islands. CHIANG-KAI SHEK commits China to a new offensive in Burma. On the 8th, 18 Japanese destroyers evacuate more Japanese troops from Guadalcanal; altogether the Imperial Navy manages to pull nearly 12,000 army and about a thousand navy personnel out of Guadalcanal. In Burma Orde WINGATE's 77th Indian Brigade, the CHINDITS, undertakes its first operation against the Japanese: Over the next few weeks its seven columns will spread out over central Burma inflicting great destruction on bridges, roads, and isolated Japanese installations before the survivors return to India. On the 9th, no organized Japanese forces remain on Guadalcanal, as US troops advancing along the northwestern and northern coasts make contact at CAPE ESPERANCE. CNO KING "invites" CINCPAC NIMITZ to consider capturing the GILBERT ISLANDS. On the 10th, Guadalcanal is secure, at the cost of 1,600 US Army and Marine Corps troops killed and 4,245 wounded, plus thousands of CASUALTIES from disease, while Japan lost at least 14,800 killed, 9,000 dead of disease, and about a thousand as PRISONERS, many of them Korean labor troops. While the naval battles off Guadalcanal and in the general area were far more numerous and, for the Allies at least, caused far more casualties than the fighting on the island, it was the land battle that decided the issue. Guadalcanal was a sobering experience for the Japanese, who had never been so decisively defeated on land. Some Japanese leaders realized that Guadalcanal would be the pattern in the future. Bill Howell leaves his billet (navy job) at the Brooklyn Armed Guard Center and reports to the Philadelphia Navy Yard to join the crew of the new light carrier *Monterey*. He is the first enlisted member of the crew to report to the ship, which already has two officers: Commander Silvius Gazze, the air officer, and Commander R. M. Oliver, the executive officer. *Monterey* (CVL-26) was originally laid down as a light cruiser (*Dayton*, CL-78) on December 29, 1941, at the New York Shipbuilding Company's yard in Camden, New Jersey. But President ROOSEVELT pressured the navy to convert nine incomplete light cruisers to light carriers and this was done. So on February 23, 1943, the converted cruiser was launched as a light carrier. Bill Howell's ship carried about a third as many aircraft (33) as the standard ESSEX CLASS carrier, and displaced a little less than a half as much at full load, about 14,000 tons to 32,000. She was a cramped ship, but an effective one. Crew size was 1,569 men, including 159 officers. On the 11th, at NOUMEA, preparations for "Operation Cleanslate," the occupation of the Russell Islands, proceed. On Guadalcanal, Marine and army troops mop up Japanese stragglers. Heavy skirmishing between Allied and Japanese troops along the Indo-Burmese frontier. On the 12th, at Noumea, a small naval task force is organized to support "Operation Cleanslate," four destroyers, four destroyer-transports, five minesweepers, and 12 LSTS, plus some smaller vessels. MACARTHUR issues plans for operations against NEW BRITAIN, New Ireland, and northeastern New Guinea. On the 13th, the Japanese 41st Division arrives at WEWAK, New Guinea, from China. On the 14th, at Noumea, elements of the US 43rd Infantry Division are embarked for Guadalcanal. On the 15th, Admiral Halsey consolidates his aircraft resources under a joint Aircraft, Solomons Command (AIRSOLS). On the 16th, US fighter aircraft begin using the new airstrip on Amchitka in the Aleutians, ending Japanese air strikes against the island. About two-thirds of the US 43rd Infantry Division lands at Koli Point, Guadalcanal, to prepare for the occupation of the Russell Islands. On the 17th, the 55th Indian Brigade attempts to capture a Japanese strongpoint on the Arakan front but is unsuccessful, and the stalemate in western Burma continues. After nightfall the New Zealand corvette *Moa* lands a small American reconnaissance team on Banika, the easternmost large island in the Russell group. On the 18th, US cruisers and destroyers shell Japanese positions on Attu, the Aleutians, for the first time. The New Zealand corvette *Moa* lands an American reconnaissance team on Pavuvu, the largest of the Russell Islands: Allied intelligence concludes that the Japanese have evacuated the island group. On the 19th, US cruisers and destroyers again shell Japanese positions on Attu. The naval forces under MacArthur are designated the Seventh Fleet. On the 20th, US submarine *Albacore* (SS-218) sinks the Japanese destroyer *Oshio* near the ADMIRALTY ISLANDS. Continued stalemate in the Arakan region of Burma. On the 21st, the first RCT of the US 43rd Infantry Division lands in the Russell Islands, the unopposed operation being treated as a large-scale training exercise. After nightfall the Royal Indian Navy lands raiding parties on the Burmese coast southwest of Akyab; they successfully raid Japanese positions before pulling out. On the 22nd, the United States commissions the battleship IOWA, the most powerful in the world, at the Brooklyn Navy Yard. On the 23rd, on Guadalcanal, the army and Marines are still coping with Japanese stragglers, most of whom refuse to surrender and fight on as snipers. On the 24th, US troops in the Russell Islands begin construction of an airfield. Heavy skirmishing between Allied and Japanese troops along the Indo-Burmese frontier; the Japanese decide to withdraw to the Burmese side of the mountains because of their tenuous logistical situation. On the 25th, the US Navy establishes a motor torpedo boat base in the Russell Islands. On the 26th, US construction projects in the Russell Islands include an airfield, three landing craft bases and repair facilities, and a base for the First Marine Division: Pavuvu becomes the division's "home" when it is not engaged in operations. Off the Burma coast light forces of the Royal Indian Navy engage a small Japanese troop convoy, sinking one vessel and damaging another. On the 27th, the veteran Ninth Australian Division arrives at SYDNEY from the Middle East, after 23 days at sea. On the 28th, escorted by cruisers and destroyers, eight Japanese transports (c. 7,000 troops) sail from Rabaul bound for LAE, in eastern New Guinea. In northern Burma the Japanese begin operations to eject small British garrisons supporting Kachin guerrillas.

March 1943

The fighting swung back and forth in Burma, as it would until nearly the end of the war. Superior Allied airpower began to assert itself in the SOLOMONS and NEW GUINEA. Japanese forces were isolated in the ALEUTIANS, where the Allies planned to clear them out in the next few months, diverting tremendous naval and air resources and slowing down buildups in the rest of the Pacific. In China, the Japanese launched a major offensive. Heavy fighting would continue in China until the end of the war.

On the 1st, aided by unusually hazy weather in the BISMARCK SEA, a Japanese troop convoy bound from Rabaul for LAE, on Huon Gulf, northeastern New Guinea, is undetected by US aerial reconnaissance. In northern Burma, British garrisons and

Kachin GUERRILLAS fall back. On the 2nd, the Battle of the Bismarck Sea: A Japanese convoy bound for Lae is attacked by USAAF aircraft, losing one transport. On the 3rd, the Battle of the Bismarck Sea continues: Off Huon Gulf, New Guinea, the Japanese convoy is attacked by over 350 US and Australian aircraft, plus light surface forces, with the loss of all transports and four destroyers, at a cost of 21 Allied aircraft. On the 4th, the Battle of the Bismarck Sea ends: In a three-day running fight, Allied air and naval forces have sunk eight Japanese transports and four destroyers, while shooting down many enemy aircraft and killing thousands of Japanese troops. In an official report to army units throughout the South and southwest Pacific, a senior Japanese staff officer criticizes American combat methods on GUADALCANAL, concluding that the Americans have many admirable qualities ("they are quite brave"), but many faults as well ("infantry forces do not engage in night attacks"), and that leadership is poor ("officers of middle rank and below possess little tactical ability"). On the 5th, the Japanese 54th Division arrives at JAVA from Japan. After nightfall, US destroyers shell Japanese positions at Vila and MUNDA, in the central Solomons. On the 6th, in the Solomon Islands US cruisers and destroyers ambush and sink two Japanese destroyers attempting to reinforce Vila, while Japanese aircraft raid the Russell Islands. Stalemate in Arakan region of Burma, but the Japanese begin preparing for an offensive. On the 7th, US and Japanese forces conduct regular naval and air patrols throughout the Solomons. The Japanese refuse a German request to join the war against Russia. On the 8th, US commanders assess the lessons of Guadalcanal; the Marines call for more firepower and special training. In China, the Japanese begin an attack across the Yangtze River between Ichang and Yoyang. On the 9th, British CHINDIT commandos in Burma advance to the Irrawaddy River. In northeastern New Guinea, Japanese aircraft conduct a major raid on Wau. On the 10th the Chinese resist the new Japanese offensive. On the 11th, the "American Volunteer Group" (FLYING TIGERS) in China is

redesignated the 14th Air Force, under Claire CHENNAULT. Adm YAMAMOTO transfers his flag to battleship *Musashi*, at TRUK. On the 12th, senior US military officials open a "Pacific Military Conference" in Washington to discuss plans. In Burma, the Japanese begin a counteroffensive against the British. On the 13th, in the Arakan region of Burma, the Japanese 55th Division undertakes an attack against the British 14th Indian Division. In northeastern New Guinea, the Australian Kanga Force presses the Japanese back to the vicinity of Guadagasel. On the 14th, there is heavy fighting in Arakan region of Burma; Japanese forces begin an arduous crossing of "impassable" mountains, which will bring them into the British rear. On the 15th, US Navy forces in the central Pacific are designated the Fifth Fleet. In New Guinea, the Japanese offer no resistance as the US 162nd Infantry occupies positions at the mouth of the Mambare River. On the 16th, US destroyers shell Vila in the central Solomons. In the Arakan region of Burma, the 55th Indian Brigade is outflanked by the Japanese, who attack across "impassable" mountains. On the 17th, in the Arakan the 71st Indian Brigade assists 55th in retiring from its outflanked positions, exposing the entire British left. On the 18th, in central Burma, the "Chindits," having already cut several rail lines, make several raids across the Irrawaddy River, while the British Sixth Brigade makes a final attempt to break the Japanese lines before Akyab; their failure, combined with increased Japanese infiltration and encirclement attacks, forces the British to begin a retreat. On the 19th, US naval forces in MACARTHUR's Southwest Pacific Theater are designated the Seventh Fleet. On the 20th, US submarine *Pollack* (SS-180) sinks Japanese merchant cruiser *Bangkok Maru* in the MARSHALL ISLANDS. On the 21st, the British rush reinforcements to their forces in the Arakan, Burma. On the 22nd, the Japanese, alarmed at their deteriorating position in the Aleutians, decide to be more aggressive with their naval patrols off the Alaskan coast, to facilitate supply of their forces there. US SUBMARINES *Grampus* (SS-207) and *Amberjack* (SS-219) are declared overdue and presumed lost in the southwest Pacific. On the 23rd, the British retreat from the Arakan region of Burma shows signs of turning into a rout, as the Japanese turn or infiltrate every position the British attempt to hold. On the 24th, the US Joint Chiefs of Staff approves a plan to retake Attu. On the 25th, US naval aircraft raid NAURU in the central Pacific, north of the SANTA CRUZ ISLANDS. On the 26th, the Battle of the KOMANDORSKI ISLANDS: In the last daylight naval shoot-out in history without interference from aircraft or submarines, US cruisers and destroyers barely beat off a stronger Japanese squadron (two cruisers and four destroyers versus four cruisers and four destroyers, with a transport) attempting to reinforce Japanese garrisons in the ALEUTIANS. On the 27th, Orde WINGATE's Chindits are ordered back to their Indian base after nearly two months of rampaging in the Japanese rear area in central Burma, where they made over 70 cuts in Japanese rail lines. On the 28th, the Japanese squadron defeated at the Komandorski Islands returns to PARAMUSHIRO, where its commander is sacked. In Washington, the Joint Chiefs of Staff directs MacArthur and HALSEY to occupy the TROBRIAND ISLANDS. On the 29th, Japanese gather hundreds of aircraft in bases throughout the northern Solomons and RABAUL, in order to launch decisive attacks on the growing Allied base on Guadalcanal. On the 30th, a US submarine sinks the Japanese cargo ship *Kurohime Maru* (c. 4,700 GRT) off MANUS, north of New Guinea: Since PEARL HARBOR the Japanese merchant marine has lost 330 ships, for a total of 1.5 million GRT, a full quarter million tons since late January, as US submarines begin to operate with greater effectiveness. On the 31st, MacKechnie Force, a task force of the US 41st Division, moves by water to secure the mouth of the Waria River and an airstrip at Dona.

April 1943

The Japanese launched a massive air offensive from RABAUL against Allied bases in New Guinea and the Solomons, which didn't do them much good.

Their offensive in China was more successful, and in Burma they continued to push British forces back toward India. Allied forces were massed in Alaska to push out Japanese bases in the ALEUTIAN ISLANDS.

On the 1st, Japanese aircraft attack the Russell Islands. On the 2nd, although TORPEDOED on the previous day by a British submarine, the Italian BLOCKADE RUNNER *Orseolo* reaches Bordeaux from KOBE. On the 3rd, elements of MacKechnie Force land at Morobe, northeastern New Guinea, near the Waria River, without opposition and begin to establish a beachhead. On the 4th, the Fourth Marine Division is activated at SAN DIEGO, using cadres drawn from the Third Marine Division. On the 5th, the British Sixth Brigade headquarters is overrun by advancing Japanese in Arakan region of Burma, who occupy the Mayu Peninsula. On the 6th, US submarine *Trout* (SS-202) begins laying MINES near Sarawak, BORNEO, late at night. On the 7th, nearly 190 Japanese aircraft from Rabaul (including aircraft landed from four carriers) attack Allied shipping at GUADALCANAL and TULAGI, sinking the US destroyer *Aaron Ward*, the New Zealand corvette *Moa*, and a tanker, damaging other vessels as well, while losing 21 of their number to the Allies, who lose seven aircraft. On the 8th, the Japanese press on with their offensive in the Arakan region of Burma. This, coupled with their recent success in the air over the Solomons and their continued hold on bases in the Aleutians, gives some Japanese cause to believe that the war is going their way. On the 9th, Japanese destroyer *Isonami* is sunk southeast of Celebes by the US submarine *Tautog* (SS-199). On the 10th, the US submarine *Triton* (SS-201) is reported as overdue and presumed lost near the ADMIRALTY ISLANDS; she is the twelfth US submarine lost in the war. On the 11th, Japanese aircraft from Rabaul raid Oro Bay, near BUNA in northeastern New Guinea, burning two merchant ships. On the 12th, Japanese aircraft from Rabaul make a major raid on PORT MORESBY in southern New Guinea, but cause little damage. On the 13th, nothing much happened. On the 14th, Japanese aircraft from Rabaul make a major raid on MILNE BAY, sinking two transports. Japanese submarine *Ro-102* is sunk by *PT-150* and *PT-152*, off LAE in eastern New Guinea. On the 15th, US convoys begin converging on Attu, in the Aleutians. The United States completes a major airfield on Banika, Russell Islands, which, with a second strip still under construction, will allow more effective use of American air power in the central and northern Solomons. On the 16th, American codebreakers discover that Japanese Navy commander-in-chief YAMAMOTO will be flying to visit bases in the Solomons: Acting on this information, senior US officers decide to attempt to shoot down Yamamoto's airplane, thereby depriving Japan of one of her most capable admirals, a risky decision since the Japanese may conclude that their codes are being broken, and change them, leaving the Allies unable to read secret Japanese transmissions, for months, at least. On the 17th, the British situation in the Arakan region of Burma is becoming hopeless, as nothing seems able to stop the Japanese, not even their increasingly difficult logistical situation. On the 18th, US P-38 fighters intercept two airplanes carrying Japanese Admiral Isoruku Yamamoto and his staff, shooting down both and killing the admiral, at Buin, BOUGAINVILLE. On the 19th, the US submarine *Scorpion* (SS-278) lays mines in Japanese waters, the beginning of an operation that will eventually prove more lethal than torpedoes or aircraft bombs in shutting down Japanese shipping. On the 20th, US submarine *Runner* lays mines off HONG KONG. On the 21st, the US submarine *Stingray* lays mines in Chinese waters. On the 22nd, Australians complain to their Allies that "Germany First" policy is putting a severe strain on their depleted resources. On the 23rd, US submarine *Seawolf* (SS-197) sinks a Japanese patrol vessel in the Yellow Sea. In northeastern New Guinea, on the Mubo front where the fighting has developed into a stalemate, the Australian Kanga Force is relieved by the Australian Third Division. On the 24th, the US Seventh Infantry Division sails from SAN FRANCISCO for Alaska, for the final assault on Japanese bases in the Aleutians. On the 25th, the US Navy launches the submarine *Dace*

(SS-247) at Groton, Connecticut: Since PEARL HARBOR 67 new American SUBMARINES have slid down the ways. While on leave, Petty Officer Bill Howell, knowing he is about to ship out for a long, long tour in the Pacific, gets married to his high school sweetheart Catherine. It will be a year and a half and several naval battles before Bill and Catherine see each other again. On the 26th, US cruisers and destroyers shell Japanese positions on Attu in the Aleutians. Off Mauritius the German submarine *U-180* transfers Indian radical nationalist leader Subhas Chandra BOSE to the Japanese submarine *I-29*. On the 27th, Chinese resistance to the Japanese advance in Huphe Province begins to stiffen. The Japanese are attacking with scant resources and depend on marginal Chinese performance to keep the offensive going. On the 28th, US submarine *Scamp* (SS-277) sinks Japanese seaplane carrier *Kamikawa Maru* off New Ireland. On the 29th, the US submarine *Gato* (SS-212) lands COASTWATCHERS on Teop, in the Solomon Islands, and evacuates missionaries. On the 30th, the submarine *Gudgeon* (SS-211) lands supplies and personnel on Panay, in the Philippines, to assist Filipino GUERRILLAS. On the 31st, after heavy fighting, Chinese troops halt a Japanese offensive in Huphe Province, ending a threat to Chungking.

May 1943

The most significant event of the Pacific War for this month occurred in the Atlantic. By May of 1943, it had become clear to the Allies that the Battle of the Atlantic had been won. From this point on, German U-boat activity declined markedly, making greater naval and shipping resources available for the Pacific. The large, increasing concentration of Allied antisubmarine forces in the North Atlantic caused the Germans to redeploy their U-boats, and they began stationing some in the Indian Ocean, where they operated in conjunction with several Italian SUBMARINES from bases in the Dutch East Indies. Meanwhile, fighting continued in New Guinea and the Solomons, and Japan launched another offensive in China, while the United States and Canada finally invaded Japanese-held islands in the ALEUTIANS.

On the 1st, the escort carrier *Coral Sea* (CVE-57, later renamed *Anzio*) is launched at VANCOUVER: Since PEARL HARBOR the US Navy has commissioned or launched 31 fleet carriers, light carriers, and escort carriers. On the 2nd, DARWIN, Australia, is bombed by Japanese aircraft based at Salamaua, New Guinea. On the 3rd, Chief of Staff MARSHALL (USA) informs General STILWELL that the United States plans to base B-29s in China for attacks on Japanese-held territory and Japan itself. On the 4th, the US Seventh Division sets sail for Attu from Cold Bay, Alaska. On the 5th, US submarines sink three small Japanese freighters, for a total of less than 7,000 GRT, but this brings the loss of Japanese merchant shipping to over 1.7 million tons since Pearl Harbor. On the 6th, Japanese hopes of a German advance into the Middle East (to meet Japanese troops moving through India) are dashed as the Allies launch their final offensive in North Africa. Within a week, all Axis troops in North Africa surrender. This will be followed by an invasion of Sicily and, before the end of the year, the surrender of Italy, one of the charter members of "the Axis." On the 7th, US destroyers mine the Blackett Strait, under cover of a cruiser-destroyer raid into VELLA GULF. In the Arakan, Burma, British forces once again withdraw, as the Japanese continue their infiltration and encirclement tactics. On the 8th, three Japanese destroyers are lost on a US minefield in Blackett Strait, near New Georgia. The Japanese battleship YAMATO puts to sea for Japan from TRUK, her first movement out of anchorage since 29 August 1942. The US Seventh Infantry Division arrives off Attu, but cannot land due to poor weather. On the 9th, foul weather continues to delay a US landing on Attu. On the 10th, Japanese intelligence informs Attu that a US assault is not imminent, and the garrison there lets down its guard, while the American invasion force rides out bad weather just over the horizon and a destroyer and a destroyer-minelayer are damaged in a collision. On the 11th, the US Seventh Division commences landings on two

beaches on Attu in the Aleutians. The Japanese battleship *Yamato* arrives at KURE for a refit. Italian submarine *Cappellini* departs La Pallice, France, on a BLOCKADE RUNNING mission to Japan. On the 12th, US cruisers and destroyers shell Vila and MUNDA and mine KULA GULF in the central SOLOMONS. In the Arakan, having driven the British back roughly to the line of the front in mid-December, the Japanese halt their advance. The Trident Conference begins in Washington, as ROOSEVELT, CHURCHILL, and the Combined Chiefs of Staff confer on STRATEGY. On the 13th, Axis troops in Tunisia, North Africa, surrender. There is very heavy fighting on Attu, as US troops are unable to advance out of their beachheads. On the 14th, Japanese minesweepers clear Kula Gulf. On the 15th, heavy fighting continues on Attu in the Aleutians, as the Japanese defenders fight to the death. Chinese troops assigned to a planned Allied offensive in Burma are diverted to the Ichang area, in the light of a Japanese offensive across the Yangtze. On the 16th, Italian submarine *Tazzoli* departs La Pallice, France, on a blockade running mission to Japan and is never heard from again (probably sunk by British aircraft in the Bay of Biscay later that day). On the 17th, Japanese forces on Attu surprisingly abandon their forward positions and withdraw into the rugged interior of the island. On the 18th, the two US beachheads on Attu link up, as additional troops land on the island. On the 19th, US troops on Attu reestablish contact with Japanese forces, and heavy fighting resumes. On the 20th, the US Joint Chiefs of Staff approves a plan for the defeat of Japan, to include simultaneous offensives through the GILBERT and MARSHALL ISLANDS, the BISMARCK ARCHIPELAGO, and Burma, preparatory to further advances, and ultimately an air and sea blockade of Japan and possible invasion. In Burma, the main body of the CHINDITS manages to return to British lines, after a three-month operation during which it lost about a third of its strength; stragglers continue coming in through early June. On the 21st, the Japanese battleship *Musashi* and a strong escort arrive at Tokyo Bay, for a possible sortie to the Aleutians, but the mission is abandoned. The Japanese open a new offensive across the Yangtze River in China. On the 22nd, the US destroyer *Caperton* (DD-650) is launched at the Bath Iron Works, Maine: Since Pearl Harbor the US Navy has lost 27 destroyers but has added nearly 160; in the same period the Imperial Navy has lost 35 destroyers and has added barely a dozen. On the 23rd, Italian submarine *Giuliani* departs La Pallice, France, on a blockade running mission to Japan. Heavy fighting continues on Attu. On the 24th, Churchill and Roosevelt agree to increase aid to China and adopt an "island hopping" strategy in the Pacific. On the 25th, elements of the Japanese Fifth Fleet (Northern Pacific) are at sea for a possible rescue of the Attu garrison. In Washington, the Trident Conference ends, having decided, among other things, to undertake a landing in France in the spring of 1944, and a major increase in Allied air supply to China. On the 26th, Japanese commence covert submarine evacuation of troops on KISKA, in the Aleutians. Elements of the Japanese Fifth Fleet go to sea for a possible rescue of the Attu garrison, which is heavily engaged with US troops. On the 27th, US forces on Attu begin building an airfield, as heavy fighting continues. On the 28th, aircraft drop surrender leaflets on remaining Japanese troops of the Attu Island garrison, with no perceptible effect. On the 29th, the Japanese abandon plans to evacuate the Attu garrison, which undertakes a major BANZAI attack in recognition of its desperate position. On the 30th, organized Japanese resistance on Attu ends. On the 31st, Chinese troops in Hopen Province halt a Japanese drive on Chungking, but the Japanese offensive gains ground elsewhere.

June 1943

The fighting in NEW GUINEA and the SOLOMONS heated up as MACARTHUR executed Operation CARTWHEEL. This plan landed US, Australian, and New Zealand troops on lightly defended islands and places, where air bases could be built. In this way, aircraft will be used to surround and neutralize the huge Japanese base at RABAUL, isolating it and

its 100,000-man garrison, which will slowly starve, as Japanese ships carrying fuel, ammunition, and food will be unable to get through. By the end of the war Rabaul will be a de facto POW camp for its malnourished garrison. Cartwheel was initially planned as a preliminary maneuver before invading Rabaul. But it was soon decided that the huge base could simply be left surrounded and bypassed. Many other Japanese island garrisons were bypassed in a similar fashion throughout the Pacific. This saved many lives, both Allied and Japanese. But the Cartwheel operation was the first, and largest, of these bypass operations.

On the 1st, the Japanese Army reorganizes the Imperial Guard, forming a second division at Tokyo, which is designated the "First," while the original Imperial Guards Division, in Sumatra since early 1942, is redesignated the "Second." US forces in the Aleutians and California begin training for the invasion of KISKA. On the 2nd, Pope Pius XII denounces air bombardment, which does not in any way delay US plans to deploy the B-29 bomber in the Pacific in 1944. On the 3rd, the Japanese offensive in China succeeds after hard campaigning, as they take control of all shipping on the upper Yangtze in western Hopeh Province, after which they will begin a voluntary withdrawal. On the 4th, the German auxiliary cruiser *Michel* sails from BATAVIA, JAVA, to raid Allied shipping in the Indian Ocean. On the 5th, the Air Battle of the Russell Islands: Over 80 Japanese aircraft from Rabaul tangle with over 100 US aircraft from Henderson (GUADALCANAL) and other fields, losing 24 aircraft to seven American ones. On the 6th, the Japanese assess their situation on Kiska, Aleutians, conclude that it is hopeless, and decide that evacuation is the only option. On the 7th, the Japanese resume air attacks on Guadalcanal, losing 23 aircraft to the Allies' nine. On the 8th, the Japanese battleship *Mutsu* is destroyed by an internal explosion while lying in HIROSHIMA harbor. In the ALEUTIANS, the United States completes an airfield on Attu, while Kiska is subjected to air and naval bombardment whenever the weather will allow. On the 9th, on convoy duty off FREMANTLE, an Australian minesweeper is sunk in a collision with a merchant ship. On the 10th, US submarine *Trigger* (SS-237) TORPEDOES the Japanese carrier *Hiyo* off Japan, but the carrier does not sink. The Japanese submarine *I-24* is sunk off Kiska by a US patrol boat. On the 11th, Japanese submarine *I-9* is sunk off Kiska by US destroyer *Frazier*. On the 12th Japan's Prime Minister TOJO grapples with the problem of how to present Japan's declining fortunes to the rest of the national leadership. It is decided to simply make an announcement to the Diet (parliament): So far in 1943, Japan has had to abandon Guadalcanal, the Aleutians, and an offensive in China, finding success only in Burma, and there only as a matter of throwing back a British offensive. Allied aircraft intercept a large Japanese raid on Guadalcanal, shooting down 31 enemy planes while losing six. On the 13th, Japanese forces in China complete their withdrawal from western Hopeh, returning to their lines of 21 May. On the 14th, Tojo meets with Indian nationalist leader Subhas Chandra BOSE and agrees to allow him to set up an Indian government and raise an Indian army, to assist Japanese forces in Burma in the "liberation" of India. On the 15th, the German merchant cruiser *Michel* sinks a 7,700–ton merchant ship west of Australia. The Italian submarine *Barbarigo* departs La Pallice, France, with critical materials and electronic equipment for Japan, and is never heard from again. On the 16th, 120 Japanese aircraft from Rabaul and New Georgia attack Allied ships in the vicinity of Guadalcanal, damaging three ships, two of which must be beached, but losing nearly 100 of their number to 104 intercepting Allied aircraft, who suffer only six planes lost. On the 17th, Italian BLOCKADE-RUNNING submarine *Giuliani* reaches the East Indies, bringing critical materials and documents for the Japanese. West of Australia, the German merchant cruiser *Michel* sinks a 9,900–ton tanker. In China, LG STILWELL briefs CHIANG KAI-SHEK on the Trident Conference. Bill Howell's skipper, Captain Lester T. Hundt, assumes command of CVL *Monterey* as the ship is commissioned into active service. Bill works with the executive officer, keeping track of personnel records and things like the Plan of the Day (the daily schedule) and legal paperwork (Captain's Mast and any courts-martial that came around). It is an important job, for Yeoman Howell handles the paperwork on everything of importance that happens on the ship. On the 18th, the 43rd Infantry Division issues its final orders for operations on Rendova and New Georgia, as part of Cartwheel. The Italian submarine *Torelli* departs La Pallice, France, on a blockade-running mission to Japan. On the 19th, Allied preparations for Cartwheel concluding, convoys begin sailing for New Georgia. On the 20th, the Japanese undertake a series of sharp attacks against the Australian 17th Brigade, on the Mubo-Lababia Ridge front in northwestern New Guinea, making little headway. The blockade-running Italian submarine *Capellini* enters the Indian Ocean, bound for the Japanese-held NETHERLANDS EAST INDIES. Gen. Claude Auchinleck succeeds Gen. Archibald WAVELL as British commander-in-chief India. On the 21st, Operation Cartwheel begins, as fast transports covertly land the US Marine Fourth Raider Battalion at Segi Point, New Georgia, to deny it to the enemy: For the next year, virtually all operations in the Solomons, BISMARCKS, and northeastern New Guinea will be related to Operation Cartwheel. On the 22nd, fast transports covertly land two companies of the US 43rd Division, and some engineers, at Segi Point, New Georgia, to reinforce the Marines, reconnoiter, and select a site for an airfield, while the US 112th Cavalry RCT (dismounted) begins landing on Woodlark Island, off eastern New Guinea, which is unoccupied by the Japanese. The Japanese submarine *I-7* is damaged off Kiska by US destroyer *Monaghan*, and puts in to Kiska harbor. On the 23rd, the US 158th RCT begins landing on Kirwina Island, in the TROBRIANDS, between Woodlark and New Guinea, which is unoccupied by the Japanese. The Japanese submarine *Ro-103* sinks two transports off Guadalcanal. In New Guinea, Japanese pressure on the

Australian 17th Brigade on the Mubo-Lababia Front eases. On the 24th, in a radio broadcast from Tokyo, Indian nationalist Subhas Chandra Bose calls for the Indian people to rise up in armed revolt against British rule, an appeal that is largely unheeded. On the 25th, US submariners finally convince the navy that there is something wrong with American torpedoes, and the brass agree to correct the problem, while authorizing temporary fixes: This, and more effective tactics, results in US subs beginning to make big inroads against the Japanese merchant marine. On the 26th the MacKechnie Force (elements of the 162nd RCT plus some Australian forces) begins moving from Morobe in preparation for an amphibious assault at Nassau Bay. On the 26th, with the sinking of three cargo ships, Japanese merchant marine losses reach approximately two million GRT. On the 27th, the US First Cavalry Division (dismounted, organized as an infantry division) sails from SAN FRANCISCO for Australia. On New Georgia, the Fourth Marine Raiders is sealifted from Segi Point to the Lambeti Plantation. On the 28th, the Marine Raiders on New Georgia begin a cross-country reconnaissance from the Lambeti Plantation to Viru Harbor, on the opposite side of the island. On the 29th, US cruisers and destroyers shell Japanese installations in the Shortlands, at MUNDA, and at Vila, to cover the movement of troop convoys. The Japanese submarine Ro-103 encounters the troop convoys and reports them, but the report is dismissed by higher headquarters. On the 30th, Operation Cartwheel begins in earnest as, in New Guinea, Allied troops feint an offensive against Salamaua with a US amphibious landing at nearby Nassau Bay while Australian troops advance from Wau, to cover Allied occupation of the Trobriand and Woodlark Islands, east of New Guinea; heavily supported by naval and air forces, elements of the US 43rd Infantry Division land at Rendova against slight resistance, while small detachments begin landing on New Georgia. In New Guinea, MacKechnie Force lands at Nassau Bay, while elements of the Australian Third Division attack overland in support.

July 1943

Japanese completed their evacuation of ALEUTIAN Island bases in Alaskan waters. Fighting continued as the noose was tightened around RABAUL.

On the 1st, Operation CARTWEEL United States lands reinforcements at Rendova; Marine Fourth Raider Battalion captures Viru Harbor on New Georgia. Japanese destroyer Hokaze is damaged by US submarine Thresher (SS-200) in the southwest Pacific. On the 2nd, Operation Cartwheel: Japanese cruisers and destroyers shell US positions at Rendova; the US 37th and 43rd Divisions and Marines, supported by artillery fire from Rendova and large naval and air forces, land on both sides of MUNDA on New Georgia. On the 3rd, Operation Cartwheel: Japanese destroyers on a resupply mission depart Rabaul; heavy fighting on New Georgia. In NEW GUINEA, the Australian Third Division links up with MacKechnie Force at Nassau Bay. On the 4th, Operation Cartwheel: Elements of the US 37th Infantry Division land at Bairoko, on KULA GULF; Japanese destroyers, landing reinforcements at Vila, on Kula Gulf, sink a US destroyer. Heavy fighting on New Georgia. On the 5th, Japan cedes five provinces of MALAYA to Siam, in order to strengthen Siamese loyalty. Operation Cartwheel: Major "Tokyo Express" supply mission departs Rabaul; heavy fighting on New Georgia. At KISKA, damaged Japanese submarine I-7 is scuttled. On the 6th, US cruisers and destroyers shell Japanese positions on Kiska in the Aleutians, a mission that is repeated several times over the next two weeks. Operation Cartwheels, Battle of Kula Gulf: Japanese destroyers attempting to land troops at Vila, on Kula Gulf, are ambushed by a US cruiser-destroyer force, but sink cruiser Helena, while losing destroyer Nagatsuki, grounded and then attacked by Allied aircraft; heavy fighting on New Georgia. On the 7th, a Japanese destroyer force sets out from PARAMUSHIRO in the KURILES to evacuate the remaining garrison on Kiska. On the 8th, heavy fighting continues on New Georgia, as US units make gains against stout resistance. On the 9th, Operation Cartwheel: US destroyers shelling

Japanese positions at Munda beat off attacks by about 100 enemy aircraft. Italian submarine *Capellini* reaches SABANG, Sumatra, bringing mercury, electronic equipment, and other items for the Japanese. On the 10th, B-25 bombers from Attu attack Paramushiro in the Kuriles for the first time. On the 11th, Operation Cartwheel: US cruisers and destroyers shell Munda. On the 12th, Operation Cartwheel, Battle of KOLOMBANGARA: eight Japanese destroyers and a light cruiser attempting to land reinforcements on New Georgia are ambushed by three cruisers (one New Zealander) and 10 destroyers, losing light cruiser *Jintsu*, while sinking a destroyer and heavily damaging all three Allied cruisers. Heavy fighting on New Georgia, where US troops are bogged down and one isolated battalion out of food. On the 13th, HALSEY reorganizes the higher command of the New Georgia operation. On New Guinea the Australian Third Division clears the Japanese from the Mubo area. On the 14th, Japanese submarine *I-179* is lost to an accident in Japanese home waters. On the 15th, a new commander takes over on New Georgia, as additional forces are landed. Major daylight air battle in the central SOLOMONS, as 74 Japanese aircraft attempt to interfere in the New Georgia battle, losing 45 of their number against three US planes shot down. On the 16th, unable to reach Kiska due to adverse weather, Japanese destroyers that sailed on 7 July return to Paramushiro. Two Australian cruisers and four US destroyers are ordered from ESPIRITU SANTO to join Seventh Fleet forces engaged off New Guinea. On the 17th, US aircraft from Henderson Field and other bases in the Solomons attack Japanese shipping off Buin, BOUGAINVILLE, sinking a destroyer and damaging several other vessels. US destroyers shell Kiska. Late in the day, the Japanese begin a series of offensive moves on New Georgia. On the 18th, desperate fighting continues on New Georgia, as the Japanese counterattacks are beaten off, while additional US forces land. On the 19th, heavily escorted, three Japanese destroyers land supplies at Vila, on Kula Gulf. On the 20th, retiring from Kula Gulf, a Japanese cruiser-destroyer force is attacked

by US aircraft, with two destroyers lost and a cruiser damaged. A Japanese submarine TORPEDOES, but does not sink, Australian light cruiser *Hobart* in the Solomons. On New Georgia, US forces relieve a battalion that had been isolated for days. The Joint Chiefs of Staff issues orders for "Operation Galvanic," the seizure of the GILBERT ISLANDS. On the 21st, the US Navy cancels an order for five new battleships. Chief of Staff George C. MARSHALL (USA) proposes bypassing Rabaul, leaving the large garrison isolated and ineffective because of a lack of supplies of fuel and ammunition. On the 22nd US battleships, cruisers, and destroyers shell Kiska and nearby islets in the Aleutians. Japanese cruisers, destroyers, and support ships sail from Paramushiro, in the Kuriles, to complete the evacuation of Kiska. Japanese seaplane carrier *Nisshin* sunk by US aircraft off Bougainville. On the 23rd, US forces on New Georgia begin a drive to capture the airfield at Munda, as a Japanese attempt to land troops by using motorized barges is frustrated by US PT-BOATS. On the 24th, US destroyers land supplies at Bairoko, on Kula Gulf. Adm NIMITZ orders US submarines to deactivate magnetic exploders on their SUBMARINES, as these are finally admitted to be defective. On the 25th, retiring from Kula Gulf, US destroyers shell Munda and Lailand. The US 25th Infantry Division reinforces New Georgia, where heavy fighting continues. Mussolini is deposed as dictator of Italy, effectively taking Italy out of the Axis. On the 26th, two ships of the Japanese Kiska evacuation squadron collide in heavy seas and are forced to turn back to Paramushiro. US destroyers shell Munda. On the 27th, "The Battle of the Pips": US battleships, cruisers, and destroyers expend hundreds of rounds against false radar blips ("pips") west of Kiska. Japanese destroyers *Ariake* and *Mikazuki* are sunk off NEW BRITAIN by US Army aircraft. In Chinese waters US submarine *Sawfish* (SS-276) sinks the Japanese minelayer *Hiroshima* and a merchantship. On the 28th after nightfall, the Japanese Kiska evacuation squadron withdraws over 5,000 troops in less than an hour and departs for Paramushiro. On the 29th, the commander of the 43rd Division on New Georgia is relieved, as his troops press on slowly. On the 30th, US destroyers shell suspected Japanese positions on Kiska. Heavy fighting continues on New Georgia, and Japanese counterattacks isolate much of an American regiment. On the 31st, the Japanese 17th Division begins moving to Rabaul from central China. Experienced troops are being steadily withdrawn from China for service in the Pacific and Burma, to be replaced (if at all) by green troops from Japan.

August 1943

The Allies poured more troops, aircraft, and ships into the New Guinea and SOLOMONS fighting. The Japanese doggedly hung on in this jungle fighting. In many parts of New Guinea and the Solomons, the Japanese will continue resisting until the end of the war.

On the 1st the Japanese KISKA evacuation squadron returns to Paramushiro in the KURILES, having suffered no losses due to enemy action. In the Blackett Strait, off New Georgia, five Japanese destroyers intent upon resupplying KOLOMBAN-GARA tangle with 15 US PT-BOATS, sinking one, *PT-109*, skippered by John F. KENNEDY. On the 2nd US battleships, cruisers, and destroyers shell suspected Japanese positions on Kiska. The US 27th RCT reinforces troops on New Georgia. On the 3rd, Fijian and Solomon Island troops join US forces in action on New Georgia, serving as scouts. On the 4th, US troops close in on Japanese airfield at Munda, New Georgia. USAAF bombers drop 152 tons of bombs on Kiska. On the 5th, US troops on New Georgia capture the Japanese airfield at Munda, after 12 days of heavy fighting. Battleship *Musashi* and her escorts return to TRUK. On the 6th, Battle of VELLA GULF: Four Japanese destroyers attempting to land troops on Kolombangara are ambushed by six US destroyers, with only lucky *Shigure* getting away. US troops on New Georgia pursue Japanese forces into the interior, as engineers begin to repair the Munda air strip. On the 7th, US troops on New Georgia break Japanese

resistance. On the 8th, fighting continues around Munda, New Georgia, the struggle for which has cost 93 US and 350 Japanese aircraft. On the 9th, the American 35th Division is ordered to make an amphibious landing on VELLA LAVELLA. On the 10th, Japanese troops on New Georgia become, effectively, GUERRILLAS, fighting on in the wild interior of the island. On the 11th, Adm NIMITZ proposes to VAdm HALSEY that Kolombangara be isolated and bypassed, a plan that is adopted. On the 12th, while the USAAF drops tons of bombs, US battleships, cruisers, and destroyers shell suspected Japanese positions on Kiska. On the 13th, flying from Australia, US B-24s bomb the oil fields at BALIKPAPAN, in Borneo. Reconnaissance parties landed on Vella Lavella determine that there are few Japanese on the island. On the 14th, Quadrant Conference: ROOSEVELT and CHURCHILL meet at Quebec for 10 days of talks concerning Allied policy and STRATEGY, definitively setting "Operation Overlord" (the landings in France) for the spring of 1944. It is agreed that the Pacific offensive will be on two fronts, one an island-hopping drive through the central Pacific, the other the ongoing advance up the Solomons toward the Philippines. On the 15th, US and Canadian troops begin landings on Kiska, heavily supported by naval and air bombardments. Five days pass before it is established that the Japanese have definitely evacuated the island. Allied CASUALTIES are a score of deaths from FRIENDLY FIRE and 75 killed on a destroyer damaged by a mine. Elements of the US 25th Infantry Division begin landing on Vella Lavella in the central Solomons, unopposed save by Japanese aircraft. On the 16th, the Fourth Marine Division is activated at Camp Pendleton. Having completed a refit, battleship YAMATO arrives at Truk. On Vella Lavella the 25th Infantry Division encounters moderate resistance. US troops who have landed on Baanga, a small island near New Georgia, encounter stiff resistance. On the 17th, Japanese light forces land reinforcements on Vella Lavella, while their covering force of four destroyers beats off an attempt by four US destroyers to intervene, with little effect on either side. Major

US/Australian air raid on Japanese installations at WEWAK, northern New Guinea, destroys over 100 aircraft. On the 18th, Nationalist Chinese complain of being left out of decision making by the Allies. China had been acknowledged as one of the "Big Four" (United States, Britain, Russia, China) Allies, but only for propaganda purposes. China wanted real power among the Big Four, but lacked the military or political clout to obtain it. US forces on Baanga Island capture Japanese guns that had been shelling Munda airfield on nearby New Georgia. On the 19th, off ESPIRITU SANTO, Japanese submarine *I-17* is sunk by US aircraft and New Zealand corvette *Moa*. Heavy Allied air raids on Wewak, New Guinea. On the 20th, Baanga Island is finally secured, at a cost of 52 Americans killed and 110 wounded, while hundreds of Japanese have been killed. On the 21st, heavy Allied air raids on Wewak, New Guinea. Japanese air raids against shipping off Vella Lavella, with little effect. On the 22nd, US destroyers shell Finschhafen, in eastern New Guinea. US Marines occupy undefended Nukufetau in the ELLICE ISLANDS. On the 23rd, Japanese submarine *I-25* reconnoiters Espiritu Santo with a small scout plane. On the 24th, British decide to appoint Lord Louis MOUNTBATTEN supreme Allied commander for Southeast Asia. On the 25th, Inter-Allied Quebec Conference ends with a recommendation that MACARTHUR and Halsey leap-frog RABAUL, occupying outlying portions of NEW BRITAIN and New Ireland to isolate the enormous (over 100,000 troops) base at Rabaul. Australian Fifth Division goes into action on the Salamaua front in New Guinea. On the 26th, operating from bases in China, US bombers attack Japanese installations in HONG KONG. Italian submarine *Torelli* reaches SABANG, Sumatra, bringing critical materials, documents, and a Japanese intelligence officer. On the 27th, elements of the 43rd Infantry Division land on Arundel Island in the Solomons unopposed. On the 28th, US Marines occupy Nanomea in the Ellice Islands unopposed, while men of the 43rd Division advance on Arundel against light Japanese resistance. On the 29th, on Vella Lavella the 25th Infantry Division

advances slowly against moderate resistance. On the 30th, US Navy Fast Carrier Task Force approaches Marcus Island to stage a raid. This type of operation is an opportunity to train pilots and ship crews under combat conditions without a great deal of risk. On the 31st, escorted by elements of the Seventh Fleet, the Australian Ninth Division sails from MILNE BAY for a landing near LAE, in northeastern New Guinea. A small task force lands US Army personnel on BAKER ISLAND, in the Central Pacific, which is not held by the Japanese.

September 1943

More fighting in New Guinea and the Solomons. First bombing raids on TARAWA (in the GILBERT ISLANDS, 1,600 miles from HAWAII), the newly designated target of a late 1943 amphibious attack. More Allied aircraft, ships and infantry entered the Pacific, increasing the pressure on the Japanese.

On the 1st, the US Fast Carrier Task Force hits MARCUS ISLAND, in the west-central Pacific, with both air and gunnery attacks. Japanese submarine *I-182* is sunk by US destroyer *Wadsworth* off ESPIRITU SANTO. On the 2nd, USAAF aircraft bomb LAE, in northeastern New Guinea, sinking a patrol vessel, while another patrol vessel is TORPEDOED near TRUK by US submarine *Snapper* (SS-185). On the 3rd, Japanese submarine *I-25* is sunk near Espiritu Santo by US destroyer *Ellet*, *I-20* in the NEW HEBRIDES by US destroyer *Patterson*. On the 4th, elements of the Australian Ninth Division land near Lae, in New Guinea. On VELLA LAVELLA the 25th Infantry Division makes gains against Japanese resistance. On the 5th, Japanese resistance on Arundel has stiffened, and the US advance is slow. On the 6th, the US 503rd Parachute Regiment airdrops 1,700 men at Nadzab, northwest of Lae, securing the airstrip, into which is flown the Australian Seventh Division. US submarine *Halibut* (SS-232) torpedoes but does not sink Japanese heavy cruiser NACHI off Japan. On the 7th, heavy fighting around Lae and on Vella Lavella. The Japanese 54th Division moves from JAVA to Burma. On the 8th, US destroyers bombard Lae in support of operations of the Australian Ninth Division. On the 9th, formal announcement is made of the surrender of Italy. The Italian sloop *Eritrea*, in Japanese-controlled SABANG, escapes to sea, eludes pursuit, and eventually reaches CEYLON, but Italian SUBMARINES *Capellini*, *Giuliani*, and *Torelli* are captured by the Japanese and turned over to the Germans, who commission them as *UIt-24*, *UIt-23*, and *UIt-25*. On the 10th, a German merchant cruiser sinks a tanker (c. 10,000 tons) in the eastern Pacific. On the 11th, the 27th Division lands on Arundel to help break Japanese resistance. Japanese minesweeper *W-16* sinks while attempting to clear MINES off MAKASSAR, in the Celebes. Japanese submarine I-26 reconnoiters FIJI. On the 12th, Australian and US troops capture Salamaua, in northeastern New Guinea, while the Australian Seventh and Ninth Divisions close in on Lae. On the 13th, Nationalist Chinese leader CHIANG consolidates his power by becoming president of China. While not an important post, it adds to Chiang's stature. On the 14th, heavy fighting around Lae. On the 15th, Japanese submarine *Ro-101* is sunk by US destroyer *Saufley* aided by two aircraft, in the South Pacific. On the 16th, Australian troops capture Lae, in northeastern New Guinea. Additional US forces are ordered to Arundel. On the 17th, US B-24s bomb Tarawa in the Gilbert Islands, from air bases on CANTON and Funafuti. On the 18th, B-24s bomb Tarawa. On Vella Lavella the US 25th Infantry Division is officially relieved by the New Zealand Third Division. On the 19th, aircraft of the US Fast Carrier Task Force and US B-24s raid Tarawa. On the 20th, in the aftermath of the previous day's attack by US carrier aircraft on their base at Tarawa, the Japanese redouble their efforts to fortify the island against amphibious attack. On the 21st, Australian raiders in six canoes enter SINGAPORE harbor, to sink two ships with limpet mines. On the 22nd, the Australian 20th Brigade Group (Ninth Division) lands near Finschhafen, New Guinea, against light resistance. On the 23rd, Allied aircraft begin operating from Vella Lavella, while in New Guinea the Australian Ninth Division presses on toward

Finschhafen. On the 24th, US submarine *Cabrilla* (SS-288) damages Japanese escort carrier TAIYO near Japan. On the 25th, the Japanese begin concentrating light craft on the north coast of KOLOMBANGARA in order to evacuate the garrison. On the 26th, Japanese counterattacks against the Australian Ninth Division before Finschhafen are beaten off. Japanese oceangoing torpedo boat *Kasasagi* is sunk off Flores, NETHERLANDS EAST INDIES. On the 27th, heavy fighting near Finschhafen, as the Australians defend against fierce Japanese attacks. On the 28th, Japanese naval forces begin evacuating troops from Kolombangara. The Japanese minelayer *Hoko* is sunk east of Buka by US Army aircraft. On the 29th STILWELL proposes that 60 Chinese divisions be reorganized, retrained, and reequipped under American auspices. On the 30th, on Vella Lavella the New Zealanders confine (c. 600) Japanese to a small pocket on the northwestern tip of the island. US submarine *Barb* (SS-220) departs PEARL HARBOR carrying the new Mark-18 torpedo.

October 1943

American carriers newly deployed to the Pacific were given training by raiding Japanese-held islands. Once such series of raids, on Wake, caused the Japanese to suspect an invasion of Wake would follow. They put the Combined Fleet to sea from TRUK. The Japanese soon realized their error and returned to Truk. The six remaining Japanese carriers were taken out of action by transferring their aircraft to RABAUL, a base attracting ever more Allied bombing raids. The Japanese carriers steamed back to Japan, there to spend nearly a year training new carrier pilots. Meanwhile, fighting continued in New Guinea and the SOLOMONS, while NIMITZ completed plans for the opening of a second drive against the enemy, across the central Pacific.

On the 1st, on VELLA LAVELLA the New Zealanders suspend offensive operations, containing the Japanese pocket on the northwest of the island. On the 2nd, Australian 20th Brigade secures Finschhafen, in eastern New Guinea. US destroyer

Henley sunk off Finschhafen, New Guinea, by Japanese submarine *Ro-103*. On the 3rd, some 9,500 Japanese troops complete withdrawing from KOLOMBANGARA. In central China, the Japanese begin another offensive, to grab as much of the local rice harvest as possible. On the 4th, in the Indian Ocean, Japanese submarine *I-37* scouts the Chagos Islands with a small reconnaissance plane. On the 5th, US carrier aircraft raid WAKE ISLAND in the central Pacific, while cruisers shell Japanese installations there; in retaliation, the Japanese execute US civilians interned on the island. On the 6th, Japanese small craft succeed in getting most of the surviving Japanese troops off Vella Lavella, leaving the central Solomons firmly under Allied control. Late that night occurs the naval Battle of Vella Lavella, as the US destroyers intercept a flotilla of Japanese destroyers trying to evacuate troops; each side loses one destroyer, and three more American ones are damaged. On the 7th, US carriers and cruisers raid Wake Island; on the 8th, Japanese leader TOJO assumes more power by taking over as minister of commerce and industry. In New Guinea the exhausted Australian I Corps is relieved by the II Corps. On the 9th, the first Allied airfield on Ellice Island becomes operational. On the 10th, the Japanese naval command concludes that the United States plans a landing at Wake Island. In the Indian Ocean, Japanese submarine *I-37* scouts Diego Suarez with a small reconnaissance plane. On the 11th, Japanese Combined Fleet is ordered to prepare for action if the United States attacks Wake Island. US submarine *Wahoo* (SS-238) is sunk by Japanese aircraft in La Perouse Strait. On the 12th, the Fifth Air Force begins heavy bombardment raids on Rabaul. On the 13th, several Japanese SUBMARINES converge on HAWAII on reconnaissance missions, but are unable to ascertain the presence of the bulk of the US fleet. On the 14th, the Fifth Air Force subjects Rabaul to a major air raid. On the 15th, Admiral Sir Andrew CUNNINGHAM is appointed first sea lord of the British Admiralty (chief of naval operations). In the Pacific final orders are issued for operations in the northern Solomons. On the 16th, the Japanese declare the Philippines an independent republic under "temporary Japanese supervision." Filipinos continue their GUERRILLA war against the Japanese. In New Guinea the Japanese begin a series of major counterattacks against the Ninth Australian Division before Finschhafen, which beats them off over the next few days. On the 17th, in the Indian Ocean, Japanese submarine *I-37* scouts Kilindini, East Africa, with a small reconnaissance plane. Japanese submarine *I-36* scouts PEARL HARBOR with a reconnaissance plane, determining that the fleet is at sea. Based on this evidence, and the heavy pounding to which Wake has been subject in recent weeks, Japanese naval headquarters feels certain the US Navy is about to conduct a landing at Wake and orders the Combined Fleet to sea. US submarine *Tarpon* (SS-175) sinks the German merchant cruiser *Michel* in the BONIN ISLANDS. On the 18th, the Japanese Combined Fleet steams northward from Truk, bound for Wake. Japanese submarine *I-19* is reported overdue. On the 19th, British, American, and Russian foreign ministers meet in Moscow and agree that Russia will enter the war against Japan once Germany has been defeated. The Japanese are not informed. On the 20th, aircraft from six Japanese carriers based at Truk are transferred to bases at Rabaul, the carriers then steam for Japan to pick up new air groups. Thus there are no operational Japanese carriers available in the Pacific, and none will be available until the new air groups are trained. This will take at least six months. The Japanese Combined Fleet steams northward from Truk, bound for Wake. On the 21st, Operation Galvanic (invasion of the GILBERTS) gets underway, as transports and escorts begin movements toward troop concentration areas. On the 22nd, Sir Archibald WAVELL is made viceroy of India, with the urgent mission of keeping India loyal and in the war. On the 23rd, the Japanese conclude that there is no American threat to Wake Island, and recall the Combined Fleet to Truk. On the 24th, the Japanese destroyer *Mochizuki* is sunk by Marine aircraft southwest of Rabaul. On the 25th, USAAF bombers based in China raid Japanese airfields in FORMOSA for the first time.

Battle of CAPE ST. GEORGE: Six US destroyers intercept six Japanese destroyers carrying reinforcements for BOUGAINVILLE, sinking three. On the 26th, Chandra BOSE proclaims a provisional Indian government in SINGAPORE and declares war on Britain. On the 27th, the New Zealand Eighth Brigade (c. 8,000 men) occupies Mono and Stirling in the Treasury Islands and the USMC Second Parachute Battalion lands amphibiously on Choiseul, against no resistance, as a deceptive measure designed to mask operations against Bougainville. The Japanese Combined Fleet returns to Truk after its abortive sortie toward Wake Island. On the 28th, the Japanese evacuation of Kolombangara ends, only about 1,000 out of nearly 11,000 men of the garrison failing to get away safely. On the 29th, USAAF subjects Rabaul to a major air raid. The newly activated Japanese 31st Division reaches Burma. On the 30th, US subs mine the waters off Indochina. Before long, Hainan Strait and the waters off SAIGON are heavily mined. On the 31st, the Japanese Second Division, withdrawn from GUADALCANAL in February 1942 for rest, reinforcement, and reorganization in the Philippines, is deployed to MALAYA.

November 1943

The drive across the central Pacific began with Operation Galvanic, the assault on TARAWA in the GILBERTS. Heavy fighting in China and Burma. On the 1st, the Third Marine Division lands at Cape Torokina, at EMPRESS AUGUSTA BAY, BOUGAINVILLE, easily overcoming initial resistance on the ground (the local Japanese garrison was only 270 men and one 75mm gun) and in the air. US destroyers shell the Japanese air base at Buka. Japanese surface forces sortie from Rabaul. US carrier aircraft raid Japanese installations at Buin and Buka. On the 2nd, Battle of Empress Augusta Bay: In a nighttime attempt to interfere in the landings at Cape Torokina four Japanese cruisers and six destroyers are intercepted by four US cruisers and nine destroyers, the Japanese being beaten off after losing a light cruiser and a destroyer and incurring

heavy damage to two cruisers and two destroyers, the United States suffering two damaged destroyers. Marine Second Parachute Battalion withdraws from Choiseul. US ships off Empress Augusta Bay are subject to a Japanese air attack, with little damage. US carrier aircraft raid Japanese installations at Buin and Buka. In China the Japanese undertake a "rice offensive" (to steal the recent harvest for their own troops) in Hunan Province. On the 3rd, major elements of the Japanese Combined Fleet (10 cruisers and about a dozen destroyers) set sail from TRUK to reinforce ships at RABAUL. Marines on Bougainville meet little resistance, since Japanese are as yet on the wrong (i.e., northern and southern) parts of the island. On the 4th, the Japanese concentrate a strong cruiser-destroyer force at Rabaul to threaten the Bougainville beachhead, and HALSEY orders air strikes. On the 5th, US submarine *Halibut* (SS–232) sinks the Japanese carrier JUNYO en route to Japan from Truk. Massive US Navy and Army air strikes at Rabaul severely damages six cruisers and several destroyers; most damaged ships promptly depart for Truk. On the 6th, the New Zealand Eighth Brigade is withdrawn from the Treasury Islands. Light action on Bougainville, where a Japanese "Tokyo Express" from Rabaul lands over 1,000 troops. On the 7th, Japanese cruisers and destroyers damaged at Rabaul on November 5 reach Truk. Japanese troops make a weak attack on Marine positions at Cape Torokina, Bougainville. On the 8th, despite Rabaul-based air strikes on its transports, US 37th Infantry Division beings reinforcing Marines at Cape Torokina, Bougainville, where VANDEGRIFT has just assumed command. On the 9th, Japanese 36th Division reaches Halmahera, northwest of New Guinea. On the 10th, Task Force 52 sails from PEARL HARBOR bound for the Gilbert Islands. The Fifth Air Force makes a major attack on Rabaul. On the 11th, major US carrier air strikes are added to Fifth Air Force attacks on Japanese at Rabaul, sinking one destroyer and damaging a cruiser and a destroyer; 41 Japanese aircraft attack US carriers with no success, only eight returning to base. Desultory action on Bougainville. On the 12th, Japanese carrier air groups landed at Rabaul on October 20 are withdrawn for reorganization after loss of 121 of their 173 aircraft. Light combat on Bougainville, while the United States lands additional Marine and army troops at Cape Torokina, despite Japanese air strikes on covering force, which cause some damage. On the 13th, Operation Galvanic (invasion of Tarawa) underway; Task Force 53 sails from the NEW HEBRIDES bound for the Gilbert Islands. US Army and Navy B-24s from Funafuti and CANTON bomb Tarawa and Makin, in the Gilberts. On the 14th, moderate fighting on Bougainville continues; US forces at Empress Augusta Bay total nearly 34,000, while Japanese forces on Bougainville and surrounding islands may total 40,000 but are unable to concentrate effectively. On the 15th, Task Force 74 (two Australian cruisers and two destroyers, plus two US destroyers) arrives at the New Hebrides from MILNE BAY. US bombers based in China attack harbor installations in HONG KONG. Operation Galvanic: Task Force 52 refuels near Baker and Howland Islands in the central Pacific, while Task Force 53 refuels near Funafuti, before resuming course for the Gilbert Islands. US Army and Navy B-24s from Funafuti again bomb Tarawa and Makin. On the 16th, Japanese minelayer *Ukishima* lost to an unknown cause near Hatsushima (possibly sunk by a US submarine later lost). US submarine *Corvina* (SS-26) sunk by Japanese submarine *I-179* near Truk. On the 17th, US destroyer transport *McKean* is sunk off EMPRESS AUGUSTA BAY by Japanese aircraft. Operation Galvanic: Task Forces 52 and 53 unite about 500 miles east of the Gilbert Islands and begin "softening up" air strikes on MAKIN and Tarawa, supported by battleship and cruiser gunfire. On the 18th, Japanese destroyer escort *Sanae* is sunk by US submarine *Bluefish* (SS-222) in the Philippines. Operation Galvanic: Makin and Tarawa are subject to intense air and sea bombardment. On the 19th, fighting continues on Bougainville. Operation Galvanic: Fast Carrier Task Force raids Japanese-held islands in the Gilberts and NAURU. US Army and Navy B-24s from Funafuti bomb Tarawa and Makin Atolls, in the Gilberts. Japanese light

cruisers *Isuzu* and NAGARA sail from Truk for Mili, in the MARSHALLS, while *Naka* departs for KWAJALIEN. Bill Howell and his ship (CVL-26, *Monterey*) see combat for the first time as they launch aircraft against Japanese forces during the Gilbert Islands (Tarawa, Makin) operation. This continues until 18 December. Bill's battle station is on the bridge, where he and another petty officer man the TBS (Talk Between Ships) radio. This short-range radio is for short commands that must be sent quickly between ships in the task force. As a short-range radio, its signals are not likely to be picked up by the enemy. Petty Officer Howell's job is to listen carefully to this radio for messages, usually course changes to ensure that the fast moving ships of the task force don't collide while rapidly maneuvering during combat or bad weather. The other petty officer manning the TBS handles the outgoing messages. When Bill is not attending to his administrative duties with the ships personnel records, he stands a four-hour "watch" each day, often in the wee hours of the morning, manning the TBS radio and listening for messages from nearby ships. On the 20th, Operation Galvanic goes into high gear: The Second Marine Division lands on Betio Island, Tarawa, while elements of the 27th Infantry Division land on Makin Island, in the Gilberts. Heavy fighting on Tarawa. Japanese air attacks on the fleet cause damage to carrier INDEPENDENCE. On the 21st, Operation Galvanic: Heavy fighting on Tarawa, troops advance on Makin, 78 Marines land on Abemama Atoll, about 75 miles southeast of Tarawa. On the 22nd, Operation Galvanic: Heavy fighting on Tarawa, where the Japanese make a BANZAI CHARGE after dark. On Makin, army personnel advance slowly; SEABEES begin construction of an air base at Abemama. On the 23rd, Operation Galvanic continues: Makin Island is secured by the US 27th Infantry Division; Marines secure Betio. In India, the Chinese New 38th Division essays an offensive into Burma across the Assamese Mountains. Chinese troops in Hunan begin stout resistance to a Japanese "rice offensive" at Changteh. Japanese light cruisers *Isuzu* and *Nagara* arrive at Mili in the Marshalls, the former then proceeds to Kwajalein, while the latter returns to Truk. Japanese light cruiser *Naka* arrives at Kwajalien from Truk. In the Indian Ocean Japanese submarine *I-37* scouts the Seychelles with a small reconnaissance plane. On the 24th, US escort carrier *Liscombe Bay* is TORPEDOED by Japanese submarine I-175 in the Gilbert Islands, sinking with heavy loss of life (including Pearl Harbor hero Dorie MILLER). Three Japanese heavy cruisers plus a destroyer squadron depart Truk for Kwajalein. The Chinese 38th Division advances across the mountains on the Burma-India frontier. On the 25th, first major Japanese operation on Bougainville, as a Japanese infantry regiment attacks the US defense perimeter, to be beaten off with heavy losses. Battle of CAPE ST. GEORGE: Five US destroyers intercept five Japanese destroyers near New Georgia, sinking three. Operation Galvanic: Japanese aircraft from Kwajalein make two unsuccessful attempts to raid the US fleet off Tarawa and Makin (one a "spectacular" night attack), as Marines eliminate final Japanese pockets on outlying islets of Tarawa Atoll. The Chinese New 38th Division continues its attack into Burma from India. On the 26th, Marines mop up Japanese pockets on outlying islets of Tarawa Atoll. Japanese submarine *I-39* is sunk near Makin by US destroyer *Boyd*. The Japanese cruiser-destroyer force that had departed Truk on the 24th arrives at Kwajalein. In Burma the Chinese New 38th Division advances into the Hukawng Valley. On the 27th, Marines eliminate final Japanese pockets on outlying islets of Tarawa Atoll. Japanese light cruiser *Isuzu* arrives at Kwajalein from Mili. The Japanese cruiser-destroyer force departs Kwajalein for ENIWETOK. On the 28th, Japanese light cruiser *Nagara* departs Truk for Maloelap. The Japanese cruiser-destroyer force arrives at Eniwetok from Kwajalein. On the 29th, US and Australian destroyers bombard Japanese positions on NEW BRITAIN US destroyer *Perkins* sunk off Cape Vogelkopf in New Guinea in a collision with an Australian troop transport. US submarine *Sculpin* (SS-191) sunk by a Japanese destroyer near Truk. Aircraft from US escort carrier *Chenango* sink Japanese submarine I-

21 in the Gilberts. The Japanese cruiser-destroyer force departs Eniwetok for Kwajalein. On the 30th, US destroyers bombard Japanese positions near Cape Torokina on Bougainville, where heavy fighting continues. The Japanese cruiser-destroyer force arrives at Kwajalein from Eniwetok. In Burma, the Japanese begin to counterattack the Chinese New 38th Division.

December 1943

Fighting continued in Burma, raids in the Pacific intensified, and Allied forces were being built up for the really big push in late 1944. For the moment, amphibious resources were being shifted to Europe to support the D-day invasion of France in June (or, as it was put at the time, "in the spring of 1944"). During November-December 1943, to release troops for combat elsewhere while still maintaining local control, the Japanese Army activated 10 "Independent Mixed Brigades" (each of four to five infantry battalions, an artillery battalion, an engineer battalion, and some services) by reorganizing occupation forces in the NETHERLANDS EAST INDIES (four new brigades), the Philippines (four), Thailand (one), and Indochina (one).

On the 1st, the Fifth Marine Division begins organizing at Camp Pendleton, California. On the 2nd, nothing much happens, except the steady grind of combat on numerous fronts, and the tedium of getting ready for more. On the 3rd, Third Phase of the Sextant Conference begins, as US and British delegates meet at Cairo; among other things, they agree to postpone an amphibious invasion of Burma. On the 4th, US Fast Carrier Task Force raids KWAJALEIN and WOTJE, sinking six transports while damaging three more plus two light cruisers and destroying 55 aircraft, at a cost of five US planes lost and an aerial TORPEDO hit on carrier *Lexington*. Japanese escort carrier *Chuyo* sunk and carrier RYUHO damaged about 250 miles southeast of Tokyo Bay by US submarine *Sailfish* (SS-192). Japanese light cruiser *Nagara* arrives Kwajalein from Maloelap, joining a light cruiser, three heavy cruisers, and a destroyer squadron, which have been there for several days. On the 5th, major Japanese air raid on port facilities at CALCUTTA, India. On the 6th, major revision of Allied plans in Burma leads to cancellation of amphibious operation designed to support Operation Tarzan, leading to concerns about Chinese reaction. On the 7th, the Japanese cruiser-destroyer force arrives at TRUK from Kwajalein, having spent a month at sea without accomplishing anything against US forces. The Sextant Conference ends in Cairo. On the 8th, a US fast battleship task force bombards Japanese positions on NAURU. Australian troops capture Wareo in New Guinea. Japanese air raids on British airfields in Assam. On the 9th, SEABEES complete an airstrip at Torokina, BOUGAINVILLE, which becomes operational. CHIANG KAI-SHEK responds to cancellation of major operations in Burma by requesting increased US financial and air assistance. On the 10th, on Bougainville, army and Marine personnel push their defensive perimeter outward, as Japanese resistance stiffens (resistance is so dogged that Japanese troops will still be fighting on Bougainville at the end of the war). On the 11th, hitherto separate British and American air forces in Southeast Asia are combined under one commander, in the Eastern Air Command. On the 12th, US and Nationalist Chinese governments cannot agree on the extent to which Chinese troops should get involved in Burmese fighting; United States wants more action, China wants more aid. On the 13th, a US Army amphibious task force sails from Goodenough bound for a landing on Arawe Peninsula off NEW BRITAIN, nearly 300 miles west of RABAUL. In Burma the Chinese New 38th Division reaches Bhamo. On the 14th, Japanese destroyer *Numakaze* is sunk by US submarine *Grayback* (SS-208) about 50 miles east of OKINAWA. Chinese New 38th Division encounters heavy fighting around *Bhamo*. On the 15th, after a major aerial bombardment the US 112th Cavalry RCT lands at Arawe, New Britain. In Burma, the Chinese New 38th Division is driven back in the Bhamo area. On the 16th, Japanese submarine *I-29* departs PENANG for France. On the 17th, Allies

battle last Japanese defenders on the Arawe Peninsula of New Britain. On the 18th, Japanese stage air raids in southern China (Kunming) to cripple Chinese forces advancing into Burma. Chiang Kaishek gives STILWELL direct command of all Chinese forces in India and Burma. On the 20th, Japanese destroyer *Fuyo* is sunk about 60 miles west of Manila by US submarine *Puffer* (SS-268). On the 21st, the Third Marine Division begins pulling out of the Bougainville beachhead. In Burma, Stilwell arrives at Ledo to assume personal direction of operations. On the 22nd, Japanese bombers again hit Kunming in China. On the 23rd, USAAF aircraft operating from bases in China sink a Japanese gunboat about 35 miles south of FORMOSA, while other army aircraft begin operating from MUNDA, New Georgia. On the 24th, in northern Burma, General Joseph Stilwell undertakes an offensive to rescue elements of the Chinese New 38th Division, which have been bottled up by the Japanese. On the 25th, US carrier aircraft raid KAVIENG, New Ireland, sinking or damaging several ships. Battleship YAMATO is damaged by a torpedo from US submarine *Skate* (SS-305) about 180 miles north of Truk. Japanese submarine *I-29*, bound for France, replenishes from the German supply ship *Bogota* in the Indian Ocean. Bill Howell's ship, *Monterey* (CVL-26), is part of a task force that launches air strikes against Japanese bases and shipping lanes in the Bismarck Islands. On 4 January 1944, *Monterey* completes its combat duty in the BISMARCKS, having accounted for an enemy destroyer and cruiser. On the 26th, the First Marine Division lands at Cape Gloucester, New Britain. US destroyer *Brownson* sunk by Japanese Army aircraft off Cape Gloucester, New Ireland. On the 27th, the First Marine Division makes a 3-mile advance at Cape Gloucester, despite monsoon rains. In Burma the Chinese New 38th Division remains heavily engaged in the Hukawng Valley. On the 28th, the US American Division completes relief of the Third Marine Division on Bougainville. On New Britain a Japanese attack against Arawe is repulsed. On the 29th, at Cape Gloucester, First Marine Division captures Japanese airfield. In Burma the Chinese New 38th Division begins breaking Japanese defenses along the Tarung River. On the 30th, the ROYAL NAVY dispatches two carriers, two battleships, a battle cruiser, and seven destroyers from Britain for the British Far Eastern Fleet. On Bougainville, FIJIAN troops reconnoiter behind Japanese lines. On the 31st, in northern Burma the Chinese New 38th Division breaks through to isolated elements and clears the Japanese from much of the Tarung River line.

January 1944

RABAUL was increasingly isolated. At the end of the month, the MARSHALL ISLANDS were invaded, only two months after TARAWA was taken. The speed of this island-hopping campaign unnerved the Japanese. Some Allied progress was made in Burma, but not enough to open the BURMA ROAD once more.

On the 1st, fighting in Cape Gloucester, on New Britain, ceases as all Japanese resistance is overcome. Allies now control western New Britain, further isolating Rabaul, at the eastern end of the island. On the 2nd, Allied troops land on Saidor, New Guinea. This isolates 12,000 Japanese troops at Sio. On the 3rd, the Chinese New 38th Division struggles to overcome last Japanese positions along the Tarung River in Burma. On the 4th, Australian forces struggle to reach Kelanoa in New Guinea, bringing them within 60 miles of linking up with US forces. On the 5th, on New Guinea, American and Australian offensives (now separated by 60 miles of jungle) struggle on to combine at Kelanoa. This juncture will greatly increase the Allied position in New Guinea, and render the Japanese position strategically hopeless. On the 6th, Nationalist Chinese government faces crisis because President ROOSEVELT demands greater Chinese operations against Japan. NIMITZ issues plan for the capture of the Marshall Islands. On the 7th, Imperial General Headquarters orders the Japanese Southern Army, in Burma, to capture the Imphal area of India. On the 8th, US Navy ships bombard Japanese base at Shortlands in the Solomon Islands. On the 9th, in the Arakan area of Burma, British troops recapture Maungdaw. Heavy fighting along the Tarung River in Burma. On the 10th, British bombers begin dropping naval MINES at the mouth of the Salween River in Burma. Major Japanese counterattacks on New Britain. On the 11th, airfield at Saidor, New Guinea, becomes operational. On the 12th, reinforcements arrive on New Britain to strengthen the Arawe beachhead. On the 13th, Chinese forces complete their operation to secure the Tarung River line in northern Burma. Nimitz issues an outline plan for operations in the central Pacific through November 1944. On the 14th, President Roosevelt threatens Chinese with loss of Lend-Lease aid if more Chinese forces are not committed to fight against Japan. On the 15th, Australian troops reach the north coast of the Huon Peninsula in New Guinea near Sio. On the 16th, Chinese reply to US threats of LEND-LEASE loss by threatening to halt all Chinese aid for US forces unless America comes across with a billion dollars in new aid. On the 17th, after desperate last ditch resistance, Allied troops subdue last organized Japanese defenders at Arawe on the southern coast of New Britain. On the 18th, the Saidor beachhead, New Guinea, is heavily reinforced. Heavy patrolling necessary on New Britain, as Japanese stragglers require mopping up. On the 19th, the Chinese New 38th Division and Japanese troops struggle for control of Taro Plain in northern Burma. On the 20th, Allies prepare to unleash thousands of commandos in northern Burma against Japanese rear-area installations. This, combined with the advance of US, British and Chinese troops, is to reopen the Burma Road to allow supply of China overland from India. On the 21st, the Chinese New 38th Division advances slowly in Burma. On the 22nd, heavy US air raids on the ADMIRALTY ISLANDS. Preparations for the occupation of the Marshall Islands end as convoys sail from HAWAII. On the 23rd, the Chinese government is caught in a quandary. Americans insist that China commit its strategic reserve of capable divisions to fighting in Burma, but this would leave

China without any reserve if the Japanese in eastern China attack again. On the 24th, US aircraft conduct long-range reconnaissance over the Marshalls, from the GILBERTS. On the 25th, major Allied air raid on main Japanese base at Rabaul results in destruction of 83 enemy aircraft. In Burma the bulk of the Chinese New 22nd Division begins supporting the 38th. On the 26th, minor diplomatic coup for the Allies. Liberia declares war on Germany and Japan while Argentina severs diplomatic relations with Germany and Japan. US bombers raid the Marshalls. On the 27th, United States issues a report on Japanese ATROCITIES (the BATAAN DEATH MARCH) against US and Filipino troops after the surrender of BATAAN in early 1942: This is the first formal public announcement of the atrocity. On the 28th, US Navy Task Force 58 (nine carriers, several battleships, many cruisers and destroyers) steams within striking distance of the Marshall Islands. On the 29th, major US Navy air offensive against Japanese bases in the Marshall Islands begins. Bill Howell's ship, *Monterey* (CVL-26) is part of the vast armada supporting the invasion of the Marshall Islands, or at least the KWAJALEIN part of the operation. This operation ends on 8 February. Between this operation and their next one, there is some time for rest and recreation on board. Along these lines, a basketball game is arranged between officers and chief petty officers (CPOs). Bill Howell is on the CPO team and he literally runs into one of the officer players during the game. The officer is Jerry FORD, later to become the president of the United States. Note that it's only in wartime that you have a lot of young men in their twenties achieving the rank of chief petty officer; in peacetime, the youngest CPOs are in their thirties. CPO Bill Howell is 24 when he makes CPO, and was doing a CPO's job soon after he arrived on *Monterey*. On the 30th, Chinese forces oust Japanese from Taro Plain in northern Burma. On the 31st, US troops land in Japanese-held Kwajalein Atoll and other nearby islands in the Marshalls. These are the first of Japan's prewar territories to fall to the Allies.

February 1944

MARSHALL ISLANDS were conquered. British won their first pitched battle in Burma. Japanese Home Islands were shelled, RABAUL and TRUK surrounded and cut off. US carrier task forces rampaged across the Pacific, pounding Japanese targets at will.

On the 1st, Japanese leadership learns that Australia has formed a commission to investigate Japanese war crimes. On the 2nd, American troops advance rapidly against light resistance on KWAJALEIN and other Marshall islands. The Soviets agree to permit US bombers to be based in Russia, "later"; nothing ever comes of this. On the 3rd, in a daring raid, US warships based in Alaska bombard the northern Japanese island of PARAMUSHIRO in the northern KURILES. This was the first time any of the Japanese Home Islands was shelled by Allied ships. On the 4th, Japanese troops launch a major offensive against British forces in the Arakan region of Burma. On the 5th, except for a few isolated holdouts, Kwajalein Atoll is conquered. The Japanese lost 5,100 troops (all dead, save for 200 POWs); American losses were 142 dead. On the 6th, Chinese troops advance from the north in Burma, while British CHINDIT irregulars to the south try to distract and delay Japanese reinforcements. On the 7th, the United States and China come to a tentative agreement on financial arrangements for Chinese support of US forces in Burma. On the 8th, STILWELL informs Washington that a major Japanese offensive in Burma is imminent. On the 9th, Americans ask Nationalist Chinese permission to send a military mission to the Chinese communists (to try to get the communists to help against the Japanese, or to frighten the Nationalists into doing so). On the 10th, Australian troops complete their takeover of the Huon Peninsula in New Guinea, and make contact with US forces near Saidor. In the Arakan region of Burma, the Japanese launch an offensive, isolating some British and Indian units that must be supplied by air. On the 11th, Japan stops using Truk (in the

CAROLINES) as a major naval base, as it has become too difficult to keep the fleet supplied there. Japanese continue heavy attacks against the Seventh Indian Division in the Arakan. On the 12th, US Marines occupy Umboi Island (off the western end of NEW BRITAIN). In Burma, the British begin moving reinforcements to support the Seventh Indian Division. On the 13th, US Marines take possession of Arno Atoll in the Marshall Islands. On the 14th, MOUNTBATTEN warns that a further Japanese offensive is likely if they win the Arakan battle. On the 15th, New Zealand troops land on Green Island in the northern SOLOMONS. On the 16th, elements of TF 58 conduct air attacks and reconnaissance of ENIWETOK. Bill Howell's ship, *Monterey* (CVL-26), takes part in a series of raids that now begin against Japanese-held islands. On 16–17 February, *Monterey*'s aircraft hit Truk. On 21–22 February, the Mariana Islands are hit, and from 30 March to 1 April, PALAU, Yap, ULITHI, and Woleai islands are all hit. On the 17th, Allies complete massive (six battleships and nine carriers) two-day attack on main Japanese base on Truk Island. Although most Japanese warships had earlier been withdrawn, Allied ships and aircraft still sink two cruisers, three destroyers, and over 200,000 tons of merchant shipping (including several tankers). The island's airstrips are destroyed. Truk is now neutralized and bypassed, leaving many of its garrison to starve before the war will end. Meanwhile, other elements of TF 58 land on Eniwetok and Engebi. On the 18th, Allied destroyers shell Japanese bases at Rabaul and KAVIENG. On the 19th, fighting continues on the Marshall Islands of Engebi and Eniwetok. On the 20th, New Zealand troops complete their conquest of Green Island. This cuts off all remaining Japanese troops in the Solomon Islands. The Allies now have an air base only 117 miles from the main Japanese base at Rabaul. This short distance permits steady aerial bombing of Rabaul, escorted by fighters. Air power on Rabaul will soon be neutralized. On the 21st, Japanese resistance on Engebi and Eniwetok ends. TOJO takes over direct control of the Japanese Army by assuming the position of army chief of staff. On the 22nd, US Navy Task Force 58 approaches the MARIANA Islands, and is attacked by Japanese aircraft, which are easily beaten off with heavy losses. On the 23rd, for the first time in the Burma war, British forces defeat the Japanese in a pitched battle; Japanese forces at Sinzweya, in the Arakan, withdraw after their attacks on the Seventh Indian Division fail. The Japanese style of warfare has been difficult for the British to deal with. The dramatic Japanese victories over the British early in the war (particularly the fall of SINGAPORE) have played a part, as has the British use of a variety of different troops (Indian and British). But there has also been the Japanese soldier's fatalistic perseverance and refusal to surrender when beaten. Eventually, the British will learn to cope. On the 24th, US carrier aircraft complete a series of attacks against Japanese positions in the Marianas (SAIPAN, TINIAN, Rota, and GUAM), the first such attacks of the war. On the 25th, British, US, and Chinese forces all advance in Burma. On the 26th, US fleet carrier *Bennington* and escort carrier *Steamer Bay* are launched. Since PEARL HARBOR the US Navy has commissioned eight fleet carriers (700–800 total aircraft capacity), nine light carriers (370 aircraft), and 43 escort carriers (729 aircraft) to its fleet, while the Imperial Navy has commissioned only three fleet carriers (c. 160 aircraft), four light carriers (121 aircraft), and five escort carriers (138 aircraft). On the 27th, US amphibious task force approaches the ADMIRALTY ISLANDS, while elements of the Alamo Scouts land on Los Negros, the Admiralties, to conduct a covert reconnaissance, and Allied aircraft attack Japanese targets there. On the 28th, the Alamo Scouts are withdrawn from Los Negros, while air attacks continue. In Burma, the British restore their earlier positions in the Arakan. On the 29th, US Army troops invade Los Negros (the Admiralty Islands) to complete the encirclement of Rabaul.

March 1944

The Japanese surprise offensive in Burma drove the British back into India. US carrier raids continued to pummel Japanese bases in the Pacific. Japanese leadership announced to the Japanese people that the war situation was not good—a bit of understatement.

On the 1st, American troops on Los Negros Island defeat Japanese attacks on their beachhead. On the 2nd, in Burma, the US MERRILL'S MARAUDERS and the British Special Air Service begin an offensive from the Ledo area, supporting Chinese troops in a drive to reopen the BURMA ROAD. The Japanese airfield at Momote on Los Negros Island is seized by US troops. On the 3rd, Japanese make a final effort to force US troops off Los Negros, which fails, a defeat involving most of the remaining Japanese combat capability. On the 4th, an airfield becomes operational on Green Island, off New Guinea. Allied forces in northern Burma continue their advance. On the 5th, US Navy ships bombard MANUS, in the ADMIRALTY ISLANDS. On the 6th, US Marines make a new landing on New Britain and establish a beachhead over a mile-deep near Talasea. US forces in Burma repel a major Japanese counterattack. On the 7th, three brigades of British COMMANDOS (CHINDITS) begin attacking Japanese rear-area installations in northern Burma; the Chindits had been dropped behind the Japanese lines two days earlier. On the 8th, while part of the Japanese force desperately struggles against Chinese regulars and British and American commandos, another Japanese force launches an offensive against British forces near Imphal in eastern India. On the 9th, US Marines seize the Talasea airstrip in New Britain, against no resistance. On the 10th, Chinese troops and Merrill's Marauders seize full control of the Walawbum Valley in northern Burma. On the 11th, Japanese counterattacks on BOUGAINVILLE threaten several airfields. On the 12th, Ireland refuses to oust Axis (Japanese and German) diplomats (who act, in effect, as spies). Britain enacts sanctions. The Joint Chiefs of Staff approaches a "dual advance" in the Pacific. On the 13th, British launch an outflanking amphibious operation in the Arakan area of Burma. On the 14th, attacking Japanese forces at Imphal (eastern India) threaten to surround retreating British units. On the 15th, US Army troops invade Manus Island in the Admiralties. On the 16th, Japanese destroyer *Shirakumo* is TORPEDOED east of Hokkaido by US submarine *Tautog* (SS-199): Since Pearl Harbor, Japan has lost 62 of her 129 destroyers. On the 17th, elements of the First Cavalry Division capture Lorengau airfield, the principal US objective on Manus. On the 18th, US Task Group 50.1 bombards Mili Atoll in the MARSHALL ISLANDS. On the 19th, TOJO and his aides debate whether to announce to the Japanese people that the outlook for the war is dire. Several days later, the announcement is made. On the 20th, US Marines occupy Emirau Island in the BISMARCK ARCHIPELAGO, without opposition. The island completes the isolation and neutralization of RABAUL. On the 21st, in northern Burma, US and Chinese forces advance toward road junctions at Inkangahrawng and Kamaing. On the 22nd, Japan's offensive in Burma gains momentum as its troops approach the Indian border. On the 23rd, Japanese troops launch attacks on Bougainville (in the SOLOMONS), which are halted by US artillery. This is the last major battle in the Solomons. On the 24th, Britain's Major General Orde WINGATE is killed in a plane crash in Burma; he had developed the commando tactics and organization used with much success against the Japanese in Burma. On the 25th, last organized Japanese resistance on Manus Island is put down. On the 26th, USS *Tullibee* (SS-284) sinks itself when one of its torpedoes circles and hits the sub; one survivor lives to tell the tale. On the 27th, the British move reinforcements to Imphal. On Bougainville, the Japanese withdraw from the EMPRESS AUGUSTA BAY beachhead. On the 28th, Merrill's Marauders and Chinese troops continue their advance. On the 29th, advancing Japanese troops in eastern India cut the road between Imphal and Kohima, threatening the entire British position in the area. On the 30th, US Task Force 58 begins several days of raids into the western CAROLINES (PALAU, YAP, and ULITHI). For a cost of 20 aircraft, the US forces destroy 150 enemy aircraft, six warships, and over 100,000 tons of shipping. On the 31st, Admiral Koga, commander of the Japanese Combined Fleet, dies in an airplane crash in the Philippines, to be succeeded by Admiral TOYODA. HOLLANDIA is bombed by the Fifth Air Force.

April 1944

US carrier raids continued across the Pacific. Japanese invasion of India faltered. Fighting intensified in New Guinea and in the SOLOMONS. TRUK was pounded into uselessness after being cut off.

On the 1st, US Navy Task Force 58's raid into the western CAROLINES enters its third and final day, with the Japanese unable to offer any effective resistance. Elements of the First Cavalry Division begin mop-up of outlying islands of the Admiralty Group, which are found to be mostly undefended. On the 2nd, US Fifth Air Force raids Hansa Bay, New Guinea. MERRILL'S MARAUDERS are heavily engaged at Nhpum Ga, Burma, where one battalion has been cut off. On the 3rd, US Fifth Air Force launches large raid on major Japanese base at HOLLANDIA, New Guinea. Over 300 Japanese aircraft are destroyed, most of them on the ground before they can take off. British juggle forces in Burma to stem the Japanese drive on Imphal, while Allied forces in northern Burma remain heavily engaged. On the 4th, in eastern India, the Japanese move on Kohima, after having cut the road from Kohima to Imphal. Heavy fighting around Nhpum Ga, Burma. On the 5th, heavy fighting continues in northern Burma, as British reinforcements reach the Kohima-Imphal front. On the 6th, after several days of US air raids, the Japanese have only 25 flyable aircraft at Hollandia. On the 7th, British forces at Kohima are brought under more pressure as advancing Japanese cut off the town's water supply. On the 8th, in a skillful, and lucky, bit of bombing, B-24s bring down the Sittang bridge in Burma, crippling Japanese railroad traffic to crucial battle areas for two months. On the 9th, Japanese offer to mediate a peace agreement between Germany and Russia. The Germans are perplexed (it was a Japanese idea) and the Russians turn down the offer. In Burma the Japanese abandon Nhpum

Ga, while the Japanese complete the encirclement of Imphal, which must be supplied by air, despite the onset of the monsoon season. On the 10th, British forces on the Imphal-Kohima front in eastern India take the offensive. The Japanese gamble everything on their offensive and soon run out of resources. The Japanese troops are left largely without food, ammunition, or other supplies. Bill Howell's ship, *Monterey* (CVL-26), gets a new skipper, with Captain Stuart Ingersoll taking over from Captain Lester Hundt. On the 11th, Japanese destroyer *Akigumo* is sunk off ZAMBOANGA, the Philippines, by US submarine *Redfin* (SS-272). On the 12th, US, British, and Chinese forces in northern Burma halt their advance, but the British airlift a West African CHINDIT brigade into central Burma. Australian light forces depart Finschhafen, New Guinea, to escort convoys carrying reinforcements to the ADMIRALTY ISLANDS and to shell bypassed Japanese positions. On the 13th, heavy fighting on the Imphal-Kohima front. On the 14th, in one of those all too common wartime accidents, the SS *Fort Stikene*, carrying 1,300 tons of TNT, explodes in Bombay. Another ammunition ship nearby explodes, and in the ensuing blast a total of 21 ships are destroyed. Nearly a thousand people are killed. On the 15th, reflecting the decreased importance of the area since the ejection of the Japanese from the ALEUTIANS, US command arrangements in the north and northeastern Pacific are reorganized. In heavy fighting, the British and Indians make important gains on the Kohima Front, in India. On the 16th, senior American military planners address the question of what must be done to defeat Japan and whether an invasion of Japan itself will be necessary, leading to preliminary studies for "Operation Olympic," the invasion of Japan. On the 17th, Japan begins its last major offensive in China as one division crosses the Yellow River. The objective is the US airfields in China that are supporting raids by long-range bombers as far as Japan itself. Chinese forces in northern Burma resume the offensive. On the 18th, fighting in NEW BRITAIN begins to die down and, by the end of the month is over save for some sporadic Japanese holdout activity. On the 19th, Japan sends two more divisions south from PEKING toward US air bases in China. On the 20th, a British division lifts the Japanese siege of Kohima in eastern India; the Japanese still hold the key road to Imphal. In northern Burma the Chinese New 38th Division ejects the Japanese from critical terrain near Kamaing. On the 21st US Task Force 58 raids Hollandia, and other points in northern New Guinea with aircraft and gunfire in preparation for the Hollandia landings. In central Burma, Allied forces are ordered to begin a drive on Myitkyina. Bill Howell's ship, *Monterey* (CVL-26), moves as far west as it will ever get, as it takes part in supporting General MACARTHUR's army troops in western New Guinea. From 21 April to 1 June, *Monterey* aircraft operate around Hollandia. On the 22nd, US Army troops make an amphibious landing near Hollandia in New Guinea. On the 23rd, staff officers at the US War Department conclude that Japan can be defeated only with an invasion of the Home Islands. This becomes an objective for the rest of the war, until the unexpected success of the ATOMIC BOMB test in July 1945 provides an alternative. On the 24th, Australian troops occupy Madang in New Guinea. This provides another airfield for the Allies, and Australian aircraft promptly begin using it. On the 25th, the First Marine Division turns over responsibility for New Britain to the 40th Infantry Division, and begins moving to Paavu, in the Solomons, for rest, recuperation, and retraining in anticipation of the PELELIU operation. On the 26th, more Allied gains in New Guinea. Australians take Alexishafen; US troops take the airfield at Hollandia. On the 27th, heavy fighting continues at Imphal, India, as the Japanese attempt to defeat the British before the start of the rainy season. On the 28th, Japanese advance in China continues. US Army Air Force planes attack Yellow River bridges in an attempt to slow down the Japanese by cutting off their supply lines. On the 29th, in Burma the 16th Brigade, Third Indian Division, a Chindit formation, is evacuated from the front, having completed a long raid behind enemy lines. On the 30th, US Navy carrier aircraft begin a two-day raid on Truk Island naval base, destroying over 120 aircraft and most of remaining fuel supplies. This effectively completes the neutralization of Truk as a naval or air base against Allied forces. US and Chinese forces begin a drive on Myitkyina, Burma.

May 1944

Heavy fighting in Burma and China. US carrier raids continued to smash Japanese bases in the Pacific.

On the 1st, PONAPE Island in the CAROLINES is worked over by US battleships and carrier aircraft. On the 2nd, STILWELL is ordered to build up supplies in China for future operations. On the 3rd, Allied aircraft begin mining river approaches to RANGOON and BANGKOK, making it nearly impossible for the Japanese to bring merchant shipping into those ports. On the 4th, Chinese troops battle to the vicinity of Kamaing in northern Burma. On the 5th, the British, feeling their military position in Burma and political position in India is now stable, release nationalist leader Mahatma Ghandi (who had been imprisoned since August 1942). On the 6th, fighting in the AITAPE area of New Guinea goes poorly for the Japanese, who, in several weeks of fighting, have lost over 500 dead to only 19 Americans killed. Allied reinforcements and supplies continue to land amphibiously. On the 7th, Allied air raids against the sea routes off Rangoon and Bangkok virtually drive Japanese shipping from the Bay of Bengal. On the 8th, heavy fighting continues in northern Burma, where the Chinese New 38th Division, supported by the 30th, presses the advance on Kamaing. On the 9th, the Japanese offensive in China succeeds in capturing Lushan, thus securing complete control of the Peking-Hankow railroad. On the 10th, Chinese launch major offensive in north Burma, the 198th, 36th, and 116th Divisions cross the Salween River and advance on a hundred-mile front. On the 11th, the new Chinese offensive across the Salween River meets little Japanese opposition. Indian troops advance on Kohima. On the 12th, Japanese troops counterattack against the Chinese forces crossing the Salween River, in northern Burma. On the 13th, one of several Japanese SUBMARINES operating outside the Pacific is sunk in mid-Atlantic by a US destroyer escort. A Japanese counterattack on the Salween front, in Burma, almost wipes out a Chinese battalion until reinforcements arrive. On the 14th, in Burma, MERRILL'S MARAUDERS begin a surprise attack on the Japanese airport at Myitkyina. On New Guinea, Japanese counterattacks briefly isolate elements of the US 127th Infantry, which are withdrawn. On the 15th, Merrill's Marauders reach within 15 miles of Myitkyina. British Indian troops finally break down the Japanese defenses of Kohima in eastern India. On the 16th, the siege of Kohima in eastern India is finally ended, with the last Japanese resistance crushed. On the 17th, US and British aircraft attack Soerabaya, in JAVA, and sink 10 enemy ships. In Burma, Merrill's Marauders capture the Myitkyina airfield in a coup de main. Preliminary phase of the WADKE Operation begin, as US troops land at Arare, Netherlands New Guinea. On the 17th, in an unusual example of inter-theater cooperation, carrier aircraft of the British Far Eastern Fleet raid the naval base at Soerabaya, Java, during the day, followed with a nighttime raid by B-24s from MACARTHUR's Southwest Pacific Theater. On the 18th, Japanese and Chinese forces engage in street fighting in the Chinese city of Loyang. Heavy fighting at Myitkyina, Burma. US Army troops make an amphibious assault on Wadke Island, off the north coast of New Guinea. On the 19th, US troops overrun most of Wadke and begin repairing the airfield. Chinese troops join battle for Myitkyina. On the 20th, US carrier aircraft begin a two-day raid on Japanese-held MARCUS ISLAND. On the 21st, Japanese resistance on Wadke Island is crushed, with over 750 dead and only four PRISONERS; US losses are 43 killed and 139 wounded. The island will support an air base that will provide air cover for the coming Allied invasion of Mindanao in the Philippines. At PEARL HARBOR, where preparations are underway for the SAIPAN landings in June, an LST loaded with fuel and ammunition inexplicably

blows up in the West Loch, near an ammunition depot. Five other LSTs alongside are destroyed and CASUALTIES are heavy—207 Marines killed and nearly 400 wounded, not to mention losses among sailors and civilians. The blast delays the movement of the Fourth Marine Division by 24 hours. On the 22nd, the campaign in the ADMIRALTY ISLANDS ends, Japan having lost over 3,000 dead, the United States 326. On the 23rd, the Japanese offensive in China is hit by a Chinese counteroffensive. In Burma, the Japanese counterattack on both the Myitkyina and Salween fronts. On the 24th, US Navy carrier aircraft attack WAKE ISLAND. On the 25th, the Japanese lose ground in fighting around Myitkyina in Burma, but reinforce their troops for a counteroffensive. On the 26th, heavy fighting develops along the Tirfoam River, on the New Guinea coast opposite Wadke. Japanese counterattacks continue on the Myitkyina and Salween fronts in Burma. On the 27th, the US Army 41st Division meets only token resistance when it lands on BIAK Island. This brings Allied troops to within 900 miles of the Philippines. On the 28th, the Chinese commit all available forces to their advance across the Salween River in north Burma, but their supplies are limited and must be supplemented by airdrops. Heavy fighting develops on Biak. On the 29th, the first tank battle of the Pacific War takes place as Japanese and American armor clash on Biak. The Japanese lose. On the 30th, despite increased Chinese resistance, two Japanese divisions force their way across the Hsiang River in their attempt to shut down Allied air bases in China. Japanese attack Arare, Netherlands New Guinea. On the 31st, Allied air attacks and airdropped MINES keep nearly all Japanese ships out of the Bay of Bengal. Heavy fighting in the Arare, Aitape, and Tirfoam areas of New Guinea.

June 1944

The British defeated the Japanese invasion of India. US Marines invaded SAIPAN, in the MARIANA Islands, providing bases from which B-29s could bomb Japan. Fighting in Burma stalled as monsoon rains began. Japanese offensive in China continued, reaching some US airbases there.

On the 1st, monsoon rains in Burma begin. Most military operations begin to slow down because of the reduced mobility, a situation that endangers Allied forces, who are far from their sources of supply. Heavy fighting continues on BIAK. On the 2nd, Japanese forces in Honan Province of China halt their operations, having achieved all of their objectives. Allied forces before Myitkyina begin to besiege the place, with Chinese troops attempting to tunnel under Japanese defenses. On the 3rd, the Battle of Kohima in eastern India ends in a British victory. Japanese forces on Biak break contact. On the 4th, US forces on Biak halt their advance after two days without serious resistance, in anticipation of a Japanese counterattack. Chinese forces on the Salween front make significant gains. On the 5th, the Japanese not having undertaken a counterattack, US forces on Biak resume the advance but still meet no resistance. In Burma, the British and Indians clear the Japanese from the vicinity of Kohima and begin operations to open the Kohima-Imphal road. On the 6th, Pentagon planners decide on 1 October 1945 as the date for the first landings on the Japanese Home Islands, setting in motion vast logistical preparations for the operation. In Europe, the Allies land in Normandy. On the 7th, Chinese forces on the Salween front in Burma reach Lung-ling, an important regional center. US forces on Biak capture the airfield unopposed, but then face intense fire from Japanese forces ensconced in the hills beyond it. On the 8th, a desperate Japanese attempt to resupply Biak Island with five heavily laden destroyers ends with one ship sunk and the other four turned back. On the 9th, heavy fighting at Lung-ling. On the 10th, the US and Chinese assault on Myitkyina, Burma, resumes. On the 11th, US Navy ships and aircraft attack the Marianas (GUAM, SAIPAN, and TINIAN), losing a dozen aircraft but destroying 200 Japanese planes and damaging installations.

On the 12th, the Chinese communists, fearful of the recent Japanese offensive, pledge support of the Chinese Nationalists in the fight against the Japanese. On the 13th, heavy fighting continues at Myitkyina, Burma. US aircraft begin limited operations from Biak, where the Japanese are still resisting. On the 14th, the Japanese offensive in China rolls on, as the city of Liu-yang falls. Heavy fighting on all fronts in Burma. On the 15th, Saipan, in the Marianas, is stormed by two US Marine divisions. The 27,000 Japanese defenders are hit by the firepower of seven battleships and 11 cruisers. Saipan, and other islands in the Marianas, will be bases for B-29 attacks on Japan. On the 16th, returning to their China bases, US B-29s have made the first air attack on Japan since the DOOLITTLE raid in early 1942. On the 17th, US Navy carrier aircraft attack IWO JIMA and the BONIN ISLANDS. On the 18th, in China, the Japanese offensive takes the city of CHANGSHA, an area the Japanese had twice reached earlier in the war and failed to take. On the 19th, the three-day Battle of the PHILIPPINE SEA begins, to end in a defeat for the Japanese, who will lose three carriers and 426 of their 473 aircraft, with no US ships lost and only a handful of US aircraft. This is a major Japanese attempt to slow the American advance across the Pacific. After their failure in this battle, Japanese senior leaders know that the war is lost. Bill Howell's ship, *Monterey* (CVL-26), takes part. In the days before the battle, CVL *Monterey* aircraft support the assault on Saipan. On the 20th, heavy fighting continues on Biak. British and Indian forces approach Imphal, in eastern India. On the 21st, US aircraft begin using Owi airfield, New Guinea; no Japanese airfields are operational anywhere on New Guinea. On the 22nd, and after 10 weeks of fighting, the battle for Imphal comes to an end as British and Indian troops open the road from Kohima to Imphal; the Japanese find they have suffered nearly 44,000 CASUALTIES, mostly dead, compared to 14,000 British Empire losses, including 2,700 dead. Chinese forces on the Salween front make significant gains. On the 23rd, Japanese forces at Sarmi, near WADKE in New Guinea, attack Allied lines. Heavy fighting on Biak. On the 24th, fighting continues at Sarmi, New Guinea, as US forces try to outflank Japanese positions. On the 25th, Emperor HIROHITO calls a conference of senior generals and admirals to discuss Japan's worsening situation. The military admit that "outer" defenses like Saipan can not be held and that emphasis must be placed on bases closer to Japan. Japanese troops begin withdrawing at Sarmi, New Guinea. On the 26th, US air base at Hengyang, China, is overrun by Japanese troops. On the 27th, Japanese forces halt the Chinese advance on the Salween front, northern Burma. On the 28th, around Hengyang, Chinese forces put up stiff resistance to advancing Japanese. On the 29th, US submarine *Archerfish* (SS-311) sinks Japanese *Patrol Boat Number 24* off IWO JIMA, while *Darter* (SS-227) sinks minelayer *Tsugaru* off Morotai: During June of 1944 US SUB-MARINES in the Pacific sink about 260,000 tons of Japanese merchant shipping, exclusive of vessels under 500 tons, not to mention two aircraft carriers, six destroyers, and these two smaller warships. On the 30th, operations on Biak enter the mopping up phase, as they do at Sarmi, on New Guinea.

July 1944

US troops battled all month to eliminate Japanese resistance in the Mariana Islands and prepare airfields for B-29 bombers. Japanese situation in Burma collapsed, mainly because of poor supply arrangements. Only in China did a Japanese offensive continue to advance.

On the 1st, as Japanese resistance on Saipan crumbles, Admiral NAGUMO commits suicide. He had led Japanese fleets to victory early in the war, until defeated at MIDWAY. He was then demoted to command of the naval forces in the Saipan area, which is how he came to end his life in a bunker surrounded by US Marines. On the 2nd, surviving Japanese forces fall back to the north end of Saipan to make a last stand. US troops land on Noemfoor, off New Guinea. On the 3rd, US Navy ships bombard IWO JIMA and the BONIN ISLANDS. Several Japanese transports are sunk. Bill Howell's ship, *Monterey* (CVL-26), takes part. A week later, *Monterey* assists in the capture of GUAM and remains in

the Marianas until 15 August. On the 4th, elements of the 503rd Parachute Infantry drop on Noemfoor to reinforce US troops already engaged there. On the 5th, Japanese commanders on the Imphal front in eastern India, discuss calling off the operation, and after several days of debate decide to withdraw: They have lost 53,000 out of the 85,000 troops committed, many due to disease and starvation caused by inadequate logistical arrangements. On the 6th, US troops make an amphibious "end run" around Japanese positions on Noemfoor, breaking enemy resistance. On the 7th, surviving Japanese troops on Saipan make a final BANZAI CHARGE, in which most of the 3,000 attackers are killed but not before inflicting heavy CASUALTIES on the defending troops. US B-29s from Chinese bases again attack targets in Japan. On the 8th, Guam is bombarded by US Navy ships, beginning a series of daily attacks in preparation for landings later in the month. On the 9th, Saipan finally falls to American forces. The Japanese lose nearly 27,000 troops, almost all dead save for a few hundred taken prisoner, while US losses are 3,200 killed, for a total of 14,200—3,700 army and 10,500 Marine. In addition, thousands of Japanese civilians commit suicide. On the 10th, cut off from supply and air support, desperate Japanese troops launch a counterattack at AITAPE, New Guinea. Heavy fighting on the Salween front in Burma, as the Chinese press their attacks. On the 11th, US vice president Henry Wallace, having been sent to China to investigate the situation, reports that Nationalist leader CHIANG KAI-SHEK is more interested in fighting the communists than the Japanese. Wallace suggests that the United States try to mediate the disputes between the Nationalists and communists. On the 12th, another Allied attempt to capture Myitkyina, Burma, fails, because Allied aircraft mistakenly bomb their own troops. On the 13th, fighting continues on Noemfoor. Japanese make small local attacks on several fronts in New Guinea. On the 14th, senior members of the Japanese government suggest that in the wake of the loss of SAIPAN it might be a good idea if General TOJO resigned as prime minister. On the 15th, heavy fighting in the Aitape area of New Guinea. On the 16th, Australian cruisers and destroyers shell Japanese positions near Aitape, New Guinea. On the 17th, the Japanese minister of the navy, Admiral Shimada, resigns, bringing down the Tojo government. Heavy fighting in the Aitape area. On the 18th, pressure from senior members of the government and from the "elders" (retired politicians and senior officers) forces General Tojo to resign his government posts (prime minister, minister of the army and army chief of staff, minister of the interior, minister of munitions, etc). A new government is formed under Kuniaki Koiso, with much the same policies as the old one. On the 19th, heavy fighting continues in the Aitape area of New Guinea, as Allied and Japanese forces make numerous small attacks and counterattacks against each other. On the 20th, American invasion force approaches Guam and begins shelling and bombing the island intensively. On the 21st, two divisions (one Marine, one army) storm ashore on Japanese-held Guam in the MARIANAS, while a pre-invasion bombardment of TINIAN commences. On the 22nd, after allowing American troops to advance a mile or so inland on Guam, Japanese launch a fierce counterattack, which is defeated. On the 23rd, from Saipan, a Marine invasion force puts to sea for nearby Tinian. Heavy fighting on Guam. Chinese troops renew their offensive on the Salween front, Burma. On the 24th, after two weeks to recuperate from the Saipan fighting, two Marine divisions land on Tinian. Only one Japanese regiment is defending. On Saipan, each US division suffers a thousand dead and over 4,000 wounded. On Tinian, each division averages less than 200 dead and 900 wounded—tough fighting, but not nearly as severe as on Saipan. In large part, the lower losses are the result of a successful DECEPTION. There was one large beach in the southern part of Tinian but only two smaller ones (65 and 130 yards wide) in the north. Going ashore on Saipan, there were heavy losses from Japanese machine guns and mortars just approaching and crossing the beach. On Tinian the Japanese were fooled, as each of these small beaches were hit by a Marine regiment that quickly pushed past the few Japanese stationed there. On the 25th, US Army and Marine units are still four miles away from linking up their separate beachheads on Guam, with Japanese resistance stiffening. On the 26th, President ROOSEVELT holds a conference in HAWAII with MACARTHUR and NIMITZ. The navy wants to take FORMOSA in order to cut Japan off from its oil and resource supplies in the Dutch East Indies (and to make it easier to supply the Chinese). MacArthur proposes retaking the Philippines, and wins the argument, even though he offers a larger and more difficult operation. On the 27th, US Marines clear most of northern Tinian and begin rebuilding the airfield they find there. On the 28th the Japanese commander at Myitkyina, Burma, orders his troops to withdraw but decides to commit hara-kiri to atone for the shame of withdrawing in the face of the enemy: The fighting has caused the Japanese nearly 2,000 casualties, including 790 dead. On the 29th, US Marines capture the Orote airstrip on Guam, despite fierce Japanese resistance. On the 30th, the US Sixth Infantry Division lands on the Vogelkop Peninsula on the northwest coast of New Guinea, as well as on the nearby islands of Amsterdam and Middleberg. On the 31st, the British assist in forming an anti-Japanese, Burmese government in exile in India.

August 1944

Japanese resistance in New Guinea and the SOLOMONS crumbled, particularly since they could no longer supply their forces there. Japanese resistance in the MARIANA Islands was crushed. Preparations moved ahead for the invasion of the Philippines. In the course of the month, US SUBMARINES sank 245,000 tons of Japanese merchant shipping, not counting vessels of under 500 tons, plus an escort carrier, two light cruisers, two destroyers, and six smaller warships, while another 50,000 tons of shipping was sunk by aircraft and surface ships.

On the 1st, US Marines crush Japanese resistance on TINIAN. Heavy fighting before Hengyang, in China, as the Japanese try to take the city. Bill Howell is promoted to chief petty officer, the top of the food chain as far as enlisted navy ranks go. For over a year before he became a "Chief," Bill did a CPO's work and took care of personnel matters for the ship's executive officer (Lieutenant Commander Frank B. Miller) and supervised six sailors (all yeomen, like himself, but of less exalted rank). On the 2nd, Chinese troops on the Salween front in northern Burma are heavily engaged before Teng-chung, to which the Japanese cling tenaciously. On the 3rd, the key town of Myitkyina in northern Burma finally falls to US and Chinese troops. This permits the reopening of the BURMA ROAD, providing a land route into China for military aid. The fierce fighting deep in the jungle costs the Allies over 5,400 CASUALTIES (including 972 Chinese and 272 Americans killed). On the 4th, US Army and Marine divisions link up on GUAM, cutting the Japanese defenders into two groups. On the Salween front in northern Burma, Chinese troops finally break into Teng-chung. On the 5th, elements of Task Force 58 attack IWO JIMA and Chichi Jima with air strikes and shellings, sinking one destroyer and two transports, and destroying or damaging many aircraft. On the 6th, Japanese troops in China advance toward Hengyang, in the face of heavy Chinese resistance. US aircraft begin raiding the Philippines from bases in New Guinea. On the 7th, Japanese light cruiser NAGARA is sunk in Japanese waters by US submarine *Croaker* (SS-246): Since PEARL HARBOR Japan has lost 16 of her 44 cruisers. On the 8th, Japanese troops finally take Hengyang, despite stiff Chinese resistance. On the 9th, the fall of Hengyang in China causes some of the warlords in the Nationalist coalition to seek to replace CHIANG KAI-SHEK as leader of the Nationalist cause. On the 10th, organized Japanese resistance on Guam is stamped out: Some 10,000 Japanese defenders have died; American casualties are 5,000, including 1,400 killed. The United States now had an island large enough, and close enough, to support hundreds of B-29 bombers with which to bomb Japan. On the 11th, US B-29s flying out of bases in India

complete the first of over 150 missions to drop marine MINES in rivers and ports in China, Indochina, MALAYA, and Sumatra. On the 12th, "mopping up" proceeds on Guam, continuing until the end of the war. On the 13th, the 14th Air Force reconnoiters Manila from Chinese bases, but MACARTHUR prohibits air attacks on the Philippines capital. On the 14th, surviving Japanese forces on New Guinea and nearby islands break contact and try to fall back. On the 15th, US troops in various parts of New Guinea and nearby islands (AITAPE, Noemfoor, the Vogelkopf) are unable to find the Japanese. On the 16th, Japanese forces on New Guinea continue to fall back on all fronts. On the 17th, the last Japanese troops to have entered Indian territory during the Imphal-Kohima offensive are killed or driven over the border into Burma. On Noemfoor, off New Guinea, US troops manage to regain contact with retiring Japanese. On the 18th, US submarine *Rasher* (SS-269) sinks the Japanese escort carrier TAIYO off Luzon: Since Pearl Harbor the Imperial Navy has lost 12 aircraft carriers of all types, out of a total of 23, with a total capacity of 525 aircraft. On the 19th, the White House announces that President ROOSEVELT has appointed a special envoy to China in order to effect a military alliance between Nationalist and communist forces. On the 20th, after three months of fighting in the jungle, BIAK ISLAND, northwest of New Guinea, is finally cleared of Japanese forces: The US Army has suffered 2,400 casualties (including 400 dead); the Japanese have lost nearly 5,000 dead, although an unprecedented 220 PRISONERS are taken. On the 21st, US B-29s operating out of bases in CEYLON begin a series of raids on Japanese installations on Sumatra. On the 22nd, the Japanese voluntarily abandon ULITHI in the western CAROLINES, not realizing that the Americans want the atoll as a forward base. Japanese troops on the Salween front in northern Burma attempt a counterattack, which is handily repelled by Chinese forces. On the 23rd, formation of the new Sixth Marine Division begins on GUADALCANAL. On the 24th, the British Far Eastern Fleet makes a carrier raid on Padang, in southwestern

Sumatra. On the 25th, US Army troops finally overcome all Japanese resistance in the Aitape region of New Guinea, in an operation that has cost the Japanese 8,800 dead and 98 surrendered; US dead number 440. On the 26th, in anticipation of the liberation of the Philippines, Filipino GUERRILLA organizations begin to receive their orders for the coming battle. On the 27th, the ROYAL NAVY doubles its submarine strength in the Far East with the arrival of the Second Submarine Flotilla at Ceylon. On the 28th, during a B-24 raid on the KURILES, Japanese *Submarine Chaser No. 77* is sunk. On the 29th, the Japanese offensive in China continues, as 11 divisions advance from Hengyang toward the major US air bases at Kweilin and Liuchow. On the 30th, the US 96th Infantry Division completes its movement from SAN FRANCISCO to HAWAII: Allied ground forces in the Pacific (Pacific Ocean Areas and Southwest Pacific) total 34 divisions (seven Australian, 21 US Army, and six US Marine divisions, plus a large New Zealand brigade and numerous independent brigades, regiments, and battalions). In these same areas Japanese ground forces total 30 divisions and about as many independent brigades, plus numerous separate regiments and battalions, plus large numbers of troops in the Home Islands. On the 31st, Chinese forces in north Burma and south China approach a linkup and re-establishment of access between the two nations severed by the Japanese in 1942. Off New Guinea, Noemfoor is declared secured by US forces.

September 1944

The BURMA ROAD was reopened, providing land access to China for the first time since early 1942. The Japanese offensive in China rampaged on. The last landing of the US Marines' cross-Pacific campaign occurred in the PALAU ISLANDS. US Army troops made more landings, bringing them closer to the Philippines.

On the 1st, the Fourth Marine Division arrives at Maui, after having invaded and conquered SAIPAN and TINIAN. The division has a 28% casualty rate (5,981 killed or wounded), most of them in the 27 240-man rifle companies. The 6,500 Marine infantry have suffered over 50% CASUALTIES. It will take several months to train the replacements up to the level of the experienced survivors of Saipan and Tinian. On the 2nd, Task Group 38.4 raids the BONIN ISLANDS. On the 3rd, US Navy ships attack the Japanese base on WAKE ISLAND. On the 4th, US Army forces on New Guinea rehearse for the Morotai operation, while the First Marine Division sails from the Solomons for Palau. On the 5th, Chinese forces moving from Burma reach the Kaolingkung Pass, to link up with Chinese forces from Yunan Province in China and reestablish the land link that had been severed by the Japanese in 1942. On the 6th, the US Navy uses 16 carriers to launch air strikes against Japanese-held islands in the western CAROLINES (YAP, ULITHI and PALAU). Bill Howell's ship, *Monterey* (CVL-26), is part of this operation. The Philippines are right to the west of the Palaus, and toward the end of September, aircraft from the *Monterey* operate in that direction. On the 7th, Chinese forces on the Salween front in Burma finally clear out all resistance, killing most of the 2,000 Japanese defenders, having lost 7,700 dead since 10 May in clearing another vital area that had to be secured in order to reopen the Burma Road. On the 8th, two and a half Japanese divisions stationed in south China join the attack on the US airfields at Kweilin and Liuchow. On the 9th, a dozen carriers of Task Force 38 begin two days of raids against Japanese bases on Mindanao. On the 10th, elements of TG 38.4 raid the Palau Islands. On the 11th, US SUBMARINES sink two Japanese transports on their way from SINGAPORE to FORMOSA. The transports carry 1,274 Allied POWs; over 300 of the POWs die, with 159 rescued by the subs and the rest by the Japanese. On the 12th, Allied leaders hold a conference in Canada where CHURCHILL and ROOSEVELT agree that emphasis should be shifted to the Pacific now that the Germans appear to be at the end of their rope. It is also reaffirmed that the first invasion of the Japanese Home Islands will take place in October 1945. On the 13th, US

Navy ships and aircraft pound PELELIU Island (in the Palaus) preparatory to an invasion. On the 14th, Japanese abandon their efforts at a counteroffensive in the Salween area of Burma; this eliminates a major threat to the reopening of the Burma Road. The United States agrees to the participation of the Royal Navy and RAF heavy bombers in the Pacific War. On the 15th, a US one-two punch as Marines land on Japanese-held island of Peleliu, 450 miles east of the Philippines (Mindanao), while the Army's 31st Division lands on Morotai in the ADMIRALTY ISLANDS, about 350 miles southeast of Mindanao, in preparation for the scheduled liberation of the Philippines. On the 16th, aided by the terrain, Japanese troops on Peleliu offer fierce resistance, although greatly outnumbered by US Marines. On the 17th, the US Army Air Force abandons major air base at Kweilin, China, as the Japanese close in. Elements of the 81st Division land on Anguar, near Peleliu. On the 18th, the Marines encounter very heavy resistance on Peleliu; army troops advance on Anguar. On the 19th, heavy fighting continues on Peleliu; army troops advance on Anguar. On the 19th, heavy fighting continues on Peleliu and Anguar. On the 20th, US troops on Morotai expand their perimeter and begin building an airfield. On the 21st, US Navy Task Force 38 launches air strikes from a dozen aircraft carriers against Japanese targets in the Luzon (Philippines) area. On the 22nd, a US Army regiment lands unopposed on Ulithi Atoll in the western Carolines. On the 23rd, the airfield on Peleliu is repaired and US Marine aircraft begin operating from it. On the 24th, elements of the army's 81st Division are sent to reinforce the Marines on Peleliu; the Japanese promptly counterattack. On the 25th, Admiral HALSEY proposes, and NIMITZ and MACARTHUR accept, changing the operational agenda and canceling the landings on Mindanao scheduled for 10 October in favor of a landing on Leyte at that date. On the 26th, Marines and soldiers make gains on Peleliu, Anguar, and Morotai, against stiff resistance. On the 27th, very heavy fighting on Peleliu. On the 28th, the British XV Corps in Burma is

ordered to resume the offensive in the Arakan. On the 29th, heeding a message from Filipino GUERRILLAS, US sub *Narwhal* (SS-167) arrives at Mindanao to pick up 81 Allied POWs who have survived the sinking of a Japanese transport (sunk by another US sub). On the 30th, US and Filipino guerrillas complete preparations to support expected American landings, having mobilized their entire strength and deployed to do maximum damage to the Japanese once the invasion gets underway.

October 1944

The Philippines were invaded by US troops, starting a battle that would still be going on when the war ended. The Japanese used KAMIKAZE attacks for the first time. Chinese troops continued to hunt down Japanese troops in northern Burma. During October Allied (mainly US) SUBMARINES in the Pacific had their best month of the war, sending 328,000 tons of Japanese shipping to the bottom. Allied aircraft and ships sunk another 186,000 tons. From this point on, the sinking of Japanese merchant shipping declined simply because there weren't many Japanese ships left to sink.

On the 1st, heavy fighting continues on PELELIU, as Allied commanders begin to realize they have seriously underestimated the number of Japanese troops on the island. On the 2nd, an American-built pipeline reaches Myitkyina from northern India, greatly easing the supply of POLs to Allied troops in northern Burma. On the 3rd, the US Joint Chiefs of Staff instructs NIMITZ and MACARTHUR that, after the landings on Leyte in October, operations are planned for Luzon in January, IWO JIMA in February, and OKINAWA two months after that. On the 4th, Task Force 38 completes replenishment and rest at ULITHI, which has been turned into an enormous navy logistical base. On the 5th, Japanese troops continue to resist on Peleliu, a battle that is turning out to be more difficult than the Marines had first thought. On the 6th, operations on Anguar enter the mopping-up phase, as the last major Japanese forces are broken.

On the 7th, US fighters begin operating from Morotai in raids against Japanese positions in the Philippines. On the 8th, Chinese forces in northern Burma begin regrouping for a renewed offensive. On the 9th, elements of the Third Fleet shell MARCUS ISLAND. On the 10th, moving ever closer to Japan itself, the US Navy launches air strikes from 17 carriers, to hit targets in the RYUKYUS (especially Okinawa). Bill Howell's ship, the *Monterey* (CVL-26), takes part in bombing Japanese bases on Okinawa. Then, attention shifts south to the Philippines and FORMOSA, where the *Monterey's* aircraft spend most of October hitting Japanese targets on Luzon and Formosa. These operations go on into December of 1944. On the 11th, the Japanese military leadership develops a series of plans for "Operation Victory" ("Sho-Go"). These plans spell out the desperate measures Japan will take when the Home Islands are threatened. Basically it comes down to, "fight to the last man, woman, child, weapon and piece of equipment." On the 12th, US Navy carrier task forces launches air strikes against Formosa, in order to destroy Japanese air power in the area. The Japanese commanders are shocked at the ineffectiveness of their air forces against the better trained and equipped Americans. On the 13th, the US Navy carrier task force launches second day of the air strikes against major Japanese air strength in Formosa. On the 14th, U.S. Navy carrier task forces completes three days of air strikes against Formosa, breaking the back of Japanese air power in the area (destroying 280 aircraft). On the 15th, Peleliu (in the PALAU ISLANDS) is finally secured after a month of heavy fighting, though some Japanese troops hold out for months longer. Japanese loses are nearly 12,000 troops killed, US over 1,200. On the 16th, Chinese forces in Burma launch another offensive to clear remaining Japanese forces that might block the BURMA ROAD between India and China. On the 17th, Admiral Nimitz announces that, during the second week of October, Allied forces had destroyed nearly 700 Japanese aircraft and over 70 Japanese ships. On the 18th, in preparation for the coming invasion of the Philippines, U.S. Army

Rangers begin landing on islands off LEYTE GULF. On the 19th, General STILWELL is relieved of his posts in China, as a result of CHIANG KAI-SHEK seeing Stilwell as the cause of all the problems with the Nationalist, American and communist leadership. On the 20th, General MacArthur returns to the Philippines, as he had promised two and a half years earlier: In the first 24 hours of the invasion, nearly 200,000 troops land on the east coast of Leyte. On the 21st, Japanese forces on Leyte counterattack, although their long-term STRATEGY is to defend, not attack. On the 22nd, Japanese naval forces close in on Leyte in order to oppose the American invasion. On the 23rd, three-day air-sea Battle of LEYTE GULF begins, as the Japanese meet the American invasion of the Philippines with a naval attack, in what becomes the greatest naval action in history. On the 24th, as US and Japanese forces close in the Philippines, the Japanese split their remaining warships between the INLAND SEA (between Honshu, Shikoku, and Kyushu) and the waters off SINGAPORE. Bill Howell's ship, *Monterey* (CVL-26), takes part in the key battles for the Philippine Islands, including the Battle of Leyte Gulf from 24 to 26 October. On the 25th, it is the decisive day of the Battle of Leyte Gulf, as Japanese forces are defeated in SURIGAO STRAIT, off SAMAR (with some difficulty), and off Cape Engaño. During the battle and the subsequent "mopping up," the Japanese fleet is smashed, losing three battleships, four carriers, 10 cruisers, and 17 other warships, while US losses are three escort carriers and three destroyers. On the 16th, the Japanese offensive in China, stalled because of logistical problems and increased Chinese resistance, starts rolling again toward the US air bases at Kweilin and Liuchow. On the 27th, the Japanese begin launching kamikaze suicide plane attacks at US ships off the Philippines. On the 28th, kamikazes draw first blood, when a US cruiser is damaged by suicide aircraft. On the 29th, heavy fighting continues on Leyte. On the 30th, covering the troops on Leyte, US Task Group 38.4 is attacked by kamikaze aircraft, which severely damage two carriers. On the 31st, Chinese troops continue to battle the Japanese in the border area of China and Burma. By the end of the year, the area will be clear.

November 1944

The Allies advanced everywhere in the Pacific, except in China, where the Japanese offensive kept moving deeper into the heartland.

On the 1st, despite the enormous US naval and air forces in the area, the Japanese are able to land reinforcements on Leyte. On the 2nd, the US Army clears Japanese troops from the central valley on Leyte. On the 3rd, the Japanese Army's "Special Balloon Regiment" begins releasing the first of over 9,000 hydrogen-filled balloons; these are expected to float with the prevailing westerly winds all the way from Japan to the west coast of North America. Each carries a 40-pound bomb that will explode on landing, injuring anyone in the vicinity or starting a fire. Over 300 of the balloons actually do reach North America, but only three are known to have caused any damage (six dead and two brush fires). On the 4th, the Japanese launch air attacks against SAIPAN and TINIAN (in the MARIANAS) to disrupt preparations for further attacks against Japan. On the 5th, B-29's, fly from Chinese bases to bomb SINGAPORE. On the 6th, the Soviet Union accuses Japan of aggression, a prelude to eventually declaring war on Japan. On the 7th, the Chinese New 22nd Division takes Shwego in northern Burma. On the 8th, Japanese transports get through US naval and air blockade to land another division as reinforcements for their troops on Leyte. On the 9th, another reinforcement landing by Japanese troops on Leyte is only partially successful: The troops get ashore, but US Navy aircraft sink the transports before the ammunition and supplies can be unloaded. On the 10th, the Japanese offensive in China finally captures the two major US air bases at Kweilin and Liuchow. The strategic situation in China is now considered critical. On the 11th, in response to the vast number of US aircraft carriers, Japan commissions its newest carrier, SHINANO, but she will be sunk in just 17 days by a US sub, giving her the shortest combat life of any major ship in the war On the 12th, Task Force 38 refuels and resupplies in the PHILIPPINE SEA, after supporting the Leyte operation and having raiding the VOLCANO ISLANDS. On the 12th, Allied forces in Burma and India are reorganized to put all ground troops—Commonwealth, American, and Chinese—under a single command, to improve operational coordination. On the 13th, US Task Force 38 begins two days of air strikes on Luzon, concentrating on Japanese shipping in Manila Bay; the Japanese will lose a light cruiser, four destroyers, and 10 transports sunk, plus a destroyer and five transports damaged. On the 14th, the Chinese New 22nd Division takes Mantha, in northern Burma, as other Chinese forces advance as well. On the 15th, escorted by US and Commonwealth warships, an American infantry regiment storms Pegun Island, near Morotai. On the 16th, US Task Force 38 refuels and resupplies in the Philippine Sea. By this time in the war, US ships are staying at sea for months on end, being replenished by fleets of cargo ships and oilers, while hospital ships and special repair ships tend to injured sailors and equipment. On the 17th, the Japanese offensive in China continues, with the next objectives being Kweiyang, then the key cities of Kunming and Chungking. On the 18th, a British carrier task force raids oil facilities, air bases, and port installations in Sumatra. On the 19th, Indian troops begin crossing the Chindwin River in Burma, opening an unusual monsoon season offensive. US troops make an amphibious landing on Asia Island (off the northwest coast of New Guinea). On the 20th, Chinese forces on the Salween front in northern Burma capture Mangshih and its airfield. On the 21st, General WEDEMEYER presents a plan to CHIANG KAI-SHEK designed to stem the Japanese drive on Kunming. On the 22nd, the British Far Eastern Fleet in the Indian Ocean is reorganized; the British Pacific Fleet is formed (four new carriers, two new battleships, plus cruisers and destroyers) for operations with the US Third/Fifth Fleet. On the 23rd, Japanese troops from Indochina move north to link up with Japanese troops approaching the Chinese city of Nanning. On the 24th, the first

B-29 raid from bases in the Marianas (Saipan) sees 111 B-29s hit Tokyo. On the 25th, Japanese KA-MIKAZE launch more attacks at US Navy carriers off the Philippines, damaging four. On the 26th, Japanese troops in central Burma begin to with-draw. On the 27th, B-29s from the Marianas hit Tokyo; B-29s from India hit BANGKOK. On the 28th, Japanese resistance on PELELIU in the PALAU ISLANDS finally ends: 14,000 Japanese troops have been killed and 400 captured, with US ground forces suffering nearly 10,000 CASUALTIES, includ-ing 1,800 dead, more than at GUADALCANAL. On the 29th, Chinese Nationalist leader Chiang Kai-shek refuses to allow US ammunition to be shipped through his territory to communist forces. On the 30th, with the Japanese closing in, most Nation-alist Chinese divisions on the Salween front in Burma are ordered north to aid in the defense of Kunming.

December 1944

The Japanese advance in China slowed from lack of supplies, and exhaustion. Fighting continued in the Philippines. Allied forces advanced in Burma. IWO JIMA was pounded in preparation for an am-phibious assault.

On the 1st, Japanese troops on Leyte exhaust their food supplies. The US blockade prevents everything except supply SUBMARINES from getting through. On the 2nd, Chiang Kai-shek again re-jects US proposals to arm some communist units for service against the Japanese. On the 3rd, the Japanese 11th Army, which had advanced into south China against orders from Tokyo, runs out of supplies and slows down. On the 4th, the new US military representative in China, General WED-EMEYER (who replaced STILWELL), requests that re-maining B-29s in China be withdrawn, since the BURMA ROAD is not yet functional and all supplies for the bombers have to be flown in over the Him-alaya Mountains. On the 5th, Chinese forces on the Salween front in northern Burma continue their advance, as the Japanese try to extricate their garrison from Bhamo. On the 6th, despite a lack

of supply, Japanese forces on Leyte continue to re-sist and even launch counterattacks. On the 7th, the Japanese attempt to resupply their forces on Leyte, but 13 transports are sunk by US aircraft. The US 77th Division lands in the Japanese rear, at Ormoc, Leyte. On the 8th, US land-based bombers and carrier aircraft begin a 72-day pound-ing of Iwo Jima in preparation for an amphibious assault. On the 9th, British troops continue ad-vancing into central Burma as they realize that the Japanese are pulling out without much of a fight. On the 10th, Japanese forces advancing north from INDO-CHINA make contact with Japanese forces ad-vancing south in southern China, a linkup that later permits the transfer of two divisions from the Indo-China garrison to southern China. On the 11th, US forces capture Ormoc, on Leyte in the Philippines, and discover the reason for the stub-born Japanese defense of the city: It was the main supply dump for the Japanese troops on Leyte; with Ormoc gone, the remaining 35,000 Japanese troops on Leyte are short on ammo and food. On the 12th, US forces on Leyte consolidate their positions. On the 13th, Chinese forces in northern Burma enter outskirts of Bhamo. On the 14th, the Third Fleet begins carrier air attacks on Japanese positions on Luzon, in preparation for the liberation of the prin-cipal island in the Philippines. On the 15th, US troops land on the Philippine island of Mindoro, meeting no resistance on the beach, but KAMIKA-ZES attack landing ships, damaging several and sinking two LSTS. On the 16th, Chinese forces in northern Burma capture town of Bhamo. On the 17th, 500 miles east of the Philippines, the US Third Fleet is caught in a mighty typhoon for two days, with losses greater than those in many naval battles. Three destroyers are sunk, over 140 aircraft destroyed, and severe damage inflicted on eight carriers, a cruiser, seven destroyers, and many sup-port ships, while nearly 800 sailors lose their lives and many more are injured. On the 18th, nearly 300 US aircraft, including over 75 B-29s, raid the Japanese base at Hankow, China, in an effort to disrupt the Japanese offensive. Bill Howell's ship, *Monterey* (CVL-26), undergoes its most harrowing moments of the war—due not to Japanese attack, but to the gigantic typhoon that pounds her and the other ships in the fleet for two days. The sustained winds are over a hundred miles an hour. There is some warning of the storm, and the crew lashes everything down with additional cables, especially *Monterey*'s aircraft. But the storm is so violent that, on 19 December, several aircraft tear loose from their ¾-inch steel cables. Before the crew can secure the aircraft, the constant movement of the planes sets off sparks, which start fires. Soon, most of the hangar deck is aflame and nearby ships think *Monterey* is done for. On the bridge, Lieutenant Commander Attard is standing watch when the fire breaks out. Bill Howell watches as Attard immediately orders the *Monterey* helmsman to turn the ship into the wind. While this will take the *Monterey* out of formation, and possibly cause a collision with another ship, it is the right decision. Heaving into the wind stabilizes the ship sufficiently so that the fire-fighting crews can do their work and the wayward aircraft can be lashed down again. There are dozens of injuries, and Lieutenant Jerry FORD will later receive a medal for his heroic actions in leading sailors in the damage control operations. On the 19th, foul weather forces postponement of a major Third Fleet carrier raid on Japanese bases on Luzon. British Commonwealth forces in Burma make steady gains. On the 20th, Japanese troops on Leyte are told by Tokyo that they can expect no further reinforcements or supplies. Bill Howell's ship, *Monterey*, damaged from the typhoon, is sent back to BREMERTON, Washington, for repairs and upgrades. *Monterey* arrives in Bremerton in early January and stays two months. On the 21st, British troops in Burma capture Kawlin. On the 22nd, the Vietnamese Liberation Army is formed in Vietnam by Vo Nguyen Giap, the core of the communist army that will eventually overcome Japanese, French, and American forces. Bill Howell manages to get word back to his wife that he is going to be on the West Coast soon. A meeting is arranged in Seattle for 22 January and despite wartime censorship and a shortage

of transportation, the reunion comes off. Another minor wartime miracle. On the 23rd, the United States opens an airfield on newly liberated Mindoro, in the Philippines. On the 24th, US cruisers and destroyers bombard Iwo Jima. On the 25th, British troops move into the Akyab Peninsula of Burma, as the Japanese withdraw. On the 26th, Japanese ships attack US beachhead on Mindoro, the Philippines. On the 27th, B-29s from SAIPAN, the MARIANAS, make their fifth major raid on Tokyo. On the 28th, Japanese assess the after-effects of five B-29s raids and find that the damage being done is not crippling. Soon the Americans realize the same thing and this leads to a switch to fire-bomb raids and a much less favorable outcome for the Japanese. On the 29th, stepping up their attack against Japanese forces on Leyte (now low on food and ammo), in less than two weeks US Army troops kill nearly 6,000 Japanese while losing only 11 of their own troops. Bill Howell's ship, *Monterey*, while undergoing repairs at Bremerton, Washington, gets her third skipper, as the executive officer, Commander Frank B. Miller, replaces Captain Stuart Ingersoll—but only on a temporary basis, as a new commanding officer is on the way. On the 30th, US Army aircraft attack Japanese shipping in the Manila Bay area. On the 31st, heavy Japanese air attacks on US shipping off Mindoro sink a PT-BOAT tender and damage a destroyer.

January 1945

The Japanese offensive continued in China, albeit less vigorously. More US landings took place in the Philippines. American carriers battled and destroyed Japanese airpower in FORMOSA and on the Asian mainland.

On the 1st, the US Eighth Army on the Philippine island of Leyte begins a campaign to clear still active Japanese troops, an effort that will continue until the end of the war. On the 2nd, as US Navy ships leave Leyte for the invasion of Luzon, they are forced to beat off attacks by KAMIKAZE.

On the 3rd, the US Third fleet stages raids on OKI-NAWA, Formosa, and the Pescadores, losing 18 aircraft, while the Japanese lose a dozen ships and over a hundred aircraft. On the 4th, the US amphibious invasion force approaching the main Philippine island of Luzon suffers heavy Japanese air attack, the CVE *Ommaney Bay* being so badly damaged by a kamikaze that she has to be sunk. On the 5th, although weakened by transfers of several divisions to China, Chinese forces in northern Burma continue to advance, with US support, crossing the Shweli River. On the 6th, the Japanese Air Force on Luzon is reduced to only 35 aircraft, down from 150 at the end of 1944. On the 7th, British troops occupy Akyab, in the Arakan area of Burma, as the Japanese situation continues to deteriorate in the region. On the 8th, heavy air strikes continue against Luzon, with a concentration on the Lingayen Gulf area, followed up during the night by the arrival of surface vessels to make the final preparations for the liberation of the island. On the 9th, the US Sixth Army lands on Luzon. Nearly 100,000 troops are landed at Lingayen Gulf, a hundred miles north of Manila in the first 24 hours. On the 10th, US forces on Luzon enlarge their beachhead. Chinese and American forces in northern Burma continue their advance. British and Indian forces capture Shwego, in the Arakan. On the 11th, the Japanese leadership examines their situation and decides to put all their remaining resources into kamikaze-type weapons. By the end of the month, all industrial and military organizations will have channeled their energies to building suicide weapons, and providing crews to man them. On the 12th, US Navy Task Force 38 sweeps the Indo-Chinese coast, its carrier aircraft sinking over three dozen Japanese ships. On the 13th, Japanese forces in the Philippines launch their few remaining aircraft against recently landed US troops on Luzon. On the 14th, British troops crossing the Irrawaddy River in Burma are hit by a Japanese counterattack, which results in a month-long battle. On the 15th, the Japanese offensive in China continues, with Japanese forces advancing

on the US air base at Suichuan. On the 16th, US carrier aircraft attack Japanese-held HONG KONG. The Japanese defenses are found to be meager, having been stripped for other fronts. On the 17th, US Sixth Army on Luzon steps up its drive on Manila. On the 18th, although "secured," fighting on PELELIU continues, with Japanese stragglers forming raiding parties to attack US ammo dumps and the air base. On the 19th, in China, Japanese troops seize control of the CANTON-Hankow rail line. On the 20th, first convoy navigates the BURMA ROAD, but the route needs repair and rebuilding before full-scale use is possible. On the 21st, US carrier aircraft attack Japanese air bases on Okinawa and Formosa, destroying some 100 enemy aircraft in the process. On the 22nd, CORREGIDOR, the island fortress guarding Japanese-held Manila Bay, is attacked by US aircraft. On the 23rd, the Burma Road is declared open, but small, scattered Japanese units in the area make travel on the route dangerous. On the 24th, in China, advancing Japanese troops cause the US air base at Suichuan to be evacuated. On the 25th, US B-29s undertake a major mining effort in the waters off the ports of SINGAPORE, SAIGON, CAM RANH BAY, and PE-NANG. This is the largest mining operation of the war, with 366 MINES dropped off Singapore alone. On the 26th, the Japanese government orders its troops in China to call off their offensive and concentrate on defending the China coast and key installations in north China. As is customary, the commanders in China do not instantly or consistently comply. On the 27th, US forces on Luzon are reinforced by the First Cavalry and 32nd Infantry Divisions, plus the 122nd Cavalry RCT. On the 28th, the Philippine island of Mindoro is declared free of organized Japanese resistance and under US control. On the 29th, the US 38th Division lands northwest of Subic Bay, on the Philippine island of Luzon, and promptly moves southward toward BATAAN. On the 30th, Task Force 63, the British Pacific Fleet (four carriers, a fast battleship, four cruisers, and 11 destroyers), refuels at sea in the Indian Ocean and then proceeds eastward to join the US Pacific Fleet. On the 31st, the US 11th Airborne Division lands—by amphibious craft—at the south entrance to Manila Bay.

February 1945

U.S. liberation of the Philippines continued. Japanese-held IWO JIMA was invaded by US Marines. The BURMA ROAD was reopened. Japanese offensive in China continued to advance toward remaining US air bases.

On the 1st, Japanese offensive in China captures Kukong, the last Chinese stronghold on the Hankow rail line. This cuts off Chinese forces to the east from the rest of China. On the 2nd, major combat operations come to a halt on Leyte Island in the Philippines, although small pockets of Japanese resistance remain. On the 3rd, on the Philippine main island of Luzon, the US Sixth Army is poised to fight its way into the Philippine capital of Manila. On the 4th, the first large supply convoy makes it from Ledo in India to Kunming in China along the full length of the BURMA ROAD. On the 5th, Australian troops effect a new landing on NEW BRITAIN, further sealing the RABAUL pocket. On the 6th, the Battle for Manila, Luzon, begins in earnest, while over 4,000 American POWs are freed from prison camps in the area, after nearly three years' imprisonment. On the 7th, the Japanese offensive in China captures another US air base, this one at Kanchow. On the 8th, Japanese resistance in Manila stiffens. On the 9th, heavy fighting continues on Luzon, particularly at Manila, Nichols Field, and the Val Verde Trail. On the 10th, Tokyo is hit with a severe earthquake shortly before a raid by nearly a hundred B-29 bombers. On the 11th, heavy fighting continues on Luzon. On the 12th, off the Philippine coast, the US sub *Batfish* (SS-113) sinks its third Japanese submarine in four days (*I-41*, *Ro-112*, and *Ro-113*). On the 14th, US troops reach the BATAAN Peninsula outside Manila as US PT-BOATS enter Manila Bay. On the 15th, US troops make a landing on the southern tip of Bataan. Japanese troops in nearby Manila are surrounded. On the 16th,

American troops make a surprise attack on CORREGIDOR Island (guarding the entrance to Manila Bay on Luzon, the Philippines), using paratroopers and troops coming ashore from nearby Bataan. Over 4,000 Japanese defenders on Corregidor are killed, with the loss of only 136 American dead. On the 17th, attempts to clear beach defenses on Japanese-held Iwo Jima encounter unexpected problems and nearly 200 US Navy frogmen are killed. On the 18th, British troops land on the Burmese coast in the Arakan region and cut off the retreat of Japanese forces. On the 19th, nearly 800 miles south of the Japanese Home Islands, 30,000 US Marines land on Iwo Jima. The Japanese have planned to use Iwo Jima to launch suicide aircraft attacks against Allied forces attempting to invade the Japanese Home Islands and also as a forward fighter base to oppose B-29 raids from the MARIANA ISLANDS. Three US Marine divisions are involved in this assault on this eight-square-mile island defended by 22,000 fanatical Japanese. Most of the Japanese are still sitting in fortified positions away from the beaches. Even so, the resistance on the beach is fierce. On the 20th, US Army troops land on SAMAR and Capul islands, giving them control of the vital San Bernardino Strait in the Philippines. On the 21st, Japanese resistance on Iwo Jima is fierce, with the invading Marines already losing half their TANKS. The fighting increases in intensity. On the 22nd, Marines on Iwo Jima make slow gains against heavy resistance. On the 23rd, on Iwo Jima, elements of the 28th Marines raise the US flag on Mount Suribachi. On the 24th, most of the Manila area on Luzon is under US control. On the 25th, in a major change in tactics against Japanese cities, US B-29 bombers switch from high-altitude daylight raids with high explosive bombs, to low-level night raids with incendiary bombs. The first raid against Tokyo, with 334 B-29s, burns out nearly 10,000 acres of the city. On the 26th, in Burma, the British begin an offensive against MANDALAY and Meiktila. On the 27th, even as heavy fighting continues on Iwo Jima, the US Navy opens a seaplane base on the island. On the 28th, US forces land on PALAWAN

Island in the Philippines. Occupation of this island effectively completes cutting off Japan from its resource areas in the East Indies.

March 1945

Japanese cities were pounded by US bombers. Japanese offensive in China slowed almost to a crawl. Recognizing its inability to provide fuel or pilots for them, the Imperial Navy laid up the last of its aircraft carriers, transferring the men to other duties.

On the 1st, US Navy ships and aircraft attack the Japanese-held RYUKYU ISLANDS. On the 2nd, Japanese resistance on CORREGIDOR Island, at the entrance of Manila Bay, ends, less than three years after the Japanese first took the island fortress from American defenders. On the 3rd, Japanese resistance in the Philippine capital of Manila ends. On the 4th, advancing British troops cut off Japanese forces in central Burma. On the 5th, US Marines have cleared most of IWO JIMA and US fighters begin operating from a captured airstrip. On the 6th, on Luzon, the US First Cavalry Division is relieved by the 43rd, as the Sixth Army reorganizes. On the 7th, trapped Japanese troops in central Burma counterattack to break out, bringing British advance to a halt. On the 8th, British troops fight their way into Japanese-held MANDALAY, Burma. In eastern Luzon the Sixth Army begins a major offensive against the Japanese Shimbu Defensive Line. On the 9th, the Japanese, having concluded a temporary armistice with Ho Chi-minh's communists, attack French garrisons in Indo-China, thus eliminating the last remnant of pro-German Vichy French rule. The Japanese fear that Free French troops will be landed (via the Allied-controlled waters around Indochina) and the Vichy troops will join the Free French. On the 10th, dawn over Tokyo reveals a manmade hell. The previous night, 279 low-flying B-29 bombers dropped 1,665 tons of incendiary bombs, which created a firestorm that killed 84,000 Japanese. This is a greater death toll than either of the later A-bomb raids. On the 11th, Emperor Bao-Dai of Vietnam,

a puppet of the French, and later the Japanese, declares Vietnam's independence from France. The Japanese ignore this and remain in control. On the 12th, heavy fighting on the Shimbu Line on Luzon. On the 13th, elements of the Indian 26th Division make an amphibious "end run" to trap Japanese forces on the Arakan coast. On the 14th, US B-29s raid the Japanese city of Osaka, inflicting 13,000 CASUALTIES. On the 15th, the British complete the recapture of Mandalay, though Japanese resistance continues in some suburban areas. On the 16th, Iwo Jima is declared free of organized Japanese resistance, but some mopping up continues for weeks. On the 17th, US B-29s raid the Japanese city of KOBE, inflicting 15,000 casualties. Bill Howell's ship, *Monterey* (CVL-26), spends the next 12 weeks operating off OKINAWA, dodging KAMIKAZE and providing air support for the American infantry on Okinawa. On the 18th, US troops land on the Philippine island of Panay and push inland. On the 19th, US Navy aircraft attack the KURE naval base area in the Japanese Home Islands. On the 20th, the last ship of a 21-vessel Japanese convoy is hunted down and destroyed. The convoy has attempted, for 10 weeks, to carry supplies from Japan to its beleaguered forces in Southeast Asia. None of the ships make it as far as SINGAPORE, being constantly harried by US aircraft and SUBMARINES. Bill Howell's ship, *Monterey*, gets its last wartime skipper, with Captain John B. Lyons taking over from Commander Frank B. Miller. On the 21st, British forces take control of Mandalay, with surviving Japanese troops in the area retreating toward SIAM. On the 22nd, Japanese offensive in China continues, with an attack toward the US air base at Laohokow. On the 23rd, a British carrier task force joins the US fleet for operations against the Japanese Home Islands. On the 24th, the last pocket of 200 Japanese troops on Iwo Jima is cornered in an area about 50 yards square. The Japanese eventually launch an attack from this position and nearly all are killed. On the 25th, the US air base at Laohokow in China is destroyed as the Japanese close in. This is the last US air base in China that the Japanese will capture. On the 26th, a US

Army division lands on Philippine island of CEBU. On the 27th, B-29s begin mining operation in the waters around Japan. In the space of a few weeks, the mining brings Japanese shipping to a standstill and makes the blockade of Japan nearly complete. On the 28th, a US Army division lands on Kerama Island, the Ryukyu Islands, providing a forward base to support an assault on Okinawa Island. On the 29th, US troops clearing Kerama Island discover 350 suicide boats, held there for use against any force that might attempt to land on Okinawa. That same day the United States informs Britain that it will probably have a usable ATOMIC BOMB in the near future. On the 30th, the British 14th Army advances against crumbling resistance. On the 31st, heavy fighting continues on eastern Luzon.

April 1945

The last major battle of World War II began, as OKINAWA was invaded. The amphibious assault was on the same scale as the one at Normandy (D-day). Okinawa turned out to be the bloodiest of the Pacific island battles. The British retook Burma from the Japanese.

On the 1st (Easter Sunday), Okinawa is assaulted by 60,000 US Army and Marine troops (two divisions of each). The island is only 360 miles south of the Japanese Home Islands. The landings on Okinawa are the last major assault of the war, and the bloodiest. On the 2nd, on Okinawa, the Japanese pull back rather than oppose the invading American troops on the beach, to await the American in fortifications farther inland. On the 3rd, Soviet Union decides to renounce the five-year Soviet-Japan neutrality pact signed in April 1941. On the 4th, US troops on Okinawa finally encounter dug-in Japanese garrison, and the bloody battle for the island ensues. The Fourth Marine Division arrives back at Maui after the IWO JIMA operation. The Marines are ordered to start training for the invasion of Japan, the first operation to take place in October 1945. The Marines will lead the way. But first the damage from Iwo

Jima has to be repaired. The division has suffered over 8,000 CASUALTIES. Over half of these are wounded who gradually returned from hospitals. The rest of the losses have to be made up by fresh replacements. While the war in Europe looks close to ending, the Marines on Maui begin retraining for the invasion of Japan. On the 5th, in the wake of the Soviet abrogation of the April 1941, five-year neutrality pact with Japan, the Japanese cabinet resigns. On the 6th, Japanese launch mass KAMIKAZE attacks on US ships off Okinawa. The 355 aircraft fly from the Home Islands (Kyushu) and only 24 of them hit anything. Six smaller ships (destroyers and support vessels) are sunk, but many more are damaged by FRIENDLY FIRE as all US ships in the area open up to stop the kamikaze. On the 7th, the Japanese Second ("suicide") Fleet is intercepted by US carrier aircraft before it can reach Okinawa: Some 900 US aircraft are involved in this battle, of which 10 are lost, while Japanese losses include the superbattleship YAMATO, a cruiser, four destroyers, and 54 aircraft. On the 8th, the battle for the Motobu Peninsula on northern Okinawa begins, as Marines probe the Japanese lines, while other Marines and soldiers on the island push southward. On the 9th, US forces land on the island of Jolo in the Sulu Sea (off the Philippines). On the 10th, British carrier aircraft attack Japanese air bases on FORMOSA to stop Japanese air raids on US ships off Okinawa. On the 11th, British forces in Burma hustle toward RANGOON (300 miles) in order to take the city before the monsoon rains begin. On the 12th, over 150 Japanese kamikaze are shot down off Okinawa, although a Baka flying bomb hits and sinks a US destroyer. On the 13th, Chinese and Japanese forces both begin offensives in different parts of China. President ROOSEVELT dies of a cerebral hemorrhage (April 12th in North America). Radio Tokyo broadcasts a dignified notice. On the 14th, Japanese forces in China are again ordered to withdraw troops for the defense of the Chinese coast and this time they comply, abandoning several captured US air bases in the process. B-29 air raid on Tokyo damages the Imperial Palace. On the 15th, in Burma, the first use of HELICOPTERS in a rescue takes place. The crew of a transport has to bail out high in the mountain jungles, then a search plane crashes during the search. When a patrol reaches an injured search plane survivor on foot, they radio back that he is too ill to move. The nearest US air base has an experimental Sikorsky YR-4 helicopter on hand for testing, and the helicopter PILOT decides to attempt the risky mission in an area where no aircraft can land. He succeeds, and thus effects the first use of a helicopter as a rescue aircraft. On the 16th, IE SHIMA, a smaller island off Okinawa, is invaded by a US Army division. On the 17th begins the last invasion of the Philippines Campaign, as US forces land on Mindanao Island. On the 18th, popular American war correspondent Ernie PYLE is killed by Japanese fire on Ie Shima. On the 19th, assisted by an enormous amount of naval gunfire and aircraft support, US Army forces launch a major offensive to break Japanese resistance on Okinawa. On the 20th, Japanese troops in Burma continue to be hunted down or trapped by advancing British forces. The British are closing in on the Yenangyaung oil fields, the largest in Burma. On the 21st, advancing British forces move to within 200 miles of Rangoon in Burma. The Japanese decide to abandon Rangoon and pull back farther to reorganize their forces. On the 22nd, the island of PALAWAN (the Philippines) is declared secure. On the 23rd, the battle for the central Philippines ends as Japanese resistance is crushed on the island of CEBU. On the 24th, around Japan, Allied airpower, SUBMARINES, and especially naval MINES begin to shut down Japanese ports. By the end of April, the port of NAGOYA becomes the first of many to cease operations. On the 25th, the Japanese Army in China still has fight left in it. At Wukang, a Chinese division is routed by Japanese forces. On the 26th, Japanese resistance on Okinawa intensifies, stalling US efforts to secure the island. On the 27th, US and Australian warships begin four days of bombarding the Japanese-held oil facilities on TARAKAN Island (off the northeast coast of BORNEO). On the 28th, Japanese kamikaze attacks on US ships off Okinawa continue. During the month

of April, over 1,000 Japanese aircraft are destroyed. But 20 Allied ships are sunk and 157 damaged, mostly by kamikaze. On the 29th, fighting is so intense on Okinawa that one US Army division has to be pulled out of the line because of heavy losses. On the 30th, the large minelayer *Terror* (CM-5) and destroyer *Bennion* (DD-662) are damaged by kamikaze aircraft off Okinawa: Since late March US naval losses off Okinawa total 20 ships sunk (14 by kamikaze) and 157 damaged (90 by kamikaze), but the Japanese have lost nearly 1,200 aircraft in attacks on the fleet. In Europe, as soldiers of the Red Army encircle his bunker, HITLER commits suicide.

May 1945

Germany surrendered. Japan was now alone against the world. Battle for OKINAWA raged. Last surface naval battle took place. Chinese counterattacked as the Japanese withdrew troops for defense of the Home Islands.

On the 1st, Australian forces land on TARAKAN, off BORNEO. The island has been held by the Japanese since early 1942. On the 2nd, advancing British troops discover that Rangoon, Burma, has been abandoned by the Japanese. On the 3rd, the Japanese attempt to reverse their declining position on Okinawa by making a pair of amphibious landings behind American lines. Nearly a thousand Japanese troops are involved, and most are quickly killed or captured. On the 4th, British warships bombard Japanese installations in the Sakishima Islands of the southern RYUKYUS. On the 5th, Japanese KAMIKAZE score a major success off Okinawa, sinking 17 ships at a loss of only 131 aircraft. On the 6th, the British declare the Burma Campaign over, although isolated Japanese units will fight on for several more weeks. On the 7th, British forces in southern Burma advance to link up with Allied units in the interior. On the 8th, the war in Europe ends with the surrender of Germany. Japan now stands alone against the massed military might of the Allied powers. With the defeat of Germany comes the announcement of a "leave plan" to determine who will get some relief now that only Japan is left and not as many troops are needed at the front. What this meant to many troops is that those who have seen the most action are eligible for transfer back to the mainland for six months of easier duty. On the 9th, as German forces lay down their arms, in the Pacific, ferocious Japanese resistance continues in Burma, China, the Philippines, and on Okinawa. On the 10th, assisted by Filipino GUERRILLAS, the US Eighth Army expands its hold on Mindanao. On the 11th, Australian troops land in the WEWAK area of New Guinea. On the 12th, heavy Japanese kamikaze attacks on US and British ships off Okinawa; battleship NEW MEXICO is badly hit. On the 13th, the US Fast Carrier Task Force begins a two-day raid against Japanese airfields on Kyushu. On the 14th, US Task Force Mars completes its concentration in China, having taken over a month to move from Burma. On the 15th, British warships and aircraft attack Japanese installations on the ANDAMAN ISLANDS. On the 16th, the most intensive use of napalm in the war occurs near the Philippine capital of Manila, where Japanese troops threaten the city's water supply. Over 300 tons of napalm are dropped over several days. US troops are then able to go in and mop up remaining Japanese resistance. On the 17th, the last surface battle of the war takes place, as the Japanese cruiser *Haguro* is sunk by five British destroyers in the Malacca Strait. On the 18th, Chinese troops take the port of FOOCHOW on the China coast. On the 19th, on Okinawa, another US Army division has to be pulled out of combat because of high casualty rates. Even the Marines are suffering an exceptionally high rate of combat fatigue losses. On the 20th, Japanese begin withdrawing divisions from China to shore up the defenses of the Home Islands. On the 21st, Marines and soldiers make small gains on Okinawa, as fighting for Shuri Castle begins. On the 22nd, Okinawa is hit with heavy rains, which stall offensive operations for nearly two weeks. On the 23rd, Japan's largest port, Yokohama, ceases operations because of Allied air and naval activity, as well as MINES offshore. On the 24th, in addition to kamikaze attacks, Japanese suicide paratroopers land on US airfield on Okinawa. Several US aircraft are destroyed before the paratroopers are all killed. On the 25th, US military planners set 1 November as the date of the first invasion of the Japanese Home Islands. On the 26th, Chinese troops reoccupy Nanning, cutting off 200,000 Japanese troops in Indo-China (who no longer have access to the sea). On the 27th, the port of Tokyo is closed because of damage to port installations and Allied military activity in the surrounding waters On the 28th, Japanese make a last attempt to reverse their situation on Okinawa with kamikaze attacks. Over a hundred Japanese aircraft are destroyed, but only one US destroyer is sunk. On the 29th, organized Japanese resistance on the Philippine island of Negros collapses. On the 30th, the Okinawan capital of NAHA is almost completely under US control. On the 31st, the United States withdraws its forces from MOUNTBATTEN's Southeast Asia Command to concentrate on supporting China, while SEAC, now entirely British Commonwealth in composition, is to concentrate on the liberation of MALAYA.

June 1945

Australian amphibious forces liberated numerous islands west of New Guinea. Japanese resistance was not as stubborn as before, a result of poor Japanese logistics and veteran Australian troops. Fighting in the Philippines wound down, but Japanese resistance went on for several more months. The battle for OKINAWA ended.

On the 1st, Japanese resistance on Luzon in the Philippines is reduced to small-unit actions. Without supplies of food or ammunition, the surviving Japanese troops begin acting like GUERRILLAS. On the 2nd, Nationalist Chinese leader CHIANG KAISHEK gives up his title of premier of the Nationalist government but remains the president and strongman. On the 3rd, in eastern Luzon the Japanese attempt to break contact and regroup. On the 4th, heavy fighting continues on Okinawa. On the 5th, a typhoon hits Okinawa, damaging four battleships, eight carriers, seven cruisers, 11 destroyers, and dozens of support ships. On the 6th, US Marines on Okinawa clear the NAHA airfield of Japanese resistance. On the 7th, in China, the Japanese are forced back to the starting point of their spring offensive. On the 8th, on Luzon in the Philippines, US Army patrols reach deep into the back country, finding only scattered Japanese resistance. On the 9th, the Sixth Army manages to isolate some Japanese forces in eastern Luzon. On the 10th, Australian troops land at BRUNEI Bay, BORNEO. On the 11th, British warships steam into the Caroline Islands to attack the Japanese base at TRUK. On the 12th, the southeastern end of the main Japanese line on Okinawa is pierced by a surprise attack by elements of the Seventh Infantry Division. On the 13th, Japanese resistance on the Visayan Islands ends. Nearly 10,000 Japanese have died, compared to 3,200 US CASUALTIES (including 835 dead). On the 14th, the Pentagon orders commanders in the Pacific to prepare plans to deal with a sudden surrender by the Japanese. On the 15th, in China, Chinese forces advance on a broad front into territory formerly held by Japanese troops (most of whom have been pulled back to MANCHURIA or Japan itself). On the 16th, British warships bombard Truk, in the CAROLINES. On the 17th, on Okinawa, US Army troops breach the final defensive line of the Japanese forces. The Japanese commander commits suicide. On the 18th, having burned out Japan's major cities, US B-29s begin attacking the smaller ones. On the 19th, British forces move out of Burma into Thailand. On the 20th, in an unprecedented event in the war, over a thousand Japanese soldiers surrender on Okinawa. Civilians, who so far have actively assisted the soldiers, also begin to surrender in great numbers. On the 21st, all of the islands in the southern Philippines are declared clear of organized Japanese resistance. On the 22nd, the United States declares the battle for Okinawa over. In 81 days of fighting, the 118,000-man Japanese garrison has been killed, except for 7,400 who have been captured (usually while wounded or otherwise incapacitated) or

have surrendered. US casualties are 49,000, of whom 12,520 are dead. Japan has lost 7,800 aircraft in KAMIKAZE attacks, as well as many ships. Allied forces have lost 800 aircraft, nearly 5,000 sailors dead and 36 ships sunk (none larger than a destroyer). Deaths among the Okinawan civilian population may have reached 150,000; we will never know for sure. It is the ferocity of this battle, more than anything else, that makes the use of ATOMIC BOMBS against Japan preferable to attempting a landing on the Home Islands. On the 23rd, on Luzon, the United States uses paratroopers, glider troops, Filipino guerrillas, and US Army troops to close the net around surviving Japanese troops. On the 24th, Australian forces capture Sarawak. On the 25th, in support of the principal operations on Okinawa, Marines land on Kume Shima, a small nearby island, meeting light resistance. On the 26th, B-29s begin night raids on Japanese oil refining facilities (to deny then aviation fuel for their remaining aircraft). On the 27th, the campaign against the Japanese on Luzon (the Philippines) is declared over, although 50,000 Japanese soldiers still hold out in the mountains of the northeast of Luzon. On the 28th, Australian troops capture Kuala Belait in the East Indies. On the 29th, President TRUMAN approves plans for Operation Olympic, to take place about 1 November. Chinese forces begin advancing into Indochina. On the 30th, although many Japanese soldiers continue to resist on Luzon, these troops pose no threat to the US hold on the island. Japanese losses in the Philippines total 317,000 troops killed, plus 7,236 captured. Total US casualties are 60,000. Philippine losses (including civilians) are far higher.

July 1945

Australian troops conquered Borneo and seized the oil fields Japan originally went to war for. Dozens of US and British carriers rampaged up and down the Japanese coast, sinking ships and bombing land targets. Chinese troops continued to push Japanese troops out of China. Japan was told to surrender or be destroyed. Already, most of Japan's cities had been largely burned out.

On the 1st, Australian troops invade BALIKPA-PAN, Borneo, the largest oil field in Asia. Japanese troops resist. On the 2nd, Japan announces that over five million of its citizens have been killed or injured in the US air raids so far; the actual figure is about 672,000 killed, with several million more injured, depending on how you count "war related injuries." On the 3rd, Australian troops take over oil fields at Balikpapan, Borneo. On the 4th, US troops in the southern islands of the Philippines, working with Filipino GUERRILLA units, continue to track down and kill isolated, but still resisting, Japanese troops, few of whom express a willingness to surrender. On the 5th, Australian troops continue their conquest of Borneo. On the 6th, Chinese forces continue moving north toward MANCHURIA. Japanese troops offer less resistance. On the 7th, Dutch troops enter the fighting in Borneo. On the 8th, Filipino troops take a major role in completing the liberation of Mindanao. On the 9th, Task Force 38 arrives off Japan; except for the rotation of individual ships to rear areas for rest, refit, or repair, the fleet (16 US carriers with escorting vessels, joined by four British carriers and escorts) will remain in Japanese waters until the war is over. On the 10th, in the largest air assault of the Pacific War to date, over a thousand US and British carrier aircraft bomb airfields and industrial installations in the Tokyo area. On the 11th, Allied bombers turn their attention to the Japanese Home Islands of Shikoku and Honshu. On the 12th, Japan asks the Soviets to assist in negotiating a cease-fire with the Allies; somehow the message doesn't get through. On the 13th, Italy declares war on Japan. Mopping up continues on Mindanao and scores of other places throughout the Pacific Theater. On the 14th, US battleships shell Kamamishi, Japan, in the first surface attack on the Home Islands. On the 16th, the first ATOMIC BOMB is tested in New Mexico. It works. On the 17th, the US Third Fleet, with the British carrier task force, engages in surface and air attacks on targets in the Tokyo area. On the 18th, Australian troops take the Sambodja oil fields in Borneo. On the 19th, surrounded Japanese units in Burma make a coordinated attack to break out of their encirclement. On the 20th, the USS *Threadfish* (SS-410) sinks Japanese *Minesweeper No. 39* in the Yellow Sea. On the 21st, US radio broadcasts demand that Japan surrender or be destroyed. On the 22nd, British troops in Burma generally defeat Japanese attempts to break out. On the 23rd, US Navy and British Commonwealth warships sweep past Japanese Home Islands of Shikoku and Kyushu, sinking over a hundred Japanese transports as they go. The first US troops land in Japan, as a raiding party off the USS *Barb* (SS-220) blows up a train on the east coast of Sakhalin Island. On the 24th, over 1,500 Allied carrier aircraft attack the Japanese naval base at KURE (on the INLAND SEA), sinking three of Japan's four remaining battleships. On the 25th, in response to a call from the Allies to surrender, Japan says it will surrender, but not unconditionally. On the 26th, British warships and aircraft attack Japanese installations on the west coast of MALAYA. On the 27th, Japan's cities are "bombed" with leaflets telling them that Japan must surrender or be destroyed. On the 28th, around midnight, KAMIKAZE sink their last ship, US destroyer *Callaghan* (DD-792) named after RAdm Dan CALLAGHAN, off Okinawa. On the 29th, US warships shell naval and air bases on Honshu. On the 30th, two British midget SUBMARINES sneak into SINGAPORE harbor and sink a Japanese cruiser by attaching MINES to it. On the 31st, malnutrition grows rampant in Japan, with the average citizen getting only 1,680 calories a day (22% less than the minimum to survive).

August 1945

Two ATOMIC BOMBS were dropped. Although these bombs killed fewer people than the earlier fire-bomb raid on Tokyo, the appearance of this new weapon, and the expectation that America has many more, made an impression on the Japanese. The Soviet Union declared war on Japan and invaded Japanese-held MANCHURIA, Sakhalin, and the KURILES. Japan surrendered.

On the 1st, mines air-dropped by the United States on the Japanese-controlled Yangtze river sink 36 Japanese transports and damage another 11. On the 2nd, B-29s drop 6,600 tons of bombs on five Japanese cities. There are few Japanese cities left to bomb. On the 3rd, the blockade of Japan is complete. Nothing gets in, nothing gets out. On the 4th, the last organized Japanese troops in Burma are killed or captured, with only 10,000 Japanese troops escaping to fight on individually or in small groups. On the 5th, Chinese forces recapture Tanchuk and Hsinning, in central China. On the 6th, a 4.5-ton atomic bomb is dropped on the Japanese city of HIROSHIMA. Over 80,000 Japanese die, with many more injured. A quarter of the dead are military personnel. On the 7th, elements of Headquarters, U.S. First Army, arrive on Luzon from Europe to begin planning for Operation Coronet, the second phase of the proposed invasion of Japan. On the 8th, the Soviet Union declares war on Japan. On the 9th a second atomic bomb is dropped on NAGASAKI, killing over 30,000 Japanese. The Red Army begins a massive offensive in Manchuria. Aircraft of the Third Fleet raid northern Honshu and Hokkaido. On the 10th, Allied carrier aircraft continue raids on northern Honshu and Hokkaido, destroying 400 Japanese aircraft and damaging over 300. The Allies lose 34 of their own planes. Bill Howell's ship, Monterey (CVL-26), takes part in the operations off the coast of Japan, hitting installations ashore and running down any surviving Japanese shipping at sea. In Japan, the war minister reminds senior officers of their obligation to obey the emperor's orders, whatever they might be. On the 11th, US and British warships shell Japanese steel mills, factories, and other installations along the eastern coasts of the Kuriles and Honshu. On the 12th, leaflets are dropped on Japanese cities calling for surrender or face "utter devastation." On the 13th, Japan's leaders offer to surrender unconditionally if the em-

peror's status is left unchanged. This is refused and the debate rages on in the Japanese government about what to do. The demand for unconditional surrender is made to avoid the mistakes made after World War I, when the German military was left intact and became the crucial factor in Germany's World War II success. Air raids on Tokyo. USS LaGrange (APA-124) is damaged by a KAMIKAZE off OKINAWA, the last US vessel damaged by direct enemy action. On the 14th, the emperor agrees to surrender unconditionally. In Tokyo, elements of the First Imperial Guard Division attempt a coup, which is put down after some bloodshed. Bill Howell leaves his ship, via a bosun's chair, a wood and canvas seat slung from a line between Monterey and a tanker. Bill has more time in service than anyone else in the crew and is eligible for rotation back to the States. The tanker is headed that way, but slowly. On the 15th, HIROHITO's surrender message is broadcast. Task Force 38 is approximately 100 miles east of Tokyo, where it beats off an attack by Japanese aircraft at 1100 hours, nearly a half-day after the emperor's surrender message. On the 16th, Soviet troops land on South Sakhalin. On the 17th, B-32 bombers on reconnaissance over Tokyo are attacked by Japanese aircraft but suffer no CASUALTIES. A new Japanese cabinet is formed under Prince Higashikuni, a general and kinsman of the emperor. On the 18th, two B-32 bombers on reconnaissance over Tokyo are again jumped by Japanese aircraft, suffering one man killed and several wounded, while knocking down three of the attackers. Soviet troops land in the Kuriles. On the 19th, a Japanese delegation arrives by air at Manila (via IE SHIMA) to negotiate details of Allied occupation of the Home Islands and of the surrender. On the 20th Japanese military authorities suppress an attempt to stage a coup and establish a "Government of National Resistance." British reconnaissance aircraft in Burma are fired upon by Japanese antiaircraft batteries. Japanese forces in China cease fire. Red Chinese forces occupy Kalgan, northwest of PEKING. Having met with MACARTHUR, a Japanese delegation leaves Manila by air for Tokyo, via Ie Shima, with instructions from the Allies on the details of the surrender. On the 21st the Asiatic Wing, Naval Air Transport Service, is established at Oakland, California, as part of preparations for the REPATRIATION of American personnel from the Pacific. On the 22nd, Mili Atoll, in the MARSHALLS, becomes the first island garrison to surrender, to the USS *Levy* (DE-162). On the 23rd, Soviet troops occupy PARAMUSHIRO, in the Kuriles. On the 24th, Red Chinese forces occupy CHEFOO and Wei-hai-wei. Nationalist China and Russia conclude an alliance. On the 25th, the last day on which specially marked Japanese aircraft are permitted to fly, US aircraft begin routine patrols over Japan to monitor compliance with terms of the armistice, and to locate prisoner-of-war camps. Nationalist Chinese forces occupy NANKING. On the 26th, Soviet troops occupy Matsuma, in the southern Kuriles. On the 27th, the Third Fleet enters Sagami Bay, south of Tokyo Bay. On Morotai and Halmahea, Japanese forces totaling over 36,000 troops and 5,000 civilians surrender to the US 93rd Division. On the 28th, a party of US personnel lands at Atsugi Airfield near Tokyo, to be greeted by a sign reading "Welcome to the U.S. Army from the Third Fleet"—erected the previous evening by a pilot from the USS YORKTOWN who had made an unofficial landing there. On the 29th, the Fourth Marine Regiment lands at Yokosuka Naval Base, near Tokyo. Japanese forces in Southeast Asia surrender to the British. On the 30th, surface combatants of TF 38 enter Tokyo Bay. The 11th Airborne Division lands at Atsugi Airfield. On the 31st, MARCUS ISLAND surrenders to the USS BAGLEY (DD-386), which has been in the Pacific since PEARL HARBOR. Additional US troops land in Japan.

September 1945

Japan formally surrendered. However, it was six months before the last of the far-flung Japanese garrisons actually laid down their arms. Indeed, Japanese troops were used as local police in many areas through late 1945, until the Allies could get their own troops in place. The REPATRIATION of former Japanese soldiers to Japan continued through 1947. And some holdouts didn't return until the 1970s.

On the 1st: Since December 7, 1941 Japan has lost nearly 700 warships of 100 tons or more, for over two million tons of warships, as well as over 2,300 merchant vessels of 500 tons or more, for some 8.5 million tons, both totals exceeding the tonnage of the Imperial Navy and Merchant Marine on PEARL HARBOR Day. On the 2nd, Japan formally signs an instrument of surrender aboard the battleship USS *Missouri* in Tokyo Harbor, as the crews of 257 other Allied warships look on. World War II is over.

Although Japan has surrendered, Bill Howell's former ship, *Monterey* (CVL-26), spends the first half of September patrolling off Japan to make sure that any Japanese ships that have not surrendered, are not tempted to go back to war.

On 19 October, Chief Petty Officer Bill Howell, after 44 months of service, is given his Honorable Discharge at Lido Beach, Long Island (New York State).

After the war, Bill Howell and his wife Catherine will have four children. Two of his sons will serve in the Far East (Vietnam and Korea) as army helicopter pilots, and survive the experience. Although the *Monterey* was scrapped in the early 1960s, the 3,000 or so sailors who served on the ship have not forgotten her and reunions are held periodically. Bill Howell begins attending some of these in the early 1980s. Although the *Monterey* is gone, the memories of wartime service on her are not. The crew remembers, and so does anyone who has ever taken any interest in the Pacific War.

Appendix 1

◆━━◈━━◆

MODERN EQUIVALENTS OF NOTABLE PACIFIC WAR PLACE-NAMES

One consequence of decolonialization and of other political changes in the half-century since the end of World War II is that many places prominent to the war now bear different names, or names spelled in a radically different fashion according to new transliterations, than was the case between 1941 and 1945. This list is limited to places that figured somewhat prominently in the war. Omitted are numerous places where the modern form is a recognizable variant of the original spelling (e.g., Lungga Point rather than Lunga Point). Note that political changes in some of these areas are fairly constant, and names have a tendency to change on short notice.

Old Name	New Name
Amboina	Ambon
Amoy	Xiamen

Old Name	New Name
Batavia	Jakarta
Bonin Islands	Ogasawara Gunto
British North Borneo	Sabah (part of Malaysia)
Burma	Myanmar
Canton	Guangzhou
Celebes	Sulawesi
Ceram	Seram
Ceylon	Sri Lanka
Charar Province	region abolished
Chengtu	Chengdu
Chosen	Korea
Chungking	Chongqing
Dalny (Dairen)	Dalian
Diego Suarez	Anteranana
Dutch Borneo	Kalimantan
Ellice Islands	Tuvalua
Efate	Vate

Old Name	New Name	Old Name	New Name
Florida Island, Solomons	Nggela	Moulmein	Mawlamyine
Formosa	Taiwan	Mukden (Fengtien, 1932–45)	Shenyang
Fusan	Pusan	Nanking	Nanjing
Gilbert Islands	Kiribati	Ndeni	Nidu
Gona	Garara	Netherlands East Indies	Indonesia
Hankow	Kankou	Netherlands New Guinea	Irian Jaya
Honan	Henan	New Hebrides	Vanuatu
Hopeh	Hebei	Noemfoor	Numfor
Hupeh	Hubei	Palau	Balau
Indo-China	Cambodia, Laos, Vietnam	Parece Vela Island	Okina Daito
Irrawaddy River	Ayeyarwady River	Pegu	Bago
Java	Jawa	Peking (Peiping)	Beijing
Jehol Province	region abolished	Ponape	Pohnpei
Karafuto (Russian: Sakhalin)	Sakhalin	Port Arthur	Lushun
Karen	Kayin	Rangoon	Yangon
Kingsu	Jiangu	Salween River	Thanlwin River
Kurile Islands	Kurilskiye Ostrova	Sapwahfik	Ngatik
Kwantung	Guangdong	Sian	Xian
Makin Island	Butaritari Island	Sumatra	Sumatera
Malacca	Melaka	Szechuan	Sichuan
Malaya	part of Malaysia, with Sarawak and the former British Borneo	Taierchwang	Teierzhuang
		Tassafaronga Point	Tasivarongo
Manchuria (Manchukuo, 1932–45)	region abolished	Timor	Nusa Tenggara
		Truk Island	Chuuck Island
Marcus Island	Minamitori Island	Volcano Islands	Kaman Retie
Moluccas Islands	Maluku Islands	Yangtze River	Joint Jung

Appendix 2

CODE WORDS AND CODE NAMES OF IMPORTANCE IN THE PACIFIC WAR

By one account the Allies used over 10,000 code words during World War II, for everything from operations to secret weapons, and from politicians to islands. And the Axis used thousands as well. Code words were coined not only for major operations and territorial features, such as islands, but also for various individuals, such as politicians and senior commanders, smaller operations, rivers, towns, military units, even different sides of the same island. For example, the Awi River in New Guinea was code-named Colabar; McGrath, Alaska, was Hacksaw; Kavieng was Forearm, later changed to Fosdick; while the Japanese Fourth Division was the Aoba Detachment. To further complicate matters, code names were sometimes changed. In addition, during combat it was not unusual for front-line forces to give code names to local features. So the total number of code names that were used during the war must surely have been in the tens of thousands. And in fact there could easily have been more, were it not for the frequent use of numerals, both Roman and Arabic, the letters of the military alphabet (Able, Baker, etc.), and even colors (such as Beach Easy Red 2) to indicate minor geographic features or to distinguish among different versions or aspects of particular plans.

Although code names were supposed to mask the identity of a person, place, or thing, they sometimes were rather transparent, such as "Gateway" for the Marianas, "Jackfrost" for Canada, and "Hotrocks" for Mount Suribachi. Occasionally they were frivolous, a practice against which Winston Churchill railed at one point, observing that it not only trivialized the importance of the operation, but was also bad for morale, both military and civilian.

What follows are some of the more important, or at least more interesting, code names. By the way, the Japanese for operation is "Go."

Allied code names were ultimately decided by the Combined Chiefs of Staff. Their working staffs drew up lists of acceptable names. Words likely to have a double meaning or deemed to be "too frivolous" were generally avoided. These lists were then distributed to theater commanders who could assign names as needed.

Ref: Faldella, *Operazioni Segrete*; Ruffner and Thomas, eds., *The Codenames Dictionary*.

Word	Code Name For
1	See Ichi Go
3	See HA Go
157	Japanese New Guinea reinforcement, Jan. 1943
A	Japanese plan for the Battle of the Philippine Sea, June 1944; used previously for a plan for a decisive air battle in the Solomons, Apr. 1943; also the designation given the Japanese atomic bomb development project
Abattoir	Netherlands New Guinea
Accumulation	Leyte
Acorn	Small USN base development unit (see Cub)
Admiral Q	Occasional name for President Roosevelt
AF	Japanese code name for Midway
Air Mica	Admiral Marc Mitscher
Alamo	US Sixth Army
Alligator	Makin Island
Amnesia	Attu
Amoeba	Goodenough Island, New Guinea
Amount	Kyushu

Word	Code Name For
Ampersand	Espiritu Santo
Anaconda	Truk
Anakim	Proposed operations in Burma, 1943
Annuity	New Guinea operations after Hotplate
Aoba Detachment	Japanese Fourth Infantry Division
Aphorism	Nauru
Apothecary	Samoa
Arabic	New Britain
Arcadia	Washington Conference, Dec. 1941–Jan. 1942
Archbishop	Jaluit, Caroline Islands
Argonaut	Malta (Cricket) and Yalta (Magneto) conferences
Artist	Ponape, Caroline Islands
Ash	Vella Lavella
B	Japanese secret radar development project
Babacoute	Eniwetok
Bamboo	Proposed operation against the upper part of the Kra Peninsula, Siam (see Clinch)
Barney	US submarine missions in the Sea of Japan, June 1945
Bataan	Headquarters of Gen. Douglas MacArthur
Baus Au	Submarine supply missions to the Filipino guerrillas, 1942–45 ("Get it back," in Tagalog)
Beefsteak	Emirau Island
Bequest	Yap, Carolina Islands
Berry	Phases in the occupation of Japan (see Blacklist); also US plan to capture Wake Island
Blacklist	Plan for the peaceful occupation of Japan, drawn up in parallel with Olympic and implemented after the surrender
Bonus	Proposed Madagascar operation, early 1942
Braid	Occasional code name for Gen. G. C. Marshall
Brewer	Admiralty Islands operation, Feb.–May 1944
Broadway	Airborne invasion of Burma, Mar. 1944
Bronx Shipment	Movement of atomic bombs to Tinian
Bu	Japanese plan for an offensive across the Chindwin River, Burma, late 1944
Buccaneer	Plan to take the Andaman Islands, 1943
Bunkum	RN recon landing on Sumatra, 23–24 Apr. 1944
Button	Major rear base on Espiritu Santo
Byproduct	Trobriand Islands Task Force
C	Japanese plan to invade India, Feb. 1944

Word	Code Name For
Cactus	Guadalcanal
Cannibal	Akyab Operation, Jan. 1945
Capital	Operations in Central Burma, June 1944–Mar. 1945
Carillon	Kwajalein
Cartwheel	Encirclement of Rabaul, Aug. 1943–mid–1944.
Cast	USN codebreaking team at Cavite, the Philippines, 1941–42; later, Frumel (see Negat, Hypo)
Catchpole	Eniwetok operation, Feb. 1944
Champion	Plan to invade Burma from the north (see Capital, Copilot)
Chervil	Fiji Islands
Chronicle	Trobriand Islands Operation, summer 1943
Clinch	Proposed operation against the lower part of the Kra Peninsula, Siam (see Bamboo)
Colleen	Occasional code name for Adm E. J. King
Collodion	Secretary of State E. R. Stimson
Copilot	Original name for Champion
Corollary	Shanghai
Coronet	Proposed invasion of Honshu, Mar. 1946
Crasher	Proposed Formosa-China Coast Operation, late 1944
Cricket	Malta Conference (see Argonaut)
Crossroads	Bikini nuclear weapons tests, July 1946
Cub	Medium USN base development unit (see Lion)
Cudgel	Operations in the Arakan, late 1943
Culverin	Plans to invade Sumatra and Malaya, 1944
Detachment	Iwo Jima operation, Feb. 1945
Downfall	Proposed invasion of Japan (see Olympic, Coronet)
Dowser	Rendova Island, the Solomons
Dracula	Plan to capture Rangoon from the sea, early 1944
Drake	Early proposal to bomb Japan from China
Dumbo	Allied program to rescue pilots downed at sea
Ebon	Espiritu Santo
Elkton	Northeastern New Guinea operations, mid-1943
Eureka	Teheran Conference, Nov. 1943
Excelsior	The Philippines
Fall River	Gili Gili, Milne Bay, Papua
Falsehood	Tinian

Word	Code Name For
Fantan	Fiji
Fat Boy	The Hiroshima atomic bomb
Ferdinand	Australian coastwatcher program
Filbert	Russell Islands
Firebreak	West Coast defensive plan against Japanese carrier raids, 1942–43
Flintlock	Marshall Islands operations, Jan.–Feb. 1944
Forager	Marianas operations, June–July 1944
Forerun	Zamboanga
Foresquare	The Panama Canal
Fourfold	Gen. G. C. Marshall
Frumel	USN codebreaking team, Australia, 1942–45 (see Cast)
Galahad	5307th CPU (Merrill's Marauders)
Galvanic	Gilbert Islands operation, Nov. 1943
Gastronomy	Schouten Islands
Gateway	The Marianas
General Lyon	King George VI
Glyptic	Soviet leader J. V. Stalin
Goodtime	Treasury Islands
Granite	Admiral Nimitz's operation plans for 1944, issued January, March (Granite I), and June (Granite II)
Granny	Manila
Gratitude	Third Fleet raid into the South China Sea, early 1945
Grew	Australia
Gymnast	A modification of Tarzan
HA Go	Japanese feint in the Arakan, Feb. 1944, to mask U Go
Hailstone	Truk Island raid, Feb. 1944
Halfterm	Manchukuo
Happy Valley	SACO HQ, near Chungking
Helen	Makin Island during Galvanic
Horror	Ulithi Atoll
Horse	Butuitari Island, Tarawa
Hotfoot	Proposed carrier raid on Japan, Oct. 1944
Hypo	USN codebreaking team at Pearl Harbor (see Negat, Cast)
Hypocrite	Japan
I Go	Yamamoto's plan for Midway
Iceberg	Okinawa Operation, spring 1945
Ichi Go	"Operation One," Japanese offensive in China, mid–1944 onward
Incredible	Tarawa
Insurgent	Proposed Mindanao operation, Oct. 1944
Integer	Visayan Island, the Philippines

Word	Code Name For
Inwall	Gen. J. W. Stilwell
Ironclad	British occupation of Madagascar, Apr.–Sept. 1942
Ironhorse	Artificial harbor for Operation Coronet
Isolator	Proposed landing in southeastern China, late 1944
Jackboot	Attu Island
Jackfrost	Canada
Jacodet	Munda Island, the Solomons
Jeroboam	Wake Island
Ka Go	Japanese reinforcement of Guadalcanal, August 1942 (Battle of the Eastern Solomons)
Kan	Japanese plan to defend Burma from amphibious attack, 1944
KE	Evacuation operations for Guadalcanal, Feb. 1943, and Kiska, July 1943
Kilting	Harry S Truman
King	Plans for the liberation of the Philippines (e.g., King II, the Leyte operation, Oct. 1944)
KO Go	First phase of Ichi Go, Apr. 1944
Kon	Japanese plan to reinforce Biak, June 1944
Kourbash	Makin Island
Kutzu	Japanese defense plan for Kyushu and Shokaku
L	Prewar Japanese espionage ring run out of Mexico
Landcrab	Attu operation, May 1943
Lawlord	Jaluit Island, the Carolines
Lawmaking	Karafuto
Leadmine	Singapore
Leech	Sunda Straits
Leguminous	Plan to develop Okinawa as a base for Olympic
Little Boy	Alternative name for Thin Man
Longchop	Manus operation
Longsuit	Tarawa operation, within Galvanic, Nov. 1943
Love I-V	Phases in liberation of central Philippines, Dec. 1944–Apr. 1945
Lucius	Ho Chi Minh
Magic	US intelligence derived from Purple
Magnet	British plan for an offensive into Siam, if Japan entered that country, 1941
Magneto	Yalta Conference (see Argonaut)

Word	Code Name For
Mailfist	Tentative plan to capture Singapore, fall 1945
Mainyard	Guadalcanal, after its capture
Majestic	Alternative name for Olympic, early Aug. 1945
Manhattan Project	Nuclear weapons research program
Manhole	Hawaii
Matterhorn	B-29 missions to Japan from China
Mike I-VII	Phases of Luzon operation, Jan. 1945
Millet	RAF raids in Southeast Asia as a diversion for the Leyte operation, Oct. 1944
Miss Kimiko	Japanese code name for President Roosevelt
Miss Umeko	Japanese code name for Cordell Hull
MO	Japanese plan to occupy Port Moresby and Guadalcanal, which led to the Battle of the Coral Sea, May 1942
Montclair	Operations in SW Pacific Theater, 1945
Mr. P	Churchill, during the Casablanca Conference
Musketeer	Overall plan for the liberation of the Philippines, Oct. 1944 onward
Mythology	Canton Island
Negat	USN codebreaking team in Washington (see Cast, Hypo)
Nutcracker	Panama Canal
Nutpine	Corregidor
Oboe	Netherlands Indies Operations, Apr.–June 1945
Octagon	Quebec Conference, Sept. 1944
Olympic	Proposed invasion of Kyushu, Nov. 1945
Orange	US series of prewar plans for war with Japan
Oxygen	Cebu Island, the Philippines
Pastel	Deception plan for Operation Olympic
Peanut	Chiang Kai-shek (not a nickname, as often said)
Peon	Samoa
Petersburg	Allied contingency plan to abandon New Guinea, should the Japanese secure the Solomons, 1942
Pigstick	Proposed landing on the Magu Peninsula, Burma
Postern	Lae-Salamaua Operation, Papua, 1943
Privilege	Eniwetok, the Carolines
Propulsion	Nagasaki
Purple	Top Japanese code broken by the United States before the war
Quadrant	Quebec Conference, Aug. 1943

Word	Code Name For
Quinine	Arawe, New Britain
Rainbow	Chinese Salween offensive, Burma, 1943–44
Rainbow I-V	US prewar plans for war
Ravenous	Proposed operation in northern Burma, fall 1943
Reckless	Hollandia operation, New Guinea, Apr. 1944
Recuperate	Ellice Islands
Red	US designation for an early Japanese naval code
Reno I-V	Preliminary proposals for the liberation of the Philippines, Feb. 1943–June 1944
RO Go	Japanese reinforcement of Rabaul with carrier aircraft, Oct.–Nov. 1943
Roger	Proposed operations against the Kra Peninsula
Romulus	Plans to occupy the Arakan and Akyab, Dec. 1944
Roses	Efate
Rover	Eleanor Roosevelt
Ruth	Siamese regent, Nai Pridi Bhanangang
San Antonio	B-29 missions against Tokyo from the Marianas
Sawbuck	Stalin
Schoolboy	Lae, Papua-New Guinea
Schoolgirl	Palau Islands
Screwdriver I-II	Landings in the Arakan, Nov. 1944
Seclusion	Bonin Islands
Seizure	Bikini Atoll
Sextant	Cairo Conference
Sho Go	"Operation Victory," the Japanese defense plans for the Philippines (Sho-1), Formosa (Sho-2), and the Home Islands (Sho-3, etc.), mid- to late 1944; Sho-1 culminated in Leyte Gulf
Shrimp	Saigon
Silverplate	Training of B-29 crews to drop the atomic bomb
Silversand	Mindanao; also Silverware
Snapshot	USN reconnaissance operations in the western Carolines, July 1944
Snow White	Madam Chiang
Spider	Sasebo

Word	Code Name For
Stalemate I-II	Palau operation, Sep.–Oct. 1944: I, Anguar; II, Peleliu
Starlit	Iwo Jima
Starvation	B–29 mining of Japanese waters, from March 1945 on
Steamroller	Manila
Stepsister	Repatriation of Australian troops from the Middle East, late 1941 to early 1942
Stevedore	Guam
Straightline	Wadke Operation, Apr. 1944
Suzu	Japanese defense plan for the Visayas and Mindanao, the Philippines, 1944–1945
Symbol	Casablanca Conference
Talon	Amphibious operations against Akyab, Jan. 1945
Tarzan	Advance on Indow-Katha area, Burma
Ten Go	Japanese plan for the defense of the Home Islands, 1944–45
Ten Ichi	Yamato's "suicide" mission, Apr. 1945
Terminal	Potsdam Conference, July 1945
Thin Man	Nagasaki atomic bomb (see Little Boy)
Thorn	Rabaul
Thunder	Chindit Operations in Burma, from March 1944
Thursday	Allied special warfare operations in Burma, 1944
TIGAR 1C	Ledo Road project
Tiger Force	RAF heavy bomber force for the Pacific, 1946
TO	Japanese Navy plan for the seaward defense of the Home Islands, mid-1944
Toenails	New Georgia Operation, mid-1943
TOGO	Second phase of Ichi Go, from May 1944
Tolstoy	Churchill-Stalin summit, Oct. 1944
Trident	Washington Conference, May 1943
U Go	Japanese Imphal Offensive, Mar. 1944
Vanguard	Similar to Dracula
Z	Japanese plan for a naval clash in the central Pacific in early 1944; evolved into A Go
Zero Zero	Adm Chester W. Nimitz
Zipper	British plan for Malaya offensive, late 1945

RECOMMENDED READING AND REFERENCES

This does not purport to be an exhaustive, or even extensive bibliography of materials on the Pacific War. There are literally thousands of books on the subject, and even a work the size of the present one would not be enough to cover items in English alone. However, some works are more important, or at least more unusual, than others, and make for particularly rewarding reading. We have omitted biographies, memoirs, most treatments of individual battles and campaigns, and "technoporn," to focus on broader topics, darker corners, and unusual perspectives.

Most of the works listed here have extensive bibliographies of their own.

Abbazia, Patrick, *Mr. Roosevelt's Navy* (Annapolis: Naval Institute Press, 1975).

Albee, Parker Bishop, Jr., and Freeman, Keller Cushing, *Shadow of Suribachi: Raising the Flag on Iwo Jima* (Westport, Conn. Greenwood: 1995).

Alden, John D., *The Fleet Submarine in the U.S. Navy* (Annapolis: Naval Institute Press, 1979).

———, *U.S. Submarine Attacks During World War II* (Annapolis: Naval Institute Press, 1989). Includes all US attacks, worldwide, as far as can be determined, whether successful or not, plus British and Dutch attacks in the Pacific Theater.

Allen, Louis, *The End of the War in Asia* (London: Beekman, 1976). An excellent summary treatment of the final phase of the war in India, Burma, Siam, Indo-China, the Netherlands East Indies, China, and Korea, stressing political developments.

Allen, Thomas B., and Polmar, Norman, *Code-Name Downfall: The Secret Plan to Invade Japan and Why Truman Dropped the Bomb* (New York: Simon and Schuster, 1995).

Angelucci, Enzo, *The American Fighter* (New York: Outlet, 1987).

Armstrong, Anne, *Unconditional Surrender: The Impact of the Casablanca Policy Upon World War II* (Westport, Conn.: Greenwood, 1974).

Australia in the Second World War (Canberra: Australian War Memorial, 1957–63). A very good, very detailed work, in five series: Army, Navy, Air Force, Medical, and Civil. The operational volumes for the Pacific War are:

  Series I (Army): IV, *The Japanese Thrust*, by Lionel Wigmore; V, *Southwest Pacific Area: Kokoda to Wau*, by Dudley McCarthy; VI, *The New Guinea Offensive*, by David Dexter; VII, *The Final Campaigns*, by Gavin Long.

  Series II (Navy): II, *The Royal Australian Navy, 1942–1945*, by G. Herman Gill.

  Series III (Air): II, *Air War Against Japan, 1943–1945*, by George Odgers.

Baclagon, Uladrico S., *Military History of the Philippines* (Manila: St. Mary's, 1975). A very good treatment of a neglected subject.

Barnett, Corelli, *Engage the Enemy More Closely: The Royal Navy in the Second World War* (New York: W. W. Norton, 1991).

Barnhart, Michael A., *Japan Prepares for Total War: The Search for Economic Security, 1919–1941* (Ithaca, N.Y.: Cornell University Press, 1987).

Beck, John Jacob, *MacArthur and Wainwright: Surrender of the Philippines* (Albuquerque: University of New Mexico Press, 1974).

Becton, F. Julian, *The Ship That Would Not Die* (Englewood Cliffs, N.J.: Prentice Hall, 1980). An account of the USS *Laffey* and her struggle against the kamikaze, by her skipper.

Bergamini, David, *Japan's Imperial Conspiracy* (New York: William Morrow, 1971). A controversial book, not without its faults, but one that raises important questions about the role of Hirohito that have never been properly answered.

Blair, Clay, Jr., *Silent Victory: The U.S. Submarine War Against Japan* (Philadelphia: Lippincott, 1975).

Borf, Dorothy, and Okamoto, Shumpei, eds., *Pearl Harbor as History: Japanese-American Relations, 1931–1941* (New York: Columbia University Press, 1973). A multifaceted look at a complex subject.

Boyd, Carl, *Hitler's Japanese Confidant: General Oshima Hiroshi and MAGIC Intelligence, 1941–1945* (Lawrence, K.: University Press of Kansas, 1993). Hitler told Hiroshi, and Hiroshi radioed the information to Tokyo, and courtesy of MAGIC, Pearl Harbor.

Boyd, Carl, and Yoshida, Akihiko, *The Japanese Submarine Force and World War II* (Annapolis: Naval Institute Press, 1995).

Boyington, Gregory, *Baa, Baa, Black Sheep* (New York: Bantam, 1990).

Brice, Martin, *Axis Blockade Runners of World War II* (Annapolis: Naval Institute Press, 1981). Unsatisfactory, but the only work available on the subject.

Brown, Robert, *Warship Losses of World War Two* (Annapolis: Naval Institute Press, 1995). A valuable compendium of all warship losses during the war, including those of neutrals. In addition to the basic chronological presentation of ship losses, with location, circumstances, and often extensive explanatory notes, there are statistical tables and sometimes extensive analysis of the causes of ship loss. Very handy for the serious student of World War II at sea.

Butow, Robert J., *Japan's Decision to Surrender* (Stanford: Stanford University Press, 1954).

———, *Tojo and the Coming of the War* (Stanford: Stanford University Press, 1961).

Carpenter, Dorr, and Polmar, Norman, *Submarines of the Imperial Japanese Navy* (Annapolis: Naval Institute Press, 1986).

Chesneua, Roger, *Aircraft Carriers of the World, 1914 to the Present: An Illustrated Encyclopedia* (Annapolis: Naval Institute Press, 1984).

Ch'i, Hsi-Sheng, *Nationalist China at War* (Ann Arbor: University of Michigan Press, 1982). The best short account of the Sino-Japanese War, with a good balance of political, diplomatic, military, and economic treatment.

Collier, Basil, *The War in the Far East, 1941–1945* (New York: Heineman, 1969).

Collins, Donald E., *Native American Aliens: Disloyalty and the Renunciation of Citizenship by Japanese-Americans during World War II* (Westport, Conn.: Greenwood, 1985).

Conway's All the World's Fighting Ships, 1922–1946 (Annapolis: Naval Institute Press, 1980).

Cook, Charles, *The Battle of Cape Esperance: Encounter at Guadalcanal* (Annapolis: Naval Institute Press, 1968).

Cook, Haruko Taya, and Cook, Theodore F., *Japan at War: An Oral History* (New York: The New Press, 1992).

Corbett, P. Scott, *Quiet Passages: The Exchange of Civilians between the United States and Japan during the Second World War* (Kent, Ohio: Kent State University Press, 1987).

Couffer, Jack, *Bat Bomb* (Austin: University of Texas Press, 1992). Worth reading.

Craven, Wesley E., and Cate, James L., eds., *The Army Air Forces in World War II*, 7 vols. (Chicago: University of Chicago Press, 1948–55).

Cressman, Robert J., *"A Magnificent Fight"; The Battle for Wake Island* (Annapolis: Naval Institute Press, 1995).

Crost, Lyn, *Honor by Fire: Japanese Americans at War in Europe and the Pacific* (Novato, Calif.: Presidio Press, 1994).

Daws, Gavin, *Prisoners of the Japanese* (New York: William Morrow, 1995).

Department of the Army, *Army Battle Casualties and Nonbattle Deaths in World War II, Final Report* (Washington: DA, 1953).

Door, Robert F., *U.S. Bombers of World War II* (London: Ian Alan, 1989).

Dorrance, William H., *Fort Kamehameha: The Story of the Harbor Defense of Pearl Harbor* (Shippensburg, Pa.: White Mane, 1993).

Dower, John W., *War Without Mercy: Race and Power in the Pacific War* (New York: Pantheon, 1986). Overstates the case, and neglects Japanese racism toward other Asians and their response in kind.

Drea, Edward J., *MacArthur's Ultra: Codebreaking and the War Against Japan, 1942–1945* (Lawrence, K.: University Press of Kansas, 1992).

Dull, Paul S., *A Battle History of the Imperial Japanese Navy, 1941–1945* (Annapolis: Naval Institute Press, 1978).

Dunnigan, James F., *How to Make War*, 3rd ed. (New York: William Morrow, 1993). Focuses on the theory and practice of warfare in the late 20th century, but contains much that is useful in helping to understand the conduct of the Second World War as well.

Dunnigan, James F., and Nofi, Albert A., *Dirty Little Secrets of World War II* (New York: William Morrow, 1994).

———, *Shooting Blanks: Warmaking that Doesn't Work* (New York: William Morrow, 1991).

———, *Victory and Deceit: Dirty Tricks at War* (New York: William Morrow, 1995).

———, *Victory at Sea: World War II in the Pacific* (New York: William Morrow, 1995).

DuPuy, Trevor N., *Great Battles of the Eastern Front, 1941–1945* New York: Macmillan, 1982).

———. *Numbers, Predictions, and War* (Indianapolis: Bobbs, Merrill 1978). A discussion of the Quantified Judgment Model, an attempt to develop a mathematical model capable of comparing the military capabilities of various military forces, based on the experience of several dozen battles during the Second World War.

Duus, Masayo, *Tokyo Rose: Orphan of the Pacific War* (New York/Tokyo: Kodansha, 1979).

Dwyer, John B., *Seaborne Deception: The History of U.S. Beach Jumpers* (New York: Greenwood, 1992). US "frogman" operations.

Eastman, Lloyd E., "Nationalist China during the Sino-Japanese War, 1937–1945," in *The Cambridge History of China* (Cambridge: Cambridge University Press, 1986), vol. 13, pt. 2.

Edoin, Hoito, *The Night Tokyo Burned* (New York: St. Martin's, 1987).

Ellis, John, *World War II, A Statistical Survey: Essential Facts and Figures for All the Combatants* (New York: Facts On File, 1993).

Feis, Herbert, *The Atomic Bomb and the End of World War II* (Princeton: Princeton University Press, 1965). Revised and expanded version of his *Japan Subdued: The Atomic Bomb and the end of the War* (Princeton: Princeton University Press, 1961).

Feldt, Eric A., *The Coastwatchers* (Oxford: Oxford University Press, 1959).

Ford, Daniel, *Flying Tigers* (Washington: Smithsonian, 1991).

Fox, Stephen, *The Unknown Internment: An Oral History of the Relocation of Italian-Americans During World War II* (Boston: Macmillan, 1990).

Francillon, Rene J., *Japanese Aircraft of the Pacific War* (Annapolis: Naval Institute Press, 1987).

Frank, Richard B., *Guadalcanal* (New York: Random House, 1990).

Friedman, Norman, *Submarine Design and Development* (Annapolis: Naval Institute Press, 1984).

———, *United States Aircraft Carriers: An Illustrated Design History* (Annapolis: Naval Institute Press, 1983).

————, *United States Battleships: An Illustrated Design History* (Annapolis: Naval Institute Press, 1988).

————, *United States Destroyers: An Illustrated Design History* (Annapolis: Naval Institute Press, 1982).

Fujita, Frank, Jr., *Foo: A Japanese-American Prisoner of the Rising Sun* (Dexter, Tex.: University of North Texas Press, 1993).

Fukui, Shizuo, *Japanese Naval Vessels at the End of the War* (Annopolis: Naval Institute Press, 1992).

Fuller, Richard, *Shokan: Hirohito's Samurai, Leaders of the Japanese Armed Forces, 1926–1945* (London: Arms and Armour Press, 1992). Though limited, this is the only biographical guide to the Japanese military available in English.

Furer, Julius A., *Administration of the Navy Department* (Washington: Government Printing Office, 1959).

Gailey, Harry A., *Bougainville, 1943–1945: The Forgotten Campaign* (Lexington, Ky.: University Press of Kentucky, 1991).

Garfield, Brian, *The Thousand Mile War* (Fairbanks: University of Alaska Press, 1995).

Garzke, William H., Jr., and Dulin, Robert O., Jr., *Battleships: Allied Battleships in World War II* (Annapolis: Naval Institute Press, 1980).

————, *Battleships: Axis and Neutral Battleships in World War II* (Annapolis: Naval Institute Press, 1985).

————, *Battleships: United States Battleships in World War II* (Annapolis: Naval Institute Press, 1976).

Giangreco, D. M., "Casualty Projections for the U.S. Invasion of Japan, 1945–1946: Planning and Policy Implications," *Journal of Military History* 61, no. 3 (June 1997), pp. 521–81.

Glantz, David, *August Storm: The Soviet 1945 Strategic Offensive in Manchuria* (Ft. Leavenworth: Combat Studies Institute, 1983).

Goldstein, Donald M., and Dillon, Katherine V., eds., *The Pearl Harbor Papers: Inside the Japanese Plans* (New York: Viking, 1993).

Greenberg, Eli, and associates, *The Ineffective Soldier: Lessons for Management and the Nation*, 3 vols. (Westport Conn.: Greenwood, 1975). Analyzes where and how the U.S. Armed Forces mismanaged its manpower, one volume is subtitled *The Lost Divisions*.

Grover, David H., *U.S. Army Ships and Watercraft of World War II* (Annapolis: Naval Institute Press, 1987).

Hallas, James H., *The Devil's Anvil: The Assault on Peleliu* (Westport, Conn.: Praeger, 1994).

————, *Killing Ground on Okinawa: The Battle for Sugar Loaf Hill* (Westport, Conn.: Praeger, 1996).

Handbook on Japanese Military Forces (London: Greenhill, 1991). Originally published by the US War Department during World War II, this should be used with that reservation in mind. A valuable source nonetheless.

Hara, Tameichi, Saito, Fred, and Pineau, Roger, *Japanese Destroyer Captain* (New York: Ballantine, 1983).

Harries, Merion, and Harries, Susie, *Soldiers of the Sun: The Rise and Fall of the Japanese Imperial Army* (New York: Random House, 1991). Although not entirely successful as a history of the Imperial Army, this comes into its own in a series of chapters that analyze the doctrine, character, equipment, and philosophy of the Japanese Army in the period of World War II.

Harrington, Joseph D., *Yankee Samurai: The Secret Role of Nisei in America's Pacific Victory* (Detroit: Nicholas Books, 1979).

Hashimoto, Mochitsura, *Sunk!* (New York: Ballantine, 1954).

Hayashi, Saburo, and Coox, Alvin D., *Kogun: The Japanese Army in the Pacific War* (Westport, Conn: Greenwood, 1979).

Heinl, Robert Debs, Jr., *Soldiers of the Sea: The United States Marine Corps, 1775–1962* (Annapolis: Naval Institute Press, 1962).

Heinl, Robert Debs, Jr., and Crown, John A., *The Marshalls: Increasing the Tempo* (Washington: US MC, 1954).

Hezlet, Arthur, R. *Aircraft and Sea Power* (New York: Stein and Day, 1970).

———, *Electronics and Sea Power.* (New York: Stein and Day, 1975).

———, *Submarines and Sea Power* (New York: Stein and Day, 1972).

Hicks, George, *The Comfort Women: Japan's Brutal Regime of Enforced Prostitution in the Second World War* (New York: W. W. Norton, 1995).

History of United States Marine Corps Operations in World War II (Washington: Government Printing Office,1956–1971): I, *Pearl Harbor to Guadalcanal*, by Frank O. Hugh, Verle E. Ludwig, and Henry I Shaw; II, *The Isolation of Rabaul*, by Henry I. Shaw, Jr., and Douglas T. Kim; III, *The Central Pacific Drive*, by Henry I. Shaw, Jr., Bernard C. Nalty, and Edwin J. Turnblodh; IV, *Western Pacific Operations*, by George W. Garond and Truman R. Strobridge; V, *Victory and Occupation*, by Benis M. Frank and Henry I. Shaw, Jr.

Hough, Richard, *The Hunting of Force Z* (London: Collins, 1963).

Howarth, Stephen, *To Shining Sea* (New York: Random House, 1991).

Hoyt, Edwin P., *Hirohito: The Emperor and the Man* (Westport, Conn.: Bergin and Garvey, 1992).

———, *Japan's War: The Great Pacific Conflict, 1853–1952* (New York: McGraw-Hill, 1986).

———, *The Last Kamikaze: The Story of Admiral Matome Ugaki* (Westport: Praeger, 1993).

Hutchison, Kevin Don, *World War II in the North Pacific: Chronology and Fact Book* (Westport, Conn.: Greenwood, 1994).

Ienaga, Saburo, *The Pacific War: World War II and the Japanese, 1931–1945*, tr. Frank Baldwin (New York: Random House, 1978).

Iriye, Akira, "Japanese Aggression and China's International Position, 1931–1945," in *The Cambridge History of China* (Cambridge: Cambridge University Press, 1986), vol. 13, pt. 2.

Irokawa, Daikichi, *The Age of Hirohito: In Search of Modern Japan*, tr. Mikiso Hano (New York: The Free Press, 1995).

Isely, Jeter A., and Crowl, Philip A. *The U.S. Marines and Amphibious War* (Princeton: Princeton University Press, 1951).

Ito, Masanori, with Roger Pineau, *The End of the Imperial Japanese Navy*, tr. Andrew Y. Kuroda and Roger Pineau (Westport, Conn.: Greenwood, 1984).

Janes Encyclopedia of Aviation (London: Janes, 1980).

Jentschura, Hansgeorg, Jung, Dieter, and Michel, Peter, *Warships of the Imperial Japanese Navy, 1869–1945*, tr. Anthony Preston and J. D. Brown (Annapolis: Naval Institute Press, 1992).

Kerr, E. Bartlett, *Flames Over Tokyo* (New York: Donald I. Fine, 1991).

———., *Surrender and Survival: The Experience of American POWs in the Pacific, 1941–1945* (New York: William Morrow, 1985).

Kirby, Stanley Woodburn, *The United Kingdom Military Series: The War Against Japan*, 5 vols. (London: HMSO, 1957–70).

Klehr, Harvey, and Radosh, Ronald, *The Amerasia Spy Case: Prelude to McCarthyism* (Chapel Hill, N.C.: University of North Carolina Press, 1996).

Koburger, Charles W., Jr., *Pacific Turning Point: The Solomons Campaign, 1942–1943* (Westport, Conn.: Praeger, 1995).

Kurzman, Dan, *Left to Die: The Tragedy of the USS Juneau* (New York: Pocket Books, 1994).

Lane, Frederic, *Ships for Victory: A History of Shipbuilding Under the U.S. Maritime Commission in World War II* (Baltimore: Johns Hopkins, 1950).

Larrabee, Eric, *Commander in Chief: Franklin Delano Roosevelt, His Lieutenants, and Their War* (New York: Simon and Schuster, 1987). The handiest treatment of the principal players in the US war effort during World War II, with excellent, and sometimes groundbreaking, word portraits of FDR, and his commanders, including MacArthur, Nimitz, and all the rest.

Larsen, C. Kay, " 'Till I Come Marching Home": A Brief History of American Women in World War II (Pasadena, Maryland: The Minerva Center, 1996).

Leasor, James, Boarding Party: The Last Action of the Calcutta Light Horse (Annopolis: Naval Institute Press, 1995).

Lewin, Ronald, The American Magic: Codes, Ciphers and the Defeat of Japan. (New York: Viking, 1982).

Liu, Frederick Fu (Liu Chih-pu), A Military History of Modern China, 1924–1947 (Princeton: Princeton University Press, 1956). Despite its age, still the best treatment of the subject.

Long, Gavin, The Six Years War: A Concise History of Australia in the 1939–1945 War (Canberra: Australian War Memorial, 1973). An excellent one-volume treatment of the Australian contribution to the war.

Lord, Walter, Lonely Vigil: Coastwatchers of the Solomons (New York: Viking, 1977). Although not entirely accurate, this remains the most available treatment of the subject.

Lorelli, John A., The Battle of the Komandorski Islands, March 1943 (Annapolis: Naval Institute Press, 1984).

Lott, Arnold S., Most Dangerous Sea: A History of Mine Warfare (Annapolis: Naval Institute Press, 1959).

MacGregor, Morris J., Jr., Integration of the Armed Forces, 1940–1965 (Washington: Department of Defense, 1981).

MacIntyre, David, The Battle for the Pacific (London: Batsford, 1966).

Marder, Arthur J., Jacobsen, Mark, and Horsfield, John, Old Friends, New Enemies: The Royal Navy and the Imperial Japanese Navy, 2 vols. (Oxford: Oxford University Press, 1990).

Masters, John, Bugles and a Tiger (New York: Viking, 1956).

———, The Road Past Mandalay (New York: Bantam, 1961). Perhaps the best book ever written about men and war. Period.

Mayo, Lida, Bloody Buna (Garden City, N.Y.: Doubleday, 1974).

Mikesh, Robert C., Japan's World War II Balloon Bomb Attack on North America (Washington: Smithsonian Institute Press, 1973).

Miller, Edward S., War Plan Orange: The U.S. Strategy to Defeat Japan, 1897–1945 (Annapolis: Naval Institute Press, 1991). Presents a superbly detailed analysis of US planning for a war with Japan, with an examination of the personalities involved and the ways in which changing world events influenced such planning; plus a look at the ways in which the various prewar plans influenced the actual development of US strategy in the Pacific War.

Millett, Allan Reid, and Murray, Williamson, eds., Military Effectiveness, 3 vols. (New York: Routledge, Chapman & Hall, 1988). A collection of essays by noted specialists on the military capabilities and limitations of the armed forces of each of the great powers during World War I, the interwar period, and World War II, with many valuable insights and much food for thought. Their Calculations: Net Assessment and the Coming of World War II (New York: Allan and Unwin, 1992) contains a series of essays on how each of the great powers dealt with the problem of evaluating the military capabilities and limitations of their opponents.

Morison, Samuel Eliot, History of United States Naval Operations in World War II, 15 vols. (Boston: Little, Brown, 1947–62). The volumes of particular interest to the Pacific War are: III, The Rising Sun in the Pacific, 1931–April 1942; IV, Coral Sea, Midway, and Submarine Actions, May 1942–August 1942; V, The Struggle for Guadalcanal, August 1942–February 1943; VI, Breaking the Bismarcks Barrier, 22 July 1942–1 May 1944; VII, Aleutians, Gilberts, and Marshalls, June 1942–April 1944; VIII, New Guinea and the Marianas, March 1944–August 1944; XII, Leyte, June 1944–January 1945; XIII, The Liberation of the Philippines: Luzon, Mindanao, the Visayas, 1944–1945; and XIV, Victory in the Pa-

cific, 1945. For those short of the leisure to read 15 volumes, Morison's *The Two Ocean War* (Boston: Little Brown, 1963) presents a shorter treatment of the subject. On Morison himself, see the entry in the main text.

Nelson, Dennis D., *The Integration of the Negro into the United States Navy* (New York: Ferrar-Strauss, 1982).

Niven, John, *The American President Line and Its Forebears, 1848–1984* (Newark, Del.: University of Delaware Press, 1987).

O'Connell, Robert L., *Sacred Vessels* (New York: Westview Press, 1991).

Ogburn, Charlton, Jr., *The Marauders* (New York: William Morrow, 1982).

Overy, R. J., *The Air War, 1939–1945* (New York: Stein and Day, 1981). A critical analytic look at the nature of the war in the air, with many valuable perspectives, such as the importance not merely of aircraft production, but also of the production of spare parts. One of the most incisive thinkers on the war, Overy's most recent volume, *Why the Allies Won* (New York: W. W. Norton, 1996), takes some startling positions on the causes of the Allied victory, an outcome that, as he effectively points out, was by no means as obvious in 1941–42 as it seems today.

Parillo, Mark P., *The Japanese Merchant Marine in World War II* (Annapolis: Naval Institute Press, 1993).

Pelz, Stephen E., *Race to Pearl Harbor: The Failure of the Second London Naval Conference and the Onset of World War II* (Cambridge, Mass.: Harvard University Press, 1974).

Perret, Geoffrey, *There's a War to Be Won: The United States Army in World War II* (New York: Ballantine, 1992). Presents a pretty good look at the US Army in the late 1930s and 1940s, weaving together the diverse trends in doctrine, organization, equipment, and planning that ultimately led to the army with which the United States fought World War II, while looking into everything from the personalities of the army's leaders, problems and surprises in weapons development, racial policies, the medical corps, the famous maneuvers of 1940–41, and, of course, the experience of battle.

Perry, Hamilton D., *The Panay Incident* (New York: Macmillan, 1969).

Polmar, Norman, and Allen, Thomas B., *America at War, 1941–1945* (New York: Random House, 1991).

Prados, John, *Combined Fleet Decoded: The Secret History of American Intelligence and the Japanese Navy in World War II* (New York: Random House, 1995). Takes a look at US codebreaking activities as they influenced the war against Japan, covering much new ground. Moreover, although the focus of the work is on cryptography, there is much material on other forms of intelligence gathering as well.

Prange, Gordon R., Goldstein, Donald M., and Dillon, Katherine V., *At Dawn We Slept* (New York: Viking, 1981).

———, *Miracle At Midway* (New York: Viking, 1982).

———, *Pearl Harbor: The Verdict of History* (New York: Viking, 1986).

———, *Target Tokyo: The Story of the Sorge Spy Ring* (New York: Viking, 1984).

At Dawn We Slept and *Pearl Harbor* provide the most detailed and exhaustive inquiry into the American disaster at Pearl Harbor, along with Goldstein and Dillon's *The Pearl Harbor Papers Inside the Japanese Plans*. Going to considerable lengths to examine the numerous conspiracy theories (some of which—such as, the attack was actually carried out by British pilots operating from a secret base on one of the other Hawaiian islands as a result of a deal between Roosevelt and Churchill—are remarkable indeed), the authors conclude that "There is enough blame for everyone," and not a little credit for the Japanese. *Miracle at Midway* carries the story forward to the series of Japanese blunders and American successes that led to the Japanese disaster just seven months later, while *Target Tokyo* looks at that intriguing aspect of the Pacific War.

Prefer, Nathan, *MacArthur's New Guinea Campaign: March–August 1944* (Conshohocken, Pa.: Combined Publishing, 1995).

Rasor, Eugene L., *General Douglas MacArthur, 1880–1964: Historiography and Annotated Bibliography* (Westport, Conn.: Greenwood, 1994).

Ravuvu, Asesela, *Fijians at War* (Suva: Institute of Pacific Studies, 1974).

Ready, J. Lee, *Forgotten Allies* (New York: McFarland, 1985). Takes an in-depth look at the role in the war of the minor powers and the numerous resistance movements, with one volume for the war against Germany and the other that against Japan. A valuable and very neglected book.

Reit, Seymour, *Masquerade: The Amazing Camouflage Deceptions of World War II* (New York: Dutton, 1978).

Reynolds, Clark G., *The Fast Carriers* (Annapolis: Naval Institute Press, 1992). Although relatively old (originally published in 1962), and rather focused on the American point of view, still the best overall treatment of the carrier war in the Pacific.

Rigelman, Harold, *Caves of Biak: An American Officer's Experience In the Southwest Pacific* (New York: Dial, 1955). Up close, and very personal.

Roscoe, Theodore, *On the Seas and in the Skies: A History of the U.S. Navy's Air Power* (New York: Hawthorne, 1970).

———, *United States Destroyer Operations in World War II* (Annapolis: Naval Institute Press, 1953).

———, *United States Submarine Operations in World War II* (Annapolis: Naval Institute Press, 1949).

Roskill, S. W., *The United Kingdom Military Series: The War At Sea, 1939–1945* Nashville: Battery Press, 1994.

———, *White Ensign: The British Navy in World War II* (Annapolis: Naval Institute Press, 1960).

Ruffner, Frederick G., Jr., and Thomas, Robert C., eds., *The Codenames Dictionary* (Detroit: Gale, 1963). A good start.

Salazar, Generoso P., Reyes, Fernando R., and Nuval, Leonardo Q., *Defense, Defeat, and Defiance: World War II in the Philippines* (Manila: Veterans Federation of the Philippines, 1993). A somewhat disorganized but very detailed treatment of the war in the Philippines, with emphasis on the guerrilla resistance.

Seagrave, Sterling, *The Soong Dynasty* (New York: HarperCollins, 1986).

Sherrod, Robert, *History of Marine Corps Aviation in WWII* (Baltimore: Nautical and Naval, 1987).

Sigal, Leon, *Fighting to the Finish: The Politics of War Termination in the United States and Japan, 1945* (Ithaca, N.Y.: Cornell University Press, 1988).

Sinclair, Thomas, *To Find a Path: The Life and Times of the Royal Pacific Islands Regiment*, 2 vols. (Brisbane: Boolarong Publications, 1990).

Skates, John Ray, *The Invasion of Japan: Alternative to the Bomb* (Columbia, S.C.: University of South Carolina 1994). The most complete treatment of Allied and Japanese preparations for an invasion of Japan. Very detailed, and with a careful analysis of casualty predictions.

Smith, Page, *Democracy on Trial: The Japanese-American Evacuation and Relocation in World War II* (New York: Simon and Schuster, 1995).

Spector, Ronald H., *Eagle Against the Sun: The American War with Japan* (New York: Random House, 1985).

Stanton, Shelby L., *Order of Battle, U.S. Army, World War II* (Novato, Calif.: Presidio, 1984). Everything you ever wanted to know about the organization of the US Army in the war. And more.

Stephen, John J., *Hawaii under the Rising Sun: Japan's Plans for Conquest after Pearl Harbor* (Honolulu: University of Hawaii Press, 1984).

Stone, James, ed., *Crisis Fleeting: Original Reports on Military Medicine in India and Burma in the Second World War* (Washington: Government Printing Office, 1969).

Stouffer, Samuel A., et al., *The American Soldier: Studies in Social Psychology in World War II* (Princeton: Princeton University Press, 1949). Summarizes the army's massive series of surveys of the common soldier's view on everything from army chow to race relations to the nature of the enemy. The volumes are subtitled: *Adjustment During Army Life, Combat and Its Aftermath, Experiments in Mass Communication,* and *Measurement and Prediction.*

Stratton, Roy O., *SACO: The Rice Paddy Navy* (Pleasantville, N.Y.: C.S. Palmer, 1950).

Tokayer, Marvin, *The Fugu Plan: The Untold Story of the Japanese and the Jews During World War II* (New York: Grosset and Dunlop, 1996).

Trota, Ricardo Jose, *The Philippine Army, 1935–1942* (Manila: Ateneo de Manila, 1992). A short, but valuable look at the organization and history of this much neglected force.

Tuchman, Barbara, *Stilwell and the American Experience in China, 1911–1945* (New York: Macmillan, 1970).

The United States Army in World War II (Washington: Government Printing Office, 1947–). The official account of the US Army in the war is probably the best official history ever written, running to about 80 volumes thus far (excluding the clinical medical history, which has been published separately in about 20 additional volumes). This is an often highly detailed account of how the war was organized, supplied, and fought. While the operational volumes are literate, well reasoned, critical, and worth reading, the really good stuff is in the technical volumes, on matters from the procurement of ammunition and aircraft to providing boots and bread for the troops. No other major-power official history comes even close to the objectivity, scholarship, and readability of this series.

The United States Strategic Bombing Survey (Washington: USSBS, 1945–1949). A 320-volume look at the war, focusing on the influence of strategic bombing, with many valuable insights.

Van Der Rhoer, E., *Deadly Magic* (New York: Time-Life, 1978).

Van der Vat, Dan, *The Pacific Campaign: World War II, the U.S.-Japanese Naval War, 1941–1945* (New York: Touchstone, 1991).

Van Slyle, Lymon, "The Chinese Communist Movement during the Sino-Japanese War, 1937–1945," in *The Cambridge History of China* (Cambridge: Cambridge University Press, 1986), vol. 13, pt. 2.

Warship International, a quarterly published for many years now by the International Naval Research Organization (5905 Reinwood Dr., Toledo, OH, 43613), is an extraordinary source of detailed historical, technical, and operational information about fighting ships, with frequent articles, letters, and reviews related to the naval war in the Pacific, marred only by lack of an index.

Webber, Bert, *Retaliation: Japanese Attacks and Allied Countermeasures on the Pacific Coast in World War II* (Corvallis, Oreg.: Oregon State University Press, 1975).

———, *Silent Siege: Japanese Attacks Against North America in World War II* (Fairfield, Wash.: Webb Research Group, 1983).

White, Geoffrey M., and Lindstrom, Lamont, eds., *The Pacific Theater: Island Representations of World War II* (Honolulu: University of Hawaii Press, 1989). For most of the Pacific islands, this is the best treatment of the effects of the war on the local peoples.

Whitman, John W., *Bataan: Our Last Ditch* (New York: Hippocrene, 1990).

Wilcox, Robert K., *Japan's Secret War.* (New York: Marlowe, 1975).

Y'Blood, William T., *Little Giants: Escort Carriers at War* (Annapolis: Naval Institute Press, 1987).

Yoshimura, Akira, *Zero Fighter,* tr. Retsu Kaiho and Michael Gregson (Westport, Conn.: Praeger, 1996).

Cyberography: World Wide Web Sites of Interest

Material dealing with World War II in general and the Pacific War in particular is beginning to become available online. The sites noted below are of special interest. Be warned that World Wide Web sites have a tendency to appear and disappear with some frequency, but the list on page 751

shows that the information you may want is out
there. All you have to do is look.

Sites of Special Interest

Bibliography:	http://www.sonic.net/~bstone
Armies:	http://www.infinet.com/~nafziger/wwii.html
Hiroshima:	http://www.cs.umn.edu/~dyue/wiihist/hiroshima/
Images:	http://www.azc.com/client/page/military.html
Japan:	http://www.cs.umn.edu/~dyue/wiihist/
Pearl Harbor:	http://www.execpc.com/~dschaaf/other.html
South Pacific:	http://life.csu.edu.au/~dspennem/MILARCH/MILARCH.HTM
USAF:	http://www.usaf.com/past.htm
USMC:	http://www.hpa.edu/CampTarawa.html
U.S. Military	
All Branches:	htt://www.dtic.mil/defenselink
US Navy:	http://www.sealion.com/
	http://www.wpi.edu/~elmer/navy.html
	http://www.history.navy.mil

INDEX

The Pacific War Encyclopedia

CB *See* large cruiser(s)
CBI (China-Burma-India) **147–149**
CC *See* battlecruisers
Cebu, Philippines **149**
Celebes Islands 342–343, 387
cemetery 250
    graves registration **250–251**
    US military 193*i*
Central Pacific Campaign **149–153,** 536
Ceron, George R. 67
Cerono, Pedro 70*i*
Ceylon **153–154**
Ceylon (British light cruiser) 622
Chang Tso-lin 167
Changsha, China **154**
    defense of 162
Charger (US escort carrier) 378
Charr (submarine) 433
Chefoo, China **154**
chemical weapons 297, 318, 509
    noncombat use in WWII 508
Chemulpo, Korea **154,** 395
Chenango (US escort carrier) 540
Chennault, Claire Lee **154,** 156
Chennault, Jack 154
Chester (US heavy cruiser) **453,** 517
Chiang Kai-shek **154–155,** 156–157,
    167, 358, 397, 533, 651
    and Stilwell 159, 581
Chiang Kai-shek, Madame **155–156**
Chiang Wei-kuo 158
Chicago (US heavy cruiser) 80, **453,** 593
Chicago Tribune (newspaper) 549
Chichi Jima 643–644
Chigusa Maru (Japanese aircraft carrier) 29
Chikuma (Japanese heavy cruiser) **611**
China 48, 129, 154, **156,** 169, 229,
    272–273, 550, 606 *See also* Manchuria
    air bases in, US raids from 108
    air force of **156,** 156*t*
    airlifts to 275, 275*t*
    American Volunteer Group in
      227–228
    armies of **157–161,** 266
      divisions of 461
      in India **163**
      medical service in 416
      notable formations **161–163**
    artillery of 63
    biological weapons tests in 96
    Burma Road and 120–121, 165
    campaigns in 147–149, **163–166**
    civilian deaths in 192, 192*t*
    defense of 162
    and Japan *See also* Sino-Japanese War
      aircraft industry 12
      collaboration with 163
      peace with **167**
    Japanese invasion of Burma and
      120–121, 474, 583
    military academy of 155, 158, **651–652**
    navy of **166**
    Peking 486, 606
    poison gas used in 508
    political developments in 154–155
    resistance to Japanese **166–167**
    and Soviet Union 156, **533–534,** 579
    and US, cooperation between 565–566
    use of cavalry in 147

China Incident 122, 157, 162, **167–168,**
    299, 533
Chindits 114, 121, 148, **168,** 274, 282
Chinese Communist Army 160
    growth of forces 160*t*
Chinese prisoners 513
    medical experiments on 96–97, 304–305
Chitose Class (Japanese light aircraft carri-
    ers) 21*t*, **169,** 560
    aircraft carrying capacity 24*t*
    manpower efficiency 27*t*
Chittagong, India **169**
Chiyoda (Japanese light aircraft carrier)
    169, 560
Choiseul Island 112
Chokai (Japanese heavy cruiser) 140, 598
Chou En-lai 651
Christie, Albert F. 494
Christmas Island (Indian Ocean) **169**
Christmas Island (Pacific Ocean) **169,**
    369 Chu Teh 160, 161
Chungking, China **169**
Churchby, Gerald 487*i*
Churchill, Winston Leonard Spencer 123,
    169–170, 214, 352, 485, 531
Chuyo (Japanese escort carrier) 133, 237,
    560, 598
CIC (combat information center) 251
cities
    German, bombing of 270
    Japanese
      bombing of 109, 109*t*, 238
      rebuilding of 315
Civil Liberties Act (1988) 47
civilians
    Japanese
      in Manchuria 394–395
      resistance to Allied forces 317,
        537*i*
      repatriation of **527–528,** 582
      Western, captured by Japanese 514
CL *See* light cruiser(s)
CLAA *See* antiaircraft cruiser(s)
classes of ships **559**
Claude *See* A5M Claude (Japanese
    fighter)
Clement, Martin 575
Clemson/Wickes Class (US destroyers)
    170, 202*t*, 425, 649
Cleveland Class (US light cruisers)
    170–171, 184*t*, 280
climate, effect on troops 118, 144, 145,
    171
CO (conscientious objector) 210
Coast Guard *See* US Coast Guard
Coast Guard cutters, converted into
    AGCs 7
coastal submarines 586
coastwatchers 130, **171–172,** 212, 254,
    343
code breaking 303, 385–386, 412, 518–519
    and battle of Midway 419, 421
coffee, consumption by US troops 231,
    535
Collins, J. Lawton ("Lightning Joe") 172
Colombo, Ceylon **172**
colonial administration of Japan 306–307
colonies
    Asian and Pacific **172–173**

    Japanese 311, **469–470**
Color plans **646–648**
Colorado (US battleship) **412,** 434
Colossus Class (British aircraft carriers)
    21*t*, **173**
Columbia (US light cruiser) 170
Columbus (US heavy cruiser) 80
combat effectiveness **173–174**
combat fatigue 4, 153
combat information center (CIC) 251
combat loading 374–375
combat psychology, of Japanese soldiers
    145, **174–175,** 191, 299, 303–305
comfort women 70, **175,** 315, 356, 430,
    514, 654
Comintern, Soviet 59
command structure, in US armed forces
    479–480
commandos
    British **175–176**
    Fiji 224
    Marine 401–402
    underwater 621
Commencement Bay Class (US escort car-
    riers) 22*t*, **176**
    aircraft carrying capacity 24*t*
    ammunition allocations to 49*t*
    aviation fuel capacity efficiency 26*t*
    manpower efficiency 27*t*
communications
    Japanese 181
    US 251, 303, 396, 437
communism, pact against 59–60
communists, Chinese 358, 391–392, 394,
    397, 533–534, 579
conferences, Allied **176**
Connally, John 638
Conqueror (British nuclear submarine) 116
conscientious objector (CO) 210
conscription **176–179,** 267
    in Australia 71–72, 73
    of Germans in Asia 247
    in occupied nations, by Japanese 356,
      510
consensus building, in Japan 307–308
constitution, Japanese 299, 312, **313–314**
Construction Battalions, US Navy 52,
    440, 546
consumption, US Army **370–371**
Conte di Cavour (Italian battleship) 85
Coogan, Jackie 639
Coombs, Russell 593
coral(s) **179**
Coral Sea (US escort carrier) **422**
Coral Sea, battle of 84, 133, 135,
    179–181, 473
Cornwall (British heavy cruiser) 344, 452
Corregidor, Philippines **181–182**
corvettes and submarine chasers (PCs) 649
Courageous (British aircraft carrier) 24*t*,
    26*t*, 27*t*, 132
Cowpens (US light aircraft carrier) **280**
Croaker (submarine) 433
cruiser(s) **182–183,** 184*t*–185*t* *See also*
    heavy cruiser(s); light cruiser(s)
    damage to 189
    fuel consumption of 648*t*
    Japanese, attrition of 183*t*